# SOUTH AFRICA

## A Modern Hist

T. R. H. DAVENPORT

*Professor of History*
*Rhodes University, Grahamstown*

*Second Edition*

M

*To Marian, Tony and Catherine*



First edition 1977
Second edition 1978

Published by
MACMILLAN SOUTH AFRICA
(PUBLISHERS) (PTY) LTD
Braamfontein Centre, Jorissen St, Johannesburg
Associated companies in
London New York Dublin Melbourne and Delhi

ISBN 0 86954 028 9

Printed in Hong Kong

Mw Logan

SOUTH AFRICA: A MODERN HISTORY

Happy birthday
Love
Sally 1980

# Contents

# List of Plates

The author and publishers have made every effort to trace the copyright holders, but if they have inadvertently overlooked any they will be pleased to make the necessary arrangement at the first opportunity.

# List of Maps, Graphs and Tables

*Maps*



*Graphs*



*Tables*

# Preface to the First Edition

The study of South African history, so dependent in the early part of this century on the work of George McCall Theal, has undergone two significant changes in the twentieth century and is now involved in the beginnings of a third.

The first resulted from the work of what may be termed the 'Macmillan School' after its pioneer W. M. Macmillan, who began to question the validity of the received version, above all in its presumption in favour of the 'colonial' as against the 'missionary' point of view in the inter-racial controversies of the early nineteenth century. Macmillan's followers have also been referred to as the 'liberal' school.

The second major change was a consequence of the revolution in the study of African history after the Second World War, with its new emphasis on the indigenous peoples of Africa, rather than on Africa as a locus for the study of the European imperial overflow. The history of Africa was 'decolonised'. The philosophical basis of this 'Africanist' school was indistinguishable from the liberal. It was largely a product of the discovery that the history of the peoples of Africa could be written in greater depth by a reflective correlation, in the writings of historians, of the findings of anthropologists, archaeologists and linguists.

This does not mean, however, that the whole of South African history has been twice rewritten, as the Soviet *Short Course* is said to have been rewritten after the elimination of the 'cult of personality' in the Khruschev era. South African historians, unlike their Russian counterparts, have not reached a series of changing unanimities in their interpretations of what happened. The traditional nineteenth-century version still has its adherents, still dominates large areas of the textbook world as if the Macmillan and the Africanist schools had never existed. Indeed, a picture emerges of conflicting schools which pursue their courses in isolation from each other. The Macmillan revision was largely ignored by the traditionalists, just as the Afrikaner nationalist rewriting of the conflict between Boer and Briton was largely ignored by English-speaking historians concerned with this imperial issue.

Yet there are some signs of change. The *Oxford History of South*

*Africa,* the pioneer 'Africanist' interpretation, of which the first volume appeared in 1969, was noticed by traditionalists as well as by the Africanists for whom it catered. Few important reviews were neutral. It started a debate among historians, the keenness of which stemmed from the fact that the rival interpretations of historians seemed to touch directly on the live public issues of the day. That remains the position in South Africa.

But the assumptions of the liberal Africanist school have also come under attack from Marxist historians who have criticised the liberals for what they term an inadequate conceptual framework, a reluctance to interpret the South African story in terms of defined categories of class conflict, or as a classic illustration of how rival power groups rationalise their actions in the light of fixed, immutable, utterly dominant economic interests.

It is impossible for the historian to escape the impact of this debate because conflicting *a priori* versions of the historical story have been pressed into the service of rival political power-groups at a moment of major confrontation in the country's history. On the one hand, the dogmatism of a white establishment assumes the perpetuation of racial difference to be part of a divine plan, or at any rate as a fixed point from which all policy calculations start. At the other extreme, a predominantly expatriate element see as inevitable the revolutionary overthrow of the existing order, on the ground that the inherent logic of the situation rules out the possibility of a peaceful transition to an acceptable social system.

If this book is to be labelled as the product of a school of thought, the author would hope to be classified as sharing the basic premises of the liberal Africanists, while admitting to inadequacy in one important respect: an inability to handle the vernacular source material which is rightly coming to be regarded as an essential tool for the historian of Africa. For this reason, above all, the best he can claim for the book is that it is an interim report, an attempt to present the current state of knowledge about a society in rapid transition. The book contains no optimistic assertion that economic growth and industrialisation are any kind of trumpet to flatten the walls of apartheid's Jericho, nor any assumption that major change will be effected through the medium of the existing political system, nor any suggestion that the opposites will happen either. Its function is not to predict, or to justify, but to look at the past in the light of tested standards, in the belief that the maintenance of such standards holds out the best hope for any society of any complexion in any age. These include adherence to the rule of law, which is not necessarily the same thing as the rule of laws, and is a very different thing from rule by decree. The rule of law is related to distributive justice, for a fair deal implies the power to pay for justice as well as the right of access to it. On the issue of political democracy versus pluralism the book takes a neutral stance. Dissimilar cultures have frequently failed to maintain harmony when grouped together in a single state; but when territorial partition has been introduced as a solvent, the solution – on the evidence of India, Ireland and Israel in our own times – is not necessarily rendered less volatile. Nor does this book recommend the overthrow of an avowedly unjust and violent society by even greater physical violence. Revolutions set a premium on power, whereas civilised government demands the taming of power. There are too many lions and foxes in the political world, but not enough people of compassion.

T. R. H. D.

*Grahamstown*
*September 1976*

# Preface to the Second Edition

Candid critics have kindly drawn my attention to errors of fact and clumsiness of style. I have sought to correct these, and to bring the narrative up to date.

*Grahamstown* T. R. H. D.
*January 1978*

# Acknowledgements

'We are the ancients', Voltaire once observed, recognising that his own generation stood on the shoulders of its predecessors. The writer of a general history depends similarly on the experience accumulated by the writers of specialised monographs. My first acknowledgement is therefore to scholars, particularly to those currently active in the field, some of whose works have not yet been published, on which I have been privileged to draw. These are either referred to in the Bibliographical Notes at the end, or mentioned at appropriate points in the text.

To those scholars who have read and commented on the book, in whole or in part, I also want to express my gratitude: Ronald Ballinger, John Benyon, Jeffrey Butler, Nancy Charton, Noel Garson, Keith Hunt, Ronald Hyam, Shula Marks, Chris Muller, Jeffrey Peires, Christopher Saunders, John Seiler, and Monica Wilson. But I would have them protected from responsibility for any of the conclusions reached.

Eric Stokes, the General Editor of the series, not only read the text but gave most generously of his candid advice and encouragement throughout. To him, to Ronald Hyam, to the managers of the Smuts Memorial Trust in the University of Cambridge, and to the Master and Fellows of Magdalene College, where I was privileged to spend a year as a Visiting Fellow, this book really owes its genesis.

The Council of Rhodes University generously granted me leave during that period.

Those who have allowed me to reproduce material include Mr Clive Algar of the Johannesburg Stock Exchange, Professor Trevor Bell, cartoonists T. O. Honiball and Don Kenyon, Dr Max Mehliss, Dr Jean van der Poel, Professor E. O. J. Westphal, the Editor of *Die Burger*, and the Republican Department of Information.

I also have a debt to Doreen Cragg, Marian Davenport, Shirley McKinnell, Jean Pote, Hilda Wells, and – last but by no means least – Ella West, for typing assistance obligingly given. Mr G. F. Walters of Rhodes University reproduced most of the photographs.

I thank Betty, my wife, as well, for helpful criticism, boundless patience, and much else besides.

# Part One
# The Prelude to White Domination

## Section I
## The Setting of the Human Problem

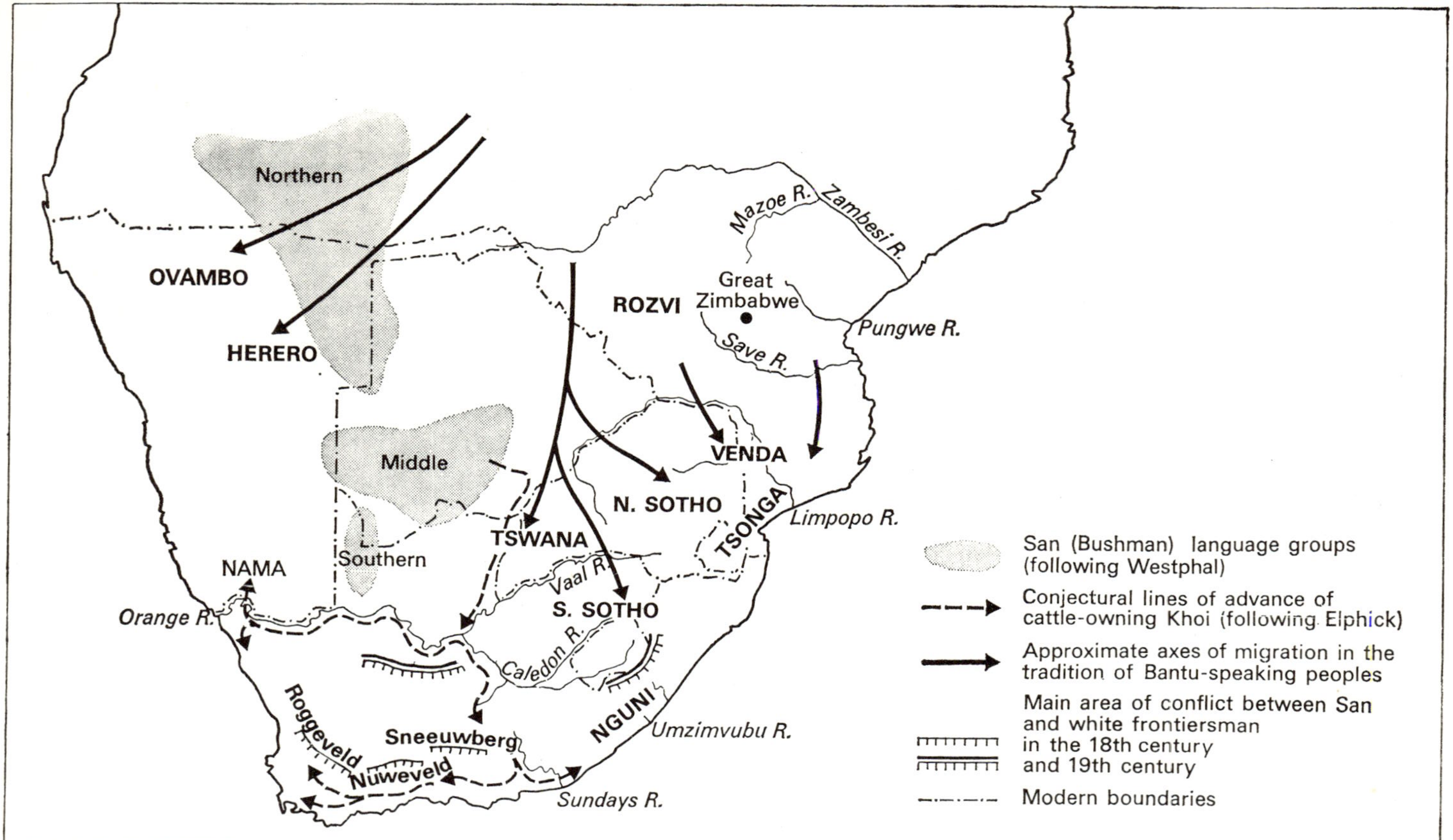
Northern
OVAMBO
HERERO
Middle
Southern
NAMA
Orange R.
Mazoe R.
Zambesi R.
Great
Zimbabwe
ROZVI
Pungwe R.
Save R.
VENDA
N. SOTHO
TSONGA
Limpopo R.
TSWANA
Vaal R.
S. SOTHO
Caledon R.
NGUNI
Umzimvubu R.
Roggeveld
Sneeuwberg
Nuweveld
Sundays R.
San (Bushman) language groups (following Westphal)
Conjectural lines of advance of cattle-owning Khoi (following Elphick)
Approximate axes of migration in the tradition of Bantu-speaking peoples
Main area of conflict between San and white frontiersman
in the 18th century
and 19th century
Modern boundaries

# 1 From the Dawn of History to the Time of Troubles

The historic distribution of people in southern Africa depended directly on the weather and the soil: the sweetveld pastures of the coastal hinterland and the Savannah of the highveld both excellent for cattle; and the reliable winter rainfall in the west and summer rainfall in the east, contrasted with the relative dryness of much of the Cape interior, tailing off into desert conditions in the north-west. But the difficulty of storing water, until this was overcome by the technology of the twentieth century, seriously inhibited intensive settlement on the land. Thus, in spite of a gentle climate ranging from the temperate to the subtropical, South Africa even in the 1970s has a population of only just over fifty persons per square mile. Apart from a very few large cities, it is even today a country of small towns and widely scattered farms. Only in the rural African homelands, where the grass is seldom long even when it is green, and in the segregated African and Coloured townships outside the cities, does it carry too many people.

The Cape was thinly populated by sallow-skinned, boskopoid hunter-gatherers and herders when the permanent white settlement began in 1652. The Dutch settlers soon drew a distinction between 'Hottentots' and 'Bushmen'. By the nineteenth century it had become usual to regard them as ethnically, linguistically, and culturally distinct peoples. Bushmen were thought to be physically smaller, and to depend upon gathering and hunting for their livelihood, whereas Hottentots were identified as pastoralists owning cattle and sheep. Both groups were thought to have migrated southwards, ahead of the Bantu-speaking peoples whose ancestral home lay well to the north.

Recent scholarship has called most of these suppositions in question.[1] The terms 'Bushman' and 'Hottentot' have been rejected by a growing number of scholars anxious to cut through the confusions they have produced and to remove pejorative associations which have developed around them. They have preferred 'Khoikhoi' or 'Khoi' for Hottentot, and the Khoi term 'San' for the Bushmen, and 'Khoisan' when a distinction between them is not required, to identify two distinct language families among these stone age peoples, whose physical attributes, religious beliefs, and material cultures were impressively similar – despite numerous problematic differences in detail – when compared with those of their Bantu-speaking neighbours.

In historic times the San south of the Orange may never have exceeded 20,000. They lived in small, loosely-knit patrilineal bands of twenty to two hundred persons. They were highly mobile on account of their dependence on game, and for the same reason widely dispersed territorially. Their political organisation was very rudimentary. Chiefs, about whom little is known, had ritual importance in rain-making and in various other ways, and were respected as the leaders of kin-groups, but had almost no institutionalised authority at all.

San languages have been variously classified. The distinction emphasised by Dorothea Bleek, endorsed by Westphal, is one between Northern, Central, and Southern groups. Geographically, these are located in south-eastern Angola, between the upper reaches of the Zambesi and Limpopo, and in the northern Kalahari on the Botswana–South West African border. R. H. Elphick has relied on the relative similarity between the main surviving Khoikhoi language, Nama, and those of the middle Bushmen group, to advance the attractive thesis that the Khoikhoi were, in origin, San groups who obtained cattle (perhaps from Bantu-speakers) while still living north of the Limpopo, and in consequence acquired a self-sufficiency which enabled them to migrate. He suggests that the main expansion of Khoikhoi was southwards along the eastern edge of the Kalahari to the confluence of the Orange and the Vaal, whence some groups (notably the Nama) moved down the Orange, branching north or south when they reached the coast, while others spread towards the eastern Cape coast, along southern tributaries of the Orange, into the Fish and Sundays river valleys, and then migrated either eastwards (the Gona) or westwards (the Attaqua, Hessequa, Chochoqua and others) in the direction of the Cape peninsula. This is more sensible than to suppose that the main Khoikhoi migration route was southwards through South West Africa to the Cape.

The largest gap in our understanding of very early southern African society remains the difficulty of correlating the Khoisan peoples with the late stone age cultures identified by archaeologists at Smithfield, Oakhurst and Wilton. Evidence of domestic animal remains is still lacking from such sites. The Khoikhoi, however, appear from other archaeological evidence to have possessed the long-horned cattle, which later attracted the attention of the Dutch East India Company, in the eleventh century AD, and sheep a thousand years earlier.[2]

The Khoikhoi, numbering at most 100,000 people when the Dutch arrived, according to Elphick's calculation (which is half Monica Wilson's estimate), were mainly located along the Orange and in the coastal belt stretching from south west Africa to the trans-Kei. The Umzimvubu river is sometimes taken as the limit of their settlement; but there is some speculation, based on the distinctive influence of Khoi clicks on the Zulu as well as Xhosa languages, that at one time they may have lived closer to what is now Natal. They had a more elaborate social organisation than the San, and were distributed in patrilineal clans of up to 2500 members, and occasionally more. It seems that before the white man's arrival they conducted a trade with their Bantu-speaking neighbours in cattle and dagga, and to a small extent in iron and copper. After the white settlement they traded their cattle for the Dutch Company's tobacco, and began to act as brokers in a developing trade between the Europeans and the Xhosa to the east. But the European advance eventually cost the Khoikhoi their land, their stock, and their trading role. Twice defeated in battle in the seventeenth century, and decimated by smallpox in 1713 and 1755, they ultimately lost their identity as a distinct cultural group and intermarried with slaves and others to form the Cape Coloured people. Most were driven into the white man's service as herdsmen, labourers or militiamen in the Colonial forces, or gained admission to one of the mission stations set up by the Europeans from the late eighteenth century onwards. Some, like the Griqua, withdrew from the western Cape to the region of the middle Orange.

There was considerable interaction between the Khoisan and the Bantu-speaking peoples in the north and east. Apart from the linguistic evidence of culture contact, there are traditions of intermarriage between the Khoikhoi and the Cape Nguni, between the Kora (Khoi) and the Tlhaping (Tswana) and other groups. The Gona (Khoi) became closely related to the Gqunukwebe (Nguni).

White South African tradition has it that the Bantu-speakers arrived as immigrants on the highveld of the trans-Vaal at about the same time as the white men first settled in Table Bay. In origin, the home of Bantu languages probably lay north-west of the central African tropical forest; but archaeological evidence suggests that the arrival of Bantu-speakers south of the Limpopo was much earlier than ethnologists once allowed for. Radio-carbon dating has provided evidence of negroid iron age settlement in the trans-Vaal as early as the fifth century AD. The reconstruction of Bantu migration patterns on the evidence of tradition and cultural affinities suggests a series of swirling currents and unexpected backwashes, rather than a steady flow of movement in a constant direction.

The southward penetration of the Bantu-speakers seems to have followed from a growth of population, which may in turn have resulted from improved control of the environment. The introduction of more nutritious foods, such as maize, is a point to which historians of

Africa have devoted considerable attention. Natural barriers like the Kalahari desert and the shifting tsetse-fly belt in the Limpopo valley and on the east coast lowveld tended to funnel settlers into the highveld regions, which were suitable for cattle-breeders, as were the well-populated sweetveld pastures of the coastal hinterland. During the Iron Age, the distribution of communities on the highveld depended also on the location of minerals – gold, copper, and above all iron ore – and on the directions followed by new trade routes between Delagoa Bay and the highveld.[3] This tended to attract a lot of people to the southern trans-Vaal.

In discussing Bantu origins in southern Africa, it is helpful to distinguish first those peoples, like the Ovambo and the Herero, who moved into south west Africa from the Congo basin, and whose association with the other southern Bantu people was so remote that they need not be closely considered here; second, the Shona-speaking communities living between the Zambesi and the Limpopo, whose association with those south of the Limpopo in historic times was relatively closer; and third, those who lived in south Africa proper.[4]

The Portuguese records throw much light on the commercial kingdom of Mwene Mutapa, which arose with the eclipse of Great Zimbabwe, the Mbire Shona trade and cult centre, during the sixteenth and seventeenth centuries. The wealth of Mwene Mutapa rested on control of the southern watershed of the Zambesi, and this shortlived dynasty controlled the gold trade in the area until this was largely wrested from it by the Portuguese, who managed to penetrate gradually into the heart of the Mashonaland plateau. To the south-west of Mwene Mutapa, in what is now Matabeleland, lay the kingdom of Butua, which always excluded the Portuguese, and was seized from the local Togwa dynasty by a rival Shona chiefdom, the Changamire Rozvi, in the late seventeenth century. The Rozvi first threw off the control of the Mwene Mutapa and then began to expel the Portuguese from Mashonaland, without however ceasing to trade with them on the Zambesi. During the eighteenth century the Rozvi developed a centralised state, sustained by the organised collection of tribute from client chiefdoms on their periphery, and by the right to ratify the succession to subordinate chieftaincies. That Rozvi rule had an unsettling effect on their neighbours can hardly be doubted, for both the Venda and the Lobedu south of the Limpopo have traditions of flight from the Changamire in the north though in the view of D. N. Beach their power has been exaggerated.

Four main groups are normally distinguished where the Bantu-speakers south of the Limpopo are concerned. These were the Venda themselves, the Sotho-Tswana, the Nguni and the Tsonga. The distinction is mainly linguistic, for the evidence points to the likelihood that at some stage there were several distinct southern Bantu cultures which subsisted for a considerable period, either north or south of the Limpopo, in isolation from each other.

The Venda of the Soutpansberg, though speaking a language akin to Shona, have cultural associations with the Sotho, and nurtured the distinctive craft traditions of the subordinate Lemba, who may have had earlier Arab associations, in metalwork, pottery and weaving. Venda traditions remain largely unexplored, but they began to flourish as a people with the southward shift of east coast trading activity during the eighteenth century, when Inhambane and Delagoa Bay began to eclipse Sofala, and iron- and copper-working spread in the trans-Vaal.

The original Sotho-speakers are not easy to identify. Among the first were the Fokeng. They built the corbelled stone huts which gave Sotho building on the highveld one of its chief characteristics. The area of Sotho dominance between the Drakensberg, the Kalahari and the Limpopo was apparently occupied by two further settler waves: first, the Rolong and the Tlhaping, who possessed similar cultures, and with whom it seems possible to associate the beginnings of iron-smelting; and subsequently those chiefdoms – the Hurutshe, Kwena, Kgatla, Ngwato, Ngwaketse, Pedi and others – which looked back to a founder named Mangope (as distinct from Morolong of the Fokeng) and which survived into the twentieth century as separate political entities.

Though Van Warmelo remains cautious, Legassick has posited a further distinction between the Kgatla and the Kwena clusters, arguing that they acquired traditions of a common ancestry only at a late stage in their development. The Kwena, following this line of argument, dispersed during the sixteenth century from a centre in the western trans-Vaal, and spread westwards towards the Kalahari and south-eastwards to the upper Caledon valley. One sub-group, the Hurutshe, who without question developed iron-smelting on a considerable scale, moved to the headwaters of the Marico river, driving the Rolong southwards. Another group of Kwena moved to the region of Swartkoppies on the Crocodile river. A third group, who have a tradition of having legitimised their occupation by intermarriage with the Fokeng, crossed the Vaal river and entered the districts of present-day Frankfort and Vrede, where they were established by the end of the eighteenth century. Meanwhile the Kgatla, who fissioned in about 1500, at about the same time as the Kwena, spread over the eastern trans-Vaal. They gave rise to chiefdoms such as the Phuting and Kgoloko (which would later become identified with the southern Sotho) and the Pedi, who moved to the Lulu mountains in the eastern trans-Vaal in the mid-seventeenth century, incorporated a large population in the eighteenth, and may well have anticipated the northern Nguni in the development of efficient state-building techniques. The Tlokwa and Lobedu were also sub-groups of the Kgatla, as were the Karanga (Kgalaka) north of the Limpopo.

At the time when the Kgatla and Kwena were spreading across the trans-Vaal, the Nguni were without any doubt well established in the coastal regions of Natal and the trans-Kei. Portuguese travellers shipwrecked off the southern African coast came across Bantu-speaking peoples in the coastal regions in the sixteenth and seventeenth centuries, and received the impression of a considerably larger settlement of people on the sweetveld pastures set back from the coast – a people they described on one occasion (1554) as 'very black in colour, with woolly hair', and on another (1593) as herdsmen and cultivators of millet, living in small villages in huts made of reed mats, practising circumcision (which was not a Khoikhoi custom), obeying chiefs called 'ancosses' (*nkosi*, a Nguni term), and being prepared to barter cattle for iron and copper.

The argument for a very early settlement of the Natal and trans-Keian coastal region by the Nguni peoples derives strength from further considerations. The Xhosa have a tradition of an ancestral home in the upper Umzimvubu valley. Some Nguni groups living in the trans-Vaal, notably the Transvaal Ndebele, who now speak Sotho, have a tradition of having arrived there very early from the south-east. On the negative side, Theal's identification of the 'Mumbos', whose southward crossing of the Zambesi is recorded in the Portuguese documents, with the Mbo of later history, seems suspect, while the arguments of A. T. Bryant, the most articulate theorist of an Nguni migration from the north, have been shown to be inaccurate in important details. Van Warmelo, the pioneer of South African ethnography, was and remains sceptical of all theories about Nguni origins. The most that can be said, perhaps, is that the migration of the Nguni peoples from the north at some early date can hardly be denied, and that – as Marks and Gray have shown with reference to the Cele, Tuli, Qwabe, Mbo-Dlamini and Zizi-Bhele among the northern Nguni, and the Xhosa, Mpondo and Mpondomisi among the southern – the main axis of Nguni migration prior to the Shakan wars was fairly consistently in a south-westerly direction.

The Tsonga, occupying the coastal area from the Save river in Mozambique as far south as St Lucia Bay, spoke a language very different from Zulu. They differed culturally from the Zulu in some respects – by being fish-eaters, for example, whereas the Nguni in general had fish taboos. Their control of the hinterland of Delagoa Bay gave them a special role in the promotion of trade during the eighteenth century, with iron and copper, ivory and slaves, as the main commodities. Tsonga trading activities ranged inland, along routes which reached the iron-smelting regions of the western trans-Vaal, involving the Pedi as middlemen. North and south along the coast, they sought ivory and introduced European ware – cloth, beads, brassware and,

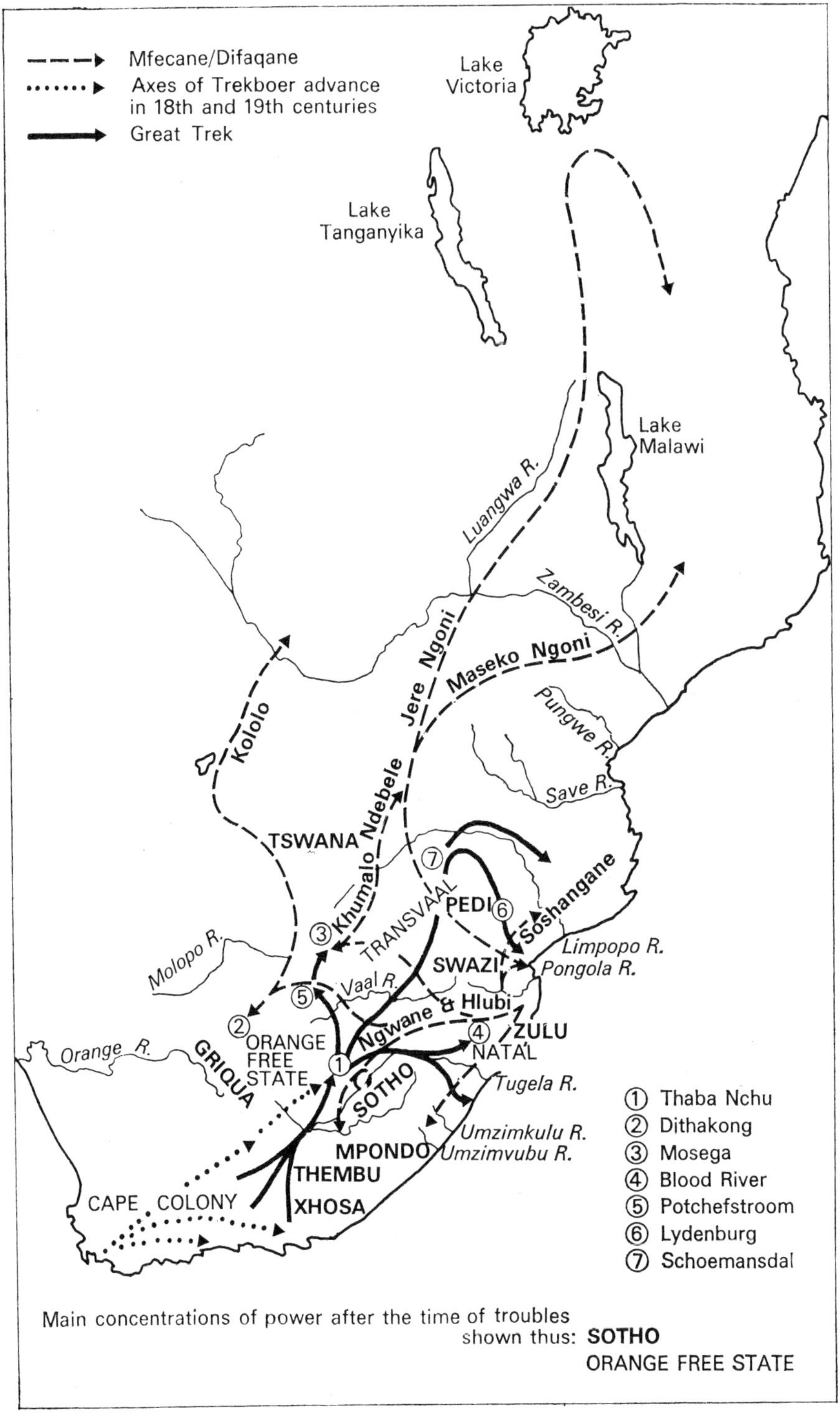


Map 2 The Mfecane and the Great Trek

later on, guns. There is evidence that ivory exported through Delagoa Bay came from Natal, and that Natal received substantial imports. Trade goods landed at Delogoa Bay were seen on the Umzimvubu, and Tsonga traders from Delagoa Bay were encountered at Ngqika's kraal in the eastern Cape. At first it was the Tsonga Tembe who dominated the trade from their base on the shores of Delagoa Bay, but in the course of the eighteenth century control was taken from them by an offshoot chiefdom, the Maputo (Mabudu), who established themselves on the Makatini Flats south of the Bay at the latest by 1794.

Before the white man's arrival in southern Africa, which will be handled in the following chapter, large areas of the sub-continent were thus unevenly peopled by Khoisan and Bantu-speaking communities whose cultural traits pointed to striking diversities of origin, but whose economic activities brought them into continuous relationships with each other. The tragedy of these communities was that, just when the European settlers had consolidated their hold on the western Cape and started to make contact with them, the same communities began to tear each other apart in one of the bloodiest of conflicts to afflict Africa in historical times.

The reconstruction of the prehistoric Bantu migrations is still largely a matter of speculation. When we turn to the great crisis of the Bantu dispersion at the beginning of the nineteenth century, however, we are on much firmer ground.[5] Known in Sotho as the *Difaqane* ('hammering'), and in Nguni languages as the *Mfecane* ('crushing', implying something like the idea of 'total war'), it was a cataclysmic event, 'one of the great formative events of African history', writes J. D. Omer-Cooper, which 'positively dwarfs the Great Trek'. In terms of geographical range and numbers of people involved, this assessment is undoubtedly true, for the Mfecane scattered African chiefdoms in fragments across half the continent of Africa. In terms of historical significance, though, there may not be much to choose between the Mfecane and the Trek.

The Mfecane started with the revolution among the northern Nguni, which has been given a variety of explanations.[6] The notion that it may have occurred simply as a consequence of a white man's influence on the Mthethwa chief Dingiswayo can be dismissed. Theories that it may have resulted from Nguni involvement in the east coast commercial revolution, or from a critical increase in population, have both attracted scholars; but the occasion was a political revolution occurring first in the Ndwandwe, then in the Mthethwa, and ultimately in the Zulu chiefdoms.

The Hlubi, Ndwandwe and Ngwane chiefdoms, which had emerged as politically independent units during the eighteenth century, had long participated in the trading activities controlled by the Tsonga chiefdoms based on Delagoa Bay. At about the same time as the Maputo overthrew the Tembe, the Ndwandwe and the Ngwane also appear to have tried, from their vantage points on the upper Pongola river, to break the Tsonga commercial monopoly. The former, under their chief Zwide, set a precedent for Shaka in the brutality of their attacks on their rivals.

The distribution of the proceeds from the ivory trade seems to have fallen more directly under the control of the chiefs among the northern Nguni than was the case among their southern neighbours, which gave the former a special interest in the expansion of trade. The desire for more trading opportunities could, similarly, provide an incentive for a military build-up. The career of Dingiswayo fits in with this supposition. As an exile among the Hlubi before acceding to the Mthethwa chiefdom, Dingiswayo had travelled to Delagoa Bay and perhaps also accompanied Tsonga traders to the Buffalo river. On accession, he immediately organised an ivory and cattle caravan to Delagoa Bay. He concluded an alliance with the Maputo, who had established their own route to the interior. He conquered a succession of clans whose territory crossed his access route to the north, and by drafting their youth into age-regiments sought to prevent any undermining of his power. At the same time the Ndwandwe expanded along the upper Pongola, perhaps also seeking an alternative outlet for trade, in view of their apparent exclusion from Delagoa Bay as a result of the Mthethwa–Maputo alliance. They attacked and beat both the Mthethwa and the Maputo in 1817 or 1818, and executed Dingiswayo.

Max Gluckman first conjectured that the Zulu revolution might have had a demographic explanation. Omer-Cooper asserted rather more confidently that 'by the end of the eighteenth century Zululand and Natal were becoming overcrowded in terms of current methods of land use', and he argued that pressure on living space could have resulted, through conflict, in a concentration of power, thus reversing the normal tendency to tribal fission. Work done by Daniel and Webb on the location of royal kraal sites in the Mthethwa, Ndwandwe and Ngwane chiefdoms in the period 1800 to 1820 has revealed something of the care with which these were selected with an eye to good rainfall, good alluvial soils, and good pastures at all times of the year, which meant the Zululand thornveld between 1500 and 3000 feet in the summer months, when nagana and malaria were lowland hazards, and the lowveld grasslands during the winter. Sites which offered all these attributes were prizes worth acquiring.

Shaka's campaigns covered the years 1817 to 1828. At first, his Zulu were an insignificant clan, who achieved prominence only after they had been conquered by Dingiswayo, who patronised their leader, Senzangakona. The latter's illegitimate son, Shaka, subsequently earned the command of the Mthethwa army through his own skill. When the

Ndwandwe fought and beat the Mthethwa in 1817, and killed Dingiswayo, Shaka took no part in the battle for reasons which are obscure. But afterwards he seized the Mthethwa chiefdom, and while continuing the war against the Ndwandwe he developed new military tactics for which he gained renown, notably the use of a short stabbing spear instead of the throwing javelin. With the help of these tactics, together with the skilful conduct of a war of attrition, Shaka beat Zwide's Ndwandwe in 1819, after two major battles at Gqokoli hill and on the Mhlatuze river. The Ndwandwe forces were shattered, and Zwide's subordinate generals, Nxaba, Soshangane and Zwangendaba, fled headlong northwards towards Delagoa Bay.

Zulu impis then moved south, penetrating Pondoland as far as the Umzimvubu river. In the early 1820s they attacked the northern Thembu of Ngoza on the Umzinyati river, driving them south into Natal. These Thembu in turn set upon the Mpondo under Faku, and Faku, whose role in checking the southward advance of the Mfecane was considerable, broke them up. But the Zulu chased a second wave of militant refugees across the Tugela, and themselves began to raid Natal in about 1822. They attacked Faku, who submitted to save what he could in 1824. Meanwhile another composite group of refugees, collectively known as the Bhaca, carried devastation southwards into the trans-Kei under the leadership of Macingwane. These fought and beat the southern Thembu of the Umtata region and the Hlubi of Mehlomakulu who had raided across the Drakensberg, as well as defending themselves against the Zulu. Another refugee group, the Mfengu, settled among the Gcaleka, still further south.

Yet to the south of Natal, the final victor was Faku. Shaka was murdered in 1828. Dingane, who had usurped power, sought to eradicate all supporters of Shaka, one of whom, Nqeto, chief of the Qwabe, found it prudent to leave Zululand. He crossed Natal in 1829, settled between the Umzimkulu and the Umzimvubu and, in a semi-independent manner, raided the Mpondo to survive. Faku quietly built up an alliance with the southern Thembu and the Xhosa, and eventually in 1830 beat Nqeto in a massive engagement at the Umzimvubu ford, inland from today's Port St Johns. The Qwabe were set upon by the Bhaca as they retreated, and Nqeto was killed. Faku and Ncaphayi of the Bhaca were now left face to face, the only significant leaders in the Natal region to survive the devastations. Though united by a dynastic marriage, they fell out. Ncaphayi was killed in action, and his followers accepted Mpondo lordship, in about 1845.

To the north of Zululand, where the commercial power of the Tsonga had been broken, the Dlamini (better known as the Swazi) were lucky to survive the vicious onslaught of the Ndwandwe under their chief Sobhuza I, after they had chased him out of his Pongola lands. Sobhuza had gradually extended his power over the Sotho-speaking people of Swaziland, allowing them to keep their chiefs, but incorporating their young men in the age-regiment system which he, like Dingiswayo, had developed in order to ensure their loyalty. Throughout Shaka's reign and the early part of Dingane's, Sobhuza was also able to preserve friendly relations with the Zulu, though periodic Zulu cattle raids troubled his later years. After this a long peace returned during the reigns of Mswati (1839–68) and his Zulu counterpart, Mpande (1839–73).

The Ndwandwe, by contrast, were scattered almost to the equator. Their exodus took place when Zwide's defeated generals Soshangane, Zwangendaba and Nxaba (Ngabe) headed for Delagoa Bay with their followers. They met resistance from the British party under Captain Owen, encamped on the southern shore, but received tribute from the Portuguese at Lourenço Marques. Throughout the 1820s these three chiefs subsisted side by side; but in 1831 conflict developed among them, and Soshangane drove out both his rivals. Before his death (in 1856 or soon after) he had made good use of the Zulu military techniques to bring the Tsonga people of Gazaland into subjection. These came to be known as the Shangaan.

The Ngoni peoples, as the followers of Zwangendaba and Nxaba came to be called, moved northwards into central Africa. Zwangendaba's Jere Ngoni attacked and beat the Changamire Rozvi kingdom based on Khami, west of the present Bulawayo. Zwangendaba thus cleared the way for Mzilikazi, who was soon to follow him. He then crossed the Zambesi near the Luangwa confluence in November 1835, and after a period of alternating settlement and migration, avoiding conflict with powerful chiefdoms like the Bemba, his people roamed through the region between Lakes Tanganyika and Malawi, one group moving almost to Lake Victoria. They had settled on the Fipa plateau to the north-east of Lake Malawi by the time Zwangendaba died in the mid-1840s. Meanwhile Nxaba, who had got the better of Zwangendaba in a battle north of the Zambesi, moved into Barotseland only to come to grief at the hands of another rampant fugitive group, Sebetwane's Kololo. Yet another group, the Maseko Ngoni, advanced up the east side of Lake Malawi into the southern part of Tanganyika, and then returned to settle in the Shire river valley, where they remained.

Mzilikazi's Khumalo (Ndebele), who should not be confused with the trans-Vaal Ndebele through whose territories they passed, had experiences of a different kind. Mzilikazi was Zwide's son-in-law. He may never have served Shaka as a subject, and apparently fled from him to avoid incorporation, accompanied by a strong following of his own kinsmen. When Shaka sent troops against Mzilikazi to demand cattle seized from the Sotho chief Somnisi, he fought his way across the

Drakensberg, and – apparently without sojourning in Pedi country as is commonly supposed – moved straight across to the region of the Apies River, where his men were occupied until 1834, hammering the Kwena and Kgatla settlements, and leaving an impression of destructiveness on the minds of visitors like Archbell, Moffat and Andrew Smith, which contrasted markedly with the impression of gentleness often created by Mzilikazi himself among those who knew him. His attacks on the Pedi are ascribed by Cobbing to 1826 or 1827, as opposed to 1823 (preferred by Lye and Omer-Cooper).

Mzilikazi retained the Zulu age-regiment system to preserve the discipline necessary for survival, but kept his soldiers on call even after they had been allowed to marry. His position necessitated this. The Kora, Taung and Rolong combined in 1829 to take revenge on him for earlier losses of cattle. The Kora had firearms, and, but for carelessness on their part, might have stripped the Ndebele of their herds. When Barend Barends of Boetsap organised a large combined commando of Griqua, Kora, Taung, Rolong and other Tswana tribesmen to attack and destroy the Ndebele, the latter saved themselves by successfully attacking their unguarded camp at night – a tactic which Moshweshwe would also employ against the Griqua. Mzilikazi's attacks and counterattacks covered vast distances. The territory he claimed, bordered by the Limpopo, Crocodile, Vaal and Molopo rivers, covered about 30,000 square miles. In 1831, he sent a force to attack Moshweshwe at Thaba Bosiu, but like all other attackers of that mountain, they failed. For security reasons, not least to get away from Dingane's Zulu, Mzilikazi moved further west and began to attack the Tswana chiefdoms of the western trans-Vaal. He persuaded the French missionaries living among Mokgatla's Hurutshe at Marico to withdraw, after which the Hurutshe fled from their town in 1835, enabling the Ndebele to move in, establish a new capital, and peg out their territorial claims by setting up further military posts. Mzilikazi then allowed the American missionaries, Lindley and Venables, to build Mosega, and agreed to a treaty with Sir Benjamin D'Urban, the Cape Governor. But he fell foul of the Voortrekkers, who began to move into the trans-Vaal in 1836. The Tregardt Trek passed through Ndebele territory unnoticed; but Hendrik Potgieter's party, mistaken by the Ndebele for marauding Griqua, were attacked and mauled. At Vegkop, the Boer laager resisted successfully, and in January 1837 their commando surprised Mosega, routing the Ndebele, who fled north. Potgieter then enlisted the support of Dingane, who attacked Mzilikazi for the third time. In October the same year, Potgieter followed with another surprise attack, routed the Ndebele, and laid claim to their lands in the trans-Vaal.

In two parties, the Ndebele retreated away from the northern trans-Vaal, crossed the Limpopo, and after the resolution of some sharp internal disputes they built a new capital, named Bulawayo, close to the Matopo hills. Sebetwane's Kololo challenged them for possession, but after a drawn contest moved away to Barotseland. Ndebele hold over the land north of the Limpopo was made easier by the prior arrival of Zwangendaba's Ngoni, who had broken the Rozvi power in the whole area south of the Zambesi. Further consolidating his position by marrying Nyamazana, a female Ngoni chief, Mzilikazi obtained for his people a few decades of peace, reaching an accommodation with the Shangaan for a boundary on the eastern escarpment, and establishing lordship over the resident Shona (Karanga) clans, until a new challenge came in the last two decades of the century, during the time of his successor Lobengula, from white land and mining prospectors and the white-controlled governments of the south.

The Difaqane on the highveld owed its origin both to an invasion across the Drakensberg from Natal and to a local conflict in Tlokwa territory which quickly merged with it. A group of Ngwane led by Matiwane (not to be confused with the Dlamini Ngwane, or Swazi), fought the Ndwandwe on the upper Pongola in about 1817, and entrusted their cattle to the Hlubi for safekeeping. They later attacked the Hlubi for not returning the cattle, and killed Mtimkulu, their chief. Meanwhile another group of related Hlubi had been attacked on the highveld, and their chief Motshodi killed by the Tlokwa of Mokotleng, ruled by their queen regent MmaNthatisi on her son Sekonyela's behalf. Motshodi's brother-in-law Mpangazita, a third Hlubi chief, crossed the Drakensberg on to the highveld a year or so later, followed by Matiwane's Ngwane in flight from Shaka. The Hlubi thus had two groups of foes in the Caledon river area, the Tlokwa and the Ngwane, with whom they had scores to settle. Anarchy resulted, as chiefdom fought chiefdom along the length of the Caledon valley. In 1825, the Hlubi risked all in an attack on Matiwane's camp, but Mpangazita was killed and all his people routed. Under a new leader, Mehlomakulu, they sought shelter for awhile with Mzilikazi north of the Vaal, and with Moshweshwe, chief of the Mokotedi Kwena, on Thaba Bosiu, before eventually settling with the Cape Government's permission in the Herschel Reserve between the Orange and Caledon rivers.

Meanwhile the Ngwane had established a base at Mekuatling, west of the Caledon, but lacked cattle for subsistence. This need brought them into conflict with Moshweshwe, who not only possessed livestock, but had already helped Matiwane's enemies, the Hlubi, against the Tlokwa. Pressed by the Tlokwa, Moshweshwe had moved from his base at Butha Buthe, at the head of the Caledon valley, to the much better fortress of Thaba Bosiu, and then spread his insurance by offering an annual tribute of crane feathers to Shaka, who was by this time master of Zululand and Natal. It is possible that, when Shaka intervened to attack the Ngwane, he did so in response to a clever diplomatic appeal by Moshweshwe; but whatever the explanation, the Ngwane fought off the Zulu, failed to take Moshweshwe's mountain in pursuit of his cattle, and accordingly resolved to move south across the Orange and raid the Thembu. While engaged in the last enterprise, the Ngwane ran into a Cape force under Colonel Henry Somerset in 1828 at Mbholompo on the Umtata river, and were routed. The survivors lost their coherence as a group and remained in Kaffraria to swell the numbers of the detribalised refugees, collectively referred to as the Mfengu. Matiwane was less fortunate still. He declined Moshweshwe's offer of asylum, and returned to Zululand hoping for shelter from Dingane, Shaka's successor; but Dingane considered him too dangerous and had him murdered.

The Hlubi attack on the Tlokwa not only intensified the conflict in the Caledon valley, but also extended it north of the Vaal. Stripped of their livestock, the Tlokwa raided desperately. It was they who attacked Moshweshwe at Butha Buthe, and forced him to move south to the better fortress of Thaba Bosiu. They also allied with Ratsebe's Phuting to attack the Ngwane. There is no evidence that the Tlokwa of MmaNthatisi themselves crossed the Vaal, and the earlier assumption that it was they who attacked the Tlhaping at Dithakong in 1823 has been shown to be incorrect. But attacks by the Tlokwa on Sebetwane's Fokeng (or Kololo) and by the Ngwane on three tribes, the Phuting, the Kololo, and the Hlakwana of Kgaraganye, drove these people across the Vaal in a starving condition to plunder the villages in those parts. It was a combination of Kololo, Hlakwana and Phuting who attacked the Tlhaping at Dithakong in 1823, only to be repulsed by a small Griqua force, who had arrived on the spot with their firearms at the instance of Moffat and Melvill of the London Missionary Society. Before attacking Dithakong, these refugee groups had previously raided as far north as the Hurutshe headquarters at Kaditshene, between the Apies and Marico rivers north of present-day Pretoria. They had travelled westwards across the Limpopo to attack the Ngwaketse, then southwards against the northern Rolong at Kunhwana on the Molopo. On arrival at Dithakong they were seen to be starving.

After defeat, these groups again divided. The Phuting suffered attacks from Mzilikazi as they retired east along the Vaal, and were eventually absorbed by Sekonyela's Tlokwa. The Hlakwana, who had been badly mauled and were now leaderless and destitute, apparently moved south, the survivors being accepted into the station set up by the London Missionary Society at Philippolis, capital of the Griqua chief, Adam Kok. Sebetwane's Kololo, by contrast, struck north and raided their way back through the Tswana chiefdoms on the edge of the Kalahari. They took a bad defeat at the hands of the Ngwaketse, who were aided by two English traders with firearms, but recovered their fortunes at the cost of the Ngwato, whom they beat at Serowe and then chased across the Kalahari to Lake Ngami. The Kololo then apparently tried to establish contact with the Portuguese in Angola, but shortage of water and guerrilla attacks by the San caused them to veer north-east along the Chobe and Zambesi rivers. They tried to settle on the highlands above the Kafue river, but after an indecisive engagement with Mzilikazi's Ndebele they moved upstream to Barotseland, where they subdued the resident Lozi at a moment of serious political division and settled in the region of Linyanti. They subsequently ambushed and beat Nxaba's Ngoni, killing Nxaba and defending themselves against renewed attacks by the Ndebele. Sebetwane died in 1851, however, and the Kololo were split apart by internal divisions afterwards, so that in 1864 the Lozi subjected them to a defeat 'so absolute' (in Mainga's words) that they could reduce the Kololo to slavery. Under Lewanika's rule (from 1878) the Lozi culture was fully restored.

# 2 The Birth of a Plural Society

European association with southern Africa began with the Portuguese circumnavigation of the Cape at the end of the fifteenth century; but, with rare exceptions, the Portuguese did not land, preferring to frequent Saint Helena and east coast havens rather than the 'Cape of Storms'.[1] Although the English, French and Dutch East India Companies all considered establishing a base during the seventeeth century, only the Dutch did so. The high sickness and mortality rate among sailors, reflected in the Company's Cape *Journal*, shows what chiefly lay behind the decision, though the continuing high death rate after the founding of the Cape station with its hospital, granary and garden, prompts the question whether the policy was successful.

The Cape was an outstation of the Company's eastern empire based on Batavia in Java, and fell directly under the Governor-General of the Indies.[2] From 1672 (regularly only from 1691) it had a governor of its own, but remained under eastern control until the end of the Company period. The Governor presided over a council of policy (*politieke raad*) consisting originally of eight senior merchants, which issued regulations (*placaaten*) and, when enlarged by one or more burghers in place of the Governor, acted as a court of justice. This governmental structure remained essentially unaltered throughout the period of Company rule, but was added to from time to time. A petty court for minor civil disputes, and a decentralised system of local government under official *landdrosts* and burgher *heemraden* were set up by High Commissioner van Rheede in 1682. A special watchdog over the administration of finance and justice, the Independent Fiscal, was first appointed in 1689. This unpopular officer would help to ensure that the Company kept effective control over the station, in the interest of maximum service to Company shipping at minimum cost to the shareholders.

The Company did not intend in the first place to establish a full-fledged colony; but once driven by economic considerations to agree in 1657 to the settlement of free burghers, and to rely on them for the supply of food which its ships required, its hands were no longer free. It gave them representation on the High Court, and its offshoots, the Matrimonial Court and the Orphan Chamber. To cheapen its costs it released potential settlers from its service, or encouraged its servants to hire themselves to free farmers as *knechts*. Settlers, in their turn, were required to do duty in the garrison, especially during the wars against Britain and against France between 1665 and 1713. During the latter part of the seventeenth century it was Company policy to encourage white settlement, and this policy led to the influx of some two hundred Huguenot refugees in 1689. Successful resistance by the free burghers to the rule of Governor W. A. van der Stel in 1705, however, led to a clamp-down on immigration from Europe, of which there was very little during the first half of the eighteenth century. After 1750, the directors tried to encourage it again, in the belief that a larger population would reinvigorate a weak economy; but even then the settlement attracted few newcomers.

The Company remained Dutch in character, though it attracted into its service men from all over central Europe. The Huguenots of 1689 might have developed into a distinct community, but Simon van der Stel dispersed them along the Berg river valley, requiring them so far as possible to learn, worship and communicate with the authorities through the Dutch language.[3] French therefore died out, and German never became established because, though more German-speakers than Dutch arrived during the eighteenth century, their numbers were not large. An originally diverse European settler population was thus coaxed into cultural uniformity, with the language of the Netherlands and the religion of the Reformed Church for cement. The Afrikaner people, an amalgam of nationalities, came gradually into being during the century after Hendrik Bibault described himself as an 'Africaander' in 1707.

The Calvinist religion enjoyed the Company's protection.[4] The Company paid the salaries of clergy nominated by the Amsterdam *classis*, and the first of these arrived in 1665. After the building of churches in the outlying districts of Stellenbosch, Drakenstein, Roodezand and Zwartland, the Company authorised a combined assembly in 1746, and set up its own political commissar to watch its activities. The Huguenot refugees helped to give Cape Calvinism its intensity and its theological awareness. Before the liberalism of the 'Atlantic Revolution' of the eighteenth century began to make its impact in the 1770s, Calvinists in the Cape interior had become intellectually isolated from new ideas coming in from outside, and inevitably made their own adjustment to the rigours of frontier life, and to the conflict with San and Xhosa, on the basis of their own traditions alone. Studies of the 'Doppers' of the Orange river frontier, who would eventually establish their own church in the 1850s, suggest that they lived within the framework of a firmly-held biblical theology, pictured themselves as wandering Israelities plagued by enemies, yet tried to live in love and charity with their San neighbours save when mastered by bouts of exasperation over their raids.

A small settlement of expatriate Europeans, many of them of humble origin, could hardly have been expected to develop rapidly into a cultural outpost of sophisticated Europe, and it did not.[5] Education was mainly limited during the Company period to the catechism (for all teachers were licensed by the Church as well as by the State) and the three Rs. At the seaport, several primary schools were established during the eighteenth century, attended in all cases by the children of the white settlers and their slaves; but, apart from an abortive attempt in 1714, there was no move for secondary education until the campaign of Serrurier and Fleck in the 1790s. Yet there was a noteworthy quickening of cultural life from the time of Ryk Tulbagh's governorship (1751–71). The colonial wars of the latter part of the eighteenth century brought periodic prosperity to the Cape, especially in the years 1756–63 and 1780–3. This was reflected in the architectural revival starting under Tulbagh, which flowered in the late eighteenth century under the stimulus of Thibault and reached its climax in the 1830s and 1840s, when money was easier to come by. With the discovery of a new architectural idiom should be grouped the baroque decorative art of Anton Anreith, and the rococo Cape furniture, European in style, though sometimes the work of Malay craftsmen.

From the start, the Cape was a place where different races met, but they generally met on terms of enforced inequality. There were a few marriages across the colour line in the early salad days of the white settlement, when company servants took Khoikhoi women to wife and fathered coloured offspring; but intermarriage between whites and blacks (though not between whites and half-castes) was prohibited in 1685, and thereafter all such liaisons became illicit – which is not to say that they did not take place.

The Company allowed the importation of slaves into the Cape settlement, and itself owned several hundred.[6] The first shipments arrived from Angola and West Africa in 1658–9; from the 1670s until 1724 they were normally brought from Madagascar, and after that date until 1730 from Delagoa Bay. Their numbers exceeded those of the white population by the early eighteenth century, because it had been found that slaves were more productive than European *knechts* on contract service from the Company, or the unwilling Khoikhoi. The importation of slaves was debated by the directors of the Company in Amsterdam in 1716, and they sought the advice of the Cape Government as to 'whether European farm hands and agriculturalists would be less expensive than slaves'. One member of the Council of Policy, Dominique de Chavonnes, in reply, proposed South Africa's first 'white labour' policy, urging an end to slave importation on the ground that white labourers were more productive, would add more to the general prosperity of the Colony, increase its security and make possible a more concentrated land settlement. But the other members of the

Council thought differently: white labourers, they urged, would be less controllable as well as more expensive, and they could not be expected to do 'slaves' work'. The continued importation of slaves was therefore allowed, and so Cape society developed on caste lines, an almost unbridgeable legal and social divide separating the free men who possessed civil rights – the right to marry, to own property, to provide for their children, to bring or defend an action in a court of law – and the slaves who, as the Roman Law enforced by the statutes of Batavia and local Cape *placaaten* made clear, possessed only the natural rights necessary for survival – the right to eat and sleep, and to cohabit, and not to be deprived of life without sufficient cause. Baron van Imhoff strongly condemned the demoralising effects of such a system on the Europeans when he reported on his visit to the Cape in 1743. A notable feature of the system was the severity of the punishments inflicted by order of the High Court on slaves who had assaulted their masters or who attempted to escape. These were clearly meant to be intimidatory as well as punitive, in an age when criminal justice in Europe was equally barbaric but just beginning to attract the attention of reformers.

Domestic slaves were generally better treated than predials or plantation slaves. They often became artisans, the craftsmen who built the houses, the carpenters who made the furniture, the boat-builders and the fishermen. Skilled slaves could hire themselves out and earn money to buy their freedom, or even own slaves themselves. A slave could earn his freedom through conversion to Christianity, though there was a tendency for this to result in fewer conversions in later times, when the suppression of the slave trade reduced the supply of slaves and put their values up. The wheat and wine farmers became dependent on slave labour. These *akkerboere* worked for a living in the shadow of the Company's trading monopoly, secure only in their quit-rent tenure, in their access to the local market, and in the cheapness of their labour force. These they tried to keep loyal, sometimes by attitudes of genuine paternalism, often accompanied by considerable familiarity within the confines of the *ménage*.

The Company intended from the start to run the Cape primarily as a supply base for its shipping, and even after it had handed over its farming activities to free burghers, it kept a firm hand on the supply of food to its own ships, and in the early years tried to prevent the sale of produce to ships of other countries.[7] It commandeered cattle, corn and wine from the burghers, at prices which it had itself laid down, though after the Van der Stel controversy of the early eighteenth century it prevented its own officials from engaging in farming. It allowed burghers to sell vegetables to visiting ships only after Company stocks had first been offered; and it limited retail activities in the port by a system of monopolies (acquired by Dutch auction) for the sale of liquor, tobacco, bread, meat and other commodities. It kept a salt monopoly for itself. There was not enough wheat for export until 1684. Thereafter, fluctuations in the size of the wheat harvest, or in the quality of the vintage, or in Batavia's arbitrary decisions as to how much Cape produce it would buy, played havoc with the burghers' calculations, though from the middle of the eighteenth century until the Anglo-Dutch war of 1780–4, Cape wheat had an assured market in the Asian colonies.

Alternative kinds of livelihood were to be found inland. Control of settlement on any colonial frontier, without surveyors' records, or roads, or effective police patrols, was difficult to enforce. At the Cape, where poor soil and scarce water encouraged farmers to scatter, and where the lure of stock-raising, hunting and barter drew people inland, control was impossible. The law of inheritance, which required equal division among a man's sons, ensured that as families grew the home farms no longer supported the next generation. Younger sons were accordingly provided with a few head of stock and a wagon, and encouraged to seek land elsewhere. Under the informal loan farm system, which came into being early in the eighteenth century, this was easy. A man could lay claim to a 6000-acre farm, provided it was not too close to another man's homestead, and keep it indefinitely on payment of an annual fee in 'recognition' of the Company's dominium. If he neglected to pay the fee, he was very unlikely to be evicted; and he could in practice bequeath, alienate and subdivide, though the law forbade these things. Attempts were made during the nineteenth century, when the Cape had become a British colony, to impose stricter controls on land tenure in accordance with the ideas of the radical reformers who were devising settlement schemes for Australia and New Zealand; but administration of the policy broke down, and the offer of perpetual quit-rent and, later, of freehold tenure, was not acceptable to Boers who already felt secure under the loan farm system, and had already acquired a taste for the ownership of wide open spaces, with farms well scattered for winter and summer grazing.

The trekboers penetrated the interior with their Khoi retainers along three main lines of advance: up the Hex river pass into the Great Karoo; or into the Little Karoo, and eventually down the Lown Kloof; or through the south-western districts to Mossel Bay, beyond which the Kaaimans river gorge made a coastal advance impossible. The establishment of drostdies at Swellendam in 1743 (when the eastern frontier was set at the Great Brak river), at Graaff-Reinet in 1785 (south-west of Plettenberg's beacon of 1778, and west of the Fish-Bushman's river line of 1775), and at Uitenhage in 1803 (shortly before the white occupation of the Suurveld), registered the efforts of the

Government to retain some control over the advancing frontier; but control was of the lightest, save where tribal resistance was strong.

In their dealings with the Khoikhoi, the Company apparently received more than value for the trade goods they paid for cattle, so that sufficient cattle to meet the fleets' requirements became harder to obtain, the Khoikhoi became more reluctant to trade, and the Company expeditions were drawn deeper and deeper into the interior. Not surprisingly, W. A. van der Stel yielded to pressure in 1700 and allowed the cattle trade to pass into private hands. The privilege was repeatedly withdrawn during the next few decades following violence against Khoikhoi by white frontiersmen and their retainers; but it proved impossible to prevent such trading contact in the long run.

Company servants noted with surprise in about 1700 that their herds were being attacked at the Berg river (near the present Paarl) by 'Bossiesman-Hottentots' armed with bows and arrows. The records refer increasingly to conflicts with 'Bushmen' as the eighteenth century advanced, though the attackers could have been Khoikhoi who had lost their stock and turned to raiding. There had been war between the Company and the Khoikhoi in 1658–60 and again in 1673–7. But by the 1770s, when the frontiers of white settlement reached the Nuweveld range in the central Karoo, it was certainly San groups who were attacking the Boer flocks. Like the Khoikhoi earlier on, the San resented alien intruders who shot the game on their hunting grounds. Moodie gives evidence of their widespread raiding for cattle and sheep, often accompanied by the killing of Khoikhoi herdsmen. Their archers directed covering fire on Boer homesteads to prevent the occupants emerging to recover their stock. Commandos of white and Khoikhoi bearing arms were organised in retaliation, sometimes on a large scale, as when three separate units of about 250 men under the overall leadership of Commandant G. R. Opperman set out in 1774, and together accounted for 500 Bushmen killed and half as many taken prisoner, in a sweep which was intended to remove the danger once and for all. But its object was not achieved. San raids continued unabated till the end of the decade. Farms were frequently abandoned by their Boer occupants, whose appeals for help often carried a note of real anguish. Rumours reached one frontier officer in 1779 that the farmers of the Camdeboo had bought immunity from the San in return for an undertaking not to interfere with the passage of stolen livestock on its way out of the Colony past their homesteads. The growing desperation of the white frontiersmen and of the authorities can be seen in the change of emphasis between Opperman's instructions of 1774 and those given to the 'Commandant of the Eastern Country' in 1780. Opperman was told 'to employ every possible means to enter into an amicable negotiation [with the Bushmen] . . . presenting them [with] tobacco and other bagatelles and trinkets, together with a promise of some farms to reside upon'. But his successor in 1780 was told to distinguish between the 'Kafirs', with whom a treaty could reasonably be concluded, and the Bushmen, who 'by their predatory proceedings, ceaselessly annoy the inhabitants and render their property insecure, and with whom we can entertain no hope of a tenable peace' – for which reason he was authorised to wage total war upon them, though – rather incongruously – without shedding innocent blood.

I. D. MacCrone advanced the proposition that white South African race attitudes hardened into a prejudice as a result of the experiences of the eighteenth century, when people with a slave-owning mentality first faced the hazards of an insecure frontier.[8] Under frontier conditions, MacCrone argued, where the desire to avoid rebarbarisation was strong, the Bible-reading trekboer easily assigned to himself the role of the elect (in Calvinist parlance), and to the black non-Christian the role of the damned. This thesis was supported by good evidence from contemporary travellers, but needs to be carefully qualified. There was social mixing as well as conflict on the frontier, as shown by the careers of men like Coenraad de Buys, who consorted intimately with the blacks, fathered a coloured progeny, and invoked Xhosa aid against his own white government. There is also evidence from the history of conflict between the Company and the free burghers that the notion of white supremacy had taken root in the agricultural districts nearer the capital.

Cape burghers in general showed a notable determination to protect their civil liberty and economic interests against Company restrictions. This came out strikingly at the beginning of the eighteenth century in their conflict with Governor W. A. van der Stel, who openly abused his official position for the sake of private profit, at their expense. Henning Husing, who had been tricked out of the meat contract by the Governor, together with Adam Tas, a well-educated Stellenbosch resident, and others, smuggled a well-signed petition to the directors in Amsterdam. The exile of Husing and three others to Holland paradoxically gave them the ear of the directors, for Van der Stel had subjected them to an irregular trial and then to torture and periods of solitary confinement (the longest for four-and-a-half months) in order to make them talk. The Governor was consequently recalled and, after inquiry into his conduct, dismissed. His estate of Vergelegen, at the foot of the Hottentots Holland mountains, was broken up, and Company officials debarred (not for the first time) from owning land and from private trading.

In a slightly different style, both *akkerboere* and frontiersmen sought to establish their liberty to deal with Khoikhoi beyond the frontiers, or with their own servants, without fear of consequences. When, in 1739, a party of settlers and Khoikhoi from Piketberg set upon a group of Nama near the Orange river mouth, killed several, and stole some cattle, the *landdrost* of Stellenbosch ordered the members of the expedition to appear before him. Though ordered to Cape Town to stand trial, the men refused and went into rebellion on the urging of Etienne Barbier, a military deserter, who accused the acting Governor, D. van den Henghel, of 'favouring Hottentots and Chinese above white men'. The rising was put down, and Barbier was executed, the first important martyr for the cause of unequal justice, and a precursor of the better known Carel Buytendag, whose case in 1779 occurred after the 'Democratic Revolution' had begun to influence the Cape.

The advance of the white frontier destroyed some Khoisan groups, absorbed others, and drove yet others deeper into the interior. Those who retreated before the whites were in many cases half-breed communities, expelled from a white society determined to protect its identity from the effects of intermarriage. Collectively, they came to be known as Bastards, which denoted, in Marais's words, a 'cross between Europeans and people of colour, with a presumption in favour of the European-Hottentot cross', though not excluding ex-slaves and free blacks. By the second half of the eighteenth century the Bastards were already becoming a distinct people. They included groups led by a succession of Adam Koks, the first of whom came from near Piketberg, and by Barend Barends, who fought the Khoikhoi leader Jager Afrikaner at the beginning of the nineteenth century. Their line of retreat ran through the Bokkeveld to the Orange river, where many of them settled on stations set up by the London Missionary Society.

When Lichtenstein encountered the Bastards in 1805, he found them an organised community, not the debauched rabble which Dr Philip later imagined. In fact, they owed much to the London Missionary Society, which encouraged them to settle at Griquatown, Philippolis and other stations, and persuaded them to adopt the name 'Griqua' in place of 'Bastard' in recognition of the Grigriqua (Khoikhoi) element in their make-up. To the missionaries, too, they owed the structure of their government and the necessary advice on how to run it.

But if the Griqua constituted the settled core of the Bastard population at the beginning of the nineteenth century, they were surrounded by splinter groups and kindred elements, some San, some mainly Khoikhoi, which were far less stable. Of these, the Bergenaars, a Griqua offshoot who moved north and terrorised the Langeberg mountains, were an example. They were joined by San groups driven northwards by the white advance, and by the Kora, a Khoikhoi people who had largely preserved their identity and got on well with the Griqua, but later became involved in conflict with the Cape Government on the Orange river in the 1860s.

What gave these elements particular significance was that in the period of the Difaqane, their general movement north-eastwards took them into the areas of Bantu dislocation, and led to conflict in which the Griqua groups enjoyed the advantage of superior weapons, notably horses and firearms. Even Moshweshwe, who eventually obtained the same weapons, placed himself under the protection of the Griqua chief, Andries Waterboer, to escape harassment from the Bergenaars in 1824. Griqua firearms defeated the desperate Sotho attack on Dithakong in 1823, while a coalition of Griqua forces, using firearms, nearly mastered the power of Mzilikazi in 1830.

Thanks largely to missionary influence, and to the statesmanship of Andries Waterboer and Adam Kok II, the Griqua settled in what became treaty states linked to the Cape Government and situated on the north bank of the Orange river. Waterboer's capital was Griquatown, Kok's Philippolis. But these states did not long survive the Trek. Pressure from white speculators north of the Orange led gradually to the erosion of their land-ownership, which Cape governors tried but failed to safeguard, so that they were in due course absorbed into the white political communities as labourers rather than peasants [see pp. 103–4].

By the middle of the nineteenth century, the separate identity of the Khoisan element in the population began to disappear through admixture with freed slaves, who, though of entirely different origin to the Khoisan, came to be identified with them as 'free persons of colour' after their emancipation in the 1830s. With this legal change, the Cape Coloured people were provided with an identity which many of them continued to regard as artificial, though it became the basis of a new and very meaningful classification during the twentieth century.

# 3 The Enlightenment and the Great Trek

Between 1776 and 1833 the settlement at the Cape, which had by that time developed into a plural, stratified, slave-owning society, was exposed to the tremors of an ideological earthquake far less painful than, but just as significant as, the agonies of the Mfecane to which the black peoples were being subjected. The change may be summarised as an onslaught by the values of the Enlightenment on white colonials whose presuppositions were explicitly Calvinist, and already moulded by a defensive desire to keep the caste structure of their small-scale society in being. The fact that this was also a period in which British rule superseded Dutch immensely complicated the situation by dividing the loyalties of the ruling but essentially insecure minority.

The ideological revolution which erupted on the opposite sides of the Atlantic in 1776 and 1789 was essentially a movement of the human spirit which embraced in its area of concern a variety of under-dogs: the victims of French religious persecution and the English-owned slaves, the Russian serfs and the inmates of Italian prisons, as well as others. Its inspiration derived partly from the non-dogmatic rationalism of the *philosophes*, partly from the humanitarianism of the evangelicals, partly from a new democratic enthusiasm among disciples of Locke and Rousseau.

The movement broke surface at the Cape in 1779, when the Buytendag affair provided a good example of how a local grievance arising out of the customary relationship between master and servant in a slave society could express itself in the universal language of European and American political liberalism, yet retain the essential ethos of a slave-owning society.[1] Buytendag, who was allegedly a brutal employer of his coloured labourers, was banished without trial to Batavia, after being arrested by armed slaves on the order of the Independent Fiscal, W. C. Boers. His arrest provided the occasion for a petition to the Directors, signed by a group of *Patriotten* whose movement had obscure beginnings, though it is known that they had contact with the leaders of the Patriot party in the Netherlands, while in their pamphlets they quoted European writers like Grotius and

Locke. Their Petition was divided into three sections. The first centred on economic grievances, suggesting that a number of the complaints of 1705 still required attention. The second enlarged on the improper conduct of officials, in particular the Fiscal, whose behaviour was said to be in conflict with 'the lawful and natural rights and freedoms of the burgher'. The final section contained thirty-seven demands, including better access to justice, greater certainty over the laws they were supposed to obey, and proper representation on the Council of Policy. Blending universal principle with a strong hint of local self-interest, they also demanded that in future white men should not be arrested by 'caffers', that burghers should be allowed to punish their own slaves without tyrannising over them, that Englishmen and Frenchmen should be denied residential rights, and that Chinese, Javanese and convicts should not be allowed to live among the burghers and run businesses in competition with theirs. Before its demise, the Company made some concessions to the burghers' demands, giving them equal representation on the Council of Justice, authorising consolidation of the law in a general *placaat*, and giving them a measure of local self-government in a body later known as the Burgher Senate. It did not pander to their demands for privilege at the expense of others, yet it was precisely this kind of demand which was renewed, with real earnestness, on the frontier in 1795, focused on the alleged misconduct of H. C. D. Maynier.

Maynier, who represented successive governments in various capacities in Graaff-Reinet between 1789 and 1801, was denounced not only for unsuccessfully leading a commando on this troublesome frontier exposed to Xhosa as well as to San depredations, but for insisting on the release of captured women and children whom the burghers coveted for labour service, and for claiming that white frontiersmen were exaggerating the rumours of Xhosa raids in order to provoke conflict with a view to seizing Xhosa stock. His accusers, who indicted him with excessive concern for the noble savage, themselves used language clothed in revolutionary slogans, greeting each other as 'Citizen [*Burger*] So-and-So', denouncing 'aristocrats', sporting tricolour cockades, and standing for the 'voice of the people' [*volksstem*] against that of authority.

The crisis over Maynier, which lasted from 1793 to 1801, resembled the Patriot movement in that the agitators availed themselves of whatever slogans of opposition were ready to hand without real concern for their original significance. It brought out clearly how independent-minded white frontier society had become, especially on racial questions over which there was already a long history of conflict. To this, however, were added three further contentious issues, which would assume greater importance in subsequent years. The first was the introduction of alien British rule during the course of the crisis. This gave the frontiersman's opposition to government of any kind a distinctly sharper edge. The second was the humanitarian intrusion, which was beginning to reach southern Africa via the anti-slavery movement and through the Protestant missionary societies, several of which would begin to work among the blacks of southern Africa at the turn of the nineteenth century. Thirdly, opposition began to gather round the tactical and strategic answers given by the governments at the Cape and in London to a new kind of frontier conflict, in which the main adversary was no longer a furtive marksman who avoided direct confrontation and could be proceeded against by punitive commandos without excessive risk, but a much more numerous, cattle-owning rival who possessed the will and appeared to possess the ability to dislodge the white settlers by direct assault.

The transfer of the Cape Colony from Company to British control took place in stages.[2] First came the temporary British occupation of 1795, which followed the French invasion of the United Netherlands at the beginning of that year, and was undertaken by arrangement with the exiled House of Orange, which continued to oppose the French. Then in February 1803, in terms of the Treaty of Amiens, the Batavian Republic (as the United Netherlands had become known) took possession. But the Batavian Republic had been in control for less than three years when, in January 1806, the British invaded for a second time, again mainly for strategic reasons, and this time with some idea of permanent occupation. But they only took formal possession in 1814–1815, during the general pacification at the end of the Napoleonic wars, as part of a triangular deal involving the governments of the United Kingdom, the United Netherlands, and Sweden.

How popular British rule was among the burghers during its earliest stages is hard to assess. The Dutch authorities under Commissioner Sluysken resisted the invasion of 1795, though Sluysken himself was an Orange supporter, but were soon forced to capitulate. Cape opinion was divided between *Jacobijnen* and *Anglomannen*, but it is not clear in what proportions. The British authorities trod carefully, anxious not to alienate more people than they had to. They guaranteed property and the Roman–Dutch legal system. They put an end to torture and monopolies, tried to control the officials by putting them on a salary basis and banning fees, and tried to buy the élite with entertainments at the castle. But they do not seem to have caught the imagination of the ordinary citizen to any degree. It was, above all, on the frontier that they found problems. The Graaff-Reinetters may not have responded to Sluysken's plead for aid; but among the '*Volksstem*' were at least some committed supporters of the new Batavian Republic, who defied General Craig. They only gave in when the prospect of a reoccupation of the Colony by the Dutch receded with the capture of Admiral Lucas's fleet in August 1796. Their opposition came alive again in 1799 when Adriaan van Jaarsveld, who had led the opposition to Maynier, was arrested on a charge of forgery. Rebels, led by Marthinus Prinsloo, released Van Jaarsveld by force, at the same time demanding permission to cross the Fish to graze cattle and apprehend runaway servants. General Vandeleur, using dragoons and Khoikhoi levies, managed to put the rebellion down.

The following year a more serious Xhosa invasion followed by a Khoikhoi rising took place. Under these circumstances, the British authorities treated the Boers as leniently as they dared. Van Jaarsveld and Prinsloo, with fifteen others, were tried in Cape Town, and the first two sentenced to death. But the Acting Governor, General Dundas, on his own authority commuted the sentences to imprisonment. Though Van Jaarsveld died in jail, the rest were subsequently released by the Batavian regime.

The Batavians in their turn were also tolerant and allowed all but the senior Orange officials to retain their posts. But they arrived expecting to remain, even if they had doubts about the long-term value of the Cape as a colony. They again made Dutch the sole official language. They also set about the overhaul of governmental institutions with conviction, turned the Council of Policy from a board of commercial management into a more compact and regularly constituted instrument of government, changed the system of accounting, and for the time being got rid of the Fiscal. They gave the Burgher Senate a more democratic basis and renamed it the *Raad der Gemeente* (Community Council). They revised the educational system with a view to training civil servants for posts of responsibility, and decentralised local government still further by establishing new *drostdies* in the troublesome frontier districts of Tulbagh and Uitenhage. If the Batavian rulers alienated Cape opinion, it was not because they could not govern or because they were seen as intruders, but because in their ideology, above all in their tolerant view of creeds other than the Reformed, in their preparedness to secularise marriage and public education, and in their liberal humanitarianism, they were innovators of a kind the colonials had been taught to view with extreme suspicion. Their reputation remained high, however, because in fact they had time to change very little.

The second British regime began negatively by restoring an autocracy even narrower than that of the Company. The Instructions to the Earl of Caledon, the first governor, subjected him to no local control at all. This situation, however, changed after the British Government had decided not merely to admit but actively to promote the settlement of British people. A substantial number of Englishmen soon settled in Cape Town, and began to play a prominent role in the life of the capital; but they were soon outnumbered by the 1820 Settlers on the eastern Cape frontier.

Apart from its military significance, as a defence against the Xhosa, the 1820 Settlement was part of the British attempt to convert the Cape into a British colony in spirit as well as in law.[3] The first of a series of attempts in the early nineteenth century to people the Empire with British subjects, it included parties from England, Scotland, Ireland and Wales. Some of them arrived in groups under wealthy leaders who received special privileges for recruiting parties of ten or more adult males. Others arrived as individuals. They numbered about 4000 in all. Most were farmers and artisans, some being victims of post-war unemployment, and there was a sprinkling of professional men – mainly soldiers, teachers and clergy. As their surviving diaries and published works reveal, they were a literate community, and their role in the struggle for press freedom was of the utmost significance for the development of independent thought and, later, of self-government for the colony. Thomas Pringle and John Fairbairn fought their political battles in the polemical language of Regency Britain, and after a few years they won them, despite the resistance of the Governor, Lord Charles Somerset. A Commission of Inquiry appointed by the Imperial Government in 1823 supported their main demands. It recommended to the Secretary of State the appointment of an advisory council which the Governor should be obliged to consult. Such a council was formed in 1825.

Oppressed in the early years by natural disasters, and by periodic Xhosa cattle raids, the 1820 Settlers became acclimatised to their new surroundings as the frontier Boers had done before them, developing the physical and moral toughness and the harder race attitudes common to the inhabitants of turbulent frontier districts, yet helping to bridge the gap between Colonial and African society, which warfare had tended to widen, and unobtrusively to weaken the bonds of African society through trade, missionary activities, and, increasingly, the employment of Africans as labourers within the settlement.

Though marriage outside the settler community did occur, and the settlers' relationship with the Afrikaner frontiersmen remained harmonious, the 1820 Settlers retained a self-awareness which the Huguenots had largely lost. This they were able to do because the Somerset regime sought to replace Dutch by English in all spheres of public life. Afrikaner scholars have commonly laid the later development of Afrikaner nationalism at the door of Somerset's anglicisation policy, and there can be no doubt that, in intention, British policy was to adjust the cultural life of Colonial society to the legal realities of British rule. English, stated the proclamation of 1822, was to be exclusively used in the courts after five years. Special incentives were given to teachers who taught through English. In due course, English would also become the sole language of the legislature. Somerset also introduced a team of Scots clergy to fill the vacant pulpits of the

Nederduits Gereformeerde Kerk. Yet before convicting the regime of oppression, it is desirable to distinguish between its intentions and the manner of their execution. Where the clergy were concerned, for example, the Scotsmen were only appointed after an attempt to obtain Dutchmen had failed. They were sent to the Netherlands to learn Dutch before going to the Cape. Their descendants tended in practice to become absorbed in the Afrikaner community which they had come to serve, and in no sense became agents of cultural conquest. Nor did they constitute any kind of liberal wing in the N.G. synod In the case of the schools, by contrast, it is clear that Dutch education suffered, both in the short and the longer term, and this fact, coming so soon after the Batavian regime had taken the trouble to place it on a sound footing, did cause resentment. Yet Dutch-medium instruction survived in the country districts at the primary level in sufficient strength to be able to underpin a successful Dutch revival in the 1870s, even though the literary Dutch of the Bible and the classroom differed from the spoken language of everyday use, which at that time had no literature of its own. In the case of the courts, it must be stressed that the Boer who had no English was always entitled to an interpreter (though he might resent betraying intimate secrets to an interpreter who was a Coloured man). His real objection concerned the abolition in 1827 of the traditional courts of *landdrost* and *heemraden*, and the removal of the judicial powers of the farmers' friends the field cornets in the interest of the better enforcement of the rule of law. These officers were replaced by resident magistrates and civil commissioners. Their titles did not necessarily mean that they had English names, but until the introduction of elected municipal councils after 1836, divisional road boards in 1843, and elected divisional councils in 1867, such local democracy as had existed now went into eclipse. The law and its enforcement were the concern of higher, generally alien authorities, who legislated in English, but gazetted the law in Dutch as well.

British institutions made inroads into the commercial as well as the political and cultural life of the Colony. Commerce had revived at the Cape during the Batavian period, when the first chamber of commerce was set up. But the scale developed markedly after the second British occupation, under the stimulus of imperial preference, and it was for the most part the British immigrants who captured the market. They also began to penetrate the interior, where the Boer was by no means entirely geared to a primitive subsistence economy, but rather to an intermediate life-style somewhere between subsistence and production for the market. He needed at least to buy gunpowder and coffee, and sold stock to enable him to do so. It was generally English-speakers or aliens who set up as shopkeepers at the centres where the Boers repaired for the quarterly *Nagmaal*, which became the first towns of the interior. After the Great Trek, the inland towns became outposts of British culture even in the Boer republics; and Afrikaner propagandists had come to caricature English culture by the 1870s as that of 'soakers, robbers and reds' – that is, of canteen-keepers, shopkeepers and red-coats – but of missionaries and humanitarians as well.

The humanitarian movement attacked and destroyed Cape slavery.[4] The Batavians, who opposed slavery in principle, had had no time to match their words with deeds. But the British Parliament made the slave trade illegal throughout the Empire in 1807, shortly after the reoccupation of the Cape. Enforcement of the legislation caused little local resentment; but it was not seen as sufficient by the abolitionists, because discretionary manumission on which they had hoped to rely did not keep us with the natural increase of the slaves. The automatic manumission of all children born to slave parents, which was seriously considered, would have taken much longer than the reformers were prepared to wait. Nor did a policy of amelioration by means of tighter control measures, such as the introduction of a slave registry in 1816, the laying down of minimum standards for food, clothing, hours of work and maximum punishments in 1823, and the compulsory recording and limitation of punishments in 1826, achieve the end desired, because these measures were treated by slave-owners as an inconvenient intrusion into their privacy and often ignored.

It was therefore against a background of slave-owners' protests that the slaves throughout the Empire were set free under a law of December 1833. This Act allowed for a period of four years' apprenticeship for domestic slaves and six for predials, before they were free to leave their masters' service, in the hope that this would cushion the shock. But there was intense resentment at the Cape, and some active opposition. The Act had been drawn up with West Indian conditions chiefly in mind, and Cape owners felt themselves not only under-compensated for the value of their slaves, but unable in many cases to draw the compensation money, which was payable only in London. Further, when emancipation did take effect in 1838–40, dislocation was considerable.

Slave emancipation was mainly the work of a pressure group in England, which achieved its end through Imperial legislation. The emancipation of the Khoikhoi and free blacks, by contrast, was much more the work of missionaries in the Colony. The interdenominational London Missionary Society began its southern African work in 1799, and had built a network of stations inside the Colony and beyond its northern border by the end of the first British occupation in 1803. The Glasgow and the Wesleyan Methodist Missionary Societies both came in on the heels of the 1820 Settlement. The former concentrated on the Tyumie valley, where Lovedale was founded in 1841. The latter built a chain of stations through the territories of the coastal Nguni in the direction of Natal, set up an important mission among the Rolong at Thaba'Nchu on the Caledon, as well as among other Sotho peoples, and in addition started work in the north-western Cape. Other societies followed. The American Board Mission sent workers to Mzilikazi's Ndebele and to Dingane's Zulu, but their arrival was almost immediately followed by the opening of hostilities between these peoples and the Boers, so that the main achievements of the American mission lay rather in its later educational work in Natal. The Paris Evangelical Missionary Society began work among the Sotho in 1833, and started to provide valuable political support for Moshweshwe.

The missionaries played a variety of roles in the frontier situation. The Wesleyan missionaries belonged to a church which was active among whites on one side of the frontier and among blacks on the other, and its white clergy sometimes found relationships difficult to work out in such a conflict situation. The Moravians, who had resumed work at the Cape in 1792 after first arriving in the 1730s, acquired the reputation among early travellers of having succeeded in their mission work without antagonising white settlers, which was not entirely true. The London Missionary Society, for its part, was conspicuous for its willingness to confront the farmers, or the Government, or both, over the treatment of the free Coloured or over frontier policy. The saintly Van der Kemp, founder of Bethelsdorp and friend of the well-known Coenraad de Buys, defied labour-hungry farmers who sought to grab his neophytes, but his mission was badly run. James Read, who took up the cases of Coloured servants who had alleged maltreatment by their employers in the celebrated 'Black Circuit' of 1812, secured some convictions but lost face and made many enemies for himself and the Society by his failure to win convictions in all cases.

It was as a consequence of the Black Circuit that in 1815 Frederick Bezuidenhout defied an order to appear in court to answer charges of maltreating a Coloured servant. After his death at the hands of Khoikhoi soldiers while resisting arrest, his brother raised a rebellion on the frontier. This was in turn suppressed, and its leaders executed; but the collapse of the gallows, followed by the re-hanging of the convicts, left a bitter memory in the minds of the witnesses, and gave the racialism of the Bezuidenhouts more favourable publicity that their actions warranted.

John Philip, who arrived in 1819 and remained superintendent of the London missions till his death in 1851, became the most controversial figure of all. He was capable of making wrong allegations as well as right ones in fluent prose, lost one libel action as a result of this, and became the *bête noire* of white settlers for the damning criticism of their labour relations in his *Researches in South Africa* (1828). His effectiveness is in dispute. Historians with as divergent views as Theal and Macmillan considered him to have been highly influential, though

Henry Cloete, the earliest historian of the Great Trek, largely ignored him in his lecture on the origins of the Trek, as did S. J. du Toit, the first Afrikaner historian. Modern historians are more inclined to see the hand of the Treasury, rather than that of the missionary lobby, behind the important decisions relating to Cape social and frontier policy, but Philip certainly did intervene, on occasion, with telling effect.

The evolution of Cape policy towards free persons of colour reached its most important stage during the early nineteenth century, when, outside the mission stations, Coloured landlessness was as good as complete. Very few efforts had been made to work out a policy for the Coloured people before the Earl of Caledon promulgated new regulations in 1809. These were aimed on the one hand to prevent vagabondage by requiring the Coloured people to carry passes when they moved about the country, and on the other to protect labourers from debt servitude, truck payments and other forms of exploitation, by means of written contracts recorded at the drostdy. Further proclamations in 1812, 1819, and 1823, governing the apprenticeship of Coloured children and related issues, brought into being a code of protective discipline for the Coloured people which, as Reyburn argued, gave them 'only a lowly status in society . . . but defended them in it'. Philip and others attacked this code on the ground that it discriminated against the Coloured people as a class, and in 1828 the Governor-in-Council promulgated an Ordinance (Number 50), which freed Coloured people from having to carry passes, made it clear that they could legally own land, and stressed their employers' continued obligation to give them service contracts – if written, for up to a year's duration, if oral for not more than a month. Whether Philip, who was in England when the Ordinance was received, helped to secure an Order-in-Council prohibiting its repeal without the authority of the British Government is by no means clear. But he did help to bring about the subsequent rejection of a Cape Vagrancy Ordinance introduced in 1834, which might have destroyed its effectiveness. The main defect of Ordinance 50, from this white farmers' point of view, was the removal of any control over vagrancy. Andries Stockenström, a member of the Council and also Commissioner-General of the Eastern Cape, upheld this criticism, and set up the Kat River Settlement on the eastern frontier in 1829, so that Coloured people who left their employment or the missions could establish themselves as smallholders. But Kat River was on a military frontier, the quality of its administration deteriorated, and when rebellion broke out among the inhabitants during the war of 1850–3, the experiment collapsed.

Government frontier policy remained a bone of contention under British rule, as it had been under Dutch.[5] The Company had tried to contain the frontier by regulating settlement, controlling trade, and imposing limits beyond which trekboers were not to proceed. But the loan farm system had not regulated settlement, control over barter had been wrested from the Company's hands, and proclamations defining the border (for example, Tulbagh's of 1770, prohibiting land grants beyond the Gamtoos, and Van Plettenberg's very rigid rule of 1780, fixing the Fish River as a border not to be crossed by anyone) had been ignored. Governor Macartney softened the approach slightly in 1797, when he ordered farmers who had engaged Xhosa as servants to discharge them within twelve months, but authorised the Landdrost of Graaff-Reinet to issue 'passports' for crossing the border to individuals. The Batavian authorities tried to adhere to a rigid frontier policy, and threatened to confiscate all the cattle of colonials who crossed the Fish-Bushmans river line, though they were not averse to some kind of passport system to regulate transit.

The Colonial authorities were unable to find a chief among the Xhosa with whom they could make binding terms. The only recognised senior chief was the Gcaleka paramount, whose great place lay beyond the Kei. His seniority was accepted by the Rharhabe chiefdoms closer to the Colonial border, but not his political authority. The Batavian authorities erred in treating Ngqika as the Rharhabe paramount, for he had no authority over Ndlambe's Rharhabe and the cluster of weak chiefdoms which occupied the disputed Suurveld.

After the second British occupation, the Government for the first time tried to impose a frontier settlement by force. Colonel Collins, sent by the Earl of Caledon to review the problem in 1809, negotiated directly with Hintsa, who had become chief of the Gcaleka in 1804. Collins proposed that the Ndlambe and Gqunukwebe be expelled across the Fish, and that the Suurveld which they were to vacate should be thickly settled by whites. Colonel Graham was sent to carry out this policy in 1812. Ndlambe, with his 20,000 subjects, was driven out, into Ngqika's territory, and the Fish frontier was fortified by a series of strong points between the villages of Cradock and Grahamstown. Like the Batavians, Lord Charles Somerset treated Ngqika as paramount, and supported him against his rivals, Ngqika having resisted white rebel attempts to involve him in the Slagters Nek rebellion of 1815. But as might have been expected, in 1818 his relationship with Ndlambe reached breaking point. Ndlambe's forces routed Ngqika's on the Amalinde Flats; but the Colony intervened on Ngqika's behalf and restored its protégé. The unsuccessful Xhosa attack on Grahamstown in April 1819 was a bid by Ndlambe's remarkable war-doctor Makanda (Nxele) to take revenge.

Somerset imposed a new settlement in October 1819 on the assembled chiefs met together at the Fish river. The Governor still treated Ngqika as paramount of the Rharhabe Xhosa, though Ndlambe was in hiding, and arranged with the chiefs that the Fish should remain the frontier, but that the area between the Fish and the Keiskamma should be regarded as a 'neutral belt' from which whites and Africans should be equally excluded. But Somerset equivocated, for in a dispatch to London on the same day he described the Fish–Keiskamma strip as 'as fine a portion of ground as is to be found, and, together with the still unappropriated lands in the Zuurveld, . . . worthy of consideration with a view to systematic colonization'. This was a bare six months before the first parties of 1820 Settlers actually arrived in Algoa Bay.

By hinting in 1817 that he would allow controlled access by the Xhosa to Grahamstown to hold fairs twice a year, Somerset had previously relaxed the rigidity of British frontier policy. During his absence from the Cape in early 1820, Lieutentant-Governor Sir Rufane Donkin authorised a fair at Fort Willshire, on the Fish river, which had become a thrice-weekly occasion by 1824. Donkin also allowed a settlement of ex-officers to be sited at Fort Frederick, in the neutral territory, in 1821, whereupon Maqoma, Ngqika's son, crossed back from the east to his home in the Kat River basin. The neutral belt had thus been entered from both sides. The Cape Government responded to Maqoma's incursion by planting the Kat River Settlement on his land. But in any case all pretence of a segregated frontier had been abandoned in the previous year when, by Ordinance 49, Lieutenant-Governor Bourke's Council gave authority for the issue of passes to Nguni migrants who wished to enter the service of Colonial farmers.

Between 1829 and 1834, tensions on the frontier grew noticeably, and the crisis broke in December 1834, when Xhosa invaders swept through the eastern Cape, destroying homesteads and seizing cattle. Dr Philip had tried unsuccessfully from the beginning of 1834 to urge the Governor, Sir Benjamin D'Urban, to visit the frontier and prescribe a new policy for the one which had broken down. Philip was particularly concerned about land shortage among the Xhosa, and provocative activities of white traders and white commandos. The evidence suggests that he tried to persuade the chiefs to keep the peace and wait for the Governor to settle their grievances.

The chiefs did not do so, however, and when D'Urban at last arrived on the frontier in January 1835, the war had already started. The Colonial forces under Colonel Harry Smith successfully repelled the invaders, and in May 1835 D'Urban annexed the whole area between the Keiskamma and the Kei as Queen Adelaide Province, and required all the defeated chiefs to remove their followers beyond the Kei. Such a policy, however, was unenforceable. Its effect would have been to create a highly dangerous and overcrowded reservoir of resentment over the Kei, with the likelihood of renewed warfare at any time. D'Urban was persuaded by the Wesleyans to abandon the 'May' policy, and in September he imposed a new settlement for which the initiative lay with Smith, though it accorded much more with Philip's ideas than the May policy had done. Queen Adelaide Province remained open for white settlement, but the African tribes (Ngqika, Ndlambe and Gqunukwebe in particular) were to be placed in locations under white resident agents, with a chief magistrate over them all. They were to be paid salaries and given responsibility for law and order. This was a radical departure from previous policies, the first plan for the direct administration of the Xhosa, with a double object of breaking up the power of the chiefs and converting their communities to European habits and the Christian religion. In view of the improvised nature of the plan, the probable lack of funds for its enforcement, and the white man's general lack of insight into the nature of African society and government, which at that time was profound, success for the September policy was at best problematic.

But before it could be applied, Lord Glenelg, Secretary of State for War and the Colonies, ordered the disannexation of Queen Adelaide Province on receipt of D'Urban's account of the May policy, not having heard as yet of the September revision. D'Urban, whose delay as a correspondent compounded the unfortunate effects of distance, obeyed the injunction without attempting to defend September, and took trouble to pose as a defender of the frontiersmen's cause. The frontier whites for their part, both Dutch and British, were wary of a colonial policy, emanating from London, which appeared to be tinged with doctrinaire assumptions, just at a time when a select committee on the treatment of aborigines had been appointed by the House of Commons, and several critics of the Cape frontiersmen (notably Philip and Stockenström), as well as Jan Tshatshu, a Bethelsdorp resident and chief's son, were due to give evidence before it.

Plans for a large-scale Boer exodus from the Colony were made a good eighteen months before the reversal of D'Urban's frontier policy, but that reversal accelerated their departure. After Dr Andrew Simth had reported favourably on his journey to Port Natal in 1832, an overland *kommissie-trek* under Piet Uys set off in September 1834 to examine the possibility of a settlement there, together with the prospects for hunting and for trading with the Africans, while other parties explored the Soutpansberg and south-west Africa. Small trekker parties left for the northern and eastern trans-Vaal under Louis Tregardt of Somerset East and Hans van Rensburg from the Graaff-Reinet region. Another, under Hendrik Potgieter of Tarka, set off late in 1835 or early 1836, and another under Gerrit Maritz in September of the latter year, after he had travelled extensively in the Colony to concert plans with other would-be emigrants. The Voortrekkers decided to concentrate in the Thaba'Nchu–Vet river area of central trans-Orangia, leapfrogging the Griqua settlements north of the Orange. On 2 February 1837, Piet Retief, originally of Stellenbosch and subsequently resident in Grahamstown and the Winterberg, published his explanatory Manifesto in the *Graham's Town Journal*, and left the Colony with a party of just over a hundred men, women and children. According to the same issue of the *Journal*, 'near the sources of the Caledon there were, a few weeks ago, 230 wagons . . . on the Orange River . . . upwards of eighty more, and . . . numerous small cavalcades, all wending their solitary way beyond the boundaries of the colony.' Most of these Voortrekkers emanated from the eastern Cape districts of Uitenhage, Albany, Somerset East, Cradock and Graaff-Reinet, a few others from Beaufort West and Swellendam. They totalled about 6000 people so far as can be calculated, including about one-fifth of the white people living in the eastern half of the Colony.

Because of the need for discretion in the planning of the Trek and the consequent paucity of records, it is not possible to give a reliable explanation of why, in detail, most of the Voortrekkers went. The Trek followed, but was not the same kind of movement as, the periodic treks out of the Colony by farmers in search of seasonal grazing, who had regularly crossed the Orange since the 1820s and always intended to return to the Colony. The *Voortrekker*, in other words, was not simply a *trekboer*, even if some trekboers, like the Kruger family, later became Voortrekkers. Muller has demonstrated the variety of ways in which a frontier Boer might feel insecure, above all through exposure to stock raids by the Xhosa, even if losses were to some extent recouped by victory in the war of 1835. Apprehension over the future security of their landholdings may have worried some frontier Boers, however, for Governor Sir Lowry Cole had threatened to put unsold lands up for auction in 1832, misunderstanding his instructions. This might have threatened the holders of some loan farms. The Cape Government, moreover, had failed to expedite the issue of quit-rent grants to many who had applied for them. But the land had not been put up for auction, loan farm occupiers had not been disturbed, and although the closing of the frontier had made new land difficult to obtain, it was not only the landless who left the Colony. The Voortrekkers included men like Gerrit Maritz, well-endowed property-owners who abandoned their farms or sold them for a song. Some Voortrekkers clearly made big financial sacrifices. Others appear to have left as debtors.

Some Voortrekkers were slave-owners, and the suggestion that the Trek was a protest against the emancipation of the slaves and the free blacks gained some currency. In a strictly economic sense, though, this may be doubted. Most of the slave-owners who suffered lived in the western Cape, and did not trek. Slave emancipation did not become effective until the end of 1838, after the Voortrekkers had already gone, though it is clear that in the transitional years of apprenticeship ex-slave-owners suffered considerable inconvenience. Further, if Khoikhoi vagrancy after 1828 and their preference for the mission stations and the Kat River Settlement made some farmers short of labour in the early 1830s (at a time when African labour had been made easier to obtain), it seems that a good many ex-slaves and free blacks left the Colony with the Voortrekkers, and continued in their service though no longer technically living in bondage. The attractions of the veld, Walker's *lekker lewe*, including the excitements and emoluments of the chase, obviously played some part, but Germanic wanderlust in itself, selected as 'first cause' of the Trek by Henry Cloete and after him by S. J. du Toit, has rightly been rejected by Muller, for whom the Trek was 'no spontaneous folk migration', but 'the best solution which a group of Afrikaner frontier leaders could devise . . . to withdraw from a situation which had become intolerable'.

The 'intolerable' conditions referred to may, as suggested, have included economic hardship or the fear of economic hardship. But it is difficult to avoid the conclusion that the Trek was, at bottom, inspired by a desire to escape from distant authorities which seemed to be both wrongly motivated and at the same time more effective than any that the frontiersmen had previously known. The burden of argument in Retief's Manifesto and in his niece Anna Steenkamp's diary was that the authorities had abandoned the proper way of handling white–black, master–servant relations, and offended the law of God as well as human susceptibilities in doing so, all at the behest of 'interested and dishonest persons' acting 'under the cloak of religion'. Slurs cast against boers for their treatment of slaves or Khoikhoi servants bit deep because they could not be shrugged off. The memory of the Black Circuit rankled, even if the executions at Slagters Nek seemed less important after the passage of a few years than they had done at the time.

There is a tradition in Afrikaner historiography which has represented the Trek as a milestone in the development of conscious Afrikaner nationalism, portraying the Voortrekkers as 'nationally aware Afrikaners' linking the Age of the Patriotten with the age of Paul Kruger. However undemonstrable, in the strict sense, this proposition may be, its existence became of great significance historically in helping to build up the Trek as perhaps the central event in the evolution of an Afrikaner mystique. But any suggestion that the Trek was a demonstration against alien government because it was alien needs to be qualified. The burden of anglicisation was, as noted above, lighter than some subsequent commentators have argued. Furthermore, if the Trek was a demonstration about Government policy, it was a demonstration in support of some aspects of it, and against others. D'Urban was the trekkers' hero, Glenelg, and those who testified on behalf of the Xhosa to the Aborigines Committee in London, their villain. In this, they enjoyed the support of frontier British opinion on the whole, as the formal presentation of a Bible by W. R. Thompson to Jacobus Uys, on the eve of his departure, was meant to symbolise.

# Section II

# Chiefdoms, Republics and Colonies in the Nineteenth Century

# 4 African Chiefdoms

In this chapter an attempt is made to set out the main characteristics of African political communities in southern Africa as they existed in the mid-nineteenth century, before their incorporation in the white-dominated political system. Characteristics common to all or most of them are first discussed and this is followed by a brief analysis of the techniques of state-building used by the more important chiefdoms.

The Mfecane, followed by the Great Trek and the penetration of white settlement into the highveld and Natal, radically redistributed power among the Bantu chiefdoms, and for a time promoted its aggregation into fewer, stronger hands. Thus Moshweshwe of the southern Sotho, who died in 1870, achieved spectacular success in building up a principality on the Caledon river out of the residue of various Sotho and Nguni peoples. Most of the Tswana chiefdoms on the edge of the Kalahari succumbed to white pressure, but Kgama's Ngwato were an important exception. Like Moshweshwe, and with just enough support from the British Government, Kgama played his cards skilfully and was able to preserve the greater part of his lands from white settlement. Together with Mswati and his successors in Swaziland, (who were far less successful in resisting white encroachment), they laid the foundations of the High Commission Territories of the twentieth century, which became independent states as Lesotho, Botswana and Swaziland in the 1960s.

Some chiefdoms were successful for a time, but later succumbed. Notable among these was the Zulu state, which survived the military overthrow of Dingane 1838–9. His successor, Mpande, refrained from risking another military confrontation before his death in 1872; but he conserved the military system for use once more against the whites by his successor Cetshwayo (1872–9), under whom it suffered destruction. Other chiefdoms which fell after resisting the spread of white settlement were the Pedi of Sekhukhune in the eastern trans-Vaal, who were overthrown between 1876 and 1879, the Ndebele of Mzilikazi and Lobengula, whose collapse resulted from the war of 1893, and on the eastern Cape frontier the Nguni chiefdoms of the Xhosa, Thembu, Mpondo and their associates, whose failure to combine, save on rare occasions, ensured their piecemeal absorption by the Cape Colony over a prolonged period.

The articulation of government in these African societies bore little resemblance in detail to that in the white-controlled states, whether British or Boer; but comparisons are instructive because all were concerned with the control of power, the rationalisation of decision-making, and issues of distributive and natural justice.[1]

Size could vary markedly in black polities, as in white. Commentators have written of 'empires' like the Zulu, or 'kingdoms' like the Swazi, and where the degree of cohesion was in doubt, of 'chiefdoms' (tribes) and 'tribal clusters', as among the Cape Nguni. There was a big difference in the size of the rambling Ngwato federation on the one hand and the minute Lobedu principality in the northern trans-Vaal on the other.

Kinship was the cement of African society. A man saw himself in the first instance as a member of a lineage, consisting of his immediate family and his known relatives and their antecedents. Beyond that, he saw himself as a member of a group – a clan in Nguni society, sharing a common 'praise name', or a totem group in Sotho, composed of people supposedly related to him, but often at too great a remove for this to be demonstrable. Membership of such a group might be valuable to him for purposes of hospitality on a journey, for they were spread across a number of chiefdoms. Totems in Sotho-Tswana society, usually some sacred animal like the porcupine of the Pedi, or the crocodile of the Kwena, or perhaps the iron (*tshipi*) of the Rolong, may have had some original connection with the economic activities of the tribe, notably hunting or iron-smelting, and most were once associated with food taboos; but in historic times they seem to have had social rather than ritual significance. To share a totem or a 'praise name' gave a person access to the fraternity of others who bore it. But whereas Sotho were encouraged to marry a partner from the same totem group, it was forbidden for the Nguni to marry within the clan.

In most societies by the nineteenth century the kinship ties had been superseded for most political purposes by territorial. The organisation of local government was by districts and wards under sub-chiefs and headmen. In the Sotho-Tswana chiefdoms, the large towns in which the people congregated were commonly divided into patrilineal wards, while Nguni village headman were normally hereditary. But there is evidence that during the late nineteenth century the concentration of particular lineages in the town wards was beginning to disappear, and the ward headman selected from among his own people was being replaced by a new official, the district headman, increasingly drawn from the royal lineage. Pauw, in his study of the Tlhaping of Taung, noted that this development started to take place at about the time of

Chief Mankurwane's death in 1892, and linked it with an attempt to check the declining authority of the chief when pressure on the land was becoming critical.

This trend is an important pointer to what was happening in the chiefdom itself, the keystone of the African political arch. Some scholars view the office of the chief as rooted in the idea of authority over persons, ruling through hereditary headmen and ward heads. Others see it as the headship of a defined territorial unit subdivided into districts and wards. It seems that there was a tendency for territorial lordship to grow, and for the office to become increasingly formalised as a result of European influences and the growth of literacy among the chief's advisers. But the coherence of tribal society always depended on the chief himself. He was the 'father' of his people, expected to govern conscientiously, wisely and generously. He was the judge of all serious misdemeanours, the lawgiver, the war leader, the distributor of land, and the universal provider, in the time of need, from the royal herds, which were largely composed of beasts levied as fines or tribute. As a Zulu proverb expressed it, he was the 'breast of the nation'. He might also be organiser of the hunt, controller of labour, and ritual rainmaker as well.

So important a figure was the chief, that rituals for strengthening the monarchy, usually connected with the first-fruits ceremonies, were common to most tribes. The Zulu *Umkhosi* ceremony, which was akin to the *Incwala* ceremony of the Swazi, and the *Ingxwala* of the Mpondo, had its parallels in Bhaca, Mpondomise and Xhosa rituals. Hilda Kuper describes the *Incwala* as more than a first-fruits festival, more than an historical pageant, and above all a 'ritualisation of the king', a device for protecting the tribe by allaying the evil forces which might harm their ruler, and consolidating the political nation around him. Among the Venda, according to Lestrade, the chief acquired an exceptionally elevated status, and could confer divinity on himself towards the end of his life. Mönnig ascribes similar attributes to the Pedi paramount, who was referred to as 'God of the Earth.'

The chief had his own councillors and officers of state. These were not in the first instance the learned clerks of a medieval European kingdom with its passion for keeping records; but the Sotho, the Mpondo and some other chiefdoms did make use of missionaries for this purpose, and by the late nineteenth century some chiefs – notably Dinuzulu, Kgama and Mbandzeni – employed literate African clerks. Councillors, however, were not so much bureaucrats as, in Sansom's words, 'leaders of followings'. From the chief's side, running government involved plying the men he valued with the plums of office – headmanships, district governorships, military leadership, and wealth in wives and cattle – and at the same time depriving those he wished to edge out. There was, however, some evidence of specialisation in the Great Place. Behind the chief generally stood the great *induna*, with a combination of viceregal and judicial authority like that of a medieval justiciar. He can be found in both Tswana and Nguni societies. Control over economic affairs was also vested in a variety of high-ranking officers, such as the *isandla senkosi* (chief's hand) of the Bhaca, the *mofa-masemo* (economic supervisor) of the Pedi, and the *modisa* (controller of pastures) of the Tswana.

In their appointment of councillors, tribal rulers might prefer either their kinsmen or commoners, sometimes a mixture of both. The proliferation of offices held in Basutoland by the sons of Moshweshwe, often at the cost of displacing other people, and almost to the exclusion of commoners, brought real danger to public peace. Swazi convention graded its aristocracy strictly in accordance with their proximity to the ruling Dlamini line, but kings avoided giving too much power to male kinsmen and reserved some key posts for leading commoners. In the Pedi and Tswana societies, chiefs tended to consult close relatives, but felt free to invite anybody whose advice could be useful to their councils, commoners included.

The councils on which the chief depended were of various kinds, formal and informal. All societies, even the Zulu in normal times, laid stress on the principle of government by discussion and consent. The *pitso* of the Sotho, the *imbito* (*imbizo*) of Nguni chiefdoms, the *libandla* of the Swazi, like the folkmoot of the Anglo-Saxons, provided a sounding-board for the ruler as he tried to determine the big issues of state. Thus Ashton describes the *pitsos* of Moshweshwe:

> Discussion, according to contemporary observers, was keen, great freedom of speech allowed, and great weight attached to the opinion and attitude of the people. The people, as often as not, followed the line they judged the chief was taking, but if, for some reason, they opposed him, and he expected their opposition to be firm, he would not often risk forcing the issue. Moshesh himself constantly asserted that he could do nothing without consulting and gaining the consent of his sons and other chiefs, and in his announcements and proclamations he usually used such phrases as 'Given with the advice and concurrence of our tribe,' or, as in his proclamation against witchcraft, 'This word is assented to by Letsie, by all my brothers and by all men of the tribe who spit on the lie of witchcraft and cover its face with their spittle.'[2]

One of the most elaborate conciliar systems was to be found among the Pedi, who had a kind of inner cabinet (the *lekgotla la teng la kgosi*), a larger 'privy council' for important but confidential business (the *lekgotla la thopa*), various special councils within particular tribes which made up the kingdom, and two types of assembly for important public business – a general assembly of adult males meeting voluntarily (the *lekgotla la banna*), and the *pitso*, at which attendance was as obligatory as attendance at a feudal great council. Similar varieties of council were to be found among the Tswana.

The decisions of a council would normally be promulgated in the name of the chief, whose task it was to ascertain the consensus of the meeting. If he ignored the advice or made a bad decision, the headmen in the wards might simply neglect to carry out his will. If he flew in the face of public opinion, he might face a political breakaway by large sections of the tribe. He had, however, certain advantages. In theory he could do no wrong. To take an extreme case, if the Queen of the Lobedu failed to make rain, it was the court official responsible for the ritual who shouldered the blame. The chief was also entitled to expect faithful service from his subjects (*khonza* in Xhosa, *khonta* in Swazi). But he could not count on continued acceptance of his authority unless he was able to exert it effectively in particular situations, and he could be tried before a tribal court for misconduct.

The councillors might sit either as a court or as a law-making body, but they were not likely to get these functions mixed up. Legislation, as distinct from the affirmation or adaptation of custom, was rare, though it did happen, especially when a king committed his tribe to the adoption of Christianity, and sought as a consequence of missionary pressure to abolish payment of brideprice, or initiation ceremonies, or the brewing of strong drink among his people. Though himself unbaptised, Moshweshwe promised the French missionaries that his own offspring would not be initiated. Kgama, Setshele and Lentswe, all Christians, introduced far-reaching changes in the above customs, but, as Dachs suggests, they found enforcement very difficult.

Succession to the chieftainship was another matter on which a good deal of uniformity prevailed. It normally passed to the eldest son of the great wife – that is, of a wife selected at a late stage in the chief's life, certainly after his accession to the chieftainship, and who was generally a member of the royalty of another tribe. The Xhosa paramount, for example, habitually married a Thembu princess, the Swazi an Ndwandwe. The chief's council nevertheless had to register its approval of the chosen heir, and the councils among the Swazi, Venda and northern Sotho could pass over an unsuitable heir reasonably easily (as the witan of Wessex had repeatedly been able to do), so long as they picked a member of the ruling house. Among the southern Sotho, it was a council of the sons of Moshweshwe who made the choice, and gave impressive backing, for example, to Lerothodi in 1891 and Letsie II in 1905. Female succession, except among the Lobedu from the time of Modjadji I, was generally ruled out; but queen-regents were not unknown, MmaNthatisi of the Tlokwa being a notable example, while the Swazi Ndlovukazi (queen-mother, literally 'she-elephant') had an important function, as the one through whom public authority was transmitted, in helping to select the heir to the chiefdom. Her role was not unlike that in which Bagehot cast Queen Victoria, for her powers included the right to be consulted, and the right to rebuke her son.

One of the main problems of chiefly government was the instability which stemmed from a number of causes inherent in the system. Assassination of chiefs sometimes occurred, generally as a consequence, not of social revolution or of ideological disagreement (though the dispatch of Shaka may have arisen out of a deep social grievance), but of a succession dispute. The mothers of a chief's sons, watchful over their offspring's claims, were quick to jump on irregularities which might keep them out of the running. Schapera notes that among some Tswana and Tsonga chiefdoms the succession was so frequently contested that the installation ceremony contained a public challenge to rivals to come forward and fight, which was 'not always an empty gesture'. Regents in the saddle were sometimes reluctant to vacate office when their wards reached manhood – a significant cause of unrest, for the fact that an Nguni chief married his great wife late in life frequently meant that his heir was a minor on accession, and what was more, surrounded by elder half-brothers from among whom his regent was likely to have been selected. Some rulers tried to make their positions secure by the murder of potential rivals, a practice in which the Zulu excelled, for Shaka and Dingane killed all their sons at birth, Dingane all his brothers.

The Tswana tribes of the Kalahari border fell into three main groups: a southern group consisting of the Tlharo, Tshidi-Rolong, Tlhaping, Hurutshe, Ngwaketse, Kwena, Kgatla (Mmanaana) and some Kgalagadi; a northern group which included the Ngwato, Tawana and the bulk of the Kgalagadi; and an eastern group to which the Malete, Tlokwa (unrelated to the Tlokwa of Sekonyela), and Kgatla (Kgafela) belonged.[3] These clusters also included a good many incorporated aliens, who constituted a substantial numerical majority in the Ngwato federation. The Tswana social structure consisted of nobles (*dikgoshana*), commoner-vassals (*batlhanka*, *bashimane*, *bagaladi*) and servants (*malata*). Unlike the Nguni, they retained not only a memory of earlier political association between chiefdoms, but some rituals in which the memories of earlier paramountcies received practical expression. Thus the Kwena, Ngwaketse and Ngwato accepted an original Hurutshe paramountcy, which was reflected in the precedence given to members of the Hurutshe tribe present at their first-fruits ceremonies, and the holding of that ceremony only after the Hurutshe chief had given permission.

Sansom has drawn a broad distinction between 'western' (Sotho-Tswana) and 'eastern' (Nguni) political systems based on the different economic systems to be found in each kind of chiefdom. Characteristic of Tswana society, he argues, was the 'tribal estate', that is, the organisation of the whole territory of the tribe into three clearly defined areas: one for residence, where the large closely settled town of perhaps 25,000 people known as the *metse* was the characteristic feature; one for the growing of crops; and one for grazing and hunting. The main functions of government in this kind of society were partly to regulate land use, making sure that the right kind of activities took place in the three regions, partly to settle the claims of rival headmen on behalf of their kin groups for access to particular areas of land, and partly to prevent the movement of townsmen away from the nuclear area of settlement and control. If residential settlements developed at the cattle posts or in the agricultural districts, perhaps twenty miles from the *metse*, then the authority of the chief might collapse, as it did among the Tlhaping of Taung when Molala succeeded Mankurwane in the 1890s. Furthermore, the defensive strategy of the tribe, which was based on the town as the strong point, would also be in jeopardy. To obviate these dangers, the regular meeting of the tribal *pitso* was necessary, so that rival interests could be harmonised and the rules of the settlement reaffirmed. 'Rulers of tribal estates were manipulators of bounds and grants,' Sansom writes, and this activity became the 'basis of political life'. The chiefdom, under such circumstances, exercised its authority behind a protective barrier of formal discussion and consultation, at the same time deriving an income from a variety of sources, of which Schapera stresses the *sehuba* (tribute of various kinds – one tusk of every elephant slain, the skin of every lion, the breast of game slaughtered), the *dikgafela* (a basket of corn from each female member of the tribe after a good harvest), the produce of public fields for which the chief had provided the seed, and so on. The chief also possessed, in his *batlanka*, an army of commoners who performed some kind of serjeanty on his behalf, such as caring for his cattle on the royal cattle posts, or repairing his homestead, in return for the right to milk those cattle, or use his wagons, and such gifts as he might shower upon them; and being dependent on the chief for their income, they were at his beck and call.

The Pedi belonged, with the Tswana, to Sansom's 'western' group of chiefdoms, but differed from them in that, living in an area of higher rainfall, their 'unit of exploitation', that is 'the largest area over which members of a given population would wish to range in furthering their productive activities', tended to be smaller.[4] Under these circumstances, state-building among the Pedi involved the chief in the amalgamation of a number of separate 'tribal estates'. The Pedi thought in terms of a hierarchical social structure, headed by the royal lineage (*bakgomana*), with commoners (*balata*), incorporated aliens (*bafaladi*) and slaves or captives (*mathupya*) as the lowest grades. The success of Sekwati (1824–60) and his heirs in absorbing other elements turned them into paramount chiefs over more than a hundred small tribes. Sekwati, who had survived the savage onslaughts of the Ndebele and skirmishing with Potgieter's Boers, played a political role among the northern Sotho not unlike that of Moshweshwe among the southern. He restored order among his people, and rooted out cannibalism. He bought Mpande's friendship with a gift of ostrich feathers and animal pelts after repelling a Zulu attack. He established a political relationship with Boer and Colonial governments, as a result of which Pedi migrants, among the first of the African tribesmen, began to seek employment in the outside world. The Pedi 'empire', writes Mönnig, 'cannot be described as a nation or as a state, or as a single tribe', but as a federation built 'by force and by marriage', that is, by conquest and diplomacy. By force, Sekwati had extended his bounds from the edge of the Soutpansberg to the Vaal river. But the Pedi rulers were also able to 'establish themselves as wife-givers to all subordinate chiefs' (Sansom). Sekwati refused to confirm in office any chief who did not marry into the royal house. He thus achieved by dynastic diplomacy the kind of extension of the paramount's influence which Shaka had achieved by the distribution of his regiments, and which the Swazi achieved by the ritual transmission of the king's medicated blood. What was more, the Pedi contrived, through the ritual of fire-lighting, to combine the assertion of paramountcy with the recognition of local autonomy among subordinate peoples. On arrival of a royal bride, for whom the tribe had given a substantial brideprice in cattle, all fires in the village were extinguished. They were subsequently relit from the fire kindled in her new homestead, thus establishing a symbolic relationship, through her, with the Pedi chiefdom itself. The tribe, says Mönnig, was then given the right to 'feed' the sons of the tribal wife, or in other words, to pay tribute to their local chief and not to the Pedi, the tribute owing to the Pedi paramount chief being limited to an annual gift of food, the *maduna*, made after the harvest [see also pp. 106–8].

Moshweshwe built a political community in the Caledon river valley in the course of the Difaqane, out of elements which were partly Sotho and partly Nguni in composition, but mainly the former.[5] The village, rather than the kinship clan, was the unit of Sotho society, even before the Difaqane. Indeed, had society been structured more pronouncedly on kinship lines, it would have been difficult for Moshweshwe, the head of the Mokotedi, a very junior branch of the Kwena, either to establish his rule over the southern Sotho in the first place, or to build up so distinctive a dynasty of his own. The creation of the Sotho state, both the achievement itself and the manner of it, testify to the statesmanship of this remarkable man [see also pp. 104–6].

Although the Sotho were among the first to possess the age-regiment system under which Moshweshwe was himself brought up, Moshweshwe did not perpetuate it as a control device, partly because the acquisition of horses and firearms gave his people an alternative military system to that devised by the Zulus, and partly because the adoption of Shaka's militarism would probably have doomed Moshweshwe's efforts to extend his influence in the crucial early years: it was sufficient that, in time of war, all his chiefs should immediately mobilise his regiments, however independently they acted at other times.

The creation of the southern Sotho state resulted from Moshweshwe's ingenuity to an unusual degree. Appeasing the strong on the one hand by strategic gifts of cattle, Matiwane, Shaka and Mzilikazi all coming in for their share, he was able on the other hand to recoup his losses by successful raids on the Thembu, Tlokwa and others, build up a livestock bank, protect it on his mountain of Thaba Bosiu, and then distribute it as occasion arose – either as brideprice on behalf of impoverished wards, his *bahlanka*, which bought their affection and tied them to him, or as *mafisa*-stock, that is, livestock taken from a defeated enemy or rebellious subordinate, which were returned to him in trust, on condition of his continued good behaviour. Moshweshwe welcomed adherents of all types, reformed cannibals included – even, to their surprise, the band under RaKotswane who had killed and eaten his grandfather. Moroka's Rolong were allowed to settle with the Wesleyans at Thaba 'Nchu in 1833. Like Sekwati, but unlike Sekwati's son Sekhukhune, Moshweshwe admitted missionaries, in his case the Paris Evangelicals, and found in Arbousset and Casalis two dedicated advisers who brought heavy pressure on him to adopt Christianity. Moshweshwe was immensely impressed by the European way of life, of which Christian values seemed to him to form an important element. His problem, as it was the problem of Sekhukhune, Setshele, Kgama and others, was to reconcile the commands of the Church, in particular Christian monogamy, with those customs of his society which held it together. For Moshweshwe's state was not an autocracy, but a loose confederation held together by two kinds of bond, the maintenance of family ties within a large ruling house, and the consent of subordinate chiefs. To disown wives, as in fact Moshweshwe did in a small measure, was both to undermine the respect of large sections of his followers, and also perhaps to undermine the extension of his own authority, and it may have been as much for this reason as any that Moshweshwe put off his baptism until in the end death came first. In general, Moshweshwe controlled his sons and his leading subordinates – the two eldest sons, Letsie and Molapo in particular – by giving them their head as much as possible, and balancing their influence in the tribal *khotla* with that of his councillors, some of whom were his own Christian younger sons.

* * *

Nguni polities, as Sansom notes, were generally distinguished by settlements of small size, fairly evenly distributed over the land, each village a self-contained economic unit, where agricultural plots and pastures were interspersed and locally controlled by headmen. Competition between villages for good land, where room for expansion was limited, could be very keen. For survival, villages needed land containing varieties of soil and climate so as to ensure year-round grazing for stock. These were conditions which led more easily to political friction, especially as cattle, on which both the economy and the social system were highly dependent, were a temptation to would-be predators. In this kind of society, the chief could control the relationship between villages, and establish his authority over them for military and fiscal purposes, only by giving constant and visible reminders of his presence. He made progresses through his domain, exercising a right to hospitality, and he levied a tribute of skins, pads and tusks of royal game, as well as receiving proceeds from the sale of privileges and justice. But the effort involved necessarily limited the area of his effective control unless – as in Shaka's case or Zwide's – extreme forms of intimidation were used as a device to compel obedience over a wide area.

The political systems of the southern Nguni, by contrast with those of the Zulu and Zulu successor states, were very loosely structured.[6] Though they possessed a common language and culture, they belonged politically to distinct tribal clusters, of which the Xhosa, Thembu, Mpondo, Mpondomise and Bomvana, all of which had occupied the area between Natal and the eastern Cape since at least the sixteenth century, were the most important. Other groups, notably the Bhele, Zizi and Hlubi (collectively known by the 1830s as 'Mfengu'), and the Bhaca, Xesibe and Ntlangwini, had arrived in the area in the early nineteenth century as a result of the *Mfecane*.

The southern Nguni never seem to have formed a single cohesive political unit. The coherence of individual tribes was in turn affected by a tendency to segmentation or fission, the former term implying the emergence of divisions within a common polity, the latter an actual break-up of the chiefdom into politically separate units. This tendency has been directly linked by Hammond-Tooke and others with the marriage customs of Nguni society, in particular the distinction drawn between the chief's great and his right-hand wife. There is plenty of evidence that the heir of the right-hand wife, who, by custom, lived at some distance from the royal kraal, could set himself up as an independent chief – perhaps as compensation for loss of seniority – and, on irregular occasions in the history of the Xhosa, Thembu, Bhaca, Mpondomise, Mpondo and Xesibe clusters, actually did so. The split between the Rharhabe and Gcaleka in about 1740 was a classic example. Secession of the right-hand house was by no means the only kind of fission to occur, however. The sons of minor wives could also move out. Sons of chiefs, in general, were enabled to build up their own entourages on the occasion of their initiation, when they also received gifts of land and stock on achieving manhood. This was an encouragement to segment, but not necessarily to break right away. Secession normally followed a dispute; and it was sometimes accompanied or preceded by violence. The ease with which it could happen militated against the rise of despotism. When secession occurred, the ability of the paramount chief to assert control of any kind over the breakaway segment, for example the right to receive tribute or military aid, could only depend on the availability of agents to use force on his behalf. If he had exceptional personal authority, a paramount might intervene in disputes between tribes which had passed beyond his control, but he had no recognised machinery for doing this. On the other hand, he was entitled to the respect of the segmented chiefs as the living embodiment of a common ancestry. Segmented tribes, for their part, had little reason for rejecting his paramountcy, since his overlordship was not exacting.

Political divisions among the Cape Nguni in the face of Settler pressure from the Cape were particularly marked between the Ndlambe and Ngqika Xhosa at the beginning of the nineteenth century, and between the Gcaleka and the Rharhabe Xhosa during the wars of the mid-nineteenth century. Divided, they eventually fell in 1878. United they might either have survived, or fallen more quickly. Among the Thembu, Ngangelizwe had difficulty in asserting paramountcy over subordinate chiefdoms, as Hintsa and Sarhili had had among the Xhosa, even when the Thembu were under Gcaleka pressure owing to shortage of land. The Mpondomise were also deeply divided between 1860 and 1886 over the rival ambitions of Mhlontlo and Mditshwa for the paramountcy, in which the latter was able to call on the western Mpondo for help. Thembu and Mpondo agreed in 1869 to allow white settlement on a buffer strip between their territories, in the hope of reducing conflict. The Mpondo, for their part, were divided into an eastern and a western branch, though the eastern Mpondo subsequently refused to recognise the split, following the secession of Faku's right-hand son Ndamase, who moved south-west across the Umzimvubu river after conflict with Mqikela, his senior.

In the history of this region the Mfengu have a special place. These refugees from the *Mfecane* found their way, first into the Thembu and Gcaleka chiefdoms, and subsequently by stages into the Cape proper. They included groups of Bhaca, victims of Shaka whom Faku took in and subordinated to Mpondo rule, as well as groups of Bhele, Zizi and Hlubi, who were victims of Matiwane's campaign of destruction, and groups of Matiwane's own Ngwane after their defeat by Colonial forces in 1828. Hintsa struggled to absorb over 20,000 of these refugees, whose nickname 'Mfengu' meant 'suppliants'. He lent them stock, treating them as his subjects ('dogs' was the expression Hintsa used, without implying servility, for they were not forced to labour for the Gcaleka). Governor Sir Benjamin D'Urban arranged for the movement of Mfengu from Gcalekaland into the Colony in 1835, hoping that they would become potential military allies and labourers. Antagonism between Xhosa and Mfengu stemmed from the fact that, like the Colonial forces after the war of 1834–5, they removed large numbers of cattle from Gcalekaland, and the estrangement lasted into the twentieth century. But as soldiers in the Colonial interest, as peasant smallholders and urban landowners under European title, as successful scholars and religious converts, and in due course as parliamentary voters, the adaptable, culturally undermined Mfengu played a very significant role as marginal people between the Xhosa-speaking and white colonial societies [see also pp. 99–103].

The Zulu and Zulu successor states made rather more progress than the southern Nguni in building and maintaining a strong, centralised chieftainship, but at a costly price.[7] Those chiefs survived best who devised techniques for extending their control over their weaker neighbours without alienating them or creating seedbeds of disaffection which they could not smother. Here the development of the Zulu age-regiment system, which was practised by all the Zulu successor states, including the Swazi, and by most of the Tswana and Sotho peoples as well, met the situation. Dingiswayo and Shaka deliberately allowed the traditional circumcision rituals to fall into disuse, perhaps because they could be used to encourage separatist dreams among ambitious princes of the blood. Instead, they drafted the youth of both sexes into separate regiments, which were located in a series of large barracks at places scattered through the kingdom. Here, till their regiments were disbanded and they were granted permission to marry, the young men worked, hunted, raided and fought for their king. The sons of conquered peoples were similarly treated, being drafted into existing regiments; and the regiments were placed under the command of the king's loyal *indunas*. Meanwhile the chiefs of defeated enemies and subordinate clans were, as a general rule, allowed to remain in office and exercise territorial jurisdiction; but they had no control over the regiments. Shaka's experience with Mzilikazi taught him the danger of leaving territorial armies under the command of their own local leaders.

The Zulu system was not broken after the death of Shaka or even that of Dingane; but under Mpande, who owed his territorial security in some measure to the good offices of the Boers and the British colonial regime in Natal, it changed in some of its externals. Mpande was not the effete, sex-ridden slug of popular legend. He wisely avoided direct confrontation with white power, but this is not to say that he allowed the Zulu military system to fall into decay. He enrolled at least thirteen new age-regiments during his reign, and probably commanded larger armies than ever Shaka had done, though like the 'Sergeant King' of Prussia he hardly ever sent them on expeditions. He murdered rivals in his own family, notably his brother Gqugqu in 1843; he took vigorous measures to discourage the emigration of refugees, especially after Gqugqu's murder had resulted in a wholesale migration from south-east Zululand into Natal. He relaxed the externals of his predecessor's despotism, however, choosing to take the advice of a council for much of the time, as was normally the Zulu practice. But this compromise position proved, in the long run, hard to hold. Perhaps through lack of vigilance he allowed opposition factions to develop in the provinces, led by Ngqengelele in the north, Maphita and his son Zibhebhu among the Ndwandwe, Uhamu the son of one of his own wives, as well as some others. This might not in itself have mattered, but for his neglect, deliberate or otherwise, to select a great wife, which led to rivalry between two of his sons, neither of whom had undisputed claim to the succession: Cetshwayo, head of the Usutu faction, and Mbuyazi of the Gqoza, whom Mpande forced to live apart on the argument that two bulls ought not to live in the same kraal. Civil war broke out between the factions in 1856. Cetswayo, with larger armies, beat his opponent and slaughtered his dependants without mercy, achieving such an ascendancy in the kingdom as a result that he became the effective ruler and left Mpande little more than titular office, before succeeding to the kingship on his father's death in 1872 [see also pp. 110–12].

The age-regiment system was retained by the Nguni chiefs who migrated to the north, but they adapted it to suit new conditions.[8] Thus Soshangane used them in Gazaland in his attempt to control and transform the Tsonga. An Nguni military aristocracy controlled the regiments and took care to preserve their identity in the midst of an alien population. They managed to retain the political loyalty of the Tsonga by these means, even though they failed to impose an Nguni language and culture on them.

Zwangendaba's Ngoni preserved their aristocratic identity among numerous subject peoples, even though they were constantly on the move. Matrimonial liaisons of the ruling dynasty were kept within the Ngoni group. As new villages were established, the arrangement of the huts was in strict accordance with the status of the householders within the clan, just as the territorial distribution of the clan-heads in relation to the king was regulated by a fixed rule. The age-regiments did not live in separate military towns, as with the Zulu, but were based on the households of the king or his relatives, though only the king could initiate major campaigns. The system enhanced the status of the king, but also lent itself to centrifugal tendencies. It did, however, encourage the conquered people to become loyal. Prisoners of war would be distributed among the Ngoni chiefs and the ordinary warriors as menials, but brought within the family, and although they remained subordinate to their Ngoni masters, they might in the course of time be granted captives of their own, and thus rise in status to the point of being recognised as Ngoni themselves.

Mzilikazi's Ndebele advanced into the trans-Vaal as an army as well as a people, but Cobbing argues that the military character of their state has been exaggerated. The king was as much ruler as general, and like other settled chiefs he was at the centre of the religious and economic life of the tribe, and the chief dispenser of justice. The military towns (*amabutho*) became, through maturation, the centres of a civil administration from which villages of settlement (*imizi*) proliferated, each under an *induna* of commoner origin, who built up his power through the incorporation of war captives and – contrary to common belief – the increase of his own cattle herds. When the Ndebele moved north of the Limpopo, the *Zansi* (that is, those who came from south of the Vaal) came to live in close association with the *Enhla* (the Sotho-Tswana elements from north of the Vaal), in proximity to the Great Place at Bulawayo. They formed the nucleus of a state, sixty per cent of whose population may have been natives of the region who accepted tributary status. Some of these spoke Sindebele and pierced their ears as a sign of allegiance, whereas others – generally those who lived at a distance from the capital – were reluctant taxpayers at best, and subject to periodic raids.

Taking African societies as a whole during their period of consolidation between the Mfecane and the imposition of white rule, one can detect the influence of forces old and new. If in some societies the authority of the chief was endowed with increased ritual significance, as among the Swazi, the Venda and the Lobedu, in others strength was discovered in new forms of military organisation – either the horses and firearms of the Sotho and Pedi, or the age-sets which so many chiefdoms adopted and used as a device for holding down conquered territory or incorporating conquered people. Less assertive devices for extending political authority were the techniques of bride-giving developed by the Lobedu and the Pedi, and the distribution of *mafisa* cattle practised by Moshweshwe. Finally, there were the beginnings of a bureaucratic breakthrough, commonly initiated by the missionaries, whose influence paved the way for a takeover by the magistrates; and this, in the case of families like the Ayliffs, Brownlees and Shepstones, meant literally a transfer of responsibility from fathers to their sons.

# 5 Boer Republics

Republicanism became, over the years, a focal point of Afrikaner political aspirations, a symbol of his group independence.[1] There were good Dutch historical reasons for this, but it was the republicanism of the 'Atlantic revolution' which revived the vogue at the Cape in 1795. Popular representation in government was the dominant note in the political demands of the *Patriotten*, just as independence to run their affairs their own way was the expressed desire of the leaders in Graaff-Reinet and Swellendam. Later, during the Great Trek, much thought was given to the question of what constitutional forms best reflected Boer customs and ensured their safety. The direct democracy of the frontier gradually gave place to articulated political systems, with the Orange Free State and the South African Republic as two contrasting end results of a varied, largely empirical tradition.[2] The Anglo-Boer war eventually ended native Afrikaner republicanism, which was superseded by a governmental system essentially British in style between 1906 and 1960. The founding of the Republic of South Africa in 1961 preserved the substance of British constitutionalism under the republican forms, but restored two things which mattered to the Afrikaner: the visual image of presidential rule, and complete independence from London.

The Voortrekkers were very concerned with group survival in the aftermath of Shaka's wars. Almost the first task which Hendrik Potgieter faced when he crossed the Vaal was the repulse of the Ndebele, who attacked his men thinking they were aggressive Griqua. Potgieter's party was organised on traditional commando lines, and controlled by a *krygsraad* (war council). Their task of subduing the Ndebele only half completed, they returned to Thaba 'Nchu in November 1836, shortly after Maritz had arrived there from the south. The Trekkers then held an open meeting on 2 December, and by ballot chose a *Burgerraad* (citizen council) of seven, electing Maritz as its president and Potgieter as their *legerkommandant* (army commander). The *Raad*, whose members were called *regters* (judges) was envisaged as a combined law-making, law-enforcing and policy-making body, though it may not have made any laws.

Personal animosity, fired by policy disagreements between Maritz and Potgieter, split this Burgerraad. Potgieter thought that the best line of advance lay northwards, with control of the highveld and access to the sea through Mozambique as the proper objectives, while Maritz saw Natal as the promised land. After the N.G. Kerk of the Cape had explicitly refused to supply a pastor for the Trekkers, Potgieter and his associates proposed the Methodist Archbell, head of the Thaba 'Nchu mission. Maritz doubted the suitability of his own brother-in-law, the elderly and rather prickly Erasmus Smit; but Smit was nevertheless supported strongly by Maritz's colleague, Piet Retief.

Maritz courted Retief's favour when the latter reached the Voortrekker base from the Colony in April 1837. In a fresh election to the Burgerraad, Retief was elected 'Governor' and Maritz 'Judge President of the Council of Policy' and 'Governor's Deputy'. Retief also took over the role of commandant from Potgieter, who, though the victor over Mzilikazi, did not gain a seat on the Raad. This was unfortunate for Voortrekker unity. Potgieter's defeat was further reflected in the Nine Articles adopted at Winburg on 6 June 1837, which purported to set up a 'Free Province of New Holland in South East Africa', and made Retief 'Overseer of our United Company [*Maatschappij*] in this camp', whose Reformed members were required to dissociate from the English missionaries (a reference to Archbell and the Methodists) on penalty of expulsion from the community. Retief sought to lay down guidelines for this new tented theocracy in his Instructions to Commandants and Field Cornets issued in July. Field cornets were made responsible, under threat of punishment, for drawing up militia lists. Failure to turn out on commando service was made a serious offence. Care of the veld, control over hunting, and supervision of subject people were placed in the hands of these semi-military officials, who were to bring to trial before *landdrost* and *heemraden* not only those who maltreated servants, but those who 'booked in' the children of Bushmen or other aboriginals for service. Good relations with the surrounding chiefdoms were essential, and in October Retief made a treaty with Moroka of Thaba 'Nchu and his Rolong.

Differences between the leaders induced them, before long, to go their separate ways. Potgieter went north to finish his fight with the Ndebele and make the trans-Vaal safe for Boer settlement. Retief, with the backing of Maritz, who followed him after an interval, moved over the Drakensberg into 'Natalia', reaching Port Natal on 19 October, 'not having met a soul on the way', and receiving a cordial welcome from the British settlers and traders already established at the port. Retief immediately wrote to Dingane, asking for the cession of territory which Shaka and Dingane had granted to white applicants on three previous occasions, and on 27 October set out for Dingane's capital of Umgungundlovu.

As the Voortrekkers had recently smashed the power of Mzilikazi, Dingane could not fail to be impressed by Boer strength. When, in the following January, Retief successfully recaptured cattle taken from the Zulu by Sekonyela, the Tlokwa chief, that impression could only have been strengthened. Retief failed to read Dingane's mind, rather presumptuously lectured him on the defeat of Mzilikazi as a sign of divine disapproval, yet walked into Dingane's prepared trap on 6 February 1838 without taking the sort of precautions which other Voortrekker leaders clearly thought necessary. After first signing a paper which granted the land between the Tugela, the Umzimvubu and the Drakensberg to the Boers, Dingane had Retief and his party murdered on the same day, and followed this up with attacks on the other Boer settlements, all but destroying the Voortrekker presence in Natal in a series of engagements between February and August. Not till November could effective relief be organised, by which time Maritz had died. But Andries Pretorius arrived with a commando of nearly 500 men in the Tugela valley, defeated the Zulu at Blood River on 16 December, and advanced to the capture of Umgungundhlovu itself shortly afterwards. The Boers accepted this as an act of divine intervention on their behalf, and built the Church of the Vow in Pietermaritzburg, which they selected as their capital, in consequence of an oath taken on 7 December, before their fight with the Zulu had begun.

The Republic of Natalia, bordered by the Black Umfolosi, the Drakensberg and the Umzimvubu, was the first Boer state properly so called, and became for five years after Blood River the main territorial base for the Trek as a whole.[3] Its constitution of March 1839 featured the principle of representative democracy, ruled by a *Raad van Representanten van het Volk*, a body of twenty-four men aged between twenty-four and sixty, elected annually in open ballot by white male adult suffrage. This insistence on an ethnically restricted suffrage, so pronounced a feature of all subsequent trekker constitutions, was not even a debating point among a self-contained *volk* living in isolated pockets on their widely scattered farms, coming together perhaps only at quarterly intervals for the *Nagmaal*, and ruling over a territory from which non-members of the *volk* had not been physically excluded. It was a natural precaution, on which group survival depended, at a time when frontiers were still improvised and the institutions of state had not yet settled down. So unthinkable did the enlargement of the franchise seem to be, that an alteration of the rules so as to include out-groups – non-Reformed, Uitlander, non-European – became almost impossible to envisage later on, even when regular government had become established. But although the principle of representation was adopted, and the Raad was given authority to decide on matters of war and peace, the allocation of land, the protection of the established Dutch Reformed

Church, and so on, controversial issues were still to be reserved for public debate, enabling a majority of the electors at a public meeting to tie the hands of the Raad. There was a profound suspicion of uncontrolled authority running through the constitution, in marked contrast to the Winburg Articles, which had made Retief a permanent head of state.

Provision was made for a vacation executive of five, to take decisions when the Raad was not engaged in its regular quarterly sessions in January, April, July and October; but all its decisions required subsequent ratification. The Raad elected a new president at each sitting, but with no executive authority independent of his chairmanship of the Raad. The Commandant-General presided over a *krygsraad* of commandants, who, with the help of field cornets, controlled military operations. But with the example of Retief before them, the Raad majority fought hard to prevent Andries Pretorius, who became Commandant-General in May 1839, from wielding independent authority, save in the actual conduct of campaigns. As a sop, Pretorius was admitted to sessions of the Raad as a non-voting adviser on 4 October 1839; but so strong was the feeling of the Raad that its own members should not hold public office, that when Pretorius went in his military capacity to demand cattle from Dingane in January 1840, he had to postpone his swearing-in as a Raad member until he was in a position to resign his military office on his return. The Raad decided in March 1840 to appoint chief commandants only on a temporary basis, though Pretorius was eventually recalled as Commandant-General to handle the conflict with the British in June 1842.

Natalia admitted to its Volksraad representatives of the highveld communities, and to cater for the needs of Voortrekkers elsewhere the Republic gradually took on a federal complexion. Potgieter had governed his Voortrekker communities on the Mooi River across the Vaal and at Winburg from November 1838 with the help of a *krysraad*, but Pretorius began to work for amalgamation when he visited the Mooi River settlement in February 1839. Two years later, after a visit by Potgieter to Pietermaritzsburg, an *Adjunkt Raad* was set up on the Mooi River, where Potchefstroom was being built, to consist of Volksraad members living on the highveld. It was not to be a separate body, but rather a committee of the Raad proper, and it was supposed to report to the Raad twice yearly, though there is no evidence that it either did so or ever accepted a subordinate role. This Adjunkt Raad became important, and a growth point in trekker constitutionalism, for the reason that after the capitulation of the Natal Volksraad to the British on 15 July 1842 – though it carried on in the shadows until October 1845 – Potchefstroom became the first successor state.

The Potchefstroom Adjunkt Raad broke away from the Natal Volksraad on 7 August 1843, rejected Natalia's submission to the British, and established a new Voortrekker republic north of the Vaal in April 1844.[4] It adopted a set of Thirty-Three Articles apparently intended as a series of supplementary judicial rules, to be taken in conjunction with the regulations of the Natal Volksraad, under which the northern Voortrekkers continued to live until the drawing-up of new fundamental laws by the Ohrigstad Volksraad in 1846. These articles were tailored for a society in which territorial government was still in the process of being created. The emphasis placed on litigation procedures and the punishment of particular misdemeanours – fraud, physical injury to persons, refusal to go on commando, encroachment on a neighbour's land, disrespect to women – reflect a community with special problems of order and security. The references to the illegal seizure of native children, which may not belong to the original document, reveal a humane if authoritarian approach to racialist temptations in frontier society, where 'bastards . . . down to the tenth degree' were excluded from membership of the Raad.

Between 1845 and 1848 the importance of Potchefstroom was eclipsed by Potgieter's decision to move to the eastern trans-Vaal. The selection of Andries Ohrigstad, named after the head of a Dutch trading company, was prompted by Potgieter's desire to establish independent commercial outlets. He also wanted to keep off territory claimed by the Portuguese, and remove beyond the reach of British authority under the Cape of Good Hope Punishment Act of 1836. The tsetse-fly, however, together with Portuguese and African opposition, killed the prospects of trade and reduced Ohrigstad to a mood of disillusionment, out of which contention sprang. Potgieter took to Ohrigstad his preference for military government, and had the title of *Hoofdkommandant* wished upon him by his supporters. This was not to the liking of J. J. ('Kootje') Burger and his associates, ex-members of the Natal Volksraad, who had migrated to Ohrigstad after the cession of Natal, and were strong in their opposition to autocracy but had the reputation of being 'sell-outs'. They wanted a Natal-style Volksraad and disliked a strong executive, and in spite of their failure in Natal they stood their ground against Potgieter, who moved off with a small following to found a new settlement in the Soutpansberg, leaving them in possession of the field.

The eclipse of Potgieter brought Andries Pretorius back to a position of influence in the Voortrekker community and he returned from Natal, where he had lived quietly until British rule, to lead Boer resistance to Sir Harry Smith's sudden decision early in 1848 to annex trans-Orangia to the British Crown. One group of Boers, led by Michael Oberholzer, had no strong desire to escape from British rule, and had reached an accommodation with Adam Kok in 1840, recognising the latter's sovereignty over their lands. Further north, however, in the region of the Modder and Vet rivers, lived a remnant of the original Voortrek, based on their laager at Winburg, whose numbers were swelled by a group of

Voortrekkers from Natal led by J. C. Mocke. This group made a brief but ineffective bid to help the Natal Voortrekkers against the British in January 1843. Rather more seriously, they tried to oppose Smith's annexation of trans-Orangia by force, and were beaten in a skirmish at Boomplaats in August 1848.

The defeat at Boomplaats reduced Pretorius's influence and brought the Volksraad party back into the ascendant, but the government of a Voortrekker community without a strong executive proved hardly easier in practice. At Hekpoort in the Magaliesberg on 9 February 1849, the Potchefstroom and Soutpansberg groups decided to set up a united Volksraad with supreme authority and not to accept British rule. This United Volksraad met at Derde Poort on 23 May, the Ohrigstaders also being present, and agreed to meet regularly three times a year at different centres; but they would not support the appointment of a single head commandant, and eventually decided in January 1851 to divide that office into four – for Mooi River and the Magaliesberg (Pretorius), for the Soutpansberg (Potgieter), for Lydenburg, where the Ohrigstaders had now established their capital (W. F. Joubert), and for Marico (J. A. Enslin), all of them to be subject to the United Volksraad. But when Pretorius tried to convene a Volksraad in September 1851, and again in December, to obtain authority to mediate between Moshweshwe and the Sovereignty is such a way as to secure British recognition of the independence of the Transvalers, on both occasions there was no quorum. Pretorius therefore had to fall back on his Krygsraad when, in January 1852, he negotiated the Convention of Sand River. The most eminent of the chief commandants thus pulled off a respectable diplomatic coup without Volksraad support. Ironically, this achievement of the military executive was followed in March by a decision that every burgher could decide to which of the military leaders he would attach himself. Some Potchefstroomers actually elected to serve under Potgieter in the Soutpansberg. This kind of attachment to personal leaders was a characteristic of Afrikaner society, born of the commando system and the experience of the Trek. It became an important bond of cohesion in later history, notably during the Anglo-Boer War, during the 1914 rebellion, and perhaps also in the political associations of later years.

Meanwhile Pretorius found himself increasingly involved in business outside the sphere of defence and diplomacy. He was consulted on questions of public religion, stock theft, the purchase of coffee beans for planting purposes, the reform of the constitution. In short, as Van Heerden has demonstrated, in the years immediately before the drafting of the Rustenburg Constitution of 1858, Pretorius, though only one of four commandant-generals, was being required to act more and more as a head of state, and appeared to like things that way.

* * *

Firm guidelines were set for Boer constitutionalism when the Orange Free Staters sat down to work out a form of government after getting their independence back under the Bloemfontein Convention of February 1854.[5] They based their decisions on Cape Dutch and Voortrekker experience, but also on American and European precedents. Typically, the Free State constitution restricted the vote to male citizens of eighteen years and over, and limited citizenship to whites; but it did not include a confessional test. It provided for a unicameral Volksraad, all members being returned from single-member constituencies, as in Natalia. Executive government was placed in the hands of a State President, chosen for a five-year term, by direct public vote, from a list drawn up by the Volksraad, and re-eligible. He was given an executive council (*Uitvoerende Raad*) of officials and unofficials appointed by the Volksraad, and he was required to report annually to the Volksraad, in which he could initiate legislation but not vote. The Volksraad was to ratify his appointments to public office and confirm or reject his decisions over war and peace and external relations. He was expected to tour his republic annually like a Prussian king, so as to maintain contact with his people. The American influence, introduced mainly through the contributions of J. G. Groenendal, the State Secretary, and J. M. Orpen, Volksraad member for Harrismith, was seen, above all, in the preference given for a rigid constitution, amendment being by a three-quarters majority in three (later reduced to two) successive sessions, with the testing right as a safeguard. Judges held office during good behaviour, and could and did use the testing right when necessary. Until the establishment of a High Court in 1867 and of an Appeal Court in 1874, jurisdiction was shared between the Executive Council and a Circuit Court of United Landdrosts (1856–74). The constitution also contained within it the rudiments of a bill of rights, with its insistence on equality before the law, press freedom, and so on. Local government in the Free State, as in other Boer republics, was conducted by landdrosts in charge of districts, which were subdivided into wards under field cornets.

A Free State parliamentarian claimed with apparent conviction in 1930 that his 'pure white country' had brought no problems with it into the Union. Geographically in the middle, the Free State acquired the reputation of being ideologically in the middle, especially during the long presidency of J. H. Brand (1864–88), where relations between Boer and Briton were concerned. It contained many moderate Afrikaners as well as strong anti-Imperialists. English-speakers were welcome, and those who chose to identify themselves with the Republic, of whom J. M. Orpen and J. G. Fraser were good examples, could expect to reach the top in public life. English was commonly spoken in town and business life, even if Dutch alone was permitted in the Volksraad. Though all six Free State presidents were Afrikaners, the last three had strong English cultural ties: Brand had an English legal training and accepted an English knighthood, while Reitz had W. P. Schreiner as a brother-in-law, and Steyn normally wrote to his wife in English. Nor do later manifestations of apparent Afrikaner extremism – the 'bitter-end' resistence at the end of the Anglo-Boer War, and the Free Staters' role in the 1914 rebellion – necessarily diminish this image. The Free State nevertheless retained an essentially Afrikaner character because it never acquired a large Uitlander element (though it might easily have done had Brand managed to gain control over Griqualand West in 1871). Without the challenge of a dominant alien culture to disturb their complacency, Free Staters found that they could preserve the political values of the armed camp with remarkable ease. It may, as Van Aswegen has shown, have been the English-speaking traders who objected most strongly to the admission of Asian traders to the Republic in the 1880s, but it was the Volksraad, an Afrikaner body in essence, which first restricted their trading rights in 1885 and then banned their admission altogether in 1890. Similarly, the Free State was the only part of South Africa where it became legally impossible for a black person to become a landowner in his own right in the period before Union. The myth of the white nation with an exclusive claim to rights survived remarkably in the Free State, where at any given moment the black population was at least double the white in size.

There was a chance during the 1850s that the Orange Free State and the Transvaal might have amalgamated into a single republic. When M. W. Pretorius succeeded his father as head commandant in 1853, he kept up a steady pressure to this end, with the aid of allies south of the Vaal, but encountered strong opposition from the supporters of Presidents Hoffman and Boshoff. He eventually gained the presidency of both republics in February 1860, but the opposition on both sides of the Vaal proved insuperable.

Transvaal politics, to a greater extent than those of the Free State, were always hampered by the antagonisms of small trekker communities separated from each other by great distances. The United Volksraad found time and again that, for pressing reasons such as farming or military emergencies, it was impossible to raise a quorum for its quarterly sessions. There was no session, for example, between June 1854 and June 1855. They began therefore to take short cuts, and to place increased reliance on the device of a *kommissieraad*, which meant the members of the Raad who lived within range of the place selected for the meeting. On two occasions a kommissieraad declared itself to be a full volksraad (and therefore competent to take binding decisions) in respect of matters which concerned the locality where it met, but merely a *kommissie* (whose decisions required ratification) in respect of matters dealing with other regions. A reduction of the number of Volksraad sessions to one a year was contemplated, but the plan eventually followed in 1855 was to abandon the peripatetic Volksraad in favour of its location in a central capital, for which the ground was prepared by the purchase of two farms on the Aapies river on which to lay out Pretoria.

The controversy which had divided Potgieter from the Volksraad party in Ohrigstad developed after the establishment of the United Volksraad into a regional conflict between Lydenburg, where opinion was led by the survivors of the old Volksraad party, notably H. T. Bührmann and J. A. Smellekamp, and the western Transvalers under M. W. Pretorius. The issue on which conflict flared up was not that of strong versus popular government which had divided Retief from Maritz, and Potgieter from J. J. Burger, but an ecclesiastical one. Although the *Nederduitse Gereformeerde Kerk* (N.G.K.) of the Cape had refrained from giving official support to the Great Trek, from a reluctance to support what the authorities regarded as rebellion, it had nevertheless built churches at Potchefstroom, Rustenburg, Lydenburg and Schoemansdal between 1842 and 1852. But in 1853 a demand for an independent Voortrekker church led to the appointment of Ds. Dirk van der Hoff as minister of the Church in the Transvaal, with the endorsement of the United Volksraad. As if to emphasise the break with the Cape, the name *Nederduitsch Hervormde Kerk* (N.H.K.) was subsequently made definitive through its incorporation in the republican constitution. The Lydenburgers, who were not represented at the Volksraad in question, rejected Van der Hoff. Later, on receiving assurances that they would not be bound by British laws, or a British oath of allegiance, or any obligation to ban racial segregation in worship, they resolved to place themselves under the Cape Synod. This was anathema to the Volksraad, which punished Lydenburg by excluding its Volksraad members. The Lydenburgers decided to go their own way, and received strong backing from the Soutpansbergers at Schoemansdal, whose leader, Stephanus Schoeman, had married Potgieter's widow. Another Boer settlement at Utrecht, on the Buffalo river between Natal and Zululand, whose landdrost A. T. Spies was one of the Lydenburgers whom the Volksraad had decided to punish, also came out in support of Lydenburg.

These eastern Transvaal communities resented Volksraad pushfulness. When it tried to plant a constitution on the other centres, and set in motion a presidential election, which Pretorius won against W. F. Joubert in a very low poll, the Lydenburgers decided to elect their own independent Volksraad, and did so with the encouragement of President Boshoff of the Free State, who was paying Pretorius back in his own coin. Schoeman actually declared war on Pretorius in April 1857. Lydenburg and Soutpansberg resolved to set up a combined Volksraad in September.

Collision was averted at this point by the tact of Paul Kruger, who, though a follower of Pretorius, maintained contact with Schoeman through his brother, Douw Kruger, and brought the two together. Early in 1858 Pretorius offered a joint inquiry to revise the controversial constitution. This was accepted, and the result was the Rustenburg Grondwet of 1858, which proved acceptable to both parties. On 12 September 1859, therefore, the Volksraad of the South African Republic met in Pretoria for the first time, and on 4 December the Lydenburg and Utrecht Volksraads were incorporated in the Republic.

The Rustenburg Grondwet was largely the work of a Hollander, Jacobus Stuart. It was an untidy, rambling document, and like the Thirty-Three Articles, contained much that did not properly belong to a constitution at all. The framework of government was similiar to that of the Free State. A popularly elected President, presiding over an Executive Council, was to lead government business in a unicameral Volksraad elected by white burghers. So concerned were the Rustenburg law-makers to preserve the authority of the *volkswil* that they insisted on a three-quarters majority for every law passed, and a minimum period of three months between the first tabling of a measure and its enactment, so as to ensure that the public had plenty of time to react. This hurdle proved too stiff, and led to the short-cut practice of making laws by *besluit* (resolution) of a simple Volksraad majority. This undermined the authority of the constitution, and led eventually to the 'judges crisis' of 1897, when Chief Justice J. G. Kotze refused to recognise legislation made by *besluit*, but chose his ground badly and was dismissed from office by President Kruger. The Grondwet was more explicitly Calvinist than its Free State counterpart. It affirmed the allegiance of the Republic to the doctrines of the Nederuits Hervormde Kerk and restricted membership of the Volksraad to those who belonged to it. By putting the Commandant-General on the Executive Council and establishing that office, at last, as a permanent institution, the Rustenburg Grondwet also brought about a polarisation of power which could not develop in the Orange Free State, whose military commander was never more than an *ad hoc* military appointee without political status. In the unified Transvaal, the Commandant-Generalship became the focus of rival power during the civil war of 1860–4, and again later during the presidencies of T. F. Burgers and Paul Kruger.

Had it not been for his decision to accept the Free State presidency, M. W. Pretorius might well have enjoyed a peaceful reign in the South African Republic. But his acceptance of the double office in 1860, in face of warnings by Sir George Grey that such a union of crowns would be treated by Britain as a violation of the Conventions of 1852 and 1854, led the Transvaal Volksraad to suspend him, not as an act of no confidence, but as an act of caution. Instead of appointing Schoeman as Acting President, however, which as the senior member of the Volksraad he should have become in terms of the constitution, the Raad gave the office to J. H. Grobler, who resigned when he found that he did not have popular support. Schoeman was in a strong position, having effectively united the Krygsraad under his own control, even though Lydenburg had been given the right to its own Commandant-General when it joined the Republic in 1860. At first he bided his time; but when signs of support began to appear, he chose the moment of Grobler's resignation to force the Executive Council, in the presence of 150 armed men, to declare himself Acting President and make W. C. Janse van Rensburg his Commandant-General.

It was around Paul Kruger, a member of the Krygsraad whose star was clearly rising, that opposition to the Schoeman coup began to gather. Encouraged by Kruger's stand, the Volksraad censured Schoeman in April 1862, and defied him by choosing Van Rensburg as Acting President and (after some difficulty) T. J. Snyman as Commandant-General. Snyman had martial law proclaimed when Schoeman refused to submit. Schoeman dug in at Potchefstroom, but was dug out by Snyman and fled to the Free State. Returning in November, however, he reoccupied Potchefstroom, and in January 1863 entered Pretoria and drove out the High Court judges who were sitting in judgment on his own misdemeanours. Kruger and his Rustenburgers, however, expelled the Schoemanites and restored the court; and the court – as part of its attempt to restore harmony – ordered new elections for the presidency and the commandant-generalship. After unduly complex proceedings, involving two elections for each office, Van Rensburg emerged above Pretorius as President-elect on a recount, with Kruger overwhelmingly favoured for the military position. The Schoeman party, however, now led by the militant J. H. Viljoen of Marico, made one further bid for power. Kruger therefore had martial law declared for a second time, but even then the supporters of the Government had a hard fight in the Magaliesberg before eventually inducing Viljoen to sue for peace. Negotiations near the Crocodile river in January 1864 then ended the civil war. A fresh presidential election was held, and this time Pretorius turned the tables on Van Rensburg to begin an unbroken period of office which lasted seven years.

Pretorius's years as President saw the beginning of a sustained period of conflict with African chiefdoms, who strongly opposed attempts to extend the frontiers of the Republic [see pp. 106–10, 126].

The Republic also experienced religious divisions in these years.[6] That which occurred in 1859, when the *Gereformeerde Kerk* under Ds. Dirk Postma broke away from the Hervormdes, had little political importance. There were some signs in the Rustenburg area during the 1850s of opposition to the use of *Evangelische Gezange* (non-biblical hymns) in public worship, which had been the occasion of troubles in the Colesberg Ring of the Church in 1841; but the establishment of the *Gereformeerde* ('Dopper') *Kerk* resulted not from this but from an offer by the *Afgeskeie* (Separatist) *Gereformeerde Kerk* of the Netherlands to help the Republic to overcome its shortage of clergy. They sent Ds. Postma to the Transvaal and the Rustenburgers took him under their wing. The Ned. Hervormde Kerk decided guardedly to work with Postma, provided that he restricted his work to white people and did not enter the mission field, that he acknowledged the Reformed articles of belief, and refrained from seeking separate recognition of the Afgeskeie Kerk under the Grondwet. These were stiff demands. Postma and his followers, who included Paul Kruger, formed a separate church rather than accept them. In the course of the negotiations, Van der Hoff, for the Hervormdes, skilfully drew attention to the *Gezange* as the main issue of public difference, and thus diverted attention from the exclusive relationship with the State which the Hervormde Kerk continued to enjoy. Yet the Hervormdes and the Gereformeerdes remained, on the whole, on good terms with each other, and the Gereformeerdes threw their weight during the political conflicts of the 1860s behind the reconciliation of the warring groups. Both parties shared a common Transvaal patriotism and a common preference for traditional Dutch forms of religion.

The Schism of 1866, which led to the refounding of a *Nederduits Gereformeerde Kerk* in the Transvaal, was far more serious for the unity of the Republic. It was primarily associated with the activities of Ds. F. Lion Cachet, a mercurial Hollander of French-Jewish descent, who had been educated in Amsterdam, and then served as a minister at Ladysmith, before moving into the Republic to take charge of Utrecht. He then attacked the credentials of the Hervormde Kerk in the Transvaal, objecting to the name 'Hervormde', objecting to the theological liberalism which he claimed to find in its discipline and in its doctrine (at a time when the Cape Church, which had recently tried three of its own clergy for heresy, was particularly sensitive to the need for doctrinal precision), and successfully reopening the rift between the Hervormdes and the Lydenburg congregation which had been cemented by careful negotiation only in 1864. After a tour of the Transvaal settlements in 1865, Cachet convened a general assembly of all malcontents and reconstituted the N.G. Kerk, which failed to gain control of the baptismal registers and funds of the established Church, but managed to take root as a rival body and build up several congregations despite its shortage of clergy.

Cachet's movement was influential for a variety of reasons. Its professed loyalty to the N.G. Kerk of the Cape, even after the Cape Supreme Court had declared in Loedolff's Case in 1862 that the

Cape Synod had no jurisdiction outside the Colonial frontiers, kept alive the notion of N.G. congregations north of the Vaal with their own independent government. The Cape Synod had already sent several deputations northwards to discourage the breakaway of the Transvalers. It sent another in 1868, and one of its two members, Ds. J. P. Jooste, remained behind to become a N.G. minister in Potchefstroom in opposition to Ds. van der Hoff of the Hervormdes. He was ordained in the Potchefstroom Methodist Church, whose minister, Ludorf, was described by the historian of the Hervormdes as a 'well-known negrophile'. Concern for the blacks, indeed, became a characteristic of the Transvaal N.G. clergy, whereas the Hervormde Synod at first took a strong line against mission work. N.G. clergy sometimes denounced Transvaal Boer race attitudes. Cachet, for example, attacked Transvaal 'slavery', as did his associate, Ds. P. Huet of Pietermaritzburg, whose *Het Lot der Zwarten in Transvaal*, published in 1869, provided ammunition for external critics of the Republic and attracted the wrath of the authorities for what they claimed to be atrocity-mongering.

The role of the N.G. predikants as 'white ants' of Republican independence was therefore of particular significance, especially after the start of the Burgers regime. Engelbrecht goes so far as to argue that they were a key factor in the fall of the Republic in 1877, suggesting the existence of an alliance between them and unprincipled fortune-seekers on the goldfields at Pilgrim's Rest and in the Transvaal towns. Cachet did argue for the overthrow of the Republic, even if he completely changed his tune in 1882, when his *Worstelstrijd der Transvalers* appeared. Others to advocate British annexation were Jooste and N. J. R. Swart. The latter, who had been trained as a Gereformeerde minister under Postma, switched in 1871 to the Anglican Church and abandoned a clerical career to become Government Secretary, first under Burgers, then under Shepstone, and was considered by some to be Shepstone's informer on Burgers's Executive Council.

The ecclesiastical picture in the Transvaal on the eve of the annexation becomes clearer once it is realised that when T. F. Burgers went to the Transvaal to conduct his presidential campaign in 1872, he was drawn towards the Hervormde Kerk. In his *Schetzen uit de Transvaal* he admitted to having arrived with some prejudice against the Hervormdes, but then noted that they had shown a lack of 'hard-necked and blind dogmatism' of the kind he had experienced in the Cape, and manifested a traditional Dutch outlook untainted by the influences of Scottish Calvinism. To the Transvaal N.G. clergy, on the other hand, Burgers was a convicted heretic. His flamboyant personality and modernist theological views hardly seemed to provide the right formula for electoral success in a Boer republic, even if his acquaintance with Charles Darwin was not generally known; but with Pretorius's diplomatic failure at Bloemhof fresh in the public mind, he won the presidential election of 1872 with only 388 votes cast against him.

Burgers failed more sensationally than any other Transvaal head of state, but his performance needs to be measured against the difficulty of his task, and neither was negligible. Without intending to divide the people on religious issues, he came in for sharp criticism from the N.G. church leaders for his Education Act of 1874, for allowing Biblical studies during school hours but permitting confessional instruction only afterwards. After the Macmahon arbitration had awarded Lourenço Marques to Portugal rather than Britain in 1875, Burgers did spend unwisely the funds which he raised in Europe the following year to build a railway from the coast. Where the Pretorius Government had faced difficulties with the Venda, Burgers had trouble with the Pedi. Paul Kruger, his Commandant-General, resigned from office in 1873, and for reasons of economy the commandant-generalship was abolished soon after – some said as a calculated bid by Burgers to destroy Kruger's influence. Burgers assumed command in the field, and failed to dislodge the Pedi from strong positions which they defended with firearms; while his attempt to raise a special war tax was widely defied. Yet in February 1877, shortly before Shepstone's annexation, Sekhukhune was persuaded to ask for peace [see p. 107].

Soon after Sir Theophilus Shepstone's arrival in Pretoria in January 1877, Burgers convened a special session of the Volksraad for 13 February, and warned against the special danger to the State's independence implicit in Shepstone's mission. He submitted the draft of a revised constitution, the chief feature of which was a plan to strengthen the Executive Council by converting it into something like a presidential cabinet, together with proposals for an improved method of raising revenue. The Raad at first rejected Burgers's proposals on the motion of H. T. Bührmann, a Hollander who had arrived at Ohrigstad in 1848 and played a prominent but perhaps irresponsible role in public affairs as a democrat who too easily found signs of executive tyranny in church and state. Before the session ended, Burgers had been granted a new Executive, into which he brought Kruger as Vice-President; but he received no authority to introduce the urgently needed tax reforms. Kruger's role was equivocal. He had not taken part in the campaign against Sekhukhune. Too good a politician and too loyal a Transvaler to allow personal antipathy alone to determine his political conduct, he had initially served under Burgers because he was head of state by popular decision, and therefore, as Kruger saw it, by divine command. But before the end of 1876 he reversed his decision not to stand for president in the election due the following year, and began to build up an organised opposition to Burgers in the early months of 1877. He took no decisive stand in support of Republican independence until after Shepstone's annexation had taken place [see pp. 129–32].

From the angle of Boer politics, the British occupation removed Burgers and his followers from the scene and promoted the political careers of Paul Kruger and Piet Joubert, but effected no more than a brief interruption in the history of the state. That occupation still awaits its historian. De Kiewiet, whose treatment is the fullest, is highly critical of its failure to set right those things which had provided the pretext for annexation, above all the financial weakness which had led the Republic's creditors to start calling in their debts. Not only was Shepstone starved of funds because, as he was told, 'Parliament does not like to have to pay even for what it theoretically approves', but the actual administration of the funds at his disposal was lax and irresponsible.

Paul Kruger's leadership of the Triumvirate, in association with Piet Joubert and M. W. Pretorius, through whom the opposition to British rule was increasingly canalised, gave him a standing in the estimation of his people which he never lost. A son of the Trek, a tough frontiersman to whom tales of valour clung rather as if he was a folk hero straight out of the *Book of Judges*, this natural man of the people was also an intense Calvinist Christian, with a basic integrity not always apparent as he twisted and turned, gave ground or stood firm, to preserve his Republic from Imperial encirclement, from materialist undermining, from English cultural domination, and from insolvency. His record of resistance to British rule gave his eighteen-year presidency an impressive start. First elected in 1883, he won three further contests in 1888, 1893, and 1898, demonstrating on the last occasion that he had an immense backing among his people, two years before his Government was brought down by defeat in the Anglo-Boer War and he left, a forlorn suppliant, for exile in Holland.

Kruger's was not a united republic, however. For a start, the religious divisions among his people persisted. In the afterglow of military victory, an over-hasty amalgamation of the Hervormde and the N.G. churches, for which the ground had been prepared under British rule, was carried through between 1882 and 1885, without full consultation of the congregations. In the resultant backlash, a number of Hervormde congregations subsequently opted out of the new *Nederduits Hervormde of Gereformeerde Kerk*, or *Verenigde* [United] *Kerk* as the amalgamated body came to be less cumbrously known. There were accompanying legal wrangles as the Verenigde Kerk insisted on its constitutional rights. Kruger tried and failed to restore harmony at a conference over which he presided in August 1891. Engelbrecht has suggested that the anti-Hollander feeling which developed in the Republic in the 1890s was in part an overspill of N.G. opposition to the Hervormdes, generated by the Verenigde Kerk, which was the spiritual home of most of Kruger's Afrikaner opponents. Its Synod attacked the 1891

Education Act of Dr Nicolaas Mansvelt with vigour, as being Dutch rather than Afrikaans in spirit.

Kruger also had to cope with the intrusion of Uitlander gold-seekers in embarrassingly large numbers, whose presence threatened to engulf the impoverished and essentially rural society over which he ruled. He tried to milk the wealth of the intruders through the sale of concessions – to A. H. Nellmapius, for example, for the making of brandy, to Eduard Lippert for the sale and distribution of dynamite, and many others. He tried to secure his regime by building up vested interests which were loyal, one being the Netherlands South Africa Railway Company, which looked after all railway-building within the Republic. It was the largest of the Dutch concessionaires. This element, on whom Kruger relied for support and service, included Dr W. J. Leyds, his State Secretary and roving diplomat, and Dr Nicolaas Mansvelt, his second Superintendent-General of Education. J. B. Robinson, however, the Langlaagte mining tycoon, whose support Kruger cultivated to provide a counterweight to the Fitzpatricks, Beits and Farrars who dominated the Uitlander community, was a son of an 1820 Settler and brother of the William Robinson who had been Kruger's choice for president in 1872.

But a policy of favourites brought enemies. Kruger's concessions became a target, not only for the Uitlander community, which resented the dynamite monopoly in particular, but also for opponents within the Boer community. General Piet Joubert, the Commandant-General, and Ds. S. J. du Toit, the founder of the Afrikaner Bond, who had been Superintendant-General of Education from 1881 to 1890, objected to Kruger's railway policy in the 1880s because they had an interest in the firm of Lewis and Marks who planned to build a railway from Kimberley to the Rand, which Kruger would not allow. They mounted an attack on the concession policy across a broad front. Kruger, for his part, had used Joubert and Du Toit as scapegoats for the failure of his attempt in 1884 to incorporate the Republics of Stellaland and Goshen. Because they were chairman and secretary respectively of the Afrikaner Bond in the Transvaal, Kruger's opposition to these two members of his Executive Council was a direct cause of the Bond's failure to establish itself in the Republic. The development of internal Boer opposition to Kruger, which C. T. Gordon has described, grew essentially out of these antecedents. Joubert, who fought Kruger in all four presidential campaigns and came within close reach of him in 1893, headed a 'Progressive' party in the Volksraad which consisted almost entirely of Afrikaners, its nucleus being Schalk Burger, Louis Botha, J. H. de la Rey, Lukas Meyer, General N. J. Smit (the victor of Majuba), Ewald Esselen and Carl Jeppe. They relied very little on English mining support, and had no tie-up with the Uitlander leaders. They could muster eight to eleven votes out of twenty-four in the

First Volksraad in 1893, and perhaps ten out of twenty-seven as late as 1899. They were clear thinkers, generally humane in outlook. They attacked concessions, favours to Hollanders, and corruption. But they had no caucus, no programme, no organisation, and in Joubert a leader who lacked Kruger's steadfastness and consistency. They showed that it was easier to reform Kruger's Government than to remove it, for Kruger did bend to some of their demands, especially by cutting back on favours to Hollanders and by giving J. C. Smuts, State Attorney from 1897, a free hand to reform the Law Department.

In a homogeneous Afrikaner community the Kruger Government could perhaps have built up a moderate reformist image, but in the shadow of the Uitlander presence this was not an easy reputation to earn.[7] From the start, the restored Republic was jealous to preserve its identity and its control over its own affairs. This can be seen, for example, in the rejection under the London Convention of 1884 of those elements of subservience accepted in the Pretoria Convention of 1881: the rejection, that is, of Imperial control over native policy, Imperial direction of the Republic's foreign relations, and the Imperial right to move troops through the Republic at will. But it can be seen, above all, in the decision to restrict Uitlander votes by the imposition of a five-year delay and a high £25 naturalisation fee which immigrants could normally be expected not to want to pay.

Uncertainty over the relative numerical strength of Boer and Uitlander voters added an element of mystery to debates over the franchise, especially as Boers were inclined to exaggerate the number of Uitlanders in order to demonstrate the seriousness of the threat, while Uitlanders inflated their own numbers to demonstrate the injustice of their not being enfranchised. The extent to which Uitlanders actually wanted the vote became a debating point as well, for many were birds of passage, while enfranchisement involved the duties of citizenship, including commando service. Kruger's Government became alarmed about the Uitlander franchise in 1890, when the flow of immigrants began to increase. It therefore reduced the naturalisation fee to £5, but increased the waiting period before a new immigrant could actually cast a vote to fourteen years from the date of arrival – by most standards an inordinately long delay. The simultaneous creation of a Second Volksraad, elected on a much less rigid franchise, was intended as a sop to Uitlander feelings. This body initated some useful legislation, but its laws required endorsement by the First Volksraad, so it was seen to be a device of the Government to avoid having to share power with a community which provided the Republic with a very sizeable proportion of its public wealth.

The Uitlanders began to challenge the Boer monopoly of power when Charles Leonard founded his National Union in 1892, from which moment serious Boer–Uitlander tensions bedevilled public life. The

Jameson Raid of December 1895 damaged their relationship beyond recall. Although Blainey's ingenious thesis that it was a desperate bid by deep-level mining interests to overthrow a regime whose policies were the direct cause of its financial losses has been shown by R. V. Kubicek to be an overstatement, it immensely heightened the mutual suspicions of the majority of capitalists and the Kruger Government. The Government not only resolved to resist their effective enfranchisement to the last, but also did its best after 1895 to drive a wedge between the capitalists and the Uitlander rank and file by giving support to a new workers' propaganda organ, the *Standard and Diggers' News*. This in turn led the Uitlander leaders to exaggerate the franchise issue in order to keep the Uitlander community together, and in doing so to appeal to the Imperial Government for help.

For the Kruger regime, policy calculations in this atmosphere were difficult to make. Fully effective political concessions would have transformed the character of the Republic. Partial concessions could perhaps have brought about a Progressive–Uitlander coalition and destroyed the basis of Kruger's power, though there was a chance it would also have split the Uitlander front since many of them were not Britishers and would have been content with a revolution which stopped short of a restoration of the Union Jack. The main disadvantage in not treating the Uitlanders fairly was that this gave the Colonial Office a cover behind which to build up its campaign for what it was really after: not so much the extension of Uitlander rights, as the achievement of paramountcy throughout southern Africa, which was not possible without the political control of its richest area.

Kruger's Republic had mellowed considerably from the cluster of warring communities of the period 1837–64. But its administration was fairly corrupt and its burghers in general were poor, relatively unenterprising, and – except for the school-goers of the 1890s – not very well educated. They had little desire to admit to equality men who did not share the Afrikaner's language, his Protestantism, and his interest in the preservation of their group power and security in a land full of potential enemies. The Republic ended by fighting and losing a war to protect itself from such a change. For reasons to be considered later, and which the Kruger Government could not have counted on, its defeated ex-burghers then won the peace and regained access to effective political power.

# 6 British Colonies

The institutions and the ethos of the Cape Colony and Natal acquired a recognisably British character; but these colonies were by no means identical. In the ethnic composition of their populations and their general attitudes over racial questions; in the cultural, religious and linguistic balance of these various elements; and above all, perhaps, in the depth of historical experience to which each could look back during the second half of the nineteenth century, the differences were profound. But their combined influence was such that, when the Union of South Africa came into being in 1910, the English language received not merely equal status with Dutch, but remained dominant in the early years; and the forms of government adopted by the Union were a much closer reflection of British than of Voortrekker institutions.

The Cape in 1850 was dominated by an English-speaking element largely urban, official, mercantile and professional in character, which rested on a numerically larger but recessive Dutch (Afrikaans)-speaking community, both depending in turn on the services of Coloured and African peoples. In the west, these comprised the Malay artisans and fisherfolk of the Cape peninsula and the Coloured farm labourers, who had been domestic and predial slaves only a few years earlier, and were still getting used to legal emancipation – the urban Coloured successfully, on account of their continuing access to the skilled trades; the rural Coloured rather less so, on account of their general landlessness, lack of schooling, and lack of bargaining power. In the east, with the line of equilibrium running roughly north-south through Graaff-Reinet, the workers on the farms were mainly Khoisan and Africans. The latter had moved in from Kaffraria and from regions north of the middle Orange, into the eastern parts of the Colony and the Cape midlands.

In the larger towns the language of public communication was English, which acquired a special protection under the constitution of 1853. In the rural areas, the laws were promulgated in English and Dutch, but colloquial Afrikaans had for years been the means of communication between farmers and their Coloured *volk*. English farmers in the east, thanks to the industry of missionary educators, were often proficient in Xhosa. Once dominant, the Dutch element was weakened numerically by the Trek. Many of the deserted midland farms were acquired by English-speakers with an eye to wool profits, and the Dutch culture went through a barren period as English came to be used more and more in public business, education, and sometimes even in the worship of the Dutch Reformed Church. But the hold of Dutch was not broken in the country districts, so that when movements developed in the western and the north-eastern Cape in the 1870s for a Dutch-Afrikaans cultural and political revival, the leaders found a ready response across a very wide constituency.

On the broader cultural plane, the addition of a Griqua element based on Kokstad and Kimberley between 1876 and 1880, and the enormous increase in the Bantu-speaking population with the incorporation of the Ciskei (1865), the Transkei (between 1879 and 1894), and for a time Basutoland (1871–84), gave the Cape considerable regional differences. This contrasted with the situation in Natal, where whites were dispersed among a relatively larger Bantu-speaking population; where very few descendants of earlier Khoi, San or slave elements could be found; and where the arrival in 1860 of the first of many shiploads of indentured Indian labourers to work on the sugar plantations radically altered the composition of the population within a few years. Natal whites sensed the numerical pressure of their African and Indian neighbours with growing anxiety, and this led them, well before Union, to place severely discriminatory political and economic legislation on their statute book, whereas the Cape whites developed a posture which came to be recognised as rather more liberal. The difference was marginal, but it was reflected in actual differences in their laws.

Liberalism, then as now, was a word of many meanings.[1] It was sometimes connected with ideas of civil liberty, sometimes with political democracy, sometimes with the notion of free trade, sometimes with freedom of thought, especially religious thought. The most distinctive feature of nineteenth-century liberalism, in the southern African experience, was a concern for the rights of other cultural groups which, being relatively rare, was treated as suspect, as a dishonest masquerade under the cloak of religion, or as an exotic plant which could not be expected to acclimatise. 'Kafferboetie' and 'Pro-Boer' became terms of abuse, though there was something impressive about the efforts of a Saul Solomon or an Olive Schreiner to defend the black underdog, of an Onze Jan Hofmeyr to reach accommodation with the English-speaking community, and of a John X. Merriman to stand up for the rights of the Afrikaner. Liberals were often paternalists, and in the late nineteenth century they found the logic of their position harder to defend: whether for example to support, or to oppose, the extension of low franchise qualifications to blacks in the Transkei who had no experience of a western electoral system, when such an extension might materially affect the political balance in the Colony; or whether to maintain, or to remove, all restrictions on the sale of the white man's liquor to Africans, when to retain restrictions was to afford necessary protection, but also to deny recognition of adulthood.

The progress of the Cape towards self-government took a course similar to that of British colonies of conquest and settlement elsewhere.[2] As in French Canada, a governor with arbitrary power replaced the military rule of the conquest era. As in New South Wales, the Governor was provided in due course with a Council of officials (1825), whose advice he could ignore, but not without explanation to the Secretary of State. After the arrival of the 1820 Settlers, who carried with them something of the political ferment of post-Napoleonic Britain, the Government at the Cape came under pressure from a small group of radical democrats in both the eastern and the western Cape, who waged a successful compaign for the freedom of the press and for some measure of political representation. The Government bent before the storm by permitting a free press and by adding unofficial nominees to the Council of Advice in 1827. It set up a new Legislative Council in 1834; but the latter body was not elective, and was given little chance to spread its wings. Governors kept the unofficial element small, and on a tight rein. When the Colonial Office persuaded the Governor in 1849 to admit a shipload of Irish ex-prisoners as settlers, this unleashed a vehement public outcry which showed British and Dutch that Cape colonials working together could have strong political opinions and make life very difficult for the Government and its supporters. After most of the unofficials had resigned rather than face public chastisement, Governor Sir Harry Smith called for an informal expression of public opinion by asking municipal and road boards to suggest the names of replacements. They voted overwhelmingly for men from the western Cape. Smith tried to rectify the balance by including one name which was lower on the list, that of Robert Godlonton, editor of the *Graham's Town Journal* and a leader of eastern separatist opinion. But this alienated some of the successful majority at a time when the Whig Government in Great Britain, in which Earl Grey was the Colonial Secretary, wanted to encourage the adoption of representative government by the Cape. It threatened again to expose political divisions between the eastern and western Cape.

Eastern Separatists stood for different things at different times. Sometimes, though only rarely, they wanted complete political separation from Cape Town. At others, as during the frontier war of 1834–1835, they wanted the removal of the seat of government from Cape Town to the eastern districts. The term could also be used to cover some kind of federal solution, involving either a straight subdivision of the Colony into an eastern and a western province, or a tripartite division which allowed for some kind of separate midland province which could hold the balance between east and west. Over and above this tendency towards fission on geographical lines, there also developed a real danger of division over colour issues, for the outbreak of the eastern frontier war of 1850, followed by the Kat River Rebellion of 1851, created a sense of nervousness even among whites of the western Cape which threatened to cut across London's insistence that there should be reasonable opportunity for the enfranchisement of blacks.

After difficult negotiations, a constitution was eventually adopted in 1853, with the approval of the Secretary of State. This tried to cater for both eastern and western interests and at the same time give some political power to indigenous blacks. It made provision for a two-chamber parliament in which the western province received fractionally greater representation in both houses than the eastern. It also laid down relatively low qualifications for the franchise, admitting to the vote males of any race who earned £50 a year or occupied a site and structure together worth £25. The Colonial Office had inclined, on balance, to a lower rather than a higher franchise qualification, which had the support both of English-speaking liberals like John Fairbairn and of Dutch farmers who hoped that they and their Coloured *volk* might together hold the balance against the richer Englishmen of the towns.

Representative government at the Cape had an easy infancy during the governorship of Sir George Grey (1854–61).[3] He was an autocrat lucky enough to rule during the prosperous years of the Namaqualand copper boom, who dominated his executive without having to fight it over the principles of politics or public finance [see pp. 101, 124–6].

Sir Philip Wodehouse, who succeeded Grey in 1861, thought, like Lord John Russell in the 1830s, that colonial self-government within the Empire was a contradiction in terms. But he paid more attention to the advice of his executive than Grey had done. He ran into trouble with his legislature, however, by proposing big increases of direct and indirect taxation to offset the deficits which hit the Colony from 1864. When he proposed to abolish the upper house as an economy measure, public opposition, suspicious of his political motives, forced him to abandon the plan. Wodehouse's popularity was not increased when the Colonial Office required him to press the annexation of British Kaffraria on the Cape, which became responsible, after its incorporation as the Ciskei in 1865, for the cost of its administration and defence.

Resistance by the Colonial Parliament to Wodehouse's policies led the Gladstone Ministry in 1869 to urge the extension of full responsible government to the Colony, if possible as the nucleus for a federated South Africa, incorporating at least Natal, Basutoland (annexed by Wodehouse on behalf of the Imperial Government in 1868), Griqualand West (annexed by Sir Henry Barkly in 1871), and the Boer Republics as well. A federated South Africa, enriched by the revenue accruing from the recent discovery of diamonds, and from a boom in wool exports, would be able to pay for its own defence and administration and relieve the Imperial Government of this burden. Boer republican opposition to British annexations north of the Orange River induced a mood of non-cooperation in the Cape legislature, which was reinforced by a natural reluctance to accept responsibility for the control of new frontiers. But Sir Henry Barkly, who had already introduced responsible government in Jamaica and operated it in the radical Colony of Victoria, was able in 1872, on his second attempt, to persuade the Cape Parliament to accept it by a narrow majority. As he had also managed to bring about the incorporation of Basutoland in the Colony in 1871, Barkly went some way towards realising the Gladstonian objectives.

Separatism, however, remained a divisive factor in Cape public life, largely because the formula agreed upon under the constitution of 1853 had not given the easterners the security which they required. A powerful Separation League grew up in Port Elizabeth and Grahamstown in 1860, and used the easterners' indignation over what seemed to be an unfair allocation of public funds for development to press for total political separation of east and west. Easterners had found it impossible during the Wodehouse era to block western schemes, even by the most determined filibusters. The stamina of the resident parliamentarians could always outdistance that of the visitors, and it was only on the occasion of the Grahamstown Parliament of 1864, called by Wodehouse as a sop to the easterners, that the westerners experienced similar treatment in reverse. By that time, however, the lines of division in Cape politics were becoming more complex. The incorporation of the Ciskei in the Colony created a new regional interest less antagonistic to Cape Town than to Port Elizabeth, which was East London's chief rival for the eastern wool trade. When the diamond fields were opened in the 1870s, a new kind of rivalry developed between Grahamstown and Graaff-Reinet, each competing for the possession of the main road and rail routes from Port Elizabeth to the interior. Graaff-Reinet became disenchanted with the easterners' cause, began to cultivate a 'midland' identity, and chose a Capetonian as one of its representatives in Parliament. But because of the new prosperity of the diamond era, when Port Elizabeth obtained a major share of Kimberley's overland trade as well as of the wool export trade, the separatist movement lost much of its drive.

It had its last formal fling in a petition drawn up in Port Elizabeth in 1872. This followed soon after Barkly's appointment of a federation commission which heard a great deal of evidence in favour of dividing the Cape into three provinces, so that the midlands could act as a counterweight to the rival pulls of east and west. Just at this time, when the Colony was in the throes of accepting responsible government, legislative subdivision was found unacceptable. The result was a compromise in 1874. The Cape Parliament carried a Seven Circles Act, which set up seven electoral provinces as constituencies for the upper house, including a midland province, and thus removed the structural reason for suspicion between east and west. A political ghost was thereby exorcised by a minor constitutional change, creating greater flexibility at the seat of power and giving an additional stimulus to country voters, who now discovered that they had a good chance of securing the election of farmers to upper house seats. Farmers' associations with an interest in political questions began to take root in the eastern Cape and the midlands. But this was not quite the end of the separatist story. The first Cape prime minister, J. C. Molteno (1872–8), represented the midland constituency of Beaufort West, and held the balance until Lord Carnarvon tried to foist a federal constitution on South Africa which appeared to involve the separation of the eastern and the western Cape as distinct units in a larger federal system. Carnarvon's plan was firmly rejected by Molteno's Government, which represented mainly western Cape interests; but Molteno was himself subsequently dismissed from office by Sir Bartle Frere, following a disagreement over the conduct of the frontier war of 1877–8, to be replaced by J. G. Sprigg, whose political base was East London, and whose ministerial colleagues all came from the east and midlands. One of his Government's first legislative acts was the imposition of an excise duty on spirits, the incidence of which could be expected to fall far more heavily on the western districts than on the eastern. The formation by Jan Hofmeyr in 1878 of a predominantly western, Dutch-speaking farmers' association, the *Boeren Beschermings Vereeniging*, to resist this tax, showed that the pattern of dominance had for the first time changed. It also marked the moment of transition in Cape politics from a period of regional tension to a period of ethnic Anglo-Boer antagonism.

The Afrikaner political and cultural revival began in the mid-1870s, at a time when the use of the Dutch language seemed to be in danger of disappearing from public life, and when confrontation between the British and Republican governments over policy in Basutoland and Griqualand West was at the same time beginning to inflame the Afrikaner's national pride. Its focal point was Paarl, where a group of clergy and teachers founded the *Genootskap van Regte Afrikaners* 'to stand for our language, our nation and our land'. The Genootskap acquired a printing press, put out the first newspaper in Afrikaans, *Die Afrikaanse Patriot*, and published its own history book, *Die Geskiedenis van ons Land in die Taal van ons Volk*, and a range of school textbooks. In 1879, the *Patriot* began to advocate the formation of a broad Afrikaner organisation to coordinate the activities of the Genootskap, Hofmeyr's B.B.V., the Transvaal *Volkskomité* which was organising resistance to British rule, and other kindred bodies. This was realised with the founding of the first branches of the *Afrikaner Bond* in 1880. The Bond originated in the Cape, but it soon set up branches in the Orange Free State and Transvaal as well, once the Transvaal had regained its independence in 1881. Its prime movers were the brothers S. J. and D. F. du Toit, the former a minister of the N.G. Kerk, the latter a schoolmaster and editor of the *Patriot*. The Bond strongly attacked the spread of British influence at the expense of traditional Afrikaner ways, and adopted the rigorous neo-Calvinism of Dr Abraham Kuyper of the Netherlands as a defence against the culture of 'liquor, lucre and redcoats' which they seized upon as the symbols of British conquest. It was directed more against Imperial rule than against English-speaking colonials, though this distinction was often lost on contemporaries. A united South Africa under its own flag, but with the Imperial navy as the first line of defence, became the Bond's advertised political goal. The tone of its propaganda offended not only Jan Hofmeyr, who saw the Bond as a rival to his own B.B.V., but also President Brand of the Orange Free State, who regarded it as subversive.

Hofmeyr, however, using the Bond's own procedures for branch formation, managed to infiltrate the movement by founding his own branch in Cape Town, and gradually gained control over its parliamentary caucus from 1883, by which time S. J. du Toit had become Superintendent-General of Education in Kruger's South African Republic. The Bond's aims were softened. A united South Africa under its own flag now became the final 'destiny' rather than the final objective; the association of the Bond with neo-Calvinism was broken, especially through the adoption of a moderate Programme of Principles in 1889; and the pan-South African character of the movement gradually disappeared, chiefly because the Bond in the Tranvaal, under the leadership of General Piet Joubert and S. J. du Toit, crossed swords with Kruger and lost its fight with him for the support of Transvaal Afrikaners.

After 1883, thanks to the influence of Hofmeyr and to changing political and economic circumstances, the antagonism between the white communities in the Cape gradually lessened. Bondsmen and the members of English-speaking farmers' congresses became increasingly aware of their common concerns as farmers and as citizens of the Cape Colony, especially after the discovery of gold on the Rand in 1886 had given the South African Republic a chance to go its own way economically, threatening to deprive the Cape of railway and customs revenue which close association with the Republic could have produced. Bondsmen, like the Cape merchants, accordingly threw their weight behind attempts to achieve a South African Customs Union; and after a short period of divided counsels, they also came down in favour of the extension of the Cape railway system into the Orange Free State and the South African Republic.

For more than a decade, the Afrikaner Bond was the only organised party in the Cape Parliament, but it did not have a majority in either house. Consequently Hofmeyr, who was its parliamentary leader from 1879 till he resigned his seat in 1895, tried to ensure Bond dominance by entering into alliance with well-disposed politicians, encouraging them to accept office on terms agreeable to the Bond. J. G. Sprigg had been opposed by both the Bond and the B.B.V. during the first ministry (1879–81), but T. C. Scanlen (1881–4) enjoyed the backing of the Bond until it went against his plans to encourage the Imperial Government to take control of the Transkei, Basutoland and Bechuanaland in 1883–4. Sir Thomas Upington (1884–7), who was Hofmeyr's next choice, fought the Bondmen's economic battles prior to the discovery of gold, just as Sprigg did during his second term (1887–90) in the matter of customs and railway policy. But Hofmeyr switched his support to Rhodes in 1890, when the latter offered good prospects for Cape farmers and speculators in central Africa at a time when the Transvaal was dragging its heels. This alliance remained firm, despite a cabinet crisis in 1893, until the calamitous Jameson Raid of December 1895. It was an alliance of mutual advantage to both Rhodes and the Bond. The former was, above all, anxious to establish a strong power base in the Cape Parliament for his enterprises beyond the Colony's borders. The Bondsmen, in addition to gaining the opportunity of participating as individuals in Rhodes's enterprises, through the acquisition of farms in Charterland or (in the case of some leaders) the acquisition of Chartered shares at par when they were unobtainable even at a great premium on the open market, found their interests as farmers helped in a variety of ways: by the creation of a Ministry of Agriculture, by steps taken to improve the Colony's breeding stock, to establish a fruit export industry, and to bring the farmers closer to their markets in the big towns through the construction of a few important rail links. Rhodes also seems to have subsidised the Bond press.

So strong were the ties between Rhodes and the Bond, that although Hofmeyr broke with Rhodes immediately after the Jameson Raid, it was only at its Malmesbury congress in 1897 that the Bond formally followed suit. Even then a small group, led by S. J. du Toit, who had apparently become dependent on Rhodes after returning from the Transvaal in 1890, refused to completely disown him. The Raid created a vacuum in Cape politics. When Sprigg formed his third, caretaker ministry in January 1896, the Bondsmen had had no time to make terms with him. Public opinion quickly polarised in the aftermath of the Raid and they soon withdrew their support. For the first time, something like a two-party system now appeared in Cape politics.

English-speaking elements set up a South African League in the Cape, Transvaal and Natal. By 1898, when the investigations into the Raid in South Africa and in London were over, Rhodes felt free to return to public life, and in the general election of that year he appealed to the voters as the leader of a new Progressive Party, the first political movement with Colony-wide organisation at the constituency level which had ever presumed to challenge the Bond. The Council elections were close, and the Progressives just pulled ahead. The Assembly elections were even closer, but this time the Bond and its allies won a narrow victory. The new governor, Sir Alfred Milner, asked W. P. Schreiner, who had served as Attorney-General in Rhodes's cabinet, to form a government. The Raid had brought Hofmeyr and Schreiner together, and they worked in close partnership with each other during the critical months prior to the Anglo-Boer War, both working hard to preserve peace between the Imperial Government and the South African Republic, or – if that were impossible – to ensure that the Cape's involvement in the conflict was minimal.

African participation in the political life of the Cape Colony was slow to develop, though many of the thousands who passed through Lovedale and the other mission schools found their way into the professions and the public service. Attempts by Mfengu to register for the vote in large numbers were not very successful in 1866, though Mfengu votes seem to have helped George Wood in the Legislative Council election of 1869. In 1871 the Attorney-General commented on the general failure of Africans to make use of their political rights.

The frontier war of 1877–8 did much to undermine the confidence of African leaders in the merits of white rule, driving some of them into rebellion. After that war, members of the traditional and educated élites were drawn increasingly into political involvement, provoked by such measures as the disarmament legislation and the tighter pass controls introduced by the Sprigg Government. McCracken provides evidence of a notable growth of interest in the vote among Africans during the middle 1880s in particular centres such as Queenstown, Victoria East, Fort Beaufort and Aliwal North. Some people built substantial homes in order to qualify. African voters numbered almost a quarter of the electorate in 1892, by which time the fall in their numbers caused by a stiff Registration Act of 1887 had been made good. As a result of the Franchise and Ballot Act of 1892, which raised the property qualification from £25 to £75, the rate of increase of the African electorate slowed down, whereas that of the European did not. The African voting strength fell to about 15 per cent of the total – about half that of the Coloured electorate, but still enough to cause candidates some concern in perhaps a third of the constituencies.

Although the Cape Afrikaners were just beginning to combine to win political power, Africans were constrained from embarking on a similar campaign, because they needed to adopt the Englishman's culture rather than break away from it, even though the founding of independent churches like Nehemiah Tile's Thembu Church of 1884 (the precursor of many others), revealed a deep desire to run their own things their own way. Asked to stand for Parliament in 1884, therefore, Tengo Jabavu declined for fear of alienating the support of his English associates. In 1886, Pambani Mzimba, subsequently the leader of a Lovedale secession movement, recommended his fellow-Africans to seek more schooling rather than more political power. It was more appropriate to awaken Africans' awareness through the classroom than to organise them expressely for politics: hence Elijah Makiwane's Native Educational Association, founded between 1879 and 1882. But some confrontation was unavoidable, even for a man like Jabavu. After taking on the editorship of *Isigidimi SamaXhosa*, the Xhosa section of Lovedale's *Christian Express*, in 1881, he abandoned the assignment after three years because the mission discouraged political commentary. He then started a new paper, *Imvo Zabantsundu*, in 1884, and used its columns to promote the election to Parliament of the liberal James Rose Innes, assisted by a Native Electoral Association which Jabavu had also founded.

Religious sectarianism tended to divide the African leadership, and a realisation that this was so apparently underlay the establishment of an 'Aborigines Association', *Imbumba Yama Afrika*, in 1882, to whose conferences Africans of all denominations were to be admitted. Its members were told to 'fight together', as the whites did, though they were members of different churches. There were special difficulties with regard to the achievement of unity in the eastern Cape on account of the deep-seated antagonism between Xhosa and Mfengu which dated from the Mfecane and the British settlement. Jabavu was Mfengu, and the Mfengu were the first Cape Africans to become politically involved. As editor of *Imvo* he used his influence to oppose movements of the *Imbumba* type which threatened, while attacking his own authority, to revive the Mfengu–Xhosa feud. In this situation, the general election of 1898 acquired critical importance. Jabavu switched his allegiance from Rhodes's Progressives to the Afrikaner Bond because his personal allies, Merriman and Sauer, had done the same. But the Progressives built up support among Jabavu's rivals, men such as the Rev. Walter Rubusana of East London, who had acquired an American doctorate for a work on South African history, and Meshach Pelem of Queenstown. They started a new African paper, *Izwi Labantu*, edited by G. W. Tyamzashe and then by A. K. Soga, to counter the influence of *Imvo*. Thus the rifts in African political loyalties had widened, each interest group attaching itself to rival white parties at the parliamentary level. The conflicts thus started survived into the period after the

Anglo-Boer War. A South African Native Congress established in the eastern Cape in 1902 stood in the *Imbumba* tradition, an umbrella designed to cover the interests of all African groups, and anticipated the Native Congress of March 1909 called to discuss the South Africa Bill (at which Rubusana was preferred to Jabavu as chairman), and Pixley ka I. Seme's South African Native National Congress of 1912. Jabavu rejected the Congress, and found his continuity rather in a conference which had met in King William's Town in 1887 to oppose Sprigg's legislation to disfranchise the owners of communal property, and agreed to meet from time to time, as need arose. These were the auspices, he later claimed, under which he had founded the Cape Native Convention in about 1908, as the representative of which he joined Schreiner's deputation to London to contest the South Africa Bill in 1909, and under which he convened his South African Races Congress in April 1912 in opposition to Seme's S.A.N.N.C.

A small settlement of Englishmen established itself at Port Natal in 1824, and by virtue of achieving a working relationship with Shaka it was just able to survive.[4] Shaka welcomed traders like F. G. Farewell just as he welcomed missionaries like Francis Owen of the C.M.S. and Adams, Lindley and Grout of the American Board. Without apparently appreciating what white people understood by the transactions, he and his successor Dingane ceded to the settlers the major part of what later became the Colony of Natal, even though they had taken under their wing a number of refugees from his own wars. The last of these cessions, that made to the Voortrekker leader, Piet Retief, in February 1838, became the basis for the establishment of the Voortrekker Republic of Natalia. But Natalia, founded in early 1840, did not last six years. A British contingent had arrived in December 1838, ostensibly to re-establish order during the confrontation between the Voortrekkers and the Zulu, but was withdrawn a year later, after the accession of Mpande promised to result in peace between the Zulu and the trekkers. A second British occupation of Port Natal took place under Captain T. C. Smith in May 1842, inspired this time apparently by concern in the Cape over the growth of unrest in Kaffraria as a result of Boer raids into eastern Pondoland. Smith's presence at Port Natal was resented by the Boers, who seized his cattle. Smith then attacked their base at Congella, failed to take it, and was himself besieged almost to the point of surrender, when he was rescued by a relieving force from the Cape sent up the coast on information delivered in Grahamstown by Dick King, South Africa's Paul Revere, who had made the five-hundred-mile overland journey to the Cape in ten days. After the siege of Port Natal had been broken, the Volksraad of Natalia submitted to British control in July 1842.

Why the British Government decided to take the territory is not clear. Sir James Stephen, Permanent Under-Secretary in the Colonial Department, did not want to annex, nor did his political heads with the exception of Lord John Russell. The suggestions that Natal was taken for its coal deposits or its cotton potential appear improbable. The Cape governor, Sir George Napier, who persuaded the Conservative Secretary of State, Lord Stanley, to change his mind, seems to have been determined to prevent further Boer raids on African border chiefdoms, which threatened to disturb the Cape's own eastern border. He announced the extension of British protection over the territory in the Cape Legislative Council on 4 May 1843. When the Volksraad submitted to the Cape's commissioner, Henry Cloete, on 9 August, it was required to agree that the laws of Natal should be colour-blind, that raids across the border were not to take place without governmental sanction, and that slavery was not to be allowed. But the formal annexation of Natal to the Cape was not proclaimed in South Africa till August 1845. After that an interregnum ensued, during which the Volksraad continued to meet but was powerless to control events, until the first Lieutenant-Governor, Martin West, reached Natal on 8 December 1845.

On a sketch-map presented to the Cape Native Laws Commission of 1883, Sir Theophilus Shepstone gave the distribution of some ninety-four chiefdoms which had occupied the whole area of Natal before the time of Shaka. Of these, about forty remained in Natal after the Mfecane, distributed mainly along the coastal belt south of Port Natal, with further clusters near the site of Pietermaritzburg and on the right bank of the Tugela. During the interregnum between the end of the Republic and the implementation of effective British rule a large influx of perhaps 50,000 Africans entered (or returned to) Natal from outside its borders, often squatting on land claimed by Voortrekkers but not yet recognised as belonging to them by the British administration. Natal now stretched only from the Tugela to the Umzimkulu.

The regulation of land policy was a pressing call on West's administration, which had the task of satisfying both of these groups. He appointed a Commission in March 1846, of which Theophilus Shepstone was a member, to define locations for African occupation. The Commission rejected the Voortrekker policy of removing all African settlements to the other side of the Tugela and Umzimkulu rivers and recommended a string of locations well within the Colony, amounting to about a tenth of the total surface area, stretching in a horseshoe along the upper and middle Tugela, then turning south parallel to but inland from the coast, with further settlements at Umlazi south of Durban (as Port Natal was now known) and at Swartkops near Pietermaritzburg.

Similar arrangements were not made in the case of the Voortrekkers, whose land claims were very extensive indeed, but generally lacking in precise delimitation. Cloete had found he could not endorse vague

Volksraad grants. West's surveyor-general, William Stanger, paid attention to the towns before he looked at the farms, and proceeded so slowly in the latter instance that a number of the trekker families lost patience, withdrew northwards in 1847, and tried to set up an independent republic under Mpande's overlordship in the Klip River district. They were experiencing the kind of delays over the registration of titles which had been common in the Cape only a few years earlier. To make matters worse, a policy of stiffness under Cloete and West was followed by one of chaotic laxity when Sir Harry Smith became governor in 1847. Smith, who came face to face in early 1848 with the Boer leaders of the Klip River insurrection immediately overrode West's tight land policy and made a provisional alienation of nearly two million acres of land to 360 heads of Trekker families, in the hope of persuading them to stay in Natal. Whitehall subsequently disallowed an ordinance abolishing restrictions on land alienation, however, and it was this, apparently, that persuaded most of the remaining trekkers to sell their claims, frequently to speculators at prices of as little as twopence an acre, and emigrate. Perhaps two-fifths of the surface of Natal fell into speculators' hands, where it lay idle, an obstacle to immigration.

Sir George Grey launched a cheap land scheme linked with military service on his visit to Natal in December 1855, hoping thereby to attract young farmers with a mere £6 a year to pay in quit-rent; but speculation remained Natal's curse, especially when Natal land became a proposition on the London stock exchange, after the founding of the Natal Land and Colonization Company in 1859. By that time fairly systematic settlement of the land, under conditions comparable with the 1820 Settlement, had begun. The Byrne scheme of 1849–50 brought some five thousand English and Scots, many of whom, like their Cape counterparts, found their land allocations far too small, and therefore moved into the towns. Pietermaritzburg and Durban began under their influence to develop a quicker commercial and cultural life. Politics too became enlivened during the lieutenant-governorship of Benjamin Pine, when the land problem entered its next controversial phase and D. D. Buchanan's *Natal Witness* assumed a role similar to that of Fairbairn's *Commercial Advertiser* at the Cape.

Pine's first term of office (1850–5) was an era of conflict between the Settlers and Theophilus Shepstone, in which the Governor took the Settlers' part. Shepstone, the son of a Wesleyan missionary, who had been made diplomatic agent to the tribes of Natal in 1845 after some years of experience in a similar post on the Cape eastern frontier, came in for the wrath of white Natal farmers on the ground that the locations his commission had set aside were too large, with the result that black workers were not coming forward to work on the farms. Pine, who resented Shepstone as an over-mighty subject, set up a commission composed mainly of land-owning colonials in 1852 to review the decisions of 1846–7. This commission proposed radical changes, criticising the size of the reserves and Shepstone's boosting of the chieftainship; but it was a dead letter because Pine's successor, Scott, supported Shepstone's view. The storm increased after the achievement of representative government in 1856, when Settler representatives in the Legislative Council mounted a sustained attack on the Government's native policy.

Shepstone respected and protected and wielded immense influence over Africans, at any rate in his early years.[5] His movement of large numbers of Africans into the designated reserves was a master-stroke of tact and influence. He would have liked to remove the bulk of Natal's Africans outside the Colony's borders, and protect them from exploitation by white landowners. With this end in view he tried to obtain first No-Man's-Land and subsequently Basutoland as annexures to Natal, but was unsuccessful in both instances. Governor Sir George Grey persuaded the Colonial Office to veto the former proposal, and in 1867 Sir Philip Wodehouse headed off the second. It was in the Natal locations, therefore, that his policy of paternal government, one of the earliest variants of 'indirect rule', came to be applied: headmen and chiefs (preferably not traditional rulers but his own appointees) worked alongside white magistrates, who were required if possible to be self-effacing. The chiefs reported to Shepstone himself as the mouthpiece of the Supreme Chief, the Lieutenant-Governor. This designation was conferred on the Lieutenant-Governor by Ordinance 3 of 1849, in a fictitious adaptation of tribal custom. Shepstone won his campaign to keep tribal Africans outside the reach of the Roman–Dutch law of the Colony, and subject to their own customs. He was prepared to allow only exceptional individuals to place themselves under Colonial law, and these under very stringent conditions, so that hardly a handful qualified during the whole period of his rule. Though anxious to protect Africans from undesirable white influences, and theoretically in favour of educating them, Shepstone paid very little attention to economic or educational development. The annual native affairs grant of £5000 from Colonial revenue, which was guaranteed under the constitution, was ridiculously small, but Welsh has shown that even in this fund a surplus of £30,000 had been allowed to accumulate by 1871. Consequently development did not take place; and because it did not, the Settlers could argue that it was better for Africans to enter the white man's service than to stagnate in the reserves, with at least some plausibility. Many, of course, did work on the farms; but the sugar plantations on the coast, with their requirement of heavy manual labour, were very short of manpower, and the sugar farmers were a growing pressure group. Far fewer Africans found their way to the towns in Shepstone's day. When they did so he was quick to recognise a potential social problem, and came out in 1874 with a schedule of 'togt' (casual labour) regulations, one of the earliest examples of modern influx control.

Shepstone's reputation as Secretary for Native Affairs was damaged in the eyes of posterity by his actions during the crisis over Langalibalele, chief of the Hlubi, in 1873–5. Langalibalele refused both to have his people's firearms registered, as the law required, and to appear personally in Pietermaritzburg for failing to do so. Instead, he withdrew to Basutoland with his cattle, possibly with the intention of going into rebellion, but he was handed over to the Natal authorities by the Sotho chief Molapo, with whom he had taken refuge. Skirmishes took place between his followers and the Natal Carbineers sent to apprehend him. The troops moved into the Hlubi location, killing over 150 in the subsequent fighting. Langalibalele was deposed, his tribe broken up, his land and cattle confiscated. After that he was put on trial in January 1874 before a special court in Pietermaritzburg, over which the Lieutenant-Governor, Pine, presided as Supreme Chief, together with Shepstone, the whole Executive Council, three magistrates and six chiefs. Langalibalele was denied defence counsel with power to cross-examine witnesses. He was found guilty, and sentenced to banishment for life. His appeal to the Executive Council was then dismissed, whereupon a special Act of the Cape Parliament consigned him to Robben Island.

The Imperial Government intervened. Pine had exceeded his authority both as Supreme Chief and Lieutenant-Governor, and was recalled. The Cape Parliament had exceeded its powers by accepting custody of a convicted person from another colony, and was ordered to bring Langalibalele back to the mainland under the British Colonial Prisoners' Removal Act (32 Vic. cap. 10) which required an address to the Queen by legislatures of both colonies where transportation was proposed. Shepstone had not in any way resisted Pine's proceedings, but may even, in Welsh's words, have 'master-minded the trial arrangements' and worked closely with a Governor who had once been his opponent. He was later deprived against his wishes of the judicial authority which had been his by delegation from the Governor, when the Legislative Council created a Native High Court in 1875. But he now began to acquire a reputation in South Africa, as the master-mind behind the policy of segregation, which was subsequently developed into the distinctive governing principle in the native policies first of Natal and later of the Union. Yet Shepstone, like Lugard, was a pragmatist rather than an ideologue, and would probably have disapproved of this trend on account of its rigidity. Though he was authoritarian to a fault, he was not a maker of systems, not even a believer in the rigid codification of African law.

* * *

The political system of Natal, which was in due course adapted to blend with Shepstone's policy of keeping blacks and whites apart, took its shape from the Charter granted by Letters Patent in 1856.[6] This gave the Colony a governor (or lieutenant-governor) who reported direct to London. He was aided by an Executive Council composed of five officials and (from 1869) two unofficials, and an elective legislative council, initially of twelve members, in which the members of the executive sat and voted. Although the structure of African administration as devised under Ordinance 3 of 1849, allowed for the government of blacks by special procedures under their own law, the Charter incorporated the franchise proposals first made by Pine, apparently admitting blacks to the vote as well as whites, if they possessed fixed property worth £50 or paid £10 a year in rent. This interpretation was challenged, even by the Chief Justice, but supported in 1863 by most members of the Executive Council. It was changed in 1864–5 on account of growing settler concern over the possibility of a widespread registration of black voters. An Exemption Law now laid down that Africans desiring to be released from native law had to produce proof of literacy and take an oath of allegiance, whereupon the Lieutenant-Governor could admit them to some of the privileges of citizenship at discretion. A second law, the Native Franchise Act of 1865, laid down that no more blacks could even petition for inclusion on the electoral roll unless they had been residents of Natal for twelve years, had held letters of exemption from native law for seven, and had the approval of three whites whose word was endorsed by a magistrate; after which the Lieutenant-Governor could admit them to the roll or exclude them at his discretion after calling for public objections. The suggestion has been made by Trapido that the Exemption and Native Franchise laws may have been the price paid by Scott to obtain a truce with the legislature in their quarrel with him over the £5000 native reserve fund, and over the continued existence of Shepstone's locations. These the Council agreed to place under the control of a new Natal Native Trust, consisting of the Governor and Executive Council, in 1864.

In spite of the tensions of the 1850s and 1860s, it was not until 1870 that the first exploratory demand for responsible government was made and withdrawn. Another such demand in 1874, following soon after the Langalibalele affair, and largely inspired by it, was understandably turned down. Indeed, in 1875 Lord Carnarvon ordered Pine's successor, Sir Garnet Wolseley, to pack the Legislative Council with almost enough nominees to swamp the elective majority. This punitive 'Jamaica' reform was given a five-year run. Wolseley managed the humiliating manoeuvre by drawing heavily on his entertainment allowance, but the demand for responsible government was revived in 1879. Those who did so had not reckoned sufficiently carefully with its implications for defence, or with the Imperial Government's likely demands over native policy. Two general elections fought on the question in 1880 and 1882 showed that the electorate at least was aware of these problems, for the 'responsibles' were well beaten, while a compromise proposal by the Durban lawyer, Harry Escombe, for the appointment of colonials to the Governor's Executive Council was either misunderstood by the Colonial Office, or ignored as unorthodox and unwise. During the late 1880s, John Robinson, editor of the *Natal Mercury*, renewed the campaign for responsible government, having won Escombe over to the cause by 1885. Natal became increasingly locked in economic conflict for the trade of the interior with its self-governing rival, the Cape. Eventually, from a desire to contain the growing strength of the Transvaal, the main political parties in Great Britain began to encourage such a step. Knutsford, for the Conservatives, was prepared to keep a garrison in Natal for five years after the change, though he looked for effective safeguards for black interests, which the Natal politicians were unwilling to provide. In the end, Knutsford sent a draft Bill for submission to the Natal electorate and, if approved in a referendum, for acceptance or rejection by the Legislative Council without amendment. A general election in 1892 resulted in the return of an 'anti-responsible' majority, but the reversal of two results following electoral petitions led Natal to accept responsible government by the same kind of precarious vote as the Cape had done twenty-one years earlier. An upper house of eleven, to be chosen by the Governor-in-Council, and a lower of thirty-seven elected on the existing franchise, constituted the new Parliament. The Colonial Office had receded from its earlier tough stand on the subject of black rights. It had managed to double the native reserve fund to £10,000; it retained the conventional powers of reservation and disallowance with respect to Bills affecting the blacks, and it insisted on the Governor retaining discretionary powers in the exercise of his authority as Supreme Chief though he was expected to keep his ministers informed.

The Imperial Government might have paid more attention than it did to the safeguarding of black interests, on account of developments where the Indian immigrants to Natal were concerned.[7] Natal's Indian population had arrived for the most part as indentured labourers destined for the sugar plantations, in a succession of shiploads since 1860. They were mainly low-caste Hindus from Madras, and more than a third of those who arrived were women. Among the Zulu, agricultural work was women's work, and the cash incentive for male labourers was still low. The Indians were brought, therefore, to supply an urgent need, on five-year contracts, at agreed low minimum wages, and at the end of their contracts were given the option of serving for another five years, or obtaining their freedom, or returning to India. Those who stayed ten years in service could get free passages home. Recruiting was steady, save for a lull in the depression years 1866–72. When the first Indian repatriates returned home in 1871 and reported on their treatment, the Government of India forbade further recruitment. The Natal legislature therefore took special steps in 1872 to put right the abuses which had been alleged – flogging of workers, and excessive pay deductions for absenteeism, for example – and appointed a Protector of Indian Immigrants. Provision was also made to allocate land to Indians who had completed their contracts, on the ground that such people had skills to contribute to the welfare of the Colony, and should be encouraged to remain. Indian immigration now accelerated, and the population rose from under 10,000 in 1875 to about 100,000 by the end of the century.

From the late 1870s, a new class of 'passenger' Indians reached Natal under their own initiative, Gujerati traders, commonly Muslim in their faith, who set up shops in effective competition with whites in the towns of Natal, the Transvaal and the Orange Free State. White shopkeepers in Natal, the Free State and the Transvaal began to agitate against the Indians, alleging unfair competition, while the dangers of the Natal Indian vote became an increasingly common electoral slogan. This anti-Indian campaign was gathering momentum at the time when Natal achieved responsible government. It resulted, after responsible government, in a legislative programme designed to restrict the political and economic power of the Indian community, and to encourage them to return *en masse* to India. On the Indian side, new techniques of resistance were worked out and set in motion, at the beginning of a career which acquired world-wide significance, by Mohandas K. Gandhi. The legislation had three main features. The first was an attempt to disfranchise the Indians, to which the British Government took exception; but, as had happened in the Transvaal in 1885, a new formula which enabled Natal to achieve the same result without appearing to discriminate on racial grounds proved acceptable: under the Franchise Act of 1896, the parliamentary vote was to be denied to people whose countries of origin did not have 'representative institutions founded on the Parliamentary franchise'. The second measure was the introduction of a £3 poll tax on Indians who neither renewed their indentures nor returned to India, levied in the first instance on the heads of families, and subsequently on all members of such families, some of which were large. In the third instance, local authorities were empowered to refuse trading licences to Indians without any risk of court actions.

Gandhi, who arrived in Natal in 1893 on a legal assignment, and very quickly experienced personal slights directed at him on account of his race, decided to remain in the Colony on learning that the disfranchisement of Indians was intended. As founder of the Natal Indian Congress and editor of *Indian Opinion*, he began to work out in the South African context the methods of *satyagraha* (soul force) derived from the teachings of the pacifist Jain sect of Hinduism in which he had been brought up: the technique of resisting the objectionable law, if need be by enduring suffering, without doing violence or ceasing to respect those who made it or enforced it [see pp. 155, 179–82].

# Section III
# The Struggle for Possession

# 7 White and Black: the Struggle for the Land

One view of the population movements which took place in the mid-nineteenth century holds that they led to an amicable distribution of the land, the black chiefdoms holding on to what had been traditionally theirs, the white settlers moving into areas which, though previously populated, had been left empty as a result of the *Difaqane*. It should be clear from the events recorded in this chapter that such a view has little historical basis, and that competition for land – an increasingly scarce commodity – best explains the history of South Africa's nineteenth-century frontiers.

The present chapter is concerned with the struggle for possession, first on the northern and eastern Cape frontiers, but subsequently on a multiplicity of new frontiers created as a result of the Great Trek. It was, almost without exception, a story of black-white confrontation, in which there was mobility on both sides, and in which the white man, with his superior weapons and his notion of individual ownership, his theodolite and his title deed, and his greater awareness of the operation of the market, generally gained at the expense of the black.

A little-documented frontier of conflict was that between the white settlers and the San, who fought their main rearguard action along the line of the Bokkeveld, Hantam, Roggeveld, Nuweveld and Sneeuwberg ranges between 1770 and 1800, and drove the frontier Boers to exasperation with their raids.

By 1809, however, Colonel Collins, who toured the eastern districts on behalf of the British authorities, found these Bushmen less intractable, and was able to recommend 'a more liberal line of policy than that which I think necessary to be observed . . . towards the Caffres'.[1] They were no longer a serious danger, though they still raided periodically. A more humane policy conducted since the 1790s and associated initially with Governor Macartney and the first L.M.S. missions had apparently reduced the tension. Restraints had been imposed upon the commandos. Frontier farmers were winning the confidence of the San in places, by giving them slaughtered game. The Bushmen could therefore be 'more safely introduced into the Colony, collected and instructed in institutions, and dispersed among the inhabitants'. There was need for the civilising influence of missions in particular areas, and Collins singled out for special attention the region of the Riet and Sak rivers, where Kicherer's L.M.S. mission had had to close down in 1806, the region of the Tarka, and the Swartberg, where there were still many Bushmen in the mountains. Collins's reliance on the missions was overoptimistic. Tooverberg, Hephzibah, Philippolis and Bethulie, all opened after 1809 to attract Bushmen, were either closed in a few years or turned over to other communities, largely because white farmers had come to look upon mission stations as hideouts for thieves and the idle. But this reaction itself reflected a changing relationship, for some San were beginning to enter into the service of white farmers. Burchell, travelling through the north-east Cape in 1816, spent some hours with a very friendly San community; but there were still whites who could think of them only as vermin, as his compatriot George Thompson found in 1823.

The Great Trek cut a swath through the San-occupied regions of the interior, isolating those of the northern Cape from those whose base of operations remained the Drakensberg mountains to the east. The former either became absorbed in the Colony, intermarrying with Khoikhoi and other groups, or they retreated gradually towards the lower Orange. Periodic friction developed on this little-publicised frontier because no steps were ever taken to provide the Bushmen with a Reserve of their own, though this had been the intention of the Government at the time of the 1774 commando, and of Macartney in 1798, while it remained the main substantive proposal of Louis Anthing when he investigated the troubles of the northern border in 1862. Because there was no Reserve, friction continued between the San and the farmers. In 1883, the *Zuid Afrikaan* considered that the troubles north of Victoria West were rather like those of the Ceres district at the end of the previous century.

The Drakensberg San retained greater independence for a time, raiding farms of Natal frequently between 1845 and 1872 along the whole length of the range from Witzieshoek in the north to No-Man's-Land in the south. Here the anarchy of the Karoo was repeated, though on a smaller scale. The raiders were far fewer – perhaps only a few hundred – but in Natal they were often mounted and therefore harder to apprehend. On the Cape frontier there were some suggestions of collaboration between the San raiders and the Tswana. On the Natal frontier, their collaboration with the Bhaca, the Phuti, the Mpondomise, and other chiefdoms seems to have endured over a long period, though it was a brittle relationship which failed to survive increased white pressure, especially when the Natal Government planted African locations on the access routes into the Colony and thus gave them a vested interest in resisting the San raids – for which purpose they were sometimes supplied with firearms. The Drakensberg San, encircled by white settlements in Natal and the Orange Free State, finally succumbed when their fastnesses in Basutoland were penetrated by the retreating Sotho in the 1860s, and when their base in No-Man's-Land was weakened with the resettlement of the Philippolis Griqua at about the same time. Lacking the cohesion and the power to resist white encroachment, they either stayed put and lost their identity, or retreated northwards in pursuit of the game. By the end of the nineteenth century few San were to be found south of the Orange river. In the mid-twentieth there may have been fifty thousand north of it.

Cape eastern frontier policy in the nineteenth century has a special interest for several reasons.[2] This was the oldest frontier between a European colony and Bantu-speakers, on which spasmodic warfare took place between 1778 and 1878. Far more than any other frontier, it was one on which policies were thought out and deliberately applied. The blockhouse system and the military village; the buffer strip, the frontier of no outlets and the trading pass; the trade fair, mission station, hospital and school; the spoor law, the treaty system, the government agent, and the magistrate – all these were tried in various combinations, in a bid to maintain order and peaceful coexistence at the meeting point of two disparate but competing cultures. Policies were debated, not only at the Cape, but also in London, where permission had to be given before the Colonial borders could be extended. Extension followed a complex double process, with the authority of the High Commissioner (exercised through Colonial magistrates) repeatedly preceding annexation to the Colony proper. On the black side of the frontier, as on the white, power was not monolithic but divided, and capable of being asserted, or broken, piecemeal but never all at once in its entirety.

The main developments in the extension of the Cape frontier were the annexation of British Kaffraria to the Crown in 1848 and to the Cape in 1865 (as the Ciskei), followed by the gradual incorporation in the Colony of the Transkei between 1879 and 1894: Fingoland, Idutywa and Griqualand East in 1879, Port St Johns in 1884, Thembuland, Gcalekaland and Bomvanaland in 1885, the Xesibe tract between Pondoland and Griqualand East in 1886, and finally Pondoland in 1894.

After winning the war of 1834–5, D'Urban proposed to make the 'neutral' territory between the Keiskamma and the Kei available for exclusive white settlement, but was prevented from annexing or admitting any white settlers by Glenelg. Andries Stockenström was appointed Lieutenant-Governor of the Eastern Cape, and he was the inspiration behind a new policy of making treaties with the individual chiefs, which defined clear boundaries between black and white territories, laid down that tribal law should operate in the former and Colonial in the latter, and provided for the appointment of diplomatic agents near the residences of the chiefs. These agents were given the task of mediating in inter-racial disputes and in all negotiations with chiefs, while the actual control of passage across the frontiers remained with the military, who could establish posts inside black territory but were not permitted to patrol on the black side of the frontier. But Stockenström's treaties failed in their object of stabilising the frontier because, as C. L. Stretch, one of his agents, made clear, the agents were too frequently ignored by the military authorities, and the chiefs not paid the kind of deference, as territorial rulers, which the system required. When Colonel John Hare succeeded Stockenström as Lieutenant-Governor in 1839, frontier relations deteriorated for this reason. Governor Sir Peregrine Maitland therefore revised the system in 1844 by insisting on a new style of treaty which provided for the trial of stock thieves inside the Colony even if they were apprehended on tribal territory, and also for the renewal of military patrols between the Fish and the Keiskamma. This angered the Xhosa still more, and after provocative acts had been committed by both sides, the 'War of the Axe' broke out in 1846.

Before the end of 1847 the Colonial forces had again broken the African resistance, and Sir Harry Smith, taking over from Maitland's unwilling successor, Sir Henry Pottinger, as Governor in December, resolved on a new policy, the basis of which was direct rule. After explaining to the assembled chiefs, with dramatic sound effects, that he proposed to get rid of the treaty system, he annexed the Keiskamma-Kei region as the Crown Colony of British Kaffraria and announced plans to appoint magistrates with authority in place of the diplomatic agents, to turn the chiefs into salaried officials, and to locate Mfengu settlers and military villages in the area to keep the peace.

Once again, however, African hostility did not take long to show itself. The year 1850 was one of drought and unrest, and the Ngqika were stirred by the utterances of Mlanjeni, a prophet who managed to awaken a spirit of resistance among the blacks to Smith's new paternalism. Though Smith agreed to try to regain the chiefs' loyalty by raising their stipends, he continued to underrate their opposition in an authoritarian manner, and his deposition of the Ngqika chief Sandile for not attending a meeting brought their resistance into the open again, this time very seriously. Taking the Government unawares, they struck against the military posts in the Tyumie valley in December 1850, and inflicted sharp defeats on Smith's reduced forces. The Kat River Khoikhoi also came out in rebellion in Februray 1851.

Smith's policy therefore went down in ruins. Sir George Cathcart, his successor, viewed the frontier primarily as a logistic problem and reverted to the strategy of creating a defensible boundary, buttressed on the Colonial side by settlements of loyal Mfengu in the Crown Reserve which he created at the foot of the Amatolas, and by new settlements of whites in the land now confiscated from Ngqika and Khoikhoi rebels. By taking more black-owned land, Cathcart increased the instability of the area; but he was also the first Governor to experiment with new forms of landholding among Africans, inviting the missions to hold their lands in trust for their African wards, with the possibility of the latter obtaining individual quit-rent title when they were ready for it.

This last aspect of Cathcart's policy was followed by his successor, Sir George Grey (1854–61), who tried to bring about the maximum socio-economic integration of black and white on the frontier, hoping to make the Xhosa 'a part of ourselves, with a common faith and common interests, useful servants, consumers of our goods, contributors to our revenue'. He therefore proposed to fill British Kaffraria with 'a considerable number of Europeans' who would settle among the indigenous blacks, teach them the Christian religion and the arts of European farming, and give them an understanding of the white man's law, as well as a vested interest through the grant of individual title. Grey miscalculated in trying to apply the land policy he had developed in New Zealand, where land was relatively plentiful, to British Kaffraria, where it was not. His plan to penetrate tribal territory with white-owned farms and military roads was as widely resented as his plan to substitute European for traditional cultural values. This resentment erupted in the Cattle-killing tragedy of 1857, when, following the prophecy of a young girl, Nongqawuse, the Xhosa people slaughtered their stock and destroyed their crops in the expectation of an act of revenge by their ancestral spirits on the white man, accompanied by the provision of food from heaven. Whether the slaughter was a spontaneous act of misguided faith or a calculated political move by Sarhili, the Gcaleka paramount, with or without the encouragement of Moshweshwe, may never be known for certain. As an episode in the history of millenarian movements in Africa, it was far from unique, and it was accompanied by signs of mass hysteria. There is plenty of evidence of bids by Sarhili to persuade other chiefdoms to fall into line, though very few outside the Xhosa chiefdom followed his lead. A Xhosa tradition which ascribes the tragedy to Grey and the missionaries lacks weight because, although the depopulation of the Ciskei made his scheme for introducing white settlers easier to carry out, it has no basis in any known acts or statements of the people concerned. The population of the affected Ciskeian chiefdoms fell from an estimated 105,000 to a mere 37,000, those who died of starvation approximating in number to those who poured into the colony in desperate search of food. The Government provided emergency relief, but also went ahead with the settlement of German immigrants – mainly Crimean veterans and peasants – on the East London–Stutterheim axis, setting aside some two hundred farms in British Kaffraria on simple military quit-rent tenure. Blacks resented his extension of politico-military control, linked with white settlement in areas cleared by the Frontier Armed and Mounted Police under Walter Currie in August 1857, which penetrated as far north as the Bashee river; but this aspect of Grey's policy collapsed because the Colonial Parliament was not prepared to pay for it.

When the next major trouble broke out, the Ciskei was under direct Colonial rule, the Cape Parliament having reluctantly accepted control in 1865. In 1877 Sarhili, perhaps remembering the fate of his father Hintsa, refused to appear before the High Commissioner to answer for an attack on the Mfengu, and as a result his Gcaleka became fully involved in conflict with the white authorities. Sir Bartle Frere deposed him without authority, and this led to a military alliance between the Gcaleka and the Ngqika, with some Thembu support. But militarily speaking, it was too late in the day.

The Thembu, situated between the Umtata and Bashee rivers, were the senior southern Nguni chiefdom, but politically very divided. After the incorporation of British Kaffraria in the Colony and the expulsion of the Ngqika and other Colonial rebels across the Kei, they also began to feel the pressure of rival Xhosa groups, above all Sarhili's Gcaleka. Ngangelizwe, their paramount chief, whose authority was not widely recognised, sought in vain to reunite the clans, some of which lived inside the Colonial borders and others outside. To protect his southern borders from Gcaleka pressure, Ngangelizwe also admitted Zizi (Mfengu) settlers, while in the north he admitted white farmers from the Dordrecht district to settle in the Slang river valley to protect his Sotho flank, offering no permanent title, but requiring a mere £6 a year in quit-rent. For the Thembu, however, involvement in the war of 1877–8 proved fatal for their independence, the Thembuland magistracy being formed in 1879.

Division also afflicted the Mpondo chiefdom, straddling the Umtamvuna river at Port St Johns. After the death of Faku in 1868, his right-hand son Ndamase in western Pondoland broke away from his heir Mqikela, and the two chiefdoms might have remained separate but for reports of German interest in that part of the coast, and the desire of the Cape and Natal each to control Port St Johns. Eventually, in 1894, Rhodes put pressure on Sigcawu, Mqikela's successor, to accept Cape rule. He had him arrested the following year, without warrant, for allegedly resisting magisterial authority.

The senior officials in the Cape Native Affairs Department were chiefly men of missionary stock, concerned to protect the Africans in their land, which they knew was in short supply. There was actually little white demand for land in the Transkei after the age of Grey. The sophisticated report of the 1883 Cape Native Laws Commission, to which all the leading magistrates gave evidence, stressed the unwisdom of pressing Africans too hard – as Grey had done – into a European mould. Cape policy avowedly aimed at peaceful change, in its own good time, towards a common society. At the same time, the growing numerical ascendancy of the blacks with every advance of the frontier produced a backlash in white opinion, and led to repeated restrictions of black political rights (but by no means their elimination), and the movement of liberal opinion away from the notion of equal rights and towards the rather more Shepstonian idea of trusteeship without fixed time limits.

From the black side, the Colonial advance presented insoluble problems. Militarily, they could not win, either by using surprise to make up for their defective weaponry, or by turning to their war doctors (as they repeatedly did) to break white power. Despite the common European belief that the black chiefdoms were coordinating their strategy to drive them back, the evidence points rather to a lack of combined effort among the chiefdoms, which also accounts for the long duration of the Cape frontier conflict. Those who accepted conquest, and the mission education that went with it, included some remarkable people; but they were no more than a few thousand by the end of the century.

The independent Griqua chiefdoms north of the Orange River, based on Philippolis and Griquatown, succumbed between the 1840s and 1870s, when the Kok and Waterboer dynasties fought a rearguard action against bids by whites to purchase the farms of their subjects.[3] Here private tenure was the undoing of the people, where communal might have afforded better protection, for individuals proved unable to resist the lure of goods, guns or liquor in return for their land. Adam Kok III of Philippolis, who had at first tried to prohibit sales to whites, accepted the arrangement proposed by the Cape Governor, Sir Peregrine Maitland, at Touwfontein in June 1845, to allow the lease of farms to whites north of the Riet–Modder line for up to forty years, but to forbid the lease of lands south of it. But not even this arrangement worked. Sales occurred even in the inalienable region without Kok's knowledge, sometimes abetted by mercenary white officials. At the time of the Bloemfontein Convention (1854), Sir George Clerk agreed with the Free State Government that when farms were sold to whites, sovereignty over that territory was to pass to the white government. Eventually, Sir George Grey, appreciating that without close protection the Griqua stood no chance, arranged in 1861 for the Philippolis Griqua to move to No-Man's-Land, to the south-east of the Drakensberg near the borders of Natal. But even here Kok failed to settle his people securely on the land. The farms were surveyed, but many of his followers were unable to pay the low registration fees because they had failed to get satisfactory prices – sometimes even payment at all – for their Philippolis lands, or lost most of their stock during their exodus through southern Basutoland. Sales were not systematically recorded; and a few white speculators were able to obtain titles to blocks of farms. So Kok's second state crumbled like his first, and his people lapsed a second time into landlessness. Griqualand East was taken over by the High Commissioner in 1875 and transferred to the Cape four years later, partly to eliminate friction between the Griqua and their resentful Bhaca, Xesibe and Mpondomise neighbours whom they had tried to dominate.

Meanwhile Nicholas Waterboer, son of the Andries who had concluded a treaty of alliance with D'Urban in 1834, fell victim to the pressure of land-seekers from the Cape, and to diamond-hunters from many parts. David Arnot, a Colesberg law agent with an eye for the main chance, undertook in 1867 to defend Waterboer's territorial claims. His price included the right to survey and settle a tract named Albania, to the east of the Vaal–Orange confluence, with whites brought up from Albany who were prepared to recognise Waterboer's authority over them. Having thus strengthened Waterboer's sovereignty up to the Ramah–Platberg line agreed as a boundary with Adam Kok in 1838, Arnot then constructed a case for his northern border on a line agreed with the Tlhaping chief Mahura in 1842 and confirmed in 1864, and successfully defended his case to the satisfaction of Lieutenant-Governor Keate of Natal in October 1871. Having secured recognition as a territorial sovereign, Waterboer then offered his territory, referred to as Griqualand West, to the Crown for protection, and Sir Henry Barkly, the High Commissioner, accepted it. This new British colony came into being within a few months of the rush to the dry diamond diggings on the site of the present Kimberley. It soon became a white speculator's paradise. The white diggers, a tough crowd whom Lieutenant-Governor Sir Richard Southey soon found he could not control, were able to ensure that diamond-mining would remain a white man's preserve. The Griqua might try to rebel in 1878, as their eastern counterparts did; but in losing their economic, they had also lost their political independence. In 1876, Judge Andries Stockenström declared in the Griqualand West Land Court that Waterboer's claim to be a territorial sovereign was also bad in law [see pp. 353–6].

Unlike the Griqua, the southern Sotho under Moshweshwe fought a relatively successful rearguard action against the Orange Free State, thanks to Imperial support. Cattle-rustling between the Orange Free Staters and the Sotho west of the Caledon river led Governor Sir George Napier, acting on Dr Philip's advice, to suggest an approximate boundary well to the west of the Caledon in 1843.[4] Disputes over cattle soon grew into disputes over land. Moshweshwe found that, within the area recognised as his by Napier, he had to defend his own both against rival black groups – the Tlokwa of Sekonyela, Taaibosch's Kora, and Moroka's Rolong, and against Boers who erected permanent structures on land to which he had given them transitory rights. Nor was the situation static on the Sotho side, for Moshweshwe also had to take into account the growing desire of his senior sons, in particular Molapo, to spread out and set up semi-independent principalities of their own.

After the establishment of the Orange River Sovereignty in 1848, the British Resident, Henry Warden, amended the Napier delimitation by recognising the Rolong, Tlokwa and Kora as independent communities between the Sotho and the Boers. Moshweshwe objected. His men also planted corn on lands claimed by the Boers, and after the restoration of O.F.S. independence in 1854 they provoked the Boers into a conflict and got the better of the encounter. Sir George Grey, negotiating the first Convention of Aliwal North in 1858, persuaded the Orange Free State to buy peace with the surrender of a stretch of territory on the Sotho south-western border.

In December 1861 Moshweshwe asked to be accepted as a British subject, but Sir Philip Wodehouse recommended no more than the appointment of a British agent at Thaba Bosiu. In July 1862 the Free State asked him to beacon off the Sotho boundary between Winburg and Harrismith. Wodehouse again demurred, but carried out the task in October 1864 in a manner so favourable to the Free State's interests that border friction broke out again, for which Lesoana and Jan Letelle, local rulers who admitted only slight allegiance to Moshweshwe and the Free State respectively, were largely responsible. Registering Free Staters' frustration, on 9 June 1865 President Brand authorised a full-scale attack on the Sotho, and sent commandos to encircle them in the north and south. This time the Boers got the better of the Sotho, and in March and April 1866 imposed on them the treaties of Mpharane (Imparani) and Thaba Bosiu, under which they were deprived of the greater part of their arable land, and of all territory west of the Caledon river, and driven back into the mountains. But although their lands were confiscated and sold, the Sotho could not easily be kept off them. Moshweshwe and his son Letsie clearly intended to disregard the terms when they recovered the ability to fight. The Sotho harvested their crops, stored them in the mountains, but stayed put, eventually inducing the Free State to allow Paulus Mopedi of Witsie's Hoek and others to remain on their lands as Free State subjects. Meanwhile Moshweshwe appealed to Natal to annex his territory.

The Natal Government, urged on by Shepstone, was fretting over lack of compensation for an earlier raid by Lesoana, and saw in the acquisition of Basutoland a means of reducing the congestion of its own blacks. Disraeli's Colonial Secretary, the Duke of Buckingham, actually assented to annexation by Natal. But Wodehouse persuaded Moshweshwe to object, and prevailed on his masters in London to place Basutoland directly under the High Commission. When fighting broke out again as a result of Moshweshwe's refusal to hand over the murderers of two Free Staters, Wodehouse cut off the Free State's access to ammunition, and annexed Basutoland as British territory.

Brand was subsequently persuaded under the second Aliwal North Convention (1869) to tear up the peace treaties of 1866 in return for the retrocession of all territory lost in 1858. He kept all territory gained on the right bank of the Caledon, and agreed to an Imperial takeover of Basutoland itself. The Free State Government was then able to go ahead with the survey and sale of farms in the 'Conquered Territory'. The Sotho began to find themselves short of living space and driven into the white man's economic system as farm labourers, servants and mineworkers; but the establishment of a firm frontier under an Imperial guarantee gave Moshweshwe the security his people needed over the territory they had retained. The land remained in Sotho hands. The Cape Government took over its administration in 1871, but after the disorders of the Sotho rebellion of 1880 (generally known as the 'Gun War' from the Cape Government's attempt to confiscate firearms, which was the occasion of its outbreak), the Imperial Government resumed authority for the territory in 1884.

The Pedi, or northern Sotho, were less successful in their conflicts with the white authorities in the Transvaal.[5] They had endured tribulation at the hands of Zulu and Swazi during the time of the *Difaqane* and the Trek, and their leader Sekwati made an agreement with Hendrik Potgieter in 1845, in which Sekwati may have ceded to the Boers the land east of the Steelpoort river. Meanwhile the Volksraad party, who thought the Pedi had been subjected by the Swazi, won recognition of their title to land west of the Steelpoort from Mswati, though it was then occupied by Pedi. As a result, hostilities broke out between the Boers and the Pedi in 1847, cattle were stolen, and the Pedi began to collect firearms. The Boers besieged their stad Phiring in September 1852; but the Pedi survived the siege and withdrew to Mosega in the shadow of the Lulu mountains. A treaty between the Boers and the Pedi followed in 1857, whereby the Steelpoort was recognised as the boundary, and the parties reached an agreement for the restoration of stolen cattle. When Sekwati was succeeded by Sekhukhune in 1861, after a civil conflict in which the heir apparent, Mampuru, was beaten, this short-lived harmony was shattered. Mampuru fled to the Swazi, and became a thorn in the side of his own people. Meanwhile Alexander

Merensky of the Berlin Missionary Society, whom Sekwati had only recently admitted to his territory, withdrew his followers to Botsabelo, outside the chiefdom, taking Sekhukhune's brother Johannes Dinkwanyane and his great wife with him. Sekhukhune accused Merensky, who was probably protecting his converts from rival separatist influences, of 'stealing his people'. He began to build up his army by welcoming Zulu and Swazi refugees, which involved him in conflict with Mabhogo, the Ndebele chief. He allowed his people to filter eastwards across the Steelpoort river and settle, which frightened the whites. He also stopped making payments to the South African Republic which Sekwati had initiated not as a token of subject status, but as a gesture of goodwill.

This Pedi movement coincided with the beginnings of the eastern Transvaal gold rush, and by early 1876 armed Pedi warriors were raiding farms in the Mac Mac district and approaching to within six miles of Lydenburg. The Transvaal Boers began war against them in May, but even with Swazi reinforcements they failed to take Sekhukhune's strong defensive positions. By switching to a war of attrition, however, they induced Sekhukhune to sue for peace in February 1877, to pay a token fine of cattle, and to acknowledge Transvaal suzerainty. But mystery surrounds the nature of the surrender, for it emerged that Sekhukhune was not fully aware of the meaning of the document he had been asked to sign by a group of over-hasty Boer commissioners, and at the same time approached Sir Theophilus Shepstone through Merensky, asking for protection from the Boers and denying that he saw himself as a subject of the Republic.

But the British annexation of the Transvaal in April did not end his troubles. Sekhukhune elected to remain in the Transvaal as a British subject and pay the war debt of 2000 cattle which he had undertaken to give the Republican Government, rather than to depart from the Transvaal with his people. Shepstone, however, refrained from applying pressure on him for the payment of the debt, with the result that Sekhukhune felt himself under no obligation to hand over more than a few occasional beasts. By the beginning of 1878 he began to appear bolder, and reports of his intention to drive out the white people living to the east of the Lulu mountains began to spread. It was suggested, but never convincingly proved, that he had been encouraged to resist British rule by either Cetshwayo or the Transvaal Boers or both. Only when his men moved against white settlements at Waterval, Ohrigstad and Krugerspost in March 1878, however, did the British authorities bring up troops. Having done so, they had even greater difficulty than Burgers had had in breaking the Pedi resistance, and eventually starved Sekhukhune out only in November 1879. Sir Garnet Wolseley, who had taken over the administration as High Commissioner for South East Africa, and himself conducted the campaign, then had the Pedi removed to two settlements, Mathebi's Kop and Maleo's Kop, fifty miles from their Lulu strongholds, and appointed Mampuru, Sekhukhune's old enemy, over the chiefdom. With the restoration of self-government under the Pretoria Convention, Sekhukhune was allowed to return to the South African Republic in 1881; but in August 1882 he was murdered at Mampuru's instigation, Mampuru himself being pursued and finally executed by the Republican authorities in November 1883, after a war of attrition conducted by General Piet Joubert.

A Pedi location of some four hundred square miles was beaconed off by the Republican Government in 1885, as a home base for workers engaged to build the Delagoa Bay railway. By this time, Pedi power was broken. Kgoloko, regent for the next chief, Sekhukhune II, accepted subordination to the white Government. In 1896 his Geluks Location was split, and this led to a political split among the Pedi leaders on geographical lines, which erupted into warfare in 1900 between the younger Sekhukhune and Malekutu, son of Mampuru.

The consolidation of Afrikaner rule in the eastern Transvaal involved the overthrow, not only of the Pedi, but of their neighbours in the Middelburg district, the Ndebele chiefdom of Mabhogo. In the words of the Berlin missionary, Wangemann, after the expulsion of the Khumalo Ndebele across the Limpopo in the 1830s, larger chiefdoms like the Pedi had managed to preserve their autonomy *vis-à-vis* the Afrikaner successor-state; but lesser chiefdoms – and he singled out the Sotho-speaking Kopa of Maleo and Mabhogo's Ndebele – had to enter into a client relationship with the Boers, make payment for the use of the land which they were assigned, and take orders from the commandant of the district. Mabhogo's lands were beaconed off in 1860, but in the same year he was accused of cattle-rustling and defied repeated summonses from the Republican authorities, who made threats but lacked sufficient ammunition to launch an attack. At this point the highly volatile nature of political relationships in the eastern Transvaal became apparent. Maleo and Mabhogo chafed under Boer domination, and joined forces to win their freedom; but war broke out, not between them and the Boers in the first instance, but between them and their old enemies the Pedi, in 1863. The Boers encouraged the conflict, persuaded their allies the Swazi to participate, and it was while fighting the Swazi that Maleo lost his life. Mabhogo survived the conflict, but was quietened for a decade. In 1876 he supported Burgers, and in 1879 Wolseley, against the Pedi. He stayed neutral in the Transvaal's war of independence in 1880–1, and it was he who handed Mampuru, the Pedi rebel, over to Republican justice in 1883. But during the same campaign, as the price for attempting once more to assert his independence, he was attacked by a Boer commando, and his lands divided among the members of the attacking force.

Further north, among the Lobedu and the Venda, the Boer Republic similarly assumed the right, as heirs of the Ndebele power, to rule and tax the tribes of the Transvaal lowveld. This task was assigned to João Albasini, helped by a force of some 2000 'Knobnose' Pedi, in 1859. The Lobedu of Queen Modjadji defied his demands for a cattle payment in 1861, so Albasini's commando went against the tribe and brought back a number of beasts together with 'about 400 little kaffir boys and girls', presumably to train as labourers. Commandos, in the execution of their duty, were told that all captured arms, ammunition and ivory had to be handed in, and all property not claimed by previous owners was to be sold on behalf of the war chest. Resistance was beyond the power of the Lobedu, though they tried it again in 1894, the year of Modjadji's death.

The Venda were initially more successful. Republican authority was not strongly entrenched in the Schoemansdal area, south of the Soutpansberg, and after the death of Ramabulana, the Venda paramount, in 1864, the authorities in Schoemansdal backed as his successor his disinherited son Davhana, who received Albasini's protection. But the majority of the tribe suspected him of having poisoned his father, and rallied behind Machado. So great was the pressure built up by Machado and his allies against Schoemansdal that, even though the Executive Council sent up a relief commando, it was decided in 1867 to evacuate Schoemansdal, which the Venda then proceeded to sack. The Soutpansberg was reoccupied by the Boers in 1868, and large farms again advertised for sale; but the episode highlighted the Republic's difficulty in maintaining control in border areas in the face of black hostility and a lack of the sinews of war. For some years, the mutual respect which prevailed between Machado and Kruger kept the peace; but after Machado's death in 1895, the Republican Government rashly backed the claims of Sinthumule to the chieftainship against those of Machado's legitimate heir, Mphephu. With Boer support, Sinthumule drove Mphephu across the Limpopo in 1898.

The Swazi, whose relationship with the Ohrigstad Boers dated back to a treaty of 1846, shared with the Griqua the experience of falling victim to concessionaries without at any point becoming involved in open conflict with the white governments.[6] Their chiefs accepted the payment for the concessions as if they were tribute, only to complain when it was too late that it was the 'documents that had killed them'. Mswati made the first major grant of land, in 1855. He gave the South African Republic a strip along his southern border to the Lebombo mountains, which cut off Swaziland from Zululand and Natal. This created a barrier against Zulu raids, but during and after the reign of his successor Ludvonga, President Burgers persuaded the Swazi to accept subject status, and this led to the signing of a treaty in July 1875, the validity of which was subsequently contested by the Swazi. Britain would only recognise it if the Republic agreed to enter into a federation. In 1889, Mbandzene signed away for a hundred years all unallotted lands and mineral rights, as well as many monopolies. Land concessions were mainly to Boers from the Transvaal, mineral ones to English-speaking prospectors from Natal.

Kruger's Government saw Swaziland as a strategic area blocking its access to the sea, and although the London Convention of 1884 set precise limits on the expansion of the Republic, it pressed hard for incorporation. To this end, Kruger, signed the first Swaziland Convention with Britain in 1890, but failed to acquire the control of the territory because his Volkraad would not join the Cape customs union as part of the price. In 1893 the Imperial Government agreed that Kruger should negotiate with the Swazi for the right to control whites in the territory, while leaving the Swazi to govern themselves under their own paramount. But the Swazi refused to ratify this arrangement. At the end of 1894, therefore, the Republican and Imperial governments agreed to dispense with the need for Swazi consent, and the South African Republic established a protectorate over the territory. Three years later the king's chief minister, Mbhabha Sibandze, was killed at the royal residence, apparently on King Bhunu's orders. Bhunu was summoned to Bremersdorp for trial. He arrived in his own good time, accompanied by his warriors, but was advised by his indunas to seek refuge in Zululand rather than directly confront Transvaal authority.

The Anglo-Boer war brought the rule of the South African Republic to an end. The Imperial Government took over the territory in 1902, and placed Swaziland under the Transvaal Crown Colony government; but when self-government was restored to the Transvaal in 1907, Swaziland was placed directly under the High Commission, under whose authority it remained after the unification of South Africa in 1909. Lord Selborne, as High Commissioner, had the concessions reviewed by a commission in 1907, but his proclamation of the same year, laying down the lines of a new policy, left only one-third of the land in Swazi hands. The remaining two-thirds were to remain with the concessionaries, in freehold now, instead of on terms of long lease with reversionary rights to the Swazi.

The Republic of Natalia had tried to establish a firm northern frontier along the Black Umfolosi river beyond the Tugela line recognised by Dingane as the limit of his cessions to white settlers in 1836 and 1838.[7] To cope with an estimated influx of 100,000 Africans into Natal after the Mfecane, the Natal authorities in 1845 agreed to the Buffalo–Tugela line, along which locations were set up; but it proved to be unstable on account of Boer–Zulu friction at its north-western end.

Mpande failed to establish a clear settlement with the Boers, for although they recognised the Buffalo as a frontier in 1848, this did not stop their slow penetration of the river valleys of northern Zululand in search of land, after they had decided to abandon their insecure holdings in Natal proper. The Zulu protested frequently between 1861 and 1876, but the Natal Government only appointed a boundary commission in 1878, by which time the Boers were already well settled. Sir Bartle Frere, who released their Report only in November 1878, thought that it was too favourable to the Zulu. It recommended the payment of compensation to the Zulu and to the Boers for land surrendered to the other party as a result of new frontiers being drawn; but Frere did not implement these proposals, not least because diplomatic relations between the British authorities and the Zulu had worsened for other reasons. A party of Zulu had crossed the Natal border, kidnapped two fugitive wives of the Zulu chief Sirayo, and put them to death. Cetshwayo was willing to compensate Natal by a payment in cattle, but not to extradite the offenders. Frere decided to break the Zulu power, and served a very stiff ultimatum on Cetshwayo, requiring not only full compensation for the Sirayo affair and another border incident, but also the disbandment of the Zulu army and of the age-regiment system, and acceptance of a British Resident in Zululand without whose assent the Zulu were not to be allowed to make war.

The Zulu rejected these demands, and in the ensuing war gained one devastating military victory at Isandhlwana, before going down in defeat at Ulundi in July 1879. Sir Garnet Wolseley dictated peace terms in September, when – after leaning on the advice of Sir Henry Bulwer, Sir Theophilus Shepstone and Charles Brownlee, ex-Secretary for Native Affairs in the Cape – he exiled Cetshwayo and divided Zululand into thirteen separate chiefdoms, some of which were based on pre-Shaken units (for example, the Mthethwa and the Ndwandwe) and others (for example, the Hlubi chiefdom under John Dunn, a white man) were new. A British Resident, without armed force, was placed over the whole. The result was disastrous. To place Cetshwayo's sons under a rival, Zibhebhu, chief of the Ndwandwe, who treated them with contempt, was in itself provocative. To remove Cetshwayo to the Cape, where the imprisonment of Langalibalele not ten years earlier had led to a public outcry, then to allow him to visit England to give momentum to an agitation for his right to return home, and then to send him back to Zululand in 1883 without proper safeguards for his status or safety, was to compound the error. Cetshwayo was restored to the Zulu throne as head of the Usuthu chiefdom, but Zibhebhu, Uhamu and John Dunn were given enough authority over their own areas to be able to cause trouble. Civil war broke out, Cetshwayo was beaten by Zibhebhu with the help of Johan Colenbrander's white volunteers, and within a year of his return he was dead.

Dinuzulu, Cetswayo's son and heir, was dependent on Boer support for the recovery of lands lost to Zibhebhu, and the Boers under Lukas Meyer exacted their full price by securing recognition of the New Republic in the Vryheid, Utrecht and Wakkerstroom districts by the British Government, without any reference to Zulu opinion. When Britain eventually annexed Zululand proper in 1887, recognising that the post-war settlement had collapsed, the New Republic was incorporated in the Transvaal. But the British authorities undermined Dinuzulu's inheritance of the Zulu paramountcy by allowing Zibhebhu to return from exile with his followers, and displacing some 5000 Usuthu from their homes in the process. There was civil war again in Zululand. British troops were used against Dinuzulu, who fled to the Boers and was interned as an embarrassing guest, but escaped and surrendered to the authorities in Pietermaritzburg on the entreaty of Bishop Colenso's daughter, Harriette. This did not save him, however, from a sentence of ten years' exile in St Helena for high treason.

Before Dinuzulu's return, which was preceded by a protracted argument between the British and Natal governments, Zululand had been incorporated (1897) into a now self-governing Natal. For a while the land was protected from alien encroachment; but a delimitation commission which reported in 1905 released 2.6 of the total 6.5 million acres for purchase, which in practice – and also, it transpired, as a matter of policy – meant purchase by whites only. This greatly increased the pressure on the land in the Reserves, and thus helped to produce the unsettlement which lay behind the Zulu rebellion in 1906, after which Dinuzulu faced a second show trial [see p. 153].

The Tlhaping of Mahura shared the good fortune of Waterboer's Griqua in being favourably rewarded by Lieutenant-Governor Keate in October 1871.[8] But they and their northern neighbours, the Rolong, who occupied the region between the Boer farms of the western Transvaal and the Kalahari desert, soon found themselves under growing pressure as the Republican Government and its subjects ignored the terms of the Keate Award. Conflict arose between the Kora of Mamusa under David Massouw, who lived on the frontier laid down by the Pretoria Convention, and Mankurwane's Tlhaping, based on Taungs. Further north, a similar conflict arose between Moswete, a Rolong chief based on Kunwana in the Transvaal, and Monthsiwa at Mafeking. Massouw and Moswete engaged white volunteers' from the Transvaal in return for promises of land. Mankurwane and Monthsiwa also engaged white supporters, some of whom came from the Cape. When the former pair, aided by covert supplies of arms from the Transvaal, were able to beat their rivals, their white allies set up two independent republics of Stellaland and Goshen, divided them into farms for themselves, and embarrassed British and Cape commercial and missionary interests by straddling the 'Road to the North', the only remaining access route from the Cape to central Africa outside the Boer republics.

This troublesome region became the centre of a double conflict: between the Imperial and Transvaal governments for the control of the strategic road, and between blacks and whites for the occupation of land. At the political level, Sir Charles Warren proclaimed the Crown Colony of British Bechuanaland and an adjacent Bechuanaland Protectorate in 1885. To deal with the land problem, a committee was first set up under the Rev. John Mackenzie. It found that Mankurwane's Tlhaping were in a state of 'extreme and increasing destitution', and recommended the setting aside of a well-watered block of land in the south of Stellaland for them. When Sir Sidney Shippard took over as Resident Commissioner, however, Mackenzie's proposal was rejected, and the Tlhaping were placed instead on a few scattered farms further north. Shippard was relatively more generous to blacks in Goshen, perhaps because it had been settled mainly by Transvalers, and set aside two reasonably large Reserves based on Kunwana and Mafeking, both considerably smaller than, and falling within, the region claimed by Monthsiwa, as belonging to his tribe. The fate of the Kora, who were incorporated in the South African Republic under the London Convention, was less happy. In 1885 they attempted to take control of a white-owned farm by force. The Boers thereupon destroyed Mamusa, which was later rebuilt as the white town of Schweitzer-Reneke, and the Kora chiefdom was broken up.

In the Bechuanaland Protectorate north of the Molopo, as in Basutoland, the establishment of British paramountcy preserved most of the land for the chiefdoms. Of the northern Tswana tribes, the Ngwato under Sekgoma and (from 1875) Kgama III, the Kwena under Setshele (1829–92), the Ngwaketse under Gatseitswe, and the Kgatla under Lentswe were the most important. Periodic hostilities had broken out between them in earlier years, notably between the Kwena and the Kgatla in 1869–76 and again in 1880, when they were at loggerheads over territory. Warren asked no permission to establish a protectorate over them. They, for their part, waited to see what would happen, and cooperated in the promotion of Christianity, to which Kgama, Setshele and Lentswe were all converts. Kgama shrewdly offered lands for settlement by whites other than Boers on his eastern borders.

Having first applied for the Queen's protection against a threatened Boer encroachment in 1876, Kgama was proof against the importunities of white 'volunteers' who sought in 1885 to interest him in a campaign against Lobengula in return for farms, though Lobengula insulted Kgama by calling him a mere tributary of the Ndebele, and a disputed frontier lay between them. In general, Kgama maintained good relations with Protectorate officials, but he kept back the power, when he saw fit, to send military expeditions against rivals who would not come to terms. The Protectorate Government at first refrained from direct administration, and when Shippard called a conference in January 1889 to discuss not only defence, but hospitals, taxation, waterways, railways and telegraphs, it failed because he did not have the means of persuading the assembled chiefs and people to accept such inroads into their sovereignty. Power to control these matters, however, were taken by High Commissioner Sir Henry Loch in 1891, on the basis of Orders-in-Council of that and the previous year. In the longer term, Kgama had little cause to regret the Imperial takeover, above all because it enabled him to escape falling into the hands of the British South Africa Company and suffering the fate of Lobengula. It was touch and go, and the pressure of the Company on himself, and on other chiefs like Monthsiwa and Ikaneng, was heavy; but with Loch's support Kgama succeeded. He went to London in 1895, accompanied by Sebele (Setshele's successor) and Bathoen (the Ngwaketse paramount). There, after being lionised by the London Missionary Society in the course of its centenary celebrations, which gave them a fine opportunity to present their case to the British public, they obtained from Joseph Chamberlain, the new Colonial Secretary, an assurance of being allowed to remain masters in their own houses, free from Company control, in return for the mere loss of a border strip which the Company required for its railway into Matabeleland, and as a launching pad for the Jameson Raid.

Kgama made a deal with the Imperial authorities and saved his lands for his people. Lobengula likewise made a deal with the Imperial authorities, but in his case it was through their sub-contractors, the British South Africa Company.[9] Within a few years he had lost both his lands and his life. Like Kgama, and like his father Mzilikazi, who had a deep if one-sided affection for Robert Moffat, Lobengula was on friendly terms with the London Missionary Society, particularly through C. D. Helm and the ex-missionary John Moffat; but in his case the association did not help him. Why this was so depends on the answers to two questions which have recently been reconsidered by scholars: what were the real terms agreed between Lobengula and his concessionaries in 1889–91, and why did war break out between Lobengula and the Company in 1893? Representatives of political and mining interests began to frequent his court from 1887, when Piet Grobler arrived on a mission from Kruger to ask for a treaty of mutual friendship and the appointment of a diplomatic representative at Bulawayo. Grobler was killed, under much debated circumstances, on his return through Bechuanaland after a fracas with some of Kgama's indunas. John Moffat had meanwhile upset Grobler's diplomatic arrangement by obtaining Lobengula's agreement to a treaty in February

1888, whereby the Ndebele ruler undertook to 'refrain from entering into any correspondence or treaty with any foreign state or power to sell, alienate or cede' any part of his territory without obtaining the High Commissioner's approval. This paved the way for C. D. Rudd and his associates, working on behalf of Rhodes, to win from Lobengula 'the complete and exclusive charge over all metals and minerals' in his kingdom, including the right to dig them up. Lobengula subsequently insisted that his verbal offer was much more restrictive, and he revoked the concession; but Rhodes used it to extract a charter from the Imperial Government for his British South Africa Company in October 1889. This gave the Company the authority to operate in the quadrant formed by the northern frontier of the Transvaal and the western frontier of Mozambique, to institute a government, issue shares, mine, and improve and distribute the land. The main limits on its power of action were the obligation to report annually to the Secretary of State, to maintain order, check slavery, and promote free trade. It could only assume such powers as were granted to it by indigenous rulers; its charter was subject to review after twenty-five years and every ten years thereafter, and all its directors had to be British subjects. But these were not onerous restrictions. Rhodes advertised farms as well as mining prospects on the strength of the Rudd concession, thus exceeding his rights, and only regularised the position in November 1891, by purchasing a land concession granted to E. A. Lippert by Lobengula, who did not know that this erstwhile rival of Rhodes had in the meantime become his associate.

The Company Pioneer Column reached the site of its new base, Fort Salisbury, in September 1890, having travelled through Lobengula's domain without his permission but also without incident. The settlement had no clear territorial frontier separating it from the realm of Lobengula, who saw no reason to renounce his sovereignty over the Shona living on the land they had taken over. Jameson, the Company Administrator, wanted to establish a firm border on the line of the Muniati and Shashi rivers, and tried to exercise control over people crossing in either direction. But the Victoria incident of May 1893, following the theft of telephone wire from the Company, provoked a crisis because the cattle taken by the Company to punish the culprits were found to belong to Lobengula, who sent men to fetch them back. Why war resulted from this episode, which was settled by negotiation, has been debated. That Lobengula wanted it appears extremely improbable, though the large raid which he subsequently mounted against the Shona near Fort Victoria showed that he was determined to uphold his authority over recalcitrant 'Mahole'. Allegations that Jameson provoked war in order to boost the Company's shares at a difficult time need to be seen in the light of his conciliatory attitude to Lobengula and the large reduction in the Company's available manpower in the year before the war broke out. Yet the Company was apparently moved by a real interest in the economic possibilities of Matabeleland and by considerations of long-term security. The suggestion that the war was brought on by agitation on the part of the Fort Victoria settlers derives some plausibility from the terms of the Victoria Agreement of August 1893, in which volunteers were promised farms, gold claims and a share of the 'loot'; but if so, it has to be recognised that these enticements were in lieu of wages, and that by 1899 only 275 of the farms obtained under that agreement remained in the hands of the original 945 grantees. Most of the rights were sold, generally for low prices, to speculators and land companies. Finally, though a force sent by the High Commissioner, Sir Henry Loch, entered Matabeleland from the Protectorate while the Company's forces entered from the east, Loch's intervention seems to have been inspired by a concern to limit the extension of Company political control.

Lobengula died in flight, the Company took over the administration of his territory, and the African population were reduced to the status of squatters, save for those who lived in Reserves set aside on the Shangani and Gwaai rivers. But the Ndebele power had not been broken, and resentment grew among the blacks at their loss of land and at the large cattle fine imposed by the victors for distribution by the loot committee. The severe rinderpest epidemic of 1896–7 increased their sense of frustration, and perhaps supplied the occasion for the Ndebele decision to reopen the war in 1896, under the leadership of Nyamanda, Lobengula's son and chosen successor. Not only did the Ndebele rise both north and south of Bulawayo, but there was even a rising among the western Shona as well, though some Shona had previously offered help against the Ndebele. Some encouragement undoubtedly came from the religious leaders of the Mware fertility cult recently taken over by the Rozvi from the Venda, and from the *mhondoro* spirit media among the Shona; but these cults did not play the dominant role assigned to them by Ranger. The rebellion was costly in lives, both black and white. The Ndebele leaders were able to buy good terms when they met Cecil Rhodes in the Matoppos in October 1896; but the Shona rebellion dragged on and was put down only in late 1897, at a far greater cost of human life, including the lives of a number of leaders who received the death penalty for participation.

The conquests described above resulted mainly from fierce competition for land, an increasingly scarce commodity, often set in motion by the oscillating rhythm of stock losses and retaliatory raids. The interests of hunting, trading, prospecting, spreading the Gospel, and protection of the strategic needs of individual states and colonies, all contributed to the elimination of black indepedence during these hectic years.

How far the trader and the missionary had been responsible for softening the black resistance before conquest has been much debated. The two activities were not unrelated. The caricature of missionaries as promoters of a revolution in social taste for the benefit of the makers of cotton piece-goods is not entirely without foundation, provided this is seen as at most a by-product of missionary endeavour.[10] There was much concern among the chiefs – well illustrated by Williams – that the missionary impact undermined traditional discipline. Chiefs resented the removal of converts from their jurisdiction, and the loss of their services in time of war. But opposition to missionary demands itself discouraged conversion, above all with regard to initiation and marriage customs. It was not easy for a chief, as the price for adopting Christianity, to have to dispense with the circumcision rituals, which were in turn connected with the organisation of age-sets, labour and soldiering, or to lay down the one-wife rule in a society traditionally polygynous, and where judicious marriages often helped to confirm or extend political control. Not surprisingly, therefore, the Christian missions at first made few converts, and they succeeded best in those communities, like the Mfengu of the eastern Cape, where traditional disciplines had broken down. The missionary breakthrough in the eastern Cape did not really begin until after the 1857 Cattle-killing tragedy. In Sekhukhuneland it took root after the conquest of the kingdom by white arms. Moshweshwe, by contrast, responded readily to the Paris Evangelicals and to the Roman Catholics. He valued their association as people and as educators without committing himself to a public acceptance of their beliefs, and made use of their know-how to resist white encroachment, just as Dingane had welcomed A. F. Gardiner as musket-instructor and preacher. Robert Moffat's writings suggest that the London missioners had little success at first among the Tswana, but in due course Setshele of the Kwena, Lentswe of the Kgatla, and Kgama of the Ngwato accepted conversion on behalf of the tribe in a manner which would have done Clovis or Aethelberht of Kent credit, and then made courageous if only partly successful attempts to overhaul the customs of their people. All three abolished male and female initiation ceremonies. Kgama, whose laws were so prolific that, in popular minds, they constituted a distinct corpus apart from that of tradition, presumed to get rid of the *bogadi* (cattle bride-price) and imposed a ban on the brewing of strong drink throughout his chiefdom. Setshele, who had been converted by Livingstone, sent all his wives home on his conversion, save one, but contrived to arrange things satisfactorily for them. The Ngwaketse prohibited polygamy altogether.

White conquest was followed by the introduction of the white man's title over conquered land, though such title was not normally imposed on Africans unless they desired some form of measured and recorded ownership. Among the detribalised Mfengu of the eastern Cape, and among the Griqua, freehold and quit-rent titles were extended to indigenous peoples. The Mfengu found security in them, the Griqua insecurity. The extension of such tenures throughout the Cape became lawful under the Native Locations Act of 1879. Under the Glen Grey Act of 1894, individual tenure was extended to Africans in such a way that their surveyed four-morgen allotments could not be alienated without the Governor's consent, but could be confiscated for non-beneficial occupation or rebellion.

There is some evidence that in the late nineteenth century a moderately prosperous African peasantry, farming under conditions of individual tenure, grew up in the north-eastern Cape; but by the early twentieth century such people were struggling, mainly from the pressure of squatters on their land, while transfers of title had so often taken place irregularly that officials were inclined to discourage further individualisation of African holdings for that reason. They also feared that to remove the right of allocating land at will from chiefs and headmen might undermine social discipline and cause resentment. The tenure provisions of the Glen Grey Act did not therefore become the blueprint for development which they might have become.

Over the rest of southern Africa regular title remained for the most part the white man's privilege, communal tenure in Reserves or on Crown land being the normal form for blacks. Individual tenure was denied, for example, to blacks in the Orange Free State, save on the Wesleyan Thaba 'Nchu mission lands among the southern Rolong. In Natal the Governor and Executive Council were constituted a Native Trust in 1864, and as such held title to all communal land on which Africans resided. The same rule was adopted in Kruger's Republic, where it was generally assumed that blacks could not hold title to land, until the opposite was established in Tsewu's case in 1905. On the strength of this case, African syndicates in the Transvaal clubbed together in a number of cases to purchase surveyed farms from whites, sometimes paying up to £10,000 for a farm, which was an eloquent comment on the scarcity of available land, for they required it for subsistence farming rather than commercial exploitation. Officials expressed alarm over the introduction of one-man-one-lot agriculture combined with communal grazing rights on such land, as well as over problems of succession in cases where a farm had been bought by perhaps fifty contributors, each of whom might be expected to want to subdivide among his heirs. Similar concern was shown over the subdivision of white-owned farms in terms of the Roman–Dutch law of succession, large numbers of uneconomic holdings being described to the Transvaal Indigency Commission of 1908. Whether for black or white, there was a shortage of farming land from the 1870s onwards. A host of problems resulted – widespread squatting, share-cropping and labour-tenancy by whites as well as blacks, and widespread over-working of the soil, from which erosion resulted. It was not until after the unification of South Africa that a systematic approach to these problems was undertaken at government level, and then the solution adopted had to satisfy the canons of political ideology, at the expense of good farming. Segregation created such overcrowding in the Reserves that individual tenure by black commercial farmers became almost an impossibility.

Although loss of land following conquest was a widespread cause of black distress, there is growing evidence that the availability of land was severely restricted by the activities of speculators and land companies who followed after the conquest. One reason for this was that Governments short of money either resorted to the distribution of real estate as a form of reward for public service (the normal procedure in the case of commando activity), or treated capital gains from the sale of public land as a form of revenue (as was done by Grey in the Cape), or used the land as security for the issue of *mandaaten* (promissory notes – a kind of *assignat*) and paper currency (as was done in the Transvaal). In these ways, large blocks were distributed. David Arnot, the law agent from Colesberg, who offered his services to the Griqua chief, Nicholas Waterboer, and to the Tlhaping chief, Mankurwane, was a notable speculator. The Natal Land and Colonisation Company, formed in 1859, was floated on the London stock exchange on the security of large acreages bought at prices of £2 per acre or less, and at its height it received income from over 650,000 acres in the 1870s. Much of this land was sold during the land boom which followed the Zulu War of 1879. Of the land which this Company bought, much was regarded as more suitable for black occupation than for white, and Shepstone stated that the Company received more than half its rent in the early 1880s, in cash or crops, from over 70,000 black tenants. These numbers fell in the early twentieth century, as the Company sold blocks to private individuals who often increased the rentals. Another company, Henderson Transvaal Estates, possessed holdings of over 100,000 acres in the northern and eastern Transvaal by the early twentieth century, and described a deal which it was negotiating with the Xananwa chief Mmalaboho (Malaboch) to the Beaumont Commission in 1916. The chief had made an offer of £3000, which had been refused, for land on which his kraal was situated in the Soutpansberg, and which was 'originally part of his stad', and negotiations over the price were still proceeding. Of 15,762,364 acres alienated in Southern Rhodesia, according to R. H. Palmer, as many as 9,276,222 were in the hands of land companies by 1899.

# 8 Empire and Republics: the Breaking of Boer Independence, 1850–1902

Successive British cabinets through the nineteenth century debated the merits of formal and informal empire in southern Africa. After many changes of policy it was eventually decided in 1899 to make war against the Boer republics in order to establish a firm paramountcy over the whole region. The events leading up to this decision have provided much fodder for the twentieth-century debate over the meaning of imperialism, in which several strands of argument may be discerned.[1] Thus the role of the humanitarian lobby, seldom if ever dominant, yet seldom so insignificant that politicians of either party could afford to ignore it, was deplored in the later writings of G. M. Theal, and commended in those of W. M. Macmillan, but neither doubted its importance. Others, notably J. S. Galbraith, have seen the hand of the British Treasury as the ruling influence in the formulation of British policy, 'reluctantly' extending the imperial frontiers, and economising in the use of governmental and military resources. Considerations of grand strategy dominated the thinking of leading imperialists, in the view of Goodfellow and of Robinson and Gallagher. Others have traced the real initiative less to the Colonial Office than to the 'man on the spot' – in South Africa, the Imperial High Commissioner. Some historians, taking their cue from J. A. Hobson's *Imperialism: a Study*, which grew out of a visit to the Transvaal, have seen in the record of British South African policy the classic example of economic colonialism – a quest by financial pressure groups for new fields of investment, to make up for an over-saturated domestic money market. All these theories have some light to throw on the turbulent politics of the era.

The Voortrekkers burst the banks of Colonial society in a surge of land hunger spiced by political protest, which had had no parallel in the *trekboerdery* of the Company era, and presented a difficult control problem for the authorities. Lord Melbourne's Government tried to assert control over regions beyond the frontiers with its Cape of Good

Hope Punishment Act in 1836, proclaiming the extension of British jurisdiction (but not sovereignty) as far north as the 25th degree of south latitude.[2] This law was of some value in buttressing magisterial authority beyond the borders, even if it did not deter the trekkers. In the same spirit Governor Sir George Napier declined on 2 December 1841 to recognise the independence of the Boers of Natal. In 1843 he annexed Natal, but many Natal Voortrekkers, after failing to obtain recognition of their land titles, moved back to the highveld, and thus attracted British attention once more towards the interior.

Napier attempted to impose a territorial settlement by treaty in trans-Orangia. Here he hoped that the Sotho and Griqua, fortified in their rights, would resist Voortrekker attempts to obtain their land. But Boers who had encroached on Sotho and Griqua territory had already called his bluff in 1842, when he had invoked the Punishment Act, while the excessive enthusiasm of a circuit judge in proclaiming British sovereignty up to the territorial limits of that Act had not helped. Napier's treaty system had further drawbacks. It placed within Moshweshwe's jurisdiction Rolong, Kora and Tlokwa chiefs who did not recognise his lordship, while Adam Kok was encouraged by it to assume British support for acts of state against whites in his territory, which was not Napier's intention. Friction between the Griqua and Boer communities resulting from Kok's enforcement of his sovereignty led to violence at Zwartkoppies in April 1845. A British force intervened on behalf of the Griqua. As a result, the Winburgers under Mocke were further alienated.

Sir Peregrine Maitland tried to work out a new basis for Boer–Griqua agreement in his Touwfontein treaty of June 1845, dividing Griqua territory into alienable and inalienable regions; but in practice the Griqua found they could not remove whites who had settled in the *in*alienable region, and gradually lost their control.

Lord John Russell's Whigs took office in July 1846, and the objections of their predecessors to annexation north of the Orange were no longer heeded. Earl Grey, the Secretary of State for the Colonies, shared his Prime Minister's enthusiasm for throwing British protection over any chief who needed it. But Governor Sir Harry Smith, who took over the office of High Commissioner from Sir Henry Pottinger (its first holder) in 1847, did not wait for orders. He persuaded Kok to surrender all authority over the alienable lands in his territory, to give up their quit-rents in return for £300 a year, and to agree not to evict any Boer on the inalienable lands without compensating him fully. He next persuaded Moshweshwe to place his chiefdom under the British Crown. Then, after negotiating with Andries Pretorius and the Boers who were in the act of leaving Natal, and giving them to understand that he would not act without evidence of their support, he proclaimed the Queen's paramount authority on 3 February 1848 over 'the territories north of the Great Orange River, including the countries of Moshesh, Moroko, Molitsani, Sinkonyala, Adam Kok, Gert Taaybosch and other minor chiefs, so far north as to the Vaal River, and east to the Drakensberg or Quathlamba Mountains'.

Pretorius, who had travelled six hundred miles to plead the cause of the Natal Boers before Pottinger in October 1847, only to be refused an interview, now emerged as the leader of trans-Orangian resistance to British rule. He discussed the proclamation with the Boers of Winburg, Potchefstroom and Ohrigstad, and on 22 April demanded from Smith 'the same privilege which you are giving to the coloured population, namely self-government', for the white Afrikaner emigrants. Boer resistance, however, did not measure up to such boldness. Other leaders, among them Potgieter and Jacobsz, the landdrost of Winburg, preferred to avoid open confrontation; but Pretorius issued an ultimatum in the name of his *krygsraad* on 12 July 1848. He sent his commandos into the southern districts of trans-Orangia, forcing Oberholzer's supporters into defensive laagers, and with his lines extended he seems to have been prepared to do a deal with Smith. But Smith, who had already outlawed Pretorius, brushed overtures aside, and with help from a force of Kok's Griqua beat Pretorius in a skirmish at Boomplaats, on 29 August, forcing the latter to retreat northwards. He then set up a provisional government for the new Orange River Sovereignty, with Major H. D. Warden as his deputy and Bloemfontein as its capital.

There was peace at first, but within four years the British retreat had begun. Smith ran into difficulties on the Cape eastern frontier in 1850–1, while on the Sotho frontier Moshweshwe was in conflict with his Tlokwa, Rolong and Kora opponents and with the white farmers of the Sovereignty over land. Moshweshwe defeated Warden at Viervoet and reached an understanding with Andries Pretorius. Prompted by news of the Cape frontier crisis, the British Government decided on caution. To work out a viable policy in the light of the military failures, Grey appointed two men with Cape experience, Major W. S. Hogge and C. M. Owen to assist Smith in establishing a secure system of government in the adjacent territories, and report directly to himself. Before long, Hogge had so undermined Grey's confidence in Smith by demonstrating that his military appraisals had been consistently oversanguine, that by September 1851 Grey and Russell had begun to think seriously of abandoning the Orange River Sovereignty, which had in any case never been properly promulgated by letters patent.

When Pretorius threatened to side with Moshweshwe against the Sovereignty unless Britain recognised the independence of the Boers north of the Vaal, the situation became very delicate. Smith agreed to revoke Pretorius's outlawry, which enabled him to enter the Sovereignty for negotiations with Hogge and Owen at the Sand river in January 1852. At this meeting the British representatives agreed to recognise 'the fullest right of the emigrant farmers beyond the Vaal River to manage their own affairs and govern themselves according to their own laws, without any interference on the part of the British Government'. They disclaimed on behalf of the Imperial Government 'all alliances whatever and with whomsoever of the coloured nations to the north of the Vaal River', while the Transvalers agreed to prohibit slavery. The balance of advantage clearly lay with the Boers, who were guaranteed access to supplies of ammunition (which were to be denied to the blacks), and granted the right to receive immigrants from British territory, as well as extradition arrangements.

The success of the Sand River negotiations reduced the urgent need to ditch the Sovereignty, but the Sovereignty itself lasted only two more years. First, its author, Smith, was recalled and replaced by Sir George Cathcart, who had been Wellington's aide at Waterloo. Cathcart was sent to devise a cheap and effective post-war settlement and, as already noted with regard to his policy for the eastern Cape, he saw his task as a simple one of logistics without philanthropy. Where the Sovereignty was concerned, Cathcart's main contribution to peace was his willingness to suffer a military setback at Moshweshwe's hands in December 1852, and then to accept his overtures for peace without having another go at so astute an opponent.

Britain was not chased out of the Sovereignty either by Boer antagonism or by inability to cope with the frontier problems, over which she had not really been put to the test. By 1854, the Cape frontier had been pacified and Moshweshwe, who had finally beaten Sekonyela in October 1853, was unquestioned master of his black rivals yet on good terms with the Imperial authorities. There were interest groups in the Sovereignty which wished Britain to continue her rule – English-speaking landowners and merchants, and whites of both language groups who feared for the security of the Caledon frontier if British troops were withdrawn. Some Boer diehards had moved north across the Vaal after Sand River, and there was no deep rift between those who remained and the Imperial authorities over frontier policy. Philanthropic pressures were now recessive. Sir George Russell Clerk, who had been sent as a Special Commissioner to work out the terms of Boer independence, was prepared to ditch the Griqua, and did so. Moreover, Hogge, Clerk and Cathcart, supported by Lord Aberdeen's Colonial Secretary (the Duke of Newcastle) and Chancellor of the Exchequer (W. E. Gladstone), and above all by Sir William Molesworth, all considered the maintenance of British rule north of the Orange a waste of resources. The decision to withdraw was taken, therefore, not as a result of any opinion poll in the Sovereignty, but primarily for economic reasons by the British Cabinet in March 1853, before Clerk had even set foot in the territory.

A Royal Proclamation renouncing sovereignty over the territory, including by necessary implication the territories of the chiefs, preceded the Bloemfontein Convention, which in turn made the 'Orange River Territory' independent without qualification. The British Government undertook not to make any treaties 'prejudicial to the interests of the Orange River Government'. Maitland's treaty with Adam Kok, which has been ineffective, was to be revised by the removal of restrictions on Griqua land sales, in return for a guarantee that the Griqua themselves would not suffer 'vexatious proceedings' and would be 'guaranteed in the possession of their estates'. Extradition arrangements, an embargo on slavery, and a guarantee of access to ammunition supplies followed on the lines of Sand River, though no mention was made of the sale of arms to blacks. Finally, the British Government undertook to station an agent 'within the Colony near to the frontier' for liaison purposes. Less than two months later, the new Orange Free State had a constitution of its own, though the repeal of the Punishment Act, which was technically necessary to free British subjects north of the Orange from the jurisdiction of the Crown, did not take place until 1863.

The appointment of Sir George Grey as High Commissioner in 1854 was a strange decision at that moment in time, for Grey viewed the settlement of Cape Colonial and extra-colonial disputes as part of a common political problem and clearly intended to turn the High Commissionership into a positive office. After first visiting the eastern Cape frontier, and receiving appeals from the Orange Free State to restrain the Sotho, he spoke in Parliament in 1855 about the need for a common southern African native policy, centrally controlled. Before the year was out, he had visited the Free State and held triangular talks with President Hoffman and Moshweshwe over unrest on the Caledon border. He had also been to Natal, drafted a constitution for that Colony, and taken its land policy in hand. But of all the problems which he had to handle, that of the eastern frontier, which he saw as a continuous line from the mouth of the Kei river to the upper Caledon valley, was the one which exercised him most. At the southern end, unrest among the dispossessed Ngqika and Gcaleka erupted in the Cattle-killing of February 1857, and a rising among the Thembu followed in its wake. At the northern end of the frontier, meanwhile, Moshweshwe and President Hoffman had failed to bring under control the raids of Witsi in the neighbourhood of Harrismith, of Molapo in the Winburg area, and of Jan Letelle and Poshuli around Smithfield. Grey believed the advisers who told him that Moshweshwe and Sarhili, the Gcaleka chief, were in league with each other against the whites.

Within his own area of control, Grey adopted tough measures

against several chiefs for criminal and political offences, and drove both Sarhili and the Thembu rebels across the Kei. But across the Orange he could not act. As early as August 1856 he tried unsuccessfully to persuade the Colonial Office that the policy of the Conventions was outdated, and that the Orange Free State should be included in a federation with the Cape in the interest of trade and defence. This would prevent the merging of the Free State with the trans-Vaal Boers, which M. W. Pretorius was trying hard to bring about. An attempted coup by Pretorius in 1857 failed; but in March 1858 Boshoff declared war on the Sotho against Grey's advice, found he could not prevent their crippling sorties against his border farms, and appealed to Pretorius and to Grey for help. The Transvaal Volksraad's price was political union, whereupon Pretorius and Boshoff met at Winburg, and arranged a truce with Moshweshwe. Grey prohibited Colonial volunteers from helping the Free State, and threatened to cancel the Conventions if the two republics amalgamated. This worked. The Free State Volksraad suspended closer union talks, while Grey went to much trouble to track down Moshweshwe and persuaded him, at Aliwal North in September 1858, to agree to peace on the basis of a new boundary giving him the Kora and Tlokwa lands, and substantial gains in the south.

While he was north of the Orange, Grey canvassed support for a federal South Africa, and on 6 December obtained a favourable vote of twelve to eleven from a Free State Volksraad anxious to escape its Sotho entanglement. He had already urged Lord Derby's new Secretary of State, Bulwer Lytton, to suport a federation of the Cape, Natal and the Orange Free State, embracing Kaffraria and perhaps other territories, under a governor appointed by the Queen, and with a responsible federal legislature elected by the people of the various states in proportion to their financial contributions, on the lines of his New Zealand constitution of 1852. But by attacking past policies he invited – and received – criticism of the cost of his own military establishment and his apparent lack of concern to cut expenditure. Grey, it was observed, had not shown how British forces could be reduced, or indicated how the Cape itself would react to being fragmented into 'two or three . . . states', as he had proposed. It was not politically easy to reverse the new orthodoxy of non-intervention north of the Orange, and Lytton did not propose to try, though he encouraged Grey to explore further the idea of federating the British coastal colonies, excluding the Free State. Grey then acted as if this was a sign that Lytton was open to persuasion on his own scheme, and recommended the Free State Volksraad resolution to the Cape Parliament in March. For this, and for what Rutherford sums up as 'a long series of past offences, great and small', Grey was recalled in June 1859, though a change of government in Britain gave him a short second term until 1861.

*     *     *

Though Grey failed to restore the Imperial presence north of the Orange, his successor, Sir Philip Wodehouse, succeeded. After showing an initial reluctance to intervene in the O.F.S.–Sotho conflict of 1865–1867, he acted vigorously to curb Free State expansion, and blocked Natal's effort to acquire Basutoland as well, by persuading the Colonial Office to let him annex directly to the High Commission. He followed this up, after the renewal of hostilities in 1867, by cutting off Free State ammunition supplies and sending his frontier police into the territory in the Queen's name. When Wodehouse and Brand later confronted each other at Aliwal North in February 1869, he persuaded the Free State, though it had no faith in the power of the Imperial Government to pacify the Caledon river frontier, to accept a major revision of the treaties imposed on the Sotho. Wodehouse was willing to restore some lands to the O.F.S., including the region lost to the Sotho in 1858, and the Volksraad ratified the agreement. Republican resentment over Imperial intervention had been rekindled, but this was not a high price to pay for letting the Republics know that from the Imperial angle – despite the Bloemfontein Convention – South African frontier problems were seen to be indivisible.

During the late 1860s the clash of Boer republican and British imperial interests began to spread, following the discovery of diamonds near the Orange–Vaal confluence, and of gold north of the Limpopo. President M. W. Pretorius of the South African Republic, who had tried unsuccessfully to gain St Lucia Bay since 1861, proclaimed new frontiers for his state in April 1868, extending west and north as far as Lake Ngami, so as to incorporate the traders' route from the Cape to central Africa as well as the gold and diamond-bearing regions, and east to include a stretch of coastline south of Delagoa Bay. The Portuguese objected, and their possession of Delagoa Bay was recognised by the South African Republic in 1869. The British Government also objected in more general terms, while the Ngwato under Matsheng, the Tlhaping under Mahura, and the Rolong of Monthsiwa, voiced their opposition through the British High Commission. The Colonial Office, by an act described by De Kiewiet as bringing about the 'virtual end' of the Sand River Convention, decided to 'disallow' the proclamation.

Behind this decision lay economic and philanthropic pressures. Cape and Natal merchants had clamoured for reannexation north of the Orange, especially during the depression years before 1868, while philanthropist agitation had grown from persistent reports – often based on hearsay – that the Transvalers were a slave-owning community, or at least guilty of black-birding on a considerable scale. Wodehouse, with the annexation of Basutoland behind him, argued that Britain had a duty to hold on to the sub-continent in the interest of order and justice, and began to revive the idea of federalism, pointing towards the reincorporation of the Boer Republics. C. B. Adderley, Under-Secretary in the Colonial Office, saw merit in the proposal, and talked his minister, the Duke of Buckingham, round. But the Tory Ministry took no positive steps. When Gladstone resumed office in December 1868, however, a new policy began to take shape, in which federalism came to be linked with the devolution of power to the Cape – which was anathema to Wodehouse – in a plan to promote economy and justice.

Sir Henry Barkly arrived as High Commissioner in December 1870, to put this policy into effect.[3] He persuaded the Cape to relieve the Imperial Government of Basutoland in 1871. He managed, on the second attempt, to persuade it to accept responsible government in 1872, with the increased defence and administrative commitments which that entailed. The only piece of the puzzle which conspicuously refused to fall into place was that territorial creation of the Colesberg lawyer David Arnot, Griqualand West.

The alluvial diggings at Pniel, on the right bank of the Vaal, first worked in 1869, were claimed not only by Nicholas Waterboer, but by the Tlhaping chief Mahura, by the South African Republic, by the O.F.S., and by the diggers themselves, who set up their own republic on territory belonging to the Berlin Missionary Society. When the dry diggings at Du Toit's Pan (the site of the later Kimberley) were opened in 1870, further dispute arose among the surveyors as to whether they were located east or west of the Ramah–Platberg line which had once divided the lands of Kok from those of Waterboer; for if they lay to the east of that line, they were in the Free State proper. In an area which contained farms granted under Sovereignty, Free State, Transvaal and Griqua title, and where evidence of effective political administration was almost non-existent, there were very strong legal arguments for granting the dry diggings to the Free State and the river diggings to the South African Republic, as well as moral ones for ensuring that the wealth of the area was preserved for the communities which lived there. The Free State Government, convinced that it had a strong case, insisted on foreign arbitration so as to demonstrate the reality of its independence, and when this was refused took no part in the arbitration court which sat at Bloemhof in October 1871. Pretorius and his attorney, Kleyn, appeared on behalf of the Transvaal, but failed to convince the court, either because their case was weak (as Agar-Hamilton argues) or because they put a good case badly (the view of Theal, supported by Van Jaarsveld). Lieutenant-Governor Keate of Natal, the chosen arbitrator, was convinced by Arnot's arguments on behalf of Waterboer, recognised the latter as territorial sovereign of Griqualand West, and upheld the Tlhaping claim by pushing the border of the South African Republic back to the Makwassie Spruit. The victorious Waterboer then asked Barkly to take over his territory, and Barkly accepted it on behalf of the Crown, expecting that the Cape would relieve it of the burden. But the Cape Parliament, despite having accepted Basutoland, was not prepared to help out. The value of the diamond mines to the Colonial economy did not depend on annexation; the administration of the area would not be easy; and acceptance could only damage the Cape's relationship with its Republican neighbours.

Griqualand West almost immediately proved an embarrassment to the skeleton government set up there under Lieutenant-Governor Sir Richard Southey. Its colour-blind authoritarianism did not suit the white digger community, who defied Southey to the brink of rebellion in 1875 and obtained his removal by Lord Carnarvon, Disraeli's Colonial Secretary. Though Carnarvon had dismissed a governor of Natal for his handling of Langalibalele, he would not support a liberal regime in Griqualand West against majority white opinion. His concern for justice was tempered by a desire to protect the Cape route to the east, which still carried more trade than the Suez Canal, and was safer in the event of war.

Carnarvon took advice from his roving ambassador, the historian J. A. Froude, who visited South Africa twice between September 1874 and November 1875, and saw one thing clearly to the obfuscation of much else: that if Britain was to maintain her influence in southern Africa, this had to be in association with the Boer governments, not in opposition to them. This meant redressing the injury caused by the annexation of the Diamond Fields and the mismanagement of native policy (above all by allowing traffic in firearms) which had gone with it. Froude urged a reversal of the Keate Award, which the Transvaal Government explicitly rejected in September 1875, whereas Carnarvon upheld it. Froude was prepared to hold on to the 'Table Mountain peninsula' and allow friendly white governments to control the rest of southern Africa, whereas Carnarvon, for whom military and naval considerations were paramount, doubted whether the Cape could be held without firm control of the hinterland. Froude later professed not to have had any enthusiasm for federating southern Africa, and though he spoke in favour of it, he certainly hindered its cause by his inflammatory speeches. Carnarvon, on the other hand, warmed to federalism by rapid stages, and on 4 May 1875 authorised the calling of a conference of delegates in Cape Town to discuss it. Unfortunately for his own plans, he alienated Molteno's Cape Government, first by suggesting names of possible delegates and including among them Paterson, the leading advocate of Eastern Cape separatism, and second, by putting pressure on the Colony to take over the running of Griqualand West, under a loose federal arrangement, as a condition for the incorporation of Walfisch Bay, which the Cape coveted. The Cape Town conference therefore never took place. Carnarvon toyed with the idea of snubbing the Cape by calling one in Pietermaritzburg instead, but eventually switched the venue to London for August 1876.

The London conference achieved little. Molteno, who refused to attend the proceedings, met Carnarvon beforehand. He was now more amenable to incorporating Griqualand West, but refused to consider federal proposals emanating from outside southern Africa. Brand, after accepting a monetary award for the loss of Griqualand West, agreed to attend the conference; but he insisted that no representative from Griqualand West should be there, and refused to discuss federation. President Burgers of the South African Republic was visiting Europe to raise a loan for a railway from Lourenço Marques to Pretoria, but was apparently not invited owing to an administrative error. Those who did attend came mainly from Natal, notably Sir Garnet Wolseley and Sir Theophilus Shepstone, while Froude stood in for Griqualand West. The conference spend much time discussing the defence of the white territories against the military threat of African chiefdoms armed with guns, and the desirability of achieving common native policies throughout the region.

Deadlock over federation, and reports of severe reverses to the Transvaal commandos in their war against the Pedi in August lay behind Carnarvon's sudden decision in September to annex the Transvaal. Wolseley had suggested that Shepstone be sent to carry out the annexation. Intelligence reports by Colonel G. P. Colley from the Transvaal and Major W. F. Butler from the O.F.S. a year earlier seemed to indicate that English influence was 'likely before long to become dominant' in the former territory, but not in the latter. To annex the Transvaal, indeed, seemed to Carnarvon a good way to promote federation. So far was he from abandoning that aim, that in December 1876 his department drafted enabling legislation very similar to the British North America Act of 1867.

But the Transvaal annexation and the Permissive Federation Bill both backfired sensationally. Shepstone entered the Transvaal from Natal with a small force of police in January 1877, with secret instructions to annex the Republic with or without popular consent. He received plenty of encouragement from the English-speaking community to take the government over. He made much propaganda out of the Zulu threat to the Republic's south-eastern border, and may have believed much of what he said. He found the Executive Council sullen rather than hostile, and divided. He saw a Volksraad unwilling to carry out the reforms which President Burgers placed before it, and a people unwilling to submit to the emergency taxation imposed by the Volksraad. Burgers, aware of the challenge of Paul Kruger to his own presidency, merely offered token resistance when Shepstone proclaimed the Transvaal a British colony on 12 April. The deed was quietly and skilfully done, but that proved to be no index to its popularity.

Meanwhile Sir Bartle Frere, who had an impressive record in India, was chosen by Carnarvon to succeed Barkly, hopefully to become the first Governor-General of a united South Africa. Frere had not been fully informed of the intention to annex the Transvaal, which happened within a few days of his arrival at the Cape. He also arrived to find that the Cape Town Government had rejected the Permissive Federation Bill while he was still on the high seas. The Transvaal Volksraad had rejected it on principle before Shepstone's annexation, and the O.F.S. Volksraad followed suit in May. Yet the measure received the royal assent on 10 August, and it was left to Frere to call a conference when the right moment arrived. His dismissal of Molteno from the Cape premierhip in February 1878 removed a major obstacle to the plan, for his successor, Sprigg, was far more amenable to federation; but not even Frere and Sprigg, working together, could make such a policy acceptable in the Colony.

The Imperial Government had taken over the Transvaal partly to right its public finances and protect it from external danger. Shepstone's financial administration, however, left much to be desired, while the Imperial Parliament contributed a mere £100,000 in financial aid. Meanwhile the Pedi, though prepared to make peace with the Republic in February 1877, had risen against their new masters and were not put down until September 1879, just three months after the Zulu armies, from whom Shepstone had been anxious to protect the Boers, had finally been beaten at Ulundi.

Despite growing Boer opposition, Carnarvon refused a plebiscite to test the popularity of the Queen's sovereignty when Kruger and E. J. P. Jorissen went to London in July 1877. A year later, by which time the initiative in the British federation policy had passed to Frere, the High Commissioner tried to sell the idea of federation to the Boers by offering them self-government linked with a single coordinated system for administering Africans. He worked for the incorporation of the whole Transkei in the Cape, for the setting up of a British protectorate over the Tlhaping and Rolong north of Griqualand West, for the destruction of Zulu military power, even for the incorporation of South West Africa and the Ngwato and Ndebele peoples north of the Limpopo. But his designs were shaken by a crisis in the British Cabinet over the Balkans, which gave the 'little England' faction the ear of the Secretary of State. They were finally wrecked in January 1879 by the disaster of Isandhlwana, at the start of a war which Hicks Beach, Carnarvon's successor, had failed to stop Frere from provoking.

It was therefore at a moment when his 'grand design' was already in tatters that Frere met the Transvaal leaders at Hennopsrivier in April 1879. The Boers had already held protest rallies in January and March. Encouraged by the signs of British military weakness, Kruger now told Frere that he did not know how much longer he could restrain his people from active resistance. Frere failed to trade self-government for a Boer acceptance of federation, but he won Boer respect by offering to forward their demands to London. Soon afterwards, as part of its retreat from the Zulu débâcle, Disraeli's Government saved Frere from the need to resign by dividing the High Commissionership and giving Natal and the Transvaal, together with the supreme military command, to Sir Garnet Wolseley. But Wolseley, expert dispenser of patronage that he was, offended the Boers by bringing them an Assembly with no representative element, and by arresting M. W. Pretorius and Eduard Bok on a frivolous pretext, as well as by his contemptuous remarks about the Boers in dispatches subsequently published. Not surprisingly, therefore, at a gathering at Wonderfontein in December the Queen's sovereignty was publicly denounced, and talk of passive resistance began, with strong support from the Dutch press at the Cape. The Liberals' election victory in April checked talk of rebellion for a while, for Gladstone had criticised Disraeli's South African policy in his Midlothian speeches; but attacks were focused on the federation policy, which was the main excuse Gladstone gave Kruger on 15 June for not letting go of the Transvaal. In April Kruger and Joubert had already started a tour of the Cape to mobilise Afrikaner opinion there. As a result, the Cape Parliament rejected Sprigg's federal motion without a division in June. Gladstone, reading the signs, recalled Frere on 1 August.

Perhaps, at this point, a generous grant of self-government might have preserved British authority in the Transvaal; but Gladstone's Cabinet was too preoccupied with the Irish crisis to give the Transvaal proper attention, while Sir Owen Lanyon, the Administrator of the Transvaal, and Sir George Colley, who had succeeded Wolseley as High Commissioner for South East Africa, had been so reassuring about the mood of the Transvalers that the issue never reached the cabinet agenda between 24 July and 30 December. Furthermore, the Cabinet was divided over policy. Humanitarians like W. E. Forster urged the retention of British rule to protect the blacks; Whig peers like Kimberley urged a strong hand so as to preserve the Imperial image; while Bright, Dilke, Gladstone himself and, above all, Joseph Chamberlain sympathised with the local Boer demand for self-determination. In the end, events moved too fast. The seizure of a Boer wagon because its owner had refused to pay a tax led to violence at Potchefstroom on 19 December, and in the next two months, the leaders of the resistence broke the myth of British military supremacy in engagements at Laing's Nek, Ingogo and Majuba, none of which need have occurred if Colley, who had commanded the British troops and was killed in action, had been clearly informed of the start of negotiations and refrained from unnecessary bravado.

These engagements on the Drakensberg escarpment did not develop into a full-scale war because the shock of Majuba enabled the moderates in Gladstone's Cabinet to gain control, and because the leaders of the Boer resistance proved amenable to the mediation of President Brand. By remaining flexible in their demands, Gladstone and Kimberley persuaded the Boer leaders to sign a Convention at Pretoria in August. This made the 'Transvaal state' independent, left its frontiers intact but prohibited Boer settlement beyond them, adjusted outstanding financial problems by defining the extent of the Transvaal's debt and the size of a small Imperial grant-in-aid, and placed a British Resident in Pretoria as local agent of the Queen's suzerainty. 'Suzerainty' was a smokescreen term, adopted after considerable Cabinet discussion, which reserved 'certain portions of sovereignty' to the Crown. Gladstone defined these in the Commons as 'those which relate to the relations between the Transvaal community and foreign countries', together with 'sufficient power to make provision for the interests of the natives'.

The Pretoria Convention, though subsequently ratified by a reconstituted Volksraad, was not a treaty between two high contracting parties, but a prerogative act conferring rights on the Transvalers. These rights did not amount to a simple return to the position of 1852, for the British presence north of the Vaal remained. The Boer leaders were consequently unable to persuade their countrymen at large that they had made the best possible bargain. They also discovered that when they or their subjects took liberties with the terms of the Convention, the British Government showed reluctance to risk a confrontation.

Kimberley and his successor, Lord Derby, in fact feared that tough action by Britain might unleash not only another war in the north, with possible Free State participation, but also a rebellion in the Cape. The Cape premier, T. C. Scanlen, could not throw his weight behind the Imperial authorities because he depended on Afrikaner Bond votes, when Transvaal Bondsmen flouted the frontier provisions of the Convention by participating in the quarrels of Tswana chiefs, as mercenaries, in return for land grants in Tswana territory. In 1882 they set up the independent Republics of Stellaland and Goshen, based on Vryburg and Mafeking respectively, but could not secure incorporation in the Transvaal, because two pressure groups in Britain stiffened the Colonial Office's resistance. One was the missionary lobby, led by Rev. John Mackenzie of the London Missionary Society. The other was the traders' lobby, led by John X. Merriman and Cecil Rhodes in the Cape Cabinet, who insisted that the Road to the North along the eastern edge of the Kalahari be kept out of Republican hands.

By the end of 1883 Kruger, who had been elected President of the Transvaal Republic in April, was back in London with Rev. S. J. du Toit and General N. Smit, engaged in talks aimed at revising the Pretoria Convention. They demanded a return to the conditions of 1852, complained that the Pretoria Convention had been imposed on them against their will, and objected to its boundary provisions, the suzerainty clause, and the financial arrangements agreed to. With the Cabinet divided by the Egyptian and Reform Bill crises, Derby played defensively, directing discussion towards the contentious issue of the Road to the North, hoping thereby to enlist the support of the Cape as an interested party, and avoiding being drawn on the other points, on which concession would be easier to make. Scanlen's refusal to step out of line with the Transvaal made Derby's task difficult, but early in 1884 Sir Hercules Robinson, Frere's successor, persuaded Scanlen to share in the cost of maintaining a British Protectorate over Bechuanaland. This offer, which amounted to very little in practice, gave Derby the chance he needed to tie Kruger down to a new definition of his western border 'which kept the Road to the North open'. In return, he agreed to reduce the Republic's debt, remove the British Resident in Pretoria, recognise the name 'South African Republic', and – all subsequent protestations by Derby, Chamberlain and others notwithstanding – abolish the Queen's suzerainty, save in so far as specific powers, not referred to by that name, were retained under the new Convention.

But unsettled conditions on the Republic's western border, persisted into 1884. Robinson secured the appointment of the Rev. John Mackenzie as administrator of Stellaland; but with the small police force supplied by the British Government his task was beyond him. Cecil Rhodes, member for Barkly West (the river diggings) and a staunch advocate of annexation by the Cape, then persuaded Robinson to appoint him in Mackenzie's place. Rhodes tried to win over the Stellalanders by generous recognition of their land titles, in the hope that they would help oust the Goshenites. In this he signally failed. Anarchy in the area persisted, and eventually, in September 1884, Kruger forced the issue by 'provisionally' annexing the two Republics to his own, on the plea that this was necessary to restore order. But when the Rev. S. J. du Toit was sent to raise the Transvaal Vierkleur at Vryburg and Mafeking, the Imperial Government reacted strongly on the ground that this was a violation of the London Convention agreed only in the previous February. Kruger climbed down. The British Government sent a force to the area under General Sir Charles Warren in January 1885, ignoring signals from the Cape Government that it was now prepared to take the initiative. Warren, with an impressive military equipage behind him, met Kruger at Fourteen Streams on the Vaal and persuaded him to accept British responsibility for the area. He then annexed the region south of the Molopo river as British Bechuanaland, and subsequently – by agreement with Kgama, chief of the Ngwato – declared a British Protectorate over the whole region south of the twenty-second parallel. Bismarck's surprise proclamation of a Protectorate over South West Africa in August 1884 had facilitated this move. He had embarrassed the British Government and the Cape, but helped Britain to establish closer rapport with the Cape Afrikaners, who had no desire to see another imperial power in their neighbourhood.

In northern Zululand the Imperial Government acted less decisively. There Afrikaner settlers in the disputed Blood River frontier district exploited divisions in Zululand after the restoration and murder of Cetswayo by recognising Dinuzulu as his successor in May 1884, when the British authorities were inclined to back Zibhebhu. In August the Boers proclaimed a New Republic. The British response was to annex St Lucia Bay (1886) and Zululand (1887), but to leave the New Republic alone. It was incorporated in the Transvaal in 1888.

The discovery of diamonds had helped to drive a wedge between Boer and Briton. The discovery of gold on the Witwatersand in 1886 tended in the first instance to cause a polarisation of interests on territorial rather than ethnic lines; but in the longer term it led to a resurgence of Anglo-Boer conflict.[4] The Boer Republics, for all their anti-Imperial fervour in the early 1880s, desired closer economic liaison with the coastal Colonies, and, above all, a share in the customs duties collected at the ports, to help stimulate their struggling economies. Both Brand and Kruger tried in 1884–5 to interest the Cape in a customs union, but the Cape Government was not interested. Then the opening of the Rand goldfields radically altered the balance of advantage. There was a rush to the Rand from the coastal Colonies as well as from abroad, and the coastal states sought to attach themselves to the Rand commercially. The Cape provincial *bestuur* of the Afrikaner Bond became as interested in a Customs Union as the various chambers of commerce of the Cape and Natal. The Cape pursued this goal with a doggedness which eventually resulted in a free trade area comprising the Cape, the Orange Free State, Basutoland, Bechuanaland, Southern Rhodesia and even Natal (which at first stood out) by 1899. But the South African Republic held aloof, fearing that economic cooperation might lead to loss of independence.

A parallel move to establish rail links between the coastal Colonies and the Rand had similar results. When E. McMurdo, an American, obtained a concession from the Portuguese Government in 1882 to construct a railway from Lourenço Marques to the Transvaal with the help of British money, the restored Republic seemed to be assured of economic independence. But McMurdo's line, which was later taken across the Transvaal by the Netherlands South Africa Railway Company holding a concession from the Transvaal Government, only reached Pretoria in 1894, after many hazards. The Transvaal and the Free State Governments discouraged the construction of lines from British colonies to the Rand. The Cape and Natal Governments, however, built lines from Cape Town, Port Elizabeth, East London and Durban to Fourteen Streams, Colesberg, Aliwal North and Charlestown respectively, hoping to wear the Republics' resistance down. Between 1888 and 1890 the Cape broke through. Sprigg, prime minister in 1888, devised a plan to extend the Colesberg line into the Free State under the threat of extending the line from Fourteen Streams into the Transvaal if the Free State refused, thus threatening to by-pass the southern Republic. If both Republics refused to admit a line, he proposed to extend the Fourteen Streams line through Bechuanaland, thus threatening to establish rail links with central Africa which left both Boer Republics in the shallows. This persuaded Kruger to put pressure on President Reitz of the Free State, who agreed to admit the Colesberg line. The subsequent extension of this line into the Transvaal resulted from the financial embarrassment of the Netherlands Company during the gold crisis of 1890. Rhodes, by that time Premier of the Cape, agreed to advance funds to the Company provided that the first call on them should be a line from the Vaal river, connecting the Port Elizabeth line to the Rand. This line reached the Rand in 1892. The Delagoa Bay and Natal lines followed only in 1894 and 1895. But then, with three competing systems at its disposal, the South African Republic could allocate the traffic as it thought fit.

A head-on collision between the Cape Government and the Netherlands Company followed, when Laing, Rhodes's Commissioner of Public Works, asked the Company for half the heavy traffic for the Cape system in August 1894. Middelberg, for the Company, offered one-third only, and raised the rates from the Vaal to the Rand in retaliation against a threatened tariff war. When the Cape merchants replied by sending goods from the river to the Rand by ox-waggon, Kruger closed the Vaal drifts for the importation of goods from overseas. This, however, was to discriminate between member states of the British Empire, in violation of the London Convention, as Rhodes and his ministers reminded Joseph Chamberlain, the new British Colonial Secretary. Together they threatened force. Kruger, as usual, climbed down – but not before he had cemented the fateful alliance between Rhodes and Chamberlain which produced the Jameson Raid within three months.

Between 1884 and 1895 imperial competition in southern Africa became more intense, as British, Portuguese and German diplomacy explored the possibility of extending right across the continent by winning control of the Zambesi valley. Portuguese *contra costa* aspirations had grown out of the Macmahon Award, followed by Serpa Pinto's journey from Angola to Mozambique in 1879. The German notion of *Mittelafrika* linked Tanganyika with South West Africa. Both these notions were repugnant to the '*Cape to Cairo*' vision of Harry Johnston and Cecil Rhodes. Both, however, were casualties of the Anglo-German and Anglo-Portuguese diplomacy of 1890–1, when the Germans added the Caprivi Strip to South West Africa but left the British in possession of the Stephenson Road connecting Lakes Tanganyika and Nyasa (Malawi), while the Portuguese obtained trans-continental telegraph rights from coast to coast, but no continuous land bridge.

The British acquisition of Rhodesia between 1888 and 1893 defeated the territorial aspirations of the South African Republic as well as those of rival European powers. The Transvaal's interest in the area beyond the Limpopo dated from the 1850s, when Hendrik Potgieter had established a treaty relationship with Mzilikazi, and was still alive when Kruger sent Piet Grobler on his ill-fated expedition in 1887 to open formal diplomatic relations with Lobengula. British and Cape activity in the region had led to the founding of a company to work the Tati goldfields in 1880, and of Lord Gifford's Bechuanaland Exploring Company in 1888. By acquiring rights under the Rudd and Lippert concession, however, Rhodes beat his rivals as well as tying up Lobengula. Whites from all parts of southern Africa, British and Boer, set off with the Pioneer Column in search of farms, while a second wave of land purchase followed the defeat and death of Lobengula in 1893. Chartered shares, like farms, found their way into Dutch as well as British hands, though the bulk of them were distributed in London, not South Africa. Rhodes's agents, Sharpe and Lochner, consolidated the Company's influence in North-Eastern Rhodesia and Barotseland, and were unfortunate not to acquire Katanga as well, while other Company servants moved east into Manicaland and tried unsuccessfully to establish control over the Pungwe River route to Beira. But the mineral wealth in Mashonaland on which much speculation was based was shown to be largely illusory by the Hays-Hammond Report of 1894. From that date it became clear that the key to the political control of southern Africa lay in the Transvaal [see pp. 114–16].

The encirclement of the Transvaal was one aim of British Imperial strategy in the 1890s. Political federation had ceased to be practical politics after the recall of Frere. Economic federation by means of a customs union and the integration of separate railway systems fell short of the target owing to Transvaal resistance in the 1890s. By revoking the provisional annexation of Bechuanaland in 1885, and by renouncing all interest north of the Limpopo in negotiations with High Commissioner Sir Henry Loch in March 1890, Kruger exposed his state to the danger of encirclement. Having made engagements, however, he honoured them, and disowned the Bowler and Adendorff treks across the Zambesi in 1890 and 1891, staking all on the acquisition of a seaport, which he never obtained. But at least his Republic was never cut off, even though by 1895 the whole coastline from the Orange River mouth to Tongaland was in British hands. When Kruger agreed to abandon the north in 1890, it was in the hope of acquiring Kosi Bay in Tongaland, but this was made conditional on the Republic's joining the Customs Union, which the Volksraad refused to do. Thereafter the emphasis of Kruger's policy, like that of Rhodes, was on the acquisition of Lourenço Marques, which seemed to be within reach after the Imperial Government had agreed to the Republic's administering Swaziland in 1895. But the Portuguese, sheltering behind protracted litigation in Switzerland over McMurdo's complicated debts, adamantly refused to sell.

British Imperial strategists who recognised that Rhodesia could not become a second Rand came to realise that the Transvaal held the key to southern Africa as a whole. On this line of thinking, the only hope of assured British political dominance was to transfer political control of the Rand to the Uitlander element. The Uitlander agitation, which first received organised form in 1892, was at least rooted in unpopular disabilities; but that it was used to further the cause of British paramountcy is clear enough, from the moment when Kruger's political reforms of 1890 put paid to the likelihood of Uitlanders winning control of the Volksraad by normal political activity. No less a person than Sir Henry Loch turned his mind in 1894 to the idea of an Uitlander rising in Johannesburg to be followed by an invasion by a British force from the Protectorate, as a means of achieving a British takeover of power less subtle by far than Shepstone's takeover of 1877. Loch's idea provided a blueprint for the Jameson Raid of 1895, with the important difference that the intention behind the Jameson Raid was that the tracks of the Colonial Office should be properly covered by the use of the Company's private army rather than men in British military uniforms.

There is no longer any reason for supposing that Joseph Chamberlain was unofficially ignorant of the planned invasion of the Transvaal, or that he had made over to the Company a force of Bechuanaland Border Police and a strip of land along the Protectorate's border without knowing that these were to be used for the Raid. Nothing could have destroyed the trust between the South African Republic and the Colonial Office in the months following the Drifts Crisis quite so effectively as an unsuccessful coup d'état. The involvement of Chamberlain, of Sir Hercules Robinson, now enjoying his second term as governor, and of other key figures, was suppressed by the Committee of Inquiry sitting in London in 1897, but this did not allay contemporary Transvaal suspicions. The Republic was given a genuine pretext for rearming in self-defence, which it now proceeded to do. But the act of rearming gave currency to the idea in British circles that Kruger aimed at the 'dominion of Afrikanerdom' (or Tranvaal republican rule) from the Limpopo to Simonstown. That he had any such aim is improbable. The case against him depended largely on the revamping of Bond propaganda utterances dating from the early 1880s, when the mood of Afrikaner nationalists had been far more flamboyant. This could have deceived Chamberlain, for it was as a member of Gladstone's government during the trying negotiations over the Pretoria and London Conventions that he had first met Paul Kruger, then an anrgy, assertive political opportunist, keen to exploit the position of strength in which he found himself, equivocal in debate but expecting to win rather than lose. He had better reason for anger in 1896–9 and the confidence his people reposed in him was now much stronger; but he was under much greater pressure than before, and if he equivocated now it was to avoid direct confrontation with skilled opponents on their ground rather than his own. They pulled him into the arena of Uitlander rights. His task was to keep the debate going on the issues related to British paramountcy, but that was not easy [see pp. 73–4].

The main thrust of the Imperial attack, however, came not from Chamberlain but from Sir Alfred Milner, High Commissioner from May 1897. Milner had a very clear picture of the way events were shaping in South Africa, and of the probable changes in the balance of power, an equally pronounced confidence in the ability of a Balliol scholar to play and beat an unschooled Voortrekker at diplomatic chess, a very fluent pen full of adjectives, and a large share of the condescension too often found among *fin de siècle* imperialists who spoke of Britain's civilising mission within earshot of the Jameson Raid. But he had little apparent understanding of the points of view of the more or less Calvinist Afrikaners. Milner was interested in power. His decision that Kruger's power had to be broken probably dated from the latter's overwhelming victory in the presidential election of March 1898, though the mounting of his diplomatic offensive was delayed by the Bond's triumph over the Progressives in the Cape lower house election in July, and by the counter-influence of General Sir William Butler, who acted as High Commissioner while Milner was in Britain at the end of the year. Milner returned in February 1899, and soon rebuilt the alliance between the Colonial Office and the anti-Government Randlords which had been shattered by the failure of the Jameson Raid. When the capitalist negotiations fell through in March, he resumed the offensive, engineered a petition from the Uitlander community to the Queen (whereas Butler had refused an earlier one for reasons of protocol in December) and tried to provoke a crisis by insisting in his celebrated 'helot' dispatch of 4 May that 'the case for intervention is overwhelming'. The Cape Government and President Steyn then undermined his strategy by arranging for a meeting between Milner and Kruger at Bloemfontein at the end of May. Milner, however, worked for public confrontation rather than private negotiation, and got it. Thereafter, events played into his hands. The 'helot' dispatch was published. The Transvaal Government made a succession of compromise offers over the controversial Uitlander franchise, realising that active support from Cape Afrikaners could not be taken for granted. Chamberlain was half persuaded by terms offered by Smuts on Kruger's behalf in August. But Milner professed to suspect a trap, the negotiations broke down, and in October 1899 both sides resorted to the arbitrament of force.

The Boers began the war on 11 October 1899 because, with an initial military advantage, they appreciated how important it was to seize the initiative.[5] Smuts had accurately calculated that they could bring about 40,000 men into the field, against a British garrison which he slightly underestimated at 15,000 at the outbreak of hostilities. A large British expeditionary force was expected, which began to arrive in November. Commandos from the Transvaal and Orange Free State moved into Natal, and after a few sharp early engagements invested Ladysmith and advanced to Estcourt and beyond. The Free Staters delayed their crossing of the Cape frontier on account of an earlier plea by Schreiner to help him maintain a non-combatant role. But faced with the prospect of attack by Cape-based Imperial troops, Steyn sent his commandos across the Orange on 1 November, and they soon brought a large number of Colonial Afrikaners out in rebellion. But there was no concentration of Boer forces for a drive into the Colony, and no determined attempt to take Mafeking, Kimberley or Ladysmith. In his discerning *Memoir* of the Anglo-Boer War, General Smuts strongly criticised this lack of offensive spirit among the Boer leadership during these early critical months, when Louis Botha and Koos de la Rey were refused permission to drive deep into Natal and the Cape respectively. The ability of the Boer forces to contain the initial British counter-offensive in tough operations on the Tugela, in the Stormberg and at Magersfontein in mid-December, perhaps lured them into a belief that defence was the best form of attack – an idea which General Sir Redvers Buller's errors encouraged. But Buller's command was taken over in December by Lord Roberts, who had volunteered to leave his semi-retirement and succeed him.

Roberts arrived from Britain in January, with Lord Kitchener as his second-in-command and brought a new plan of campaign: to advance up the line of rail from Cape Town to the Modder river, and then send his main force eastwards to cut the Free State line south of Bloemfontein, thus threatening to isolate the Boer forces in the south, while Buller, who had meanwhile relieved Ladysmith with the help of troop reinforcements, completed the reconquest of Natal. British forces advanced with relative ease into the Free State and Transvaal, taking Bloemfontein on 13 March after capturing Cronje's large commando at Paardeberg, Johannesburg on 5 May and Pretoria on 6 June. Roberts proclaimed British sovereignty over the 'Orange River Colony' and the 'Transvaal Colony' on 24 May and 1 September respectively. Kruger left via Lourenço Marques for Europe in a vain bid to seek Continental aid, and Boer resistance dwindled as the commandos began to trickle home, leaving a mere 8000 Free Staters and 7000 Transvalers under arms (in the calculations of De Wet and Smuts).

It was the determination of a few leaders at this point which brought the commandos back into the field, notably President Steyn and General de Wet in the Free State, Botha, De la Rey and Smuts in the Transvaal. The leaders reappraised their tactics. Cronje's defeat had destroyed the glamour of the traditional laager. The experience of Diamond Hill, fought soon after the fall of Pretoria, showed the folly of allowing manpower losses in set-piece defensive actions. The accent now was on a war of movement with local commandants operating on their own initiative under centrally coordinated plans. Botha took charge of the eastern Transvaal, while De la Rey returned to the western. In the Free State, De Wet was elected Commandant-General in June. He organised the return of commandos to the Cape led by J. B. M. Hertzog, Kritzinger, Gideon Scheepers and (very briefly) himself. These invasions spread the war deep into the Cape. Smuts wrote on 3 February 1901 that 'the Afrikaners are rising everywhere', the Free State commandos having reached beyond Willowmore, Fraserburg and Carnarvon (all in the Karoo), with Colonial rebels active at Clanwilliam, Van Rhynsdorp and Tulbagh.

The Boer commandos proved a match for the British military machine, which was provided at first with far too few mounted men, and was quite unused to this kind of warfare. Under the inspiration of Danie Theron they quickly became masters of scouting, sabotaged the railway lines, and learned how to turn flight into an offensive weapon by suddenly turning on their exhausted pursuers. Smuts detected in the British field commanders a lack of confidence in themselves comparable with that which he had earlier noticed in the Boer veterans, Piet Joubert and P. A. Cronje – a weakness particularly discernible in Baden-Powell, the popular hero of Mafeking.

Faced with a type of warfare for which they were unprepared, the British commanders reacted with a good deal of unfeeling brutality. S. B. Spies has shown that the farm-burning started before the departure of Roberts in November 1900, so that the full responsibility cannot be placed on Kitchener. His calculation that about 30,000 farmsteads were destroyed during the course of the war, and approximately twenty villages, bears out Smuts's report to Botha from the northern Transvaal on 22 September 1900 that

> whenever the enemy now appears, he carries out indescribable destruction. All houses are burned down, all fields and gardens utterly destroyed, all cattle and foodstuffs carried off and all males taken prisoner!

Margaret Marquard's letters from Winburg tell a similar story with reference to one district in the Free State.

Because farms were in the front line in a war of movement, burnings could be militarily justified; but they led to the spread of atrocity stories, the truth of which is in the nature of the case very difficult to assess. Some involved high-ranking British officers, like General French. The stories became the fuel for a women's protest movement in the Cape, led by Olive Schreiner and Marie Koopmans de Wet. When the Opposition newspapers took up the stories, their editors were tried and convicted on charges of seditious libel, and the newspapers themselves were suppressed.

Train-wrecking became so frequent – Spies notes 135 incidents between December 1900 and September 1901 – that it was treated as a criminal offence, and in a vain attempt to stop it the military authorities made Boer hostages ride on the trains, or destroyed homesteads close to the places where sabotage had occurred. De Wet's accounts of successful attacks on trains passing through the Free State show how vulnerable the British supply lines had become.

Boers caught wearing British military uniforms were sometimes executed, the shooting of Jack Baxter of Klerksdorp being a case in point. Miscarriages of justice for which the military courts were held responsible formed the theme of G. Jordaan's later *Hoe Zij Stierven* (1915) and of Gustav Preller's edition of the diary of the colourful Boer martyr, Gideon Scheepers. The first work in Afrikaans to defend these military tribunals on the ground that they did what was expected of them under circumstances of martial law, appeared only in the very different climate of 1962.

To deal with the elusive Boers, the British authorities cordoned off enormous areas of South Africa with fences guarded by blockhouses, and then carried out organised sweeps. At first the commandos generally managed to cut their way through the obstacles, but by the end of the war Kitchener's 'new model' sweeps were making evasion extremely difficult, and even De Wet was fully extended to break out of his cordon in February 1902.

The British also made use of surrendered Boers as peace propagandists. Burgher Peace Committees were promoted by brothers of De Wet and Cronje from December 1900. The same A. P. Cronje was the moving spirit behind the National Scouts, composed of Boers who had 'hands-upped' from conviction that their cause was hopeless and only surrender could bring relief. The diary of P. J. du Toit, a member of General Liebenberg's Transvaal commando, reveals clearly the mental anguish of such people.

National Scouts and their families were particularly vulnerable to Boer retribution, and it was in the first instance to protect them that the British military authorities decided in the second half of 1900 to set up concentration camps. But before the end of the year the concept was enlarged to include civilians cleared from their homes as a result of farm-burnings and military sweeps. Two categories of camp inmate were soon distinguished: those who were non-partisan or had taken oaths of allegiance to the Queen, and those whose husbands or sons were on commando and were regarded as hostile to the Imperial cause. The former received more considerate treatment. Some forty-four camps for whites were set up altogether, most of them in the Transvaal and the Orange River Colony. They were transferred to civilian control in November 1901, after Milner had protested to Kitchener about the harshness of the system and the high mortality rate, which had risen to 344 per thousand during October. The camps became a public scandal an account of the high incidence of disease in them (mainly measles and amoebic dysentery), and their administrative defects to which Emily Hobhouse drew attention during her visit in January 1901. As the war drew to a close, conditions in the camps improved until the death rate was not abnormal, but by then 26,000 inmates had died, of whom about 20,000 were under the age of 16. Milner criticised the camps because of the adverse publicity which they gave to the British cause. The military authorities, however, would have had fewer problems if they had been allowed to make peace with the Boers and leave them some measure of independence.

Demands for peace on such terms split and then destroyed the Schreiner Government at the Cape in June 1900. Merriman and Te Water campaigned against martial law and against the disfranchisement of rank-and-file rebels. They found an ally in the South African Conciliation Committee, which had been set up in January with branches in England and at the Cape, and organised a massive public meeting at Worcester, Cape Colony, in December, as a result of which Merriman and Sauer tried unsuccessfully to deliver a 'grand remonstrance' to the House of Commons in March 1901. The Conciliation Committee deplored the inroads made by the war into the rights of the subject, denying – as Sir Edward Coke might equally have done – that reason of state justified any action done under martial law. In doing so, they struck a common chord with the British Liberal left, who deplored the Tory victory in the Khaki election of October 1900, and were so shocked by Emily Hobhouse's revelations concerning the camps that their parliamentary leader, Sir Henry Campbell-Bannerman, could blast A. J. Balfour's defence of British methods on the ground that the war was really over with the rhetorical question: 'When is a war not a war? When it is carried on by methods of barbarism in South Africa.'

People throughout the land experienced real loss of liberty and material deprivation in 1901. Farmers in the Cape did not know whom to fear more, the Boers who moved in and commandeered their stock, or the military authorities who took their stock and destroyed their crops to prevent them from falling into Boer hands. Relations between Dutch- and English-speaking communities in the towns deteriorated. Boer supporters dressed provocatively in Republican colours. Supporters of the Empire joined Vigilance Associations or enlisted in the Natal-based South African Light Horse or in the (Cape) Colonial Volunteer Corps, whose members were freed for active service by the formation of town guard units from December 1899.

Militarily the year was indecisive. Invasions by Boer commandos at the beginning of the year had helped to bring about a second Cape rebellion, which resulted by mid-year in most of the north-west Cape falling into rebel hands. In February Kitchener offered to meet Botha at Middelburg, Transvaal, to discuss terms of peace. Botha accepted the invitation but negotiations broke down because Kitchener had refused to offer elective self-government, let alone independence, to the Boers. On 10 May, however, the Transvalers asked the Free Staters to agree to seek Kruger's advice on future policy. Though Steyn was strongly opposed, Smuts cabled Kruger after getting Kitchener's permission. He painted the situation of the Boers in gloomy colours. Kruger's reply indicated that foreign support could be discounted, but that so long as the Cape rebellion looked promising they should fight on. Eventually, on 20 June, the two governments managed to renew contact with each other and publicly renounced all thought of making peace unless their independence was assured.

The situation in the Cape remained fluid. The Boer Central Peace Committee had corresponded with T. P. Theron, then chairman of the Afrikaner Bond, in February, trying to get the 'Afrikaner Party' to support its peace efforts by publicly refusing to assist the commandos. Theron declined to negotiate with them, and would only work through the 'constituted authorities'. The times were out of joint, with the treason courts sitting in the north-east Cape, the editors of *Ons Land* and the *South African News* behind bars for publishing seditious libel, and the Progressive campaign for the suspension of the Cape constitution beginning to get underway. In August came Kitchener's 'paper bomb', requiring the commandos to surrender by 15 September on pain of life banishment. Three commando leaders, Lötter, Kritzinger and Scheepers, were all caught by the British in the eastern Cape in September and October. But Smuts also arrived there in September, eluded capture and moved down into the western province, where he eventually linked up with Maritz's rebels in the north-west, who controlled the whole area except for Kenhardt and Upington. Yet Smuts's field report of 16 December, optimistic though it was as to the mood of Colonial Afrikaners, made it clear that the rebellion could not become mobile because of the scarcity of horses. Meanwhile Kitchener's drives in the northern Free State and eastern Transvaal were placing De Wet and Botha under severe strain, forcing De Wet to quit the eastern Free State and move westwards. De la Rey's capture of Lord Methuen in March was an insignificant if spectacular reversal of fortune.

Devastating attrition was the brute fact underlying the Boer situation. Understandably, the numbers ready to make peace grew. On 4 March Kitchener was instructed to pass on to the Boer leaders a dispatch from Lord Lansdowne which, in rejecting a Dutch offer to mediate, made it clear that the Boer governments were once again recognised by the British as the spokesmen of their people. Schalk Burger, acting president of the Transvaal, asked for a safe conduct, and managed to persuade even Steyn to talk. The two Boer governments therefore met at Klerksdorp on 9 April, in tents supplied by the British. On 31 May they agreed to terms and the war ended.

The Anglo-Boer War was fought to determine which white authority held real power in South Africa. In scale and in temper, it was vastly different from all previous Anglo-Boer military encounters. A British subaltern might publish his diary under the title *The Last of the Gentlemen's Wars.* De la Rey might give point to this by handing over the wounded Lord Methuen to the British and then sending a personal message of condolence to his Lady. But these were at best civilised moments in a war of considerable brutality. Kipling, lionising De Wet in his *Five Nations*, reflected this mood. But his vitriolic attack on the Cape partisans in his *Science of Rebellion* and Leipoldt's tragic *Oom Gert vertel* were more in keeping with the dominant mood of the war.

Because it was a war between whites, it was not allowed, save in a marginal sense, to become a black man's war. What was total war for a fifth of the population was therefore no war at all, in theory, for the other four fifths. This was symbolised by Sol Plaatje's description, in his diary of the siege of Mafeking, of Rolong herdboys openly guarding their stock in the no-man's-land between the Boer and British lines, and casually picking up the fragments of shells which burst nearby. Yet the role of blacks was by no means as passive or as immune as this description suggests.

Republican laws forbade the carrying of arms by blacks, and Breytenbach affirms that the Boer authorities enforced this rule, limiting blacks who accompanied the commandos to the roles of wagon-drivers or servants. Blacks were also commonly required to stand in on the farms of commandeered burghers. On the British side, Roberts and

Kitchener used blacks from the farms and the mines as labourers, drivers, convoy guards, dispatch riders, watchmen in blockhouses, and scouts. The black residents of the Mafeking *stadt*, who could move into and out of the town more easily than the whites, often carried messages and raided Boer farms for cattle, which they brought into the town, sometimes after armed clashes with groups of Boers. Further north, where Colonel Herbert Plumer fought a war of movement with the Boer commandos, in competition for the loyalty of the Tswana chiefdoms, mutual raiding occurred between the Boers and Lentswe's Kgatla, whose initial disposition was apparently pro-Boer. Boer relations with black chiefdoms depended in large measure on the degree of their economic distress. At the beginning of the war, black levies stationed on the borders of the Transkei, with a stiffening of Cape Mounted Rifle detachments, successfully deterred the commandos from moving into the area; whereas the arming of Zulu in the Nqutu district with 'sticks and assegais' was not sufficient to deter a big Boer cattle raid in September 1901. General Kemp, urging his compatriots to fight on at Vereeniging, claimed to have no problem where food supplies were concerned because he 'took what he wanted from the Kaffirs'. There were, on the other hand, many Boer complaints that the British armed the blacks in order to cause trouble for the Boers. Thus Smuts, in a propaganda letter to W. T. Stead on 4 January 1902 alleged that all the tribes in and around the South African Republic, had been armed by the British military authorities and had 'committed horrible atrocities on fugitive or peaceful women and children'. Ben Viljoen's *Reminiscences* likewise deal with black violence in the Lydenburg district, in association with a troop of white thugs known as Steinacker's Horse. The truth of such reports is hard to ascertain, but increasing deprivation was likely to make Boer–black relations more tense, and in proportion as Boer fortunes declined, so their fear of black molestation grew.

Blacks also found their way into concentration camps, without the same amount of publicity as the white because neither Emily Hobhouse, who was aware of their situation, nor Dame Millicent Fawcett's Ladies' Committee had the time to pay much attention to them. The British created camps for blacks from the start. In general, African locations were not disturbed, but Africans living on Boer farms were removed, the women and children into camps, the men into labour service. A separate Native Refugee Department was set up in June 1901, and about 4000 (largely ex-mine workers) drafted into the Army Labour Department for railway maintenance – of whom De Wet captured three hundred in June 1900. Maintenance in African camps was calculated at 4½*d* per day, as against 8½*d* for whites, partly because Africans were encouraged to grow their own food and build their own huts. There were twenty-nine African camps housing 107,344 by the end of the war. The death toll was not as high as in the white camps during the early months, but at the end of the war it was considerably higher, for the figures did not drop as they did in the white, and rose to the very high figure of 372 per thousand (as against the highest white figure of 344 in October 1901). The African camps remained under military control after the white had been transferred to civilian. The official figure for African camp deaths was 13,315, though Spies asserts that 'considerably more' must have died.

# 9 The Shaping of a White Dominion

When the Boer leaders met at Klerksdorp in April 1902 to consider making peace, they rallied to the exhortations of the ailing Steyn and proudly approached Kitchener with a peace offer which took their continued independence for granted.[1] They would demilitarise the republics but asked for a treaty of friendship which would settle future economic relationships and political rights, and provide for the arbitration of disputes, equal language rights, and a mutual amnesty. Kitchener agreed to relay their offer to London, knowing that the British Government would not contemplate such a basis for talks. He insisted that the annexation was a *fait accompli.* They retorted that they had no authority to sign away their independence. But Kitchener allowed them facilities for convening a representative assembly of the people with plenipotentiary powers. The two Boer governments accordingly met again on 15 May at Vereeniging, in company with thirty delegates representing the commandos of each republic. These reported on the situation in their districts, which in many cases was critical. Those who still had cattle, grain and horses were generally prepared to fight on, and De Wet in particular, keeping faith with his diehard president, brushed aside obstacles in a rousing speech. But it was Botha and De la Rey who best represented the majority view, as they weighed logistic possibilities, and concluded that to continue a hopeless fight might well weaken their bargaining position in the long run. On the 17th the delegates decided that they could accept a British protectorate, surrender control over foreign policy, and if necessary give up some territory – for example, the Rand and Swaziland.

For a second time Kitchener, who was now joined by Milner, rejected the basis of the Boer offer. This time they insisted that the Boers return to the Middelburg terms as a starting-point for talks. These had treated the annexation of the Republics as irreversible, but included the honouring of war debts incurred by the Republican governments among their own people, loans for the reconstruction of destroyed farms, and an undertaking by the British Government not to enfranchise 'kaffirs' before granting representative government to the Boers, and even then with securities for 'the just predominance of the white race'.

Conversion of the Middelburg terms into those eventually agreed to in the Treaty of Vereeniging was assigned to a committee consisting of Smuts, Hertzog, Kitchener and Sir Richard Solomon, whose work was then reviewed by the British Government. The log-jam among the Boers was largely broken when Botha and De la Rey approached De Wet, to whom Steyn had handed over his authority, and persuaded him in private to agree to peace. The Boer leaders then agreed by 54 votes to 6 to surrender their independence in return for the repatriation and release of prisoners of war, the limited protection of their language in court and school, the expectation of ultimate political autonomy with no target date set, and certain economic safeguards – the right to their property, protection against a land tax to pay war expenses, the honouring of republican war debts to a maximum of £3 million, and the provision of extensive relief for the victims of war. The British also promised not even to consider the enfranchisement of 'natives' until self-government had been introduced, thus giving the Boers a decisive say in the matter.

South Africa was at last at Milner's feet. He had already moved with the high commissionership to Johannesburg in February 1901, and then received a peerage in England before returning in August to preside over the reconstruction of British South Africa.

Natal, under Sir Henry McCallum, presented no problems where Milner's plans were concerned. Its northern boundaries extended by the incorporation of the Vryheid district of the Transvaal, it remained faithful to the Imperial cause during the successive premierships of Sir Albert Hime (1899–1903), G. M. Sutton (1903–5), C. J. Smythe (1905–6) and F. R. Moor (1906–10).

In the Cape, the possibility of a Bond majority seemed to Milner to endanger the British character of South Africa as a whole. For this reason he had urged the suspension of the constitution since early in the war, with considerable support from the Progressives, whose campaign reached a climax with a well-signed petition on 10 May 1902. But the movement was killed by the resistance of a few Cape parliamentarians, led by Sir Gordon Sprigg, who won the ear of Chamberlain and of the Colonial Conference of 1902. So serious was the rift which had developed between Chamberlain and Milner on this issue that it must be seen as one of the main reasons for Chamberlain's visit to South Africa in November 1902. But suspension ceased to matter in practice because the disfranchisement of Cape rebels by the military courts ensured a Progressive victory in the Cape elections of 1904, despite signs of an electoral swing in favour of the Bond.

Jameson's victory postponed the political crisis; but ironically it did not preserve that sure base for British power which all parties had expected of such a premier. In a fairly successful bid to befriend Afrikanerdom, he carried out a redistribution of parliamentary seats with mathematical objectivity which only gave his party a very slight advantage, and then reduced the disfranchisement of rank-and-file rebels from a lifespan to five years, thus preparing the ground for his own defeat in 1908. For the rest, he tried to secure financial compensation for the victims of war damage (until this was killed by the financial crisis in 1907), worked hard to satisfy the farmers' interests by irrigation and agricultural credit legislation, coupled with protective tariffs, and sought popularity with the white electorate by measures to curb Chinese immigration and entrench white privilege in the government schools.

As Governor of the Transvaal and the Orange River Colony, Milner had the help of Lieutenant-Governors Sir Arthur Lawley and Sir Hamilton Goold-Adams respectively, each with an executive council which took over from the military authorities in June 1902. Legislative councils consisting of officials and nominees were appointed soon afterwards, both holding their first sessions in 1903. In June that year an Inter-Colonial Council of four nominees (later raised to twelve) and fourteen officials came into being. This was Milner's brainchild, and it was given special responsibility for certain key agencies which straddled both the new colonies in a calculated bid to break down the provincial spirit – notably the Central South African Railways (an amalgamation of the Free State governmental and Transvaal private companies), Baden-Powell's South African Constabulary, repatriation, and schools. For administrative skill, Milner relied on the talented but controversial group of Oxford bachelors dubbed by Merriman his 'Kindergarten'.

To achieve the political conversion of the new colonies Milner attached great importance to their economic recovery. This meant bringing the mines back into full production as quickly as possible, getting the farmers back on to the land and their desolated farms restocked, building up railway communications for the proper flow of goods, and completing the drive towards a customs union which had stopped short before the war.

He received authority to raise a loan of £35 millions under Imperial guarantee, and this, with the imposition of a 10 per cent tax on mining profits which was expected to net at least £500,000 a year, served to prime the pump, though only £10 millions were available for development as distinct from other commitments. Mining returned to its pre-war production level by 1904, and expanded steadily thereafter, the value of gold mined rising from fractionally over £1 million in 1901 to £20.9 millions in 1905 and £32 millions in 1910. This happened in spite of a serious labour crisis which Milner resolved, first, by a not very advantageous *modus vivendi* concluded with the Governor of Mozambique in December 1901 for the engagement of Shangaan workers, and second, by the introduction of indentured Chinese labourers from 1904. The Chinese made it possible for expansion to take place while the machinery for the recruitment of African labour was getting into gear again; but the demand for labour remained greater than the supply, largely on account of the need for labourers to man the railway construction projects as well as rebuild the farms [see pp. 357–9].

The establishment of the Central South African Railways at the Bloemfontein railway conference in March 1903 resulted, during the next few years, in the completion of a line from Kimberley to the Rand, and of another joining the Natal and Orange River Colony systems between Ladysmith and Kroonstad, as well as the doubling of the line from Lourenço Marques to Witbank. At the same time an experimental pan-South African Customs Union was set up in 1903, all internal customs dues abolished, and a 10 per cent *ad valorem* duty imposed on imports from outside, with 25 per cent Imperial preference – all for a two-year trial period.

Restoration of the farms and the repatriation of Boer prisoners was the task of a central committee operating through local commissions. The £3 million allotted under the terms of Vereeniging were to be divided among the ex-burghers of the Republics who could prove war losses, whichever side they had fought for. The actual sum spent on relief and repatriation amounted to over £16 millions, in grants and loans. Complaints among the Boers that those who had supported the British were favoured at the expense of those who had not were frequently made. But in practice the new administration worked hard to provide the Boers with ploughs, seed, and rations until they could feed themselves, and introduced veterinary services to deal with stock disease. By the end of 1902, most of the people were back on the land, and the problem of planting food for the following year more or less solved. What Milner could not have reckoned with, however, was the sustained drought conditions of 1903–8, which made rural recovery very difficult.

Milner hoped also to place English-speakers on the land so as to break down the sharp occupational division between rural Afrikaners and urban British. He wanted a massive infusion of English-speakers into the new colonies – 'a good class of settler – not "tommies" but men with farming experience and a little capital – Australians, Canadians, Scottish Lowland farmers, the best of the Yeomanry, and the best of the young British Colonists from the Cape and Natal', arriving he hoped at the rate of 10,000 settlers 'within a twelvemonth'. Schemes for land settlement started by the Duke of Westminster, Lord Lovat and Sir Percy Fitzpatrick received his support. But he complained to Chamberlain in January 1902 that the means at his disposal for acquiring land were 'quite inadequate' because it was difficult to allocate the money needed for land purchase from the funds available, and he lacked sufficient power of expropriation. All told, Milner's immigration policy settled only about 1300 English-speaking heads of families on the land, and therefore failed in its political purpose.

Milner denied that his purpose was to plough the Afrikaner under: 'I no more want to exterminate the Dutch than I want to exterminate the British,' he wrote; but he wished to ensure the dominance of the British element, politically and culturally. Therefore instruction through the Dutch language was not to be allowed in the government schools: 'Dutch should only be used to teach English, and English to teach everything else.' He attached special importance to school textbooks, in particular, history books:

> A good world history would be worth anything. . . . Everything that makes South African children look outside South Africa and *realize the world* makes for peace. Everything that cramps and confines their views to South Africa only . . . makes for Afrikanerdom and further discord.

An Englishwoman, Bertha Synge, obliged with a *Story of the World* in five substantial volumes of equal length and difficulty, covering everything from the ancient world to the Victorian Empire (which formed the theme of the final volume). The tone was conciliatory towards the Boer, flattering his physique and his courage but not his culture, and setting out a new political orthodoxy: 'Today Boer and Briton stand shoulder to shoulder, "forged in strong fires, by equal war made one", both members of one great Empire, and as time rolls onward into space, they may feel

> The touch of human brotherhood, and act
> As one great nation, true and strong as steel.'

In the final resort, Milner intended to withhold political power from the whites of the new colonies until British ascendancy was assured, arguing that 'if, ten years hence, there are three men of British race to two of Dutch, the country will be safe and prosperous. If there are three of Dutch to two of British, we shall have perpetual difficulty.' But, rather like Lord Durham on French Canada, Milner miscalculated. Possessing in Stokes's words, 'faith in a planned society conceived and ordered by the scientific intelligence', he ran into serious opposition from those who lacked his kind of confidence, and from those who objected to their allotted place in his scheme of things. Afrikaners, in general, intensely resented his programme, but also discovered a way of defeating it. The English-speaking whites were divided over his aims, and ended by failing to give him the degree of support which he required if his policies were to succeed.

Meanwhile Africans, Asians and Coloured people experienced during the Milner era a series of attacks on their position in society which effectively cut them off from access to full citizenship. They did not discover an effective style of resistance, so that the achievement of Union in 1910 left them no better off.

Black access to political power was blocked by Article 8 of the Treaty of Vereeniging, which made the enfranchisement of non-white people in the new colonies dependent on the consent of the white majority. This was a victory for Milner, for Chamberlain had at first insisted on the enfranchisement of blacks as a condition for self-government. In December 1901 Milner had privately rejected the desirability of political equality for blacks, and recommended that they should be represented in the legislatures by whites nominated for the purpose. He told Chamberlain that the blacks should not be forced to change their ways or to work for whites, but that the whites should teach them 'habits of regular and skilled labour' and keep them severely away from strong drink. He placed blacks low on the Great Chain of Being, as people to be 'well-treated' and 'justly governed'.

To achieve uniformity in native policy, Milner appointed a South African Native Affairs Commission in 1903 to make recommendations to the various governments 'with the object of arriving at a common understanding' against the day when South African federation would be achieved. Sir Godfrey Lagden, his Commissioner for Native Affairs, presided over this almost exclusively English-speaking body. It produced a report in 1905 which reflected the High Commissioner's own concern for social planning, and introduced new rigidities into South African thinking about race relations which had an immense influence on later political debate. The Lagden Commission formalised the idea of segregation in a new way. It envisaged the territorial separation of black and white, for purposes of residence and ownership, as a permanent mandatory feature of public life. It gave its approval to the establishment of segregated 'locations' for urban Africans, at a time when the governments of all the colonies were busy setting them up. It also urged the separation of blacks from whites in political life, with Africans represented only by whites in the federal legislature of the future.

There was a good deal of open violence between black and white during the first decade of the twentieth century, for which the Zulu rebellion of 1906 provides the chief focal point. The suppression of the Herero and the Maji-Maji by the Germans, and of the Zulu by the Natalians, involved the shedding of a lot of blood. Whether these risings were coordinated in the Rand mine compounds seems at best doubtful, for they were set in motion by identifiable local causes. The Zulu rebellion took the authorities by surprise, but ought not to have done so. Shepstonian authoritarianism, streamlined and consolidated in the Natal Native Code of 1891, had given the Governor almost unlimited powers over blacks, which he used on the advice of the Executive Council rather than as a reserve power as was originally intended. This power had already been used to dismiss chiefs without trial, and to enforce the *isibalo* (labour tax), a *corvée* imposed arbitrarily on nearly a tenth of the male black population in return for rations and a small wage. Land shortage aggravated discontent, especially in Zululand, where the final report of the Delimitation Commission in 1905 had set aside 2.6 million acres for white settlement (mainly for the extension of sugar plantations), leaving only 3.9 million acres in tribal hands. Stock and crop diseases compounded the rural distress, while in 1906 the Government imposed a poll tax of £1 on every male not liable for the hut tax, hoping thus to catch the young (who were frequently the ones who raised the cash to pay the hut tax anyway).

Against a background of rumour, much of it relating to the supposed restlessness of the evergreen but not irresponsible Dinuzulu, the Zulu rebellion developed out of a series of small incidents initially connected with refusals to pay the poll tax. After the killing of two white Natal policemen at Byrnetown, the Government imposed martial law, and over a dozen men who had resisted were summarily executed, despite remonstrations by the British Government which caused the Natal ministers to resign in protest. When Bambatha, a petty chief in the Greytown area, rose in April and fled across the Tugela to Sigananda's kraal in the Nkandla Forest, the black resistance assumed more serious proportions. But Bambatha, the head of an impoverished tribe (the Zondi), had a long history of conflict with the authorities, and left no reason for going into rebellion, or even any indication of what he hoped to achieve, beyond what can be inferred from his actions: he had refused to pay the poll tax, failed to report that some of his men were armed, and then reacted to his own deposition by kidnapping his successor, before fleeing across the Tugela to avoid capture by Colonial forces. Sigananda, his Cube host, a man reputedly in his nineties, who had served Shaka, helped to increase the rebel force. But the rebels had no apparent plan of campaign. They were defeated with heavy losses in the Mome Gorge, near Cetswayo's grave, by Col. D. Mackenzie, Bambatha himself being killed and Sigananda captured. Only after they had been defeated did rebellion flare up in Natal proper, in the Mapumulo district. There, too, the resistance was weak, the rebels' strategy directionless, and the slaughter massive in relation to the losses on the Colonial side. Altogether, only twenty-four white soldiers and about six white civilians were killed, during the rising, as against over three thousand blacks.

Black protest took other forms than that of uncoordinated civil disobedience. Independent churches had begun to spread as vehicles of religious enthusiasm and political protest, at least since Nehemiah Tile's Thembu Church had been set up in 1884. The founding of Magena Mokone's Ethiopian Church in Pretoria in 1892 was an important occasion. He was joined four years later by James M. Dwane (like Tile and Mokone, an ex-Methodist minister), and they both affiliated to the African Methodist Episcopal Church, an American foundation, in 1896. Two years later, Bishop H. M. Turner of the A.M.E.C. visited South Africa, consecrated Dwane an assistant bishop, and ordained over sixty priests. So rapidly did the movement spread that it claimed 10,000 members by 1898. Dwane led his followers out of the A.M.E.C. after a dispute with its American leaders, and after joining the Anglicans they were recognised as an autonomous Order of Ethiopia. Other groups then split away from the A.M.E.C. in quest of black autonomy. Loosely connected across the sub-continent from the Cape to Nyasaland, above all by the efforts of the radical British missionary, Joseph Booth, who visited the Cape and Natal in 1896–1897, and published his pamphlet *Africa for the African* in the latter year. Ethiopianism was accepted as legitimate in the Cape and the Transvaal but denied legal status in Natal and the O.R.C., where the term became a synonym for irresponsible black nationalism in official eyes. The contemporary assumption that 'Ethiopianism' lay behind the Zulu rebellion has been shown, however, to be an over-simplification.

Ethiopianism did not, on the whole, run in step with the more deliberately political movements, of which there were several in all colonies before Union. In the Cape, a Native Congress founded in 1902 existed alongside a Transkei Native Vigilance Association. Martin Luthuli described a Natal Native Congress, of which he had been chairman, to the Lagden Commission in May 1904. It had close mission associations, a secretariat based on Verulam, a scattering of branches and an ability to draw up to 100 people to its meetings, which had tried to put pressure on the Natal Government over such issues as political representation, education and forced labour. The O.R.C.'s Native Vigilance Association of 1904 (which was apparently sometimes known as the O.R.C. Native Congress) had an executive composed of Africans from all four colonies and one Coloured man. It was described by one of them as 'more or less governed by the Church' laws (two of its members belonging to the A.M.E.C.), and it joined issue with the Government on industrial education, location self-government and urban property rights. The Congress stressed political rights and civil liberty in the urban areas, above all its opposition to casual labour regulations about to be imposed and to the carrying of passes by African women. In the Transvaal there was a Transvaal Congress, a Bapedi Union and a

Basuto Association, while a Native United Political Association of the Transvaal Colony petitioned for the franchise under Article 8 of the Treaty of Vereeniging in April 1905, and protested generally against discriminatory legislation. In addition to all these African bodies, there was the African Political (later People's) Organisation. Though founded only in 1902, the A.P.O. owed its origin to the upsurge of Coloured interest in politics following their marginal participation in political contests during the late nineteenth century. The A.P.O. was divided in 1904 over whether to support Jameson's Progressives or the Bond-dominated South African Party, and elected Dr A. Abdurahman, a Cape Malay doctor, to avoid a split between rival factions. Under his leadership it fought against the Cape School Board Act of 1905 which made schooling compulsory for white but not for Coloured children, and sent a deputation to London to canvass for political rights in the Transvaal, but without success. Its division over which white party to support persisted at its congress in 1908, when a majority favoured the Progressives against the view of Abdurahman himself.

The decade also witnessed the early stages of conflict between the Indian community of the Transvaal and the Colonial Government, in which M. K. Gandhi developed his technique of non-violent non-cooperation in protest against the restrictions imposed on Indian residential and trading rights. It was in protest against amendments to the Gold Law and the Immigration Law, above all to the indignity of carrying passes bearing their fingerprints, that the Indian community indulged in 1908 in a pass-burning demonstration, as a result of which Gandhi himself was imprisoned. While in prison he worked out an acceptable formula with Smuts for the registration of Indians, only to fall out with Smuts afterwards, following a misunderstanding over the nature of their unwritten agreement.

The Afrikaners took less time than might have been expected to organise their opposition to Milner's regime. Chamberlain's visit in November 1902 gave Botha, Smuts, Hertzog and others an opportunity, which they used, to cross swords with a long-standing adversary. On 2 July 1903, Botha and Smuts, supported by Emily Hobhouse, addressed a protest meeting at Heidelberg, held with Milner's permission and in the presence of a good spread of ex-commando leaders as well as the South African Constabulary. Their mood was basically unconciliatory. They subsequently refused to serve on Milner's nominee Legislative Council, on the ground that nothing short of self-government would satisfy them. In May 1904 several hundred Boer representatives met in Pretoria to establish their own political organisation, *Het Volk*, which was formally constituted on 28 January 1905. This movement, built up in its early stages under cover of farmers' associations, spread through the activities of ex-Republican leaders who went through the districts in pairs, sometimes the same districts they had toured in 1900 to bring the commandos back into the field. In the O.R.C. a congress met at Brandfort on 1 December 1904, to act as a sounding board for Boer grievances against the post-war settlement, and this led to the founding of *Orangia Unie* in July 1905.

These meetings displayed a good deal of pent-up anger, above all over the introduction of the Chinese, over the administration of relief funds (for a very large number of Afrikaners could now be described as poor whites) and over the restrictions on the public use of the Dutch language. They produced, on the rebound, a movement for the establishment of private Christian National schools, in which the language of instruction was to be Dutch, and the educational rationale was the cooperation of Church, school and family in the upbringing of the child. Out of Christian National education the Second Language Movement was born, a far more mature movement than its predecessor of the 1870s. Once again, the rival merits of simplified Dutch and Afrikaans were earnestly debated, with Onze Jan Hofmeyr maintaining his earlier conservative line, and others like Gustav Preller urging the recognition of Afrikaans. This time the supporters of Afrikaans, with the poetry of writers like Jan F. E. Celliers and Eugene Marais behind them, spoke with more confidence, and ran a campaign which gained steadily until Afrikaans eventually became an official language of the Union in 1925.

But if the mood of the Afrikaner revival had remained exclusively bitter, or exclusively preoccupied with questions which concerned the Afrikaner alone, it could have produced a series of barren confrontations, leading perhaps to another trial of strength with the British, and achieved nothing. It developed into a dynamic movement because its more sophisticated leaders realised the importance, in context, of conciliation. Conciliation was necessary to heal the rifts within Afrikanerdom between the *bittereinder* and the National Scout. It was necessary, further, to destroy the ill-feeling between Dutch- and English-speaker on South African soil, to say nothing of the gulf that had to be bridged between the Imperial Government and its new subjects north of the Orange. The Cape Bondsmen were the first to appreciate the value of a change in tactics, which they put into practice with great success during Chamberlain's tour in February 1903. At the emotional level they showed that concessions could follow from ostentatiously burying the hatchet. Before long, however, Afrikaner leaders began to realise that it was not merely possible to de-claw the lion by gentle words: one could actually divide the South African British and derive political advantage from the exercise, by exploiting the growing opposition between capital and labour. Het Volk and the Orangia Unie began to open their doors to the English-speaking artisan, and the latter began to respond. The issue of Chinese labour was at first ideally suited to this purpose, for while the Afrikaner viewed the Chinese as an unnecessary complication of an already difficult racial problem, the English worker saw him as a potential rival.

Botha and Smuts developed the new tactics with real finesse. While setting their sights firmly on responsible government, they cultivated a thoroughly reasonable approach to the British authorities, and were careful to suppress potential manifestations of republicanism. This, in turn, reassured those English-speakers on whom the Afrikaner leaders depended as allies.

The political behaviour of the Transvaal British in the period after the Anglo-Boer War is much better understood, as a result of the work of Denoon and Mawby, than was the case a few years ago. The British victory in the war raised the expectations of the returning Uitlanders, as they re-established themselves in Johannesburg and elsewhere, and expected Milner to promote them to positions of power. They tended to resent the young bachelors from Balliol who obtained the top administrative jobs, as well as the absence of an elected element in the Legislative Council of 1902; and if they accepted municipal government for Johannesburg in 1903 as a palliative, they were disappointed that Johannesburg was not made the capital. Uitlander dissatisfaction over the slowness of reform found expression in 1902 in the founding of a Transvaal Political Association, identified by Denoon as at first enjoying the support of 'virtually the whole English-speaking white community'. But this association was soon weakened by the withdrawal of several of its leaders – not so much gold magnates with deep-level interests, as Denoon initially supposed, but 'the leading men of Johannesburg of all walks of life, mining, professional, commercial and other men', in the words of Mawby. They were not anxious for self-government until they could be sure that, as a community, the English-speakers could retain control of the Colony, and for that reason would not be drawn into open confrontation with Milner.

The rump of the Transvaal Political Association, whose leading member was the diamond magnate Dale Lace, remained in being; but in 1904 a new move for the creation of a political organisation to agitate for self-government came from E. P. Solomon, brother of Sir Richard, with the backing of another diamond magnate, T. P. Cullinan, and others. This resulted in the establishment of the Transvaal Responsible Government Association in December 1904, which clearly attracted leading diamond interests as Denoon and Mawby both emphasise, even if the divisions within the diamond industry – some mines being independent, others (like De Beers) having close relations with the Chamber, and others (like the Premier Mine) subject to controlling pressure from the Transvaal Government – make generalisations dangerous. With safer profit margins and a consequent ability to pay better wages, the diamond industry did not need the services of a body like the Chamber, while the industry was sensitive to a 67 per cent profits tax as against the 10 per cent levied on gold production. There is evidence of discontent over the Diamond Law from within the ranks of Het Volk as well, but related to its restrictions on landowners rather than its fiscal demands, and it seems likely that what brought the Responsibles and Het Volk together was not so much a common policy over diamond legislation as a common desire for responsible government. When the two movements reached a partial agreement in March 1905, Het Volk agreed to refrain from criticising Chinese labour, to which the Responsibles were committed, while the Responsibles agreed to withdraw their support for Milner's policy of anglicising the educational system.

Meanwhile on 22 November 1904 a Transvaal Progressive Association had come into being. Its leaders were Sir Percy Fitzpatrick, George Farrar, and other prominent English-speaking Johannesburgers, several of them survivors of the pre-war Uitlander Council and of the earlier Reform Committee. The suggestion that they had a special relationship with the Chamber of Mines needs to be qualified by the statement that the Chamber was precluded by its very nature from party political involvement. The Progressives came into being with a six-point manifesto which included a demand for representative government (as distinct from responsible). They quickly expanded into a large organisation, claiming forty-three branches scattered through the Rand and Pretoria, and 32,000 members by February 1905. The Responsibles, by contrast, remained Johannesburg-based, and in May that year had a mere 5000 members. Neither was technically a political party, and Transvaal Britons commonly looked on both as subdivisions of 'our party'. But disagreement over the form of government and over relations with the Afrikaner, which became important issues during the closing months of Milner's period of office and the early months of Selborne's, drew them apart.

English-speaking white labour had its own political organisations, notably the Transvaal Labour Party (formed in November 1904) and the Political Labour League of the Witwatersrand Trades and Labour Council, established under the presidency of W. H. Andrews in August 1905. But these groups were still small and politically insignificant, and there was some movement by English-speaking artisans into the predominantly bourgeois T.R.G.A., whose desire for full self-government they shared.

British policy towards the new colonies after the Peace of Vereeniging articulated fully with these trends in Afrikaner and British politics. Milner knew well before his recall in March 1905 that his bid to establish British dominance north of the Vaal had failed. On 2 May

1904 he suggested to Alfred Lyttelton, Chamberlain's successor, that electives might replace the nominees in the Transvaal Legislative Council. Lyttelton agreed in principle in July, so in December Milner outlined proposals for representative government, based on £100 property, £10 rent, or £100 income qualifications, which were low enough to admit most adult white townsmen, but too high for most white rural squatters. For the electoral divisions, Milner put forward two alternatives: either a system of equal constituencies, each returning three members (Scheme A), or a system of single-member constituencies corresponding approximately to existing magisterial districts (Scheme B). He envisaged a legislature of thirty under Scheme A, and thirty-five under Scheme B, plus six to nine officials. He evidently did not anticipate the reactions which greeted his plan. The Colonial Office, which already looked askance at his Inter-Colonial Council, felt that it would give the electorate enough power to make government impossible. Het Volk and the Responsibles protested that the scheme did not go far enough, while the Progressives expressed fears of an Afrikaner takeover, and only gradually began to change their tune as the possibility of winning an election under Milner's rules occurred to them. Disillusioned, Milner reverted to a defence of the *status quo*, but Lyttelton felt that withdrawal was now impossible, and the British Government came out with a new constitution for the Transvaal, to take effect on Milner's retirement at the end of March 1905.

The Lyttelton Constitution provided for a legislative assembly of up to thirty-five white members, elected by whites only. It was to be constituted according to Milner's Scheme B, and contained new criteria for the regular adjustment of constituency boundaries to replace the very unequal ones of the old South African Republic. But for technical reasons the new constitution could not be implemented immediately. Meanwhile the Unionist Government fell from power in Britain in December 1905, and the new Liberal Ministry under Campbell-Bannerman considered modifying Lyttleton's document, and ended by granting full responsible government instead.

The Liberals appointed a Cabinet committee under Lord Loreburn to review the Transvaal question, and it became clear during January 1906 – despite the influence of Milner and Selborne in the opposite direction – that they were beginning to favour full self-government. Churchill, Under-Secretary of State for the Colonies, was arguing that representative government was indefensible in the Transvaal context, Loreburn that it was necessary to decentralise power completely so as to exonerate the British Government from having to take responsibility for the introduction of Chinese labour. Elgin, the Colonial Secretary, was more inclined to retain the Lyttleton constitution in revised form, but he was swayed by his colleagues.

Smuts visited London in January and February 1906, bearing a memorandum in support of responsible government with the authority of Het Volk, and after meeting Campbell-Bannerman came away with the feeling that he had convinced the Liberal premier that this was the way to settle the future of South Africa. But did his conviction represent the true facts? The Cabinet had been put on its guard against Smuts by Selborne. It had decided, even before Smuts's arrival, to grant responsible government. The only doubts still to be cleared up were procedural and tactical: how to set about the dismantling of the Lyttelton constitution, which was technically in force, and whether to present the policy of the new Government as a stage in a continuously evolving bi-partisan colonial policy, or as a dramatic break with the past, intended to bring about a miracle of reconciliation. It does not seem necessary to belittle the personal impact of Smuts on Campbell-Bannerman, or – as Le May stresses – that of Campbell-Bannerman on Smuts. The rapport which clearly grew between them, nurtured on Smuts's side by the memory of the 'methods of barbarism' speech, gave Campbell-Bannerman encouragement to present his government's policy in the shape of a dramatic new deal, a 'magnanimous gesture' for the world (and above all the imperialists in his own party) to take note of. There was a stormy cabinet meeting on 8 February, the day after the interview, when Campbell-Bannerman argued in favour of sending a Royal Commission to South Africa in face of Elgin's resistance. But it was Elgin who told Selborne on 18 February that the Lyttelton Constitution had been abandoned, and that the intention was to give the Transvaal full self-government. The magnanimity of the offer received wide acclaim, even if to Milner's supporters it was a 'great betrayal'. It was less widely realised that the British Government was 'absolutely determined', in the words of a secret memorandum by Churchill, 'to maintain . . . a numerical majority of a loyal and English population', and that it had come to see the grant of self-government as the only possible way of retaining influence, short of the uneconomical use of force, in a part of the world where Afrikaner power was bound one day to reassert itself.

The Committee of Inquiry which the British Government decided to send to South Africa was led by Sir Joseph West Ridgeway, an ex-Governor of Ceylon. They were to take soundings of opinion in the Transvaal and supplement the not altogether welcome communications of Lord Selborne, who was fighting a rearguard action on behalf of the Transvaal British. The West Ridgeway Committee first interviewed Het Volk's leaders in Pretoria, and was struck by their moderation, and their preparedness to accept a constitution which did not give them an immediate majority in the legislature, if only control were not allowed to pass into the hands of the Chamber of Mines. (Smuts had also taken this line in his February memorandum.) The Progressives, by contrast, appeared disunited, and by stressing the danger of Boer dominance were adopting a line which did not tally with the direct impressions the Committee had received from Het Volk. When the Responsibles and the labour representatives endorsed Het Volk's fear of the Chamber, the Committee adopted the strategy of trying to turn these moderate English-speaking groups into a balancing force between Het Volk and the Progressives. Much depended on the distribution of seats between the Rand, the platteland and Pretoria, especially when the Committee overruled Het Volk's objection to 'one vote one value', but agreed to single-member constituencies and a variation of up to 15 per cent from the norm, upwards or downwards, in the number of voters per constituency. After hearing evidence in secret from all parties – a procedure rightly criticised by Mawby, for it did not expose their representations to public comment – the Committee decided, against the advice of the Progressives but in accordance with that of Het Volk and the Responsibles, to use the 1904 census figures as their guide to delimitation, rather than the voters' rolls drawn up under the Lyttelton scheme, which the Progressives were accused (but only accused) of having packed. On this basis, they recommended 33 seats for the Rand (later raised to 34), 6 for Pretoria and 30 for the platteland. They calculated that this would give the Transvaal British a small majority if they all pulled together, but recognised that otherwise 'the result cannot be by any means certain'. The only other safeguard provided for the British was the device of a nominated upper house for four years, after which the legislature would be empowered to make it an elective body. The Lyttelton Constitution might have given the British element a majority, as Mawby argues, above all if the Progressive delimitation proposals had been adhered to. His further argument, that the West Ridgeway Committee misjudged the real intentions of Het Volk, overrated the capacity of the British Transvalers to work together, and overrated their capacity for winning seats outside Pretoria and the Rand, was borne out by the election results of 1907, when Het Volk was returned with 37 seats against 21 for the Progressives, 6 for the National Association (the new name of the Responsibles), 3 for labour and 2 for Independents. The Committee had in fact recommended an electoral system which deprived the Responsibles of the moderating role for which it had cast them.

The constitution framed for the Transvaal in the light of the West Ridgeway recommendations provided for an elective Legislative Assembly of 69 members and a Legislative Council of 15, nominated in the first instance. The English and Dutch languages were both made official, but English was to be the language of record. The electorate was limited to whites, the Liberal Government having decided that to attempt to impose conditions on the new Transvaal Government for the safeguarding of blacks was likely to alienate Transvaal white opinion to the ultimate disadvantage of the blacks. The Liberals were subsequently accused of having defaulted on undertakings made by the Unionists, in terms of Article 8 of the Treaty of Vereeniging, for the enfranchisement of blacks on the grant of self-government. In defence of their actions, however, Hyam has noted Elgin's concern to do justice by the 'natives' (a term taken in context to include Coloured and Indians) in his minute of 5 April 1906, as well as Elgin's interviews with those who sought ways of entrenching black rights. All the Government eventually did was to confer formal powers as Supreme Chief on the Governor, to provide for the reservation of legislation affecting blacks, to provide for the convening of assemblies of chiefs if the Governor thought fit, and to place Swaziland directly under the High Commission instead of under the Governor of the Transvaal. The political climate which had developed in South Africa in the aftermath of the Zulu rebellion was not one in which rights could easily be extended to blacks. Nor, as Mansergh argued, could black rights be easily defended from London, once self-government had been granted to a South African colony, unless there was a substantial body of white opinion in the Colony determined to maintain those rights.

The Orange River Colony likewise received self-government, on the recommendation of the West Ridgeway Committee, on 5 June 1907. Selborne had ingeniously proposed a restoration of the old Republican Grondwet with a mere substitution of a nominated governor for the elected president, but this was strongly attacked by the Afrikaner leaders on account of the real powers previously enjoyed by the president, which would thus be placed outside political control. A constitution on the lines of that of the Transvaal was consequently introduced, with a nominee upper house of eleven, which would be subsequently elected, and a Legislative Assembly of 38. In the first elections, held in 1908, Orangia Unie won thirty lower house seats, to the eight won by Sir J. G. Fraser's Constitutionalists.

When Milner created a South African Customs Union for an experimental period of two years, and amalgamated the Transvaal and O.R.C. railway systems into a single Central South African Railways, his hope was that these arrangements would justify themselves, and thereby further the federal cause. The Transvaal would be drawn into an already existing common market, while the possession of a considerable length of rail traversing the O.R.C. would incline the C.S.A.R. to do as much business as possible through the Cape ports. But two awkward facts stood in the way of Milner's plans. One was the growing economic dominance of the Transvaal, and the danger that, when it achieved self-government it would follow its own interests, if need be by cutting economic ties with the south. The other was the Portuguese stranglehold over the Rand's rail traffic, linked with Mozambique's power to give or withhold labourers for the gold mines.

On the customs front, the Transvaal needed to impose high duties for revenue purposes at the end of the Anglo-Boer War, and began in 1902 to tax Natal sugar and Cape wines. The Customs Convention of 1903 stopped this practice, and the Transvaal Government began to rely on an increased gold profits tax, which amounted to approximately three-quarters of the annual railway revenue from 1906 onwards. But on achieving responsible government Botha's ministry came under very heavy pressure to protect the Colony from Cape farm products and in June 1907 gave notice of its intention to withdraw from the Customs Union. The customs dispute suggested that the only way to eliminate harmful inter-colonial competition was to unite the colonies politically.

On the railway front the problems were more intricate. Milner had allocated money for railway expansion, and set in motion the construction of lines from Witbank to Springs, and from Ladysmith in Natal to Kroonstad in the O.R.C., as well as from Fourteen Streams in the Cape to the Rand. These works were completed by the middle of 1906. But the creation of new lines brought fresh friction. Thus the entry of goods into the O.R.C. from Natal led to so much bitter competition between the Cape and Natal systems that Selborne had to threaten to impose countervailing tariffs on the Free State sections in order to offset attempts by either colony to undercut the other. A similar conflict developed between the Cape and the O.R.C. over the C.S.A.R.'s plan to build a line from Bloemfontein to Kimberley, which threatened to admit goods landed at Durban into the Kimberley market. Meanwhile deadlock developed between the High Commissioner and the Portuguese authorities when the former insisted that the privileges guaranteed to the Portuguese under the *modus vivendi* of 1901 did not apply with regard to the Springs–Witbank line, and the other routes to the Rand which had not existed at the time of that agreement. This became a cause of bitter dispute on account of the relative growth of rail traffic between Lourenço Marques and the Rand as a result of the *modus vivendi*: it had increased from 30.9 per cent of tne total in 1903 to 51.5 per cent in 1905, during which time Durban's proportion had fallen from 44 per cent to 36.5 per cent and that of the Cape ports had fallen to a mere 12 per cent.

The bitterness behind these quarrels ran deep, and formed the subject matter of Lord Selborne's Memorandum of 1 January 1907, with its urgent plea for political federation as a means of staving off economic catastrophe. Conferences at Johannesburg (1905) and Pietermaritzburg (1906) merely bought time. It was therefore a matter of great significance that when the representatives of the Colonies met again at Pretoria in May 1908 they should have adopted Smuts's proposal to seek a political solution of their economic divisions, by calling for a National Convention. As this Pretoria conference failed like its predecessors to reach agreement on the economic issues, the adoption of Smuts's proposal was timely. As a by-product of Union, the National Convention managed to set up a central Railways and Harbours administration taking over all the railway systems and running them on a commercial basis under a separate budget. At the same time it accepted a new agreement concluded by the Transvaal with the Portuguese, which gave Lourenço Marques the lion's share of Rand traffic but guaranteed minimum percentages of the traffic for Durban (30 per cent) and the Cape (15 per cent).

It had always been unquestioningly assumed that if the political unification of southern Africa was to be brought about this would have to be done on federal rather than unitary lines, on account of the cultural differences and regional disparities, which seemed to require the maximum possible devolution of power. So Milner thought. So thought the Afrikaner Bond when it reviewed its political objectives in 1903. F. S. Malan and Jameson moved a joint motion to the same effect in the Cape Assembly in July 1907. Lionel Curtis was a federalist, and chiefly responsible for the content of Selborne's Memorandum of January 1907, the document through which, in Thompson's words, the Kindergarten took the initiative which led to the Union of South Africa. But the Kindergarten was not allowed to retain the initiative, for the leaders of the Afrikaner movements began to suspect that their schemes would place power in unfriendly hands. Hence the decision, taken by Merriman, Steyn and Smuts in the course of 1906, to discourage any closer union movement until self-government had been restored to the new colonies, and until power had passed to Het Volk and the Orangia Unie, and returned to the South African Party in the Cape.

By February 1908, with the South African Party's victory in the Cape general election, these conditions had been realised. The leaders of the Afrikaner movements had also reached the conclusion that a unitary rather than a federal form of government would suit their interests best. Lionel Curtis and other members of the Kindergarten began to move in that direction too. Federalism still had its supporters; but its most convinced spokesmen, W. P. Schreiner, his sister Olive, and J. H. Hofmeyr, were not at the Convention, while the Natal delegates, who wanted as decentralised a constitution as they could get, and actually produced a draft federal scheme at the Convention, had neither the skill nor the bargaining strength to force their views on to the other delegates. The triumph of unitary over federal thinking is to be explained primarily by the convictions of Smuts and Merriman, who led from the time of the Pretoria conference onwards. Both men were attracted by British constitutionalism, while Merriman was driven by his abhorrence of over-government to favour a centralised system, and Smuts became convinced that it was necessary to concentrate power at the centre to prevent the structure from being shaken apart:

> What we want is a supreme national authority to give expression to the national will of South Africa, and the rest is really subordinate.

Together with Sir Henry de Villiers, Chief Justice of the Cape, who presided over the Convention, they examined and took what lessons they chose from the federal constitutions of the United States, Canada and Australia, looking to the American civil war and to Australian inter-state wrangles as powerful arguments against federalism, and ignoring the proffered advice of expert defenders of these constitutions.

The National Convention was primarily concerned with the distribution of power. In this sense, it must be seen against the background of confrontation between the racial and ethnic groups which had battled for possession throughout historic times in the sub-continent, but more especially during the preceding hundred years. The power situation was reflected in the actual distribution of delegates. There were no Africans, Coloured People or Asians present. The Government and Opposition white parties of the four Colonies were represented in almost equal proportions and in the numbers agreed at the Pretoria Conference, though there was rather greater cohesion among the Governmental representatives of the Cape, O.R.C. and Transvaal than among the groups of Opposition leaders. Southern Rhodesia, still a non-self-governing colony, was represented by observers with speaking but not voting rights, two appointed by the British South Africa Company and one by the Legislative Council; but Rhodesian settler interest in joining the Union was at best marginal.

After the completion of preliminaries, Merriman moved on 13 October in favour of a legislative Union of South Africa, of which the existing self-governing Colonies were to be constituted provinces, with provision for the incorporation of 'all such parts of South Africa as are not included from its establishment'. He and Smuts put their case for a unitary constitution, basing it on the correspondence which they had shared since August over a 'Suggested Scheme for South African Union' drafted by Smuts, on which Merriman, Sir Henry de Villiers and Steyn had passed comments. This scheme had been revised by Smuts and R. H. Brand, who became secretary of the Transvaal delegation. Having cleared up the constitutional flaws in his proposals, Smuts had then summarised them for the members of the Transvaal delegation, who had discussed them during the week before the Convention met and arrived with their differences ironed out. As the Transvaal and Cape Opposition parties arrived in Durban without alternative schemes of their own, and the Natal delegates were taken unawares by Merriman's opening motion and had not canvassed their federal alternative, the Merriman-Smuts proposal was carried without dissentient voice after a Natal amendment to place residual powers in the 'states' had been voted down. As a result, the Convention settled for a sovereign central Parliament with authority to amend the powers of Provincial Councils, or even remove them altogether, by ordinary simple majorities, and it made short work of attempts by Natal to increase the scope of Provincial Councils. Their authority was carefully circumscribed, while the provincial Executive Committees were placed under Administrators appointed by the Governor-General, rather than under provincial premiers.

Thompson pertinently observes that the Natal delegates missed an opportunity, after losing the battle for federation, by not insisting on the entrenchment of Provincial rights with special majorities for their removal. To obtain this alternative security, however, they would have had to vanquish the strong disposition to favour a flexible rather than a rigid constitution in South Africa at the time, rooted in the somewhat irrational notion that full autonomy required full flexibility. What emerged from the Convention was a flexible constitution like the British, albeit a written one, in which sovereignty (subject to the limitations of the Colonial Laws Validity Act of 1865 and the safeguards for the Royal prerogative) lay with the Union Parliament. Any part of the constitution could be amended by a simple majority of each House, but for the section protecting the voting rights of the non-white people of the Cape (Section 35), on which the Cape delegates dug in their heels, and the section defining the equal status of the English and Dutch languages (Section 137), over which the O.R.C. delegates were adamant. These could only be amended by a two-thirds majority at the third reading in a joint session of both Houses. Whether this involved granting a testing right to the courts, as had existed in the O.F.S. but not in the Transvaal, was not clearly stated in the Act, though by implication such a power had to exist.

The Convention agreed that the executive government should be headed by a Governor-General as the representative of the King, aided by an Executive Council composed in practice of the Ministry of the day. It settled for a two-chamber Parliament without great enthusiasm. This was to comprise, first, a Senate of forty members with a ten-year term (eight for each province, elected collegially by proportional representation, plus eight nominated by the Governor-General, of whom four were to be chosen for their 'thorough acquaintance . . . with the reasonable wants and wishes of the coloured races'). The House of Assembly was to have an initial membership of 121, rising to 150, as the size of the electorate increased. Each Province could aquire extra members as its total voters increased by multiples of the Union quota (obtained by dividing the total number of electors by the total number of seats).

The composition of the House of Assembly involved crucial decisions over the distribution of power. After sustained debates it became clear that on the question of black representation neither the northern Colonies nor the Cape was prepared to compromise. Walter Stanford of the Cape, supported by several of his colleagues, tried to have the political colour bar removed. De Villiers and Fitzpatrick proposed a civilisation test for blacks, while Botha and Moor adamantly refused to admit blacks to political rights in the Transvaal and Natal respectively. Rather than break up the Convention, the delegates therefore agreed that the franchise system in operation in each Province should continue. The Convention refused to allow the election of non-white people to Parliament. On this point the Cape gave ground for it had never admitted them in the past, though it kept the door open for black membership of the Cape Provincial Council.

In determining the allocation of seats between the provinces, several criteria were discussed. The basis of total population, which would have greatly favoured Natal with its large black population, was rejected. The Cape would have stood to gain from a distribution on a basis of total voters, on account of its relatively greater black electorate. But the basis eventually agreed on was that of the total white adult male population, which was a voters' basis in the northern colonies. The 1904 census returns were apparently taken as the basis for calculation, save that the delegates allowed the Transvaal an upward adjustment of its figures on account of the sizeable immigration to that colony since 1904, and allowed the Orange Free State (as the O.R.C. was renamed) and Natal an inflated number of 17 seats each for ten years, as against the Cape's 51, and the Transvaal's 36. The upshot was that the Cape had an initial average of 2791 voters per constituency, the Transvaal 2715, the O.F.S. 2131, and Natal 1647.

When it came to distributing the seats within the provinces, the main problem was to balance the interests of town and country, which largely corresponded with those of the English- and Dutch-speaking populations. The Afrikaner parties, on the whole, favoured unequal constituencies and the loading of the urban electorate, for which strong precedents already existed in all colonies, whereas the Progressives of the Transvaal, mindful of the Uitlander franchise wrangles and keenly led by Fitzpatrick, wanted 'one vote one value' and regular redistribution to ensure that constituencies remained equal. After one of its toughest debates, the Convention appointed a committee which recommended that Delimitation Commissions of three judges should be empowered to vary the size of constituencies up to 15 per cent either way from the provincial average (or quota), applying any of five criteria in the process: community or diversity of interests, communications, physical features, existing electoral boundaries, and sparsity or density of population. This allowed a measure of judicial discretion, and the guidelines were by no means precise, but at this stage in proceedings the delegates accepted Smuts's proposal for large multi-member constituencies linked with a system of proportional representation, as likely to protect minority interests. It was only at the final Bloemfontein session of the Convention in May 1909 that proportional representation was dropped in favour of single-member constituencies and simple cumulative voting procedures on account of the fear of Cape Bondsmen that Smuts's plan and the principle of equal constituencies might be to their disadvantage. At this late stage, too, came the Transvaal Progressives' first determined insistence on 'one vote one value', sparked off by the Cape resolutions. When the Convention was close to breaking up, De Villiers suggested the abandonment of proportional representation. The Progressives tried to insist on the entrenchment of 'one vote one value'. For several days the delegates deadlocked, before compromising on the acceptance of equal constituencies (subject always to the principle of loading), the abandonment of proportional representation, and the reservation for the royal pleasure of any bills to alter the sub-chapter dealing with the House of Assembly.

The federation of Australia had taken about ten years from the initial moves in 1890, and the federation of Canada took three. With relatively much bigger differences to bridge, the South African National Convention completed its work in less than a year. After a brief Durban session, it had moved to Cape Town in November 1908, and deliberated there (with a Christmas recess) until February. The draft legislation was then submitted to the Colonial Parliaments in March, and the proposed amendments then debated at the Bloemfontein session between 3 and 11 May. The Colonial Parliaments approved the amended draft at the beginning of June, and it was approved in Natal by a referendum on the 10th. The draft South Africa Bill, having gone through all the formal procedures thought necessary, was then taken to London by a delegation from the Convention (in which Hofmeyr was also present) and went through all stages in the British Parliament between 22 July and 19 August, eventually receiving the royal assent on 20 September.

But although the South African Convention had bigger difficulties in its path, it overcame these as much by avoiding them as by facing up to them. The decision over the capital was a case in point. This, above all, was the issue on which local pride was most intimately touched. But a decision which made the Mother City the seat of Parliament, gave the most economically active Province the seat of administration, and placed the judicial capital in the centrally situated Bloemfontein did justice of a kind to all save Natal, at the cost of sending the civil servants on an expensive annual trek.

Far more consequential was the agreement to differ over the treatment of blacks. The dissatisfaction of Africans, Coloured people and Indians over the South Africa Bill was widespread and made known at the time. The A.P.O. held a big meeting in Cape Town on 5 March, and communicated its disapproval of the proposed political colour bar to the National Convention. A South African Native Convention met in Bloemfontein on the 24th, and resolved similarly, but deliberately pulled its punches so as not to spoil the chance of a favourable response at the final session of the National Convention. Ultimately, when their pleas were ignored, and after the Cape Parliament had voted against making the extension of black rights a matter of principle, W. P. Schreiner led a delegation consisting of Abdurahman, Rubusana and Jabavu to London, where it published an appeal through the press but got little editorial support outside the *Manchester Guardian*. They obtained an interview with Lord Crewe, the Secretary of State, but as the British Government deemed it improper to interfere materially with the agreed decisions of the National Convention, they returned home empty-handed. Gandhi also visited Britain to protest on behalf of the Indian community. It would have been very difficult for the British Government to interfere on behalf of the blacks without wrecking the Closer Union movement, for experience had already shown how sensitive the South African electorate was to attempts to determine their future from London, especially if the treatment of blacks was the point at issue. The Liberals were not in fact insensitive to the problem. Hyam has made it clear that the Territories were withheld, and barred from incorporation save under the stiff conditions of Section 151 and the Schedule to the Act, to provide some kind of lever on white South African opinion. The South Africa Act, however, had created something rather different: it had given South Africa that 'supreme national authority to give expression to the national will' which Smuts originally desired, and provided a boxing-ring in which the contenders for different principles could confront each other until the palm of victory went one day to the stronger.

# Part Two
# The Consolidation of a White State

## Section I
## The Road to Afrikaner Dominance, 1910–48

# 10 Union under Stress: Botha and Smuts, 1910–24

General Louis Botha's Government took office on 31 May 1910 in the sunshine of Imperial approval, and dedicated to conciliation between Briton and Boer.[1] The ministry contained almost as many British as Dutch names. In choosing it, Botha had drawn carefully from all provinces. Because of the manoeuvrings which had preceded his own appointment and the pressure inside his own party for the spoils of office, Botha could neither abandon party lines and choose a ministry of all the talents, nor divide the nation along lines which he would probably have preferred – with Jameson and the Unionists on the government benches, and Hertzog in opposition. This was ironic, for when the electorate went to the polls in September 1910 the policies of the South African and Unionist parties were difficult to distinguish. As Thompson has noted, both stressed the idea of a single South African nation (white by implication), both professed a non-doctrinaire native policy, both wanted white but not Asian immigration, material development, and Imperial preference, and neither sought special protection for the Afrikaner. Both hoped, in effect, that the spirit of tolerance would continue to grow in an atmosphere of ethnic peace. Problems arising from the relationship between blacks and whites did not appear to cloud the scene, for all save a few discerning thinkers like Abdullah Abdurahman, Olive Schreiner and M. K. Gandhi were inclined to leave these for the broader shoulders of the future. The bitter memories of the Anglo-Boer war, which was still less than a decade away, were probably much more present in their minds, as wounds to be healed by gentle medication and the passage of time.

But Botha reckoned without Barry Hertzog, and the elements which he represented. Though Hertzog had won his campaign at the National Convention for the equal status of Dutch and English in public business, and for a bilingual public service, he was not convinced that equality would be achieved in practice unless both languages were used as media for the instruction of all white children. Two principles were at issue here: the right of parents to choose the language medium of their children's education, and the right of society to expect pupils to have those linguistic skills which would make for proper social understanding, which was Hertzog's main argument, as it would be for the proponents of dual-medium education in later years. The atmosphere was poisoned by the memory of the recent controversies arising out of Hertzog's Education Act in the Orange Free State, and by Botha's feeling that it was Hertzog's campaigning which had caused his personal defeat by Fitzpatrick in the Pretoria East constituency during the general election of September 1910.

Because of his performance in the election, Hertzog's cabinet colleagues regarded him as a cuckoo in the nest, but recognised his power as the leading representative of latent Afrikaner republican sentiments which, for reasons of expediency, had been suppressed since the end of the Anglo-Boer war. He was not consistently immoderate. The Fremantle Commission, which investigated the working of the provincial education laws in 1912, vindicated the O.F.S. system as the only one which did not discriminate against Dutch. The Commission recommended a margin of choice for parents over the language medium, but Hertzog signed the Report for sake of cabinet unity, though he did not agree with this policy and he resented Botha's subsequent attempts to identify him with the majority view. His controversial public statements about the Imperial connection were of special importance, however, for acceptance of that connection had been a central feature of the conciliation policy since Vereeniging, though in places it was deeply resented.

The constitution of 1910 united South Africa under a single government but did not make her in all respects a sovereign independent state. Above all was this the case with reference to external affairs, for South Africa was bound by the decisions of the King, acting on the advice of his British ministers of state, on questions of war and peace. South Africa was represented by Botha at the Imperial Conference of 1911, at which Sir Joseph Ward, premier of New Zealand, moved for the setting up of an Imperial Council of Defence. Acting on the assumption that the United Kingdom could commit the dominions to participation in war, he sought collective participation in the making of Imperial external policy. Botha led the attack on this plan, which was withdrawn in the face of general opposition. The Union's Defence Act of 1912 accordingly provided for a completely autonomous defence force, limited to military operations in any part of South Africa whether within or outside the Union. When Asquith, the Prime Minister, invited Dominion representatives to attend meetings of the Committee of Imperial Defence the same year, the principle of consultation over policy decisions was established. It was extended when Dominion governments were represented in the Imperial War Cabinet, but consultation had not made the King's declaration of war against Germany in August 1914 a collective Imperial decision.

Hertzog embarked on a campaign to assert South Africa's right to control her own international destiny in 1912. Speaking at Nylstroom, Smithfield and De Wildt at the end of the year, he insisted on the priority of South Africa's interests without insisting on a severance of the Imperial tie. This kind of utterance would hardly have caused a ripple if it had been uttered after 1931, but it provoked a strong reaction at the time, because he described Sir Thomas Smartt, ex-Afrikaner Bondsman and leader of the Unionists, who had recently been urging contributions to the British navy, as a 'foreign fortune-seeker', just when Botha was about to campaign among English-speakers, whose leaders controlled the mining, industrial and commercial assets of the country, and whom it was important for Botha's entire strategy not to antagonise.

There had already been a Cabinet crisis in May 1912, when the Treasurer, H. C. Hull, had crossed swords with J. W. Sauer, Minister of Railways and Harbours, for failing to coordinate the railway budget with the Treasury, and resigned. After Hertzog's De Wildt speech, Sir George Leuchars, the Minister of Public Works, asked Botha to accept his resignation. Botha tried to persuade Hertzog to resign as well, and when the latter refused he resigned himself. Asked to form another government, he then left both Hertzog and Leuchars out. But the dropping of Hertzog stirred up the feelings of fellow Free Staters. In November 1913, Hertzog and General C. R. de Wet walked out of the S.A.P. congress in Cape Town, taking a handful of the parliamentary caucus with them. In January, a congress of dissidents in Bloemfontein decided to form a new National Party, on a platform of South African self-sufficiency, dual-medium education, and compulsory bilingualism in the public service. At their first Transvaal congress in August 1914, they opposed South African participation in the Great War and any contemplated attack on South West Africa.

If the international crisis had not arisen, perhaps the Government might have come to terms with Hertzogism. But once the threat of war appeared, it was to the magnates' party, the Unionists rather than the Nationalists that the Government had to look for support. This in turn helped to revive anti-capitalist sentiments among the Afrikaner rank and file. The Government experienced a head-on collision with the power of Afrikaner nationalists and white workers on two occasions, first in 1913–14, before and after the outbreak of the First World War, and again in 1920–4. These were significant moments in the evolution of the South African political system, rare occasions when a struggle for power clearly cut across the lines of racial division. But these conflicts acquire their proper meaning only if one realises that they took place against the backdrop of another political struggle – that between the white community as a whole and the African and Asian communities for political and economic control.

* * *

In its attitude towards the African people, the Government was strongly influenced by the segregationist arguments of the Lagden Commission; but the pattern of its policies was not uniform, for the rules of segregation, whether economic, social or political, were less rigid in the Cape than in the northern provinces.[2] Botha's Government was dominated by northerners; but on the details of policy they were still feeling their way and, as Kallaway has shown, for most of the period between 1910 and 1924 the key portfolios of Mines and Industry (generally combined), were held by F. S. Malan, who also had a great deal to do with the running of the Department of Native Affairs, and, as a Cape man, used his influence to moderate the rigours of policy.

The differences in outlook of the South African and Unionist Parties, which dominated Parliament between them, were not marked where 'native policy' was concerned. Both disapproved of racial miscegenation; both regarded the idea of a black political majority as unthinkable, though the Unionists may have been less antagonistic to the retention of the Cape non-white franchise than the S.A.P.; both desired to see the restriction of African land ownership to the Reserves, and both wished to see African urban immigrants segregated in locations. In their various ways – some as farmers, others as mine-owners or industrialists – S.A.P. and Unionist politicians were anxious to safeguard their supplies of black labour. If this meant deliberately depressing wage rates, or preventing the growth of labour's bargaining power, or playing off white against black workers, or keeping land for Africans in short supply to force men on to the farms or down the mines, the power balance arrived at in the South Africa Act made it possible to do these things.

The South African Party's programme extended the pattern of segregation. In the 1911 session it shackled African labour by prohibiting strikes by contract workers, and in regulations promulgated under the Mines and Works Act it reserved certain categories of work for white people. Its Defence Act of 1912 provided for a white active citizen force. The 1913 Natives Land Act laid down the principle of territorial segregation. The Native Affairs Act of 1920, carried after Smuts had succeeded Botha to the premiership, enacted the substance of an earlier Bill of 1917, and sought to implement the Lagden principle of segregated political institutions for Africans, which Smuts himself had applauded in 1917 in a speech at the Savoy Hotel in London. It built on the Glen Grey system of district councils, which by then extended across the greater part of the Transkei (excluding Pondoland), by providing for their extension throughout the Union, and their grouping into general councils as at Umtata. The Act also set up a Native Conference of African leaders to be nominated by the Government and meet annually in Pretoria, together with an all-white Native Affairs Commission of experts, who were to maintain contact with the

## VERSIONS OF THE NATIONAL ENEMY: CAPITALISM AND COMMUNISM

**1 An Afrikaner Nationalist view of Capitalism, 1915**

D. C. Boonzaaier of *De Burger* depicts 'a full Cabinet meeting' comprising (clockwise from l.) 'Hoggenheimer', Sir T. Smartt, J. C. Smuts and Louis Botha.

**2 An Afrikaner Nationalist view of Communism, 1948**

T. O. Honiball of *Die Burger* depicts 'Ghosts out of the Red Past', commenting that 'the same Field Marshal Smuts who once blessed Russian weapons and doffed his hat to Stalin, is currently making an urgent appeal for the stopping of Communist imperialism'.

**3 An Afrikaner Nationalist view of Liberalism, 1948**

T. O. Honiball of *Die Burger* depicts Smuts and Hofmeyr enticing the voter towards their web. He comments that Smuts had told a Johannesburg meeting that the voters had no need to fear Hofmeyr.

**4 A Liberal view of Afrikaner Nationalist ideology, *c.* 1970**

By Don Kenyon of the *Daily Dispatch*.

**5 An African view of Imperialism, 1936**

From *Umvikeli-Thebe. The African Defender*, January 1936. The caption, 'Tata amakatango ako. Angiwafuni', means 'Take away your chains. I do not want them'. Mussolini's invasion of Ethiopia and Hertzog's 1936 legislation are equated.

**6 An Afrikaner Nationalist view of Imperialism, 1948**

T. O. Honiball of *Die Burger* depicts Smuts, Hofmeyr and Colin Steyn on the S.A. Party nag, Smuts's *Century of Wrong* having fallen on the ground. Steyn asks: 'Daddy, is the snake really dead, or is he just lying and digesting his prey?' Smuts replies: 'No, my child, I'd say he's been dead for years'.

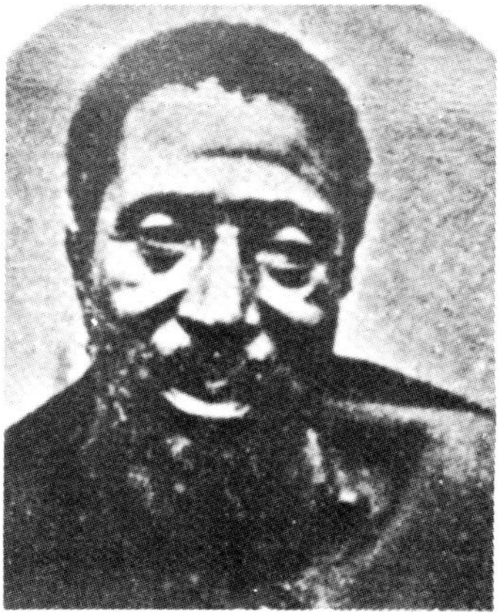

7 Sarhili

8 Sir George Grey

9 Moshweshwe

10 President Brand

11 President Burgers

12 Sekhukhune I

13 Cetshwayo

14 Sir Theophilus Shepstone

15 Kgama III

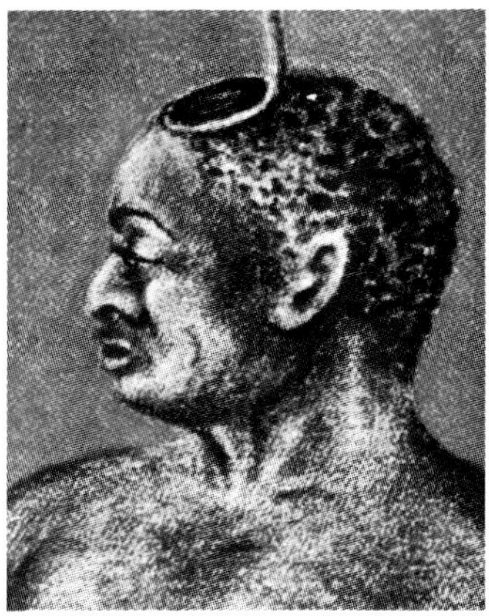

16 Lobengula

17 M. K. Gandhi

18 J. C. Smuts

**27 The Malan Cabinet of 1948**

*Front row, l. to r.*: C. R. Swart, E. G. Jansen, D. F. Malan, Governor-General G. B. van Zyl, N. C. Havenga, J. G. Strijdom, P. O. Sauer. *Back row, l. to r.*: B. J. Schoeman, F. C. Erasmus, T. E. Dönges, A. J. Stals, E. H. Louw, S. P. le Roux, official

**28 The Verwoerd Cabinet of 1958**

*Front row, l. to r.*: T. E. Dönges, P. O. Sauer, H. F. Verwoerd, Governor-General E. G. Jansen, C. R. Swart, E. H. Louw. *Back row, l. to r.*: J. J. Serfontein, M. D. C. de Wet Nel, A. J. R. van Rhijn, Senator J. de Klerk, B. J. Schoeman, P. M. K. le Roux, F. C. Erasmus, J. F. T. Naude

African population through its leaders, report annually to Parliament, and act as a liaison between the white legislators and African opinion. Before relinquishing power in 1924, the South African Party also made access to skilled trades safe for the white community by insisting on minimum educational qualifications for entry to apprenticeship which youths of other race groups could not easily attain (1922). It also carried a Natives (Urban Areas) Act in 1923, which provided in a single instrument for the administration, financing and policing of African locations as segregated residential areas. Finally, its Industrial Conciliation Act of 1924 restricted the use of new collective bargaining machinery to white and Coloured people only [see pp. 332–44].

Most of these measures were highly unpopular among politically conscious Africans, who tried to build up organs of political and industrial opposition. The establishment of Union was seen, by African political leaders as by white, as the right moment for consolidation across provincial frontiers. Disappointment over the outcome of the Convention, combined with anger at the racist tone of some of the Union Parliament's first new laws, provided a sufficient stimulus for the convening of 'representatives of provincial associations and vigilance committees, Chiefs, delegates and other leading men in the High Commission Territories and the provinces' to Bloemfontein on 8 January 1912. The chief mover was Pixley Seme, a lawyer trained at Columbia, Oxford and the Middle Temple, who had met Schreiner's deputation in London and later prepared the way for this conference in a letter to *Imvo* of 24 October 1911. Seme wanted a Congress formally constituted, office-bearers installed, the Government and the Natives' Senators formally recognised, and wide-ranging discussions on the important problems of African life. These things were done, but the meetings went unnoticed in the press. Seme was made treasurer of the new body. The office of president was given to Dr J. L. Dube, an American-trained Zulu disciple of Booker T. Washington, who had returned to Natal to edit *Ilanga lase Natal* in 1904, and later set up an African industrial school, the Ohlange Institute, at Inanda in 1909. Rubusana was chosen vice-president, and Sol Plaatje, the journalist from Kimberley, secretary. The speakership of Congress went to Thomas Mapikela, a builder from Bloemfontein who had fluent Sotho, Zulu and English. The executive also included Meshach Pelem (Cape), Sam Makgatho (Transvaal) and Alfred Mangena, a lawyer who had defended Bambatha's associates in Natal. A committee under Richard Msimang was appointed to draft a constitution for the South African Native National Congress. It did so, though its first report was rejected, and the constitution providing for a two-chamber association formally adopted only in September 1919.

Tengo Jabavu did not become involved in the S.A.N.N.C., but in

April 1912 set up his own South African Races Congress as a separate body. He seems to have been reluctant to surrender the position of leadership which he had gained as the father of African political movements, and by a desire to maintain good relations with the white government, above all with his personal friend J. W. Sauer, who would shortly succeed Hertzog as Minister of Native Affairs.

Jabavu's real test, which he failed, came over the issue of government land policy. To understand why, it is necessary to appreciate the extent to which unnecessary distress was caused by this cruel and misleading law, especially in the Orange Free State, an assessment of which is given in Chapter 18. Jabavu's trust in Hertzog and Sauer led him and the Races Congress to support the 1913 Land Bill, on the assumption that the Government's intentions were above suspicion and that real advantage was to be gained from fair territorial segregation. The S.A.N.N.C. was divided over the merits of segregation, though a majority in opposition to it emerged over the next three years. It was far from satisfied with Sauer's Land Bill of 1913. It sent four deputations to remonstrate with Sauer, tried to persuade the Governor-General to refuse his assent, and ended by sending Plaatje and Mapikela to London on a fruitless deputation to the Imperial Parliament. When the issue was reopened in congress after the publication of the Beaumont Commission's Report in 1916, offering an extension of land to Africans in each province, the members divided behind Dube, who had no objection to segregation in principle, and Makgatho, who did object. Makgatho succeeded to the presidency in 1917.

One side-effect of the general anguish over the Land Act was a proliferation of the independent churches, products of a vigorous search for new forms of black autonomy. The most dramatic manifestation of this on South African soil was Enoch Mgijima's Israelite sect, who squatted on the Ntabelanga commonage at Bulhoek, near Queenstown, in 1921, and defied all government attempts to persuade them to depart. In the end they suffered grievous loss of life when blind faith in their leader's words drove them to attack the police. This seems to have been a tragic example of group resentment among landless blacks, seeking an outlet in the millenarian teachings of a leader whose message drew on Jewish and Christian symbolism, and was first inspired by the passage of Halley's comet.

Apart from continued expressions of opposition to the Land Act, and to the segregationist features of the Native Administration Bill of 1917, African politicians restrained their utterances during the war years, and generally gave support to the Allied cause, although the Defence Act made no provision for the arming of black troops, and Rubusana's offer to recruit Africans for armed service was rejected. Considerable numbers served in the South West African, East African and Western Front campaigns in non-combatant roles, and when the troopship

*Mendi* sank on the way to Europe in 1917, 615 Africans lost their lives.

Not unreasonably, therefore, some hope that the fruits of victory would fall into African mouths touched their feelings at the end of the war. Meshach Pelem's Bantu Union, which emerged in 1919 from a Native Convention held in the Transkei shortly before, was a naïve pressure group nurtured on this sentiment, and it never spread beyond the eastern Cape. The S.A.N.N.C., by contrast, took on a more aggressive air under the presidency of Makgatho between 1917 and 1924, sponsoring both a passive resistance campaign against the pass laws on the Rand and a spate of strikes.

Charlotte Maxeke, science graduate of an American college, wife of an A.M.E.C. missionary and founder of the women's section of the S.A.N.N.C. had conducted a moderately successful campaign against the carrying of passes by African women in the Orange Free State in 1913. After the war, Witwatersrand branches of the Congress, taking a leaf out of Gandhi's book, organised the collection of passes in sacks and persuaded thousands, without the use of picketing or physical force, to hand themselves over to the police for disobeying the law. These demonstrations were broken up by the authorities, however, amid considerable violence, which Makgatho angrily denounced in his presidential address in May 1919. The Government's subsequent appointment of the Godley Committee to review the pass laws seemed at first to vindicate the organisers of the campaign; but that committee's recommendations in favour of simplification of the system were not implemented, and failure cost the S.A.N.N.C. some support.

More serious for its image, however, was the overall failure of African strike activity. The consolidation of an industrial colour bar by the legislation of 1911 did not prevent but did inhibit African strike action. African gold miners came out in support of the Kleinfontein whites in July 1913, but arrests and an official inquiry followed. African diamond miners came out at Jagersfontein in the Orange Free State, following the killing of one of their number by a white man in 1914; but this resulted in the shooting of several more black miners. In 1918, the S.A.N.N.C. took a lead in organising a strike of the poorly paid Johannesburg sanitary workers, but the strike leaders were arrested. The following year Selby Msimang, a lawyer and Congress member, engineered another wage strike in Bloemfontein which for a change was partly successful, but Msimang was arrested though not convicted. In 1920, a strike of the Port Elizabeth municipal workers organised by Samuel Masabalala of the Cape Provincial Native Congress resulted, after a riot in which the police failed to control would-be strike-breakers, in nineteen deaths. In the same year, some 71,000 black miners struck for higher wages on the Rand, incidentally putting over 8000 whites out of work. The police, profiting from the recommendations of Commissioner Buckle's report on African grievances after the

1913 strike, dealt with the mine compounds piecemeal, and broke the strike by destroying communications between them. There was some loss of life when the strikers at the Village Deep compound resisted the police intrusion.

The failure of this industrial action caused new divisions in the African political movements. Clements Kadalie, an expatriate Nyasalander who had taught and held clerical posts in Southern Rhodesia and Mozambique before going to Cape Town, organised a moderately successful strike of African and Coloured dock workers, members of an Industrial and Commercial Union of which he was honorary secretary, in 1919. They refused to load maize for export at a time when it was in short supply, and received some backing from the white Railways and Harbours Servants. They also won higher wages, but not as a direct result of the strike. Following this limited success, wage demands among unskilled workers there and elsewhere began to proliferate. Kadalie in Cape Town and Msimang in Bloemfontein accordingly discussed the establishment of a general workers' union for skilled and unskilled, industrial, domestic and rural workers, which could organise industrial action and provide a wide range of benefits. At a conference in Bloemfontein in May 1920, they established a new Industrial and Commercial Workers' Union (I.C.W.U.) which, if more widely supported, might have formed the nucleus of a formidable labour movement. But there was no representation from Natal, where African labour was still very poorly organised, or from the Transvaal where workers on the Rand were still licking their wounds after the 'bucket' and mineworkers' strikes and the pass-law demonstration. To make matters worse, the I.C.W.U. suffered loss of face from the Port Elizabeth riot in October, for Masabalala's workers had joined the new labour organisation. Partly for personal reasons, the alliance between Msimang and Kadalie became strained. The I.C.W.U. disintegrated, Msimang withdrawing from trade union politics, while Kadalie reconstituted his earlier I.C.U. which became essentially a Cape-based organisation, and began to take on the character of a political movement rather than an industrial pressure group. According to its historian, P. L. Wickins, the I.C.U. lacked the three essential qualities of a successful general union, namely a firm base in large-scale industry, recognition by employers, and a record of successful strikes. These deficiencies were plain to see during the critical period 1920–4.

Smuts and Gandhi had reached an uneasy truce when the separate existence of the Transvaal Colony came to an end.[3] Gandhi, like the Coloured and African leaders, went to London to object to the draft South Africa Bill, which gave no political rights to Indians at all. He returned at the end of the year to Tolstoy Farm, but also kept in touch with Indian leaders, notably G. K. Gokhale, a prominent member of the Viceroy's Council, about the disabilities which continued to plague his fellow-countrymen – the £3 contract labour tax in Natal, for example, the personal registration certificates and the restrictions on the ownership of property in the Transvaal, and the restrictions on freedom of movement through the country as a whole. Gokhale helped to bring about the Indian Government's prohibition of further emigration to South Africa, in the hope that Natal's continued dependence on contract labour would force the Government to effect some improvement in the circumstances of Indians in South Africa. He and Gandhi had the £3 tax especially in mind, both because of its intrinsic unfairness – it did not apply to any save Indian contract labourers and their families – and because it was not effective either as a means of raising revenue or as a means of encouraging the repatriation of Indians not on contract.

Gokhale visited South Africa in October 1912, and returned to India under the impression that the Government had agreed to abolish the Natal tax, in return for his own acceptance of Union legislation which would informally restrict Indian settlement in South Africa. But the Union Government, anxious to retain the backing of its Natal supporters when the dispute between Botha and Hertzog was reaching its climax, admitted no such commitment. At the same time it proceeded with an Immigrants' Restrictions Bill which avoided crude racial definitions, but employed a European language test and provided for discretionary exclusion by the minister of 'any person or class of persons deemed . . . on economic grounds or on account of standard or habits of life to be unsuited'.

This double offence provided the catalyst for Gandhi's last and most effective South African Satyagraha. In negotiations with the Government, Gandhi had laid his emphasis on four issues, of which the head tax was not one: property rights, Indian entry into the Cape under the restrictive Immigration Act of 1906, restrictions on Indians in the Orange Free State dating from the 1880s, and the legality of Indian marriages (arising out of recent judgments in the Transvaal and Cape Supreme Courts, in which the courts had made it progressively harder for Indians to bring into South Africa, first more than one wife of a polygamous marriage, then any such wives, and finally – by Judge Searle in Cape Town on 14 March 1913 – any wives who were not Christians). But as Gandhi later recorded, 'The undertaking given to Gokhale cleared the way for the satyagrahis.' Some moved out of Natal across the Transvaal border and were arrested under the Transvaal Immigration Regulation Act of 1908. Others moved from the Transvaal and went to the Natal collieries, where they organised the non-payment of the £3 tax by those liable to it, and a strike until the tax was withdrawn by those who were not liable. Gandhi himself was arrested and released on bail several times before being sent off to prison in Bloemfontein. But the demonstration was publicised across the world. The Government of India and the Viceroy, Lord Hardinge, were outspoken in their criticism. After Lord Crewe had proposed an informal inquiry into the South African Indian problem, Botha appointed a Commission chaired by the South African judge, Sir William Solomon, to which Sir Benjamin Robertson was attached to represent the Government of India, after the inclusion of an Indian had been refused by Botha. Smuts and Gandhi met on 16 January 1914 and with the help of Robertson and Gandhi's missionary friend, the Rev. C. F. Andrews, the terms of a compromise were hammered out which came to be embodied in the Indian Relief Act of the same year. This Act abolished the £3 tax entirely, recognised marriages performed by accredited marriage officers of any Indian religion, and made it possible for children of Indians domiciled in South Africa to join their families; but it did not remove restrictions on Indian residence, land ownership and trading where these existed.

When Gandhi finally left South Africa in July 1914, to the great relief of Smuts, he had made a few explicit gains, but knew that the legislation of that year could not be the end of the story. Very soon renewed friction developed under the existing restrictive laws. Thus, in the Transvaal, Indians discovered that it was possible to evade the Gold Law and Townships Act of 1908 by establishing businesses under the Transvaal Companies Act of 1909, and to evade Law 3 of 1885, respecting the ownership of property, by registering it in the names of companies, which was declared lawful by the courts in 1916 and confirmed on appeal in 1920. The number of Indian private companies in the Transvaal grew from three in 1913 to 103 in 1916. Whites of Krugersdorp initiated a South Africans' League in 1919, under the chairmanship of Sir Abe Bailey, the local M.P., to work for the expropriation of Indians who had acquired property in defiance of the Gold Law, and an Anti-Asiatic League congress met in Pretoria in September that year, attended by twenty-six local authorities, thirty chambers of commerce, nine agricultural societies, twelve religious congregations and forty trade unions. A Transvaal Asiatic Land and Trading Amendment Act of 1919 exempted Indians with businesses in mining areas if they still occupied the sites, but prohibited the ownership of fixed property by companies in which one or more Asians had a controlling interest. Smuts appointed a commission under Judge J. H. Lange, to which Sir Benjamin Robertson was again attached. In 1921 this body rejected suggestions that Indian traders be required to live 'at some distance outside the town proper', considering it 'unjust and unreasonable to force men who had been trading in the centre of the town for many years, and established businesses there, to remove to an outside location'. It recommended voluntary segregation, and voluntary repatriation to India. It thought that the Transvaal Land

and Trading Act of 1919 should be retained, and that Indian land purchases in Natal should be restricted to the coastal belt. But white public opinion was beginning to demand radical solutions, and the extent of their pressure can be gauged from Smuts's willingness, even after a serious clash with Dr Sastri at the 1921 Imperial Conference, and with Sir Tej Bahadur Sapru at the conference of 1923, to allow Patrick Duncan to introduce the segregationist Class Areas Bill in 1924. Not surprisingly, political organisations which had been set up to represent Indian interests in Natal, the Cape and the Transvaal amalgamated to form the South African Indian Congress in May 1923. But like the African people, the Indians found no effective way of asserting their power. It had been established by 1924 that the direction of South African public life was in the white man's hands. But over the question of which whites were to do the controlling, there was still room for doubt.

White workers tried to seize power in 1913–14, and failed.[4] In July 1913 the white miners at the New Kleinfontein mine came out over Saturday afternoon work. The Government had not yet organised its Active Citizen Force under the Defence Act of 1912, and incurred hostility by allowing Imperial troops to fire on the strikers. Some 18,000 whites came out on sixty-three mines on the Rand as a result, and syndicalist leaders tried to turn the strike into an attack on capitalism itself. The Government and the Chamber, who lost control of the situation, bought peace by recognising the white labour unions' right to participate in collective bargaining. Smuts and Botha were exposed to crowd hostility as they returned from the settlement with the strike leaders, and this experience profoundly affected Smuts's handling of the next outburst of labour unrest six months later, when he showed a determination not to be caught out again.

Confrontation between the Government and the labour unions resulted in a growing polarisation of forces, in which English-speaking labour enjoyed support from rural as well as urban Afrikaners, whose anti-capitalist posture was at least as old as the Jameson Raid. Afrikaners were beginning to join the trade unions even before the 1913 strike, despite some opposition from Dutch Reformed clergy. Afrikaner-dominated branches of the Labour Party were coming into existence at the same time.

The 1914 strike hastened the process. It started on 8 January, on the heels of a government threat to lay off Railway and Harbour employees, and the Federation of Trades backed the railwaymen with a call for a general strike on the 13th. Smuts, as Minister of Defence, was now able to bring ten thousand troops to the Rand. He proclaimed martial law on 14 January, and commandos under General Beyers and De la Rey, with supporting artillery, were moved into position against the strikers. The Johannesburg Trades Hall was surrounded, and the executive of the Federation of Trades, along with many other strikers, were arrested. These included Creswell and Boydell of the Labour Party (both cabinet ministers under Hertzog after 1924), and W. H. Andrews (then Labour Party chairman and later leader of the Communist Party). Smuts deported nine strike leaders on 30 January, and then carried an Indemnity and Undesirables Special Deportation Bill. To maintain public order, he then introduced a Riotous Assemblies Bill, which prohibited recruitment to unions by force, banned strikes in public utility services, permitted magistrates to prohibit meetings thought likely to endanger public peace, and greatly widened police powers of law enforcement.

In March 1914, the Labour Party won a majority of seats in the Transvaal Provincial Council, when predominantly Afrikaner electorates in constituencies like Krugersdorp and Pretoria West returned English-speaking Labour candidates. Even Free State constituencies like Ficksburg and Edenburg developed strong Labour Party branches. The outbreak of war in 1914, however, checked the growth of Labour power and of Labour influence in rural Nationalist constituencies, for the party split on the issue of participation in the war. A minority of convinced socialists, led by D. Ivon Jones, S. P. Bunting and Colin Wade, set up a War on War League in September 1914 and carried an anti-war resolution at the Party conference at East London in January 1915. But the majority under Colonel Creswell, who favoured participation in the war, soon regained control over the Party, and in doing so lost the contact with the rural Afrikaner which their Rural Propaganda Committee had cultivated assiduously.

There was real opposition in the Afrikaner camp to war directed against South West Africa, the colonial territory of a friendly power. In August 1914, the Imperial Government asked the South African Government to invade German South West Africa, to immobilise radio stations serving the German naval forces in the South Atlantic. Botha was told that, if South Africa did not act, other Imperial forces would be sent. The Government therefore had to view the matter in the light, not only of immediate military necessity, but also of longer term national interest, with incorporation of the territory in the Union as a possibility. The opponents of invasion took various stances.[5] Hertzog was not prepared to admit that South Africa was legally involved in Britain's war. General C. F. Beyers, who was commander of the Active Citizen Force, J. H. de la Rey, who was now a Union senator and still a close friend of Botha, and General de Wet, who was now a Nationalist, were all opposed to the invasion of German territory, and all may have thought that the time was ripe for a restoration of republican independence. Others, of whom General S. G. ('Manie') Maritz was the most prominent, quite clearly desired a republican restoration, if necessary with German support. Maritz, whose commandos had ranged over the north-western Cape with those of Smuts at the end of the Anglo-Boer war, was in command of the military district which covered the South West African frontier, and had been appointed, like Beyers, by Smuts.

Botha and Smuts underrated the opposition to the proposed campaign, which a special session of Parliament had agreed to by 12 September with big majorities in the Assembly and in the Senate. The Nationalists opposed invasion at their August congress. The Transvaal and Free State commandants dissented at a special briefing, and there was an excited republican demonstration at Lichtenburg in the Western Transvaal on 15 August, apparently inspired by the dreams of a local 'prophet', Van Rensburg. The Government therefore stated that only volunteers would be asked to cross into German territory, but this assurance was not punctiliously carried out. On 15 September, Beyers resigned his commission. That night, after failing to stop at a road block in Langlaagte while he and Beyers were on their way to Potchefstroom, De la Rey was shot and killed (accidentally, according to Judge Gregorowski, who made the official investigation) by troops who were under orders to intercept the criminal Foster gang. The shooting of De la Rey may have delayed the outbreak of a planned rebellion. But on 9 October, cornered by Smuts into admitting treasonable intentions, Maritz went over to the Germans, who were embarrassed by his action because they were not anxious to provoke hostilities on their poorly defended frontiers. Beyers and De Wet then faced a hard choice. Beyers rebelled after being physically assaulted while addressing a meeting in Pretoria. De Wet also went into open rebellion. Soon afterwards his son was killed by Government forces while he himself was on his way to seek ex-president Steyn's mediation.

The rebels were put down in a few weeks, and Botha was careful to use only Afrikaner commandos against them. De Wet's defeat at Mushroom Valley demonstrated that evasive commando action was less easy to contrive in the age of the motor car. Beyers perished while in retreat across the Vaal river. General J. C. G. Kemp, who crossed the Kalahari in a vain attempt to join Maritz, surrendered in January 1915. Maritz himself escaped to Angola. The sentences imposed on the rebels were generally lenient – seven years for the ringleaders, but none served more than two. Yet the rebellion added to the Afrikaner hall of fame, producing more legends and martyrs to inspire a new nationalist movement in the 1930s. De la Rey was held to be a murder victim; Beyers came to be seen as a martyr to his conscience who had died without having fired a shot in anger, symbolically uniting Transvalers and Free Staters by his death in the river which divided them; while Jopie Fourie, who had not resigned his commission before rebelling, and had been executed for shooting at Government forces under a flag of truce, excited feelings rather by the manner of his death – facing his executioners without a blindfold, on a Sunday, singing a psalm, after Dr D. F. Malan had tried unsuccessfully to find Smuts to intercede on his behalf. Not surprisingly, the rebellion consolidated Nationalist forces behind Hertzog, who himself stood up to a severe grilling by a parliamentary select committee under Patrick Duncan, and cleared his party of the allegation of collective treason. To help pay the fines of the rebel leaders, the *Helpmekaar* society was born. Competitive giving to a popular cause, which had created *Helpmekaar*, was extended in 1916 to the subscription lists of the first Nationalist newspaper, *De Burger*. The Nationalists made impressive gains in the 1915 general election, taking 16 out of the 17 Free State seats, as well as 7 in the Cape and 4 in the Transvaal, and netted 77,000 votes to the S.A.P.'s 95,000. Despite the victory of Union arms in South West Africa, the S.A.P. lost eight seats and the Unionists (if one includes the Natal Independents of 1910) a further ten.

The war brought and held the S.A.P. and the Unionists together in competitive enthusiasm for the Allied cause.[6] The organisation of the South-West African campaign, which was over by 15 July 1915, was essentially the work of the Government. Botha himself overran the north. Smuts, taking over from Van Deventer, completed the conquest of the south, and then – after some initial reluctance to assume command – began the conquest of German East Africa in February 1916. Botha had meanwhile responded to pressure from his Unionist allies and offered to send a South African contingent to Europe. A brigade of 6000 men was accordingly sent to Britain in December 1915. It was almost immediately switched to Egypt to help defend the Suez Canal against Turkish attacks, but after successfully concluding the Egyptian campaign it was sent to France in April 1916, where it took part in the battle of the Somme in July, and won great military distinction by taking and then holding Delville Wood on an exposed salient of the British line, losing over two-thirds of its strength in the process. After playing a prominent part in the advance into Belgium in 1917, the South African brigade was almost exterminated before it surrendered during the German offensive of March 1918.

Despite the Nationalist successes in the 1915 election, the Unionists and the S.A.P. could not afford to amalgamate with each other, even though no party had a clear majority. The loss of electoral support which the Unionists suffered, accompanied by widespread resignations by their leaders (Farrar, Jameson, Chaplin, Phillips, Abe Bailey, and ultimately Fitzpatrick) in the period 1911 to 1920, induced a mood of frustration among men who had neither the desire to oppose nor the electoral support to form a government. The few who hung on, like

Smartt, Duncan and Jagger, became increasingly amenable to talk of coalition, which Merriman had resisted so firmly and Botha so deviously, on the eve of Union. The South African Party had little incentive to trade with the Unionists, since their support against the Nationalists was assured, the desire to bring the Hertzogites back into their fold was always present, and the fear that Afrikaner working men might move across to Labour was always real.

At the end of 1919 the Unionists and the S.A.P. could do no more than flirt discreetly with each other. Smartt reverted to the 'best man' theme at his party congress in October, and spoke favourably of 'fair amalgamation' without surrender of identity by his own party. Smuts replied at the S.A.P. congress the same month with a carefully limited request for their 'hearty co-operation'. The general election of March 1920 made the Nationalists, with 44 seats, the largest party in the Assembly. The S.A.P. dropped back to 41 seats, the Unionists to 25, while the Labour Party, profiting from triangular contests and from popular discontent during the post-war depression, won 21 seats as against the four previously held. Smuts, after failing to persuade the other parties to form a non-party government, decided to woo the Nationalists again, for the desire for reunion among sections of his party was strong. A private congress at Robertson, however, followed by a public one at Bloemfontein in September 1920, broke down over the definition of South Africa's relationship to the Empire, chiefly because the Nationalists had decided in 1919 to make republicanism a permissible article of faith, and sent a deputation to Versailles in a futile bid to ask for a restoration of freedom. At the end of the month Smuts circularised all S.A.P. branches with a call for the establishment of a new centre party 'which all moderate South Africans of whatever race can join with every confidence', and dedicated to support of the British Commonwealth. A special S.A.P. congress at the end of October accepted a resolution standing in Smuts's name, which proposed that major constitutional changes should only be made on the basis of a clear popular mandate, recognised the priority of South African interests as a condition for the maintenance of the Imperial bond, and asserted the equality of the two white language groups and the need for them to work together. The Unionists accepted this overture, and, at a special congress in Bloemfontein at the beginning of November, gave their executive discretion to act. Most delegates were willing to join the S.A.P. on the latter's terms, after Smuts had appealed through Smartt for an understanding of his special difficulties. Although Sir Edgar Walton wanted fusion on equal terms, Smartt thought that the strengthening of the S.A.P. was necessary to keep the Nationalists out of power. The Unionist Party was accordingly dissolved, and its members encouraged to join the S.A.P. as individuals. Smuts announced publicly that there had been no amalgamation of parties, but that the

Unionists had joined the S.A.P. 'unconditionally and without bargaining'. He told Hofmeyr privately that 'the dissolution of the party of Rhodes and Jameson is one of the greatest victories ever obtained on the road to "het Zuid Afrikaanderisme" '. He then had Parliament dissolved, and in the 1921 election the enlarged S.A.P. was returned to power with 79 seats, won mainly at the expense of Labour, who were cut back to 9, while the Nationalists increased their holding to 45. Smartt, Jagger and Duncan received posts in the new Cabinet.

Among the factors which aided the rapprochement of the S.A.P. and the Unionists must be included the contributions made by Botha and Smuts at the Paris peace conference, and to the debate on the nature of the emerging Commonwealth, and their attempts to secure an extension of South African influence on the African continent.[7]

Lloyd George had appointed Smuts to the British War Cabinet in January 1917 in the hope that he might be able to deal with pressures on the Government by the General Staff. Smuts's military advice proved to be of little consequence; but the ideas expressed in his pamphlet of 1917, *The League of Nations: a Practical Suggestion*, had a direct influence on the formulation of President Wilson's plans for a post-war settlement. Wilson took from Smuts several key features of his League proposals, among them the idea of a strong League Council composed of the Great Powers, joined by representatives of smaller states in rotation, and the device of a veto to restrain the League from acting if three council members exercised it.

Smuts's influence at the peace conference, as a member of the British delegation, had one serious result not intended by himself. He recommended that war widows' pensions be made a charge against the German reparations account, thus extending substantial compensation to Britain as well as to France. This pushed the sum demanded as reparations to such a high figure that Smuts only signed the peace treaty with great reluctance, for, with the memory of Vereeniging still green, he saw no virtue in a peace which fostered resentment.

Smuts gave Wilson the idea of the League Mandate system, but intended that it should be applied to the satellite provinces of the broken Central Powers. Wilson adopted the idea, but insisted that it be applied to all conquered colonial territories such as German South-West Africa, which Smuts intended to annex. Smuts countered with a proposal for three categories of mandate, and was able to arrange that the 'C' class, in which South-West Africa fell, allowed for the government of the territory under the laws of the mandatory power, an arrangement stopping just short of annexation. The extent to which Smuts and Botha had taken part in the war in Africa in order to be able to extend South Africa's influence on the Continent, and that with Colonial Office approval, was not clearly revealed until the 1970s.

Apart from the incorporation of South-West Africa, Smuts had hoped that the conquest of German East Africa might lead to its being exchanged for southern Mozambique, including Lourenço Marques and Beira. This might have the further effect of inducing Southern Rhodesia, once compelled to trade with the outside world through Union ports, to amalgamate with the Union. In view of rising difficulties over the 1909 tariff agreement with Portuguese East Africa, and the need to negotiate a new agreement in 1923, South Africa had economic as well as strategic reasons for seeking such a line of advance.

Smuts tried but failed to incorporate Southern Rhodesia. Successive amendments to the original Order-in-Council had resulted in an elective majority in the Southern Rhodesian Legislative Council, and Settler support for Chartered Company rule had diminished on account of the Company's assumption of vested rights in unappropriated land, which a Privy Council judgment in 1918 declared to be vested in the Crown. Meanwhile Charles Coghlan, who had originally favoured incorporation in South Africa, founded his Responsible Government Association to press for political autonomy for Southern Rhodesia. By 1923 the two main alternatives offered to the electorate in a referendum were self-government and incorporation in the Union. Strong pressures were applied in favour of incorporation. Milner and then Churchill in the Colonial Office threw their weight behind it, as did the *Argus* press. From the South African side, Smuts desired it for reasons of political strategy – the extension of Union influence northwards, and the incorporation of a territory likely to support the S.A.P.–Unionist fusion against Hertzog's Nationalists. The incorporationists found a Rhodesian leader in Drummond Chaplin. Smuts offered attractive terms: incorporation as a fifth province with ten members in the Assembly, the promise of railway and harbour development, the establishment of a land settlement board to bring in a large white settler population, and respect for the borders of existing native reserves. But the Southern Rhodesian voters were apparently frightened by Afrikaner Nationalist successes in the South African election of 1920, and by a fairly narrow majority of 8774 votes to 5989 in an 80 per cent poll, voted in favour of independent self-government.

The High Commission Territories, excluded from the Union under the National Convention on account of the British Government's reservations over white South African ideas on native policy, continued to attract the interest of Botha and Smuts in spite of this initial rebuff. Botha had begun to urge their incorporation even before the outbreak of the First World War. He first made a special plea for Swaziland on the ground that it was already extensively occupied by white people, in face of a warning by the Secretary of State, Lewis Harcourt, not to alienate African feelings by trying to force the pace. Botha also put in a bid for Bechuanaland, acting on information (which proved unreliable) that the B.S.A. Company might be about to extract land rights there from the British Government under the terms of its charter. The Colonial Office steadily refused to part with any of the Territories, on the ground that African opinion was strongly opposed to transfer. After the First World War, Botha raised the question of Swaziland's transfer again, claiming that this territory was best suited of the three for an experimental takeover, and urging that this would make it possible to give whites in Swaziland political representation, and at the same time enable the Union Government to extend rail communications from the Transvaal through the mining districts of Swaziland to the coast. Smuts kept up the pressure after Botha's death. Lord Buxton, the Imperial High Commissioner, was more sensitive to African desires than his predecessor, Lord Gladstone, had been, and it was partly to meet his objections to transfer that Smuts introduced his Native Affairs Bill of 1920, which provided for a statutory Native Affairs Commission of the kind defined in the Schedule to the South Africa Act. Once the Bill had become law, Smuts asked for the transfer of Swaziland, offering immediate railway development and representation for whites. But the newly installed Paramount Chief, Sobhuza II, led a deputation to London at the end of 1922 to protest against transfer and fight the British Government's land apportionment of 1907 before the Privy Council.

By the time of its fall from power in 1924, therefore, the South African Party Government had achieved most of what it wanted in relation to South-West Africa, but failed to obtain either Southern Rhodesia, or the Territories, or any portion of Mozambique. In the last resort, these bids for territorial expansion had failed because Imperial support had been withdrawn. The new doctrine of the paramountcy of African interests, which had been clearly expressed by the Duke of Devonshire in relation to Kenya in 1923, lay behind the British attitude. It formed no part of Smuts's vision, for Smuts had come to look upon the extension of 'a great White Africa along the Eastern backbone, with railway and road communications connecting north and south', as a necessary guarantee for the long-term security of the white south. His correspondence with Lord Delamere during the 1920s, and his Rhodes Lectures at Oxford in 1929, amply demonstrate this point.

It is now recognised that, by his performance at the Imperial War Conference of 1917 and at the subsequent Imperial Conference of 1921, Smuts went a long way towards bringing about the definition of dominion status for which General Hertzog received most of the credit in 1926. There had been a tendency for Commonwealth solidarity to grow during the war years. Smuts himself strongly supported the idea of the Commonwealth, as a comity of nations held together by consent, in stark contrast to the Hohenzollern, Habsburg, Romanov and Turkish

Empires, which had not been based on government by consent, and had also failed to survive the war. But, with the lesson of Ireland much in mind, he warned against over-centralisation, and spoke in support of Sir Robert Borden's Resolution Nine at the 1917 conference. This Canadian proposal called for a special conference after the war to readjust the constitutional relationships of the component parts of the Empire, stressing Dominion self-government, and proper participation by the Dominions, as autonomous states, in the framing of a common foreign policy by means of continuous consultation. At the Prime Ministers' Conference in 1921 Smuts put in a plea for 'the practical recognition of the equality of statehood of the Dominions with the United Kingdom', and for legislation by the British Parliament to remove both the restrictions of the Colonial Laws Validity Act on dominion law-making powers, and also the right of the British Parliament to legislate in respect of the dominions, as well as to limit the Governor-General's powers to those of a viceroy. The Prime Ministers, however, swayed by the rhetoric of W. M. Hughes, who spoke for Australia, rejected Smuts's proposals, which covered in their main features the subsequent provisions of the 1931 Statute of Westminster.

But if Smuts plotted the course towards dominion autonomy without managing to steer the British Commonwealth in that direction, his government also had the misfortune of helping to steer South Africa into the minefield of international disapproval over racial policy. In 1921 it became involved in the suppression of the Bondelswarts, inhabitants of South West Africa, whose hopes for redress of grievances when the Union Government took over the territory were soon disappointed. They complained about the non-restoration of their captain, Jacobus Christian, about continuing white penetration of their land, and – above all – the new Government's imposition of a graded dog tax which severely limited their ability to keep packs of dogs for purposes of hunting game. Christian was arrested without proper cause, while he was on his way to the police station to report his return from exile. Abraham Morris, who had led the Bondelswart resistance to the Germans, had fled to the Union for sanctuary, and returned in May 1922, still a popular hero, with a group of armed companions. Violence broke out between the Government and the Bondelswarts because Morris's followers would not allow him to surrender their guns, and because Christian and the new Administrator of South West Africa, G. R. Hofmeyr, failed to reach a proper understanding about their surrender a fortnight later. Hofmeyr resolved on a punitive expedition, but aircraft used to bomb the Bondelswart flocks killed some women and children, and drove the menfolk into rebellion in the mountains. They were soon suppressed by Union troops and aircraft; but the affair was given widespread international publicity and was debated over a full year in the Permanent Mandates Commission of the League of

Nations. Smuts attempted in private to restrain Hofmeyr, but defended him in public at the cost of his own reputation.

It was at the 1917 conference that the Government of India first gave clear warning that it intended to press for fair treatment for Indians in Commonwealth countries. Smuts played for time. In 1921 and 1923 his encounters with Dr Sastri and Sir Tej Bahadur Sapru carried the controversy deeper. Most dominion prime ministers accepted that their policies towards Asians were capable of improvement. Smuts alone took the line that, because of the peculiar racial balance of his country, and the difficulty of granting rights to Asians without extending them also to the African majority, his Government was not in a position to make concessions. For Sapru, it was a matter of honour (*izzat*); for Smuts, a question of the white man's position in society, and in the last resort of his continuing presence in southern Africa. But it was Sapru who won the battle of words, and he made one remark which threw a long shadow:

> I tell him frankly that if the Indian problem in South Africa is allowed to fester much longer it will pass . . . beyond the bounds of a domestic issue and will become a question of foreign policy of such gravity that upon it the unity of the Empire may founder irretrievably.

The absorption of the Unionist Party in the S.A.P. was accompanied by a blending of attitudes towards the Commonwealth and world affairs by the leaders of the Afrikaans- and English-speaking communities. But this led to a new polarisation of outlooks, for it brought into the open again that clash of interests based on status and class which had erupted before the war and was for a short while to become the most strident of all South African issues. For even allowing for the escalation of black political activity after 1918, the main conflict between 1920 and 1925 was between white owners and white workers, in which black workers found themselves unable to play a positive role on account of the restrictions under which they had to operate.

The enlarged S.A.P. had a deceptively safe majority in the light of the troubles which were about to assail it. At the end of the First World War the sterling value of gold rose sharply when it was made possible to trade gold for dollars on the open market. But between the beginning of 1920 and the end of 1921 deflationary policies in Britain and South Africa restored the relative value of their currencies at the expense of gold. The South African mines found it difficult to face the fall in the gold price because of a marked increase in costs since 1914, and when the Low Grade Mines Commission reported in May 1920 it warned that with the decline in prosperity which was expected to continue, some twenty-one mines, constituting about half the Rand gold industry, and employing over ten thousand whites and over eighty thousand Africans, were in danger of becoming unprofitable. These facts, set against the imbalance between white and black wages on the mines (in 1920, according to Hancock, 21,455 whites earned £10.64 millions per annum, whereas 179,987 blacks earned £5.96 millions) forced the Chamber of Mines to review the *status quo* agreement of 1918 under which the existing allocation of work to the different race groups had been frozen. In November the Chamber gave notice of its intention to abandon the *status quo* agreement, and on 28 December suddenly announced that some twenty-five semi-skilled jobs previously performed by whites would be brought within reach of black workers from the beginning of February, though Smuts was able to obtain a public assurance that this was not intended as an attack on white employment as such, and that a limit of two thousand white men would be retrenched in the first instance as a temporary measure.

The white miners reacted to this announcement, which Hancock has labelled 'a precipitate response to the accelerating fall in the price of gold', with suspicion and alarm. Tempers were already stretched by an unofficial strike at Consolidated Langlaagte in February, after the Union's executive had punished the leaders to forestall heavier discipline by the Chamber. Some of those punished were Communists with a penchant for direct action (notably Ernie Shaw and Percy Fisher). The Mineworkers' Union also contained followers of Hertzog bent on establishing a separate Afrikaner *mynwerkersbond*. Fisher, the irregularly elected and subsequently deposed secretary of the S.A.M.W.U., announced the formation of a new and militant Miners' Council of Action, which had managed by January 1922 to infiltrate many of the unions and set up a Red International of Labour Unions with revolutionary intent. Their chance came when the Chamber's decision to abandon the *status quo* agreement coincided with a new bid by the coal-owners to depress wages to make South African coal prices competitive, a threat by the engineering firms to reduce wages to meet rising costs, and a refusal by the Victoria Falls Power Company to agree to higher wage demands. It would have been possible at this stage, Hancock argues, for the South African Industrial Federation (on which the various unions were represented) to ask for a board of conciliation under the Industrial Disputes Act, which would have been bound to freeze existing arrangements until it had completed an inquiry. Instead, however, the S.A.I.F. ballotted its members and brought the coalminers out on 2 January, and the goldminers, engineers and power workers out on the 10th.

The Labour and Nationalist Parties were quick to identify themselves with the cause of the strikers. On 14 January the former publicly backed the S.A.I.F.'s action, while the *Vaderland* carried a letter by Tielman Roos, the Transvaal Nationalist leader, urging Active Citizen

Force members to disobey the call-up, if it were made. Meanwhile unofficial commandos were organised by the strikers on the Rand and in the country districts to meet force with force. Immediately after the start of the goldminers' strike, Smuts arranged for direct negotiations between the Chamber and the S.A.I.F., under the chairmanship of Judge Curlewis; but after two weeks of bargaining, these meetings broke up in failure on the 27th. The Chamber now insisted, instead of abrogating the *status quo* agreement, on an employment ratio of two whites to twenty-one blacks for a two-year period, which implied more white dismissals than would have been the case under their earlier offer. The Federation demanded nothing less than two whites to seven blacks, which was an abnormally high ratio of whites, and followed the breakdown of the negotiations with a public attack on the Government on the 29th, alleging that it was in collusion with the owners. This was to turn an industrial struggle into a political conflict. An unofficial 'Parliament' convened by Nationalists and Labour members in Pretoria on 30 January heard an appeal by R. B. Waterston on 5 February to proclaim an independent republic.

These developments cut across a new round of negotiations between Smuts and the moderate members of the S.A.I.F., which made some progress. On 5 February, Smuts accordingly persuaded the Chamber to modify its earlier terms by agreeing that the *status quo* arrangements could continue on all save the low-grade mines until an impartial report had been considered by the Government. The S.A.I.F. rejected this concession on the 6th. Next day Crawford, the moderate Mine-workers' leader, backed the strike committee's approval of the use of commandos against scabbing; but this itself showed that the workers' feelings were beginning to waver. The augmented executive of the S.A.I.F. rejected a call for a general strike on 8 February, even after the arrest of Fisher and Shaw for incitement.

On 11 February Smuts came down clearly on the side of the owners with an 'abrupt change of front' (Hancock). He called on the owners to restart the mines, and on the workers to go back on the owners' terms, with an assurance that the Government would protect those who did and that Parliament would see that right was done. He then returned to Cape Town to attend Parliament, whose opening had been deferred until 17 February to enable him to take charge of the Rand crisis on the spot. He justified his actions to Parliament during a debate on a confused motion by Hertzog; but the tough line he took against the commandos by declaring them to be unlawful assemblies on the 22nd and authorising police action against them on the 27th, led to the death of three men at Boksburg. The Nationalists demanded an official inquiry. From that moment the crisis escalated fast, yet probably need not have done so. On 2 March, in view of the general move by the miners back to their jobs, the augmented executive of the

S.A.I.F. asked the Chamber for a conference without conditions in order to try to end the strike. The Chamber returned an unqualified refusal on the 4th, and in doing so created the conditions under which the revolutionary Miners' Council of Action could seize the initiative and force the S.A.I.F. to proclaim a general strike on the 7th. Smuts mobilised the A.C.F. on the 9th, after violence had already broken out on the Rand, and proclaimed martial law on the 10th. It took several days of bitter fighting between the A.C.F. and the commandos before the insurrection was put down on the 16th. Smuts then followed this at the end of the month with an Indemnity and Trial of Offenders Bill, which set up a special court to try those accused of murder. All other accused were given jury trials. In retrospect, Smuts rejected the Opposition charge that the Government had sat idly by while the rising got out of hand, contending that before declaring martial law the Government was 'bound in the interest of the country to let the situation develop, . . . because it was possible that the situation might develop peacefully'. Hertzog misrepresented Smuts's claim to have 'wanted the situation to develop', by deliberately portraying him in a miscast Krugerian role of 'sitting behind the tortoise to stick his fork into its head when it should put its head out', which was proper treatment only for the likes of Jameson. The trouble, from Smuts's point of view, was that Hertzog's mud stuck, because his handling of the strikes of 1913 and 1914, and of the Afrikaner rebellion, and of the shooting of Africans at Port Elizabeth in 1920 and Queenstown in 1921 made it easy to caricature him as one whose footsteps 'dripped with blood'.

African mineworkers had more to gain from supporting the mineowners in 1922 than from supporting the white mineworkers, for abandonment of the 1918 *status quo* agreement which the owners desired would have made twenty-five extra categories of semi-skilled work available for black and Coloured workers. African coalminers in fact continued to work, and with the help of a few officials brought up the coal while the white miners were on strike. But the Chamber sent large numbers of black goldminers back to the Reserves when the strike started, in a necessary move to reduce working costs. The white Mineworkers' Union, consisting largely of men whose past relations with African workers, as Simons has shown, gave them little enough reason to feel a sense of class solidarity with them, had struck with the primary purpose of maintaining the colour bar, and the communist leaders of the strike justified the slogan carried by the Fordsburg commando – 'Workers of the World Unite, and Fight for a White South Africa' – with the special plea that the struggle would build up class-consciousness among the white workers, opening the way for the disappearance of the colour bar at a later date. Meanwhile it was necessary to build up an alliance between white townsmen and countrymen to break the Rand tycoons, on whatever terms this could be arranged. Even

S. P. Bunting, who later became a dedicated supporter of black emancipation, thought like this. Not surprisingly, the A.P.O. and the I.C.U. both condemned the actions of the white workers in strong terms. There was a good deal of violence between white strikers and Africans, and perhaps thirty Africans lost their lives from the actions of white strikers' commandos.

The growing unpopularity of the South African Party regime, which was reflected in several by-election defeats, encouraged Hertzog and Creswell to conclude an electoral pact in April 1923.[8] The two leaders condemned the Smuts regime as a tool of 'big finance' and harmful to the country, and stressed that they wanted to save South Africa from a minority government after the next election. They admitted that Nationalist secessionism and Labour's 'bolshevism' were mutual stumbling blocks, but Hertzog assured Creswell that his party would not change existing constitutional relationships with the British Crown if it were returned to power at the next election. The two leaders rejected party fusion, and limited their agreement to an electoral pact under which they shared out controversial seats to avoid mutual contests, and undertook to support each other's candidates. By killing secession as an immediate prospect, Hancock writes, Creswell and Hertzog 'sank the ship which had brought Smuts triumphantly to port in the elections of 1921'. Their alliance also profited from the hard times of 1923, when the mine-owners were trying to turn their victory after the strike of the previous year to good account, and white workers in both language groups looked to government to secure them in their jobs at rates of pay which would enable them to keep up their 'white' standards.

Meanwhile Hertzog had started to make a strong bid for Coloured and African support. In preparation for the election, the Nationalists now proposed to release the Coloured people from the economic colour bar, while Hertzog even proposed the extension of the vote to Coloured people in the northern provinces. His appeal played on their cultural ties with the Afrikaner and on the natural desire of many to rise in status by dissociating themselves from the Africans. At a time when the A.P.O. normally supported the South African Party, or at least opposed the Nationalists, Hertzog's overtures brought into being an Afrikaner Nasionale Bond, a Coloured organisation led by W. H. le Grange, which offered him electoral support. He also won the support of M. A. Gamiet's Cape Malay Association. The Nationalists derived some benefit from this Coloured support in every election between 1920 and 1929, notably in 1924, when Dr W. B. de Villiers captured the Stellenbosch seat.

Hertzog also obtain Kadalie's support. At its 1923 and 1924 conferences, the I.C.U. decided not to align itself with either white party, and when it convened a 'united Non-European congress' in Cape

Town after the dissolution of Parliament in April 1924, its neutral stand alienated both the A.P.O. and the Cape Native Voters' Association, both of which inclined to the S.A.P. The African National Congress (as the S.A.N.N.C. had renamed itself in 1923) went further in its May conference, by urging the black electorate 'to vote solidly for a change of government', and a mixed deputation of I.C.U. and A.N.C. leaders (Kadalie, Thaele, Masabalala and Dlwati) then called on Hertzog in Bloemfontein. Apart from Hertzog's contribution to I.C.U. funds in 1921 and his offer to cover the costs of an election edition of their *Workers' Herald*, there is no evidence that the Nationalists made any specific undertaking to Kadalie in return for the support he then offered.

Smuts, sensing the swing of opinion against the S.A.P., resigned after the loss of a by-election at Wakkerstroom on 5 April 1924. In the ensuing general election, victory went to the Hertzog–Creswell Pact. The Nationalists won 63 seats and Labour 18, giving a total of 81, against the 53 won by the S.A.P., and one by an Independent. This represented a gain for the Nationalists of 16 seats, mainly in the Transvaal and Cape rural areas, a gain of 5 by Labour on the Rand, and a loss of 19 by the S.A.P.; but in terms of votes cast, the S.A.P. polled 47.39 per cent of the total (over 150,000) whereas the Nationalists polled only 36.34 per cent (under 120,000). This was because the Cape, where the S.A.P. won most of its seats, had numerically inflated constituencies, and because the S.A.P. was most successful in the urban constituencies, some of which had been loaded in the 1923 delimitation by as much as 10 per cent. On top of this, the Pact won the propaganda battle. Its call for more segregation, its playing down of the secession issue, its defence of white workers against black competitors and the capitalists, its overtures to Coloured voters and its charges of bloodthirstiness, or lassitude, or economic stringency, levelled against the S.A.P. cumulatively produced the swing which carried Hertzog to power.

The fall of Smuts left big questions about the direction of South African history, perhaps even the viability of Union under the terms of 1910, still largely undecided. On the inter-white front, the coalition rejected by Botha in 1910 had been accepted by Smuts in 1920, but no longer satisfied the electorate on account of the revival of discontent among Afrikaners, which the fathers of Union had tried very hard to avert. From this angle, the Great War could not have come at a worse time, for it had widened the alienation of capital from labour as well as of Nationalist Afrikaner from Briton. On the front of black–white relations, the Botha–Smuts ministries had insisted on white political and economic hegemony, and placed segregationist legislation on the statute book without being entirely convinced of its desirability, which had led them to suppress black discontent rather than seriously try to satisfy it. The resultant growth of inter-racial tension, as reflected in the violence of 1919–22, made the removal of inhumanity in the law harder to contrive, and this fact played into the hands of the more ideological politicians who took over the reins in 1924. At the international level, the first clouds of isolation began to gather, but the weather prophets were not yet insistent with their warnings.

# 11 The Afrikaner's Road to Parity: Hertzog, 1924–33

The government which took office on 30 June 1924 was almost devoid of men with cabinet experience, but several of them had won reputations as public figures. Hertzog himself, the stormy petrel of South African politics for over a decade, had sat on the Free State bench with distinction, and led a commando during the war of 1899–1902, before becoming Minister of Education in the O.R.C. J. C. G. Kemp, Piet Grobler and N. C. Havenga were also Anglo-Boer War veterans, while Dr D. F. Malan, who had an important assignment as Minister of the Interior, Education and Public Health, had already displayed a variety of skills as philosopher, cleric and editor of the *Burger*. Tielman Roos, leader of the Party in the Transvaal, was a personable but volatile lawyer. The two Labour men in the coalition cabinet, Colonel Creswell and Thomas Boydell, had both been imprisoned for leading the 1914 strike.

These ministers set about a busy legislative programme. Havenga, as Minister of Finance, made the South African economy fully protectionist in a succession of budgets and tariff bills, each geared to the market needs of the moment, but all designed to pull South African industry on to its feet. Creswell brought the Iron and Steel Corporation (ISCOR) into being in 1927 as a public utility, in face of opposition criticism that this profit-making enterprise should have been entrusted to a syndicate of steel producers. Kemp (Agriculture) and Grobler (Lands) together looked after the farmers with measures to improve the overseas marketing of fruit and other produce, to regularise dairy marketing, to establish agricultural credit associations operating under the aegis of the Land Bank even for farmers who lacked the security for raising normal loans; laws, too, to regularise irrigation and overhaul water rights, and to facilitate the settlement on the land of whites without capital or skills, and to set up work colonies for those in need of social salvage. The white working class, looked after by Creswell and Boydell who successively headed the new Department of Labour, enjoyed a period of growing prosperity and industrial peace. The Government increased the protection of tenants against eviction at a time when houses were short, overhauled the law on miners' phthisis, and brought the Factories Act into line with current international standards with regard to the length of the working week and the employment of child labour. More controversial were the Wage Act of 1925 and the 'Colour Bar' Act of 1926.[1] After being rejected in the Senate in 1925, the latter measure was opposed at every reading when it was reintroduced in the Assembly in 1926, but the Government forced it through by 83 to 67 votes in a joint sitting. The former law was designed to help unskilled white workers, in particular poor whites, whereas the Colour Bar Act was meant to protect the skilled and semi-skilled [see pp. 360–3].

The Afrikaner, whose cultural needs Botha and Smuts had played down, was also made to feel that he mattered to the new regime. Malan began a campaign for bilingualism in the civil service, and in so doing opened job opportunities for his people in a new and important field. In 1925, the meaning of 'Dutch' in the constitution was extended to include Afrikaans, which thus became an official language for the first time. It had already been adopted in the schools and by the Dutch Reformed Churches, whose Afrikaans Bible was completed in 1933.

Hertzog followed up the work of Smuts between 1917 and 1923 by tackling the question of dominion status with great singleness of aim, asserting South Africa's right to full international sovereignty, and within two years of taking office he had contributed substantially to the formula agreed at the 1926 Imperial Conference.[2]

'South Africa first' was a satisfactory election slogan for Hertzog's Nationalists in 1915 or 1920. Under the Pact with Creswell he was obliged to treat the Imperial relationship with circumspection during the election campaign of 1924; but, in his own view at least, he held to a consistent policy from the De Wildt speech of December 1912 until his participation in the 1919 deputation to Versailles, and beyond. Much of what Hertzog said was by implication secessionist, though whether he would at that time have seceded from the Empire had he been in a position of power could be debated. During the 1925 budget debate, he described secession as a right, but went on to say that for South Africa to secede from the British Commonwealth would be 'a flagrant mistake and a national disaster'. He made two key speeches in April and May 1926, the first in the Assembly, the second at Stellenbosch, before going to the Imperial Conference in London in November. These indicated that he regarded South Africa as already in practice 'completely independent . . . just as free as England itself', but he rounded on Smuts in Parliament for having questioned South Africa's right of secession from the Commonwealth, saying that this committed Smuts to a view of the Commonwealth as 'a kind of super-authority . . . a super-State'. For Hertzog, the only legal tie was the 'personal bond of a common king', as distinct from the formal bond of King-in-Parliament. He contended that the Dominion Prime Ministers should have recognised this in 1921; but instead they stuck to 'the idea of the unity of the Empire group', envisaging 'nothing less than a quasi-federal Empire, with the highest authority vested in the Imperial Conference', and with Great Britain enjoying the decisive voice as the only member with accepted international standing. But, Hertzog continued, events since the peace conference had shown that the international standing of the Dominions remained ambiguous, while the non-participation of the Dominions in the Locarno treaties had shown that the idea of a common foreign policy was a myth.

Smuts referred to the Stellenbosch speech as one of 'first-class importance', but in certain respects 'contentious'. He asked Hertzog for an assurance that if the forthcoming Imperial Conference did not reach agreement on the status of the Dominions, he would not publish a declaration of South Africa's external sovereignty without reference to Parliament. Hertzog reassured him, replying that international recognition of South Africa's independence was an important consideration, and that if the Imperial Conference did not reach agreement 'then we shall have to wait and see whether it cannot be got later'.

An important feature of the prepared speech which Hertzog gave to the secret session of the Committee of Prime Ministers at the Imperial Conference in London in November 1926 was the central position which he gave to Smuts's memorandum of June 1921. Picking up the sense of urgency in Smuts's memorandum, he stressed the need both to clarify and to publicise the equal status of the Dominions, while insisting that it would be 'monstrous, and certainly disastrous, if the freedom of one Dominion, or its exercise of the rights pertaining to that freedom, were made dependent upon the will of, or upon the exercise of similar rights by, the other[s]'. His warning of the dangers of separatist movements if a clear definition of equal status were not achieved and made public, and his references to the confusion of foreign governments over the Dominions' legal position, had an important influence on the deliberations. They were of major importance in the drafting of the Balfour Declaration which stated that Great Britain and the Dominions were 'autonomous communities within the British Empire, equal in status, in no way subordinate one to another in any aspect of their domestic or external affairs, though united by a common allegiance to the Crown and freely associated as members of the British Commonwealth of Nations'.

Intelligent discussion in Parliament of the report of the Imperial Conference was delayed until March 1928, chiefly on account of the extremely acrimonious reaction of members to Dr Malan's Nationality and Flag Bill, first introduced on 25 May 1926, shortly after Hertzog's Stellenbosch speech. The definition of South African nationality and the achievement of a distinctive national flag could not be separated from the issue of Dominion autonomy, from which in the view of Hertzog's Government they flowed naturally. Contention arose, however, because the Government's proposal to adopt a flag which contained neither the old republican colours nor the Union Jack seemed to the Opposition to have secessionist implications, even though Dr Malan, when introducing the second reading, referred to the Union Jack as the 'flag of the Empire', to be displayed 'officially on all occasions which are intended specifically to represent or indicate our relationship to the British community of nations'. The Government decided not to proceed with the measure in 1926, and deferred it. But when the measure was reintroduced in May 1927, fur flew once more. It was only in October, after Hertzog and Smuts had held private talks, that the Prime Minister climbed down. He now offered to incorporate both the Union Jack and the Republican flags in a new Union Flag, and to accept the Union Jack as a flag to be flown alongside the new Union flag as a symbol 'giving expression to our relationship with the other members of the commonwealth of nations'. Smuts congratulated Hertzog on 'the most important, statesmanlike and wise speech he has just made to the House'.

When Hertzog introduced the debate on the Report of the 1926 Imperial Conference on 8 March 1928, he laid stress on the attention paid by the Conference to the practical aspects of Dominion participation in international affairs – procedure to be adopted over international treaties, their representation at international conferences, the practical conduct of foreign policy, the granting of authority to foreign consuls, and means of communication between Dominion and foreign governments. He then switched to the question of Dominion neutrality in the event of British involvement in war, arguing eloquently (as Botha and Smuts had done with Lloyd George in 1919) that if the right to neutrality did not exist, then equality of status meant nothing. These remarks were controversial, because the question of Dominion neutrality had been deliberately avoided at the Imperial Conference on account of its potentially disruptive side-effects. Smuts warned of these in his reply to Hertzog, referring to the unresolved legal problem of the divsibility of the Crown which had not yet been fully faced, but which was implicit in Hertzog's stance, and, above all, the danger to Commonwealth solidarity if hypothetical discussion of neutrality were to get out of hand. 'So long as our cause is just and good', Smuts said, 'and the danger is really one of first-class character, it will be practically impossible for any dominion to declare its neutrality in a great war in which Britain is involved.' Smuts also picked on Hertzog for his emphasis on Dominion independence, on the ground that the Conference had not discussed this either, but dwelt rather on the need to ensure the voluntary co-operation of the Dominions as equal members of the Commonwealth.

The Balfour Declaration of 1926 gave the green light for the creation of a South African Department of External Affairs, of which Hertzog assumed the portfolio on 1 June 1927. This was followed by the appointment of ministers plenipotentiary at the Hague, Washington and Rome, together with the raising of the London High Commissionership to diplomatic rank, and the establishment of a network of trade commissioners in Europe and North America. The Union was also represented at the League of Nations Headquarters in Geneva, notably by Charles te Water and E. H. Louw.

Separation of the offices of Governor-General and Imperial High Commissioner followed logically if the King's deputy as head of state were not also to hold a British ambassadorial role. Smuts warned against such a separation in May 1927, on the ground that a combination of these offices made it easier for the Union Government to deal with Britain on matters affecting the High Commission Territories. But the change was effected in December 1930, at the end of the Earl of Athlone's term of office, when the Earl of Clarendon was appointed Governor-General, and Sir Herbert Stanley High Commissioner. Once this step had been taken, it became more appropriate to select a local person as head of state. Hence Hertzog's choice of a resident South African, Patrick Duncan, as Governor-General at the end of Clarendon's term. Smuts later trumped this move, on Duncan's death in 1942, by securing the appointment of Gideon Brand van Zyl, a Governor-General who was an Afrikaans-speaking South African by birth.

Botha and Smuts had shown considerable enthusiasm for territorial expansion in Africa. Hertzog's designs were less wide-ranging, but at least he desired to consolidate the Union's control over the southern end of the continent by obtaining the High Commission Territories, while he accepted as a *fait accompli* the mandate over South-West Africa. Hertzog wasted no time in asking for the transfer of Swaziland and Bechuanaland to the Union in 1924, but his lack of finesse made it relatively easy for the High Commissioner, Athlone, to turn his demand. From 1926, when the Territories were placed under the Dominions Office in London, Hertzog's case for incorporation became harder to defend on account of the unpopularity of his colour bar legislation both among the residents of the Territories and in London. L. S. Amery, as Secretary of State for the Dominions, toured South Africa in late 1927, and began to urge the development of the Territories, to preserve them as bases of continuing British influence in an Afrikaner-dominated region, and because he realised that the Territories were in urgent need of development as Sir Alan Pim's reports of 1932–5 were later to make clear. His visit stiffened the British Government against early transfer, and no more was heard from the South African Government until 1932.

Hertzog did not help his cause in that year by demanding the incorporation of the Territories on the argument that, if this were denied, the Union might have to withdraw economic favours to protect herself from competition. This threat of economic pressure, to which Smuts gave some support after joining Hertzog's Government in 1933, was turned by the British Government into an argument for promoting economic cooperation, and London's refusal to talk of transfer remained obdurate. It remained a live issue, however, enlivened further by a debate in *The Times* between Margery Perham of Oxford, who opposed incorporation, and Lionel Curtis, who supported it. An *aide-mémoire* presented to Hertzog by the Dominions Secretary, J. H. Thomas, in May 1935 seemed to break the deadlock by offering the Union Government an opportunity to cooperate with the territorial administrations economically, so that an appetite for incorporation in the Union could be whetted among the African populations. Hertzog made an offer of £35,000 for aid to the Territories, but spoiled the effect of this by asserting on at best dubious grounds that Thomas had agreed to a definite transfer in 1937. He was persuaded to withdraw this assertion, but not before it had done its damage by implying that the South African offer of money was a Trojan horse. Malcolm Macdonald, who succeeded Thomas in 1937, was keen to effect transfer if at all possible. Hertzog met him in June, while in London for the Imperial Conference; but he again spoiled a promising atmosphere, this time by an untimely press interview. Macdonald gave him an opportunity to recover by suggesting that the Union prepare a policy statement indicating what it would do in the Territories after transfer had taken place. Hertzog's Government accordingly did so, in a memorandum completed in August 1939; but by offering to maintain rather than to extend the services started by Britain, and by failing to over-trump the British record of expenditure under the Colonial Development Act of 1929, it did nothing to counter black fears generated afresh by its own restrictive legislation for Union Africans of 1936–7. African opposition was in fact becoming more and more public, even if King Sobhuza of the Swazi seemed to flirt with incorporation from time to time. Against such a background, Smuts's bravado in attempting to wrest the Territories from British control, by an appeal to the Dominions Office to relinquish them in October 1939, could hardly have been expected to succeed.

Compromise, which unlocked the tensions over the Flag Bill, also provided an 'Open Sesame' for Hertzog's Indian policy during his early years of office.[3] When Dr Malan introduced his Areas Reservation Bill in 1925, to stiffen the Class Area proposals of the Smuts Government and make the repatriation of Indians easier to effect, this threatened to ruin the atmosphere for round-table discussions which had been proposed both by the Indian Government and by J. H.

Thomas in the Colonial Office. But the South African Government agreed in 1925 to receive a fact-finding commission from India, led by G. F. Paddison, Commissioner of Labour in Madras, and containing two Indian members of the Council of State. At the same time the S.A.I.C. sent a deputation to India led by Dr A. Abdurahman, to interview the Viceroy and put its case to the Indian National Congress, over which Mrs Sarojini Naidu, who had recently visited South Africa, presided. The two missions crossed each other at sea. Abdurahman's won world-wide publicity for the South African Indians' cause, while Paddison's negotiated patiently for the holding of a round-table conference, which eventually took place between the South African and Indian governments over four weeks from 17 December 1926. The subsequent Cape Town Agreement was the product of an exceptionally harmonious encounter. It contained provisions for the assisted emigration of South African Indians, for the entry into South Africa of the wives and minor children of Indians with domiciliary rights, and included an undertaking by the South African Government to withdraw the Areas Reservation Bill. What was more, the policies of Hertzog's Government continued to reflect the afterglow of this encounter for several years, as it agreed to condone illegal entries of the past and to radically overhaul the Indian educational system. This mood disappeared in the early 1930s, when the repatriation provisions of the Agreement proved unworkable, the attitude of white Natal and Transvaal townsmen gradually turned sour, and backbenchers renewed the onslaught on Indian trading and property purchases in those two provinces, and tried to make the marriage of Indians with whites illegal.

Hertzog also took the portfolio of Native Affairs, which he had previously held until Botha dropped him from the Cabinet in 1912. Though committed in general terms to a policy of segregation, he marked time for over a year before giving any details. 'This Government has no native policy at this moment,' he asserted defensively in in 1924. In March 1925 he criticised the Smuts Government for not purchasing land released on the recommendation of the local committees of 1918, and affirmed that 'territorial segregation of the natives is the only sound policy that can be followed both for the natives and the Europeans in South Africa'. It depended, he said, on the African's learning how to develop the Reserves both agriculturally and industrially; but he linked this with the notion that in the towns, on the railways, in existing industrial undertakings, the white man was entitled to first consideration: 'the native cannot blame us if in the first place we try to find work for our own class.' Thus the reverse side of segregation (which was conceived as a favour conferred on the black man) was the industrial colour bar, which Hertzog saw in 1925 as a means of redressing wrongs done to the white worker in 1922, even if –

as he disingenuously admitted in the second reading debate on the 1925 Mines and Works Bill – such a policy was morally below par.

But the balance of right was to be restored by making the extra land promised to Africans available as the basis for a final settlement. After giving advance notice of his intentions in a speech at Smithfield in November 1925, Hertzog tabled three bills on native affairs and one dealing with the rights of Coloured people, on 23 July 1926.[4] The Native Lands Further Release and Acquisition Bill was to make land available in terms of the 1913 Act, by setting aside the land recommended for the purpose by the local committees of 1918, as released land which Africans as well as whites could buy. The Union Native Council Bill aimed to establish a Council of fifty Africans, of whom thirty-five were to be elective, as a substitute for the Native Conference set up under Smuts's Native Affairs Act of 1920. The purpose of the Representation of Natives in Parliament Bill was to remove the African voters from the common roll in the Cape, and as an alternative to give seven white representatives in the House of Assembly to Africans from all provinces, with the power to vote on measures affecting Africans only. Hertzog hoped to make this legislation bi-partisan, and approached Smuts on 23 January 1926; but when the latter asked to see the draft legislation before committing himself Hertzog alleged that Smuts was dragging his heels and closed the correspondence. In August, Smuts criticised the Bills severely in a memorandum which found the land proposals far less generous to Africans than his own Government had been in practice, but then – with the electorate perhaps in mind – went on to criticise the proposal to give Africans separate representation in Parliament as an attempt to weaken the political influence of the white man.

On 28 March 1927 the House agreed to send the Bills to a select committee, which reported on 17 June, too late for them to be handled that session. Meanwhile Parliament took through all its stages a Native Administration Bill, which extended over Africans in every province except the Cape the authoritarian powers enjoyed by the Governor-General in Natal under the Natal Native Code of 1891. He was made Supreme Chief over all Africans, with authority to appoint native commissioners, chiefs and headmen, define tribal boundaries, alter the composition of tribes, and move tribes or individuals at will 'from any place to any other place within the Union upon such conditions as he may determine' (provided Parliamentary approval was obtained if a tribe – as distinct from an individual – objected). His powers were also made to cover the registration and ultimate control of African-owned land, and all judicial procedure affecting Africans, both civil and criminal, through a separate system of courts surmounted by a Native Appeal Court, which was given the right to refuse appeals from its own judgments to the Appellate Division in Bloemfontein. The Governor-

General was also empowered, subject to Parliamentary veto, to legislate by proclamation for the scheduled Native Areas, such legislation to have effect unless and until abrogated at the request of Parliament. He was also given authority, in this portmanteau law, to impose rules on Africans governing censorship, control of weapons, wearing of clothes, carrying of passes – and, in a controversial Section 29, he could punish 'any person who utters any words or does any other act or thing whatever with intent to promote any feeling of hostility between Natives and Europeans'. This law, together with the Mines and Works Act and the Riotous Assemblies Amendment Act of 1930, provided the legal rampart behind which Hertzog's supporters acquired the courage to extend African land rights in return for a reduced ration of political power.

Meanwhile pressure from his own supporters caused Hertzog to modify the Parliamentary Representation Bill by offering Africans from the northern provinces two senators in place of five members of the Assembly. In a series of private conversations in February 1928, Smuts pushed him the other way, urging him to consider 'a common franchise all over South Africa, based on occupation and income or salary which was to apply to all, black and white alike', but be high enough to exclude the bulk of the African population, together with a civilisation test from which white people would be exempt. If he could not accept that, then Smuts suggested that 'the least he could do would be to offer the Cape natives representation according to their present voting strength' – perhaps five or six seats in the Assembly, and five in the Senate for the northern provinces, the Cape seats to increase as the number of qualified voters increased, until a permitted maximum was reached. Hertzog appears to have been attracted by Smuts's idea of a high uniform non-racial franchise, backed by a civilisation test, but he did not follow it up, on the ground that the time was not yet ripe. Smuts also criticised the proposed Native Council by expressing the fear that it would 'collect all the Kadalies and Communist agitators in South Africa into a body which might have a very unsettling effect on the native mind'. He urged Hertzog 'to let the General Council stand over, to establish councils under the Act of 1920 in the various territories, and when these were in full and efficient working order, then to consider the question of a General Council based on them as a superstructure'. Hertzog took this advice, and dropped the Native Council Bill during a joint sitting called before the 1929 election.

The South African Party decided to oppose the Natives' Parliamentary Representation Bill and the Coloured Persons' Rights Bill at the joint sitting, in the knowledge that Hertzog had timed the sitting with an eye on the forthcoming election, and that they could prevent him from getting a two-thirds majority. For Hertzog it was an unhappy moment. He was obliged to recognise, and did, that his attempts to consult African opinion had brought an adverse response. In 1926 the Transkeian Bunga had given signs of equivocation. But the Native Conference was outspoken: Selope Thema said that under the Representation Bill 'all hope of getting full citizenship rights was closed', and carried a motion for its rejection by a big majority. He carried another for the extensive modification of the Land Bill, in a debate in which one speaker said it reminded him of 'lysol', and another called it a 'jackal trap'. The Union Native Council Bill, the only one to fall by the wayside was, ironically, found to be acceptable. Now, in 1929, Hertzog contended that the Africans had been more than adequately consulted by the Native Affairs Commission and by himself, but because they had refused to accept any alteration of the Cape system only Parliament could resolve the difference. The Coloured Rights Bill now came under Smuts's attack as 'a raw uncouth immature scheme' which threatened surreptitiously to undermine the security of Cape voters by placing their registration under the scrutiny of magistrate and Minister for the first time. He repeated a proposal first made in 1925, for an inquiry into the economic and other relations of the European, Coloured and African population of the Union by 'a national commission or convention' on which the views of all sections of the people should be represented. Although the Nationalists held together in the divisions (Roos being absent), only one backbencher from a northern constituency, who was provoked, actually spoke in favour of enfranchising Coloured people in the northern provinces. When the third reading division on the Native Representation Bill failed to produce a two-thirds majority, Hertzog announced the withdrawal of the Coloured Bill, since the measures had been made interdependent.

The Government's failure to carry the Native Representation Bill set the stage for the 1929 general election, when questions of native policy were placed before the voters as never before. In fact, the election battle had begun before the joint sitting, sparked off by two speeches at Ermelo, Transvaal, the first by Roos in September 1928, the second by Smuts in January 1929. Roos selected native policy, and in particular the restriction of the Cape African franchise, as the issue on which he hoped the election would be fought. Smuts, who was particularly disturbed by the paramountcy accorded to black interests in Kenya by the Colonial Office, spoke of a 'great African Dominion stretching unbroken throughout Africa' as 'the cardinal point in my policy'. His opponents reacted, in the words of a manifesto put out by Hertzog, Roos and Malan, by pouring scorn on 'the apostle of a black Kaffir state'. It was a bitter election, in which the Nationalists and the S.A.P. fought each other almost to the exclusion of Labour. That Party had begun to fall apart through internal dissension in 1928, after Hertzog had dismissed Madeley from the Cabinet following a dispute over the latter's close relationship with Kadalie. Nationalist slogans notwithstanding, the S.A.P. stood for the policies implicit in the Land Act, the Native Affairs Act and the Natives (Urban Areas) Act, involving a substantial measure of segregation on the land, in politics and in the towns. Segregation was not in fact the issue which divided the major parties, and when Smuts delivered his Rhodes Memorial lectures at Oxford in November, he laid special emphasis on the need to prevent the excessive integration of the black man in white society. The aims of the National Party were hardly different from this, but as they relied almost entirely on white votes they could pose as the more robust defenders of white security. Emphasis on justice for the black man was therefore played right down.

On polling day the Nationalists picked up fifteen seats to give them 78, the S.A.P. eight to give them 61. Labour, which had split, lost ten, five of the eight they won going to Creswellites, who supported the Nationalists, while the other three went to supporters of the Labour National Council under Madeley.

The cordiality which had prevailed between the Nationalists and selected Coloured and African organisations had already worn thin. Coloured people, even if pleased at being distinguished from Africans in the Coloured Persons Rights Bill, tended to resent being equally clearly distinguished from Europeans. Their leaders had begun to draw away from Hertzog when the Transvaal Nationalists resisted the meagre extension of their political rights (one white representative in Parliament for all the northern provinces) which Hertzog proposed to allow. Despite the letter of the Colour Bar Act, Coloured people also began to find that, like other non-white groups, they were being eased out of jobs on the railways and in other public and private concerns, as a result of governmental pressure, to make way for unemployed whites. After the 1929 election this became pronounced, as it had been for Africans (but not Coloured people) between 1924 and 1927.

The A.N.C. and the I.C.U., which had made gestures to Hertzog in 1924, had even less reason for supporting him. Those who accepted territorial segregation doubted whether the proposed land distribution was fair. Very few thought that the loss of parliamentary representation in the lower House was a fair price for communal representation in the upper. And the Native Administration Act of 1927 called forth angry denunciation, both for the extension of arbitrary powers which the Governor-General could exercise over Africans, and for the 'race hostility' clause which gave the Government power to act against people or organisations deemed (without judicial testing) to have acted in an inflammatory manner.

Overtaken by the stronger government initiative in racial matters during the early years of the Hertzog era, the African organisations adopted a variety of defensive tactics but failed to act together. The I.C.U. and the Communists fell out, while the A.N.C. was torn asunder through marginal involvement in the conflicts of the other two.

The I.C.U. went in for mass organisation, but did so without whole-hearted conviction. It enlarged its organisation by adopting a new constitution in 1925. In the same year it scored minor strike successes in East London and Johannesburg, and in 1926, after strongly opposing the Colour Bar Bill, Kadalie approached the British trade union movement. Working through Mabel Palmer, Ethelreda Lewis and Winifred Holtby, he made contact with the Fabian movement, and applied for I.C.U. membership of the International Federation of Trade Unions. There was a notable increase in the number of I.C.U. branches in 1927 and 1928, those in the Transvaal and Natal growing fast under the respective influences of Thomas Mbeki and A. W. G. Champion. A membership of over 50,000 was claimed – not unreasonably – in January 1927, rising to about 86,000 in the next few years. This included a marked increase in the rural areas, resulting from opposition to the poll tax, to land shortage, and to Hertzog's threat of 1926 to double the labour tenant's obligatory service to 180 days.

But the I.C.U. could not keep up its pressure. Kadalie's bid to secure international recognition of his union was defeated as a result of opposition from the South African Department of Labour. This was matched by a variety of I.C.U. failures at home – either to launch successful strikes among the Durban dockers, Natal coalminers and Johannesburg railway workers in 1927; or to protect I.C.U. farm workers from eviction by their landlords, or to launch an alternative scheme of buying land for the homeless; or even to reach agreement at a special conference called in Kimberley in December 1927 over the I.C.U.'s relationship with white labour unions and the Communists. Soon afterwards a personal feud developed between Kadalie and Champion, which focused on Kadalie's refusal to charge the I.C.U. with the costs of Champion's semi-private litigation, and on Champion's counter-allegation that the head office had regularly failed to present proper financial statements. Kadalie probably felt Champion had too much power over the Natal section of the Union; but his attempt to humiliate the Natal leader resulted in the latter's decision to break away and establish a rival *I.C.U. yase Natal*, in May 1928. Meanwhile the national council of the I.C.U. sought the help of a financial organiser from Britain; but William Ballinger, the Scottish trade unionist eventually selected, found the affairs of the Union were in a very bad state, and in the course of trying to impose discipline on its operations he antagonised Kadalie, who broke away to form an Independent I.C.U. in March 1929. The I.C.U. proper held its last congress at Kroonstad in June 1929, and thereafter led no more than a twilight existence until its final disappearance in 1933. The first mass movement in the history of black South Africa, it died essentially of its own weaknesses in the face of steady but not overbearing pressure from outside.

There had been very little effective liaison between the African political leaders and left-wing political thinking before the general strike of 1922. The Labour Party had given only grudging admission to non-white people in 1913, while the International Socialist League (established in South Africa in 1915) had failed to build up meaningful contact with the black masses. During the 1922 strike the Communists had obviously put skin colour before class. After 1922, however, they began to pay more attention to the Africans, without at first abandoning the hope of influencing white labour. They tried to affiliate with the Labour Party in 1923, in accordance with instructions from the Comintern and in defiance of the facts of the South African scene, even at a time when the passions generated during the Rand rebellion had given rise to a good deal of superficial left-wing propaganda on the platteland. The Communists failed to make headway with white labour, and in 1926 began to cross swords with the I.C.U. as well. In the Communist view, Kadalie had become a 'respectable trade union bureaucrat', who was financially corrupt and had refused to launch a proper mass movement. From the angle of the I.C.U., the Communists' profession to give priority to black interests was suspect. It was Champion rather than Kadalie who took the initiative against Communist influence in the movement, though personal animosity between Kadalie and Bunting played its part. When James la Guma, general secretary of the I.C.U., accepted the Communist Party's nomination to attend a Congress of Oppressed Nationalities in Brussels in 1927, without consulting his executive, the National Council of the I.C.U. decided to make its officers relinquish Communist Party membership. The Communists came worst out of the quarrel. They tried to set up their own trade unions in opposition to those affiliated with the I.C.U., but in the South African Federation of Non-European Trade Unions, established in 1928, they fathered an organisation which committed itself to the separation of black from white workers. Their South African Trades and Labour Council of 1930 was non-racial; but under pressure from the Government the key Mineworkers Union refused to join.

Following the Comintern line, the Communists began in 1928 to work for a black Republic in South Africa, dissociated from the British or any other Empire, in accordance with Lenin's Colonial Theses of 1920. The classless society, as La Guma saw it, was to be introduced via a period of African rule, and African nationalism encouraged as the first stage of a social revolution. Bunting resisted the implications of such a strategy, which he feared would result in race conflict and the elimination of the whites, but subsequently accepted Comintern discipline and preached black republicanism when he contested the Tembuland seat in the 1929 election – unsuccessfully, it was alleged, owing to police interference with his campaign.

The professedly political African movements reacted cautiously to Hertzog's policies at first. Davidson Jabavu, who took over his father's mantle as leader of a Cape Native Voters' Convention, tried hard to keep lines of communication with the Government open, and petitioned Hertzog to withdraw his bills in 1928. The A.N.C., under the presidency of the Rev. Z. R. Mahabane from 1924, strongly attacked the bills in 1927, but refrained from protest activities or passive resistance. It relied on deputations, sought at the same time to build bridges with the Coloured and Indian movements, and participated in the conciliatory work of the Joint Councils of Europeans and Natives which had been established since 1921.

Black republicanism of a Leninist kind appealed to Gumede, the next A.N.C. President, as a result of his trip to Europe (which included Moscow) in 1927–8. In 1928–9, the Communist Party attracted several capable leaders of the A.N.C., like J. B. Marks and Moses Kotane, into its ranks. But liaison between the Communists and the A.N.C. barely survived the 'white terror' of Pirow's campaign against left-wing political activity during the 1929 election and afterwards, particularly when he armed himself with new powers under an amended Riotous Assemblies Act in 1930. Pressure to dissociate from the Communists now built up within the A.N.C. Z. R. Mahabane, John Dube and Thomas Mapikela managed to remove Gumede from the presidency in April 1930, though Gumede could call on the personal support of Champion and several other prominent leaders. Pixley Seme's election in Gumede's place heralded a return to caution in the African Congress.

Hertzog made few cabinet changes after the 1929 election. Oswald Pirow took over the Department of Justice, because Roos was ill and critical of Hertzog's agreement with Labour. Roos argued that Madeley's office should have gone to a Nationalist, not to H. W. Sampson, defied Hertzog almost to the brink over the allocation of the Brakpan and Germiston seats to Labour in the election, and found a rather unhappy release on the Appeal Court Bench. Hertzog also abandoned Native Affairs to E. G. Jansen of Natal. A new head was perhaps needed, as in 1930 the Native Bills went to another joint sitting, and from there to a Joint Select Committee of both houses, from which they did not emerge until 1935.

The Government now had to face the Great Depression of 1931–2.[5] After the Wall Street collapse of 1929, the outside world found it increasingly hard to pay adequate prices for South Africa's main export products. Consequently South African diamond exports fell in value from £16.5 millions in 1928 to £1.4 millions in 1934, and although South African wool exports did not vary much in quantity during the period 1926 to 1934 – never less than 235 million pounds weight, never more than 336 million – the world price of wool fell from 16.6 pence in 1927–8 to 4.4 pence in 1931–2. At 1932 prices, therefore, it would have been necessary to export four times as much wool as in 1927 to earn the same amount of foreign exchange. World wool prices had started to fall in August 1929. Australia, whose product amounted to about three times that of the Union, devalued her currency in February 1931, and Great Britain followed suit in September. At the end of the year and in early 1932, £100 sterling bought £125 Australian but only between £70 and £75 South African. With the South African pound valued at nearly double the Australian, competition on the world wool markets became almost impossible for South African growers. Havenga announced on 20 November 1931 that 'South Africa is on the gold basis and will remain on the gold basis'. He and his young Opposition counterpart, J. H. Hofmeyr, were both orthodox financiers who disapproved of devaluation. Gold-producers feared that higher import prices would force wages up, and perhaps cause marginal mines to close down. So instead of devaluing, as the Opposition urged during the Finance Emergency Regulations Bill debate, and as Smuts strongly urged while overseas, Havenga clapped duties of up to 12.5 per cent on nearly all imports and offered a bounty of 10 per cent rising to 20 per cent on nearly all exports, hoping to achieve a balance of payments by fiscal measures. Prompted by Hertzog and Havenga, a select committee appointed in January 1932 recommended that South Africa stay on the gold standard. But fiscal measures could not stop a flight from the South African pound, if this looked like a promising speculative risk. People began to gamble on the possibility of the South African pound following sterling, and bought extensively on the London stock exchange, thus creating a currency famine in South Africa itself. It was a situation in which, as Schumann observed, 'political and psychological issues may emphatically not be neglected by the economist'.

At this point, after a young S.A.P. politician, and protégé of Smuts, J. G. N. Strauss, surprisingly beat the Nationalist and Labour candidates in a triangular by-election at Germiston, Tielman Roos suddenly embarked on a flamboyant personal crusade for devaluation on 16 December 1932. On the 22nd he resigned from the Bench, and people supposed, on good grounds, that he was making a bid for the premiership. His actions increased the speculation to such an extent that on the 28th Havenga was forced to announce the abandonment of the gold standard. Within a month, emancipated from the control of the Reserve Bank, the South African pound had fallen to parity with sterling, and many fortunes had been made.

Roos's return to politics came as no surprise to Hertzog, who had expected it for several years. Early in 1933 Smuts, who depended on Hofmeyr for information about Roos's intentions, was persuaded by him to offer Roos the deputy premiership under himself and three additional cabinet seats. Roos replied with an offer of equal representation in a cabinet of ten, under supposedly himself as premier. Smuts learned from his parliamentary colleagues in Cape Town in mid-January that party feelings in favour of coalition were strong, but that the idea of serving under Roos was not popular. Roos improved his offer to a ratio of seven to four in favour of the S.A.P., with himself still as premier, shortly afterwards; but when the party caucus debated the question between 27 and 31 January, Smuts resolved the dilemma in which it found itself by personally deciding to reject Roos's offer.

At the same time, Smuts was moving in the Assembly for a new start in politics, calling on Hertzog to resign, not, suggest Blackwell and Paton, as a motion of no confidence, but as a gesture of reconciliation. Hertzog rejected the overture. But things were moving behind the scenes. Hofmeyr claimed, in a memorandum written at the time, to have dropped the hint to 'Pen' Wessels, the Nationalist member for Frankfort, that Smuts was willing to cooperate, and to have received an encouraging response which he passed on to Smuts. Pirow claimed to have received a conciliatory message from Hertzog for Smuts, and to have passed it on through Duncan. Although the Cabinet was divided, with D. F. Malan strongly opposing coalition, and Havenga, Grobler, Kemp and Pirow in favour, on 31 January Hertzog authorised the approach to Smuts to be made. Hofmeyr noted Smuts's difficulty in agreeing to serve under Hertzog, but he nevertheless persuaded Smuts to meet the premier in mid-February. Havenga and Duncan were brought into the discussions.

The advantages of coalition were clear to both parties, though the Roosites would be the losers, their market value having slumped the moment devaluation had been approved. An election was due at the latest in 1934. Hertzog might count on his followers to close their ranks to some extent, but on the evidence of by-elections at Germiston and Roodepoort, which the Nationalists had lost, and at Colesberg which they had only just won, he could not be sure of victory. Disenchantment over the Government's handling of the economic crisis was real. Hertzog also knew he had lost the support of the I.C.U. and of his erstwhile Coloured allies. On the other hand, the passage of the Statute of Westminster through the British Parliament seemed to give South Africa in general, and the Afrikaner people in particular, real security – greater by far than Kruger had received under the London Convention – enabling Nationalist Afrikaners to risk lowering their defences. Equally important, a coalition with the S.A.P. could result in an agreed measure on the African vote, which alone could overcome the hurdle of the two-thirds majority. The S.A.P., for its part, may or may not have smelt electoral victory. It is not clear how much Smuts wanted it. He later told Gilbert Murray on 20 April 1933 that he wanted 'a cessation of the orgy of racial politics which has been the stock-in-trade of our public life'. He was currently troubled, too, by a schismatic movement in Natal, represented by Stuart Helps's Devolution League, which had been formed in 1931 to give expression to Natal fears for the future of the provincial system. This mood was only contained by the Natal Congress's acceptance in 1933 of a memorandum by F. C. Hollander, proposing the extension of provincial control over such areas as immigration, higher education, native affairs and the police. Furthermore Smuts had accepted the machinery of a Select Committee, on which his own party was well represented, for ironing out the native bills, and they were not yet free to walk out of its deliberations.

In March 1933, therefore, Hertzog and Smuts formed a Coalition Ministry, on a basis of seven agreed points, some clear, some opaque: the maintenance of South African autonomy as defined in the Statute of Westminster; acceptance of the national flag; equal language rights for Afrikaners- and English-speakers; the safeguarding of a 'sound rural population'; acceptance of a 'white labour' policy; the solution of the 'native question' through the maintenance of 'white civilisation' and political separation; and the protection of South Africa's currency and economic assets. In the distribution of Cabinet offices, which were shared equally between the parties, Hertzog kept External Affairs, while Smuts received the deputy premiership and the portfolio of Justice, which he had last held as a young man in Kruger's Republic. His protégé Jan Hofmeyr took over the Interior, Education and Public Health, and Duncan was given Mines and Industries. On the Nationalist side Pirow, a personable white supremacist and versatile outdoor man with something of Roos's opportunism, moved from Justice to take Defence and the Railways from Creswell, who, despite Hertzog's desire to find him a post, went out of office with his defeated Labour colleague, Sampson. Jansen, the recently appointed Minister of Native Affairs, gave up that portfolio and was in due course elected Speaker, so that Grobler (Nationalist) could have Native Affairs and give Lands to Deneys Reitz (S.A.P.). It was not a coalition which satisfied all, and Esselen gave Smuts a full catalogue of Cape S.A.P. frustrations, centring on the disappointment of F. S. Malan, for whom nothing had been found. His namesake, Dr D. F. Malan, refused a post. He and his followers met in special congress on 15 March and decided to accept coalition, however, for this would enable them to take part as coalition candidates in the general election which Hertzog called in May, thus avoiding likely defeat, for Hertzog and Smuts had agreed that sitting members had first option on the seats they currently held.

The coalition parties were returned with a massive majority of 144

(75 Nationalists and 61 S.A.P. men) to 14 (only two of whom were Roosites). Some thirty Malanites were among the Nationalists returned, and they soon chafed at having to work with Smuts. Hertzog did his best to reassure them, through meetings with W. Visser, M.P. for Senekal, in August, and Dr N. J. van der Merwe, a prominent Free State Malanite, in September, telling the latter that he would not agree to fusion with the S.A.P. as it was then constituted 'without differentiation', nor accept a ban on the making of republican propaganda which Smuts appeared to be demanding as his price for closer association with the Nationalists. Having apparently been able to satisfy Malan's supporters on all the points that mattered, Hertzog was taken aback when Malan, after carrying a motion at the Cape Nationalist congress at Port Elizabeth against fusion of the parties by 142 votes to 30 at the beginning of October, then turned up at the meeting of the Federale Raad in Bloemfontein later in the month to say that negotiations with Smuts could not be entertained by his section of the party. If Pirow (who was a Hertzog supporter) is right, Malan shifted his ground in his talks with Hertzog. He behaved, Hertzog thought, as if he was subject to pressures that he was not prepared or at liberty to divulge.

Hertzog, in the end, agreed to fusion with the S.A.P., but on terms which contradicted his statement to Malan, for he laid down no conditions as to which members of Smuts's party were acceptable, nor could he reasonably have done so. A desire for fusion grew in both Nationalist and S.A.P. circles during the middle months of 1933. Even Tielman Roos, whose small Centre Party, formed since the election, remained in the wilderness, agreed in December to put the idea of party amalgamation to his own followers in January, after Pirow and Esselen had prepared the ground. This induced Malan to approach Hertzog again. They met at Groote Schuur on 4 February, and Hertzog sought to reassure Malan on three controversial issues: the right to make republican propaganda, the abolition of appeals to the privy council, and the selection of a South African as the next Governor-General. It seemed, momentarily, as if the Nationalist rift had been healed, at the expense of the Hertzog–Smuts alliance. But, as he told Malan, Hertzog was not free to turn his back on a partnership which had brought his coalition an impressive electoral victory. He also took seriously a letter which Smuts addressed to him on 18 February, seeking clarification over their agreement in earlier talks, and raising three issues over and above the seven points of coalition, on which cautious drafting was necessary in the preparation of a joint programme of principles, which Smuts assumed was to go ahead. These were, not surprisingly, points on which Malan differed: first, the definition of South Africa's sovereign status, but so as to avoid explicit standpoints on the divisibility of the Crown, the right of neutrality, and secession; second, the formulation of a doctrine of nationality which recognised 'our common status within the British Commonwealth'; and third, safeguards against the undermining of South Africa's status in the Commonwealth by excessive propagation of republican doctrines. Hertzog met all Smuts's points the same day, and in the course of the next few weeks the leaders of the Nationalist and S.A. Parties together nursed the Status of the Union and the Royal Executive Functions and Seals Bills through Parliament. These measures, by which the South African legislature helped itself to the legal freedoms offered by the Statute of Westminster, put the reality of South African autonomy beyond reasonable doubt, and for the time being closed the debate between Smuts and Hertzog on the relationship between South Africa and the Empire. Not only had the South African Parliament become a completely sovereign legislature, but the placing of a Great Seal for the Union in the custody of the Prime Minister, for use by the Governor-General, who was now to be regarded as the King's complete *alter ego*, ensured that all acts of state, even the making of war and peace, even secession from the Commonwealth, could now be performed legally on local authority alone.

The Programme of Principles of the combined party was published in the press on 5 June 1934. Fusion was accepted by the Nationalist Federale Raad later in the month, and by the S.A.P. congress in August by a massive vote of 453 to 8. In December the United South African Nationalist Party (more familiarly, the United Party) was brought into being. Malan immediately broke away with his followers to establish the Gesuiwerde Nasionale Party. They became avowed republicans in 1935. The published principles of the United Party, and in particular their flexibility on the topic of constitutional change, drove out Colonel Stallard and a handful of supporters for reasons diametrically opposed to those which had driven out Malan. The members of Stallard's new Dominion Party saw a danger to the Imperial connection in the statement that 'while the Party stands for the maintenance of the present constitutional position, no one will be denied the right to express his individual opinion about or advocate his honest convictions in connection with any change of our form of government'.

# 12 White Unity, Black Division, 1933–9

The Fusion Government was born of a common desire to settle the constitutional relationships within the Empire and to pull South Africa out of economic crisis. The Status and Seals Acts, carried without any recrudescence of party hostility within its ranks, had taken care of the first issue by the middle of 1934. The economy had taken a remarkable upswing after devaluation, with gold shares well over twice their January 1931 listed prices by May 1934, and manufacturing industry booming in a variety of fields – food and drink, metals and engineering, clothing and textiles in particular, both on the Rand and in the main coastal cities. If the English-speaking community was growing rich on the proceeds, Afrikaners and Africans were moving to town in large numbers, and the former were building up their influence through the trade unions.

There remained one task of special difficulty, which could have broken the coalition, but which the amalgamation of the parties was able to bring to a conclusion – whether that conclusion was a settlement, as Hertzog saw it, or the 'new unsettlement' of which Smuts complained. This was to complete the work of the Joint Select Committee of 1930 on the Native Bills.[1] Heaton Nicholls, who at first dominated the Committee's proceedings, claimed that its deliberations were inhibited by Fusion, arguing that at that point the Cabinet took over the decision-making and destroyed its initiative; but without Cabinet intervention, it may be doubted whether any agreed decisions would have been reached at all.

With the Natives' Parliamentary Representation Bill and the Natives' Land Bill of 1929 before it, the Committee also invited its members to submit individual proposals. Those submitted fell substantially into three groups. F. S. Malan proposed the enfranchisement on the common voters' roll in all provinces of all Africans who passed a high qualification test, and his proposal was modified by J. H. Hofmeyr, who urged, rather incongruously in the light of his later attitude – that the level of the qualifications should be altered periodically to ensure that the African electorate did not exceed 10 per cent of the total. Second, there were proposals by G. B. van Zyl and by Smuts that the representation of Africans should be developed through the establishment of further General Councils in the Reserves, which should be politically correlated, and the parliamentary vote restricted to Africans who passed a test of civilisation. Third, there were proposals related to Hertzog's, of which those put forward by Heaton Nicholls on 2 May 1930 were accepted by the Committee for discussion.

Nicholls moved two bills. The first provided that, apart from the Governor-General's nominees, Africans should elect four representatives to the Senate, namely one each for Natal, for the Transvaal and Orange Free State, for the Transkei, and for the rest of the Cape. These were to take the place of elected African representatives in the lower ('democratic') house, for Nicholls asserted that democracy was alien to the African outlook, and that their representation in the Assembly, if conceded in principle, would undermine his objective of preserving white supremacy 'for all time'. He suggested that Africans might elect black senators in the Cape, and in other provinces too if, after ten years, both houses of Parliament were agreeable; but he later withdrew this proposal. He also moved a Native Land Development Bill, the object of which was to make it easier for Africans actually to get the land voted to them, by empowering the Governor-General to buy it on their behalf with funds supplied by Parliament. In 1931 he proposed, as an alternative, that the Government set up a South African Native Trust, on the analogy of the Natal Native Trust, to buy and hold land on behalf of the African people.

To these proposals, Stallard added the idea of a Senate Grand Committee on Native Affairs, consisting of 'all native representatives and at least an equal number of Europeans with a chairman', to consider and, if it desired, also initiate legislation and tax proposals affecting Africans, together with matters referred to it by the Minister of Native Affairs or by any General Council under the Act of 1920.

The Committee accepted the Nicholls–Stallard proposals in principle, but rejected proposals by Stallard to include in the package deal an amended Urban Areas Bill to restrict African access to the towns according to the availability of work. This notion, which he had first propagated in 1922, was subsequently denounced by a departmental committee under J. M. Young and A. L. Barrett in 1935, but reappeared in the Native Laws Amendment Act of 1937 – too late for the 1936 legislative programme.

The year 1932 was difficult for the Committee, not only on account of the prevailing economic crisis, but because, as both Hancock and Nicholls have noted, the S.A.P. minority were losing enthusiasm for the proposals. Nicholls sensed that the South African Party members were being told to undermine the Committee's proceedings. Smuts told his English friends that 'the Native Bills Committee is getting worse and worse. We shall not arrive at an agreement and the Natives will be deprived of such scanty rights as they still possess.'

There was no progress in 1933, the year of election and political crisis. In 1934, the achievement of fusion may have robbed the Committee of its freedom, but it gave additional weight to the views of the majority, despite a brave attempt by the drafters of the United Party's programme of principles to leave the door open as wide as possible, by laying down that the 'solution of the political aspect of [the Native] question might be on the basis of separate representation of Europeans and Natives "or otherwise"', and that consensus was to be sought through 'the free exercise of the discretion of individual members representing the party in Parliament'. Therefore the Nicholls–Stallard formulation remained in tentative possession of the field; but there was room for change, and the Cabinet's new initiative brought some fresh surprises.

The first of these came in 1935, when Hertzog moved the rejection of Stallard's Grand Committee, and proposed instead the establishment of a Natives Representative Council of twenty-two, presided over by the Secretary for Native Affairs. It was to be attended by the five Chief Native Commissioners (non-voting), and include four nominated Africans and twelve Africans elected by colleges in the Transkei, in the rest of the Cape, in Natal, and in the Transvaal and Orange Free State together, some of the representatives being chosen by the urban Advisory Boards. This was a much smaller body than that originally proposed by Hertzog in 1926, and because the Natives' Representatives could attend, it has been described by Tatz as a 'compound' between Stallard's Grand Committee and the original council of 1926. The influence of Smuts may be discernible here; but if so, he and the minority continued to oppose the Natives Representation Bill in which it was incorporated, for it still embodied Nicholls's rejection of African representation in the lower house.

The Nicholls Bill, then, as amended by the inclusion of Hertzog's plan for a Natives Representative Council, was the measure published on 31 December 1935 for debate in the Joint Sitting of February 1936. There was doubt, however, as to whether it could gain sufficient support. The efforts of men such as Sir James Rose Innes (ex-Chief Justice of the Union) and Eric Walker (Professor of History at the University of Cape Town) had helped to build up a hostile climate of opinion in urban Opposition circles, and Hertzog had reason to fear for his two-thirds majority if Smuts's followers withheld support. Smuts himself had constantly voted with the minority in the Joint Select Committee.

Despite the apparent disarray of the African political organisations in the early 1930s, the African reaction was, in the words of Karis and Carter, 'unequivocal in its opposition and Unionwide in its expression'. On the one hand the A.N.C., the Cape Native Voters' Convention,

I.C.U. remnants, advisory boards and vigilance committees uniformly damned the proposed land legislation which was intended to compensate Africans for loss of common-roll voters' rights. Their opposition to the proposed abolition of Cape African representation in the lower house was equally widespread. Even conferences of black leaders which had been arranged by Hertzog at best tried to buy time. The decision to set up an All African Convention in December 1935, so as to coordinate resistance to the legislation, stemmed from consultation between D. D. T. Jabavu, leader of the Cape Native Voters' Convention, and Seme, president-general of the A.N.C.; but they were able to attract to their conference in Bloemfontein some four-hundred-odd representatives of many different kinds of organisation who reached a high degree of unanimity, and ended by sending a deputation to Cape Town led by Jabavu, with a petition of protest and an instruction to seek an interview with the Prime Minister.

Before meeting Hertzog, however, on 7 February, members of Jabavu's deputation met a number of Eastern Province and Border M.P.s and discussed the idea of a compromise measure, on the lines of the 1929 Bill, which adhered to the principle of a separate voters' roll but allowed for some black representation in the lower house. They wired Jabavu, after he had returned to Alice, to convene the A.A.C. executive in Cape Town, so as to obtain a mandate for negotiating with Hertzog on these terms. But the arguments of Mofutsanyana, Xuma and Moroka, all members of the A.A.C. executive, as well as the concern of white liberals associated with the Institute of Race Relations, seem to have convinced Jabavu that compromise would be a mistake. Consequently, when the deputation met Hertzog on 13 February it knew it had no mandate, though Hertzog insisted that it was they who had brought up the idea of discussing the 1929 proposals, not himself. A memorandum by D. L. Smit, Secretary for Native Affairs, drawn up on the 14th, makes it clear that this was the basis of their negotiations. Hertzog gave the African leaders until the following Wednesday (the 19th) to come up with positive proposals, which he agreed to submit to his colleagues. On the day after the interview, however, he went ahead with his December Bill, which made no provision for black representation in the lower house, while Jabavu and his associates tried to have their case presented at the bar of the Assembly through the good offices of F. S. Malan and Sir James Rose Innes.

Hertzog surprised the House on the 17th by withdrawing the controversial Bill and replacing it by a second, which would give the Africans three white representatives in the Assembly. This drew the fire of D. F. Malan and the Purified Nationalists, who now moved an amendment to place Coloured as well as African voters on a separate roll, while Colonel Stallard tried in vain to disinter his Senate Grand Committee proposal from the archives of the Joint Select Committee. But neither of these extreme groups had much influence on the debate. What Hertzog apparently did was to accept overtures from the group of eastern Cape members who had negotiated with Jabavu on the 7th and were prepared to do a deal with the Prime Minister even without African support, perhaps not realising that Jabavu had failed to get the mandate from his executive which such a deal clearly required. L. D. Gilson justified the support of this group for Bill Number Two on the ground that the decision of the Purified Nationalists to support Hertzog meant that they had no prospect of voting Bill Number One down if Hertzog decided to revert to it. Bill Number Two, he argued, at least provided for the 'retention of the individual vote', and still made it possible for black men's advocates to sit and debate in the Assembly. For Smuts and his S.A.P. followers who had consistently voted against the Nicholls proposals in the Joint Select Committee, retreat still had merit. Smuts saw himself as a 'Fabian', seeking to delay the complete exclusion of African representation from the lower house.

Only eleven members voted against the third reading, which received 169 supporting votes – a result greeted by spontaneous cheering, in defiance of convention, as members recognised the triumphal ending of Hertzog's ten-year campaign. The eleven opponents consisted, in about equal numbers, of S.A.P. liberals like F. S. Malan, Morris Alexander, and, above all, J. H. Hofmeyr, and Dominion Party representatives – liberals like C. W. A. Coulter on the one hand, and the segregationist Stallard on the other. Unlike Malan's Nationalists, Stallard preferred to throw the whole matter back into the melting pot rather than abandon Bill Number One. Hofmeyr's third reading speech made an impact because he was a cabinet minister, though he had arranged with Hertzog beforehand that his action would not be construed as involving an issue of confidence. He tore into the principle of communal representation on the ground that it involved inferior citizenship, and objected to the destruction of the 'vested right' of Africans in the existing political system because it involved a breach of faith by the white man which was likely to destroy the trust of the black. He accused Hertzog of lack of courage, as he retreated by stages from the relatively generous Bill of 1926, and prophesied that there would be no end to the retreat.

Whether to reject the new institutions imposed on the African people, or to make use of what was offered in the hope that it could be turned to some good purpose, greatly troubled the A.A.C.[2] The moderates prevailed, and Jabavu, with understandable inconsistency, was among them. In December 1936, the Convention damned the Government's policy but authorised its executive to investigate how common citizenship could be restored and extended. A disenfranchised African,

Ndlwana, took his case through to the Appeal Court in 1937, in an unsuccessful bid to have the Representation Act invalidated. Counsel argued on his behalf that he had been wrongfully removed from the common roll on the ground that Parliament had been incorrect to follow the unicameral procedure after the Union's adoption of the Statute of Westminster; but the Court ruled that the Union Parliament, being fully sovereign, could adopt any legislative procedure which it thought fit. Recourse to the law having thus proved fruitless, some leaders of the A.A.C. decided to stand for the new Native Representative Council, and some (though not Jabavu himself) fought for and obtained seats. They also backed white candidates for the Natives' Representatives' seats in Parliament and the Cape Provincial Council. Finally, in December 1937, despite opposition from Seme and others, the A.A.C. adopted a constitution which turned it into an umbrella for any African organisations, political or other, which wished to affiliate. This action made it a potential rival to the A.N.C., which had clearly lost the initiative to it. But the A.N.C.'s longer history and the wide range of its African membership, together with some measure of built-in sensitivity to a Jabavu challenge, led men with as differing views as James Calata (Anglican priest and Cape president), Selope Thema (Representative Councillor and editor of the *Bantu World*), on the one hand, and the communists J. B. Marks and Moses Kotane on the other, to propose a silver jubilee revival conference in 1937. This took place. The re-election of Mahabane as president-general did not rebuild the organisation's fighting efficiency, but at least it filled it with a bit more potential fire and helped prepare the movement for a new lease of life during the Second World War.

An important pointer to the strategy and fortunes of the Communist Party, whose only positive achievement to date had been to establish the S.A.T.L.C., is the fact that, throughout the thirties and forties its headquarters were in Cape Town, which gave it a close relationship to political developments among the Coloured people, for only about a tenth of its membership was drawn from the whites. In the mid-1930s, it attracted prominent Coloured leaders to its ranks, especially those members of Abdullah Abdurahman's family who reacted against his conservatism, and who set up a National Liberation League in 1935, under the presidency of Zainunissa ('Cissie') Gool (Abdurahman's daughter), with James la Guma as secretary, and a programme demanding complete equality in all spheres, irrespective of race or sex. This was a bid to state a programme which would give the Coloured intelligentsia a controlling position in the development of black nationalism as a whole.

The Communists promoted the National Liberation League's trade union conference in March 1938 to establish a Non-European United Front against the colour bar, and backed the Front's fiery demonstrations in Cape Town on 27 March 1939, when Mrs Gool attacked a Cape ordinance empowering local authorities to segregate public places, public transport and residential areas. A riot ensued and the police intervened; but the Government vetoed the Ordinance.

Mrs Gool toured Natal and the Transvaal in June and July 1939, encouraging the Indians of Johannesburg to begin a passive disobedience campaign in August, in opposition to the Transvaal Asiatics (Land and Trading) Bill, which gave two years' grace only to Indians living in areas exempted from the provisions of the Gold Law, empowered the Minister of the Interior to refuse trading licences, and pegged the Indian occupation of land to existing bazaars, save with ministerial consent. The Indians themselves were divided. Conservatives hoped that the Government would accept the findings of the Feetham Commission of 1934–5, which recommended a slight extension of Indian land rights; but the militants led by Dr Y. M. Dadoo favoured a passive resistance campaign, and – despite Gandhi's discouragement on account of the international situation – won the general support of Indian opinion when friction between the two sides erupted in violence.

While backing the United Front, the Communists also approached the A.A.C., urging it to fight the Hertzog bills by refusing to pay taxes. They hoped to transform it from within and persuade the A.A.C. and the A.N.C. to affiliate. This involved a return to their earlier tactic of joining hands with African nationalism, but even though men like E. Mofutsanyana sat on the executives of both bodies, they failed.

The African organisations proved to themselves between 1935 and 1937 that they could not hold up the will of a determined white parliament either by political demonstration and a direct appeal to the Government, or by seeking to defend their rights in the courts. The Purified Nationalists (*Gesuiwerdes*) under D. F. Malan could at least make a noise in Parliament; but Malan could not count on more than twenty votes in the Assembly, and the prospects for his Gesuiwerde followers seemed bleak in the middle thirties, a mere fifteen years before they became the government of the country in 1948.

It is not possible to explain the rise of Malan nationalism from these unpromising beginnings without taking into account the large number of new agencies in the political, cultural and economic fields which stood behind them, stiffened their morale, provided their funds, and brought them the votes they needed at election times.[3] These agencies had been built up over several decades, in the aftermath of defeat and distress, but were developed by men of exceptional astuteness, who knew how to harness their people's extraordinary capacity for self-help, and how to turn what started as a series of rescue operations patronised by large-hearted men like J. I. Marais of Stellenbosch and the Rev.

J. D. Kestell, into self-supporting organisations which expanded and in doing so built up the prosperity, pride and power of the *volk*.

About a fifth of the Afrikaner population could be loosely classified as 'poor whites' in 1930, in the sense in which J. F. W. Grosskopf of the Carnegie Commission used the term. He defined a poor white as 'a person who has become dependent to such an extent, whether from mental, moral, economic or physical causes, that he is unfit, without help from others, to find proper means of livelihood for himself or to procure it directly or indirectly for his children'. The incidence of poor whiteism, which was regularly discussed at Afrikaner Bond congresses in the 1890s, increased markedly as a result of the rinderpest epidemic of 1896–7, the burning of farms by the British army during the Anglo-Boer war, and the sustained drought of the years 1903–8. These catastrophes led to the eviction of white *bywoners* in considerable numbers, many of whom migrated to the towns in search of livelihood, but without qualifications for jobs. At first the authorities hoped to rehabilitate such people by enticing them back to the land; but land was short, and too many poor whites lacked sufficient initiative, as the Transvaal Indigency Commission stressed in 1908. In 1916 the N.G. Kerk convened a conference at Cradock, which concerned itself with a variety of remedial measures, including the provision of sheltered employment combined with suitable training, where possible, in the towns, on the railways, and in organisations where the discipline was strict (as in the police force). Eventually the Carnegie Commission of 1929–32 carried out a Union-wide investigation, again on the initiative of the churches, and its report in five volumes, dealing with rural impoverishment, the psychology of the poor white, and with educational, health and social aspects of the problem, suggested leads which the Hertzog Government began to follow up, offering privileged employment for white workers, setting up a Department of Social Welfare in 1937, and in other ways.

The Afrikaner was helped by the expansion of opportunities in the towns. Some had moved into the mines after the strike of (mainly British) workers in 1907, and by 1922 perhaps half of the white miners on the Rand were Afrikaners. As already noted, this brought the Afrikaner workers into close association with English-speaking workers, from whom they were able to pick up the techniques of industrial organisation which would enable them at a later stage to take control of the industrial unions and turn them to their own purposes. One immediate result of this contact was the establishment of close links between urban and rural Afrikaners and the Labour Party, which had notable results in the capture of the Transvaal provincial council by Labour in 1914, and in the electoral victory of the Pact in 1924. But a fully bilingual labour party, capable of drawing on the support of large numbers of Afrikaans- and English-speaking workers, never emerged.

'Aristocrats of labour' could not combine under the banner of socialism, while common cultural ties between Afrikaans- and English-speaking workers could hardly grow in the face of determined efforts by politicians to divide them.

The Botha–Hertzog split, the neo-republicanism of the Nationalists after their breakaway in 1913, the Afrikaner rebellion of 1914 with its new list of folk heroes, and the deeds of community self-help which saw the establishment of the *Helpmekaar* (mutual aid) movement in 1915, the launching of *De Burger* in 1916, the creation of the *Arme Blanke Verbond* (poor white alliance) in 1917 to facilitate job-seeking by poor whites, and in 1918 of *Ons Eerste Volksbank* (our first people's bank) for savings, S.A.N.T.A.M. (for insurance) and S.A.N.L.A.M. (for investment and endowment), were key developments in a popular *risorgimento*. 'Jong Suid-Afrika', which came into being in May 1918 and soon changed its name to the *Afrikaner Broederbond*, began as a modest attempt to 'propagate the Afrikaans language and bring together serious-minded young Afrikaners in Johannesburg and along the Reef' and was 'nothing more than a semi-religious organization', according to L. J. du Plessis, who later became its chairman. But it was already developing some of its latter-day characteristics by 1921, as a body which deliberated in secret, worked for the cultural isolation of the Afrikaner as the formula for his survival, and therefore pressed for single-medium schools (as distinct from the bilingual schools which Hertzog had tried to foster). It was a growing force in public life, the full extent of whose actual influence must necessarily be guessed at rather than accurately described. As had been the case with its prototype, the *Genootskap van Regte Afrikaners*, it saw the need to branch out into the cultural and economic fields, and achieved important breakthroughs with the establishment of the *Federasie van Afrikaanse Kultuurverenigings* in 1929 and the launching of the *Ekonomiese Volkskongres* in 1939. The former was a coordinating body for a wide range of cultural organisations, which numbered perhaps three hundred in 1937. The latter represented a landmark in the build-up of Afrikaner economic power, which could already boast, in addition to the important foundations of 1918, the first major Afrikaner-controlled bank, *Volkskas*, established in 1934, the beginnings of a powerful Afrikaner gold-mining group under the enterprising Willem Boshoff, and a prototype Afrikaner industrial union in the *Spoorbond*, established as a rival to the National Union of Railways and Harbours Servants in 1933.

How early the Bond began to engage directly in politics was never disclosed by its members, nor the manner in which this was done. But it followed from its first premises that it should seek to dominate the public life of South Africa, since only in that way could it ensure the restoration of authentic Afrikaner republican and Calvinist institutions to a position of ascendancy. People who thought in this way deplored the pact with Labour in 1922, alleging that it involved 'the continuous trafficking in principles, . . . the violation of consciences, . . . double-heartedness', and other undesirable things. Under coalition, Malan said, problems could not be tackled or solved 'in a manly way'. Strong, purposeful action, *kragdadigheid*, came to mean a great deal to the neo-Nationalists. Hertzog's fault, whether his compromise was with English-speaking labour or English-speaking capital, was that he had diluted the Afrikaner cause. His gesture of bilingualism in education was looked upon as a risk not worth taking because the English-speaker did not want to learn Afrikaans or identify himself with South Africa, and would continue to try to preserve the towns as bastions of his culture, and keep alive and spread among Afrikaners the humanitarian (but, as they would urge, unpractical) notions regarding colour policy which had marked official British attitudes from the start. Hertzog's faith in the Statute of Westminster was subject to the same criticism: it was satisfactory as far as it went, but until the right to contract out of the Empire, and the right to stay out of Britain's wars, and the right to have a South African head of state, and to dispense with judicial appeals to the Privy Council were all clearly asserted, the Afrikaner cause was not secure. Coalition with Smuts's half-English S.A.P., or worse still fusion, therefore put much at risk.

With the support of the Broederbond, which Malan joined in 1933, the Gesuiwerdes attacked boldly, but at first made a poor showing as the official Opposition in Parliament. Malan's 'no confidence' speech on 15 January 1935 was long-winded, vague and trivial. He did not repeat the tactics in the years immediately following. But there were moments during the sessions of 1934–7 when his party took a distinctive stand. Thus they rejected Hertzog's demand for sanctions against Italy during the Abyssinian war. They drew Hertzog's fire by demanding a bilingual chairman for the select committee on public accounts in 1936, and they explicitly demanded an amendment to the Aliens Bill in 1937, asking for a ban on the immigration of 'persons or classes of persons or races, who, such as among others the Jewish, cannot be readily assimilated', together with the abolition of Yiddish as a specially recognised European language. But on the whole they were unable to make the Government take them seriously.

Change came, though, in 1938. In the general election in May they increased their strength in the Assembly to twenty-seven. They managed, also, to win the initiative in the stage management of the Voortrekker centenary celebrations, which were sponsored by the F.A.K. and placed under the control of the Afrikaanse Taal en Kultuur Vereeniging, under the chairmanship of H. J. Klopper, a leading figure in the Broederbond. By this time they were able to exclude even Hertzog from a promiment role in the celebrations, seemingly mindful of his attack on the Broederbond at Smithfield on 7 November 1935, and in Parliament in 1936, when he had accused the Bond of being a self-elected élite in unholy alliance with the *Gesuiwerdes*, playing politics in the guise of a cultural organisation, and arrogating to themselves a monopoly of patriotism. During the organisation of the Voortrekker centenary celebrations J. D. Kestell, the much-respected commando chaplain of Anglo-Boer war days, appealed to save the living descendants of the Voortrekkers, and this led, under the auspices of the F.A.K., to the calling of an *Ekonomiese Volkskongres* in Bloemfontein in October 1939 to discuss the future of the Afrikaner. New ground was broken here, and the speakers who broke it were in a number of cases men who later played a prominent role in public life: among them Dr C. G. W. Schumann, the Stellenbosch economist, who spoke on the economic position of the Afrikaner; Dr T. E. Dönges, later cabinet minister and State-President elect, and M. S. Louw, later chairman of the *Ekonomiese Instituut*, who both spoke on the mobilisation of capital; Dr H. F. Verwoerd, who spoke on consumer cooperatives; Dr Albert Hertzog, critic and son of the Prime Minister, who spoke on the organisation of labour and made a strong attack on communism in the trade unions; and others who dealt with peoples' banks, the Afrikaner's role in manufacturing, and other topics. The *Reddingsdaadbond* which grew out of the proceedings was a far more ambitious organisation than Kestell had apparently intended, for the relief of the poor whites was now viewed merely as an incidental by-product of an economic advance intended for the Afrikaner people as a whole.

The *Ossewa Brandwag* was another movement to grow out of the Voortrekker celebrations. Rather like the Broederbond itself, it started as a cultural organisation officially founded under the leadership of Colonel J. C. C. Laas in Bloemfontein on 4 February 1939. But in the context of a tense international situation, marked by the rise of Nazi Germany, it underwent a fundamental change, becoming a para-military body with its own storm troopers under a new commandant-general selected in December 1940, the ex-Administrator of the Orange Free State, J. F. J. van Rensburg, who would soon be fighting Malan for control of the nationalist movement.

The *Nasionale Instituut vir Christelike Onderwys en Opvoeding* (National Institute for Christian Education and Instruction) was established under the F.A.K. in July 1939, under the chairmanship of Professor J. C. van Rooy of Potchefstroom, who was also chairman of the F.A.K. and a leading Bond member. Its aim was to apply in the schools the culturally separatist doctrines which had been developed in Purified Nationalist circles, involving a revival of the defensive educational strategy which had been developed in the Transvaal and Orange River Colony in opposition to Milner's anglicisation policy after 1902.

A third of the Broederbond's members were teachers, wrote I. M. Lombard in the *Transvaler* in December 1944.

Teaching, broadly conceived, involved also the means of propaganda. By the outbreak of the war in 1939, the Nationalists could rely on a spread of newspapers in the main centres. Since the founding of the *Burger*, they had established or gained control of the *Vaderland* (1935) and the *Transvaler* (1937), the latter edited by the dynamic H. F. Verwoerd. Behind the newspapers were the publishing houses, notably the *Afrikanerpers*, the *Nasionalepers* and the *Voortrekkerpers*, in the founding of the last of which Malan had played a leading role. These Houses put out a series of volumes, some commemorating the Afrikaner's historical past, like Gustav Preller's *Voortrekkermense* series, some to boost the Afrikaans language and literature; while the political tracts of the *Tweede Trek* series put across the programme of the Afrikaner revival in handy pocket editions.

As the Malan Nationalists grew in confidence from 1938 onwards, the United Party found it increasingly difficult to hold together in face of their attacks. At first, the issues which divided it were domestic, but it was the decision to enter the war against Nazi Germany which eventually drove Hertzog and Smuts apart. Tea-cup storms over the national anthem plagued 1938 – when *Die Stem van Suid-Afrika* was played together with *God Save the King* at the opening of Parliament, when *Die Stem* was played at military parades on Union Day and *The King* was not, and when, because the organisers of the Voortrekker Centenary would not allow the playing of *The King* at their celebrations, the Governor-General (and therefore the Prime Minister) felt unable to take part. But these storms were damaging to government morale, for on the second occasion Richard Stuttaford temporarily resigned from the Cabinet, while Leslie Blackwell, a leading backbencher, openly dissented from his leader's policy. A ministerial decision, taken without Hertzog's knowledge, to give Roberts Heights, the military base south of Pretoria, the new name of Voortrekkerhoogte in December 1938 had similar repercussions, appropriate though the gesture may have been to the occasion. Rather more serious were the effects of Hertzog's decision in 1938 to appoint A. P. J. Fourie, the ex-Minister of Labour, who had been defeated in the general election, as a senator selected for his knowledge of native affairs. Hofmeyr resigned from the Cabinet in protest, and Sturrock followed, believing Hertzog had forced Hofmeyr out. Smuts, who felt strongly about Hertzog's choice of Fourie, lost face in some quarters for not resigning, but made it clear that he was still more concerned over the implications of the current crisis in Czechoslovakia, and saw this as a compelling reason for staying in office.

* * *

Slowly the right to conduct an independent foreign policy was coming to mean something in practice, and the Union Government began to assert its point of view, often hesitantly but occasionally with firm conviction, during the years of international crisis after Fusion. Both Hertzog and Smuts were League of Nations men in that they saw the League as a necessary instrument of peace. This meant that their foreign policy was bi-partisan in character even though Hertzog kept the decision-making largely to himself and left Smuts to operate only on the private, unofficial level, in correspondence with L. S. Amery, Gilbert Murray, Tom Lamont of New York, Chaim Weizmann, and other leaders of opinion in Britain and elsewhere. In the early 1930s, before the Disarmament Conference had ended in failure and while Hitler's Germany was still in the League, both men inclined to optimism. After 1934, both continued to see support of the League as a necessary condition for peace, above all when the Italian invasion of Abyssinia brought the crisis nearer home. Through Te Water in Geneva, Hertzog threw South Africa's weight firmly behind the collective security clauses of the League of Nations Covenant. Te Water said to the League Assembly on 1 July 1936 that 'the destruction of Ethiopian sovereignty by Italy and the annexation of the territory of a country which at no time menaced the safety of Italy creates now the exact state of affairs which this League was designed to avoid', and he pledged his government to support the collective action resolution of 10 October 1935, agreeing to sanctions. But if Italy was to be regarded as an aggressor in an African setting, could the same be said of Germany in Europe?

Hertzog and Smuts reacted in rather different ways to the growth of German assertiveness, and this mattered for local reasons because of the pull exerted on Hertzog by his ex-colleagues, the Malan Nationalists, some of whom saw in Hitler's racism a credo which could be adapted to South African needs. Both Hertzog and Smuts had reacted against the severity of Versailles, Smuts as a participant who had had to shoulder more of the blame for the harshness of the treaty than his role at the peace conference warranted, Hertzog with the uninhibited judgment of one who had not been involved in the settlement. Smuts tended to see the rise of Hitlerism as a monstrous consequence of an unjust peace, Hertzog as the legitimate reaction of a downtrodden nation. Hertzog was prepared to trust Hitler's undertakings right down to the outbreak of the Second World War, whereas Smuts, who shared Hertzog's feeling that the posture of neutrality in a European conflict was desirable, felt unable to recommend neutrality after the rape of Czechoslovakia. Their differing assessments of the international danger became tied up, in the course of time, with their differing attitudes to the role of South Africa in the British Commonwealth, above all the right of South Africa to participate or not, at will, in any war in which

Britain became involved. For Hertzog, even after the Sudeten crisis of September 1938, neutrality was a right which it was still prudent to exercise. For Smuts, too, it was a legal right; but he denied that South Africa had the political right to use it in the international crisis of 1939. Both men probably realised the dangers to white South African unity involved in making war against Germany for the second time in less than twenty-five years, when the unpleasant memories of the first occasion were still green; but for Smuts the international dangers outweighed the domestic, whereas for Hertzog it was the other way round.

Hertzog considered that a statement which he had placed before the Cabinet in September 1938, setting out a firm neutralist line in the event of Britain becoming involved in war against a European power, was still binding on Smuts, who had originally approved it, a year later. Smuts, whose public utterances reflected a growing anxiety for the preservation of civilised values, rejected this argument. A special session of Parliament was called for 2 September 1939, primarily to prolong the life of the Senate, which was due to expire on the 5th. On the 4th, Hertzog moved a motion to reaffirm South Africa's policy or neutrality in the European war, but Smuts carried an amendment in favour of breaking off relations with Germany, by 80 votes to 67. The Cabinet was split down the middle. Hertzog asked the Governor-General, Sir Patrick Duncan, for a dissolution; but Duncan refused on the ground that a viable alternative government could be formed. On the 6th, Smuts was entrusted with the formation of a new ministry, and did so with the cooperation of the Labour and Dominion parties. The outbreak of war thus brought Fusion to a dramatic end.

# 13 Smuts and the Liberal–Nationalist Confrontation, 1939–48

Smuts took South Africa into the Second World War out of concern for the future of the human race, and in particular for that of Europe, 'this glorious mother continent of Western civilization – the proudest achievement of the human spirit up to date', which seemed to be in danger of destruction in the short term by Hitler, or in the longer term by Stalin.[1] It was a choice, as he put it, 'between the Devil and Beelzebub', since Hitler was 'another Attila', whereas Stalin and the communists, the 'looters' who grabbed half of Poland, had taken the wrong turning, 'for man is primary, not society'.

The team which he selected to take South Africa into the war consisted largely of survivors of the Fusion Government who had remained with him in the September division – notably Harry Lawrence (Interior), Claude Sturrock (Railways), Deneys Reitz (Native Affairs), Stuttaford and Clarkson. He brought Hofmeyr back (Finance and Education), put Collins and Conroy, ex-Hertzogite colleagues from the Anglo-Boer War, into Agriculture and Lands respectively, gave Justice to Colin Steyn, son of the last O.F.S. president, and found places in his coalition for the Dominion Party leader, Stallard, and the Labour leader, Madeley. They were men of uneven competence, though some – notably Hofmeyr and Sturrock – achieved much during their period of office. What mattered most to Smuts was that he should be able to devote his energies to the winning of the war. The management of parliamentary business was therefore left mainly to Hofmeyr, while Louis Esselen took charge of party affairs. Smuts himself concentrated on external affairs and defence, the military aspects of which were handled through the Chief of General Staff, Sir Pierre van Ryneveld, and the economic through Dr H. J. van der Byl, the first chairman of ISCOR, who was made Director-General of War Supplies.

The needs of war required changes in the methods of administration, though parliamentary government, including the contesting of elections, was kept going and served as a lightning conductor for the release of public emotions, which – as will be shown later – were extremely volatile. Indeed, one of the outstanding characteristics of the Smuts wartime government was the coolness with which it handled threats to the security of the State. Like all belligerents, it armed itself under a War Measures Act of 1940, with the power to intern suspects and enemy aliens, and used them; it called in all firearms; and it helped itself to a range of arbitrary powers, including powers to control supplies and curb industrial unrest. But, profiting from the lessons of the First World War, Smuts pulled his punches in handling the most provocative opposition to his war policy, and refrained from the use of the death penalty even for blatant acts of treason.

The Treasury was required to relax its controls over defence expenditure by acceding as a matter of routine to all requests made by a new combined Defence Authorities Committee. Thus released from the economics of peacetime, the Department of Defence spent close on £650 millions between 1939 and 1945 on the war against the Axis. The demands of war, in consequence, resulted in considerable industrial expansion, above all in mining, steel and textiles, as factories turned to the manufacture of armoured cars, artillery pieces, munitions, boots and uniforms, using a good deal of unskilled black labour, diluted with that of white artisans, in order to meet production targets.

Defence of the Cape sea route was South Africa's first duty to her allies, and Smuts cast South Africa, in the first instance, for an otherwise passive military role, while raising sizeable forces against contingencies elsewhere. But once France and French seapower had been lost to the Allies, and Italy had entered on the German side, the continent of Africa became directly involved. The Defence Act limited the operational area of South African forces to 'any part of South Africa whether within or outside the Union'; but in 1940 the Smuts Government made it possible for volunteers to offer their services anywhere in Africa. Only white troops, however, were permitted to join combat units, the Coloured and African soldiers being confined to auxiliary services. Union forces took part in the reconquest of Ethiopia from the Italians in 1940–1. They seized Madagascar which had thrown in its lot with Vichy France, in 1942, in order to forestall any possible landing by the Japanese. Three South African divisions took part in the north African campaigns against German and Italian forces in Egypt and Libya, the second being captured by Rommel's Afrika Korps in Tobruk. After taking part in the battle of El Alamein in September 1942, and the final expulsion of the Axis forces from Africa, the 6th South African Armoured Division was sent to Italy as part of the American Fifth Army, its members having volunteered to serve anywhere in the world, and fought its way up the peninsula from Salerno to the Po valley. Altogether some 200,000 uniformed South Africans took part in the war, of whom close on 9000 were killed.

Although the Government's reliance on volunteers for all operations outside the Union was intended as a means of avoiding the provocation of its opponents, the world-wide ideological conflict cut deep into South African public opinion. Those people, black and white, who adhered to traditional notions of civil liberty and deplored racial fanaticism were concerned to ensure the victory of the western Allies. But whites who felt that the preservation of the existing South African race–caste structure was necessary for European survival in the sub-continent, or who were emotionally drawn to the Germans as to near-kinsmen, or who were excited by the energy or the doctrines of Nazi Germany, either backed the Axis or demanded a return to neutrality. Few but the Marxists, who saw the war as a civil conflict between rival sections of the capitalist order, were neutral by conviction. During the period of the 'phoney' war (until May 1940), and during Hitler's *Blitzkrieg* of May and June, however, though the Opposition gave the Government cause for anxiety, it restricted its activities to propaganda.

The Nationalists had advertised a republican demonstration on Monumentkoppie, outside Pretoria for 9 October.[2] The occasion was used to celebrate the impending reunion (*hereniging*) of the Nationalists under Malan and Hertzog, thirty-seven Hertzogites having crossed the floor of the Assembly to vote with the Malanites for neutrality. *Hereniging* was a difficult assignment, however, for in five years the U.P. and the G.N.P. had drifted apart in sentiment and objectives; but it was achieved in December 1939, so far as a form of words could do this, and announced in January. Hertzog agreed, for the first time ever, to a Republic outside the Empire, while Malan agreed that it could only be allowed to happen 'on the broad basis of the people's will', and with proper consideration for the equal language and cultural rights of the two sections of the white population. This, however, was an awkward formula, for the more rigorous Nationalists like J. G. Strijdom and H. F. Verwoerd of the Transvaal, and N. J. van der Merwe and C. R. Swart of the O.F.S., firmly believed that an Afrikaner Republic had to be created as a precondition for the build-up of a right relationship between the two white groups, and that remained anathema to Hertzog. Malan and Hertzog, working together, put pressure on the Government to leave the war; but they could not stop the Free State Nationalists, in the heady atmosphere engendered by Hitler's campaigns of May and June, from calling a republican rally in Bloemfontein on 20 July against Hertzog's express instructions. They used the occasion to propagate not only republicanism but also Christian National (unilingual) education, of which Hertzog strongly disapproved, and to attack the party fusion of 1934 as a product of

'British–Jewish capitalist' influence. An anonymous attempt was made at about this time to smear Hertzog and Havenga by 'discovering' evidence in a freemason's private suitcase which suggested that they had connived with Smuts to make South Africa (including English-speaking Rhodesia) a Republic within the British Empire. This rumour helped to erode Free State Nationalist confidence in Hertzog. With Malan's firm support, Hertzog could probably have survived this kind of attack; but from about August 1940 the Nationalist hawks began to put pressure on Malan as well. Hertzog tried, as co-leader of what had become a federal party, to reassert his authority by submitting a draft programme of principles for the Free State section of the Party to the provincial congress in October. Swart moved an alternative draft which stood in the name of the Federale Raad, and got this accepted as the basis of discussion. Hertzog, ducking a fight on the procedural point, later asked Swart to explain the omission from the federal draft of any reference to the equality of rights for the English-speakers, such as appeared in his own. Swart's answer did not satisfy him, so for the second time in his career, Hertzog stormed out of the party congress with a small group of followers (among them Havenga), this time not to found a nationalist party but to dissociate himself from the Free State section of a party of which he intended to remain a member. But he could not remain a member, for shortly afterwards the Transvaal congress, on Strijdom's initiative, quietly withdrew its support. Malan did not defend him. His contribution at this stage, by drawing a smokescreen in public over what had happened at the conference in Bloemfontein, was to ensure that when the Hertzogites rallied at the end of the year and went on to form their breakaway Afrikaner Party in January 1941, only a small number of the H.N.P. supporters went with them.

In the distractions of the *Hereniging* crisis which lasted through 1940, the H.N.P. missed an opportunity to strengthen their own hand, by turning their backs on a new and popular movement, Gert Yssel's *Handhawersbond*, which might have given them the equivalent of an *Ossewa Brandwag*, within their own ranks. But Yssel did not enjoy the confidence of the Broederbond leadership. As a result, Malan's party was faced right through to the general election of 7 July 1943 with the problem of coordinating rival groups which doggedly retained their own identities rather than combine, some committed to peaceful change, but others appearing to welcome violence.

Despite the precedent of Hertzog's deposition, personalities remained important, among them Malan's chief rival, J. F. J. van Rensburg, ex-Administrator of the O.F.S., who succeeded a discredited Colonel Laas as Commandant-General of the O.B. in January 1941. The O.B. was committed broadly to the maintenance of the Afrikaner values, the nurturing of patriotism and group pride, and the vigorous defence of their way of life, through participation in festivals, heroes' days, wreath-layings, target-shoots, *jukskei* matches, public lectures on folk history and folk literature, camps, and in other ways. Its leaders were doubtful whether the Afrikaner cause could be adequately served by orthodox political action alone, and some of them, like Van Rensburg himself, were sufficiently influenced by developments in Europe to doubt the value of the parliamentary system at all. In this they differed fundamentally from Malan. They gambled on a victory for the Axis, encouraged from 1942 by Zeesen radio's support for Van Rensburg against Malan. Malan, however, insisted on constitutional procedures, arguing that they alone were capable of producing the right results, whichever side eventually won the war. On 29 October 1940 he obtained from Dr C. R. Kotze, chairman of the O.B. Groot Raad, a document subsequently known as the Cradock Agreement whereby the H.N.P. was to operate on the party political level and the O.B. on the non-political, the latter to refrain from subversive activities or force directed against friendly political movements. Van Rensburg had not been elected Commandant-General when this agreement was drawn up, and the O.B. already had an élite body of *Stormjaers* whose potential danger to public security had led Smuts to order the general surrender of rifles. Members of the O.B. tended not to commit acts of sabotage and public violence until 1942, and then they were denounced by the H.N.P. for so doing, but their attraction to Nazism and what they termed 'the revolution of the twentieth century' and their liking for the Nationalist virtue of *kragdadigheid* made the restraints of the Cradock Agreement wise policy from the H.N.P.'s point of view – if they could be enforced.

Of the H.N.P.'s other rivals, the least significant in terms of actual power was the Afrikaner Party, now without its leader Hertzog, who had gone into almost complete retirement after he and Havenga had lost by-elections to contest their own seats. They retained ten members in the lower House and a few senators, but lacked an audience as they struggled to keep faith with Hertzog's now apparently outdated policy of Anglo-Afrikaner accord. Weakened by desertions to either the government benches or the Nationalists, they cast around for political allies, sometimes in unlikely places, such as the O.B., which at least shared a common dislike of the H.N.P., but Havenga failed to reach an agreement with Malan before the 1943 election and the Party failed to win more than a handful of votes.

The most original member of the Hertzogite diaspora was Oswald Pirow, ex-Minister of Defence, who had travelled in Nazi Germany on government business and expressed in his *Nuwe Orde vir Suid Afrika*, which was frequently reprinted between December 1940 and May 1941, what he later described as an attraction for the national socialism of Salazar. Pirow remained in the Nationalist Party, but his propaganda embarrassed the H.N.P. and Malan began to move against him in August 1941. Verwoerd's *Transvaler* attacked him for his Nazism. Pirow established a separate New Order Group so as to be able to continue his propaganda. In January 1942 he and his parliamentary followers left the Nationalist caucus without formally seceding from the Party, but they would not attach themselves to the O.B., with which they had ideological loyalties in common, and soon faded out. In any case, Pirow had become disenchanted with the parliamentary system.

Malan's offensive against the New Order was important because it initiated a period of open conflict between the H.N.P. and the O.B. Van Rensburg reacted to the attack on Pirow by throwing down the gauntlet to Malan. Owing to a misunderstanding, the O.B. had distributed 100,000 copies of a draft republican constitution throughout the land on 3 July, thinking that Malan, whose Party had been involved in its preparation, had given his authority for such a step. But Malan had not done so, and the O.B.'s action violated the terms of the Cradock Agreement. At first, the leaders acted with restraint. Malan accepted van Rensburg's apology. But when Malan attacked Pirow, Van Rensburg in a speech at Elsburg on 9 August assumed public responsibility on behalf of the O.B., not only for publishing the constitution but for its contents as well. He presented the O.B. to his audience as a national movement which all could join, and made a bid for Afrikaner leadership by proclaiming that in the issue between Malan and Pirow his movement did not take sides.

For some months peace had been kept between the rival bodies by a *Volkseenheidskomitee* (People's Unity Committee), the creation of Professor L. J. du Plessis of Potchefstroom, a Calvinist political philosopher and member of the Broederbond executive, whose thinking had begun to move – out of disillusionment with democracy – in the direction of some combination of nationalism and socialism. Thanks to Du Plessis's efforts, Malan had been accorded the title of *Volksleier* (Leader of the people) in June 1941, with an invitation to coordinate the activities, not only of the H.N.P. and the O.B., but of the F.A.K., the R.D.B., and the churches. The *Eenheidskomitee* tried in September to patch up the dispute between Malan and Van Rensburg, using ingenious formulae which granted the essence of Malan's case but enabled Van Rensburg to cover up for the O.B., in the matter of the embarrassing publication. But the O.B. had not eaten its pie with sufficient humility for Malan's liking, and he resolved to break Van Rensburg as he had broken Pirow. Zeesen's support for Van Rensburg stimulated Malan's determination. The *Eenheidskomitee* soon found it could no longer hold the ring. In September 1941 Malan sought to increase his control still further by instituting a shadow cabinet of his own choosing, to be called the *Nasionale Komitee*. Later, in January

1942, after further abortive attempts to close the breach, he purged the O.B. members from the Cape H.N.P. ranks, and publicly declared war on the movement for carrying out acts of sabotage.

By the time of the general election of 1943 the H.N.P. had clearly emerged as the dominant political mouthpiece of Afrikanerdom. Malan's ruthlessness and his rejection of para-military activity were much resented. There were many, notably Professor J. C. van Rooy of Potchefstroom, who would have preferred an electoral alliance between the various groups, rather than allow an H.N.P. victory by *force majeure*; but events played into Malan's hands in spite of this. The O.B. found it could not refuse to support H.N.P. parliamentary candidates, especially after the H.N.P. had shown, in a series of by-elections in 1942, that it was beginning to make ground against the ruling U.P. This trend continued in the 1943 general election. The United Party retained a massive majority, as was to be expected, and was returned to power with 110 seats. Malan's party had a mere 43, which meant that 23 opponents of the war policy had now disappeared from the Opposition benches; but all those defeated were Afrikaner Party supporters or members of Pirow's New Order, which had been swept from the board. The H.N.P., as the only Opposition party facing the Government coalition, had won two extra seats and polled 362,000 votes against the 640,000 polled by the government parties, and cut the U.P.'s share of the Afrikaner vote from 40 to 32 per cent.

One reason for the electoral success of the H.N.P. had been the manner in which it shifted its attack away from the war policies of the Government, on which it began to realise that it had been wasting its breath, to domestic issues, especially those touching on race relations, which could not fail to increase in importance and urgency.

On assuming power, the United Party coalition had inherited the Hertzogian racial policy, with its five defensive bastions against African pressure: communal representation under the 1936 Representation Act, territorial segregation under the 1936 Native Trust and Land Act, urban segregation with influx control under the 1937 Native Laws Amendment Act, authoritarian rule under the Native Administration Act of 1927, and the Riotous Assemblies Act of 1930 as a security back-stop.[3] In the case of the Indian population of the Transvaal and Natal, the restriction of land and trading rights remained the dominant features of government policy, and there was no thought of extending political liberties to Indians anywhere. Hertzog's policy for the Coloured people was in the process of formation. Its main lines were not yet intelligible, for although his political and economic 'new deal' had been a casualty of the debates of 1926–36, the Willcocks Commission had reported in 1937, urging that the Coloured people merited better jobs, better trade unions, better schools, better health services and pensions, more opportunities for owning land and a chance to learn how to farm it, and even a parliamentary vote in the northern provinces if they were well qualified. But no legislation had been tabled before Hertzog fell from power.

The alteration of these policies was not at issue when Smuts assumed office. The Government was committed to a policy of segregation, of which nearly all parliamentarians wanted more rather than less. But instead of developing the policy systematically the Smuts Government allowed it, to some extent, to run down, and perhaps even contemplated its reversal. Unanticipated difficulties were partly responsible for this. Industrial growth, already remarkable during the 1930s, proceeded even faster during the war years, as South Africa began to manufacture munitions and military equipment. The systematic enforcement of influx control had begun only in 1938, and even then the municipal labour censuses carried out under the Native Laws Amendment Act of 1937 showed that there were relatively few able-bodied African workers in the towns who could reasonably be driven out to work on the white-owned farms, because of growing industrial labour demands. The labour shortage became still more noticeable during the war years when, to keep the war industries going, the dilution of skilled with unskilled labour was increasingly practised in government factories.

Another reason for the slowing down of segregation was the appearance in Parliament in 1938 of a well-coordinated group of white Natives' Representatives, whose influence was strong enough to transform the debate over native policy from a discussion of control techniques into a discussion of immediate and long-term welfare. Margaret Ballinger and Senator Edgar Brookes led this team, the former spearheading their attack in the Assembly, while Brookes concentrated his efforts mainly in the Native Affairs Commission, and put his constituents' case in the Senate with consummate tact. Together they saw to it (in a way which Hertzog had perhaps never calculated) that a case for their African constituents was continuously and accurately put. In 1941 Senator J. D. Rheinallt Jones set a precedent with a motion commending the resolutions of the Natives' Representative Council to 'the careful consideration of the Government'. It produced a hostile reaction in some quarters, but ensured that the statutory tabling of the resolutions on this occasion was more than a formality. A corresponding change of outlook began to appear in the Department of Native Affairs, through the initiative of its Secretary, Douglas Smit.

The Government's appointment of a Social and Economic Planning Council to devise blueprints for post-war reform, and of an Inter-Departmental Committee under Smit's chairmanship to investigate the social, educational and health conditions of urban Africans in 1942, gave promise of important reforms. The Government introduced improvements in the fields of workmen's compensation, pensions, unemployment insurance, public health and secondary education in particular. While none involved the spending of large sums of money, they established areas of public responsibility where this had not been acknowledged before, extending to other races benefits which the Hertzog Government had introduced for white (and sometimes Coloured) people. In May 1942, following ministerial consternation at the increase in the number of Africans arrested for technically infringing the pass laws, the abolition of which had in any case been recommended by the Smit Committee, the Departments of Justice and Native Affairs agreed to restrain the police from demanding the production of passes save by individuals who seemed to be breaking the law. There was a dramatic reduction in the number of pass arrests in the second half of 1942. At about the same time Madeley, the Minister of Labour, let it be known that he was considering the inclusion of African workers in the collective bargaining procedures of the Industrial Conciliation Act, and he personally opened the inaugural conference of the Congress of Non-European Trade Unions.

The liberal reforms adumbrated in 1942, however, unleashed a predictable reaction, and the Nationalist counterattack started in Parliament as the two sides squared up for the general election. In the Assembly, Malan moved a highly eclectic social security motion on 19 January 1943. He dissociated himself from both Nazism and Communism, attacked the Social and Economic Planning Council as 'neither representative nor competent' and professed a faith in segregation while at the same time identifying himself with the current interest in general social welfare. A week later, Eric Louw asked the House to deplore the spread of communism (Soviet Russia being by this time an ally of the West and under strong German attack), and this produced heated exchanges which had obvious electioneering value. Mrs Ballinger counterattacked with a motion urging a new beginning in native policy, through the adoption of the Smit Report; but the new Minister of Native Affairs, Major Piet van der Byl, countered with a defensive amendment asking the House to endorse 'the Native Policy envisaged in the 1936–'37 legislation' as well as the policy of providing 'improved health, housing, education and other social services for the Non-European population'. Brookes, whose approach was more conciliatory, had a similar experience in the Senate. The task of the Natives' Representatives in this changed atmosphere was beginning to require the avoidance of collision with the United Party, for fear of losing the chance of influencing its majority.

Between 1943 and 1946 the African population suffered many new hardships. On the Witwatersrand a committee under S. H. Elliott, Chief Magistrate of Johannesburg, recommended a return to pass law enforcement in 1943, not because it could demonstrate a causal connection between policy relaxation and the increase in crime (which was the field of its inquiry) but because it was able to show that the relaxation of the policy had led to fewer Africans registering for work on arrival in the municipalities, and therefore threatened to undermine the policy of influx control itself. The measure of African disappointment at this reversal of their hopes can best be seen in the determination with which an Anti-Pass Campaign was set in motion in Johannesburg in May 1944. The organisers made repeated approaches to the Government and obtained no concessions, save that the pass laws were eventually placed on the agenda of the 1946 Fagan Commission.

An acute housing shortage for Johannesburg Africans reached crisis point in 1944 when the first of seven substantial squatter movements was launched. It could not be resolved with any speed owing to the shortage of building materials, and the ban still imposed by the white builders on the training of Africans in their trade. A handful of African leaders, of whom James Sofasonke Mpanza was the most noteworthy, defied the law and moved their followers on to the Orlando commonage, provided hessian for shanties, employed camp guards to prevent looting, sold trading rights and levied an *ad hoc* rate from the squatters. They eventually forced the central Government and the Johannesburg City Council to set up emergency camps. But the episode left a bitter legacy, above all in the relationship between urban Africans and the police, which eventually led to riots in August 1947, the climax of a series of confrontations which had in recent years alone produced violence at Vereeniging in September 1937, at Marabastad in December 1942, in Sophiatown in October 1944, and at Springs in July 1945.

A rapid spread of African trade unionism characterised the middle war years. This owed a good deal to Communist Party influence. By the 1930s African workers, realising they could expect little support from white artisans, had formed their own African Federation of Trade Unions, which had been incorporated in a Council of Non-European Trade Unions by November 1941. There were frequent African strikes during the second half of 1942, and a good many resulted in redress of grievances, especially where it could be shown that employers had been paying low wages; but, so far from Madeley's hint of collective bargaining rights being extended, successive war measures tightened the controls over black workers. Of these, War Measure 145 of January 1942, which outlawed strikes by Africans under threat of heavy penalties, and required them to accept arbitration of disputes at ministerial discretion, was regularly renewed until permanently embodied in a statute (the Native Labour Settlement of Disputes Act of 1953). Both the parliamentary Labour Party and the Trades and Labour Council opposed the extension of bargaining rights to Africans, and when the Council of Non-European Trade Unions secured an interview with Madeley in October 1943, it came away empty-handed. Though it appointed the Lansdown Commission to investigate the wages of African mine and power workers in 1944, the Smuts Government never hit on a black labour policy which won general acceptance. This was significant, for it was a dispute with the African mineworkers that led to a breakdown in its relations with the political as well as the industrial leaders of African opinion in 1946.

The mineworkers' basic wage of two shillings a shift was low because families had to be maintained in the Reserves under the mines' scheme of deferred pay, and because the miners had to buy their boots, blankets and any supplementary food at normal prices. They had tried as early as 1943 to obtain four shillings a day, plus better food and free equipment, but failed to persuade the owners. In August 1941 the African Mineworkers' Union was formally constituted under the energetic leadership of S. P. Matseke (chairman of the Transvaal A.N.C.), Gaur Radebe and J. B. Marks (Communist members of the A.N.C. executive). The energy they put into their recruiting campaign enabled them to claim over 25,000 members in 1944. In that year the Lansdown Commission recommended that African miners should receive an extra fivepence per shift plus threepence cost-of-living allowance, together with a boot allowance, overtime pay, and, in the case of permanent workers, increased cost-of-living and two weeks' paid leave. The Government and the Chamber accepted the overtime proposal, and rejected cost-of-living and boot allowances, but agreed to a wage increase of fourpence and fivepence for surface and underground workers respectively. This cut the extra expenditure recommended by Lansdown from £2,642,000 to £1,850,000. The Lansdown Commission also advised against the recognition of the African Mineworkers' Union, though it recommended the recognition of African trade unions in principle. Its case was based on the arguments that 'no movement . . . has emanated from the mine native labourers themselves', and that the Communists had manipulated the workers. The Commission therefore looked rather to the appointment of suitable welfare officers under the control of the Department of Native Affairs, who should keep close contact with the workers and report their needs to the Department and to the mine managements.

The miners were dissatisfied on both counts, and soon had other grievances. By War Measure 1425 of 1945 the Government then sought to contain union resistance by prohibiting gatherings of more than twenty people on mine property. The Union-wide famine in that year necessitated a cut in mine rations and violence resulted at the Modderfontein East compound. In April 1946 the Mineworkers' Union put in a claim for a basic wage of ten shillings a day and demanded the repeal of War Measure 1425. The Chamber repeatedly ignored the wage demand on the ground that the union had no *locus standi*. Eventually, on 4 August, over 70,000 African miners went out on strike. It was put down by the police, as the strike of 1920 had been, at the cost of several lives lost and many injured. It was soon followed by the arrest and trial of leading communists, notably W. H. Andrews (the national president), Moses Kotane (the general secretary), and Betty Radford, editor of the *Guardian*, which had supported the strikers and incurred a libel action for publishing extracts from the African Mine-workers' Union's evidence before the Lansdown Commission.

Two days after the start of the miners' strike, the Natives' Representative Council reassembled in Pretoria, each of its members having been asked on 26 July by Xuma, as president-general of the A.N.C. and chairman of the Anti-Pass Committee, to adjourn their session unless the Government agreed to abolish the pass laws, recognise African trade unions under the Industrial Conciliation Act, and repeal the oppressive sections of the Native Administration Act of 1927 which permitted banishment without trial. The action next taken by the Natives' Representative Council, therefore, seems to have been deliberate rather than spontaneous. The Under-Secretary for Native Affairs opened the Council because the Secretary, Dr G. Mears, was absent on account of the miners' strike. He made no reference to the strike in his opening address, and had no information for members when he was pressed by them. The Council reacted angrily. Dr Moroka, who in any case thought there was no substitute for direct representation in Parliament and had no love for the Council as an institution, moved the adjournment of the session with a motion that was antagonistic in tone and obviously intended to be so. Significantly, his motion was supported unanimously by radicals, moderate intellectuals, and even chiefs.

The Natives' Representatives tried to bring the parties together, without avail. Brookes approached the Native Affairs Commission and Hofmeyr (the acting Prime Minister), urging them to consider a meaningful programme of reform, and not take umbrage as Hofmeyr was inclined to do. The pass laws, the educational system, the status of the N.R.C., the recognition of African unions and the miners' strike, Brookes urged, were all nettles that needed to be grasped in a new initiative. Hofmeyr discounted this advice, telling Smuts, who was at the United Nations Conference in Paris, that he thought the whites would look on such proposals as surrender. He preferred 'a friendly and conciliatory but firm statement of government policy as at present followed', with an offer that went no further than Lansdown on the subject of trade unions. Smuts, however, saw something in Brookes's proposal, and asked for a draft on those lines to be approved by the Cabinet and sent to him, remarking that 'our native policy would have to be liberalized at modest pace but public opinion has to be carried with us. . . . Practical social policy away from politics as stated by me still holds, is being carried out, and will be so more and more as finance permits.'

The Native Affairs Commission agreed that Hofmeyr, rather than the less popular Van der Byl, should address the N.R.C. on 20 November to give the Government's reply; but the reply given dwelt more on the Government's past record than its future plans, and above all offered no collective bargaining concessions to the African miners. The N.R.C. accordingly replied on the 26th, repudiating Hofmeyr's censure on its earlier action, indicting the Government with responsibility for lives lost during the miners' strike, and rejecting Hofmeyr's defence of government action because it 'made no attempt to deal with . . . the Pass Laws, the colour bar in industry, the political rights of Non-Europeans' and did not recognise the miners' union. It ended by demanding direct African representation at all levels from the municipal councils to Parliament.

Smuts said on his return to South Africa that he understood that the N.R.C. would be satisfied with nothing less than effective political power, which to him was an unthinkable concession; but he did listen to Mrs Ballinger's suggestion in February 1947 that if he were to recognise the existence of permanent African communities in the towns, make some plan for the better training of increasingly scarce African farm workers, set about the establishment of efficient labour exchanges so that the pass laws could be dispensed with, give the N.R.C. a promise of proper consultation in the future, and extend African representation in some form to the municipal and provincial councils, he might buy ten years in which to persuade the white electorate to adjust to a sharing of power. Much of this was already being considered by the Fagan Commission, appointed before the strike. The Native Affairs Commission was now asked to prepare proposals for constitutional reform; but when Smuts met a group of members of the N.R.C. on 8 May, he was not yet in a position to make them a meaningful offer.

The constitutional plan proposed by the Native Affairs Commission, which resembled Smuts's advice to Hertzog in 1928, was for the democratisation of African government downwards rather than for an extension of African influence upwards. It suggested a council of fifty (as Hertzog had proposed in 1926, only this time all members were to be elective) which was to be the apex of a country-wide representative system, based on General Councils in the Reserves (as established under the Native Affairs Act of 1920), and on an official Location Advisory Boards Congress for the representation of African interests in the urban areas (as distinct from the unofficial congress which had met annually since 1929). But without the Fagan proposals, which were not available until February 1948, the constitutional offer looked singularly meagre, while on the trade union front the Departments of Labour and Native Affairs were still unable to improve on Lansdown. Consequently Smuts's overtures proved unacceptable, and although Smuts urged Parliament in January 1948 not to break off relations with the N.R.C. he gave the Council no real reason for expecting better things at the political level.

The Fagan Report, which was eventually published in February 1948, contained much that was acceptable to moderate black opinion. Its proposals for a Union-wide system of labour bureaux, which might eventually provide a substitute for influx control, can be traced back to the Smit Report. Its proposals for the stabilisation of African labour in the towns, which meant encouraging workers to bring their families with them, was an idea which the N.R.C. had been pressing very hard. Fagan did not think that the system of migrant labour could be legislated out of existence, or stopped by administrative decree, any more than he thought stabilisation of labour could be forced on employers. But he urged that they be encouraged to experiment, for example on the new O.F.S. goldfields. At the same time, his recommendation that villages should be built in the Reserves for the concentrated settlement of the landless aroused apprehensions on account of the overcrowding of the Reserves and the constant demand of the white farmers to be relieved of their black squatters. On the pass laws, the Fagan Report was strangely equivocal, for it recommended the retention of passes as a control device, while at the same time proposing that under the new name of identity cards they should be voluntarily applied for on account of the security in employment which they were to be made to provide. The Report did recommend a change of direction, as Smit had done in 1942. It represented the most considered view of which the combined thinking of the Smuts ministry, prodded by the Natives' Representatives, were capable under conditions of extreme political stress. Published two years earlier, in time to enable the Government to put some of its ideas into practice, there was an outside chance that it might have changed the direction of South African policy; but appearing so near the end of the Government's term, with none of its recommendations yet tested in practice or in public debate, it offered the electorate a liberal aspiration rather than a policy, and if the choice for voters was between aspirations, the Sauer Report of the Nationalists, with its early spelling out of the gospel of *apartheid*, seemed to offer more security on more familiar lines.

The N.R.C. was demanding 'a policy which recognizes that Africans are citizens of this country and not things apart'. How to give content to such an aspiration was the difficulty which the Smuts Government could not surmount. It required that they should take a chance on the good faith of the black man, and assume that the moderate leadership of black political opinion both meant what it said and was able to hold in check such radical elements as there were in their rank and file. They saw this as at best an open question, for the mood of the black political organisations was far more purposeful after 1945 than it had been before 1940.

When Dr A. B. Xuma became president-general of the A.N.C. in December 1940, he worked hard to transform it into an efficient, centralised national body. He refused to allow provincial branches to step out of line in the formulation of electoral policy, as the Cape Congress discovered in 1942, and stepped in to take over the running of the Transvaal Congress when rifts developed among its members on ideological grounds. Under his supervision, Congress adopted a new constitution in December 1943, which allowed it to include people of other races, eliminated the House of Chiefs (which had proved largely ineffective, especially since the Native Affairs Department had discouraged chiefs from participation in Congress activities), provided for the election of the secretary and treasurer by a free vote at the annual conference, instead of from a list submitted by the provincial presidents, and set up a working committee consisting of members living within fifty miles of the national headquarters, with power to take day-to-day decisions. The 1942 conference initiated a million-member campaign. This failed to achieve its object because the A.N.C. could not sustain its drive, owing to the fickle and uneven enthusiasms of its local organisers; but it was good for Congress morale. Another of Xuma's contributions was to introduce regularity into Congress's accounting procedures. It never became a wealthy organisation, and the balance of £800 which it achieved on one occasion was hardly enough to sustain any kind of political campaign; but the fact that it could collect subscriptions and have them transferred to the centre made it potentially a force to be reckoned with.

On the propaganda front, Xuma's A.N.C. encouraged the hope of better times in the post-war years. The 1942 conference empowered Xuma to set up a committee to study the Atlantic Charter and draft a Bill of Rights to present to the peace conference at the end of the war. Xuma interested some thirty leading African intellectuals in the task, and aroused public interest by inviting individuals to submit essays for the committee to consider. Professor Z. K. Matthews of Fort Hare was chairman of the committee, which included conservatives like Selope Thema and Richard Godlo, and left-wingers like Kotane, Marks and Mofutsanyana. The Bill of Rights which they eventually issued demanded the 'freedom of the African people from all discriminatory laws whatsoever', as well as something very like adult suffrage – a more ambitious claim than the 'equitable' representation asked for in 1919, or the 'equal rights for all civilized men' asked for in an earlier bill of rights in 1923. The pamphlet *African Claims*, which embodied this Bill of Rights, was adopted by conference in December 1943, but turned down by the Government as unrealistic. It was, however, a demand couched in the moderate language of western liberal thinking.

As was the case with the Afrikaner Nationalists, who divided over the rival merits of parliamentary methods and direct action, so the African Nationalists, for whom the option of parliamentary methods was scarcely available, tended to divide into those who relied on the Natives' Representatives and the N.R.C., supported by well-signed petitions and deputations, and those who wanted to force the hand of the Government by strikes, boycotts and passive resistance. In the first group fell nearly every member of the N.R.C., with a few possible exceptions like Dr J. S. Moroka, together with the 'old guard' of the A.N.C., Xuma himself included. In the second group were the Communists, who had opposed South Africa's entry into the war in 1939, while taking care to remain aloof from the Nationalists, but changed their tune when Soviet Russia, the 'motherland of socialism', was attacked by the Germans in June 1941. But they failed to make much headway with the A.N.C., who rejected their anti-war stand just as the Communists rejected the exclusive Africanism of some A.N.C. elements. Though prepared to go some way with a Non-European Unity Movement, supported by the A.A.C. and a section of the Coloured people, the Communist Party (which had a small white membership) could not persuade these bodies to become involved in direct action and mass demonstrations, while on the political front it had no success save when Sam Kahn and Betty Radford were elected to the Cape Town city council in 1943.

Between these extremes stood the African Democratic Party of Paul Mosaka and Self Mampuru, founded in 1943 with the encouragement of Senator H. M. Basner, a provocative ex-Communist Natives' Representative for the Transvaal and Orange Free State. It developed loose Trotskyite leanings (largely as a result of a conflict with the Communists) but never developed a policy of boycott, never pressed for Non-European unity, and maintained friendly contact with whites through liberal bodies like the Institute of Race Relations and the Friends of Africa; but it soon wilted before the attacks of Xuma, who, with the instincts of a Malan, berated it for trying to divide African loyalties and took care that the Transvaal A.N.C. did not fall into its hands.

The A.N.C. Youth League, established in 1943–4, differed both in calibre and objective from the A.D.P. Its founders were for the most part products of the mission schools, as the original founders of the A.N.C. had been, talented professional men in their early manhood, some still trainees. Their posture was originally anti-communist, the committee which drafted their manifesto recording 'the need for vigilance against Communists and other groups which foster non-African interests'. The group originally came together to lobby for Self Mampuru as Transvaal A.N.C. presidential candidate in 1943, before Mampuru joined the A.D.P. It owed something, too, to Xuma's encouragement in December 1943, though Champion's warning that a youth league would destroy Xuma's presidency seemed prophetic when the group attacked Xuma's new constitution at the 1943 conference as 'collaborationist'. The group consisted of the charismatic Anton Lembede, who was to die aged only 33 in 1947, and many who acquired celebrity in later years, notably Jordan Ngubane (who later joined the Liberals), W. F. Nkomo (a doctor attracted to Moral Re-armament, whose long career ended when he died in office as president of the S.A. Institute of Race Relations in 1972), Walter Sisulu and Nelson Mandela (who were sentenced to life imprisonment in 1963 for their part in the Rivonia conspiracy), A. P. Mda and Robert Sobukwe (men of strong 'Africanist' inclinations, one the brains of the movement, the other the founder of the Pan-Africanist Congress in 1959), the lawyer Duma Nokwe, Joseph Matthews (son of Z. K. Matthews), Congress Mbata, the others. In March 1944 the Youth League published its Manifesto, a document designed to make Africans prize unity and maintain high standards of conduct, Christian by implication. They aimed, says Johns, to become an élitist pressure group within the A.N.C., analogous to the Afrikaner Broederbond. Not until 1949, when their Programme of Action was endorsed by the A.N.C. conference proper, did the Youth League commit itself to challenging white power, and this was after the League had witnessed the actions of the Indian passive resisters in Natal. The League subscribed to the slogan 'Africa for the Africans', and like the Afrikaner Bond's 'Afrika voor de Afrikaanders' in the early 1880s, the phrase was not given a narrow ethnic interpretation by League spokesmen. The idea of driving whites into the sea was explicitly disavowed, though the League expected whites to accept majority rule.

The Cape Coloured people, left unscathed by Hertzog's legislation of 1936–7, were awakened by the Smuts Government's decision to set up a Coloured Affairs Department in 1943. The decision to administer them as a separate people gave birth to Dr Gool's National Anti-CAD movement to campaign for the abolition of the Department and its new Coloured Advisory Council. The Anti-CAD looked to the A.A.C. as the agency to bring all non-Europeans together to resist further erosion of their rights. The A.A.C.'s triennial conference in December 1940 had tried to establish a committee to coordinate its activities with those of the A.N.C. but a year later its leaders objected to a scheme to make the A.A.C. a mere coordinating body for all manner of African organisations, while the A.N.C. concentrated on politics. Consequently the A.N.C. and the A.A.C. stayed apart even though men like Z. R. Mahabane were office-bearers in both.

A.A.C. and Anti-CAD delegates held a 'unity conference' in Bloemfontein after the A.A.C.'s triennial conference of December 1943, and drew up a Ten-Point Programme, which was not so much a programme of action as a list of demands, including demands for political power and a fairer division of the land. They hoped to bring the Indian Congresses to the conference; but the Natal Indian leaders were currently engaged in their own battle with the Union Government over the Pegging Act of 1943, and still attempting under A. I. Kajee's leadership to win concessions by a policy of non-provocation. The Indians therefore agreed to cooperate on specific issues such as the pass laws, the Pegging Act or the Coloured Advisory Council, and rejected an attempt to make the whole Ten-Point Programme the basis of an alliance. They stayed away from the Second Unity Conference in July 1944. Although they attended the third in January 1945, they never built up a close association with the Non-European Unity Movement, as the A.A.C.–Anti-CAD alliance had come to be called, and eventually found their closest ties were with the A.N.C. This was partly because the N.E.U.M., consisting largely of Coloured intellectuals who wanted to direct and broaden the ambitions of the potentially much more powerful African nationalists, preferred to take part in peaceful protests well within the law, rather than to defy the law by means of organised passive resistance. It was primarily in their mutual preparedness to defy the law that the Indian congresses and the A.N.C. found that they could make common cause; but this became true only after the radicals under Y. Dadoo and G. M. Naicker had captured the Indian congresses in late 1945, and set in motion the Indians' passive resistance campaign.

At the beginning of the war, when it was rumoured that the Transvaal land and trading legislation affecting Indians was to be extended to Natal, the Natal Indian leaders put pressure on the Government to settle questions of property transfer informally, and to this end a Committee under H. G. Lawrence was appointed in March 1940.[4] But pressure from Durban whites induced the Government to appoint an Indian Penetration Commission under Judge Broome in May. In his first report, Broome found no significant penetrations by Indians in any area of Natal or the Transvaal which could be said to have precipitated a white exodus. His second report, published in 1943, demonstrated that there had been a significant Indian takeover of a small section of the Durban Berea, though for investment rather than residential purposes. What it did not make clear was that this was an area of 'white' Durban which the building societies had decided to regard as suitable for Indian settlement, and where they were therefore prepared to advance loans, and that the Indian population of Durban, which was not far short of the white in total numbers, owned a mere 4 per cent of the land in the Old Borough.

Against this background, the Government's decision to introduce 'pegging' legislation in April 1943 (shortly before the general election) caused a sharp reaction. All white-Indian property transactions in Durban were to be frozen for three years, and the Transvaal land legislation extended for a similar period. Objections were widespread, and Hofmeyr, the Deputy Prime Minister, contemplated resignation. The Natal Indian Congress protested vigorously. The Government of India protested, got nowhere, and began to consider economic sanctions against the Union. The South African Government immediately tried to damp down the crisis by putting Judge Broome at the head of another commission to investigate the 'uplift' provisions of the Cape Town Agreement, and as a result of a compromise gesture by the N.I.C., sponsored by A. I. Kajee and P. R. Pather, the Pegging Act was suspended in terms of the Pretoria Agreement of 18 April 1944, whereby a board consisting of two whites, two Indians and a lawyer as chairman was to control inter-racial property transactions. This, however, proved no more than a brief respite. The Natal Provincial Council was allowed under the agreement to legislate to prohibit whites and Indians living next to each other. It accordingly drafted an ordinance, which was withdrawn after N.I.C. objections. It drew up a second, to which whites took exception. Its third attempt, a Residential Property Regulation Draft Ordinance, was regarded by the N.I.C. as a violation of the Pretoria Agreement in that it provided for the control of purchase by Indians, whereas the Pretoria Agreement was concerned only with occupation, and because it extended beyond Durban. The Natal Provincial Council was also seeking to restrict Indians in other ways, by means of Housing Board and Expropriation ordinances which were enacted with the Residential Property Ordinance in November 1944. So sharp was the public outcry that the Broome Commission found it could no longer hold public hearings. The Indian Government immediately began to apply retaliatory legislation against white South Africans. A deputation of the N.I.C. saw Smuts at the end of the month, drawing from him the comment that the Pretoria Agreement was now 'stone dead'. Shortly afterwards the N.I.C. split into a militant section under Dr G. M. Naicker and a moderate under Kajee and Pather, who later broke away to form the Natal Indian Organization. Smuts's response to the collapse of the Pretoria Agreement was to introduce new legislation in March 1946, the Asiatic Land Tenure and Indian Representation Bill, which would restrict Indian ownership and occupation to particular 'uncontrolled' areas of Natal, but attempt to buy their support back by an ironic reversal of Hertzog's tactic with the Africans – the offer of token political representation in place of land rights: three white representatives in the Assembly and two in the Senate, plus two provincial councillors who could be Indians.

The N.I.C. scorned the offer and went for world-wide publicity for its cause, through the Government of India and the United Nations. When the Union Government refused to alter its course and allowed the 'Ghetto Act' to become law, the N.I.C. began a passive resistance campaign, when some two thousand went to prison for squatting in batches on a vacant 'controlled' site in Durban. It was during this passive resistance campaign that the N.I.C. leaders began to find common cause with African and Coloured movements. In March 1947 a 'Joint Declaration of Co-operation' was drawn up by Naicker of the N.I.C., Dadoo of the T.I.C., and Xuma of the A.N.C., to work together for full franchise rights, equal industrial rights, the removal of land restrictions, the extension of free compulsory education to all non-Europeans, freedom of movement (involving the abolition of passes for Africans and of restrictions on inter-provincial travel for Indians), and the removal of all discriminatory legislation.

It was unfortunate for the United Party, but fortunate for the Nationalists, that the development of robust opposition by African, Coloured and Indian elements should have occurred at the same time as the beginning of the Government's serious difficulties on the international front. Together they created the strong impression that the Government could not control the situation, and when the results of the general election on 26 May 1948 became known, Malan's Nationalists had won 70 seats to 65 by the U.P., 9 by the Afrikaner Party and 6 by Labour. The Nationalists had in fact prepared the ground far better than their opponents. In place of the latter's cumbersome campaign organisation of provincial head committees and regional general councils, they had a small steering committee consisting of the provincial party leaders only; they had professional organisers in place of the U.P.'s reliance on voluntary help; and they had an active cell system, copied from the O.B. in 1941, as against the relatively inactive branch system of the U.P. The lethargy of the U.P. organisers was noted by its candid friends before the election, but the lesson does not seem to have been appreciated sufficiently, even by Smuts himself.

The Nationalists had also prepared the ground politically by reversing their stand of 1943 and entering into an electoral pact with Havenga and the Afrikaner Party. There was still tension within Afrikanerdom over the role of the A.P.'s allies, the O.B., whom some, like Verwoerd and Dönges, wanted to conciliate, while others, notably Diederichs and Albert Hertzog, did not. The Broederbond itself was divided. According to B. M. Schoeman, when Malan and Havenga met to discuss terms in March 1947, Havenga at first insisted that all political groups, including the O.B. and the New Order group, should be included, and that Verwoerd should be removed from the editorship of the *Transvaler.* But he ended by agreeing with Malan that the Afrikaner Party, which was to be allowed to contest eleven seats, would not put up any candidates who held prominent posts in the O.B. Friction resulted when it chose an O.B. General, B. J. Vorster, as its candidate for Brakpan. He therefore stood as an independent, but was narrowly beaten by A. E. Trollip, the U.P. candidate. Havenga's support not only ensured that O.B. votes would be cast for the Nationalist candidates, thus avoiding triangular contests, but it enabled the Nationalists to form a government with A.P. support when the election was over. Further, by starting negotiations with Havenga as early as March 1947, Malan had minimised the possibility of Havenga's followers drifting closer to the U.P. E. G. Malherbe urged Smuts to persuade Havenga to change sides after the general election was over; but at that stage it was too late to make the attempt. Against this alliance between Malan and Havenga, a similar agreement reached between the U.P. and the Labour Party was of relatively little significance.

Although the Smuts Government had successfully won the war to its credit, and demobilised its military volunteers efficiently, on the domestic front some resented the slow progress of its housing programme, others the lack of tax relief for wage-earners in Hofmeyr's budgets, others the irritations of wartime controls on food distribution. More seriously, its racial policies aroused opposition. Where they were illiberal, they came under pressure at the U.N. In so far as they were either liberal or unsuccessful, the Nationalists knew how to capitalise on this, and set out to convince the electorate that the U.P. either consorted with or was not tough enough with the Communists, and that the Communists were a danger to South Africa. They fastened their attention on the Springbok Legion (the more socialist-inclined of the two main ex-servicemen's organisations), and on Jan Hofmeyr, the Deputy Prime Minister and Smuts's presumed successor, as a man of dangerous liberal purposes. With the help of a dedicated press and some brilliant cartoonists, they won the propaganda battle even though their opponents had a call on the loyalties of newspapers with far greater circulations. They won this battle, in the second place, because they stripped their policy of its prickly attributes, explicitly refrained from asking for a mandate for a Republic, stressed their change of front in the matter of the rights of English-speakers, and undertook to honour all obligations entered into by the Smuts regime towards ex-servicemen.

They also launched on the electorate their new doctrine of *apartheid*, which was really Hertzogian segregation elevated to the status of a system, but also modified in certain particulars.[5] The Malanites had not agreed with all aspects of Hertzog's policy in 1936–7, standing out in particular against the continued presence of Coloured people on the Cape electoral roll, against the purchase of more land for Africans in released areas by the State (as distinct from purchase by individuals), and against the watering down of the provision in the Native Laws Amendment Bill of 1937 to prohibit the establishment of churches and schools for Africans in white urban areas. According to M. D. C. de Wet Nel, who later became a leading exponent of the doctrine as Minister of Bantu Administration under Dr Verwoerd, the *apartheid* concept originated in the mid-1930s, among Afrikaner intellectuals who wanted some 'vertical' separation of the races and founded a *Suid-Afrikaanse Bond vir Rassestudie* (South African League for Racial Studies) in 1935, with Mrs E. G. Jansen as chairman and De Wet Nel himself as secretary. During the war years, as racial integration speeded up, the Nationalist intellectuals worked hard on the problem. From 1946 the *Burger* became, in N. J. Rhoodie's words 'the mass-ventilator of apartheid theory', while active thinkers like Professor G. A. Cronje of the University of Pretoria, who published *'n Tuiste vir die Nageslag* ('A Home for Posterity') in 1945 and *Regverdige Rasse-apartheid* ('Justifiable Race Separation') in 1947, helped create the intellectual climate for the founding of the *S.A. Buro vir Rasse Aangeleenthede* (South African Bureau for Racial Affairs, S.A.B.R.A.) in 1948. Meanwhile, with a view to the general election, the National Party appointed a committee under P. O. Sauer to draft an *apartheid* policy. The Sauer Report converted the *apartheid* concept into a political programme, though much detail still needed to be supplied.

At the time of the general election, the Malanites stood for a policy which treated the Reserves as the proper homelands of the African population, where their welfare agencies should so far as possible be concentrated, and where alone they would properly enjoy rights of citizenship, under a political system based on the example of the Transkei Bunga, only with more safeguards for the power of the chiefs. Educational facilities were to be separate at all levels for all groups. African administration was in all matters to be canalised through the Department of Native Affairs, even African education; and Coloured administration similarily, through a Coloured Affairs Department. There was also to be segregation for Coloured people with regard to residence, amenities, transport, education and politics. Indians were to be restricted in all ways legally possible, and their repatriation stepped up. The strength of the Nationalist manifesto lay in its simplicity, and in its appeal to the voters' desire for security in a world which seemed to be moving too fast in a liberal direction and turning its wrath against South Africa as it did so. Its weakness, considered as a contribution to South African development, lay in the way in which it made the country's problems seem easier to resolve than they were, and in the way it rode roughshod over the feelings and the dignity of those who were at the receiving end of the policy. In this it differed in degree and direction, rather than in kind, from the policies which had gone before.

# Section II

# The Designing of a New Model State, 1948–76

# 14 The Age of the Social Engineers, 1948–60

Dr Malan's coalition Government was the first fully bilingual government in the history of the Union, and the first to consist of Afrikaners only. Its members had resolutely opposed taking part in the war against Nazi Germany. It was not easy under these circumstances for ex-soldiers and English-speakers to see that some members of the ruling party had been less attracted to Nazism than others; nor was it easy for the Nationalists, who had been bred on resentment at the treatment of their own people by Imperial Britain, to understand the revulsion with which their wartime attitude was regarded by Europeans (Continental as well as British) who had suffered as a result of the war.

From the start, parliamentary relations between the Government and the Opposition got off on the wrong foot.[1] The Government broke with tradition by failing to consult with the Opposition over the choice of a Speaker. In the first two sessions of the new Parliament, despite the care taken by Malan to reassure English-speakers that they were not destined to second-class citizenship, the Government took steps to weaken their dependence on the Commonwealth association. A United Party plan to recruit British immigrants was immediately suspended, and although the Government sponsored white immigration again after a short interval, it tried to give Continental Europeans at least equivalent encouragement. The South African Citizenship Bill of 1949 resulted in an acrimonious series of debates because, though Canada and Great Britain had both revised their own citizenship legislation, the South African measure made it considerably harder for immigrants to acquire citizenship, and as expensive for them to do so as it had been in Kruger's Republic between 1890 and 1899. It also narrowed almost to vanishing point the advantage previously enjoyed by British subjects (including all white citizens of the Commonwealth) over aliens. This seemed ominous to English-speakers, in view of the development of separatist republicanism in J. G. Strijdom's wing of the National Party. The Strijdom challenge was in fact a serious matter. He rejected the stand taken by Malan, made possible by a decision taken at the Prime Ministers' Conference of 1949, that South Africa should become a Republic and stay within the Commonwealth. Their disagreement lasted until the middle of 1951, when Malan and Strijdom were persuaded to agree that the issues of Republican status and Commonwealth membership were separable, and that the latter should be considered in the light of circumstances when the Republic was introduced.

The new Government also showed from the start that it intended to check and eliminate the trends towards inter-racial integration.[2] One can distinguish here between legislation to establish distinct biological categories among the population groups, and legislation to prevent their residential mixing when the biological sorting had been done. The Prohibition of Mixed Marriages Act of 1949, which made all future marriages between whites and members of other groups illegal, rested on a Hertzogian precedent banning marriages between whites and Africans. It was followed by a Population Registration Act in 1950, designed to allocate everybody to a racial group, and by a stiffening of the Immorality Act to make extramarital intercourse a more serious offence if indulged in across racial frontiers. Later on, when members of all races were required to carry identification documents which clearly stated the race they belonged to, the sorting procedures became more foolproof than they were at first, when they often depended on the impressionistic decisions of officials. But 'trying for white', and the harrowing social consequences which it entailed for the Coloured community through the severing of contact between close kinsfolk, was not eliminated by these new rules.

The Group Areas Bill, introduced by Dr Dönges in 1950, to empower the Government to proclaim residential and business areas for particular race groups, incorporated much of the machinery devised for the restriction of Asians under the Smuts Government's Asiatic Land Tenure Act of 1946. A Land Tenure Advisory Board was created (later renamed the Group Areas Board, and later still the Community Development Board), consisting of white officials responsible to the Minister of the Interior, who could recommend the setting aside of particular areas for the sole ownership or occupation (or both) of particular race groups. Provision was made for representations to be made by local authorities and other interested parties; but the object of the legislation was nothing less than a complete unscrambling of the residential patterns in South African towns. Africans were barely affected, for they were already controlled under the Urban Areas Act. But the Indian and Coloured communities were brought under strong pressure in ways which quickly became apparent. Dönges asserted that he had received many petitions from whites objecting to penetration by Indian and Coloured people into white residential areas, resulting in the depreciation of property values, though he was not prepared to divulge confidential details. When committees of the Land Tenure Advisory

Board later visited towns in the Transvaal and Natal, they were generally presented with proposals by the local authorities for the removal of Indian homes and businesses a mile or more out of town, and occasionally for the elimination of Indian homes and shops altogether. Indian and Coloured opposition to the measure, at both the local and national levels, was intense. The United Party, which opposed the Mixed Marriages Bill at all stages, attacked the Group Areas Bill as well, for its members viewed it either as unnecessary, or as improper, or as likely to lead to unfair speculation in real estate on a grand scale [see pp. 350–1].

The new Government also began to dismantle the political structures set up by the United Party regime to cater for the African, Asian and Coloured peoples. The token enfranchisement of Indians allowed for in Smuts's unpopular package deal of 1946 was reversed with no waste of time in 1948, after Indians had themselves rejected it as inadequate. In 1951, the Government abolished the Native Representative Council, which had persisted in its refusal to do business with the Nationalists, as it had previously with the United Party.

The Nationalists wanted to remove the Coloured voters in the Cape from the common roll, but they met resistance from Havenga, who, out of loyalty to Hertzog, did not favour such action save on the basis of a statutory two-thirds majority in a joint sitting of Parliament. He apparently felt that if the constitutional objections to the creation of a separate roll for Coloured people were met, the question of a branch of trust did not arise. The constitutional point did not in itself trouble Malan. He accepted the view of the Government's law advisers that the decision of the Appeal Court in Ndlwana's Case (1937) was definitive, and that after the passage of the Statute of Westminster the Union Parliament was sovereign over its own affairs, and therefore able to ignore the special procedures laid down for the amendment of the entrenched voting rights of the Coloured people. But rather than override Havenga, on whose party's votes the Nationalists were still dependent for survival, Malan let the Coloured vote issue lie dormant in 1949. On 14 October 1950 he and Havenga agreed to go ahead with legislation the following year, to place the Coloured voters on a separate roll with power to elect four members to the Assembly, one to the Senate, and two to the Cape Provincial Council – whites only in the first two categories, but not explicitly so in the last, for on Malan's insistence it was decided in caucus to leave this detail unresolved. A Separate Representation of Voters Bill was duly published and introduced by Dönges in the Assembly on 8 March 1951. On 10 April the Speaker rejected the Opposition's submission that a joint sitting was necessary under the constitution, and the Bill went through all stages as a bicameral measure, to receive the Governor-General's assent on

15 June. A group of Coloured voters, however, contested the legislation. They lost their case before the Cape Provincial Division, but were vindicated by the unanimous decision of the Appellate Division in *Harris* v. *Dönges* on 20 March 1952. The court fully accepted the validity of Stratford's earlier judgment in Ndlwana's case where the sovereignty of Parliament was concerned, confirming that as a sovereign body Parliament could legislate in any manner it chose; but it also insisted that, in terms of the constitution, Parliament, for purposes of amending the entrenched clauses, could only be defined as a legislative body which functioned unicamerally: if it functioned in any other way, it could not be regarded as Parliament. Strauss moved in the Assembly on 16 April that the judgment of the Appellate Division be accepted; but the Government was unable to accept such a rebuff, and on the 22nd Dönges moved a Bill for the reconstitution of Parliament itself as a High Court with power to review all cases in which the Appellate Division declared legislation invalid. Despite Opposition protests, this legislation was then taken through all stages; but the same four Coloured voters appealed against this law too. The 'High Court of Parliament' duly sat in Pretoria and solemnly set aside the Appeal Court's judgment on 25 August, but the High Court itself was declared invalid by the Cape Provincial Division on the 29th, and subsequently by the Appellate Division on 13 November. The judges had no hesitation in rejecting such a court, as badly conceived in history as it was in law, and the Government discreetly dropped this constitutional fantasy.

Malan could then have forced the issue by interfering with the judges or by packing Parliament, or he could have worked to obtain a two-thirds majority and thus lift the vote legislation above legal controversy. What he could not do, having once accepted the jurisdiction of the courts, was to ignore that jurisdiction and proceed with the disfranchisement of the Coloured voters. He decided to use the Coloured vote as a platform for the 1953 general election. He did not get his two-thirds majority that way, but his government survived a tough confrontation.

The Nationalists had already increased their bare majority in Parliament by creating six new seats for South West Africa in the lower House and four in the Senate – ingeniously, without incorporating the territory in defiance of the Mandate – and then winning them. But they were now confronted by the War Veterans' Torch Commando, an ex-servicemen's extra-parliamentary movement which was established in April 1951 by Louis Kane-Berman, 'Sailor' Malan (an ex-Battle of Britain ace pilot) and others, explicitly to oppose the Government's Coloured vote policy. It achieved a paid-up membership which ran into six figures, and showed that it could bring very large crowds together to protest against the Government's policy. By joining a United

Democratic Front with the United and Labour Parties in April 1952, it was within reach of being able to endow the political Opposition with a winning combination of organising skill, political dedication, and an incisive political programme which catered for the main traditional fears of the white electorate without shedding the idealist mood of the post-war world or losing sight of the demand that in a politico-moral crisis right had to be done. But its political campaign became blunted. Rioting, followed by injury to well over a hundred people, occurred in the wake of a procession to Parliament to deliver a protest petition to Dr Malan on 28 May 1951. The angry exchanges between the Government and the Opposition which followed failed to establish how far this was the work of the Torch's supporters, and how far the work of provocateurs, but enabled the Government to brand it as a force for anarchy. The Torch, having taken up the political cause of the Coloured people, failed to agree over the admission of Coloured people as members, with the result that in November 1951 the Coloured ex-servicemen withdrew. It also allowed itself to be drawn into the politics of Natal separatism, which arose again over the Government's threat to ignore the spirit of the constitution, and this in turn weakened its links with the United Party. It also made the mistake of trying to split the Nationalists by attributing their racism to Nazi influences, which was an ineffective tactic because so much of it was traditional white South African practice. Moving on to the scene in force to help the U.P. in a by-election at Wakkerstroom in June 1952, the Torch failed to prevent the Nationalists from increasing their majority. The same year it failed to win U.P. support for its determined lobbying of the Tenth Delimitation Commission in favour of equal constituencies. The U.P. preferred, as Smuts himself had done in 1947, to propose a slight loading of the urban seats in the vain hope that the more radical loading proposed by the Nationalists would be rejected by the three judges of the Commission. When, after all this, the Nationalists won the general election in April 1953 with an increased majority, taking 94 seats to the U.P.'s 58 and Labour's 4, the Torch Commando faded out. Its divided spirit lived on in the U.P. and in two new political parties, both formed in May 1953: the Union Federal Party, with its main base in Natal and the devolution of political power as its main platform; and the Liberal Party, which aimed to establish a common South African citizenship irrespective of race.

Malan's Nationalists monopolised the government benches after the 1953 election, for after the Nationalist and Afrikaner Parties had formally merged in October 1951, all the former A.P. members save Havenga were eliminated at the nomination meetings. The Government claimed that the increase in their following gave them a mandate to go ahead with their Coloured vote legislation, even though they still did not have a two-thirds majority. Undaunted, Malan announced a joint sitting for 14 July. He let it be known that if the requisite majority were not forthcoming, the Government would legislate to amend the constitution of the Appeal Court. Despite this threat, he was still sixteen votes short at the third reading on 16 September. An Appellate Division Quorum Bill was therefore introduced on the 18th by Swart, its purpose being to expand the court and divide it into three separate panels for constitutional, civil and criminal appeals. But rather than proceed with the second reading as planned on 28 September, Malan unexpectedly postponed the debate, reconvened a joint sitting on the Coloured vote Bill on 1 October, and immediately had that legislation referred to a Joint Select Committee. His tactic now was to try to persuade dissidents in the U.P. to vote with the Government on an agreed measure, and thus defuse the constitutional crisis. A small group of U.P. members led by Bailey Bekker and Arthur Barlow showed signs of willingness to compromise with the Government, provided Coloured Voters then on the common roll were left on it. Despite a great deal of opposition in the Nationalist caucus, which they handled firmly, Malan and Dönges, who were confident of a majority in the Cabinet, decided to make a deal with the U.P. rebels. But this gamble did not pay. Malan had reckoned without Strauss, who saw his own leadership of the U.P. threatened, and reacted by urging his party to rethink the fundamentals of its race policy, and in doing so to take a stand on the moral as well as the constitutional issues at stake. The United Party stood almost solid and the Joint Select Committee therefore reached deadlock when it began its work in February 1954. Even though the Bill which it produced for the consideration of yet another joint sitting in May was tailored to meet the susceptibilities of the Bekker group, half of whom supported it, it failed by nine votes to obtain a two-thirds majority on 14 June. Malan apparently began to consider the enlargement of the Senate as a way out of the deadlock at this stage, but his own resignation from office on 30 November left the next step in the hands of his successor.

All non-white groups – Coloured, Africans and Indian – had grounds for feeling that their interests were under attack under Nationalist rule, to an even greater extent than they had been under previous regimes.[8] In face of this pressure, twelve African leaders, of whom half belonged to the Representative Council, met at Bloemfontein in October 1948 and issued a 'Call for African Unity'. The A.N.C. was represented by Xuma, Matthews, Bokwe, Godlo, Baloyi, Champion and Thema; the A.D.P. by Mosaka; and the A.A.C. by Jabavu, Moroka, Ntlabati and Mahabane; but although it was decided to adopt the Youth League proposal to start a 'mass struggle for national freedom', the meeting was divided over organisation and aims. In December Xuma and Jabavu met again to work out a basis for amalgamation between the A.N.C. and the A.A.C.; but negotiations broke down in

April 1949 after the A.A.C. had elected W. M. Tsotsi as its new president. The A.N.C. leaders wanted an all-African body, and the A.A.C. a federation which African, Coloured and Indian organisations could all join. In July, the Youth League published a Programme of Action, which rejected the use of petitions and deputations to the Government, and proposed the use of direct action through boycotts, strikes and civil disobedience. Despite reservations on the part of older Statesmen, the Programme of Action was endorsed by the A.N.C. annual conference in December, when the change of policy was marked by the election of Moroka, the Youth League's candidate, in place of Xuma as President-General. Although there were three Communists on the A.N.C. executive at the time (Tloome, Marks and Kotane), the decision of the A.N.C. to go over to some form of direct action seems to have resulted mainly from a failure to discover any alternative form of action which stood a chance of succeeding. Direct action required the kind of know-how which the Communists had already aquired in previous confrontations. Success also required the sinking of differences between Africans and other racial groups, and that too was a Communist objective.

How deep those differences could be was shown by the Durban riots of January 1949, when 142 people were killed and over a thousand injured, after an African youth had struck an Indian shop assistant, whose employer in turn beat and inflicted accidental injury on the youth near a crowded bus terminus at the end of the working day. The riots exposed a serious measure of tension between the two black communities in Durban, for which a variety of explanations were offered, some stressing Indian commercial exploitation, others urban African indiscipline, yet others the oppressiveness of the social situation in which Durban's black folk found themselves. But if the riot was a tragic episode, the black leaders – Champion and Xuma in particular on the African side, and Naicker and Dadoo on the Indian – were able to use it as the starting point of a new relationship between their respective communities, and in the new atmosphere the African and Indian congresses began to work cautiously together on a basis of non-violent non-cooperation with the authorities, towards the partnership which led in 1952 to the launching of a joint Defiance Campaign.

Having by its policies precipitated an association between the black nationalists and the Communists, the Government then attempted to eliminate the latter. This task was allocated to C. R. Swart. On becoming Minister of Justice in 1948, he appointed a Departmental Committee to investigate the influence of communism in South Africa, and told the Assembly in February 1949 that it had indeed found communism to be a 'national danger'. In May 1950, he brought in an Unlawful Organizations Bill, at first not explicitly directed against

Communists; but it was soon withdrawn and replaced by a Suppression of Communism Bill designed to grant the minister very wide powers to deal with communism and a good deal else besides. This was one of a series of measures over the next few years which, on the plea of national security, ignored the principles of civil liberty on which the public law of South Africa was theoretically grounded. It made the Communist Party unlawful. It empowered the Minister of Justice to declare any kindred organisations unlawful too, and to 'name' the office-bearers and active supporters of such bodies (subject to their right to make contrary representations), and to prohibit named persons from taking part in their activities. He could also restrict the movements of named persons and prohibit any gatherings likely in his view to further the ends of communism. The Bill defined communism to mean not only Marxist-Leninism, but also 'any related form of that doctrine' which sought to establish the dictatorship of the proletariat, or to bring about 'any political, industrial, social or economic change within the Union by the promotion of disturbances or disorder', whether in association with a 'foreign government' or not, or by encouraging hostility between Europeans and non-Europeans. Both sides of the House, with the exception of one Communist member, Kahn, and at best a small handful of others, were antagonistic towards communism. This was not surprising in a society where wealth was so unevenly divided and at a time when the intensification of the cold war made Communist activity appear particularly subversive. The Opposition based its resistance, not on any defence of communism itself, but on the implied violation of civil rights which the Bill contained, in particular the recourse to arbitrary action in place of the usual reliance on the courts. J. G. N. Strauss, who succeeded to the leadership of the Opposition shortly before Smuts's death, confused the issues by introducing a personal amendment which aimed to preserve the role of the courts, yet placed the onus on the accused to show that he was not a Communist, and argued that Communist activities be declared treasonable and liable to the death penalty. The Government, which enjoyed the backing of the Afrikaner Party, stood up to the vigorous opposition of bar councils, English-language newspapers and the S.A.T.L.C. The Communist Party dissolved itself on 20 June 1950, shortly before the Bill was due to become law. It seemed likely that this action would keep its property out of the hands of the liquidator provided for in Swart's Bills, and also make it possible for Kahn and Carneson to keep their seats in the Assembly and the Cape Provincial Council. But in the following year the Government amended the Act to extend the definition of 'communist' to include any who had ever professed communism, and to make its operation retroactive. Kahn and Carneson defended themselves before a select committee on which the United Party had agreed to serve, but were turned out by the House in a straight party vote on 26 May 1952, the United Party opposing such action. Two other Communists, Brian Bunting and Ray Alexander, who were successively elected to follow Kahn in Parliament in 1953, were both prevented from doing so. Meanwhile the Communist *Guardian* was suppressed, to reappear successively as the *Clarion*, the *People's World*, *Advance* and *New Age* until its final spark was extinguished in 1962.

Aided by the Suppression of Communism Act, the Government also began to move against multi-racial trade unions, and more particularly against Communists in their ranks. The establishment of a number of breakaway Afrikaner unions under the auspices of the *Blankewerkers-beskermingsbond* had prepared the way for this, and the S.A.T.L.C. was further weakened in 1949–51 by the secession of several English-speaking craft and other unions, some of them as a result of the passage of the Act. Although some sixteen mixed-racial unions then formed a South African Federation of Trade Unions in a bid to continue their struggle, they could not resist the new ministerial powers effectively, though Solly Sachs, General Secretary of the Garment Workers' Union, immediately defied the ban imposed on him in May 1952 by addressing a public meeting outside the Johannesburg city hall. Over fifty union officials, several of them office-bearers of the S.A.T.L.C., were banned before the end of 1955, and all unions were compelled to segregate their membership in 1957.

It was the Communist Party which initiated the May Day strike of 1950, as a protest against the Unlawful Organizations Bill, and it resulted in the deaths of eighteen Africans following tough counter-measures by the police. It was the kind of incident needed to dispel the mutual suspicion between African nationalists and Communists, the former inclined to believe that the Communists were trying to manipulate the forces of African nationalism in the interests of ideological class warfare from which the Africans might not benefit, the latter tending to regard the Programme of Action as a blueprint for wealthy Africans to squeeze their own people under a free enterprise economy. After the dissolution of the Communist Party on 20 June, however, the organisation of the Day of Mourning called to honour the May dead on 26 June was taken over by the A.N.C. The two sides were beginning to discover that the achievement of their immediate objective, the destruction of unbending white supremacy, did not require complete identification of their ultimate aims.

This was the mood which characterised the outlook of the African, Indian and Coloured groups as they began to prepare for the next major confrontation with the Government, planned to coincide with the tercentenary of Jan van Riebeeck's arrival at the Cape, on 6 April 1952. Mass protest meetings were held in many parts of South Africa on that day, and the A.N.C. and S.A.I.C. capitalised on the enthusiasm aroused by them to set up a Joint Planning Council to organise a more ambitious demonstration on the next 26 June – not a general strike, for which they calculated the African workers to be unprepared, but a civil disobedience campaign on Gandhian lines, aimed at the removal of particular grievances, especially the pass laws, the Group Areas Act, the Coloured vote legislation, the culling of stock in the Reserves. Many Africans and Indians defied the *apartheid* laws. Africans threw away their passes and courted arrest, or invaded the 'Whites Only' public rooms at railway stations; and by mid-December over 8000 people had been arrested, the Africans of the eastern Cape playing a leading role. As had sometimes happened during Gandhi's *satyagrahas*, on which the tactics of the Defiance Campaign seem to have been largely based, violence broke out in some places, twenty-six Africans and six Europeans losing their lives, including a nun in East London, Sister Aidan, who was brutally murdered. Some demonstrators were arrested for occupying premises reserved for whites, and won their cases in the Supreme Court by arguing that separate facilities should be equal. After losing the case of *Rex* v. *Lusu*, however, the Government came back with a Reservation of Separate Amenities Act in 1953, which invalidated this construction. It also carried further draconian legislation – a Public Safety Bill which empowered it to declare a state of emergency over all or parts of South Africa and then to bring in emergency regulations to deal with any contingencies that might arise, and a Criminal Law Amendment Bill which imposed heavy sentences of fines, imprisonment and corporal punishment for breaches of the peace or incitement. Because of the imminence of a general election on 15 April, the United Party did not oppose these bills, though urged to do so by the leaders of the Torch Commando.

The early years of the Malan Ministry were thus marked by bitter conflict, giving an aspect of unrelenting toughness to the face of *apartheid* which hardly tallied with the idealistic image which its devotees wished to foster. Malan himself had little interest in native policy, and significantly neglected this topic in his memoirs. The Department of Native Affairs was still controlled by officials appointed by the Smuts Government, notably the Secretary, Dr Gordon Mears, who, with Dr Edgar Brookes on the Native Affairs Commission, continued to maintain the liberal approach they had held during the previous administration. The Minister himself, Dr E. G. Jansen, who had previously held this portfolio under Hertzog between 1929 and 1933, was not an ideologue. His policy statements in the Senate in 1949 and 1950 were almost empty of the jargon of *apartheid*; his approach was flexible, and he seemed mainly concerned with practical administrative problems, notably the rehabilitation of the Reserves and the shortage of housing in the townships. The native affairs group in the Nationalist caucus, however, consisting of men such as M. D. C. de Wet Nel, P. W. Botha, W. A. Maree, and Albert Hertzog, began to agitate for Jansen's removal, and his replacement by the dedicated Dr H. F. Verwoerd, whose omission from the Cabinet had angered some Transvalers. In self-defence, Jansen did get rid of Mears and Brookes; but the crusaders of *apartheid* won their way, and Malan, after appointing another *apartheid* enthusiast, W. W. M. Eiselen, to succeed Mears, brought Verwoerd into the Cabinet as Minister of Native Affairs on 18 October 1950. The atmosphere and the pace of the Native Affairs Department now began to change.

As chairman of the Bantu Education Commission appointed in 1949, Eiselen moved against the control over African schooling achieved by the Christian missions, Catholic and Protestant, after over a century of work in the field. In its Report, tabled in 1951, the Commission argued the case for a separate educational system for the Bantu, controlled by the central government rather than the provinces, and – in contradistinction to Hofmeyr's reform of 1945 – by the Department of Native Affairs rather than by the Union Department of Education. It also argued a differential syllabus for Africans, designed to prepare them for their special place in society, rather than give them what Heaton Nicholls had described in 1937 as 'a little clerkly instruction in individualism'. This meant, as Eiselen saw it, a greater emphasis on the use of the vernacular medium than was practised in any colonial territory in Africa, so as to anchor the African child in his own culture, combined with basic instruction in both the official languages and special emphasis on manual training, to provide an avenue to employment in the white-controlled economy.

Verwoerd did not lag behind Jansen in noting the measure of distress in the Reserves and the urban locations. By 1952 he was beginning to expound a coordinated long-term policy to deal with it, undertaking to show the Senate 'how the various Acts, Bills and also public statements which I have made all fit into a pattern, and together form a single constructive plan'. He wanted to establish economic farming units in the Reserves, cultivated by 'full-time stock-farmers or agriculturists' producing for the market and resale to 'large non-farming native communities in the native areas' engaged in 'the rural type of urban development'. He had appointed a socio-economic commission under F. R. Tomlinson to look into this, as well as an Inter-Departmental Committee to investigate the location of industry near the Reserves so as to cut down the black invasion of white urban areas. Two other Departmental Committees were investigating ways of reducing livestock and exploiting mineral deposits in native areas. Verwoerd also said he was 'training the Bantu for possible forms of self-government, based on their own traditions', and on the principle that 'sound evolution depends on starting with small responsibilities within a limited sphere'.

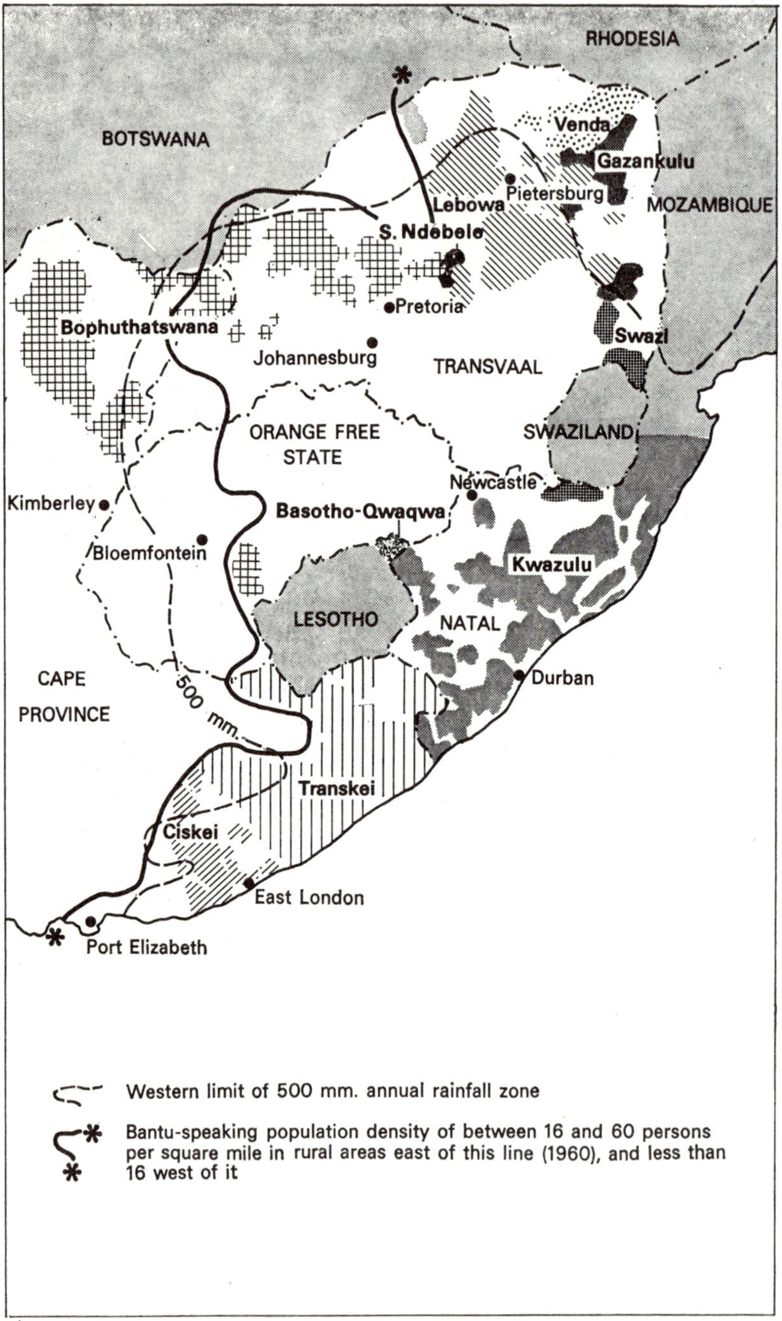


Map 3 African homelands established on the recommendation of the Tomlinson Commission

In place of the Smuts system of 1920, which was in conflict with Hertzog's system of 1927, and in place of Hertzog's N.R.C. which was 'an umbrella authority without proper props to keep it up', he planned a pyramid of Bantu Authorities in town and country, rooted in tribal custom. Starting from the Stallardian position that blacks in white towns could not have political rights, he argued that they could not complain if they were given adequate residential areas, adequate housing, and conditions for an orderly social life. It was therefore necessary to provide 'in every town, and particularly in every industrial area, a potentially comprehensive location site, virtually a native group area', large enough to house all Africans in the area, so that peri-urban and backyard squatting could be eliminated. He elaborated on general conditions to be observed in the siting of locations – above all their separation by a *cordon sanitaire* from the white urban area, and provision of easy rail transport to industrial sites, all of which required planning at the regional as well as municipal levels. He now saw the site-and-service scheme, under which Africans were allowed to build their own homes on surveyed plots, under the supervision of the local authority, which provided water and sanitary removals, as a complete answer to housing difficulties. With home-ownership (but never site-ownership) by Africans as an incentive, there was also a prospect of such housing schemes becoming economic, so that transfers from general municipal revenue to urban location revenue accounts (which in 1950 had amounted altogether to £358,774) could be reduced. Finally, Verwoerd announced a campaign to eliminate black land ownership in white farming areas, and to get rid of African squatting and labour tenancy on white farms through the conversion of all farm workers to wage labourers, and the revision of the anti-squatting provisions of the 1936 Land Act to make it an effective measure.

Verwoerd's policy resulted in a crop of legislation. His Bantu Authorities Act went through Parliament in 1953, though the Urban Bantu Authorities Bill was a casualty of the debates, and became law in a revised form only in 1961. A Prevention of Illegal Squatting Act in 1951 empowered the Minister of Native Affairs to compel Africans to move off public or privately owned land, at the same time authorising local authorities to establish resettlement camps where squatters could be concentrated. The Native Building Workers' Act of 1951 and the Native Services Levy Act of 1952 took care of location housing policy, creating jobs for blacks, thus cutting costs, and ensuring that employers could be made to pay their share in the construction of location housing. The Native Laws Amendment Act of 1952 limited Africans with a right to live permanently in the urban areas to those who were born there, those who had lived there continuously for fifteen years, and those who had worked continuously for the same employer for ten. In the same year a Natives (Abolition of Passes and Coordination of Documents) Act required all Africans (including those exempted under the pass laws, and women for the first time, as well as men) to carry 'reference books' containing their photographs, and information about their places of origin, their employment records, their tax payments and their encounters with the police. This created the means of ensuring that control over African influx into the towns could be exercised. In the Bantu Education Act of 1953, which resulted from the work of the Eiselen Commission two years earlier, the Department of Native Affairs obtained control over all African schools. This involved financial pressure on the missions to hand their schools over to the Government. It also placed the immediate management of Bantu schools in the hands of African school boards, enforced vernacular instruction in the junior schools, made both English and Afrikaans compulsory subjects in the higher primary, and laid down a differential syllabus for Bantu schools, geared to what the Government considered African educational needs to be.

With a capacity for imagining social change greater even than that of Milner, and with more self-confidence than ever Milner possessed, Verwoerd imparted a crusading zeal to his fellow devotees of *apartheid*. That static term soon gave place to *aparte ontwikkeling* (separate development) in Government parlance. By May 1956, so systematic had been the development of his policy across a broad front that he felt able to set out his achievements against the declared goals of 1952, as evidence that 'the solid and sound foundation of a great reformation' had already been laid. It took him two hours to say what had been achieved. As for the future, Verwoerd saw the total separation of white and black as 'an ideal to aim at', but estimated in 1956 that it would take twenty years before the integrationist tide could be seen to have turned. There was more to *apartheid*, though, than the territorial separation of the races, for as he said in 1954,

> Apartheid comprises a whole multiplicity of phenomena. It comprises the political sphere; it is necessary in the social sphere; it is aimed at in Church matters; it is relevant to every sphere of life. Even within the economic sphere it is not just a question of numbers. What is of more importance there is whether one maintains the colour bar or not.

As the ideology took hold, Verwoerd himself became its leading glossator.

It became possible to take stock of the Verwoerdian claims for the first time in 1956, after the publication of the massive report of the Tomlinson Commission. This commission was required 'to conduct an exhaustive inquiry into and to report on a comprehensive scheme for the rehabilitation of the Native Areas with a view to developing within them a social structure in keeping with the culture of the Native and based on effective socio-economic planning' – terms which appeared to be open-ended, but which precluded proper correlation in the Commission's Report of policy proposals for African life in both the white areas and the Reserves. The Commissioners pointed this out, but only one of them felt free to suggest that the policy of separate development should itself be regarded empirically, and abandoned if found to be impracticable. The Commission as a whole took as its starting point the view 'that there is little hope of evolutionary development' towards a common society, and 'not the slightest ground for believing that the European population, either now or in the future, would be willing to sacrifice its character as a national entity and as a European racial group'. It considered that this should be accepted as 'the dominant fact in the South African situation'.

It accordingly tried to discover how far the Bantu Areas were capable of carrying the Bantu population, and reached the conclusion that, if a gross income of £120 per annum per farming family were taken as a guide (being, on average, the figure preferred by witnesses), only 20 per cent of the families living in the Reserves could be adequately provided for on the land. That was too few. It therefore took as its standard an annual gross income of £60 for mixed and pastoral farming, and £110 for irrigation and cane farming, as being in practice 'large enough to attract a Bantu to full-time farming', but urged that with improved methods the land could be made to yield substantially better profits. As pastoral economic units required 275 morgen and agricultural units 52.5 morgen to yield the requisite income, this meant that there was enough land in the Reserves to support 51 per cent of the Bantu Reserve population as it stood at the time of the 1951 census. With a further three million morgen still to be bought under the 1936 Act, the Commission calculated that the Bantu Areas would ultimately be able to house 2,142,000 people in households engaged in commercial agriculture. This left some 16,300 pastoral farmers and some 282,000 mixed farmers in the Reserves for whom alternative means of livelihood had to be provided.

The Commission put in a plea for improved marketing methods for farmers, better credit facilities, better farm-planning and stabilisation of tenure, with limited encouragement for successful farmers to buy a second lot if they had paid for their first, and the canalisation of funds through a development corporation for the introduction of valuable plantation crops – sugar, fibres and timber in particular. They saw good prospects of mining development in the northern Transvaal and, to a lesser extent, in Natal. They also underlined the need for industrial development both in the Bantu Areas and on their borders. In the Bantu Areas, they wanted to encourage Bantu entrepreneurs, who could receive assistance from the same development corporation, which might itself initiate its own enterprises. A majority argued that white-sponsored industries should be allowed in the Reserves, in order to increase the carrying capacity of the Bantu Areas sufficiently, create a better balance between urban and rural employment, and encourage Africans to acquire skills. As part of the process of establishing industry, the Commission had its eye on the twenty-six towns and villages of the Transkei, on thirty-four centres in Natal and Zululand, on the various *statte* of the Tswana in the western Transvaal, and other well-spread centres, as likely nuclei for town-building. Only in the Vaal triangle, the industrial heartland of South Africa, was it unable to find a satisfactory Bantu homeland, and concluded that 'the Bantu population of this largest development complex will, therefore, have to be concentrated chiefly in urban residential areas for Bantu . . . on a regional basis'. The Commission hoped, however, to draw African workers away from the existing industrial centres by encouraging industrial firms to decentralise their activities and set up factories on the borders of the Reserves, where labour was cheaper and basic resources (above all, water) presented fewer problems.

The Tomlinson Commission took the widest view it was allowed to take of its task, and included the provision of health, welfare and educational services in its recommendations. The churches were encouraged to do missionary work, even if they could no longer teach. The Commission calculated that £104,486,000 should be spent on development of the Bantu Areas in the first ten years, of which £55 millions would be recoverable in due course. The largest single item of proposed expenditure was £27.4 millions for soil reclamation. The budget of the Department of Native Affairs, which the Commission desired to see highly centralised, and as much revenue as possible derived from African sources, would have to rise from about £9 million in the next financial year to about £20 million at the end of the decade. Then, if the right tempo were kept up, the population of the Bantu areas could be expected to reach ten million by the end of the century (including dependants of migrant workers in the white areas), through the provision of 50,000 new jobs per annum, of which 20,000 were to be in secondary industry and most of the remainder in commercial and professional employment. In the Bantu areas there would also be local self-government under the Bantu Authorities Act. In the white areas, political power would remain in the hands of the whites; and there the Bantu population, with no political rights, would not be larger than the white.

When Dr Malan resigned on 30 November 1954, he was 80 years old; but the need to replace him by a younger man was not the only consideration for the National Party. Malan's Government, as first appointed, had contained seven Cape men to two Free Staters and three Transvalers, and there were strong feelings in the northern provinces both over this imbalance and over the apparent intention of Malan to determine his own succession. It was common knowledge that he favoured Dr Dönges; but Dönges's reputation had suffered from his introduction of the unfortunate High Court of Parliament Bill, while for Group Areas and the population register he was better liked in his own party than outside it. Malan therefore worked for the election of Havenga as a night watchman, hoping that he could keep the succession warm for Dönges and keep out Strijdom, whose health was not robust, and who was distrusted by Malan for his direct but unsubtle approach to public issues. Strijdom's supporters, mainly Transvalers such as Albert Hertzog and Verwoerd, felt that Havenga, who was not a dyed-in-the-wool Nationalist, was mainly responsible for the Government's failure over the Coloured vote issue. Malan resigned the Cape leadership in November 1953, so as to give Dönges, who became his successor, greater stature in the Party, but although he announced his pending resignation from the premiership on the eve of Strijdom's visit to Europe a year later, the latter's allies in the caucus saw to it that his name was canvassed among the members, and eventually secured his election.

The choice of Strijdom meant that Havenga followed Malan into retirement, and Parliament lost two devotees of constitutional restraint. Strijdom saw political problems in much simpler terms, as a succession of Gordian knots to be cleanly severed. Examples of this approach were his bland announcement in 1957 that *Die Stem van Suid Afrika* would henceforth be the only national anthem and his unopposed legislation of the same year that the Union Jack ceased to have any standing as an official flag of the Union. Issues which had led to displays of great political emotion in 1927 and 1938 were now settled arbitrarily and without a major outcry because there were more important matters to think about. Perhaps surprisingly, these issues did not include the introduction of a Republican constitution, to which Strijdom was dedicated. But a steamrollered Republic could have removed all chance of incorporating the High Commission Territories, on which he had also set his heart. Nor could he assume, even in 1958 after he had enfranchised eighteen-year-old whites, that the Nationalists were in a position to win a referendum on the republican issue.

Lacking Malan's concern for constitutional propriety, which seemed to him much less important than the vindication of the sovereignty of Parliament, Strijdom also brought to an end the long-drawn-out crisis over the Coloured vote. Without taking the caucus into its confidence, the Cabinet worked out a new strategy. The first step was to reform the constitution of the Appeal Court, not on the lines of the earlier bill moved by Swart, but by increasing its membership to eleven judges and requiring a full quorum of eleven for constitutional appeals. The second was to enlarge the Senate so as to ensure that the Government would get a two-thirds majority in a joint session of Parliament, and then to bring the Coloured vote Bill to a joint sitting of the enlarged Parliament. The Government made sure of appointing a majority of judges who favoured its case, even if all members of the existing Appellate Division handed down hostile judgments. Its second aim was achieved by increasing the membership of the Senate to 89, by giving the larger provinces proportionately more members than the smaller (in defiance of the federal principle of equal representation), and ordaining that the party which could muster the majority of votes in the electoral college in each Province (that is, the majority of Assembly plus Provincial Council members) could elect all the senators for that province. This involved a rejection of the other federal principle of proportional representation, and was to the advantage of the Nationalists, who commanded a majority in all provinces save Natal. There followed a rush for the plums of office. The constitution thus altered to suit its purposes without actual breach of the law, the Government validated the Coloured vote legislation with a manufactured two-thirds majority during the session of 1956. In Collins's case, heard before the eleven judges of the new Appeal Court in November, the Government won its fight, the only dissenting judgment being that of Judge O. D. Schreiner, who considered the legislation invalid because the intention behind it had been to circumvent the rules of the constitution. The Government did not deny this, but claimed to have acted on the higher morality of a popular mandate. It was not deterred even by the efforts of the Women's Defence of the Constitution League (more familiarly known as the Black Sash), which was established in May 1955 to propagate respect for the constitution, and sought to do this by doggedly 'haunting' cabinet ministers through the holding of silent stands on public occasions.

During Strijdom's Ministry residential *apartheid* began to affect all dark race groups, even urban Africans living in those few suburbs like Lady Selborne, Pretoria, where they could still own property in spite of the Urban Areas Act. Under a Native Resettlement Act of 1954 the Government moved the African residents of the western suburbs of Johannesburg to a new area called Meadowlands twelve miles from the city. Sophiatown was re-zoned for whites and renamed Triomf in 1956, and the southern part of the district for Coloured ownership and occupation in 1957. The removals were carried out with the precision of a military operation, and left over a thousand 'unlawful' residents of Johannesburg homeless. In Cape Town the City Council boycotted a public hearing of the Group Areas Committee in August 1956, because of the many Coloured homes and institutions affected, when it was proposed to zone the whole of the Table Mountain area to the west of the suburban railway line from Cape Town to Muizenberg for white people; but the main features of this proposal were put into effect during the next few years, the loss to the Coloured people of District Six and the Kalk Bay harbour settlements being particularly severe. Many Group Area determinations had the support, or had been initiated by, white local authorities or pressure groups. Thus the removal of Coloured people from the centres of Paarl to the area of the Berg River, was endorsed by the white Ratepayers' Association. Proposals for the removal of Indian shops and residencies from the central business areas of many Transvaal towns were made to the Group Areas Board by local authorities, and adopted, notably in Lydenburg (1952), Balfour and Carolina (1953), Nelspruit and White River (1954), Ermelo, Wolmaransstad and Klerksdorp (1955), and Pretoria, involving the removal of the wealthy Asiatic Bazaar area (1956). Meanwhile experience led the Government to increase its powers under the Act in a series of amendments between 1952 and 1957. It set up a Group Areas Development Board in 1955 to control the disposal of affected properties, and overcame numerous legal snags with regard to the racial classification of individuals and the meanings of 'occupation' of property which had arisen in the administration of the Act [see pp. 350–1].

Cultural *apartheid* was extended during the Strijdom era. A State-Aided Institutions Act of 1957 empowered it to enforce segregation in libraries and places of entertainment if they were controlled by public authorities, whether the audiences gathered to read, to watch boxing or to listen to Brahms. The Native Laws Amendment Bill of the same year contained a clause to empower the Government to prohibit the holding of classes, entertainments and even church services if they were attended by Bantu in white Group Areas. The public protest was sharp – a good deal sharper, in fact, than had been the case in 1937 when the Hertzog Government had introduced a not dissimilar proposal. Even in the Nationalist caucus it was argued by a minority that the Bill violated the Reformed principle of the sovereignty of the Church within its own sphere, while the Anglican episcopal synod informed the Prime Minister that its members would not be able to advise their clergy to obey a law which excluded people from a church on racial grounds. The terms of the Bill were modified but only so as to leave the initiative with local authorities and to expose the offending African rather than the Church concerned to the risk of prosecution. It became increasingly difficult for whites to hold night schools for urban Africans, which were also brought under the Bantu Education Act and had to be held in African locations, and less easy than before for domestic servants to hold religious services in private suburban garages on Sunday afternoons [see pp. 347–50].

It was also in 1957 that the Government went ahead with its plans to attack integrated higher education, in the face of strong opposition from those universities (all of them English-medium) which were not already uniracial. Acting on the Report of the Holloway Commission, which had investigated the administrative aspects but not the principle of university *apartheid*, the Government made alternative provision under an Extension of University Education Act for four ethnic university colleges in addition to Fort Hare at Bellville, Ngoye, Durban and Turfloop, for Coloured, Zulu, Indian and Sotho-Tswana students respectively. Objections to its policy were overridden, whether these were based on the argument that segregated education was wrong if publicly endowed, or on the much more widely supported view – at least among whites – that the Government's proposals were an invasion of university autonomy. The measure was eventually carried only after widespread demonstrations and an all-night sitting on 11 June 1959.

The work of the designers was not quite complete after the segregation of higher education in 1959. Governmental structures for the subordinate ethnic groups were given a radically different purpose in the same year, when the Government envisaged the political break-up of South Africa into a White State and some eight black satellite 'Homelands' for the first time. Further, the decision to establish a Republic outside the Commonwealth was only taken in 1960. Both these developments will be discussed in the following chapter; but the dominant characteristic of the era to which they belong was a marked increase in physical violence on the part of groups seeking to resist government policies, and on the part of the Government in suppressing them.

# 15 Internal Combustion, 1956–64

South Africa is a country of many baffling contrasts. There have been few societies in history in which so much dedicated enthusiasm for the promotion of a cause had been manifested by one section of society, while another section complained so persistently to be suffering from a sense of indignity and pain as a result of policies ostensibly designed for their long-term benefit. Between the euphoric vision of Dr Verwoerd and the resigned apathy of a pass-law offender on his rapid progress through the magistrate's court stood a vast gulf of apparent incomprehension.

Police counter-measures, aided by the sanctions of the Public Safety and Criminal Law Amendment Acts, had brought an end to the Defiance Campaign of 1952. But the grievances which had produced the disturbances remained, and it was not long before the peace was broken again.

There was a considerable increase in peasant violence during the Strijdom era, stemming from the enforcement of laws both old and new.[1] The resistance of the Mamathola tribe to removal from their farm in the Wolkeberg mountains of the north-eastern Transvaal affords one kind of example. They had had title to their land on this watershed since 1907, and claimed a much longer occupation; but the beginning of soil erosion on their watersponge made remedial action urgent. In September 1956 they were given two weeks to move to another farm, but they objected and were then given until the end of June 1957 to move to the farm Metz, thirty miles away on the lowveld, so that their original Reserve could be planted with trees. Metz was well provided with amenities to receive them; but there was outspoken opposition to the removal, which grew when Chief Mamathola was himself deposed for non-cooperation. The tribe was eventually obliged to settle at Metz, but a third of them went off elsewhere. A migration which was probably necessary for ecological reasons had proved a disaster for good public relations on account of deep-seated opposition to the 1927 Native Administration Act, in terms of which they were moved, and on account of suspicion of the new Bantu Authorities system.

Opposition to Bantu Authorities took another form in Sekhukhuneland, where, in April 1957, the Government deported two Pedi councillors, Arthur Phetedi Thulare and Godfrey Sekhukhune, to Natal after they had begun to agitate against to rumoured deposition of their chief, Moroamoche Sekhukhune. The Government subsequently set up a Tribal Authority under Moroamoche in July, but dissensions persisted in the tribe, and were attributed by the authorities to the A.N.C. Moroamoche was suspended in November. He successfully appealed against suspension in the following March, whereupon he was deported to Cala in the Transkei in terms of the Native Administration Act, and superseded by Kgobalela Sekhukhune, a retired policeman with whom the Pedi refused to cooperate. Riots broke out in May 1958, and to ease the tension the Government suspended the Tribal Authority. Over three hundred arrests followed the rioting, and twenty-one people were convicted of murder; but all sixteen of the death sentences imposed were commuted on appeal.

Further dissension arose all over South Africa when the Government began to compel African women to carry reference books (as the consolidated passes were now known) in 1956. As might have been expected from the Orange Free State experience of 1913, this led to widespread acts of protest, to the burning of reference books by the women, often with the encouragement of their menfolk when they returned from working in Johannesburg at weekends, and to the stoning of officials sent to distribute the books. There were many arrests between November 1956 and February 1959. The violence was particularly severe in the Hurutshe Reserve in the Western Transvaal, particularly in the location of Chief Moiloa, who was deposed in April 1957. The protest did not avail in the long run. In his *Brief Authority*. Charles Hooper, the Anglican priest at Zeerust, captured much of its pathos.

The climax of rural violence was reached in Pondoland between 1957 and 1960. It began, as in Sekhukhuneland, with opposition to the introduction of Bantu Authorities. The chosen agent of the new system, Chief Botha Sigcawu, had been controversially appointed in 1939 under the old. Rioting broke out in the Bizana district in 1958, and the rebels formed an 'Intaba' (Mountain) Committee and took to the hills, where they set up a rival administration and sought to enlist popular support by burning the huts of government informers, and intimidating the waverers in unofficial courts. People serving on school committees under the Bantu Education Act were required to resign, and the 'selfish' were fined to provide defence funds for those charged with public violence by the police. The Government brought in mobile armoured units and aircraft, and beat down the resistance in a series of clashes culminating in a police onslaught on the rebel headquarters at Ngquza Hill on 6 June 1960, when between eleven and thirty Africans were killed. Inquiries conducted by the Government and by

Mary Draper of the Institute of Race Relations revealed that much of the opposition could be ascribed to peasant conservatism in face of official attempts to introduce not merely Bantu Authorities but agricultural betterment schemes; but as in Sekhukhuneland and the western Transvaal, the atmosphere was vitiated by fundamental suspicion over Government intentions. Significantly, the Mpondo peasants kept up their opposition for several months, and were successfully politicised by urban black leaders, to the point of including in their demands the terms of the Congress of the People's Freedom Charter.

Meanwhile the urban African leaders had been forced by the defeat of the Defiance Campaign and by the Nationalists' victory in the 1953 general election to rethink their strategy.[2] Here they received some encouragement from the support of Liberals, for one consequence of the Campaign had been to bring some whites out in support of the African resistance. A very few, like Patrick Duncan, son of the former Governor-General, had taken part fully and been arrested. The Liberal Party was committed to the support of a qualified non-racial franchise. At its congress in July 1954, it adopted the principle of adult suffrage, subject to suitable transitional safeguards, and was thus able to hold the support of a small section of moderate black opinion, of elder statesmen like Selby Msimang, and younger men like the Natal journalist, Jordan Ngubane; but in the western Cape it could not compete for African loyalties against candidates put up by the Congress of Democrats, who inherited the mantle of Kahn and Bunting.

The Liberals and the African, Indian and Coloured organisation did not find it easy to make common cause, because voteless blacks often had difficulty with the Liberals' insistence on safeguards for the franchise. Liberals, white or otherwise, began by being suspicious of Nationalist and Marxist ideologies. Socialists saw Liberals as defenders of the existing economic order. Cooperation between the African and Indian congresses, however, grew after the end of the Defiance Campaign. The N.I.C. invited Albert Luthuli, President-General of the A.N.C., to open their conference in Durban in July 1954. There had been a huge escalation in A.N.C. membership during the Defiance Campaign, rising it was said to 100,000, and this led some of its leaders, notably J. L. Z. Njongwe of Port Elizabeth, to see it still as a potential mass movement. But this was to underrate the effects of attrition caused by the banning of several of its effective leaders, and the fickleness of its branch offices which Xuma had tried and failed to overcome, and which was subsequently stressed by Feit after examining A.N.C. material in the Treason Trial records. It proved difficult to concentrate on humdrum organisational and fund-raising activities when dramatic public issues like the Western Areas Removal and the Bantu Education Act invited political action; and it was bad for the morale of Congress when large numbers of Africans put security before principle by settling for homes in Meadowlands rather than find themselves in the streets, or chose Bantu education rather than no education at all. The numbers of Congress stopped growing. In this situation the notion of a mass national conference to adopt a charter of liberties was very attractive.

The idea of an assembly of the people seems to have been first proposed by Z. K. Matthews at the A.N.C. conference in Queenstown in December 1953. In the following March, executive members of the A.N.C., S.A.I.C., S.A.C.P.O. and the Congress of Democrats met at Frasers on the Lower Tugela in Natal, so that Luthuli, who was under a restriction order, could take the chair. After further meetings in Johannesburg, Durban and elsewhere, a Congress of the People was called for 26 and 27 June 1955. The Congress of Democrats made the running on this occasion. Luthuli did not suspect their good faith; but the Liberal Party, though invited to participate after the initial plans had been laid, suspected an attempt by Communists to capture control of the A.N.C., and withdrew. The Congress took place at Kliptown, outside Johannesburg, some three thousand people attended, and a Freedom Charter was adopted clause by clause before the police broke up the meeting. This Charter affirmed that South Africa belonged to all its inhabitants, black and white, and demanded a non-racial, democratic system of government, equal protection for all groups before the law, nationalisation of the banks, mines and heavy industry, land redistribution, equal work and educational opportunities and the removal of restrictions on domestic and family life. Because of its provenance, the Liberals did not adopt it. The A.N.C. did in March 1956, but with some difficulty, for its Africanist wing led by Robert Sobukwe was loath to accept the idea of nationalisation.

For the authorities, the Congress gave a warning of how successfully the Congress of Democrats had moved into an alliance with the black organisations. Police raids on the homes and offices of those who had participated therefore followed in September, and at dawn on 5 December 1956 the police arrested 156 people from all races and all walks of life all over South Africa and held them in the Johannesburg Fort pending an arraignment for high treason. Then began one of the longest and largest trials in the history of mankind.[3] By August 1958 the Government had reduced the number of the accused to 91, and these were committed for trial in the Johannesburg Drill Hall, which was specially prepared for the purpose. Bail had meanwhile been allowed despite the nature of the charge. By November 1960 the number of the accused had been further whittled down to 30, and all without exception were eventually acquitted of the charge of treason by three judges of the Supreme Court on 29 March 1961. Interpreters of the trial ranged from those who thought that – even without convictions –

it demonstrated that there were many operating close to the edge of treason, to those who considered that the Government had abused its own authority, and prematurely cried 'Wolf'.

Strijdom died in office on 24 August 1958, a man respected by his followers for the long and initially lonely stand he had taken on behalf of his party in the Transvaal. Though he had opponents in the party, above all in the Cape, he had controlled his Cabinet, stood up to the Broederbond in a way Malan had not, and left his mark on the policy of the country through his capacity for taking resolute decisions.

Dr H. F. Verwoerd emerged the victor over Dönges and Swart in the subsequent lobbying for the premiership, but although his victory in the caucus was fairly decisive, he had the greatest difficulty in winning the personal loyalty of Strijdom's cabinet and in rearranging the portfolios so as to placate disappointed supporters. But by giving Dr N. Diederichs Economic Affairs, releasing Dönges from the Interior and giving him Finance, and persuading Dr Albert Hertzog to take Health and Posts and Telegraphs, rather than Mines, he was able to minimise the tensions in a difficult team. A Hollander by birth, though he had lived in South Africa since early childhood, Verwoerd had received university training in pre-Hitlerian Germany before taking up a chair in social psychology at Stellenbosch. He edited the *Transvaler* during the war years, provocatively enough to lose a court action brought against an opponent for alleging that his editorials had supported the enemies of South Africa. Verwoerd had actually supported Malan's attack on Pirow and the New Order. Intellectually, he stood head and shoulders above most of his parliamentary supporters, while his self-assurance and his didactic manner led many to believe that he really could wish into being the political objectives of his fertile imagination. Relatively few parliamentarians, among them Mrs Ballinger, queried his genius.[4]

The Verwoerd era began with two major changes in the political orientation of South Africa. One was the firm commitment of the Government to a policy of some kind of independence for the Bantu areas, which brought in its train a realignment of the forces of parliamentary opposition. The other was the decision of the Government to go for a Republic, which led to South Africa's departure from the Commonwealth. Both these developments occurred against a background of increasing tension between the white authorities and the black political organisations, leading to widespread violence which reached a climax at Sharpeville in March 1960, but continued thereafter to make the Verwoerd era the most unsettled in the country's history between 1922 and 1976.

As Minister of Native Affairs, Verwoerd had never committed himself to independence for the Reserves, always limiting his promises to self-government under Pretoria at the level of the Territorial Authority.[5] Dr Eiselen, the Secretary for Native Affairs, stated very explicitly in *Optima* as late as March 1959 that the grant of independence was never intended, and confirmed that this had been the case in a press interview in October 1972, urging that he had always attached more importance to the economic development of the Bantu areas than to their political autonomy. As late as January 1959, Verwoerd hedged over the political future of these areas, referring to their ultimate independence only as a remote, unforeseeable possibility. When asked on 5 September 1958 about a related topic, the abolition of African representation in the House of Assembly, Verwoerd replied that the matter had not yet been considered. But during the 1959 session the Government introduced a Promotion of Bantu Self-Government Bill, the negative feature of which was the termination of African elected representation in Parliament, rounding off the policy for the elimination of African political influence in the white areas which had already led to the abolition of the N.R.C. and to the break-up of the Location Advisory Boards Congress in 1956–7. There was opposition in Nationalist circles, however, chiefly from Japie Basson, the member for Namib, who had crossed over from the United Party in 1948. Basson argued that only the grant of genuine political independence to the Bantu areas would justify such disenfranchisement. He was expelled from the party caucus in May. Meanwhile the new Bill made provision for the restructuring of the Bantu Authorities system on a framework of eight Territorial Authorities, and Verwoerd allowed the suggestion of eventual independence for these Territorial Authorities to creep into his introductory and second reading speeches. He repudiated Eiselen's *Optima* article, saying it had been written 'long before the latest official Government statement was made'. In reply to a question by the leader of the Opposition, Sir de Villiers Graaff, whether the Union Government would retain control over the foreign affairs of the Bantu areas 'forever or merely temporarily', Verwoerd explicitly referred to the possible development of these areas to full independence. He saw analogies between the direction South Africa could take and that being taken by Europe – a combination of national sovereignties with economic interdependence. He also repudiated the fear expressed by Graaff that independent Bantustans might provide footholds for Communist powers and hostile armed forces by saying:

> My belief is that the development of South Africa on the basis of this Bill will create so much friendship, so much gratitude, so many mutual interests in the propulsive development that there will be no danger of hostile Bantu states, but that there will arise what I call a commonwealth, founded on common interests and linked together by common interests in this southern part of Africa. In other

words, I believe that these dangers of foreign ideologies, of foreign navies and so on, will not materialize.

The decolonisation of Africa was then in its very early stages, and Harold Macmillan's 'Winds of Change' speech was not delivered to the South African Parliament until 3 February 1960. But Verwoerd's vision of a South African commonwealth, in the framework of which the independence of the Bantustans was to be considered, had the merit of being something into which a new policy for the High Commission Territories could be made to fit: they were in any case about to become independent, but might also become Bantustans, perhaps even with boundaries adjusted to mesh with South African Reserves on their borders, and the whole question of transfer be allowed to fall into abeyance. This possibility was certainly noticed by Verwoerd, De Wet Nel and Eiselen at the beginning of 1959. The legislation of 1959, while it demolished the Hertzogian political settlement of 1936, and silenced the African voice in the legislature, therefore plotted a new course which could help to inaugurate a new system of international relations in the sub-continent.

While the thinking of the Nationalists moved in the direction of a multinational South African commonwealth based on the conversion of the African Reserves into eight 'independent' units to be consolidated so far as possible into territorial states, some extremely fragmented, the United Party retorted that the partition of South Africa was unthinkable.[6] After emancipating itself in 1948 from the toils of Hertzog's policy of 1936–7, and adopting the Fagan proposals as its guidelines, the U.P. had discovered by 1954 that its lack of positive objectives placed it at a disadvantage in face of Nationalist propaganda. Under Strauss's initiative, the party adopted a new statement of policy at its Union congress in November 1954. This accepted the African as part of a single South African political community, and justified white leadership only if the white man was prepared to share his civilisation with the African. It affirmed, as in 1948, the fact of economic integration, but now described political rights for the black man as 'an inevitable historical corollary to an increase in economic power', once he had undergone a 'long period of training in the ways of democracy' and after 'a decisive majority of the European electorate' had agreed that such rights should be conferred. This was a cautious, empirical approach with almost no electoral appeal at all, though it indicated a direction opposed to the Nationalist line of advance, and admitted the principle of greater African participation in parliamentary politics one day, which might be difficult to shrug off. The U.P. rejected the non-racial democratic ideas of the Liberals as electorally non-viable, which they were, and it rejected federalism as a device for the protection of minorities, no doubt because all the federal thunder had been stolen by the Union Federal Party, whose posture was closely linked with the historic 'Natal stand' of the early 1930s, and had more to do in their hands with provincial rights than with the solution of racial problems. After the 1958 election, when the Federal Party collapsed after winning a third of the Natal votes but failing to take a single seat, the federal option became more available, but it was the new Progressive Party and not the U.P. which then snapped it up.

Overtaken by Verwoerd's partition proposals, the U.P. reacted by asserting that it would oppose the transfer of any further land to the African Reserves if the destiny of such land was to be lopped off the Union. But the liberal wing dissented, and the issue split the Party, eleven of its fifty-three M.P.s seceding in 1959 to form the Progressive Party. They contended that the obligation to find more land for the Africans was unaffected by Verwoerd's change of policy, and, once freed from the constraints of the U.P. caucus, they subjected their own standpoints to fundamental review. A new constitutional policy was adopted, known as the Molteno plan, for the protection of minority interests through a two-tier multi-racial common-roll franchise for the lower house, giving nine-tenths of the seats to people possessing minimal educational and wealth qualifications. It also recommended the direct representation of all races in the upper house, through special voting procedures to ensure that no candidate could win a seat without receiving support from voters of all race groups. This was intended to ensure that the Senate would be disposed to veto racially discriminatory legislation. The Progressives also proposed to entrench a Bill of Rights, and to bring about a considerable devolution of power to bicameral provincial legislatures, each one a replica of the federal Parliament and possessing wider powers than the existing Provincial Councils. Despite the originality of these proposals, however, the urban voters rejected Progressive candidates in the general election of 1961, enabling the U.P. to recapture all their seats save that of Mrs Helen Suzman in Houghton, Johannesburg.

Having survived the Progressive challenge, but failed to prevent the Nationalists from increasing their seats by three, the U.P. came out with a new policy, described as 'Race Federation', in 1963. This envisaged a three-stage plan after the party's return to power. In the first stage, it would study and then dismantle what it could of the controversial *apartheid* laws. It then planned to restore the Coloured voters to the common roll in the Cape and Natal, and give those in the Transvaal and Orange Free State some representation in the Senate, to restore and enlarge African representation on a separate roll in both houses (up to eight seats in the Assembly, and up to six in the Senate), and to seek some formula for the representation of the Indians after consultation with them. In the third phase, it would set up a number of communal councils for each race, building on the structure outlined by Smuts in 1947 for the Africans, and allowing for the representation of each group, indirectly through these councils, in a central Parliament. As later elaborated in 1972, the U.P. policy allowed for the adaptation of the existing Provincial Councils and of the Territorial Authorities in the Bantu Homelands (assuming that the latter could be persuaded to reject independence) to become communal councils under this race federation plan; and the Party insisted that the white electorate, which was in possession of the field, should be able to control the evolution of the policy, and if need be stop it, at every stage.

Thus the whites debated about the future of the blacks. But it was a debate conducted in a political whirlpool, and had almost no relationship to the thinking of the black leadership, save in so far as a few thinkers like Ngubane were toying with a new kind of federal map. The unrest in Sekhukhuneland and the western Transvaal was still simmering, while the situation in Pondoland was highly volatile. Active opposition to reference books for African women, to Bantu education (especially, now, to its higher manifestations in the 'tribal colleges'), and to the new Bantu Authorities was still widespread. The A.N.C. was beginning to send emissaries into the rural areas to coordinate opposition, though it did not at this stage encourage violence. There were ugly scenes at Lady Selborne, Pretoria, in February 1959, when police broke up a protest meeting of African women. In June there was serious rioting in Durban's African townships sparked off by three rather more traditional irritants – low wages, shack removals, and liquor raids – during an epidemic of typhoid. Feelings there exploded again in the following January, when nine policemen were murdered in a riot after a liquor raid in Cato Manor.

In this situation of unremitting tension, divided counsels began to appear within the African leadership. The Congress Alliance left wing had persuaded Luthuli to give A.N.C. support to a stay-at-home demonstration before the general election of 1958. The demonstration was not a success. Recriminations between the two wings, the leftists and the Africanists, resulted. Luthuli, Matthews and most of the leadership tried to hold the two sides together, and reassure the Africanist malcontents that the Communists were not trying to divert the stream into the wrong channels. But the Africanists were not to be convinced, and at the Transvaal A.N.C. conference, in November 1958, Robert Sobukwe led a walk-out with the intention of reverting to the authentic tradition of the Congress before it had become 'contaminated' by non-African elements. In March 1959 the Pan-Africanist Congress was formed, with Sobukwe as its chairman, Potlako Leballo as its secretary, and the Youth League's Programme of Action and the Defiance Campaign as their main points of reference for the struggle they planned to continue.

Sensing competition from this breakaway activist movement, the A.N.C. conference at Durban in December 1959 decided to hold massive demonstrations on 31 March 1960 against the pass laws, linked with a national campaign for a minimum wage of £1 a day. But on 18 March, the P.A.C. pre-empted this plan by announcing a campaign to defy the pass laws on the 21st, linked with a demand for a slightly higher minimum wage. Sobukwe and his followers, true to their word, defied the pass laws on the 21st and were arrested, as were many of their followers all over the country. Though the Government used aircraft in one place to scatter the crowds, the police reaction to a non-violent demonstration was itself in most places non-violent. At Sharpeville in the Transvaal, however, sixty-nine Africans were killed and 180 injured when the police opened fire on a crowd of demonstrators, some of whom, according to a statement by Nyakane Tsolo, their spokesman, had arrived without reference books and merely wanted to be arrested. Some witnesses at the subsequent judicial inquiry regarded the crowd as noisy but not hostile, and composed largely of people who had gone to the police station expecting to hear an important announcement about the pass laws. The police, on the other hand, thought that the crowd was getting out of hand, and that the fence round the police station was in danger of collapsing under their pressure. What followed was not a calculated massacre like the slaughter of Indians at Amritsar in 1919, but a panic reaction, barely two months after the Cato Manor murders, by undisciplined police, who were probably not told to open fire before the first shot went off, and then went on firing after the crowd had been put to flight. The shooting was immediately condemned throughout the world, primarily because it exposed the harshness of a system of controls which the rest of the world condemned as inhumane, just the kind of bloody confrontation which could have been expected during what was, after all, not the first major protest movement against the pass system since Union, but the seventh. A similar tragedy, on a much smaller scale, occurred at Langa, near Cape Town, later the same day [see pp. 345–6].

As the ripples of shock spread across the country, the Government banned public meetings in all the disturbed centres. Luthuli identified himself with the P.A.C. protest even though he had not been involved in its planning, and on the 27th, after the Commissioner of Police had announced that Africans were not to be arrested simply for not carrying reference books, Luthuli publicly burned his own. He also declared the 28th a day of mourning for the victims of the 21st, asking people to stay at home, which many of all races did. On the 28th, the Government introduced legislation to declare the A.N.C. and the P.A.C. illegal organisations, and acted to control the situation in other ways before this ban became operative on 8 April. Thus at dawn on 30 March and on subsequent days, a total of over 18,000 people were detained under new emergency regulations. Many of these were released after screening, but over five thousand were convicted and sentenced for various offences, and others held for several months in custody. (Sobukwe was subsequently given a three-year jail sentence but was actually detained for a further six years on the annual decision of Parliament. Over a hundred P.A.C. leaders were given the alternative of three years' jail or a £300 fine, but the sentence was subsequently halved. Luthuli and the A.N.C. leaders who had destroyed their reference books were sentenced to one year's imprisonment or a £100 fine.) The atmosphere of crisis was further heightened on 30 March, when rioting broke out in several centres in reaction to government measures. The P.A.C. staged protest marches in Durban and Cape Town. In Cape Town Philip Kgosana led about 30,000 Africans to the Caledon Square police station to demand the release of their arrested leaders. They dispersed peacefully at Kgosana's request after the latter had demanded and thought he had been granted an interview with the Minister of Justice, F. C. Erasmus. (Kgosana was young and uncynical, Erasmus was a seasoned campaigner and a Machiavellian, who instead of interviewing Kgosana had him arrested. Kgosana later levelled the scores by estreating bail and leaving the country.) The same afternoon a state of emergency was proclaimed in altogether 122 of the Union's 265 magisterial districts. This empowered the authorities to prohibit gatherings, impose curfews, detain suspects, impound publications, search premises and do whatever was necessary to maintain public order. The Active Citizen Force was mobilised in strength, and used to cordon off the African townships of Langa and Nyanga in the Cape.

On 9 April there was an attempt to assassinate the Prime Minister, Dr Verwoerd, while he was opening the Rand Easter Show. He was shot in the head and badly injured by a white man who was subsequently declared to be mentally disturbed.

The South African state was shaken by these events, not least because the economy itself came under heavy pressure. Because of the danger that a mass stay-at-home by African workers might paralyse the industrial system, one of the tasks allotted to the police and to the troops during the crisis was to propel African workers out of the townships and back to their jobs, not to besiege them in their homes. Since 1957 there had been a net outflow of capital from the Union of over R20 millions; but in the eighteen months to June 1961 a total of R248 millions left South Africa, while the gold and foreign exchange reserves fell from R315 millions in January 1960 to R142 millions in June 1961. A major loss of confidence by investors in the South African economy had been inspired by the disturbances and by the chain of events, during the same period, which led to South Africa's withdrawal from the Commonwealth.

But the Government managed within a few years to nurse the economy back to a level of unprecedented growth and prosperity. It imposed new controls on imports to take care of the balance of payments deficit; it blocked the repatriation of distributed profits earned by foreign investors, and imposed tight controls on the export of capital in general. This in turn built up reserves of private capital inside the country, and led to an expansion of economic activity and rising share prices as more and more public and private investors were attracted to the stock market. The upswing was discernible before the end of 1962, and by 1966 the prosperity was so marked that increased imports were already beginning to create inflationary conditions. There was a net capital inflow of R235 millions in 1965.

The full significance of the final stages of the Republican movement can be appreciated only if they are seen in the context of the political and economic crisis. Before both the 'Winds of Change' speech and Sharpeville, and before the onset of the economic crisis, Verwoerd had already indicated on 20 January 1960 that he intended to submit the Republican issue to a referendum of white voters (excluding, he said, those of South West Africa), and to accept the decision of a bare majority either way. The Commonwealth Prime Ministers' Conference in May 1960 would not take a decision in advance on whether a Republic of South Africa would be allowed to remain within the Commonwealth, so Verwoerd indicated before the referendum, which was held on 6 October, that he intended to apply for continued membership should the Republicans win a majority. The Government had also decided in March to extend the poll to South West African whites, but to exclude Coloured voters everywhere from the referendum.

The outcome of the referendum was a majority in favour of a Republic of 76,117 in a total poll of 1,632,583 votes cast: 52.14 per cent voted 'Yes' as against 47.42 per cent who voted 'No'. In the Orange Free State, Transvaal Cape and South West Africa, majorities of 76,733, 81,091, 3771 and 7921 respectively voted in favour of a republic, and in Natal a majority of 93,399 voted against, the results in individual constituencies corresponding closely to those which might have been predicted in a general election. The United Party told its supporters to oppose a Republic, while the Progressives urged theirs to 'reject *this* Republic' on the argument that the referendum was sectional and therefore invalid as a test of opinion.

Verwoerd accordingly took South Africa's application to remain in the Commonwealth as a Republic to the Prime Ministers' conference in March 1961. He worked hard for a final communiqué which South

Africa could accept, without the inclusion of a partisan statement critical of *apartheid* and therefore repugnant to South African public policy. For the sake of obtaining such a formula, and because he did not want to throttle debate, Verwoerd did not insist on the exclusion of domestic political issues from the discussion. When it became clear, however, that South Africa's remaining in the Commonwealth would probably lead other members to leave it, he formally withdrew South Africa's application. The Union became the Republic of South Africa on 31 May, and its membership of the Commonwealth therefore ceased forthwith.

A draft Republican constitution had meanwhile been debated in Parliament and received the Governor-General's assent on 24 April. It bore little resemblance either to a traditional Boer Republican constitution or to the draft of 1941, either as to the form of government proposed, or as to its provisions for the relationships between the white communities. Its form was essentially that of the South Africa Act, with the new office of State President combining those of the Queen and the Governor-General: a head of state without a political role, elected by the legislature, not by popular vote, though like Paul Kruger he would wear a top hat and presidential sash on state occasions. The equality of the white language groups, and of the English and Afrikaans languages, remained. Political power remained as before almost exclusively in the hands of the whites, who retained their monopoly of the seats in the two-chamber Parliament.

The Republic invited a new start, and this meant different things to different groups. For the Nationalist Afrikaners it was, perhaps only in passing, the annulment of the defeat of Vereeniging; but it was also a step towards the creation of white unity, which meant that offence should not be given to the white English-speaker by introducing too radical a change in the form of the constitution. Politically conscious English-speakers, for their part, were divided. Some resented the severing of the umbilical cord whch tied them to Britain – that, rather than the institution of a Republic, for it meant that they had to decide whether to remain British or become South African citizens. Others were driven into the arms of the Nationalists by Britain's decolonisation movement in Africa and Macmillan's famous speech. Verwoerd was soon able to exploit this sentiment by persuading two English-speakers, Frank Waring and A. E. Trollip, to join the National Party and the Cabinet.

The Government had excluded all non-white people from any share in the making of the Republic. Although it took steps after 1960 to promote the economic and educational development of Coloured people, and gave recognition to Indian South Africans as citizens of the Republic for the first time in 1963, it did not give either of these communities a defined territorial base for even local self-government. Its apologists considered, however, that by setting up the Bantu Authorities system, and above all by giving a form of self-government to the Transkei in 1963, it was restoring to the Africans a governmental system as rooted in their own soil as republicanism was in that of the Afrikaner. The Transkeian constitution, however, was drawn up in Pretoria, not in Umtata, at the request of a recess committee of the Territorial Authority, and Verwoerd himself had a great deal to do with it. It provided for a dyarchical system of government under which this 'self-governing territory within the Republic of South Africa' was to have a cabinet elected by a ballot in the Legislative Assembly, with initial control over the portfolios of Finance, Justice, Education, the Interior, Agriculture and Forestry, and Roads and Works. The Assembly in turn was to consist of the four paramount chiefs of the Transkei, together with the sixty chiefs of the Transkeian regional authorities and forty-five elected members chosen by adult suffrage, giving a clear majority of chiefs over commoners. This enabled the Government of the Republic to ensure that its own favourite for the premiership, Chief Kaiser Matanzima, was provided with a safe majority, though nearly all the elective seats in the first general election in 1963 went to supporters of Matanzima's opponents, the Paramount Chiefs Victor Poto and Sabata Dalindyebo. Something of the atmosphere of a democratic election was achieved, though it was contested in the shadow of emergency regulations proclaimed in November 1960 to deal with the Pondoland rising. Matanzima later founded his Transkeian National Independence Party, (T.N.I.P.) which professed allegiance to separate development, while the opposition Democratic Party opposed the fragmentation of South Africa and favoured full African representation in the Republic's Parliament. The T.N.I.P. gave the Republican Government something that it had failed to get under the 1936 system of representation – a black political ally committed to its own policies. To grasp and sustain the initiative which the Republican Government handed to them by promising them 'independence' presented a challenge to the Transkeian Government, and Matanzima's team were able to show from time to time that they could stand up to Pretoria, even without the power to make their territory economically independent or militarily strong.

For the leaders of the black organisations outlawed after Sharpeville, the birth of the Republic became the occasion not for rejoicing but for going underground. Towards the end of 1960, when the Union-wide state of emergency had ended except in the Transkei, a group of African Liberals and ex-members of the A.N.C. and P.A.C. called a consultative conference at Orlando, to work for a non-racial democracy and the continuance of non-violent pressures against *apartheid*. This in turn sponsored an African leaders' conference in Pietermaritzburg the following March, at which plans were developed for the calling of a new national convention – a different kind of fresh start altogether, and involving all races. Several of the organisers of this conference were arrested on charges of promoting the aims of the A.N.C. but were cleared of guilt on appeal. Under the pressure of events, however, the rifts in the African leadership were not healed. Ngubane, one of the leading promoters of the conference (and, incidentally, one of those arrested) deplored the ease with which other elements could take over the running after Luthuli had been restricted to Groutville in Zululand by a government banning order. The conference chose Nelson Mandela, a Witwatersrand University law graduate and ex-Youth Leaguer, who had been born in the Transkei, as leader of a new National Action Council. This council put out a demand for a convention of all races, but coupled it with a threat that if the Government did not respond favourably it would call a general strike between 29 and 31 May, during the inauguration of the Republic. The Government spurned the challenge and the strike took place, with uneven effect because the strikers failed to gain the support of the Opposition press. Mandela himself went underground and began actively to establish a new militant wing of the A.N.C., Umkonto we Sizwe (Spear of the Nation), with a plan to sabotage installations without taking human lives. Their first acts of sabotage took place on the Day of the Covenant, 16 December 1961.

Umkonto's sabotage activities were directed against such targets as electric pylons, post offices, Bantu Administration premises, jails, and railway installations, and some twenty separate acts were eventually admitted by its leaders. Their activities were supplemented by those of a white student group, the African Resistance Movement, Cumulatively these were at least as widespread, and at least as destructive, as the sabotage acts performed by the militants in the Ossewa Brandwag during 1942.

The P.A.C. also sponsored an underground movement, Poqo ('We go it alone'), which turned to tactics of intimidation and did not shrink from taking lives. Judge J. H. Snyman, in his report on the Paarl riots of 20–22 November 1962, listed eleven murders of constables and suspected informers in the western Cape in 1962–3, as well as a succession of attempts, some by armed parties travelling from the western Cape, to kill Chief Kaiser Matanzima and other chiefs and headmen associated with the Bantu Authorities system, all of which he attributed to Poqo adherents. The Paarl riots themselves were the reaction of Poqo members to the arrest of some of their number who were thought to be responsible for the killings.

While the Umkonto and Poqo campaigns developed in the townships, both the A.N.C. and the P.A.C. set up headquarters outside South Africa. Both established missions in Dar-es-Salaam and London, and set up offices in Cairo, Algiers, and elsewhere. Oliver Tambo directed the activities of the A.N.C. The P.A.C., led by Potlako Leballo, who had moved from his exile in Lesotho to Lusaka, remained a divided body, weakened by the desertion of some of its leaders, and was eventually excluded from Zambia in 1968. Together with African émigré political groups from South West Africa and Southern Rhodesia, these bodies became involved in the African summit conference at Addis Ababa in May 1963, which set up an African Liberation Committee. They began to exert pressure on the United Nations and on the World Council of Churches, aiming at the moral isolation of South Africa prior to the political or military overthrow of white rule. They could count on the support of refugees and political exiles calculated variously at between one and five thousand by 1964.

The embattled South African Government had both a new kind of internal security problem and an external logistic problem of unpredictable long-term proportions. It tackled the former with a wider range of security laws touching many aspects of life. Wide discretionary powers were given to a new Publications Control Board in 1963 to prohibit the importation of works and films considered offensive, harmful to public morals, blasphemous, or prejudicial to state security or good order. The press escaped direct governmental control by drawing up its own code of conduct and establishing its own Press Board of Reference in 1962, to deal with complaints of misreporting. The South African Broadcasting Corporation, a public utility, changed its neutral political stance after Sharpeville for an 'editorial' policy more openly favourable to the policies of the Government. The Defence Act was amended in 1961 to enable the Government to handle the threat of internal disorder more effectively. The period of military training was extended, and provision made for the creation of a police reserve, in the same year. When B. J. Vorster took over the Department of Justice in 1962, the power of the police in the interrogation and control of suspected persons, and even over potential state witnesses, were greatly widened to help them uncover plots and obtain convictions. By successive stages, authority was granted to the police to detain suspects without putting them on a charge, and under conditions of solitary confinement, for single or successive periods of twelve days (1962), ninety days (1963), one hundred and eighty days (1965), and later for an unlimited period if authorised by a judge (1966), and even without such authorisation (1976). Sabotage and terrorism were defined as statutory offences: in 1962 the former was made to cover tampering with property, the illegal possession of offensive weapons, and unlawful entry, as well as acts of wilful destruction; while terrorism was defined in 1966 to include training for terrorist activity, furthering the objects of communism, and committing acts of sabotage. The Government took power in 1962 to place individuals under partial or total house arrest, and this, when added to its existing powers of banning, banishing and listing individuals or organisations, gave it an overwhelming advantage in its conflict with active opposition movements within the frontiers. Restrictions imposed under the Prisons Act of 1959, which made the unauthorised reporting of conditions in prisons illegal, together with the power of the State to hold suspects incommunicado, made it impossible to corroborate or refute allegations of third-degree treatment of prisoners, except in a very few cases, though such allegations were commonly made and as commonly denied by the authorities. Some detainees committed suicide. The story of Adam Tas no longer made sensational reading.

Before long, the new draconian legal system achieved the results intended. Umkonto we Sizwe was broken after the capture of Mandela in August 1962, followed by the seizure the following July of its other leaders at Rivonia, near Johannesburg. They were tried in 1964, and sentenced to life imprisonment on conviction for sabotage, the State having withdrawn the charge of treason. Those members of the African Resistance Movement who had failed to flee the country were sentenced shortly afterwards to jail terms of up to fifteen years. In 1964 the security police also managed to infiltrate the underground Communist Party, and secured the conviction of its leaders for belonging to an unlawful organisation. One of them was Bram Fischer, a member of a prominent O.F.S. Afrikaner family, who had himself defended the Rivonia trialists. Fischer, after being allowed out of South Africa on bail to fight an important case for his country before the Privy Council, returned honourably to stand trial. When it became clear that police infiltration of the movement had established the State's case, he estreated bail and went into hiding to continue his fight, a Marxist for whom treason, patriotism and humanity were synonymous terms in the South African context. He was recaptured in November 1965 and sentenced to life imprisonment, to be released on compassionate grounds only shortly before his death from cancer in 1975.

After the retrial in 1966 of a number of Africans previously convicted and imprisoned for A.N.C. activities in 1963–4, the wave of political trials began to peter out, though from time to time members of political movements in exile who had managed to return to the country were captured and put on trial in subsequent years. Under the next government, moreover, the machinery for the detention of political suspects would be further strengthened and periodically used.

In the general election of 1966, the National Party increased its majority to 86, winning 126 seats to 39 won by the U.P. and one by the Progressives. The fifth anniversary of the Republic occurred two months later. The country was experiencing unprecedented economic growth, and to some extent overseas confidence in South Africa as a stable society seemed to have returned. But on 6 September, just before he was due to make a major policy speech, Dr Verwoerd was stabbed to death by a white parliamentary messenger as he sat at his desk in the House of Assembly. As with the earlier attempted assassination, the man was declared insane. To the nation at large, it seemed as if the architect of public policy had been suddenly removed, for although Verwoerd's critics within the National Party had become more outspoken of late, both on the right and on the left, there was a disposition on both sides of the House to view the recovery since Sharpeville as in a real sense his personal achievement.

His sudden removal, however, left no political vacuum and hardly caused a hiatus in the continuity of government policy. The succession passed, by unanimous vote of the caucus after B. J. Schoeman, the Party's elder statesman, had withdrawn, to the Minister of Justice, B. J. Vorster. And the new Government would soon show clearly that Nationalist policies did not depend, in essence, on the brainwaves or idiosyncrasies of individuals, but on the collective determination of Party leaders and of top civil servants who had themselves advanced to positions of authority only after careful ideological screening.

# 16 The Era of Maintenance and Modification, 1964–76

The credibility of the Nationalist Government depended at all times on its ability to find a workable solution to its population problems which would enable the white people to survive as a distinct community and at the same time permit other communities to share the decencies of life. The existence of a long-term plan, encapsulated in the Tomlinson Report, was a source of confidence to it. Although Professor Tomlinson appears to have doubted Verwoerd's enthusiasm for the work of his own Commission, the recommendations of that Commission had for the most part become official Government policy in 1956, when Verwoerd was still Minister of Native Affairs. The Government published a White Paper in that year, in which it dissented from the Report in sertain important particulars, but the bulk of it was accepted without question. With regard to land policy, it rejected Tomlinson's proposal to allow individual tenure in tribal areas, or give preference to it in the released areas, or to allow the purchase of more than one lot by an individual, because it was not anxious to encourage commercial farming by individual Africans at the cost of 'the proper settlement of many'. It also held its hand over the immediate development of mining enterprise, and over the immediate setting up of a development corporation for the Reserves, but saw these as long-term projects. It strongly supported the principle of labour-intensive industries on the European side of the borders, but rejected absolutely the idea of allowing white-owned capital into the Bantu areas, thus siding with Young and Prinsloo, two of the commissioners, against the majority. But what was accepted by Strijdom's Government and by Verwoerd's was the decision to reorganise the economy so as to enable the Reserves to house the 'surplus' black population of the white urban areas and the white farms. Verwoerd accordingly took the first hesitant steps towards the implementation of the Tomlinson Report.

The Tomlinson Commission thought that industrialists could be attracted to the neighbourhood of the Reserves to provide work for Bantu taken off the land, by the lure of cheaper transport, power, water and African housing. It took the Verwoerd Government until

1964 to realise that Tomlinson had underrated the difficulty. The Government therefore tried to speed up industrial decentralisation by offering significant tax concessions, help over the erection of factories, and exemptions from minimum wage determinations and statutory restrictions on the use of motor transport, to those industrialists who were willing to move to the border areas. By the end of 1966, rather less than 45,000 new jobs for Africans had been created in the border areas and the Reserves, a slower rate of progress in ten years than the Tomlinson Commission required in one. This was in spite of the passage of a Bantu Investment Corporation Act in 1959 and a Bantu Homelands Development Corporations Act in 1965, enabling the Government to set up and capitalise individual entrepreneurs and a Development Corporation in each of the Bantu homelands. By prohibiting white-owned risk capital, in opposition to the recommendations of the Tomlinson Commission, the Government prevented the rapid diversification of the economy within the Reserves, and therefore their capacity to absorb more people.

To win the propaganda battle, Verwoerd had needed to be able to demonstrate that his policies could be effective in turning the flow of African migration back from the urban areas; but on his own statements it was too early for this to have happened. On the eve of his assumption of the premiership, he said in Parliament that it would take twenty years before the urban African population started to decrease. He did little before 1966 to help bring about that result, though an attempt was made in the Bantu Laws Amendment Act of 1964 to extend influx control beyond the urban areas to include peri-urban districts, (now known collectively as 'prescribed areas'), in order to plug gaps in the control machinery. His Urban Bantu Councils Act of 1961, by allowing for the democratic election of new bodies, with African chairmen and some administrative duties, to replace the Advisory Boards, was a measure curiously at variance with the terms of his Promotion of Bantu Self-Government Act of 1959, which aimed to give authority in urban locations to representatives of Homeland chiefs so as to promote awareness among residents of their identity with homeland areas in the Reserves. Because the Urban Bantu Councils Act seemed likely to promote rather than undermine the Africans' sense of belonging to the urban area, it tended to lose favour with the white Institute of Administrators of Non-European Affairs, which had a growing voice in the detailed formulation of policy.

The Vorster Ministry was the first government which had to live with the implications of the Tomlinson Report, whose predictions of black population growth were shown to be extremely inaccurate by the evidence of the 1970 census.[1] Projections made in 1972 on the basis of that census report gave a total African population of 36 millions at the very least by the year 2000, as against the outside figure of 21.36 millions calculated by the Tomlinson Commission.

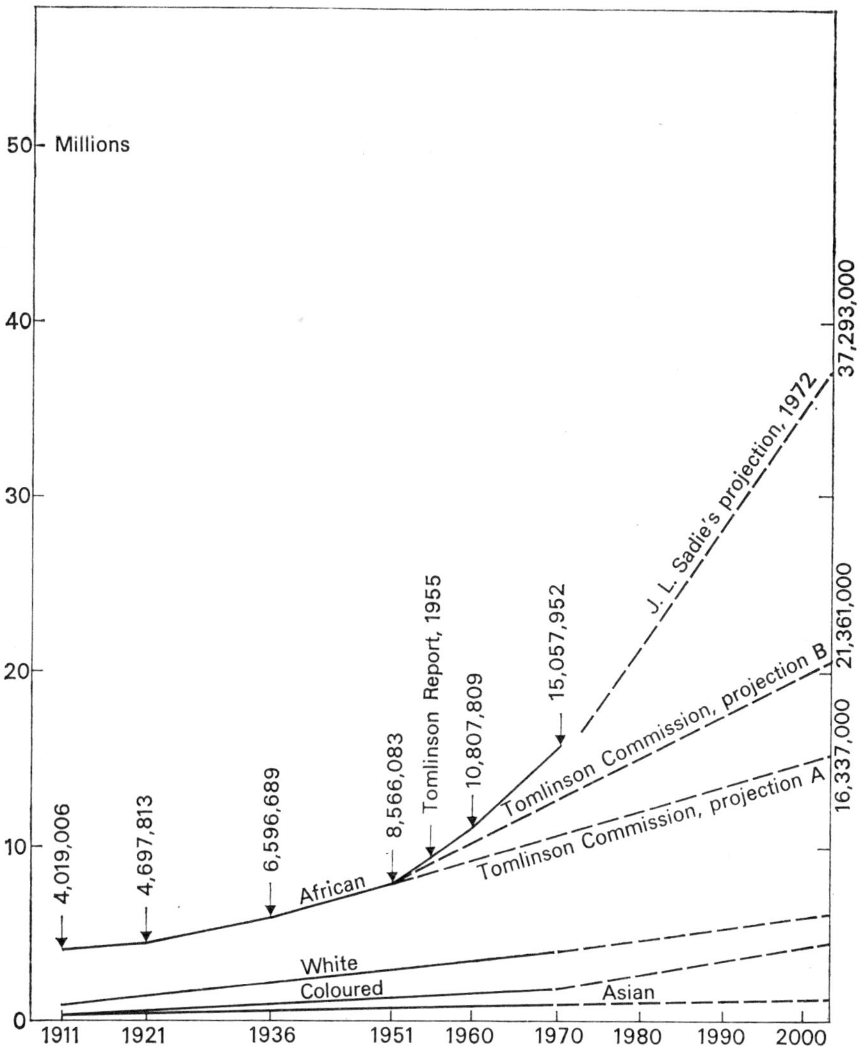


| | 1911 | 1951 | 1970 |
|---|---|---|---|
| African | 4,019,006 | 8,560,083 | 15,057,952 |
| White | 1,276,242 | 2,641,689 | 3,752,528 |
| Coloured | 525,943 | 1,103,016 | 2,018,453 |
| Asian | 152,203 | 366,664 | 620,436 |
| Total | 5,973,394 | 12,671,452 | 21,448,169 |

Sources: H. Sonnabend, in E. Hellmann (ed.), *Handbook on Race Relations* (1949) p.13; *Report* of the Tomlinson Commission (summary) p.29; M. Horrell (ed.), *Survey of Race Relations* (1973) p.49; *Monthly Bulletins of Statistics*

Population growth

Aware of the previous government's failure to achieve rapid industrial decentralisation, Vorster's Cabinet turned to the device of industrial licensing and carried a Physical Planning and Utilization of Resources Act in 1967, under which they could hold up any new industrial development in what were termed 'controlled areas', or impose conditions regarding the employment of labour, the building of houses, and the utilisation of water or other resources in them. The southern Transvaal and the Port Elizabeth–Uitenhage regions were soon proclaimed as controlled, and applications for the employment of Africans in new enterprises in these areas were turned down or reduced in scale, employment for 61,908 extra individuals being refused to the end of March 1973. Meanwhile decentralisation was further encouraged by the positive offer, to industrialists who set up in the border areas, of up to five years' income tax exemption, together with specially favourable loan rates, road and rail tariff rebates, and other concessions. The Government, abandoning the policy of the 1956 White Paper on the Tomlinson Report, also offered to consider requests to develop industries inside the Homelands by white entrepreneurs who were prepared to operate on an agency basis, without acquiring ownership of land or establishing links with foreign interests, and who would accept fixed-period agreements only, and give preference to the employment of Africans over whites. In consequence of these and earlier concessions, new jobs for 85,554 Africans were found in the border areas and the Homelands in the years 1960–72. But this figure of under 8000 jobs a year was well short of the 50,000 jobs a year deemed necessary by Tomlinson, and it caused the Government concern because there was no evidence of acceleration in the latter years in the rate of employment, nor even as rapid a growth rate in these areas as in the country as a whole.

The Government tried at the same time to restrict the African presence in the white areas by whittling down residential rights and encouraging labour migrancy. An Act of 1970 empowered the Minister of Bantu Administration to prohibit the employment of an African in any specified area, or in any specified class of employment or trade, or in the service of any specified employer or class of employer. In terms of these powers, the Minister gave a month's notice on 3 April 1970 of his intention to ban the employment of Africans as counter assistants in shops and cafés; as professional or commercial receptionists; as telephone operators in shops, offices, factories and hotels; or as clerks, cashiers or typists in shops, offices and factories, save in municipal African townships, Bantu Homelands and Border areas. Requests for exemption were invited, but some employers immediately dismissed their African employees on the mistaken assumption that the Government Notice required them to do so. In fact, the Minister revised his policy in the light of a widespread public outcry, first by making a series of detailed amendments to the original notice on 7 August, offering to exempt Africans employed under strictly segregated conditions or outside normal working hours, and those employed in farming and domestic service, or as street news-vendors, petrol pump attendants, waiters and delivery workers. A six months' adjustment period was to be allowed after the publication of a final notice confirming these rules; but no final notice was issued. It was made increasingly difficult, however, for qualified Africans – shopkeepers, technicians, lawyers, doctors – to obtain permission to work in white areas, even if they desired to serve their own people, by making residential permits dependent on the availability of housing, and keeping houses in short supply. The success of the Government in solving the urban Bantu housing crisis in the 1950s by means of its 'site-and-service' scheme, and by authorising municipal housing loans was largely undone after 1966 by the new policy of trying to prevent the growth of African locations in white areas without also preventing the natural increase and the migratory influx of many more people. Enforcement of Section 10 of the Urban Areas Act through the 'endorsement out' of 'surplus' dependants of working people did result in a slight reduction of the total African population of the Cape Peninsula in 1967–8, and may well have helped to peg the growth of the urban African population in the Republic as a whole, for over 450,000 Africans from the white areas were resettled in the Homelands down to the end of 1968, and any Section 10 rights they may have had were thus forfeited. But the Government dropped the plan, put forward, in a Bill of 1969, to prohibit the further acquisition of Section 10 rights by anybody, on account of strong opposition from the municipalities. Though the number of Africans increased in the white areas, however, they came to consist more and more of contract workers without residential rights, living in hostels or 'bachelor' quarters rather than private homes, or – on account of the growing housing shortage – as lodgers in the homes of others.

To accommodate Africans endorsed out of the white areas, whether from the towns or from the farms, where the squatter population was steadily increasing, the Government accelerated the development of Bantu towns and resettlement villages in the Homelands, laying down the main lines of this policy in instructions to magistrates issued in December 1967. R44.5 millions were set aside for the development of rural townships in the Bantu Administration budget of 1966, representing just over half the total Departmental budget. Municipalities were given authority to make contributions from local revenue to Bantu Homeland development, and 80 per cent of the profits of municipal liquor sales to Africans were earmarked for this purpose. In 1968 it was officially stated that plans for 105 such villages had been approved, and that 54 were under construction, 55,000 houses having been built so far at a cost of R31 millions. Though seen by the Government as necessary to the implementation of its policy, the resettlement villages received a great deal of adverse publicity, above all as a result of the publication of Cosmas Desmond's *The Discarded People* in 1970; but the banning of Desmond in 1971 helped to scotch public debate by rendering his book unquotable. Critics of the policy focused attention on the manner of the removals (above all at Limehill, Natal, in 1968), and on the lack of amenities in the villages, especially in the early stages of settlement, on the general lack of jobs other than low-paid unskilled work, on the inadequacy of the statutory old-age pensions for Africans, which then amounted on average to R4.725 a month, and on the insufficiency of the rations supplied to non-pensioners for sustaining health. There was evidence by 1973 that in some of the villages, notably Sada, Ilinge and Dimbaza in the Ciskei, amenities and job opportunities were beginning to improve; but in the case of the great majority of settlements little information had been published. In its public utterances, however, the Government began to profess the intention of providing proper amenities in the future before it started to move people. Verwoerd's dictum that the care of the black aged was the responsibility of the extended family was quietly abandoned, but the scale of relief remained very low in relation to the rapidly increasing cost of living.

The Vorster Ministry made two important changes in the government of urban blacks. The first was an Act of 1971, which vested all urban Bantu administration in sixteen boards spread throughout the Republic, all reporting directly to Pretoria. This Act entirely removed responsibility from the town councils over their own African locations, but required them to contribute the income from their Bantu Revenue Accounts in the normal way, and to make the services of their officials available to the Boards on a *pro rata* payment basis. When this law came into force in July 1973, the duality of control which had characterised urban African administration since 1910 was removed at a stroke, and the Government had an instrument in its hands for controlling the growth of urban African townships, directing the flow of contract workers (which was simplified by the Act), and overcoming either opposition or inertia in the local authorities. The second development, occurring after the Soweto riots of 1976–7 (see pp. 310–11) was the replacement of Urban Bantu Councils by new Community Councils, in an attempt to give urban blacks more local power (for example, control over their troublesome schools) as a pretext for excluding them from a new political deal to be worked out for the Coloured and Indian peoples.

By way of compensation, the African control over the government of the Homelands was increased, as attempts were made through the Bantu Homelands Citizenship Act of 1970 to attach the citizenship of one or other of the Homelands to every African in the Republic (for domestic as distinct from international purposes), even if he had never lived outside the white area. The Bantu Homelands Constitution Act of 1971 was enabling legislation, to empower the State President to confer self-government on any of the eight Territorial Authorities by proclamation, as had happened in the Transkei. In terms of this law, the Ciskei became a self-governing territory on 28 July 1972, with a Legislative Assembly of fifty and an elected Cabinet under the leading Mfengu chief, Justice Mabandla. Zululand became the self-governing though fragmented territory of Kwazulu on 30 March 1972, under its own King, Chief Zwelithini Bhekuzulu; but the Territorial Authority forestalled a bid by the Department of Bantu Administration to endow the King with the historical authority of the Zulu monarchy by depriving him of the power to select his own chief minister, and themselves electing Chief Gatsha Buthelezi to the position. The sprawling territory of Bophutatswana, stretching in eight main territorial enclaves from north-east of Pretoria across to the borderlands east and south of Botswana, and taking in the Thaba 'Nchu enclave in the eastern Orange Free State, became self-governing in May 1972, with Chief Lucas Mangope's Bophutatswana National Party clear victors in the first election. Lebowa, Homeland of the Lobedu of the north-eastern Transvaal, followed in September. Eventually, political independence was extended to the Republic of Transkei in October 1976, and to the Republic of Bophutatswana a year later. The policy of Homeland self-government had to be seen to be on the move, under the dedicated direction of M. C. Botha, Vorster's Minister of Bantu Affairs.

In granting self-government to the Territorial Authorities, the Government of the Republic had no intention of sowing dragons' teeth, and there was no real indication by the eleventh year of the Vorster Ministry that they had done so. But the black leaders of the new Homeland Governments, like chiefs in the past who had had the difficult task of interpreting their peoples and the authorities to each other, frequently found themselves walking a tightrope. The two most prominent, Chief Kaiser Matanzima and Chief Gatsha Buthelezi, at first reacted very differently to the Bantu Authorities system. Matanzima, head of a subordinate Thembu chiefdom, was prepared to use Bantu Authorities as an avenue to personal promotion, and became not only Chief Minister in 1963, but a paramount chief in 1966. By contrast, Buthelezi at first looked on Bantu Authorities with suspicion. Matanzima had pushed through the Transkeian Territorial Authority a constitution which gave great power to the chiefs, whereas Buthelezi, who belonged to the family which traditionally supplied the Zulu King's chief minister, was the choice of a Territorial Authority which had rejected the Republican Government's bid to set up something like a rejuvenated Zulu autocracy. Matanzima backed separate development and initially desired the removal of whites from the Transkei; Buthelezi, while accepting the principle of an independent Kwazulu, had no intention of requiring members of other race groups to leave or abandon their rights. Matanzima, who had himself used the powers of banishment given to him under the Transkeian emergency regulations, and experienced both the political attacks of the integrationist Democratic Party and the more violent attempts of Poqo to eliminate him, was identified with the National Party's policy in a way that Buthelezi, who was deprived of a passport between 1966 and 1971, could hardly be.

But as time passed, the approaches of these two leaders became less distinguishable. Matanzima, like other Homeland leaders, pressed the Republican Government to revise its policy of excluding white-owned capital from the Transkei at least as early as 1967, while Buthelezi devoted much energy in the 1970s to discouraging overseas firms from contemplating the withdrawal of capital from South Africa. By 1968, Matanzima was beginning to agitate for the incorporation in the Transkei of the border districts of Elliot, Maclear, Mount Currie and Matatiele, and he continued to ask for these areas, and for Port St Johns, despite rebuffs from the white government, arguing in 1972 that the 1936 land settlement had not been made with political frontiers in mind, and asserting (until he changed his front two years later) that he would not settle for independence until adequate extensions of territory had been conceded. In 1975 Port St Johns was zoned for African ownership, and Matanzima – apparently falling out of step with the other Homeland leaders – decided to negotiate with the Republican Government for full independence, a date for which was agreed upon: October 1976. Buthelezi, meanwhile, was conducting a similar campaign, asking for the incorporation in Kwazulu of the new port of Richards Bay, as well as Empangeni, Eshowe and other white towns, and using the expulsion of large numbers of Zulu labour tenants from northern Natal to resettlement villages at Nqutu and elsewhere as his justification for demanding more land. It was in 1972, as well, that Matanzima spoke out in support of a 'Greater Xhosaland', involving the amalgamation of the Transkei and the Ciskei with the white-owned region as far as the Fish River, and including the port of East London, urging now, as Buthelezi might have done, that the white people should be allowed to remain in the area with full citizenship rights. He visited Britain with Buthelezi in 1971, and then went to the U.S.A. On their return they began to propagate the idea of a federation of the African Homelands. This idea was resisted. The Republican Government stood firm in opposing any extension of the Transkei; the Ciskeians themselves voted against amalgamation; while the leaders of Bophutatswana rejected the Transkei–Kwazulu federation plan by expressing a preference for associating with Botswana.

But it was clear by 1973 that the leaders of the two largest Homelands had kept the initiative and were putting the white Government's policy severely to the test. Vorster himself, appreciating the need to react imaginatively, set a precedent by holding summit discussions with the Homeland leaders, thus establishing direct personal contact with the hand-picked agents of his Government's policy, who were by no means simple 'yes'-men. Buthelezi even talked in 1971 of holding another national convention, with encouragement from Sonny Leon and A. M. Rajab, the (Coloured) Labour Party and Indian Council leaders, and took part in 1974 in Round Table discussions in East London with the Progressive Party and other groups over the possibility of a federal constitution for the white Republic and the Bantustans.

Criticism of the Government by the agents of its own policy had to be allowed. M. C. Botha, the S.A.B.C., and other pillars of the establishment could therefore be slated by the Bantustan leaders with impunity. But outspoken criticism from groups ideologically at variance with the Government, especially the English-language churches, the English-language press, English-speaking student organisations (black as well as white), and the Liberal and Progressive Parties were harder for the Government to tolerate. Immediately after taking power, Vorster attempted to break the inter-racial contact fostered by organisations hostile to his own policies. His Prohibition of Improper Interference Bill of 1966 was a measure to block probable Progressive victories in the forthcoming elections for Coloured seats in the Cape Provincial Council and in Parliament. The Government tried to take more power than it needed for this purpose, and phrased the Bill so as to make it illegal for a person to belong, not merely to a mixed political party, but to any kind of mixed racial organisation, the objects of which were to propagate, discuss, study or encourage political views. There was a public outcry, in which the *Burger* shared. The Government covered its tracks by appointing a select committee, and the Bill, as revised, was enacted as the Prevention of Political Interference Act in 1968, its terms now limited to membership of political parties and attendance at political meetings, which in either case was to be uniracial. Rather than continue under conditions which made nonsense of its basic values, the Liberal Party, several of whose leaders had been served with banning orders, decided to dissolve. Though deprived of the prospect of winning the Coloured seats, the Progressives had retained a toehold in the white constituencies and felt justified in continuing as a white Party, but it was not until the general election of 1974 that they were able to extend their representation.

After preventing the election of Progressives as Coloured representatives in the Cape Provincial Council and both houses of Parliament, the Government set about establishing a completely segregated political system for the Coloured people, centred on a Coloured Persons' Representative Council. Legislation to this effect became law in 1968. Unlike the Transkeian constitution, the measure allowed for a majority of elective members (40) over Government nominees (20). Most of the elective seats were won by the opposition Labour Party of M. D. Arendse in the first general election, held on 24 September 1969; but the pro-*apartheid* Federal Party of Tom Swartz won just enough seats, with the support of the Government nominees, to accept office. The nominees included thirteen men who had been defeated in the election, and this destroyed the faith of many Coloured people in the future of the Council, which had a stormy apprenticeship, the opposition Labour Party making no secret of its disapproval of this substitute political system. In 1974 the Opposition carried a motion in favour of direct representation in Parliament, went on to defeat an important financial measure, and eventually, after personal confrontations with the Prime Minister in August and September, they won an outright majority in the election of 1975. This time the Government invited Sonny Leon, the Labour leader, to take office. He did so, but there was much opposition in his own party to devices put forward by the Prime Minister to break the deadlock. These included a mixed consultative cabinet council under the Prime Minister and the appointment of Coloured people to a larger number of administrative and advisory bodies. But the Labour Party remained dissatisfied, and in October 1975 its members in the Coloured Representative Council decided not to appropriate funds allocated to the Council on the ground that the budget was racially discriminatory. Leon was removed from his post by the Government in November, and replaced by an independent Government nominee, Mrs Alathea Jansen, who approved the budget.

The feelings of Coloured people were further strained by developments on the Group Areas front. The extent to which Coloured and Indian families bore the brunt of the compulsory removals under the Group Areas Act was revealed by the figures released by the Minister of Community Development in the Assembly on 21 February 1973. He then stated that, whereas only 1513 white families had had to move because they lived in the wrong group area, 44,885 Coloured and 27,694 Indian families had been moved by the end of 1972: 135 white families, 27,448 Coloured and 10,641 Indian still had to move, as well as 1162 Chinese. In terms of geographical realities, the Coloured people of the western Cape had seen the central city area of Cape Town proclaimed for the white group in 1965, which meant that permits had to be obtained for Coloured people to attend the traditionally multi-racial occasions – concerts, receptions, public meetings, and so on – in the Cape Town city hall or on the Grand Parade. District Six, Kalk Bay and Simonstown were all proclaimed white Group Areas in 1966–7, which involved the displacement of families whose ancestors had lived there since the days of the Dutch East India Company, and the removal of fisherfolk from their homes near the sea to new homes on the Cape Flats. The construction of substitute Coloured townships went ahead at Factreton, Kensington, Bonteheuwel and Bishop Lavis on the Flats, and longer-term plans were laid for large Coloured settlements behind Strandfontein on False Bay, and near Mamre to the north of greater Cape Town; but the new settlements developed many of the problems of displaced communities, and a massive housing shortage (authoritatively calculated at over 43,000 houses in 1971) was in part the result of the enforced sale of Coloured homes in proclaimed white Group Areas. Several large shanty towns developed on the Cape Flats. The Coloured people were given generous opportunities for finding wage-earning employment in the western Cape through the proclamation in January 1957 of the area west of Aliwal North and the line of the Fish and Kat rivers as a Coloured labour preference area. This meant that Coloured employees were to be appointed in preference to Bantu wherever possible, even in Port Elizabeth, where the Coloured population was a small fraction of the Bantu, and the latter was growing fast. In 1972, the Government abolished Coloured representation on Cape municipal councils by means of a provincial ordinance, and substituted nominated consultative committees, provided for under a Cape ordinance of 1963. Some of these were replaced by elective management committees, with a view to the eventual separation of Coloured and white municipalities in each urban area. This was a step which made more practical sense in larger urban settlements than it did in smaller, where the task of finding people qualified to perform the work of senior municipal officials proved difficult. These bodies provided a sub-structure of a kind for the Representative Council; but in spite of several constitutional amendments in its early years, the Representative Council remained a body in a vacuum, unattached to any defined territory which it might one day be allowed to call its own.

The Government's policy towards the Coloured people had thus led to a considerable estrangement between the two sides. Like Hertzog in the 1930s, therefore, and for very similar reasons, Vorster appointed a commission, this time under Professor Erika Theron of Stellenbosch, to look at the problems again.

The Vorster era was marked by increased pressure on the English-speaking churches, newspapers and universities, as the repositories of surviving liberalism; but these attacks cannot be seen in perspective unless they are first set against the background of a new and bitter conflict within the Afrikaner world itself. Between 1966 and 1969 the spirit of dissidence which had been fairly mute during the Verwoerd era returned with vigour, and resulted in the first major split in

Afrikanerdom since 1948. Vorster had acceded to the premiership as a junior in the Party hierarchy, apparently conscious of the void left by the charismatic Verwoerd, but determined – if the Party wanted him as leader – to assert his authority. It began to appear to his more outspoken critics that the Government would only recognise the Church and the Party as the authorities with the right to speak for the Volk, and looked on all other bodies as mere supporting organisations. Leaders of some of these bodies resented such relegation, in particular those of the *Afrikaner-Orde* (a Republican organisation dating from 1929, containing many Broederbonders, and in which Albert Hertzog had a measure of influence), *Christelike Kultuuraksie* (a body established in 1964 to oppose the influence of the liberal *Sestigers* in literature), and the *Genootskap vir Handhaving van Afrikaans*. Confrontation between the Party leaders and these bodies came to a head in 1968, and was reflected in a struggle for the control of the *Akademie vir Wetenskap en Kuns*. The Prime Minister himself played a leading role in the struggle, and in August 1968 dismissed Albert Hertzog (Health), P. M. K. le Roux (Interior) and A. E. G. Trollip (Indian Affairs) from the Cabinet, in a more direct manner than this was usually done. At about the same time the *Afrikaner-Orde* was dissolved on a decision of the Broederbond. Some argued that if Hertzog had resigned from the Cabinet at an earlier date and tried to build up his influence in the caucus as an ordinary member, he might have been able to avoid political exile; but this is at best doubtful. As it was, he and his '*verkrampte*' (narrow) associates pulled out of the Party in September 1969 and reconstituted themselves the *Herstigte* (Restored) *Nasionale Party*, devoted to the old racial rigidities as necessary to the survival of the Volk, in opposition to their rivals, the *verligtes* (enlightened). Vorster managed to contain their challenge. He advanced the general election a year, and eliminated their influence from Parliament in 1970 before they had time to organise. The Broederbond came down strongly on the side of the National Party, though it has been suggested that its constitutional duty was to remain neutral. At bottom, the issue seems to have been one of incompatibility between the ideologues who saw *apartheid* as a self-contained system to be defended in its totality, and the politicians who, faced with mounting pressures in the outside world, required room to manoeuvre on such issues as mixed sport, the admission of black diplomats, and the defence of South Africa's position at the U.N. To beat its internal enemies, the Government was prepared to use the machinery of intimidation normally turned against opponents outside Afrikanerdom, even using the Security Police to trace the source of anonymous correspondence addressed to the Cabinet. Election contests between the Nationalists and Herstigtes in 1970 and 1974 were very bitter. But the success of the Government's campaign against the *verkramptes* also required constant assertiveness against the liberals on its other flank, for it could not be seen to lack the courage of its convictions and still hope to stay in power.

The English-language press, described by Elaine Potter as the real Opposition in the South African political system, had long been under attack in the National Party. The leading monument to this was the twelve-volume Press Commission Report of 1964, which had taken fourteen years to produce. By accepting the establishment of the Press Board of Reference in 1962, newspapers published by members of the Newspaper Press Union had avoided the threat of censorship. In 1967, however, the State placed the editor of the *Rand Daily Mail*, Laurence Gandar, and a senior reporter, Benjamin Pogrund, on trial for publishing statements about conditions in the Republic's prisons which, though attested on oath before publication, were held to be false. The sentences on conviction were nominal, but the legal fees incurred by the newspaper in what had become a show trial amounted to about R250,000, and Gandar, like ffrench-Beytagh after him, subsequently retired from his post under strain. On occasion, decisions of the Publications Control Board to ban books and periodicals were successfully contested in the courts, one magazine winning its eighth appeal against a decision of the Board in 1973. The Government then appointed a Commission of Inquiry, and followed this with legislation to remove the decisions of the Board from judicial review. In 1974 a new chapter opened with the first banning of a literary work in Afrikaans – André Brink's *Kennis van die Aand*.

The censorship of literary works could be counted on to arouse very strong criticism in South African writers' circles. This was hardly surprising, in view of the quality of the best South African writing to emerge from the tensions and the tragedies wrought in so many lives by the toughness of the legal system – works of which Alan Paton's *Cry, the Beloved Country* was the pioneer. To it were soon added the graphic descriptive novels of Peter Abrahams and Ezekiel Mphahlele, the sensitive writing of Nadine Gordimer, the calculated defiance of convention by the Afrikaans-speaking *Sestigers* (School of the Sixties), of whom André Brink was one, and the stage plays of Athol Fugard, to mention only a few. They revealed a society in which the leaders of opinion were not only wrestling publicly with the moral issues presented by their situation, but were also free to do so in a manner which would not have been possible in Nazi Germany, and could only be done at considerable risk in Soviet Russia.

The English-language universities had fallen foul of the Government over the admission of non-white people as students in the 1950s, and lost this fight but not their objection to this kind of interference by the State in their affairs. Student opposition to government policy, both in relation to the universities and to public affairs in general, remained vocal, above all, in ranks of the National Union of South African Students (N.U.S.A.S.), though hardly at all in the Afrikaans universities, whose Afrikaanse Studentebond (A.S.B.) was committed to the support of government policy. Some ex-N.U.S.A.S. leaders became involved in the African Resistance Movement before 1964, though N.U.S.A.S. itself explicitly condemned acts of sabotage. N.U.S.A.S. successfully invited Senator Robert Kennedy of the United States to South Africa in 1966, but its president, Ian Robertson, was served with a banning order on the eve of his visit. Thereafter, Government attacks on N.U.S.A.S., combined with pressure on the English-language universities, began to intensify. There was a world-wide upsurge of student radicalism at the time, by which the conservative English-medium universities in South Africa were marginally affected. They proved vulnerable to Government attacks because their criticism of the country's racial policies, combined with their rejection of some aspects of conventional morality, made it possible for the Government to draw a response from the much more conservative Anglo-Afrikaner electorate to its cry of 'the nation in danger'. In February 1972, the Prime Minister appointed a Select Committee under the chairmanship of A. L. Schlebusch, on which both the National and the United parties agreed to serve, to investigate N.U.S.A.S. along with the University Christian Movement, the Christian Institute and the South African Institute of Race Relations. It started by investigating N.U.S.A.S. and held its hearings in camera. On the black campuses 1972 was a year of unrest. There the South African Student Organization (S.A.S.O.) had recently been formed to give expression to the principle of 'black power' rather than that of non-racialism in its public policy. When O. R. Tiro, a black student at the University of the North, was expelled for a public attack on the white control of black universities, a wave of support for him developed in the other English-language universities, black and white. N.U.S.A.S. identified itself with the black demands and held protest stands in June. Those in Cape Town and Johannesburg were broken up by the police, using batons and tear gas. Some students subsequently paid fines for unlawful marching or unlawful assembly, but all charges under the Riotous Assemblies Act, under which 118 persons were arraigned, either failed or were withdrawn. Early in 1973 the Schlebusch Commission issued an interim report on N.U.S.A.S., in which it recommended no action against the union as a body, but named eight leaders whom it regarded as dangerous to internal security. These, including the N.U.S.A.S. president, Paul Pretorius, were very soon served with banning orders, as were eight leaders of S.A.S.O., including their president, Jerome Modisane. The student demonstrations prompted a series of intimidatory attacks on the homes of some of their leaders, which resulted in the prosecution of one man. Tiro was subsequently murdered by a car bomb in Botswana, but his assassin was not identified.

The English-speaking churches were not easy to assail on account of the adverse effects of international propaganda likely to follow acts of persecution, and they had remained largely immune from attacks by the State since their defiance of the 'church clause' in 1957. But a full-scale judicial onslaught on the Anglican Dean of Johannesburg, G. A. ffrench-Beytagh, in 1971, on a charge of possessing subversive propaganda material and of having attempted to incite audiences to violence, got as far as the Appeal Court before the evidence of state witnesses was rejected and the Dean found not guilty. But this trial, helped by a decision of the World Council of Churches to make contributions for non-military purposes to guerrilla organisations operating in southern Africa, built up the atmosphere for a more direct confrontation. The withdrawal of passports from, or refusal of visas to, clergy (many of whom were not South African citizens) became more frequent. In 1972 the Schlebusch–Le Grange Commission forced the liberal University Christian Movement into dissolution. It also investigated the inter-denominational Christian Institute, a body best known for its sponsoring of the Study Project on Christianity in Apartheid Society (Spro-Cas), one of the fullest public airings of South African ethnic problems ever to appear. The Institute, some of whose members were prepared to commit contempt of Parliament rather than appear before a secret quasi-judicial inquiry, was heavily censured in the final report of the Commission in 1975.

Before waiting for the result of the Schlebusch–Le Grange inquiry, the Government introduced an Affected Organizations Bill during the early part of the 1974 session. This measure empowered the State President to declare any organisation 'affected' if he considered it was dangerous to the security of the State, and it prohibited affected organisations from receiving foreign funds. N.U.S.A.S. and the Christian Institute were declared 'affected'. Organisations thought by those in authority to be subversive had been subjected to a non-judicial form of inquiry from which penalties could ensue. The Government had outmanoeuvred the official Opposition, by inducing it out of concern for public security to participate in the Schlebusch Commission and endorse procedures which ignored normal judicial safeguards. At first the United Party was able to conceal its divisions, and it went into the general election of 1974 with its front unbroken, though it lost some ground. During 1975–7, however, the Party split twice and disintegrated. First, Harry Schwartz and his splinter Reform Party joined the Progressives in 1975. Then in 1977 Sir de Villiers Graaff tried and failed to reunite the Opposition. But so divided were his followers that his right wing broke away to form a new South African Party, the centre group renamed itself the New Republic Party in June 1977, while Japie

Basson's liberals joined the Progressives under Colin Eglin, to form the Progressive Federal Party.

While the Opposition was thus fragmenting, the external and the internal situations became less stable. To counter new threats beyond the frontiers (see p. 326), Vorster removed all judicial restraints from the 1966 Terrorism Act, allowing commissioned officers to detain suspects in solitary confinement, at will, for as long as they deemed it necessary. It took steps to tighten border control and extended compulsory military service to all young whites, making provision in 1967 for the training of Coloured cadets as well, and sending African as well as white police to patrol the borders. The military budget was greatly increased, and a factory set up for the production of jet aircraft. Legislation was passed to enable the Government to procure and conserve essential military supplies. The search for oil, started in the Verwoerd era, was continued, with special attention to off-shore exploration. Between 1969 and 1972 the Government brought into being a Bureau of State Security attached to the Prime Minister's office, and its members were accorded an unusual measure of protection from public discussion. A Security Services Special Account was set up, to enable the Government to invest funds secretly for the defence of the Republic.

It was a common boast of South African Governments in the post-Sharpeville era that, however much might be thought to be wrong about the South African economic and social system, it was at least a society in which order prevailed, and in which investors could therefore safely invest. Unrest which developed during the middle months of 1976 disturbed this complacent assumption. Just before the Prime Minister went to Europe to meet the American Secretary of State, Dr Kissinger, major violence broke out in Soweto from 16 to 24 June, during which 176 people died, over 1200 were wounded, and scores of administrative buildings, beer halls, schools, hostels and police vehicles went up in flames. Immediately before the Prime Minister's second departure, again to meet Dr Kissinger, unrest erupted among Coloured people in Cape Town. The Government had very recently published the completed Erika Theron Report on the Coloured people and had accepted in principle its recommendations on a number of important issues; but it had rejected out of hand the demand – endorsed by the Report – for the reintegration of the Coloured people into the white political system. Whether the Theron Report was any kind of catalyst for the Cape Town unrest, or – as was alleged – compulsory instruction through the medium of Afrikaans lay behind that in Soweto, the violence spread to many other centres. Predictably, it was described as the work of agitators. What appeared to be at issue, however, was the rejection by a rising generation of African and Coloured youths of a social system and a political philosophy which the outside world, as well as the domestic opponents of white racial dominance, had been criticising for years.

Unrest spread in 1977, especially among high-school pupils in Soweto and the eastern Cape. There were acts of urban terrorism on the Rand. Then in September the much-respected Steve Biko, president of the Black People's Convention (a black consciousness organisation founded two years earlier) died in police detention. Evidence at his inquest suggested that he had died, after humiliation, from either violence or neglect or both. The disclosures were immensely damaging to South Africa's reputation, and led directly to the West's decision to support a mandatory arms embargo against the Republic in the U.N. The Government, however, made a virtue of order even if it undervalued law. It banned a long list of 'black consciousness' organisations, together with the Christian Institute and its leaders, and in its most serious onslaught on the press to date, suppressed the Johannesburg *World*, detained its editor, Percy Qoboza, and banned Donald Woods, the outspoken editor of the *Daily Dispatch*, who was a personal friend of Biko.

The Prime Minister then called a snap general election, dangling before the electorate the bare bones of a new constitution, providing for an executive State President, aided by a white-dominated multi-national Council and separate parliaments for the White, Coloured and Indian (but not African) communities – all to replace the supposedly inadequate 'Westminster system'. But Vorster's real appeal was for white unity in face of growing pressure from the outside world. He gained eleven seats, most from split Opposition votes, but he also won nearly 70 per cent of the electoral votes, as against the 17 per cent which went to the Progressives, who now became the largest Opposition party.

# 17 Salesmanship: *Ethnasia contra Mundum*, 1945–76

Ethnasia,
A country which emerges when Ethnosis
Has been applied a hundred years or two
And those with similar skin and hair and noses
Are grouped according to the Race Who's Who.

A. R. Delius,
*The Last Division, Canto* II, x.

As a leader of one of the victorious Allied powers, and an elder statesman in international affairs, Smuts attended the opening conference of the United Nations Organization at San Francisco in April 1945. It was he who drafted the original declaration of aims in the preamble to the United Nations Charter, with its emphasis on fundamental human rights, the value of the human personality, and non-discrimination between the sexes.[1] But as Hancock has shown, he went to the conference in a pessimistic mood. It then looked as if the U.S.A. and the U.S.S.R., though at loggerheads with each other, were nevertheless agreed in their opposition to European-style colonialism. Smuts considered it essential that the Commonwealth (which he regarded as in essence an association of the White Dominions) should act as a third force in the post-war world, especially at a time when western Europe was down and out. He hoped also to gain recognition for the incorporation of South West Africa in the Union, and thus obtain by lawful means what some thought he should have got by simple annexation during the war years. He had conducted an opinion poll among the chiefs of South West Africa and their board members, asking them to state that they supported Union rule and desired incorporation. Most of them did so, but the validity of such a referendum was questionable and the General Assembly rejected it. Smuts could not have foreseen, at this stage, that his critics would not merely forbid incorporation, but insist that South West Africa should be brought under a United Nations trusteeship agreement like all the other territories which had been allocated under a League of Nations mandate.

Forced on to the defensive, Smuts tried, with almost no room to manoeuvre, to alienate as few powers as possible, and therefore agreed to administer South West Africa 'in the spirit of the Mandate', and submit reports to the Trusteeship Committee for information. He also tried from the start to model the U.N. Organization on the pattern of earlier peace-keeping bodies by limiting effective control to the great powers working through the Security Council, and trying to ensure that the General Assembly remained a forum for debate between governments, from which private individuals would be rigidly excluded. During his own term of office the Security Council retained effective control, and Smuts found solace in the veto which any Permanent Member of that Council could use. But the General Assembly was not precluded by the Charter from listening to criticism of the domestic policies of member states, or from hearing the plaints of representative individuals against their own governments. In December 1946, Mrs Pandit of India made a scorching attack on South Africa's Indian policy at the second session of the General Assembly, while Dr A. B. Xuma of the A.N.C. lobbied Assembly delegates in New York, and Smuts found – as he had found at the Imperial Conference of 1923 – that he was precluded by pressures at home from bending before the gale of criticism. By the time he fell from office pressures had developed at the international level which he could not divert with the argument that these policies were South Africa's private domestic concern.

Having had time to see the direction in which world opinion was moving, the Malan Government, which took over in 1948, decided to act on the assumption that South Africa's interests would best be served by the vigorous assertion of sovereignty rather than by compromise. It told the United Nations in 1948 that the South West African mandate had lapsed, announced its intention to discontinue sending courtesy reports, and in 1949 it gave South West Africa representation in the Union Parliament. It rejected an advisory opinion of the International Court in 1950 that the Union Government was obliged to submit to U.N. supervision to the extent that it had been obliged to submit to that of the League, and proposed instead that it should negotiate a new agreement with the three remaining Principal Allied Powers (the United States, the United Kingdom and France). The U.N. in turn found this unacceptable, and decided to receive petitions against Union rule in the territory from the Rev. Michael Scott, and – though this would not have been permitted under the Mandate system – listen to the Herero, Nama and Damara chiefs whose case he had presented. In 1954 the Union Native Affairs Department was given direct control of South West African native affairs. In 1955 the Union Government withdrew from UNESCO on the ground that it had become an anti-South African agitators' forum, and in 1957 it decided to retain only token membership of the U.N. At a point when South

African withdrawal seemed imminent, however, the Government resumed active participation in 1958, asserting that the attitudes of some governments had changed for the better.

Whereas Smuts had taken a cautious line on the influence of Soviet Russia in the post-war world, hoping to limit that influence by bringing the Commonwealth into line with the United States so that they could be *à deux* in a world of three great powers, the Malan and Strijdom Governments saw their greatest security in a posture of unequivocal opposition to the Soviet Union and to communism, first clearly implemented on the home front with the passage of the Suppression of Communism Act in 1950. In February 1956 the Soviet Government was required to close down its Consulate-General in Pretoria, on the ground that it had 'cultivated and maintained contact with subverse elements in the Union' and disseminated Communist propaganda. No person could have presented the Union's anti-communist case at the U.N. more vehemently than E. H. Louw now proceeded to do. The Communist states were in the forefront of the attack on South African domestic policies in the General Assembly. To that extent the Union Government's campaign could be seen as self-explanatory, but it found itself in a predicament when non-communist states like India voted against the same policies for the same reasons. The vehemence of the Government's anti-communism may even have helped to increase the Union's isolation, for other governments distinguished more clearly between those things which were undesirable in Soviet behaviour, and those which were not, while critics could not help noticing that the Union Government's domestic policy was becoming as indifferent to traditional notions of civil liberty as the Russian.

A count of U.N. resolutions directed against South Africa would show those relating to South West Africa to be far more numerous than those directed against South Africa's internal policies. But it was the Union's treatment of her Indian population which first drew international attention to her domestic record, and resolutions on that theme were passed nearly every year after 1946.[2] In 1952 the U.N. extended its concern to cover the policy of *apartheid* in general. It was not a straightforward matter to bring what appeared to be a purely domestic issue before the international body, but certain clauses in the U.N. Charter were accepted with growing readiness by the bulk of the member states as appropriate for such a purpose, in particular Article 55 (c), under which the U.N. undertook to 'promote . . . universal respect for, and observance of, human rights and fundamental freedoms for all without distinction as to race, sex, language or religion'. The other heads under which intervention was justified were Article 14, empowering the General Assembly to 'recommend measures for the peaceful adjustment of any situation . . . which it deems likely to impair . . . friendly relations among nations', which was used by India in 1946; and Article 39, requiring the Security Council to 'determine the existence of any threat to peace, breach of the peace, or act of aggression', and to take appropriate steps to avert these things.

It was perhaps an unavoidable weakness of Malan's foreign policy that he followed an uncompromising line without making sure that he remained the close associate of a major power bloc.[3] Like Smuts, he accepted the utility of the Commonwealth association; but like Hertzog, he did so without enthusiasm, supporting Nehru's plea in 1949 to retain Indian membership of the Commonwealth even after becoming a Republic, because he hoped to loosen ties between Great Britain and South Africa in a similar way; revising governmental immigration policy in a manner which reduced the British and increased the Continental element; and destroying the advantages enjoyed by Commonwealth citizens in applying for South African nationality – all quite legitimate actions for which a strong case could be made, yet none of them likely to strengthen South Africa's international position. The support of Britain and of western European states at the U.N. was welcomed by the Union Government during the 1950s, but the price it was prepared to pay for that support was low because there appeared to be little danger of hostile U.N. resolutions being translated into meaningful action. Thus the defence budgets during the early years of Nationalist rule remained at the level of less than £10 millions annually, escalating to between £20 and £30 millions during the Korean war, in which South Africa participated as an anti-communist gesture.

At the same time, the Government tried, with only mediocre success, to become involved in regional defensive alliances. NATO, however, was not designed to operate south of the Tropic of Cancer, though Portugal, a member state, had colonies bordering on South Africa. The ANZUS treaty was designed for the defence of the Pacific rather than the Indian Ocean. The Union Government offered to join Britain's abortive Middle East Defence Organization (MEDO), which was abandoned for want of Commonwealth support, and it did try to bring into being an alliance for the defence of Africa at conferences in Nairobi in 1951 and Dakar in 1954, which were attended by the major Colonial Powers in Africa as well as by South Africa, Southern Rhodesia and the United States. Between 1945 and 1953, Malan made reference from time to time to an 'African Charter', the object of which was to be the protection of Africa from Asian domination, the preservation of Africa for the Africans (including the resident white Africans), the development of the Continent along Western and Christian lines, the exclusion of communism, and the demilitarisation of the southern part of the Continent. But this was a project more likely to commend itself to Colonial powers in their heyday than to Colonial powers in the process of decolonising, and it had little outside appeal. Malan's 'roving ambassador' in Africa, Charles te Water, had little diplomatic success. The establishment of the ill-fated Central African Federation in 1953 had the Malan Government's strong endorsement, but this fact in itself helped to widen the gap between the Union Government and black opinion.

The Simonstown Agreement of 1955 was the one breakthrough made by South Africa, and this occurred during Strijdom's premiership after correspondence between F. C. Erasmus, Minister of Defence, and the British Foreign Secretary, Selwyn Lloyd. The South African Navy took over Simonstown, which had been a British base, but the Royal Navy was still allowed to use its facilities, and to maintain a headquarters at the Cape. The South African Navy was to be expanded by the purchase of six frigates, ten minesweepers and four other coastal defence vessels from Britain, as part of a joint plan for the defence of a new maritime strategic zone running from the northern end of South-West Africa to a line joining the southern border of Mozambique and the southern tip of Madagascar. South Africa would look after her own internal defence, while Great Britain would take steps to keep the Suez route open from her eastern Mediterranean and Red Sea bases.

The Suez crisis of 1956 destroyed much of the effectiveness of the latter arrangement. South Africa's public disapproval of the Anglo-French attack on the canal zone, following the outbreak of an Arab-Israeli war, was perhaps forced on her by what Barber has called a 'classic example of a breakdown of Commonwealth cooperation'. Sir Percivale Liesching, the British High Commissioner in South Africa, explained on 6 November 1956 that there had been no prior consultation before the seizure of the Canal because it was a decision taken in an emergency; but early the next year E. H. Louw, the South African Minister of External Affairs, insisted that the Egyptian nationalisation of the Canal, which had shortly preceded the Anglo-French action, was a domestic Egyptian issue in which South Africa had no interest as either user or shareholder. It was a significant moment in South Africa's external relations, for the Suez crisis led to the first effective steps by the Soviet Union to extend its influence into Africa, an influence channelled through support for Nasser's Egypt, Nkrumah's Ghana which became independent in 1957, Sékou Touré's Guinea which left the French Community in 1958, and Algeria, which obtained its independence from De Gaulle the same year.

Recognition of the fact of black independent states in Africa required a considerable shift of attitude on the part of the South African Government. It wasted no time in uttering the necessary courtesies once its efforts to prevent the 'blackening' of the Commonwealth had failed, but missed an opportunity to make contact with black Africa by turning down Dr Nkrumah's invitation to the first conference of independent African states in Accra in 1958, on the ground that colonial powers should have been invited as well. The prospects of achieving rapport with the black states were ruled out at this stage by black distaste at Union policies on the one hand and South Africa's reluctance to admit black ambassadors on the other, even though the Reservation of Separate Amenities Act of 1953 had punched a hole in the colour bar for the benefit of black representatives of foreign governments. South Africa tried to gain influence in the new states through participating in the Council for Technical Co-operation in Africa (C.C.T.A.), the Foundation for Mutual Assistance (F.A.M.A.), the Scientific Council for Africa (C.S.A.) and other bodies, thus maintaining contact within a limited sphere of activity, but in the early 1960s she was forced not only out of these bodies, but also out of the Food and Agricultural Organization (F.A.O.) and World Health Organization (W.H.O.) on account of her racial policies.

Soon after taking office in 1958 Dr Verwoerd managed, by a clever shift of emphasis, to end the long wrangle with the Imperial Government over the future of the High Commission Territories, which in due course received self-government under the names of Lesotho and Botswana in 1966, and Swaziland in 1968.[4] On assuming power, Malan had reverted in 1949–51 to the slightly peevish tones of Hertzog, and understandably got nowhere with the British Government, while Strijdom had made a similar demand for their incorporation in the Union in 1955. Verwoerd, however, realising that Britain could not agree to incorporation in view of African opposition in the Territories to such a move, gave support to the British plans for their independence and began to look upon them as African homelands analogous to those which he began to establish in the Republic under the Promotion of Bantu Self-Government Act of 1959, with independence for the first time as their declared destiny. This was an ingenious rationalisation which made both political and economic sense. The Bantu Homelands, among them Botswana, Lesotho and Swaziland, would – so Verwoerd hoped – become satellites of a southern African Commonwealth, of which the Republic was destined to be the planet.

But in all other respects the spread of decolonisation made the Government's task progressively harder, so that the problems facing Verwoerd were considerably tougher than those which had faced Malan and Strijdom. By 1960, not only was a large part of northern Africa decolonised, but pressure was developing on the white Settler communities of East Africa, and this was soon followed by the unexpectedly sudden Belgian withdrawal from the Congo. Decolonisation in turn changed the balance of forces in the General Assembly of the United Nations, where the Afro-Asian element had risen from fifteen out of fifty members in 1946 to seventy-three out of 125 in 1965. The newly independent member-states of the Third World looked increasingly to the Soviet Union for support – and, outside the U.N., to Red China, whose influence in Africa began to be effective from about the time of Chou En-lai's visit to Zanzibar in 1964. The Western powers found themselves under a growing strain, as they were forced into the position of having to support for strategic and economic reasons the surviving colonial regimes of southern Africa, whose policies offended their sensitivities but not their interests.

When Harold Macmillan, Prime Minister of Great Britain, addressed the combined South African Houses of Parliament in February 1960, his speech registered this tension. He offered South Africa continued friendship on the basis of Christian values, racial non-discrimination and the rule of law, and gave an undertaking not to support an economic boycott against her. But his dissociation from South African policies was clear, just as Verwoerd made it clear in his reply that South Africa would abandon accepted values if the survival of the white race in southern Africa seemed to warrant so doing.

The era of U.N. resolutions condemning South Africa's policies wholesale, with massive majorities and almost no defending votes now began. The boycott of South African products was encouraged. In 1962 the General Assembly urged member states to break off diplomatic relations with South Africa, and close their harbours and airports to South African ships and planes. In 1963 the Security Council resolved to ban the sale of arms to South Africa, and the United States and Great Britain were among the powers which complied with the resolution, though West Germany, France and Canada were not. The formation of the Organization of African Unity at Addis Ababa in the same year provided the decolonization crusade with a central organisation, if not a high command. In 1964 a large conference in London debated the feasibility of imposing sanctions.

An essential part of the background to this intensified international campaign was the growth of confrontation between South Africa and the United Nations over South West Africa.[5] The General Assembly had appointed an *ad hoc* committee to negotiate with the Union Government in 1951. In 1952 it failed in its object, and the Union Government withdrew from the Trusteeship Committee in protest against continued U.N. intervention. It was persuaded to return in 1957 after the General Assembly had set up a Good Offices Committee under Sir Charles Arden-Clarke, which held general discussions with the Union Government on its proposals to partition South West Africa; but such a solution was not acceptable either to the Trusteeship Committee or to the General Assembly. In November 1959 the Assembly noted with grave concern that the Union was administering the territory in a manner contrary to the Mandate, the U.N. Charter, the Universal Declaration of Human Rights, the advisory opinions of the International Court, and earlier resolutions of the Assembly itself. Riots among Africans at Windhoek in December 1959, following government attempts to remove them to a new location, led in turn to the appointment of a one-man judicial commission by the Union Government, which defended the use of force by the police. But it also led the Conference of Independent African States meeting at Addis Ababa in June 1960 to institute proceedings against South Africa in the International Court. Ethiopia and Liberia, the only other independent African states which had been members of the League were the plaintiffs. Meanwhile pressure continued at the United Nations. The Trusteeship Committee required South Africa to revoke all *apartheid* laws which applied in South West, and called on its own South West Africa Committee to visit the territory, if necessary without the cooperation of the Union Government. This proved difficult to do, as Professor Enrique Fabregat, the chairman of that committee, found after arriving in Salisbury in July 1961. Denied access even to Bechuanaland, from which it proposed to enter South West Africa, by the British Government, the party returned via Dar-es-Salaam and reported failure. Thereupon the Trusteeship Committee, instead of retreating, proceeded by an impressive majority of 86 votes to one (Portugal's) to appoint a seven-nation committee with instructions to visit South West Africa before 1 May 1962, conduct investigations on the spot, see to the removal of South African control, prepare for democratic elections leading to the establishment of an independent government, arrange U.N. technical assistance, release political prisoners and repeal discriminatory laws. Brazil, Burma, Mexico, Norway, the Philippines, Somalia and Togo accepted membership of this new committee. The South African Government, deeming it wise not to trail its coat, invited the chairman and secretary of this committee, Victorio Carpio of the Philippines and Dr Martinez de Alva of Mexico respectively, to visit South West Africa. They did so, and announced that they had not found evidence of either genocide or any militarisation of South West Africa in violation of the mandate, nor any threat to international peace consequent upon South Africa's administration of the territory. After leaving South Africa, however, the same two men affirmed that *apartheid* was being rigorously enforced in the territory (as would indeed became clear with the publication of the Odendaal Report in 1964), and that South Africa was administering it in violation of U.N. principles, and had revealed no intention to abandon its policies or prepare the peoples for self-government or independence. They also asserted that the African people desired direct administration by the U.N. But it was difficult to recommend further action, not only because the initial Carpio–De Alva Report appeared too favourable to South Africa and was later repudiated by Carpio himself, but because the South West African case was all the while *sub judice* at The Hague.

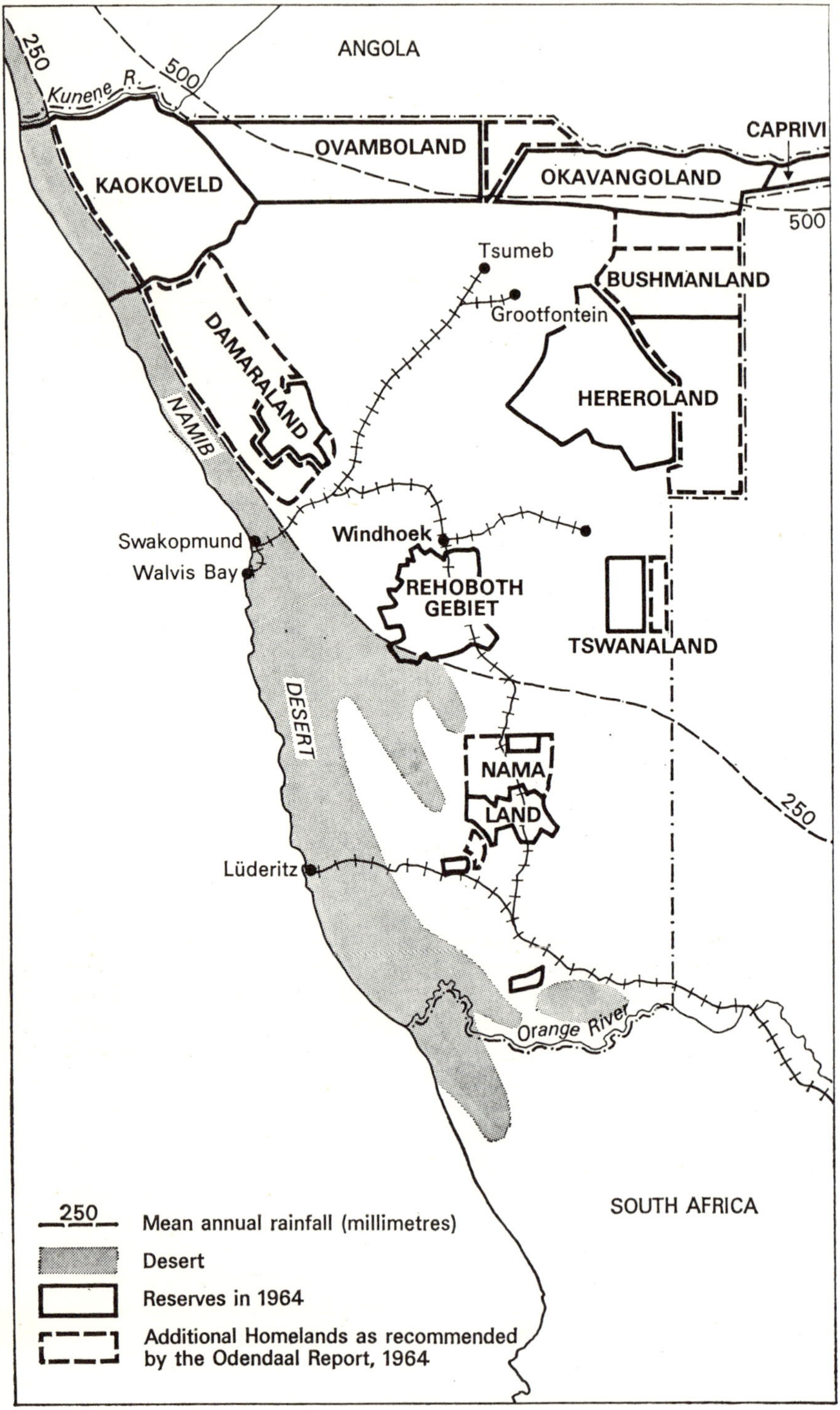


Map 4 South West Africa (Namibia)

The court decided in 1962 that it had jurisdiction to try the case, and rejected the South African contention that Ethiopia and Liberia had no *locus standi*. From then on, argument at The Hague turned on the South African administrative record, and the case of the plaintiffs was made to rest on the Union Government's restriction of the franchise to whites, its failure to provide adequate educational facilities, its introduction of travel passes, its ban on political party and trade union membership by blacks, its policy of racial segregation, its exclusion of non-white people from certain defined occupations, its exclusion of non-white people from the right to landed property over large areas of the territory, and the forcible deportation of individuals on the orders of the Administrator without any right of appeal. When judgment was given in 1968, however, after a six-year hearing during which one judge had died and a successor with different views had been appointed, the Court by a narrow majority of eight opinions against seven reversed its earlier decision and, without examining the substance of the plaintiffs' case, accepted the South African contention that the plaintiffs had no standing. This narrow decision bought time for South Africa, and put off a situation in which the Security Council might have found itself in the position of having to initiate either sanctions or stronger action against the Republic. It also inflamed the majority in the U.N. General Assembly, which now began to put pressure on the Security Council to compel South African compliance.

The Security Council first took cognisance of the South West African dispute in January 1968, when it demanded the release of thirty-seven South West Africans on trial in Pretoria on political charges. The following year it recognised a resolution of the General Assembly taken in 1966, formally terminating the mandate, and called upon the South African Government to withdraw its administration from the territory. It subsequently called South Africa's refusal to do so 'an aggressive encroachment on the authority of the United Nations'. On 30 July 1970 the Council asked the International Court of Justice for an advisory opinion on the legal implications of South Africa's continued presence in Namibia – as South West Africa was coming to be called – and received the reply that the U.N. resolution of 1966 was valid in law, and that all states, in their dealings with Namibia, should explicitly indicate that they did not recognise the validity of South African rule there. South Africa's offer of the same year to hold an all-races plebiscite under joint supervision of the Republican Government and the International Court, to test the relative popularity of South African and United Nations administration, was not accepted by the U.N. The following year the Security Council asked the Secretary-General, Dr Kurt Waldheim, to make contact with all parties concerned in order to establish conditions under which the people of Namibia could exercise their right to self-determination. Invited by the

South African Government, Dr Waldheim arrived in Cape Town in March 1971, and made a brief tour of South West Africa. He held discussions with Vorster, the Republican Prime Minister, but they reached deadlock on the question of whether 'self-determination' could include South Africa's plan for balkanisation on the lines of the Odendaal Report. As that report had been partly implemented, for example by the establishment of representative assemblies for the Ovambo and other groups, since 1967, this point was of more than academic interest. Those parties in South West Africa which favoured South Africa's immediate withdrawal and the creation of a unitary Namibian state, met in convention at Rehoboth in November 1971. They included the Baster Volksparty, the National Unity Democratic Action (a Herero movement under Chief Clemens Kapuuo), the South West African People's Organization (SWAPO), and the South West African National Union (SWANU). Dr Waldheim's personal representative, Dr A. M. Escher of Switzerland, visited southern Africa at the end of the year and met representatives of this Convention as well as the Prime Minister. The latter now undertook to form an Advisory Council for South West Africa. When this Council first met in March 1972, it included two whites nominated by the Legislative Assembly, two Coloured men nominated by the Coloured Council (a nominated body then in the process of becoming partly elective), two representatives each from Ovamboland, Okavango and East Caprivi, and a single representative (or observer) from each of the Tswana, Bushman, Herero, Rehoboth Baster, Damara and Nama groups. It met behind closed doors.

But deadlock between the Security Council and the South African Government was fully restored in 1973 when the former body resolved unanimously to call a halt to Dr Waldheim's mediation. Chief Kapuuo of the Convention, who had been allowed to leave South-West Africa by the Republican authorities, urged upon the Trusteeship Committee the need for an immediate South African withdrawal. On 17 December 1974, the Security Council unanimously called on South Africa to transfer power to the people of Namibia in accordance with the International Court ruling of 1971, and immediately adhere to the Universal Declaration of Human Rights by releasing political prisoners, ending discriminatory practices and allowing political exiles to return in safety. A deadline was set at 30 May 1975, whereupon the Council would meet again to consider its next step. It duly did so, but a proposal to enforce positive economic sanctions by authorising the seizure of South-West African products on the high seas was vetoed by the combined decisions of Britain, the United States and France.

In the meantime the Republican Government continued to consult with the Advisory Council, made public profession of its acceptance of self-determination for the territory, and announced on the eve of the

Security Council's resumed session that some discriminatory measures – notably the pass laws – were to be withdrawn.

Rhodesia's Unilateral Declaration of Independence in 1965 increased South Africa's difficulties on the international front, for without wishing to appear to back white supremacy outside her borders, she felt bound to ignore the instruction of the Security Council to impose economic sanctions on the territory.[6] It was politically impossible to alienate the upstart Government of Rhodesia, to which the white South African Government felt drawn by ties of common interest. From the outset, therefore, the South African Government treated the dispute between Britain and the Smith regime as a private dispute, and recognised the Smith Government *de facto* but not *de jure*. It also refused to apply sanctions on the ground that it was opposed to such action on principle. The ties between the South African and Rhodesian governments were drawn tighter in 1967 by the dispatch of South African police units to help combat guerrillas on the Zambesi border. Two years later a two-thirds majority in the Security Council voted for the application of sanctions to South Africa and Portugal for the assistance they had given to Rhodesia; but the United States and the United Kingdom vetoed implementation. The situation became more tense with the closure of the Zambian–Rhodesian border in January 1973, and tenser still after the success of the Frelimo guerrillas in taking over Mozambique following the overthrow of Dr Caetano's Government in Portugal in April 1974. This left the Republican Government in the difficult position of having to decide whether Rhodesia could be defended indefinitely against guerrilla attacks from the east as well as from the north, or whether it was better to accept the inevitability of black rule north of the Limpopo and strengthen its own bastion further south. Vorster withdrew the South African police from Rhodesia, but kept his options open, refusing on the one hand to prescribe policies for a neighbouring state, but applying all the diplomatic pressure at his disposal to bring the Smith Government and Bishop Abel Muzorewa, leader of the African National Council, to the conference table. The policy was effective because Vorster and the Zambian president, Dr Kenneth Kaunda, were able to overlook an earlier contretemps on account of their common desire to avoid a southern African bloodbath, which, as Vorster said in the Senate on 23 November 1974, could produce consequences 'too horrible to contemplate'. The convening of a Rhodesian constitutional conference at the Victoria Falls in August 1975 showed that Kaunda and Vorster could at least bring their respective horses to the water, if that was all.

As South Africa's external dangers seemed to be increasing, her diplomacy was becoming noticeably more flexible. Verwoerd had rejected a request by Sir Abubakar Tafawa Balewa of Nigeria to be allowed to visit South Africa in 1962, and an offer by Dr Banda of Malawi to establish diplomatic relations with the Republic in 1964, in the first instance because he doubted Balewa's bona fides, and in the second because the offer had been made from a political platform. Vorster, by contrast, arranged personal meetings with the heads of Lesotho, Chief Jonathan, in 1966, with the President of Botswana, Sir Seretse Khama, in 1968, and with Prince Makhosini Dlamini of Swaziland in March 1971. Diplomatic relations with Malawi were opened in 1967 (the Malawians appointing a white representative), while Dr Banda paid a state visit to South Africa in 1971. But these were essentially set-piece manoeuvres in which neither side was prepared to give ground, and the distance which still stood between Vorster and the leaders of the black states was shown by his early attempts to score points at the expense of Dr Kaunda, and by his Government's rejection of the Lusaka Manifesto of April 1969. Fourteen East and Central African states were represented on that occasion at a conference which affirmed its disapproval of racialism, but agreed to recognise South Africa as an independent African state like themselves. The governments represented at Lusaka refused to abandon their plan to liberate the blacks in the south, but they affirmed their desire to do this by peaceful means rather than by war. The Lusaka Manifesto, rejected by South Africa, was adopted by the O.A.U. and subsequently by the United Nations. In June 1971, the O.A.U. summit meeting at Addis Ababa decided that South Africa's rejection of the Manifesto justified the abandonment of dialogue with the white regime, and it was left to South Africa to save what she could of the policy by maintaining unpublicised contacts behind the scenes.

Economic links between South Africa and her black neighbours prevented too wide a rift from developing. The direct offer of aid by South Africa, for example her offer to build a new capital for Malawi at Lilongwe, and her investment in the Cabora Bassa dam project in Mozambique helped here. The mutual interdependence of South Africa, Malawi, Zambia and Portuguese East Africa on the long-standing system of labour migrancy was one such bond. Of 381,000 blacks employed by the Chamber of Mines in 1972, about one-third were drawn from north of Latitude 22° South, while another third came from Mozambique. The total number of 'tropicals' had risen from 3000 to 119,000 between 1936 and 1972. It was no matter for surprise, therefore, when the governments of states within South Africa's economic orbit contracted out of O.A.U. attempts to impose an economic boycott of the Republic, as Dr Kamuzu Banda of Malawi and Sir Seretse Khama of Botswana did in 1964, and the Government of Zambia did in 1965. In spite of a tendency for states north of the Limpopo, and above all Lesotho, to reduce the number of migrants to the South African mines in 1974–5, and of a corresponding effort by the Chamber of Mines to make do with less foreign labour, the pattern of interdependence was not significantly altered.

Business interests in the outside world were also closely tied to business interests in South Africa, despite a tendency for South African business houses and their foreign counterparts to bring about a formal separation of their assets and management. British industry was particularly heavily committed, with close on £2000 million invested in the Republic in 1970, and over 500 commercial companies with associates or subsidiaries there. At that time about 60 per cent of overseas investment in South Africa was British-owned, about 20 per cent West European, and about 15 per cent American. Trade between South Africa and Japan escalated massively between 1955 and 1969, the total value of exports and imports between the two countries rising from R31 millions in the former year to R411 millions in the latter. The investment of private capital in South African enterprises aroused great controversy in Western countries during the late 1960s and early 1970s, on the argument that such investment was propping up the system of *apartheid*. Supporters of such investment argued that the creation of work opportunities in the Republic was making the implementation of *apartheid* less inhumane, and forcing the South African Government, from the shortage of trained artisans, to connive at the employment of blacks in fields of work from which they were excluded by law. But whichever argument was the stronger, there was a tendency during the 1970s for the scale of overseas investment to increase, and in doing so to build up the interest of Western countries in the continued stability of the Republic under whatever conditions that stability was maintained.

From the strategic side, the same tendency was not so easy to discern. During the mid-1960s strategists in Britain came round to the view that the Simonstown naval base was of little importance to the Western powers, on account of growing détente with the Soviet Union, and on account of the development of long-range missiles and nuclear-powered long-range submarines, which together made bases more vulnerable and less necessary. By 1969 this view was not shared so firmly in NATO strategic circles, for it was now clear that Soviet Russia aimed to become a world naval power, and that the projected withdrawal of British naval units from the Indian Ocean (in which the United States had never established itself as a naval power) was creating a power vacuum into which Russia could move, helped by Egyptian permission to move warships through the Suez Canal and permission from Somalia to establish a supply base at Berbera. The United States eventually reacted to this new Soviet threat to the West's oil supply lines in the Indian Ocean by deciding to set up a naval base on Diego Garcia. But at almost exactly the same time France withdrew from Diego Suarez in Malagasy, and Britain decided to terminate the twenty-year-old Simonstown Agreement.

Whether South Africa's strategic value to the West appreciated significantly, as a result of these developments, therefore depended less on bases (which the Republic could hardly have denied to the West in a crisis), than on the presence in southern Africa of key strategic raw materials – notably uranium and chrome. The West relied on these, and might therefore wish to deny them to potential enemies (see Map 5, p. 377).

Efforts were made by the South African Government from about 1968 to build up a system of joint defence for the southern oceans. This resulted only in the opening up of diplomatic contact with Argentina and Paraguay, for the main effort of the Republican Government was devoted instead to rearmament. In 1950 South Africa's defence budget had stood at a mere R16 millions. It had grown to R38.5 millions by 1960, to R230 millions by 1966, and to R1350 millions by 1976.

The beginnings of guerrilla infiltration into South Africa's territory had occurred shortly before Vorster came to power. In 1966–7 a few guerrillas belonging to the South West African People's Organization (S.W.A.P.O.) had entered South West Africa from Tanzania via Zambia and Angola, and it was known that perhaps 2000 had left South Africa for training in various countries, mainly in the Communist bloc. In 1969 to 1972 there were several clashes between police and guerrillas in the Caprivi Strip, but guerrilla pressure became significantly greater in Rhodesia and Mozambique in 1972–3. They managed to penetrate the north-eastern frontier districts of Rhodesia, while members of Frelimo, one of the Portuguese African liberatory movements, periodically cut the Umtali–Beira railway and put pressure on Tete. South Africa was directly involved on account of her participation in the construction of the Cabora Bassa dam and hydro-electric scheme, power from which was destined for the Rand. Despite the growth of terrorism in the rest of the world in the early 1970s, there was a disposition in international circles, in particular in the World Council of Churches, to exempt guerrillas of southern Africa from their general condemnation, even to give them moral and other support.

South Africa's defensive preparations were more than adequate to deal with any challenge thought likely to appear, but the Angolan crisis of 1975–6 threatened to cause a serious escalation of the conflict. When the Portuguese authorities withdrew in November 1975, leaving the territory in dispute between rival Marxist and non-Marxist factions, the former already enjoying some support from the Communist world, South African troops became involved in helping the advance of the non-Marxist Unita–F.N.L.A. forces right to the outskirts of Luanda, the capital and main base of the Marxist M.P.L.A. When the arrival of Cuban regulars, equipped with sophisticated Russian weaponry, enabled the M.P.L.A. to turn the tables on its black opponents, the South African forces were withdrawn, first to defensive positions still inside Angola, to shelter political refugees and protect the half-completed Calueque dam on the Kunene river, and later – after the M.P.L.A. had guaranteed the safety of the construction workers – to within the South West African borders. The Government apparently withdrew its forces on account of two considerations: the refusal of the U.S.A. or the NATO powers to take active steps to prevent an M.P.L.A. victory, and the hostile reaction of other African governments to South African involvement in the war.

By the time the M.P.L.A. had become the Government of Angola in February 1976, recognised by the O.A.U., by Portugal, and by many Western as well as Communist states, the damage done to Vorster's détente policy became apparent. Zambia could no longer count on the use of the Benguela railway for the export of her copper, at a time when the Rhodesian debate had reached an apparent stalemate, and the prospect of reopening traffic via the Victoria Falls had receded. Soon after the Victoria Falls conference, Bishop Muzorewa had broken off negotiations with the Smith Government, and the external wing of the now split Rhodesian African National Council had begun to organise an intensification of guerrilla war from Mozambique, which closed its border with Rhodesia on 3 March. Smith continued to negotiate privately with the rump of the A.N.C., led by Joshua Nkomo (leader of Z.A.P.U.), in Salisbury, but these negotiations broke down the same month. Meanwhile the South West African constitutional conference continued to meet behind closed doors, offering very little information to the outside world about progress made. When the Soweto riots broke out in June, adding internal violence to external deadlock, the prospects for a peaceful future in southern Africa seemed bleak indeed.

Vorster, however, still had a role to play: to help the outside world in defusing the tensions of an area which now began to look as if it might actually erupt in racial war, and thus really threaten the peace of the world. His visit to Israel in April, though it caused some surprise, made good diplomatic sense. For the first time in nearly thirty years, a South African prime minister was cutting a figure outside his own country. The visit served as a diplomatic prelude for his visits to Europe to meet Dr Henry Kissinger, the American Secretary of State, in June and September. In the latter month, Kissinger also visited southern Africa, including Pretoria, where he agreed to meet Smith of Rhodesia at the Prime Minister's official residence, 'Libertas'. As a result of this meeting, Smith announced his acceptance of an Anglo-American scheme for bringing peace to his borders and an ending of international sanctions, at the price of an immediate multi-racial interim regime to be followed by majority rule within two years. The scheme proved abortive, however, because it had not actually won the support of the 'front-line presidents' (as the leaders of Tanzania, Zambia, Botswana, Angola and Mozambique were now described), nor received the backing of the 'Zimbabwean' leaders in exile, Joshua Nkomo and Robert Mugabe, who joined forces to form a Patriotic Front. After a year's negotiating through the medium of British, American and South African representatives, Smith decided in November 1977 to work for an internal settlement with African leaders who had not gone into exile, led by Bishop Abel Muzorewa, on the basis of adult suffrage with built-in safeguards for the white minority. The South African role throughout was a double one: to keep the doors open for negotiations, and to refuse to comply with U.N. mandatory sanctions.

Meanwhile the South West African constitutional conference at the Turnhalle in Windhoek, which had met initially behind closed doors, responded to an approach by the ambassadors of five Western powers – Britain, the U.S.A., France, Germany and Canada – to work towards a unitary constitution (as opposed to the fragmented scheme outlined in the Odendaal Report of 1964), to agree to S.W.A.P.O. participation in elections to the constituent asembly, and to accept 31 December 1978 as a firm target date for independence. Dirk Mudge, the chairman of the Turnhalle conference, was defeated in the S.W.A. National Party's leadership elections, and immediately resigned from the Party to form a new multi-racial Turnhalle Alliance. South Africa also insisted on retaining an effective military force in the territory to prevent guerrilla incursions, despite S.W.A.P.O. protests. But at the end of 1977 there was a real chance that the logjam there, and perhaps even in Rhodesia, could be resolved by negotiations.

This did not make the Republic's policy of separate development any more acceptable internationally, however, as was shown, symbolically, by the universal refusal of other States to recognise the independence of Transkei.

# Section III
# The Problem of Perspective

# 18 Segregation and *Apartheid*

The characteristic international image of the South African system is more commonly summed up by the word *apartheid* than by any other single term. This chapter aims simply to explain what is meant by the term as it has evolved historically, and to illustrate it with reference to some of the more important legislation which has been promulgated in its name, or in the name of segregation (*segregasie*) or separate develop ment (*aparte ontwikkeling*) with which it is commonly associated.[1] Semantic experts have sometimes distinguished between these terms, and sometimes the distinctions drawn by them are helpful. Thus Professor Hoernlé stated in 1941 that 'Segregation ... is most perfectly realized in a multi-racial caste society. Separation, falsely called "segregation", is most perfectly realized when the diffent racial groups are sorted out into their own territorially distinct societies' (*Race and Reason*, p. 160). Definitions have tended, however, to differ according to whether they are defensive or propagandist. The position taken in this chapter is that all represent a common phenomenon, as well described as anywhere in Dr H. F. Verwoerd's words spoken in the House of Assembly in 1954. The mystique of *apartheid*, as elaborated by its exponents after 1948, came to mean separation in all possible fields, political, territorial, residential, cultural and economic. The policy is best understood if these elements are looked at individually; but it is desirable first of all to discuss origins.

Ever since Van Riebeeck planted his hedge, there have been people in southern Africa who wished the races to live together, and people who wished them to live apart. They became easier to identify in the nineteenth century. A contrast is commonly drawn, for example, between the frontier farmers who encouraged the settlement of blacks on their land in order to obtain their services as labourers, and the missionaries who tried to protect the Griqua and Bantu-speaking chiefdoms from white encroachment and cultural contamination, much as the Jesuits of Paraguay had sheltered the Amerindians in their Reductions. The rival outlooks of Governor Sir George Grey (1854–61) and Sir Theophilus Shepstone (Secretary for Native Affairs in Natal, 1848–75) highlight a similar distinction. Grey, opening the Cape Parliament in March 1855, envisaged an integrated, multi-racial society under white patronage, when he allowed himself to imagine

> a fertile and populous country, filled with a large population, partly European, partly native . . . the natives won by our exertions to Christianity, trained by us in agriculture and in simple arts, possessing property of their own, and a stake in the country, accustomed to our laws, and aware of their advantages, – attached to us from a sense of benefits received, – respecting us for our strength and generosity.

Shepstone for his part master-minded the establishment of segregated locations for Africans in Natal, and devoted much of his energy to preventing contact between his African wards and white labour-seekers, hoping thereby to check the contamination of the weaker culture by the stronger. But Shepstone was a pragmatist rather than an ideologue. The elevation of 'segregation' to a political doctrine was a product, not of the nineteenth century, but of the early twentieth, and appears to owe its 'take-off' to the decade between the Anglo-Boer war and the establishment of the Union.

Central to the thinking of that decade was the Report of the South African Native Affairs Commission under the chairmanship of Sir Godfrey Lagden, appointed by Lord Milner after the Inter-Colonial Conference of March 1903, with the task of working out an agreed native policy for all southern Africa. Nearly all the members of that Commission were English-speakers. They made proposals for the separation of blacks and whites politically and territorially, planning to leave the substance of political power in the hands of white legislatures, and to have the land demarcated into black and white areas 'with a view to finality'. The extent to which subsequent South African legislators looked back to the Lagden Commission as the inspiration behind the segregation policies of later years was set out in detail by C. M. Tatz in his *Shadow and Substance in South Africa*. The importance of the same decade is further underlined by the enactment, in one colony after another between 1902 and 1909, of laws which either enabled local authorities to establish 'locations' for African townsmen, or entrusted a similar responsibility to the central governments. It was also the decade in which the 'Jim Crow' laws began to gather momentum in the United States of America.

But if the decade before Union was important for the clarification of ideas, it was in the period 1910 to 1924 that the first definitive legislative steps were taken which placed 'Segregation' metaphorically on the cover of the statute book, politically, territorially and residentially.

On the political plane, the Act of Union set an important precedent with its restriction of black and Coloured voters to the Cape alone, and the exclusion of blacks everywhere from Parliament.[2] This process of political segregation was taken a step further by the Native Affairs Act of General Smuts, which extended the principles of the Glen Grey Act to the territorial level by enabling the Governor-General to appoint local and General Councils in the Reserves, from which emerged the United Transkeian Territories General Council in 1931. It also set up a nominated 'Native Conference' which was to meet annually in Pretoria and keep the Union Government informed of African aspirations through another statutory body created under the same Act, the Native Affairs Commission.

Political segregation received further elaboration through General Hertzog's legislation of 1936, removing Cape Africans from the common to a separate voters' roll, for the return of three white members to the House of Assembly, and three to the Provincial Council, and also making provision for the election of four whites to the Senate by African voters in all provinces. The conversion of Smuts's Native Conference into a predominantly elective Native Representative Council with advisory powers completed the 1936 political changes.

The experiment was unhappy, save in so far as the whites elected to Parliament were able to give greater publicity to African needs than had been the case before, and – as Margaret Ballinger explained in her autobiography – extend some marginal benefits such as workmen's compensation and pension rights to Africans during the Second World War. But the Natives Representative Council reached a deadlock with the Smuts Government in 1946 and was abolished by the Nationalists in 1951. The system of African representation in Parliament by whites was abolished by Verwoerd's Promotion of Bantu Self-Government Act of 1959. This law crowned the National Party's Bantu Authorities' system, which dated from 1951, by defining eight Bantu Homelands and offering them, for the first time, the goal of independence. The Government's bona fides on this matter was long subject to doubt, above all as most of the Homelands, even if further consolidated, did not seem substantial enough for any meaningful kind of autonomy. But the Transkei took a further step in 1963 when it was given a dyarchical constitution and some of the decorative trappings of autonomy – a flag and an anthem. There was talk among the Homeland leaders of collective action and a refusal to ask for independence until all was ready; but in 1974 the Transkeian Government decided to go the whole way, having reached an agreement with the Republican Government over its boundaries, and other issues in preparation for full nominal independence in October 1976. This represented a considerable change of policy from that first put forward by the Nationalists when they took power. But the policy of white domination remained their objective for the white area. Hence the Government's refusal to allow meaningful forms of local government for African locations – even for a city of three-quarters of a million people like Soweto – in the white area, for neither the Advisory Boards nor the Urban Bantu Councils, introduced as a substitute in 1961, were ever allowed to do more than advise their white masters.

Coloured people, left on the common roll in 1936 by the Hertzog Government, were removed after a bitter parliamentary and legal struggle between 1951 and 1957. Like the African population, they then enjoyed a brief period of separate representation by whites, until in 1969 their representation in Parliament was likewise abolished, and they were given instead a Coloured Persons' Representative Council to which the Government nominated a minority of the members. The Indian population had no representation in Parliament at all until, under the Indian Representation Act of 1946, the Smuts Government offered them token representation in both houses of Parliament by whites, and in the Natal Provincial Council by one of their own number; but this legislation was removed from the statute book as soon as the Malan Government took over in 1948, the Indian community having previously decided to ignore the concession. They also received a separate advisory Council, meeting in Durban and well removed from the seat of power. All in all, therefore at the political level segregation and *apartheid* came to mean the concentration of power in the hands of the white community, save in so far as individual African homelands received a modicum of local self-government through the Bantu Authorities system, with the prospect – very real in the case of the Transkei and Bophutatswana, rather less so in the case of other Homelands – of substantial independence in the future.

Territorially, the ends of segregation were first served by the Natives Land Act of 1913.[3] Apart from the ideological compulsion which underlay it, this Act was prompted by two significant changes which had presented themselves in recent years. One was the purchase of surveyed farms by black syndicates, the other a growth in the incidence of African squatting, both of which were products of land shortage. The area of land under African communal tenure had shrunk by the early twentieth century to critical limits, and there is evidence that, in their search for land on which to settle, Africans had started to pool their resources and buy surveyed farms from Europeans. The practice was especially prevalent to the north and west of Pretoria in the region north of the Magaliesberg, where there had been a great deal of farm-burning during the Anglo-Boer war, and where a number of white farmers had come under an economic necessity to sell. Africans began to move into the Transvaal property market after it had been decided, in Tsewu's Case in 1905, that they were not precluded from land ownership by the old Republican rule which had made the Native Location Commission trustee of all tribal land. White farmers became concerned over the growth of this new practice by Africans, not merely because it seemed to them to threaten white control over the land to which they attached high symbolic value, but also because of the expected chaos resulting from subdivision of such farms on the deaths of their multiple owners.

But outside the western Transvaal and south-western Natal, there was little outright purchase of farming land by blacks. African squatting was a far more common phenomenon in all four provinces, as is witnessed by the existence of restrictive squatter legislation on every law book – colour-blind in the Cape, colour-oriented elsewhere. Squatters, black and white, had generally reached an accommodation with the owners of the land, as the evidence before the Beaumont Commission of 1916 and the Transvaal Indigency Commission of 1908 made plain. For the most part, they were either share-croppers, 'sowing on shares' or running stock and paying their landlords a stipulated proportion of the increase; or they were labour tenants, owing their landlord a fixed amount of work each year. The leading complaints of white farmers were that where share-cropping prevailed, it tended to cause a labour shortage and to disturb the traditional master–servant relationship which had become the norm across the colour line. As the Beaumont Commission was later told, 'the half-share system is a pernicious system, because it takes away from your neighbour natives who ought to be servants'.

The Land Act of 1913 was an attempt to get rid of those features of African land-ownership and share-cropping thought undesirable by whites. It accordingly set aside the existing African Reserves as 'scheduled areas' reserved for black ownership and occupation, and prohibited any purchase of land by Africans outside them. But in order to fulfil the Lagden Commission's objective of finalising a land settlement on a basis satisfactory to both parties, it included a provision for the enlargement of the Reserves, to which end the Beaumont Commission was set up and given two years in which to investigate and make a report. The remainder of the Act defined its segregationist provisions. Thus the Cape was excluded from the operation of the Act, because to interfere with African land rights in the Cape was to interfere with their qualifications for the franchise, and this required recourse to the special amending procedures in the constitution which the Government was not prepared, at that early stage, to bring into use. African squatters living in Natal and the Transvaal were also spared from eviction 'until Parliament has made other provision'. But where the Orange Free State was concerned, existing legislation which restricted squatting was explicitly confirmed, and the general stipulation that existing share-cropping agreements could remain in force for the time being was incorporated in other sections of the Act, in which the Cape, Transvaal and Natal were mentioned but the O.F.S. was not. Many farmers in the Orange Free State proceeded to evict their squatters, rightly thinking that the law required them to do so. The sudden uprooting of large numbers of Africans from Free State farms, and the migration of many of them northwards across the Vaal, to the accompaniment of widespread forced stock sales at bargain prices, were described in evidence before the Beaumont Commission and by Sol Plaatje in his memoirs.

Despite the hardships caused by the 1913 Land Act, it does not seem to have been the Government's intention to cast large numbers of squatters adrift before alternative provision was made; but having started the dislocation, the authorities appear to have done little about it. Hertzog, who had relinquished the portfolio of Native Affairs shortly before his successor, J. W. Sauer, introduced the Land Bill, criticised the measure because it was not severe enough on squatters; but even he would later decide that the tough Chapter IV of his Native Trust and Land Act of 1936, making squatting illegal, was unenforceable for the time being, because there was nowhere for the squatters to go.

Hertzog's main criticism of the policy of the Smuts Government, however, was that it had failed to carry out the undertaking of the Land Act to make more land available for African ownership and occupation, in the decade between the passage of that law and its fall from power in 1924. Delay in implementing the Government's policy resulted, in the first instance, from public criticism of the Beaumont Commission's detailed recommendations, made in 1916, for the setting aside of eight million morgen for African purchase. The Government reacted by appointing five local committees – one each for the Cape, Natal, Orange Free State, the Eastern and the Western Transvaal – which reviewed the Beaumont findings and made alternative proposals in 1918 for the setting aside of about seven-and-a-half million morgen. The Smuts Government decided in 1922 to accept the findings of these local committees as the basis of the released areas, but fell from power within two years before any decisive changes had been made, though not before the purchase of released land by Africans had started.

General Hertzog's proposals in 1926 aimed to release the land for African purchase which the Smuts Government had decided to make available, but made it possible for whites also to buy that land, which the Smuts proposals had not. Between 1913 and 1936, one-and-a-quarter million morgen of released land were in fact bought by Africans, though what proportion of this was bought before 1926 has not been disclosed. Hertzog's Native Trust and Land Bill of 1936 did introduce a new point of principle by abandoning the earlier preference for individual purchase by Africans, as favoured by the Lagden Commission in 1905 and by Parliament since 1913, and substituting the Natal principle of trust tenure. At the suggestion of Senator Heaton Nicholls, a South African Native Trust was established, on the model of the Natal Act of 1864, to purchase land on behalf of the Africans and exercise control over the farming of that land once purchased. This had the advantage of providing direct government financial aid for the purchase of released land, and the Government agreed to set aside £1 million a year for ten years to this end. In conformity with the urgent recommendations of the Native Economic (Holloway) Commission of 1932, it also tried to ensure that good husbandry followed transfer. The Government now attached importance to the setting up of 'betterment areas' under professional supervision to check the spread of soil erosion, which was beginning to scar the reserves as a result of over-population, drought, lack of modern equipment and general lack of scientific know-how among the African farming population, a high proportion of whose menfolk were absent in the towns as migrant workers. Against these advantages, however, trust tenure was precarious, unlike quit-rent tenure, and was unpopular for that reason among peasants who regarded their land as an investment. If it gave the agricultural officers an opportunity to secure the eviction of bad farmers, which was necessary in a community which was short of land, it also helped to prevent the emergence of a new class of African 'kulaks', or rich peasants, by rigidly adhering to a combination of communal grazing and one-man-one-lot agriculture. The adoption of 'Segregation' had greatly restricted the choice of farming methods open to the African population. The Tomlinson Commission in 1955 felt obliged to recommend a departure from the policy of 1936, and urged the abandonment of the 'one-man-on-lot' principle in the interest of increasing the agricultural productivity of the Reserves to enable them to absorb a large influx of people from the white areas under the 'Apartheid' policy of the Nationalist Government. They proposed to absorb this larger population by providing opportunities in the Reserves for businessmen, industrialists and tradesmen, while granting full-time African farmers economic units under freehold title. The Government, however, refused then to allow the acquisition of more than one farming unit by a single individual, and confirmed its refusal in 1971, when the Minister of Bantu Administration and Development argued in Parliament that to individualise African land-holding and allow the emergence of kulaks would be to undermine the tribal system by undermining the chief's control over the distribution of land.

One of the paradoxes of the South African land problem was the continued presence of many more Africans in the white farming areas than the white population desired to see there, together with an enduring shortage of farm labourers. Agricultural wages were seldom competitive with industrial, and white farmers accustomed to the system of labour tenancy frequently contented themselves with the employment of very cheap inefficient casual labour of the kind provided by squatters, because it was available on their doorstep, rather than engage more skilled men at competitive rates of pay. In doing this, they were to some extent victims of the policy of segregation, for the application of influx control in the towns, and in particular the very strict rules against the urbanisation of African women after 1937, had turned the farms into outdoor relief centres for a growing number of homeless persons – the wives and children of migrant workers for whom there was no room in the Reserves, and who were not allowed in the towns, refugees driven from the Reserves by shortage of food, and so on.

Understandably, therefore, the intensity of white farmers' opposition to squatting grew as the numbers of squatters increased. This was reflected in official policy in the withdrawal of official support for labour tenancy, which had been acceptable at the time of the 1913 Land Act. The Native Economic Commission of 1932 poured its wrath on labour tenancy, and started a campaign for the re-establishment of the farm economy on a basis of properly controlled wage labour. This was to increase the pressure on the squatters, and although the anti-squatter provisions of the 1936 legislation were not enforced, after the end of the Second World War the National Party (which had taken a strong line against squatting while in opposition in the 1930s) introduced enabling legislation by its Prevention of Illegal Squatters Act of 1951. This empowered the authorities to remove squatters from public or private land and send them elsewhere at discretion, and gave every local authority the right (or the duty, on ministerial command) to 'establish ... an emergency camp for the accommodation of homeless persons'. The resettlement policy of the 1960s and 1970s was based mainly on this law. A policy statement in December 1967 outlined three categories of Bantu who could be removed to the Homelands – first, the elderly, the unfit, and those (mainly women and children) who did not qualify for residential rights in the towns under the Urban Areas Act; second, 'surplus Bantu' on white-owned farms or in pockets of black settlement in white areas whose removal was suggested by the desire for cartographical order; and third, professional people who were thought to be of more use to their own people in the Homelands than in the white areas. Various types of settlement were provided for, from full-scale 'Bantu towns' with fairly advanced amenities, such as public transport, tarred roads and water-borne sewerage, like Mdantsane outside East London, to very rudimentary settlements in the veld, almost entirely devoid of amenities at the time of their establishment, as at Sada and Ilinge in the eastern Cape, or Limehill in Natal. The establishment of settlements in the Reserves was necessary if the policy of territorial separation was to have any meaning; but villages of old people and children, with little more than a nucleus of able-bodied men, were an unlikely combination for making a success of virgin settlements, especially as there was little work available in many of the areas selected, so that the residents were largely dependent on old age pensions which had barely increased since their introduction during the

Second World War, and on sometimes regular but dietetically inadequate public rations.

A further paradox of the land problem was that, at a time when the pressure of population on the Reserves was increasing at a steady rate under the twin pressures of natural increase and political repatriation, the white population of the 'white' rural areas was on the decline. There were already clear signs that this was happening in the Karoo at the time of the Drought Investigation Commission in 1923. The Du Toit Commission of 1960, investigating European occupancy of the rural areas, found that many farms had been deserted by Europeans, especially in the south-east Orange Free State – the 'Conquered Territory', as it is commonly called, in memory of the Free State conflict with Moshweshwe – and in north-western Natal. This was partly a result of agricultural consolidation, as successful wool farmers expanded their sheep runs, but partly a natural consequence of the more attractive conditions of town living: better security, higher wages, more amenities. The Commission also found that, where whites had moved out, blacks had moved in – as foremen and bailiffs, taking over from white men, or as squatters in defiance or ignorance of the law. It also drew attention to the emergence of yet another variety of landlord–tenant relationship, the labour farm, where landowners, instead of using the labour of their own squatters, to which they were entitled, had begun to sell that labour to other white farmers in the neighbourhood at considerable profit to themselves.

Within the broad sweep of segregation policy, the demarcation of separate territorial bases for black and non-black South Africa, it was thought necessary to set aside special residential areas for each group within the territory of the other. In the case of the African Reserves, centres where white magistrates, traders and missions established themselves had often come to acquire the status of autonomous enclaves within the Reserves before 1910. Umtata and the other urban centres of the Transkei were examples of this.

But in the white areas the establishment of 'locations', as the places of African settlement on the edges of towns came to be called, became a matter for explicit legislation.[4] Locations were provided for under some Cape municipal statutes during the nineteenth century, but by no means in all, while in the South African Republic the first locations were designated for the settlement of Asians rather than Africans, the accommodation of African servants being restricted by a regulation of 1899 to rooms in the back yards of white homes. At the beginning of the twentieth century, however, the Cape Parliament carried a Native Reserve Location Act (1902), authorising the Government to set up and control African residential areas outside towns. Natal carried a Locations Act in 1904, empowering local authorities to set them up and control them.

The Transvaal Municipal Corporations Ordinance and the Bloemfontein Municipal Ordinance, both of 1903, formed the basis of a new system of urban African administration on segregated lines in the ex-Republics.

Elimination of slums, control of crime, control of disease, and in general the segregation of black from white people, were the main influences behind the decision to establish separate residential areas for Africans. The Reports of the Commissions on Assaults on Women (1913) and Tuberculosis (1914) helped to coordinate the thinking of the Union Native Affairs Department, which hesitated to introduce a policy of urban segregation before the First World War, at the time of the passage of the Land Act, because it was not yet confident that the principle of segregation had been 'fully accepted by the country'. After the war, however, came the 1918 influenza epidemic and, four years later, the report of Colonel Stallard's Transvaal Local Government Commission, which gained some following for its idea that the urban areas were the white man's creation, and that Africans had a right to be there only in so far as they were ministering to the white man's needs. After false starts in 1918 and 1922, the Department went to considerable trouble to consult both African and white municipal opinion before bringing in the legislation in 1923, which reached the statute book in much amended form as the Natives (Urban Areas) Act. The Act later underwent major amendments in 1930, 1937, 1944, 1952, 1957, 1964 and 1971, as well as consolidation in 1945, and grew into one of the most complex pieces of control legislation ever devised anywhere.

The Urban Areas Act was a portmanteau law covering a great variety of issues. One objective of the legislators was to clear Africans out of the mixed residential areas which had grown up in some of the larger towns, notably Johannesburg, and re-house them in locations. Because these mixed areas were also slums, the policy was not entirely unconventional; but the task of providing homes for blacks in locations proved far more complicated in the long run than the authorities first envisaged. What followed was a saga with many unexpected turns, mainly tragic. To begin with, the authorities found that, instead of moving to locations, Africans evicted from backyards often preferred to move into other backyards. When Orlando Township was built outside Johannesburg in the 1930s, it contained numerous empty houses until as late as 1937, when the pressure of continuing townward migration filled them – too late to enable the Johannesburg Municipality to adjust its sights to the enormous extension of housing demands during the Second World War, when both materials and trained builders to deal with the emergency were lacking. Squatter movements on a big scale resulted from this bottleneck in 1944–7, as gifted leaders like James Sofasonke ('We shall all die together') Mpanza emerged to take their followers on to the Orlando commonage, sign them up as members of the Sofasonke Party, distribute hessian for homes, levy fees for elementary services, and then wait for the local authority to attend to sanitation and – it was hoped – build houses over their heads. The housing crisis of the 1940s in turn produced new legislation for the training of African builders, and an energetic slum clearance programme in the 1950s, as shanties in the larger centres gave place to new, professionally laid out locations like Daveyton outside Benoni, which were provided with communal amenities as well as well-constructed homes. An emergency measure, the 'site-and-service' scheme worked out in the Department of Native Affairs, went a long way towards a solution of the problem. The scheme was based on the provision of water points and sanitary services by the local authority, and a requirement that African residents should build shanties for their immediate use at one end of their plots. Meanwhile the building of more solid homes at the other end of their plots took place under municipal supervision. In Johannesburg's South Western Native Township (Soweto) municipal effort, aided by substantial financial contributions from one of the mining houses, resulted in the proliferation of small but well-built, if architecturally monotonous, 'little boxes' for about three-quarters of a million African residents. Nyanga outside Cape Town and New Brighton outside Port Elizabeth were similar.

But a change of emphasis in government policy during the late 1960s upset the rhythm of this urban development. This was the decision to give priority to the building of homes in the Homelands, as the Reserves had come to be called. Mdantsane near East London, Ga Rankuwa near Pretoria, Kwa Mashu near Durban, and other 'Bantu towns' now consumed the building energies of the Government. There was an enforced cutback on municipal housing. The policy of the Government required a reduction in the number of Africans permanently residing in the urban areas and an increase in the number of workers migrating from the Homelands and living as contract workers in hostels or 'bachelor quarters' (a highly misleading term) while 'temporarily' in the urban area doing the work which – under the Stallard doctrine – legitimised their presence in the town. The parallel policy of relocating industry in the border regions under the Physical Planning Act of 1967 also required the building of houses in the Homelands rather than in the existing urban locations. As a consequence of this redirection of energy, housing shortages in the urban locations again became acute, for African workers proved less resilient than the law required them to be, with the result that slum conditions began to reappear in many urban locations, large and small. The housing backlog in Johannesburg in 1972 was even larger than it had been on the eve of Mpanza's squatter movement in 1944. An exceptional increase in the black birthrate and some irregular influx from white farms also helped to make the situation critical.

Underlying the policy of urban segregation was a desire to reduce the power of the black man in the urban areas by making it difficult for him to acquire a stake in the town or, indeed, in his own location, for – as the Stallard Commission emphasised – the man of property could hardly be denied the municipal vote. Thus, although the original Urban Areas Bill of 1923 contained a provision for some Africans to own property in freehold, this provision was removed, largely on General Hertzog's insistence, before the Bill became law, and without consultation with the Africans. During the Second World War, thirty-year leases were made lawful, and though location plots tended to be small, some African leaseholders built substantial properties, for example in Dube Township, Soweto. In 1968, however, local authorities were pressed by the Government to buy in these leasehold properties on the expiry of their leases. Significantly, Prime Minister Vorster relented on this point after his personal encounter with Homeland leaders in 1974; but the Government made itself unpopular by insisting that new leaseholders accept Homeland citizenship first.

A similar history underlay the related issue of African trading rights in urban locations. The Act of 1923 empowered local authorities to grant trading licences to African location residents. This was widely done, but strong resistance developed, especially in the Orange Free State, so that the Minister of Native Affairs took extra powers under the 1930 amendment to the Act. The Government was reluctant to use these powers, and did not do so openly; but during the Second World War the principle of African trading came to be accepted by local authorities in the Orange Free State as well as elsewhere. It remained Government policy, however, to prevent the expansion of African businesses in urban locations, in the hope that these would move to the Homelands – for which reason it was thought better that blacks should frequent the central business areas for shopping purposes, where in any case goods bought in chain stores tended to be cheaper. In 1963, a Government circular required local authorities to limit African trading in the locations by imposing a rule of 'one-man-one-shop', prohibiting African trading in all but 'daily essential domestic necessities' (which could not include the sale of petrol, for example), and banning the establishment of African companies in white areas.

There were certain residential areas which, though peopled by Africans, did not fall under the scope of the Urban Areas Act, and it became Government policy to regularise these wherever possible. Thus a Natives Resettlement Act was carried in 1954, to enable the Government to remove the African residents of Johannesburg's western suburbs of Sophiatown, Martindale and Newclare, where much property was black-owned, to a new Government settlement at Meadowlands. This move, carried out in 1957, was hailed by government officials as a triumph of social engineering, and the new white suburb which arose from the rubble was named Triomf. The action was criticised by many of the residents, by welfare bodies, and notably in Trevor Huddleston's *Naught for your Comfort*, as the break-up of a community, albeit a community in which crime, poverty and disease abounded.

Another feature of the Urban Areas Act of 1923 was the provision of a system of local government on segregated lines. African representation on town councils was rejected. African representation on council committees was never seriously considered, and the location was never permitted either to become a municipal ward or to develop into a separate municipality with its own council. But under the stimulus of the Act, municipal native affairs departments began to acquire a separate existence, employing as location superintendents – or in the larger centres as managers of native affairs – men who had frequently served in the police or acquired administrative experience elsewhere, and who governed the locations with the aid of partly elected Advisory Boards, usually of six members. Potentially capable of development into either political or responsible executive bodies, the Advisory Boards were prevented from so developing by the ambiguous position of the location as a black enclave in a 'white' area. Some managers, concerned over the developing frustration of Advisory Board members at their own powerlessness, experimented with a policy of downward democratisation, by developing a 'ward' or 'block' system of electoral responsibility within the location itself, but opposition among whites precluded the extension of their powers, though the Native Representative Council frequently asked for this. In 1961, the Government started the replacement of Advisory Boards by a new system of Urban Bantu Councils, the chairmen of which were to be Africans instead of white councillors or officials, as was the case in the Advisory Boards. These Councils could also be given various administrative and financial powers by the local authority with the assent of the Minister; but in practice such powers were not extended, and it became clear by the early 1970s that supporters of the Government were less enthusiastic about the Urban Bantu Councils as centres of urban African responsibility than about the appointment, under the Promotion of Bantu Self-Government Act of 1959, of representatives of the Homeland chiefs in the urban locations, whose function would be to maintain and develop links between Africans living in the urban locations and the Homelands whose 'citizenship' they were in the process of acquiring.

Municipal control over the urban locations was fundamental to the system established in 1923, though the establishment of a separate Native Revenue Account, which was supposed to be self-balancing, was an important feature of the law. In so far as local authorities had made profits from the running of their locations, this had to come to an end. By the time of the Second World War, more and more local authorities had begun to realise that revenues from 'Kaffir beer' sales (a lucrative source of municipal finance first discovered by Durban at the beginning of the century), and from rents and fines, were not sufficient for the provision of basic amenities in the locations, and they had begun to contribute to the Native Revenue Account from the general rate fund. When the self-balancing principle was revived after the Second World War, therefore, the emphasis of the policy had changed: the intention now was to reduce the dependence of the location on the general rate fund, and to return so far as possible to a policy of economic rents (as opposed to the sub-economic rents subsidised by the central Government during the war years, which had been made available to municipal tenants in all race groups). Where rents were not sufficient, local authorities were encouraged to raise lodgers' fees. By 1971, only twenty-one of over 450 local authorities still contributed funds from general revenue to their Bantu (Native) Revenue Accounts. Yet another device for regulating the financing of locations was contained in the Native Services Levy Act of 1952. This law amplified a provision in the original 1923 Act that it was the duty of the employer to look after the proper housing of his African employees – a provision which had proved very difficult to enforce. Monthly levies were now imposed on employers of African labour to subsidise location development. But as the emphasis of government policy shifted, so the expenditure permitted from the Native Service Levy Fund came to be restricted to the provision of capital amenities (for example, roads and drainage) in new African townships in the Homelands and for the provision of transport at subsidised rates between the Homelands and the towns from which Africans commuted to work. Another regulation which served the same purpose was the obligation imposed on local authorities, after it became lawful for Africans to consume 'European' liquor in 1961, to pay 80 per cent of the profits from municipal liquor outlets (as distinct from beer profits) to the central Government for purposes of Homeland development. Further, and in the interest of giving the central Government even fuller control over the running of urban locations and the direction of urban areas policy, new Bantu Affairs Administration Boards were established in July 1973, under legislation carried in 1971. These boards covered much larger areas than the individual local authorities, and took over responsibility for the detailed running of the locations from the local authorities, which were required to pay over to them all moneys received from the locations, and to provide the services of their own officials to the Boards as required, on a *pro rata* basis. The officials of the municipal native affairs departments, whose appointment and dismissal had all along been subject to approval in Pretoria, were now taken over as employees of the central Government, and all control by the town councils over the locations was legally severed.

* * *

The policy of the Urban Areas Act, it was realised from the outset, was likely to stand or fall on the ability of the Government to control the movement of people within the frontiers of the state.[5] Control over people was already a notable feature of the South African legal system, for in spite of the celebrated abolition of passes under Ordinance 50 of 1828, all kinds of controls over the movement of Africans, in particular, had returned by the time of Union, and some existed in all provinces: travel documents, labour documents, residential documents, curfew documents, the non-production of which, when they were asked for by officials, carried penalties of various kinds. The variety of documents which Africans were required to possess was complex to the point of unfairness, even if – within a narrow compass – passes could in some instances serve as a security device. In 1920, following widespread demonstrations against the pass laws in the previous year, an Inter-Departmental Committee of inquiry met to consider their simplification, and recommended that all necessary pass information be coordinated in a single document, made of parchment, to be carried by males from the age of eighteen whenever they were outside the ward of issue, but explicitly not by women on account of the strong feeling against the registration of African women which had been shown by Charlotte Maxeke's demonstration in the Orange Free State in 1913. These proposals were included in a Native Registration and Protection Bill tabled at the same time as the Urban Areas Bill in 1923; but the two measures were amalgamated in Select Committee, the controls retained, and the proposed simplifications ignored – as they would be ignored again when the Holloway (Native Economic) Commission made similar proposals in 1932, following widespread anti-pass demonstrations in 1929–31, and when J. M. Young of the Native Affairs Commission made them again in 1939 after further criticism from the Native Representative Council.

The impact of these repeated rejections of proposed improvements in the pass laws acquired special colour from the fact that the original proposals of 1920 had received the guarded support of the Native Conference appointed under the Native Affairs Act. There was no recovery from the damage done to African confidence by these rejections. During the Second World War, so sharply had the number of arrests under the pass laws increased on the Witwatersrand that the Ministers of Justice and of Native Affairs agreed to issue instructions in May 1942 that the police were not to arrest Africans simply for not having their passes on them, unless they suspected that such Africans were engaged in criminal activity. A sharp fall in actual arrests resulted; but unfortunately for this experiment, the Elliott Committee appointed by the same two departments to examine the problem of crime on the Rand came to the conclusion that relaxation of pass controls had resulted in large-scale non-registration at the labour exchanges by

Africans entering the towns. Searches were therefore resumed. Within a few months a well-organised Anti-Pass campaign was under way, with the African, Coloured and Indian movements acting together. By endorsing the Fagan proposals of 1948 for softening the impact of pass restrictions, the Smuts Government hoped to turn away black indignation; but by then it had lost political contact with black leaders. Its successors, who were in any case less well disposed towards the emancipation of Africans from existing controls, inherited the problem. Black opposition to the pass laws therefore continued, and found further expression in the Defiance Campaign in 1952, when large numbers courted arrest by deliberately destroying their passes. The Natives Abolition of Passes and Coordination of Documents Act of the same year belied its title, for it retained control documents and merely renamed them 'reference books'. It did embody the proposals for a simplified system which characterised the suggestions of 1920, 1932 and 1939; but it provided for the extension of reference books to African women, and when this part of the Act was put into operation it led, as in 1913, to racial violence, this time mainly in the western Transvaal. At the end of the decade, it was anti-pass demonstrations mounted by the new Pan-Africanist Congress and by the A.N.C., that resulted in the shootings at Sharpeville and Langa of March 1960. After Sharpeville, the instruction went out again to the police to demand the presentation of passes only when they suspected that a crime was being committed. The figures for pass arrests again diminished; but they gradually returned to previous levels, and by the early 1970s arrests under legislation restricting the movement of Africans had climbed to an annual figure of well over 600,000.

The normal way to maintain social control in towns all over the world is to rely upon the local police to enforce municipal by-laws and deal, as need arises, with vagrants, drunkards and other offenders. Normal social controls, though, were found to be insufficient by the South African legislature because the Urban Areas Act was required to do abnormal things: to make rules for blacks which did not apply to whites; to enforce a segregationist legal system; to restrict the urbanisation of blacks in strict proportion to the availability of work; to expel blacks from town (but not whites) for vagrancy, idleness, disorderliness, failure to pay rent, and other causes. Control over African influx was not an important feature of the original Act, and no special machinery was provided for enforcing it. But the first restrictions on the urbanisation of African women were enacted in 1930, chiefly in an attempt to limit prostitution and illicit brewing, and these were stiffened in 1937. The 1937 amendment was the first to restrict the number of blacks in town according to the availability of work. Local authorities were required to send to the Minister of Native Affairs regular estimates of local labour requirements in relation to the number of Africans living in the area. The measure also restricted the African immigrant to fourteen days in which to find work in the town, or return to the Reserve – later cut down to 72 hours in the 1952 amendment. Influx control regulations were applied systematically for the first time in 1938, but largely fell into abeyance during the war because of the scarcity of all kinds of labour in the urban areas. In 1952 Parliament enacted the notorious 'Section Ten' provisions, which denied the right to live in an urban area to any African who was not born there, male or female, unless he had either lived there continuously for fifteen years – lawful holidays excepted – or served under the same employer for ten. The law, as enforced, could and did split husbands and wives if only one of them qualified; but it was less effective as a means of excluding blacks from town than the Government hoped, because those who could qualify – and there were by then many of them – now had a statutory as well as a common law right to be in the urban area. Thus, although the rustication clauses grew markedly longer with each new edition of the Act, as the offences which could earn this penalty multiplied, the number of Africans in the towns steadily grew. But the legal status of urban Africans began to change after the passage of the 1964 Bantu Labour Act: the proportion of migrant workers under contract of service grew, and the proportion with rights under the Urban Areas Act diminished.

The Black Sash started advice offices in Cape Town, Johannesburg and elsewhere in an attempt to mitigate the social distress caused by the break-up of homes resulting from the strict enforcement of Section Ten. Its monthly reports and records of case histories soon grew into a formidable corpus of evidence for the social historian. The Government followed with experimental aid centres designed to provide Africans who had infringed the influx control laws with employment rather than prison sentences, and in 1975 it announced a plan for rehabilitation camps in the Homelands for the same purpose. These private and public counter-measures, however, left it in no doubt that influx control caused widespread social pain.

The physical separation of the races was powerfully reinforced by a segregated educational system.[6] This had not always been the case. Cape schools in Company days normally contained the children of slaves as well as of their white masters. The mission schools established in the eastern Cape during the nineteenth century, which received strong support from Governor Sir George Grey, were mixed. But Government schools, wherever they were established, developed into institutions for white children only, and there were few if any exceptions to this by the time of Union. This applied even in the Cape, where agitation inspired by fear of Coloured competition led Parliament to pass the School Boards Act in 1905, limiting attendance at Government schools to children of 'European parentage and extraction', which was interpreted in Moller's Case (1911) to mean white children only. This legislation gave white pupils a headstart when educational qualifications were tied to industrial apprenticeship in 1922, especially in view of the very high wastage among non-white pupils after the fourth year of schooling and again at the end of the primary school, Government expenditure on the education of children of other race groups was provided for under the Financial Relations Act of 1922; but although that expenditure increased over the years, it was never sufficient to enable the Government to make schooling compulsory for any group save the whites (though a start was made with Coloured pupils in 1973) and expenditure per head for white and other children reflected enormous discrepancies throughout the period under discussion. In 1971–2, for example, the per capita costs for white children were R366 in primary schools and R624 in high schools, for Africans R21 and R113 respectively, with Coloured and Indian pupils marginally above African. Very few secondary schools were built by the Government for African pupils before the Second World War, when – despite other calls on Government funds – Hofmeyr's department took energetic steps to increase the number of such schools. Even in 1973, however, there were 728,772 African children attending school in the lowest standard, but only 170,711 in the lowest forms of secondary schools, 4073 in the matriculation class, and 7845 at university.

School education was made a provincial matter under the Act of Union, while the administration of native affairs was vested in the Governor-General-in-Council. At first, African education fell under the Provincial education departments, though attempts were made from early days to have it transferred either to the Union Department of Education or to the Department of Native Affairs. This developed into an ideological dispute. Jan Hofmeyr set up a Union Advisory Board on Native Education in 1945, the members of which were appointed by his own Education Department. But the Native Affairs Commission in 1936 had urged greater differentiation between black and white schools, and this line of argument was further developed by the Eiselen Commission in 1951, when it came up with a new concept of 'Bantu Education', tailor-made for the special place of the Bantu in South African society and brought into operation through the Bantu Education Act of 1953. Bantu education involved a different syllabus, vernacular instruction throughout the primary school, and the simultaneous introduction of both English and Afrikaans as media of instruction in the lower secondary school.

Although the South African Native College at Fort Hare was established in 1916 as an institution primarily for Africans, university education fell under the Union Government from 1910, and universities were entitled by law to admit students of any colour. Cape Town and the

Witwatersrand universities admitted non-white students; but in 1959 the Government carried legislation to compel the segregation of higher education, and then established separate institutions for Xhosa, Coloured, Indian, Zulu and Sotho-Tswana students to attend.

Although it became customary to group all white people together for statistical purposes, the merging of the Afrikaans- and English-language school systems was not allowed to happen. As with black educational policy, this developed into an ideological issue. General Hertzog, the pioneer of dual-medium instruction, ran into heavy weather when he tried to make both Dutch and English the media of instruction in Orange River Colony schools; but he held to the ideal of an educational system designed to bring Afrikaans- and English-speaking children into the same classroom, if need be at the expense of parental rights. The United Party adopted Hertzogian principles and adhered to them after the split with Hertzog in 1939, and the merits of such a system were cogently argued in the published researches of Dr E. G. Malherbe. The Nationalists, however, preferred mother-tongue instruction as a means of preserving the identity of the Afrikaans-speaking population, reverting in principle to the ideas of Christian National Education as propagated by the Genootskap van Regte Afrikaners in the 1870s, and by the opponents of Milner after 1903, with their insistence on the coordination of church, school and home influences in the total education of the Afrikaner child. This approach had special relevance for the National Party after 1948, as a device for containing the non-exclusive, non-dogmatic, liberal values implicit in the British educational system, which it regarded as a threat to its own race policies.

'Unwritten codes of behaviour', in the view of N. J. Rhoodie and H. J. Venter, underlay a customary *apartheid* 'in the field of public transport, entertainment, recreation, and so on'.[7] This is a simplified statement of what had been substantially true before 1948 over nearly the whole of the country. The very fact of geographical distance between white-run towns and their locations would have ensured this result, even if there had been no language or cultural barriers between black and white. But after 1948 the cultural isolation of the races from each other became a matter of public policy. Not only was this brought about in education at all levels, but it was very largely true of religious worship, in the case both of churches like the Dutch Reformed and Presbyterian which were organised into separate black and white bodies, and churches like the Anglican, Roman Catholic and Methodist, which were not. Outcries in 1937 and again in 1957 prevented the Government from enforcing religious separation by law; but the relationship between the Government and the churches which rejected the *apartheid* policy on the ground that it was un-Christian took on the form of a simmering *Kulturkampf* with growing international implications.

Much of the tension after 1948 stemmed from attempts by the Government to make the custom of separate activities uniform throughout the country, and where this was not the case to enforce it by law. To take one example of many, Cape Town had not previously segregated either its buses or its city hall for public performances. It was required to segregate both. Great controversy followed the building of the Nico Malan theatre in Cape Town, by the Cape Provincial Administration, as an entertainment centre for whites only. After a great deal of public pressure the theatre was made available for mixed audiences in 1975; but the Government made it clear at the same time that the principle of segregated audiences for public entertainment in general was to be maintained, and that special permits would still be required from Pretoria for every proposed performance before a racially mixed audience in nearly every theatre in the Republic.

Machinery for this kind of regulation depended on powers granted to the Government under the Group Areas Act of 1950, and its frequent amendments, to which we must now turn.

Control over the movement and residential rights of Africans was made relatively simple by the existence of the pass laws. In the case of other non-white race groups it was rather more complicated.[8] Indians could be prevented by existing laws from moving from one province to another, and from residing in particular areas, and were barred from the Orange Free State altogether; but they could not be made to carry passes. Coloured people were not controlled at all as to their movements, could live in any province, and carried no passes.

As a result of pressure from its own followers, the Smuts Government in 1946 carried an Asiatic Land Tenure Act to restrict Indian residence to particular parts of Natal, as they had already been restricted in the Transvaal since the early 1930s. To do this, special machinery was set up which included the appointment of a Land Tenure Advisory Board with power to screen potential buyers and occupiers and advise on the issuing of permits. In 1950 the principle of setting aside particular areas in towns for the ownership or occupation of particular race groups was adopted by the Malan Government as the central feature of its Group Areas legislation and the machinery of the Asiatic Land Tenure Act adopted for this purpose. In his second reading speech Dr T. E. Dönges, the Minister of the Interior, claimed to be responding to pressure from all parts of the country, and advertised the measure as an attempt to eliminate race friction and to ensure 'the paramountcy of the white man and of Western civilisation in South Africa ... in the interests of the material, cultural and spiritual development of all races'.

This Act underwent important revisions in 1952, 1956, 1957, 1961, 1962, 1965, and 1969, and was consolidated in 1957 and 1966. Its primary purpose was to segregate all race groups, and if need be sub-groups (for example, Cape Coloured and Cape Malay) in urban areas. The Land Tenure Advisory Board (later renamed the Group Areas Board, and later still the Community Development Board) consisted of white officials responsible to the Minister of the Interior (later, the Minister of Community Development). It could recommend the setting aside of particular areas for the sole ownership or occupation (or both) of particular race groups. Provision was made for representations to be made by local authorities and other interested parties; but the object was nothing less than the complete unscrambling of the residential patterns of South African towns. Africans were barely affected, for they were already controlled under the Urban Areas Act, save in a handful of centres like Alexandra Township, Johannesburg, or the Fingo Village, Grahamstown. But the Indian and Coloured communities were brought under strong pressure in ways which quickly became apparent. When committees of the Land Tenure Advisory Board later visited towns in the Transvaal and Natal, they were generally presented with proposals by local authorities for the removal of Indian homes and businesses a mile or more out of town, and occasionally for the elimination of Indian homes and shops altogether, and the delimitations which they advertised generally conformed to such proposals. Similar delimitations affecting the Coloured people were made in the western Cape, and the relative incidence of the legislation on particular race groups can be seen from figures previously quoted in relation to the white, Coloured, Indian and Chinese communities [see p. 304].

The complexities of the Group Areas Act derived largely from the fact that it had to deal with the expropriation of real estate. But alongside the expropriation of property, the Board was given power under a succession of Group Areas Development Acts and Community Development Acts to buy and sell, administer and develop properties on an enormous scale. For the property which it held in February 1971 the Board had paid R84,141,477. As a body which had the power to expropriate as well as enter the property market, it was placed in a position to take advantage of rises and falls in property values determined by its own decisions, and the profitability of its own transactions under such conditions gave it the capacity to extend its own activities. As a result, the whole Republic had been covered by the racial zoning plans of the Board and its regional subdivisions by the mid-1970s, and in almost all respects these zoning plans had been finalised [see pp. 274–5].

Like the Urban Areas Act, the Group Areas Act provided the basis for a new system of local self-government for the Coloured people; but, as previously indicated, the machinery was too cumbrous for smaller Coloured communities

The extent to which aspects of *apartheid* so far dealt with were concerned with issues of a non-economic kind will be readily apparent. But Verwoerd's definition of *apartheid* laid special emphasis on the 'economic sphere' and the colour bar. In the following chapter, these aspects are singled out for special treatment.

# 19 The Colour Bar in the Economy

Such a big prosperity gap developed over the years between the blacks and whites of South Africa, that some scholars argued in the 1960s that the policies of successive South African Governments were inspired rather by economic than by racial ideology. They were held, that is, to represent the self-protective action of an economic interest group which happened to be white, rather than of a white group which happened to prosper under the system. Thomas Hobbes suggested in the seventeenth century that competition and diffidence – or, as we might say, acquisitiveness and mistrust of those unlike ourselves – formed two of the three 'principall causes of quarrell' among men. In South Africa, the peculiarities of *apartheid* may have resulted in an over-exclusive emphasis on racial explanations of political conflict by purveyors of what is sometimes called the 'conventional wisdom'. It is important, therefore, to set the social system against its economic background if the influence of ideology on policy-making is to be seen in perspective. This means, in particular, an examination of the colour bar in the evolving South African economy.[1]

The Cape's early economic progress rested mainly on the development of merino wool production from the 1780s. Wool exports accelerated during the 1830s, and increased steadily until their value topped £3 millions in 1872, exclusive of the produce of other colonies. Agricultural prosperity led to the development of an embryonic road system from the 1840s, during the Colonial Secretaryship of John Montagu, when a number of important mountain passes were built by engineers such as A. G. Bain. The growth of chambers of commerce dated back to the Cape Commercial Exchange of 1822, but they began to proliferate only after 1860, which was also the moment when local banking enterprises, which had begun to appear in the 1830s, began to give way to the larger Imperial banks like the Standard, with access to the London money market.

The Diamond Fields contributed in a variety of ways to the shaping of South Africa.[2] At the time of Union, this very important industry accounted for over 98 per cent of the world's total diamond production, and still accounted for more than half at the time of the Great Depression of 1929. It gave a boost to capital investment in the early years, to artisan immigration, and to railway construction. It also had a decisive influence on the growth of labour patterns, promoting the immigration of artisans and helping to reinforce the socio-economic stratification between the races, which had already begun to develop into a rigid pattern on the farms. After the discovery of the dry diggings, black and white prospectors moved to the Fields to stake their claims, though many of the blacks went there as servants of their white masters. Before the installation of Sir Richard Southey as Lieutenant-Governor of the new Colony in January 1873, the diggers had set up their own committees as an informal government. In theory they had to comply with Cape law, which contained no barrier to the pegging of claims by blacks. But in practice the diggers' committees applied pressure to have the allocation of claims limited to whites, urging that to admit blacks as claimholders would be to destroy the possibility of controlling diamond smuggling. They never obtained a colour bar as such from the Colonial Government; but they achieved the same result by means of master-servant legislation administered by white officials sympathetic to their aspirations, under a proclamation dated 10 August 1872. Claimholders were made to require a certificate of good character from a magistrate; persons found loitering within range of a mining camp could be accosted by any registered claimholder and asked to produce a pass, which – if they were servants – they were obliged to carry. When the diggers took their opposition to Southey's regime almost to the point of violence in 1875, this was not because Southey had encouraged claimholding by Coloured people, though he would have liked to be able to do so, but because under the Constitution of 1873 the diggers had not been given as much power in the Legislative Council as they wanted, and because some of the diggers' leaders on the new Mining Board (constituted in July 1874) had developed a personal hostility to Southey and to J. B. Currey, his Colonial Secretary, and thought – it seems, erroneously – that Southey had been involved in corrupt land deals. Southey and Currey were recalled by the Secretary of State, Lord Carnarvon, as scapegoats for a social policy whose failure they had not been given the resources to prevent. But the *de facto* colour bar over mining claims remained, and was subsequently consolidated by two further developments: the emergence of a widely differentiated labour force, and the introduction of the compound system.

As the complexity of mining operations grew, it became necessary to attract skilled miners from Britain at rates of up to £8 per week; but the bulk of the labour force continued to consist of Africans hired in the tribal areas through their chiefs on short-term contracts of three to six months, commonly for wages of about 10*s* per week plus (until

1877) a gun. Coming at first from nearly all parts of South Africa, the migrant labourers on the diamond fields came increasingly from northern regions chosen by white agents who operated in the tribal areas under the authority of the Griqualand West Government, in succession to the less responsible touts who in the early years had lain in wait for migrants and 'sold' them to individual diggers. The Southey Government did what it could to facilitate the transit of migrant Africans, some of whom had walked 600 miles from their homes; but it proved difficult to arrange satisfactory staging posts in Republican territory, though the Boer Republics insisted on the purchase of transit passes. The confiscation of firearms on the return journey through the Republics, and the theft of wages and clothing, were further hazards. After 1880, when the ownership of the claims had begun to be concentrated in fewer hands, the role of the Government in labour recruitment diminished, and that of the companies increased. But the main areas of recruitment remained unaltered. The Sekhukhune Pedi ('Mahawas'), whom John Edwards had first approached in 1873, provided most of the labourers; Shona workers were first induced to go to Kimberley in 1874; and the recruitment of Ndebele and Tswana labourers followed as a result of A. C. Bailie's expedition of 1876 to Mankurwane, Gaseitswe, Setshele, Kgama, and Lobengula. But wherever they came from, as short-term migrants they were not well placed to acquire the skills or achieve the kind of break with their own traditions which could turn them into the white man's competitors in a strange society which the white men controlled.

The other differential factor which came to matter was the success of the white workers and the failure of the black to resist the search of their persons for concealed diamonds on the orders of the white managements. After the consolidation of claims had begun to make progress in the 1880s, the whites defended their liberty by effective strike action. The blacks not only failed to do this, but were obliged to submit to a regime of closed compounds from 1885 onwards, thus placing themselves under very close supervision and control.

Opinions about the compounds ranged from the severe strictures of John X. Merriman to the enthusiasm of J. W. Matthews and Gardner Williams. They enabled the mining companies, during the years of business consolidation in the late 1880s, to provide amenities such as recreation and health supervision as well as industrial control. Black miners had occasion to resent their loss of liberty, while Kimberley shopkeepers objected to the loss of business resulting from establishment of canteens run by the companies in their own compounds.

As a control device, the lesson of the Kimberley compounds was not lost. The Durban municipality discovered at the beginning of the twentieth century that an open compound system could be used for the control of casual ('togt') labourers. It was a short step from the municipal compound to the 'native hostel', which became a common feature of municipal locations in the larger centres under the stimulus of the Urban Areas Act of 1923. The open compound system was also adopted on the gold mines, not to prevent the theft of gold but to provide a method for maintaining police control over the much larger number of Africans (and for a short time the Chinese) who went to the Rand mines on contract. When Commissioner Buckle conducted an inquiry into the grievances underlying the African strike at Kleinfontein Mine in 1913, he stressed this feature of the compound system, and with good reason, for the isolation of African strikers in their compounds later broke the serious African miners' strikes of 1920 and 1946.

Gold-mining never became as closely controlled an industry as diamond-mining became with the establishment of the De Beers monopoly in 1888–9; but the setting up of the Chamber of Mines in 1887, the year after the discovery of the Main Reef outcrop, resulted in a high degree of uniformity between the mining houses in the matter of labour policy. The extraction of the gold-bearing reef was a costly process even after the discovery of the Macarthur–Forrest cyanide process in 1891, which was 95 per cent efficient and for the first time made deep-level mining seem an economic proposition. The cost structure of the industry was critical, for the lower the costs, the greater the possibility of mining the less lucrative seams; the higher the costs, the smaller the amount of recoverable gold. During the 1890s, therefore, the Chamber repeatedly attempted to reduce costs by cutting the wages of its African workers, and to put pressure on its member companies to keep in line, well aware as it did so that a balance had to be found between too high a wage (which was thought to lead to long gaps between contracts) and too low a wage (which was thought to divert workers from mining to other forms of employment). But the harder management tried to reduce wages, the more white miners began to fear that their jobs were in jeopardy. Their suspicion of the motives of the mining capitalists, so easily discernible in D. C. Boonzaaier's 'Hoggenheimer' cartoons in the years immediately after the Anglo-Boer war, ran deep; it was embittered by the high mortality rate from miners' phthisis, and fortified by the fellow-feeling of Afrikaners who, though hardly connected as yet with mining activities in significant numbers, had unpleasant memories of the performance of Rand capitalists at the time of the Jameson Raid.

After the Anglo-Boer war, the tension between the capitalists and the white workers increased, as the former came under pressure from Milner to provide the profits out of which the policy of reconstruction was to grow, and the latter began to resist the apparent threat to their own job security by forming their Mineworkers' Union. A critical shortage of African labour now occurred. The rhythm of pre-war labour recruitment collapsed, though the establishment of the Witwatersrand Native Labour Association ('Wenela') in 1900 helped to revive activity in the African areas. But African resentment at the Chamber's policy of wage reductions, at commandeering by the British army during the war, as well as over the bad conditions in the mine compounds, injured recruitment. Meanwhile the Portuguese authorities, who controlled Gazaland where the mines' Shangaan labourers came from, imposed stiff conditions on Milner when he negotiated the resumption of labour contracts under a *modus vivendi* in December 1901. Yet they were unable to raise the number of recruits Milner required, owing to African resistance to enforced recruitment, and Milner was frustrated by the paucity of the recruits because he needed workers not only for the mines, but to build railways and rebuild the farms as well.

Two rival lines of argument for solving the labour problem were aired in 1903. One, associated with Colonel F. H. P. Creswell, manager of the Village Main Reef mine, was nicknamed the 'white labour policy'. Its aim was to replace black labour by white, at any rate on some mines, and to provide them with more machines, on the argument that a relatively few white artisans with machines could bring up the rock more economically than a much larger number of blacks without. Creswell persuaded his Johannesburg board that he was right, but failed to convince either his London board or the Chamber, for experiments on other mines produced results contrary to Creswell's. The other line of argument, associated mainly with the magnate, George Farrar, had the backing of Milner's Transvaal Labour Commission and of Milner himself. It was to find substitute cheap labour by looking outside southern Africa. Remembering its Natal experience, the Government of India responded adversely. But Imperial China agreed to send contract labourers on terms very favourable to the mining companies, so that – in the teeth of opposition from Liberals in Britain who denounced 'Chinese slavery', from English-speaking miners who feared a plot to undermine their own jobs, and from Transvaal Afrikaners who deplored the infusion of yet another racial strain into an already unpalatable Uitlander brew – the importation of Chinese on contract began in 1904, and over 60,000 arrived in the course of the next few years. Contracts imposed on the Transvaal Chinese were far more restrictive than those which had been imposed on the Natal Indians in 1860. They were rigidly excluded from the performance of skilled work in order to reassure the immigrant white miners; they were very strictly housed in compounds to reassure those who feared they might prove lawless; and they were engaged at wage rates even lower than those currently paid to African mineworkers – 37*s* 7*d* a month in 1905, against an African wage of 51*s* 9*d*.

The Chinese labourers were systematically returned to China on completion of their contracts, after the accession of Botha's Government to power in the Transvaal in 1907. By that time they had served Milner's purpose of expanding the productivity of the mines, even if that had not brought the political consequences which he intended. More important, they helped to save the colour bar on the gold mines. Restrictions imposed on the range of work which the Chinese might do, the first legalised system of job reservation, were subsequently applied to Africans. Without imported labour, the owners would have been under heavy pressure to extend Creswell's experiment, which enjoyed much more support than the magnates and Milner were prepared to admit. If whites had been employed at unskilled as well as skilled levels on the mines, this could in turn have led to a narrowing of the wage gap between skilled and unskilled rates; and if the gap had been closed in the mines, it would have been harder to reopen when secondary industries began to proliferate during and after the First World War.

The Chinese were expendable once the machinery for the recruitment of Africans was in working order again. By 1910 there were 183,793 Africans at work on the gold mines, which was double the number employed in 1899, and half the number employed in 1972. 'Wenela' and the Native Recruiting Corporation struggled to eliminate competitive recruiting by individual mining companies, and gradually to extend their recruiting networks further afield. Health hazards, notably the vulnerability of African miners to pneumonia, at first discouraged the Government of Northern Rhodesia and Nyasaland from allowing the Union to recruit mineworkers north of the twenty-second parallel. Southern Rhodesia discouraged Wenela because it wanted the workers itself. Between 1912 and 1937 the Union Government barred recruitment beyond its northern borders, but relaxed the embargo for the gold mines when new vaccines had brought the health dangers under control. Wenela then extended its recruiting stations beyond the Transvaal and Mozambique to take in Nyasaland, Northern Rhodesia, Bechuanaland and South West Africa (where stations in the Caprivi Strip were intended to draw in workers from Angola). The N.R.C. concentrated on Basutoland, Swaziland and the African areas of Natal and the eastern Cape. As had been the case with the diamond mines, the main areas of recruitment had moved north. By 1972, nearly four-fifths of the African labour employed by the Chamber of Mines was recruited outside the Republic of South Africa – 25 per cent from Lesotho, Botswana and Swaziland, 21 per cent from Mozambique, and 32 per cent from beyond the northern borders, of whom most came from Malawi (Nyasaland). But disputes between the mining houses and miners from Malawi and Lesotho in 1974, together with growing uncertainty over the long-term prospects of continued recruitment from an independent Mozambique, led the mining houses in 1975 to look for ways of increasing recruitment from the Republic itself.

The mines had set a pattern for South African industry by organising their labour on the migratory system. Its chief advantages were the cheapness of the labour itself, for employers were not involved in the expense of providing family accommodation, and in the way it undercut the workers' bargaining power. The latter was a sensitive point. But the leaders of industry were able to obtain from the first Union Parliament a legislative programme which ensured that the industrial power of black workers remained weak. Thus the Mines and Works Act of 1911 was mainly concerned with industrial safety; but regulations issued under it restricted certain categories of work to white people, on the ground that they carried special responsibility – for example, the handling of explosives. There were already a few examples of racially restrictive industrial legislation on the Transvaal statute book; but this kind of legislation was thrown out as *ultra vires* in 1923 by the Transvaal Supreme Court in the case of *R.* v. *Hildick Smith.* Another law of Botha's Government, its Native Labour Regulation Act of 1911, reduced the industrial power of black workers by making strike action by them a criminal offence.[3] It did not have the immediate effect of preventing strikes by Africans, for African miners came out in 1913 during the strike of whites at the Kleinfontein mine, while in 1919 Clements Kadalie's newly founded Industrial and Commercial Workers' Union had a short-lived success in organising a strike in the Cape Town docks. But the dice were loaded against African strike action, which was negligible between 1920 and the Second World War because it proved easy to put down. Kadalie's Union subsequently paid more attention to political than to industrial action. Having lost the right and the apparent ability to strike, African workers then found themselves excluded in 1924 from the new collective bargaining procedures laid down in the Industrial Conciliation Act of the Smuts Government. This Act excluded pass-bearing Africans (that is, African males) from the definition of 'employee' for conciliation purposes. (African women were excluded under the 1937 amendment, and the definition was amended in 1953 to include members of 'any aboriginal tribe of Africa'.) This left no machinery for the adjustment of African industrial claims until Hertzog's Wage Act of 1925 set up a Wage Board with power to make determinations, and that body was of little use to them in the early years. Africans could still form trade unions, or be members of trade unions along with workers of other races, however, and the possibility of the recognition of African unions was considered by Smuts's wartime Government between 1942 and 1946. During this period a large number of small strikes by African workers occurred, and in a high proportion of the cases, thanks to the appointment of arbitrators under emergency war measures, this unofficial strike action resulted in the improvement of their conditions. But after a serious African miners' strike in August 1946 the Government refused (following strong representations from the Chamber) to give official recognition to the African Mineworkers' Union which had been formed in 1941, and in doing so helped to precipitate the political deadlock with the African leadership which marked its last two years of office.

National Party policy after 1948 tightened African bargaining procedures in two ways. Its Native Labour (Settlement of Disputes) Act of 1953 provided for the establishment of regional native labour committees composed of African workers, who could approach the industrial councils through a Central Native Labour Board, which promised a better opportunity for the presentation of grievances but still fell short of collective bargaining. Then in 1956 a further amendment to the Industrial Conciliation Act required racially mixed trade unions to segregate their membership into distinct branches or to split into separate unions, so that bargains concluded in the interest of one race group did not necessarily affect another. The Native Labour Regulation Act of 1911 was finally repealed in 1964, but the Bantu Labour Act which replaced it contained a very tight rule prohibiting breach of contract by black workers. Periodic African strikes nevertheless continued, reaching a climax in 1973, when the combined effects of inflation and widespread publicity given to the low level of African wages resulted in industrial action in several parts of South Africa, notably in Durban. Like the strikes during the war years, these sometimes led to wage improvements, and the Government made guarded concessions to African unions but still refused to grant official recognition. The Durban textile workers' strike of January 1974 showed, however, that the position remained anomalous. Ten thousand workers struck for higher pay, and as a result of mediation by the Kwazulu Homeland Government received an award which met their claim in part. Some two hundred of the strike leaders were prosecuted for breaking the law by striking, and fined a total of over R1000. The fine was in turn paid by the white Garment Workers' Union, a body which had itself been compulsorily segregated under the legislation of 1956.

A colour bar was implicit in the restrictive legislation described above, but it was also made explicit in the field of job opportunities as a result of the mining crisis of 1922.[4] Economic difficulties not unlike those which had provided the background for the debate over white labour and Chinese labour in 1903 recurred in the wake of the First World War, and their seriousness was underlined by the Low Grade Mines Commission of 1920, which reported that twenty-one mines employing about ten thousand white and eighty thousand black workers, comprising approximately half the Rand gold-mining industry, were making a profit of two shillings or less on every ton of rock mined. This was a critical profit margin, and in order to cut costs the Chamber of Mines declared its intention of abandoning a *status quo* agreement reached with the European mineworkers in 1918, and increasing the ratio of black to white workers to ten-and-a-half blacks for every white. The South African Industrial Federation, on behalf of the miners, replied by insisting on a ratio of only three-and-a-half blacks to one white. The Rand rebellion of 1922 grew out of the strike which followed the breakdown of negotiations, commandos of rural Afrikaners arriving to help the mineworkers against the management at a time when over half the white mineworkers on the Rand were now South African-born, a growing number of them Afrikaners who, like their English-speaking counterparts, had lost none of the anti-capitalist sentiments which had begun to bring them together before Union. Government forces suppressed the rebellion after there had been considerable loss of life. But the white Labour Party, now led by Creswell, took part in the general election of 1924 as junior partner to Hertzog's Nationalists. They won the election and, as the 'Pact' Government, began to implement an industrial policy more in tune with the wishes of European workers.

The industrial policy of General Hertzog's Government aimed to do three things in particular: to protect South African industry against outside competition and thus conserve foreign exchange, to protect poor whites against black and Coloured competition in the unskilled field, and to protect skilled white workers from undercutting by black competition in the higher trades. The Government's attempt to nurse the industrial sector took the form of high tariffs against imported goods which threatened to compete with local manufactures, special favour being shown in 1925, for example, to locally produced 'bacon and ham, cardboard boxes, cheese, clothing bespoke, confectionary, fish, buckets household and sanitary, jam and jellies, mica manufactures, varnishes, printed matter, coir mats, embossed steel ceilings'. Tariff concessions were also offered to firms whose labour policies were 'satisfactory' – that is, if they were trying to place white workers in employment, if necessary by putting them into jobs previously done by black or Coloured.

This related to the second leg of government policy, the protection of poor whites, who were said to number perhaps 220,000 persons by the Carnegie Commission of 1929–31, the vast majority of them being Afrikaners. The Government set up a Wage Board in 1925, with the task of making wage determinations in industries where no provision for collective bargaining existed. The principle on which this board was to operate was 'the rate for the job', a principle which gave the appearance of complete fairness, but which has been described by W. H. Hutt as 'the most powerful yet most subtle colour bar that has ever operated'. In a society where racial prejudice played an influential role, where access to training by members of different race groups was unequal, where the customary gap between skilled (white) wages and unskilled (black) wages was unusually wide, and where competitive under-cutting by those with lower living standards was prohibited by law, Hutt's argument was correct. Once set up, the Wage Board directed its attention in the early years to the upgrading of wages in unskilled work normally done by whites, and paid little attention to categories of work normally the preserve of Coloured or African workers – all this in the interest of 'persons whose standard of living conforms to the standard of living generally recognized as tolerable from the usual European standpoint', and against the interest of 'persons whose aim is restricted to the bare requirements of the necessities of life as understood among barbarous and undeveloped peoples'. These were the classic definitions of 'civilised' and 'uncivilised' labour put out by the Union Department of Labour on 31 October 1924.

The Mines and Works Amendment (or 'Colour Bar') Act of 1926 was Hertzog's way of securing the interests of the white skilled worker. This law simply reserved the grant of certificates of competency in skilled trades to white people and Coloured people, placing Indians and Africans on the wrong side of the fence and giving the force of law to a principle which the Supreme Court had declared invalid. Job reservation appeared to favour the Coloured man, but in practice did not do so. The combined pressures of the Cape School Board Act of 1905, which had made primary education compulsory for white children but not for others, and of the Apprenticeship Act of 1922, which had for the first time laid down minimal educational qualifications for entry into specific trades, had reduced the relative opportunities for Coloured people to qualify as artisans. Their hold over the skilled trades in the Cape actually fell from about half the total in the late nineteenth century to about one-thirteenth of the total by 1961. The effect of these combined employment policies of the Hertzog Government can be illustrated by one clear example from the public sector, where the policies also applied – namely, employment on the railways. Between 1924 and 1933, the number of Africans employed by the South African Railways and Harbours as labourers fell from 37,564 to 22,008, and the number of Coloured people from 5628 to 4663, while the number of Europeans rose from 4760 to 17,683.

Whether the 'civilised labour' policy was of actual economic advantage to the white worker was questioned by the Economic and Wage Commission, which was appointed only after the passage of the Wage Act, for that commission argued that to subsidise unskilled white wages was to reduce profit margins in the undertakings where this was done, and thus to inhibit the expansion of those undertakings through the creation of more jobs.

But if the 'civilised labour' policy did not protect the white worker, there can be no doubt that the devaluation of the South African pound in December 1932 did. During the middle thirties, under the stimulus of new capital in search of outlets, industries sprouted in the main centres of South Africa, above all on the Rand, and at Durban, Cape Town and Port Elizabeth. Full employment for whites followed, while growing numbers of whites and Africans moved to the towns from the Reserves and from the white-owned farms. Poor Whiteism, the preoccupation of an important commission at the beginning of the decade, was hardly noticed when the *Ekonomiese Volkskongres* of Nationalist Afrikaners met at Bloemfontein in 1939 and decided to pool their resources in a bid to win a foothold in commerce and industry. Poor blacks remained a problem, and the Native Economic (Holloway) Commission of 1932 could still think in terms of directing the Government's main efforts to the rehabilitation of the Reserves; but by the end of the decade the increased demands of the urban labour market made that emphasis questionable, especially when an acute labour shortage in industry followed the outbreak of the Second World War.

The war made the colour bar largely redundant, at a time when the creation of a variety of new semi-skilled jobs involving machine-minding of various kinds rendered the old categories of 'skilled' and 'unskilled' increasingly obsolete. Because of increased competition for artisans, the Government was compelled to authorise dilution of labour, allowing unqualified workers to do skilled work under supervision, above all in the engineering industry, but also in textiles, furniture, leatherwork and other fields, in all of which the employment of Coloured and black workers greatly increased. At the end of the war the serious shortage of housing forced the Government to permit the training of African builders to construct houses for Africans in urban locations, and this policy was later consolidated by the Malan Government through the Native Building Workers' Act of 1951.

In order to reassure the white electorate, however, the appearance of job reservation was preserved, and its reality maintained wherever it was practicable to maintain it. The amendments to the Industrial Conciliation Act in 1956 and 1959 had these objects in view. Under the former, the Minister of Labour was granted blanket powers to safeguard the economic welfare of employees of any race in any industry or trade by requiring an industrial tribunal to reserve particular kinds of work for particular race groups in particular areas. At first the powers were used for the protection of white people. Skilled work in the clothing industry was reserved for whites in 1957, but the determination was withdrawn when it was declared invalid by the courts, and replaced in 1960 by a new determination designed to stabilise racial percentages as they stood in August 1959. In 1958, the positions of ambulance driver and fireman and most ranks in the traffic police in Cape Town were reserved for whites. In 1959, the operation of lifts in Bloemfontein, Johannesburg and Pretoria, and all kinds of lifts everywhere (unless they were for the conveyance of non-Europeans only, or for goods only) was reserved for whites. A range of other determinations followed.

The policy proved increasingly difficult to implement because of the unexpectedly rapid growth rate of the economy in the years following the Sharpeville shootings, when the value of industrial share prices rose from a mean figure of 65 in March 1960 to about 290 on the *Rand Daily Mail* index (see the graph opposite). The ability of the white community to supply the manpower required for the types of work normally reserved for whites steadily receded. This appeared, on the surface, to justify the argument (considered in the following chapter) that economic pressures were bound to destroy the *apartheid* ideology. But the system proved to be more flexible in practice. The manner in which the white community could adjust to this changing situation without having to abandon the advantages accruing from the retention of the colour bar can be illustrated from developments in the gold-mining industry. In 1964 the owners of twelve gold mines, embarrassed by the white labour shortage, reached an agreement with the unions to allow small inroads by black workers into jobs legally reserved for whites. The experiment resulted in increased productivity and was profitable to all concerned; but when white miners on mines not involved in the experiment objected, the Government, after appointing a commission, decided to block the experiment. The Chamber of Mines subsequently changed its tactics and tried to bargain with the white miners by offering productivity bonuses in return for concessions to black workers; but the radical right-wing miners organised a series of strikes in 1966 in protest against the feared inroads into the colour bar. Eventually, in 1967, a compromise agreement was reached: the white miners agreed that blacks could do some 'white' jobs, such as handling explosives or driving engines slowly; but in return they obtained guarantees against retrenchment and the lion's share of the proceeds from the resultant increase in productivity.

Thus blacks were enabled to move upwards in the employment scale, by conferring even greater benefits on whites, under very unequal arrangements which were mutually not disadvantageous. Understandably, the opposition of the white trade union movement to black inroads became less monolithic under arrangements of this kind, and a notable feature of the early 1970s was a tendency for the liberal wing of that movement, represented by the Trades Union Congress of South Africa, to encourage the unionisation of black labour on the supposition that the reason for antagonism between black and white unions was disappearing. Meanwhile government policy paid increasing attention to methods for improving the efficiency of black labour, setting up

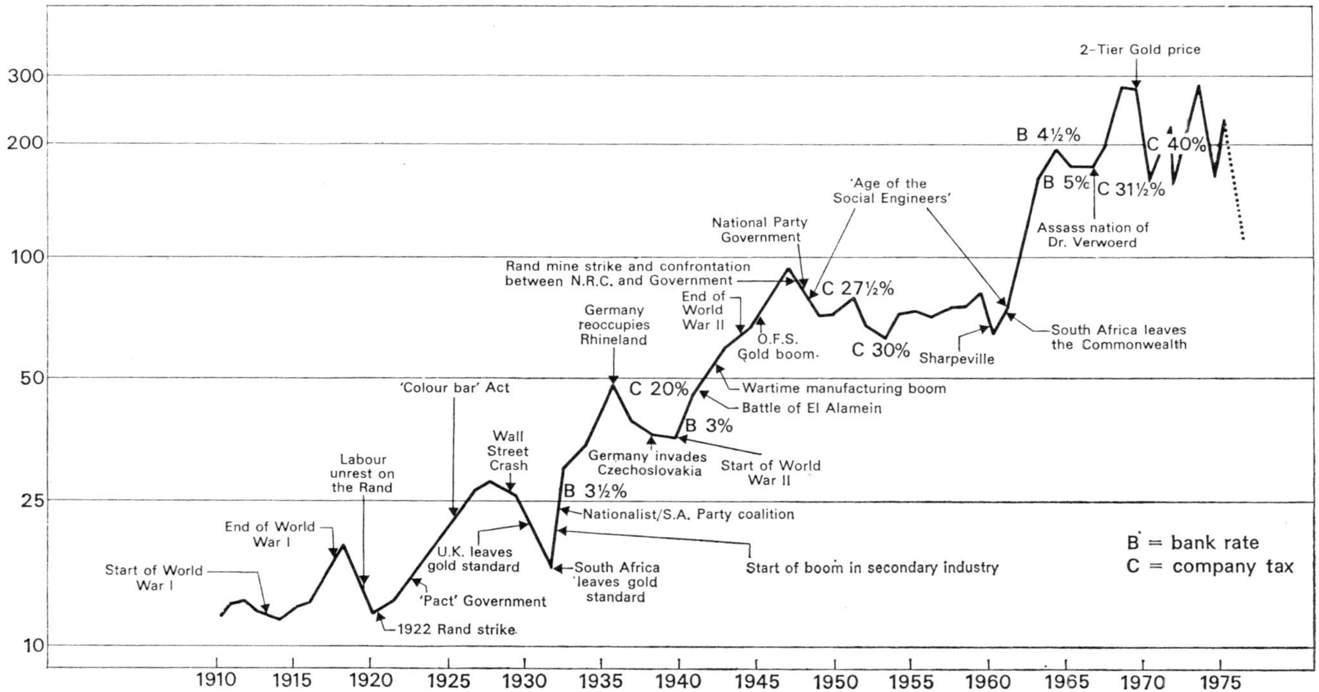


This chart shows the course of industrial share prices on the Johannesburg Stock Exchange, 1911–75. The index plotted is the Rand Daily Mail 100 (from 1958) correlated with an index compiled by the Bureau of Economic Research, Stellenbosch (1910–51) and with calculations done by Sanlam (1949–58). It is based on a representative sample of the major listed industrial companies weighted relative to size.

South African Industrial Share Prices, 1911–75

labour bureaux in the new administrative 'prescribed areas' under the Bantu Labour Act of 1964, and establishing 'aid centres' to which Africans found guilty of contravening urban influx control regulations could be referred, so that they could be directed to employment in town or country where labour was needed, instead of being punished by short unproductive terms of imprisonment. The Physical Planning Act of 1967 initiated an attempt by the Government to divert industrial development from the larger centres to the border areas on the edge of the Bantu Homelands, with a view to the creation of new growth points where factories, established with the prospect of tax rebate incentives and cheaper labour, could attract workers direct from the Homelands, to which they could return nightly or at frequent intervals, thus in theory diverting the flow of labour from the 'white' towns and at the same time cutting down the social evils of labour migrancy.

Labour migrancy helped to reinforce the colour bar by ensuring that, in general, African workers remained a peasant proletariat with one foot in the Reserves.[5] It thus acted as a drag on the urbanisation of the black worker and on his acquisition of skills which might fit him for more responsible employment. Its growth during the nineteenth century had been gradual, and it hardly developed at all on the farms until the mid-1960s, when farm labourers from the Transkei and Ciskei were taken to the sugar farms of Natal and the fruit farms of the western Cape by farmers' cooperative societies on short-term labour contracts. The practice received a boost from the railway construction programmes in the 1880s onwards, but it was the diamond and, above all, the gold mines which placed migrant labour on an organised basis and turned it into the characteristic South African mode of labour recruitment, to which – under governmental encouragement – more and more industrial firms went over after 1950. There was a chance during the late 1940s that the Government might have abandoned the migrant labour policy, at least in part, on the recommendations of the Fagan Commission, which came out with cautious proposals for the encouragement of a settled urban labour force, the workers being allowed to bring their families to town. The opening of the Orange Free State goldfields also gave the mining houses a chance to reconsider their labour policies, especially as the stabilisation of mine labour had already been successfully carried out in the Congo since 1927 and on the Northern Rhodesian copper belt since 1940. Sir Ernest Oppenheimer, opening a new shaft at the Welkom mine, felt sure that the Company's ultimate aim should be 'to create, within a reasonable time, modern Native villages which will attract Natives from all over the Union, and from which the mines will ultimately draw a large proportion of their Native labour requirements'. The Nationalist Government, however, opposed this suggestion, fearing the establishment of irremovable 'black spots' far away from the existing Bantu areas if it were adopted, and insisting on the provision of as little married accommodation for African mineworkers as possible.

One feature of government policy which stressed the importance attached to migrant labour therefore was the switch to hostel-building in the urban townships, in place of earlier schemes during the 1950s for the provision of single-residential accommodation. Provision was made during the 1960s for the housing of approximately 60,000 migrant workers in 'bachelor' quarters on the Rand, and for the housing of the same number under similar conditions in Alexandra Township, Johannesburg, an area previously occupied by the homes of African married couples. Steps were also taken to reduce the number of town-based African employees, and to increase the number of Homeland-based employees working temporarily in the urban areas under short-term contracts of up to a year's duration, or, under special arrangements, for longer periods.

Restrictions imposed on blacks entering the urban areas as workers are more easily to be explained in terms of a desire to maintain segregation than of a desire to eliminate black competition. Where questions of restricting property ownership and trading rights were concerned, however, the interpretation is not so straightforward. Historically, this issue first presented itself in relation to the Indian immigrants of the 1880s. Many of these were not indentured workers, but traders who had paid their own passages, and began to arrive in sufficient numbers to alarm white traders in Natal and the Boer republics. Indians were accordingly excluded from the Orange Free State by stages between 1885 and 1890, largely on the insistence of English-speaking shopkeepers. These years also saw the first attempts in Natal and the South African Republic to restrict their residential and trading rights in the towns, and in Natal to restrict their political influence. (In the longer term, fears arising from Indian business success led whites to oppose the introduction of the Chinese to the Transvaal after 1903, in case they might be allowed to compete with whites in industry.) Eventually, Indians were placed on the 'wrong' side of the colour bar under the Mines and Works Amendment Act of 1926. A widespread onslaught on their economic power began with the Transvaal pegging legislation of the 1930s, the Asiatic Land Tenure Act of 1946, which had special reference to Natal, and the Group Areas Act of 1950. Even if people sometimes denied an economic motivation for these laws, there can hardly have been a more important reason for restricting their right to invest in fixed property in Natal, or for moving their shops well away from the central business districts of towns in the Transvaal. In the case of Africans, black businesses in urban locations were theoretically permitted under the Urban Areas Act, but it was left to urban local authorities to grant or refuse trading licences, and in a number of centres they were refused to Africans, notably in the Orange Free State. Even though the Minister of Native Affairs took powers under the 1930 amendment of the Act to enable him to compel local authorities to fall into line, he never invoked these powers, and it was only in 1944 that the O.F.S. municipalities were persuaded to allow blacks to trade in their own locations. After 1948 it once more became Government policy to restrict black trading in urban areas so far as possible. In 1963 a Government circular accordingly required local authorities to limit African trading in the locations by imposing a rule of one-man-one-shop, prohibiting African trading in all but 'daily essential domestic necessities' (which could not include the sale of petrol, for example), and banning the establishment of African trading partnerships in white areas. It was thought better that blacks should frequent the central business areas for shopping purposes, where in any case goods bought in chain stores tended to be cheaper than in the townships, and where crowd control on Friday afternoons could be maintained, if necessary, by police using trained dogs.

The Government regulations controlling black trading in white areas, however, cover only part of the picture. Trade in the Reserves was governed by a different set of laws. A proclamation of 1922 banned the opening of a new trading store within five miles of an existing one. This played into the hands of the white traders already established there, and evoked much resentment from blacks, especially in the Transkei. To help African traders, the law was changed in 1934 to allow stores within two miles of each other. One of the first acts of the Transkeian legislature after taking power in 1964 was to abolish this kind of geographical restriction, with the result that black-owned stores began to proliferate and it became necessary in 1970 to suspend the issue of new licences. Meanwhile the setting up of the Bantu Investment Corporation in 1959, and of subsidiary Homeland development corporations to promote African entrepreneurship, canalised further government and – in due course – white agency capital into the Homelands. This helped to produce a growing number of African commercial trainees, if rather fewer capitalists, and some complaints that too much responsibility and initiative remained in white hands, and too little in those of the Bantu. This was, however, a step towards African economic emancipation, especially when the development corporations began to buy the stores of white traders. The number of African traders in the African areas continued to grow, though not at the rate produced by the 1934 proclamation, save in the larger Bantu towns near white urban centres – Soweto, Mdantsane, and others, where an urban wage-earning clientele proved able to support a large and growing number of small businesses – as many as 1460 in Soweto in 1969, for example.

Without native expertise to draw upon, African business enterprise spread through contact with the commercial civilisation of the white man. Business values acquired in the town gradually found their way into the outlooks of Reserve Africans, who began to look upon livestock and services rendered (such as ploughing for others) in terms of cash rather than customary values. But this enterprise, restricted as it was by special rules, and prohibited save on a very small scale over most of the surface of the land, could hardly be said to enjoy conditions of freedom.

# 20 The Current Debate

South Africa's isolation arose from social policies which came to offend not only black South Africans but the independent African states, the communist world, and the liberal democratic states of the West. The Government's commitment to these internationally unpopular policies – a commitment endorsed by the plebiscite of half a dozen general elections since 1948 – has elicited various kinds of explanation. These tend to fall into two main groups: explanations which see racism as the chief determinant of white South African attitudes, and explanations which attribute them to a clash of class interests.[1]

Writers who have seen government action as inspired by racial assumptions, the holders of what has come to be referred to as the 'conventional wisdom', included both proponents and critics of racialism. Racial segregationists like Gert Cronje asserted that individual race groups had the moral right to ensure the survival of their separate (divinely ordained) identities, and that separation was the only practical solvent to racial friction. Liberal segregationists like Alfred Hoernlé tended to deny the validity of the first of these propositions, but to accept the second. Both kinds of theorist were not so much innovators as elaborators of a segregationist line of thought which went back into the nineteenth century, and had enjoyed the support of most of the articulate commentators on South African affairs from the Lagden Commission of 1903–5 onwards, whether their postures were white supremacist or liberal.

The segregationist position was enthusiastically adopted by the Purified Nationalists in the 1930s. Leading liberal thinkers moved away from segregationist ideas at the same time, but saw no reason to abandone the frame of reference within which the public debate had been placed. Whether segregation was good or bad, they saw racism as the great divisive factor in South African life, the phenomenon which needed to be eliminated above all others if the right public policies were to be prescribed. Hence the significance of works like I. D. MacCrone's *Race Attitudes in South Africa*, which looked for reasons for the evolution of race prejudice and claimed to find them on the Cape frontier in the eighteenth century. Liberals who looked for the origins of racist thinking were seeking to explain a phenomenon of which they disapproved, and it was no accident that they should have been doing this in the decade when Hitler's Germany was in the making. But their grounds of objection to segregation varied. Some saw it simply as economic moonshine, and therefore not viable. Others saw it as politically immoral (whether viable or not) and therefore insufferable. Therefore both the main traditional schools of liberal thinker – the devotees of free enterprise and the guardians of human rights – found reasons for attacking the system.

As Yudelman has stressed, the economic liberals who believed that the pull of the market would crush ideological racism and its supporting structure of pass laws and colour bars all wrote during the period after 1933, which was one of relatively uninterrupted growth for the South African economy. Economic historians in the 1930s, notably H. M. Robertson, had shown that the degree of integration at the economic level was already so far advanced that racial separation was no longer a serious possibility. Such an argument appeared to be even stronger after the Second World War, as black urbanisation and the movement by blacks into the white economy accelerated, and was watched with approval by the Smuts Government's Social and Economic Planning Council. Indeed, economic pressure was breaking down the barriers of segregation to such an extent that the devotees of *apartheid* began to insist on a tougher policy of job reservation to keep lucrative urban employment in white hands.

When W. W. Rostow, the American economist, published his *Stages of Economic Growth* in 1953, urging that periods of disequilibrium and labour exploitation necessarily occurred where an industrial society reached 'take-off', and before it had achieved the stage of mass consumption, some South African economists – notably D. Hobart Houghton and M. C. O'Dowd – took his model very seriously. O'Dowd considered in 1964 that large-scale exploitation of labour was probably unavoidable at first, but that the stage of mass consumption would arrive well before the end of the twentieth century. He still adhered to this view in 1974, when he contributed to Leftwich's anthology on political change in South Africa. Another clear expression of confidence in the ability of the market economy to break *apartheid* was Ralph Horwitz's *Political Economy of South Africa* (1957), which concluded with the assertion that 'the South African economy is inescapably integrated in the pursuit of productivity. Economic rationality urges the polity forward beyond its ideology.'

The Rostow thesis carried an element of economic determinism, however much the South African economists who made use of it might resist those implications. But not all political economists were prepared to predict the victory of the market over racial ideology as a matter of course. Herbert Blumer's chapters in Guy Hunter's *Industrialization and Race Relations* was important for this reason. Blumer, drawing particularly on the work of the South African economist, Sheila van der Horst, concluded that on the evidence available the demands of industry would not necessarily destroy *apartheid*, but that industry would rather adapt itself to the political order and content itself with less than optimal profit margins for the sake of preserving industrial peace and maintaining the security of the white ruling group. 'Industry can and does tolerate a wide latitude of inefficient operation and still achieve acceptable production and profit,' he wrote, in spite of very good *a priori* reasons for thinking that industrialisation must 'break through and break up the racial scheme'. He saw industrialisation as neutral in a situation of racial confrontation, 'an incitant to change, without providing the definition of how change is to be met'.

Faith in the power of the market to destroy *apartheid* thus gave confidence to some critics of segregation (*apartheid*) but not to all. There were others who judged the South African scene in terms of liberal political values which had evolved in the experience of the Western democracies. Accepting racist aberrations as lying at the root of the disease, they prescribed political reform in the expectation (or perhaps no more than the hope) that the introduction of political liberty and an ending of injustice would sufficiently defuse the situation for peaceful change to be made possible. Their stand has to be seen against a particular background: the steady abandonment of liberal political principles over the years, with a tendency for the already well-advanced process to accelerate after 1948, by means of inroads made into the rule of law over a wide area, the narrowing of the political rights of all black groups, and of the civil liberties of all groups, both black and white, unequal treatment in nearly all situations where separate amenities were laid down for the different races, and the continuing insistence on unequal access to economic opportunity. It was, above all, the proven inequity of the system of segregation that drove leading liberals like Edgar Brookes, W. M. Macmillan, Leo Marquard, Margaret Hodgson (later Ballinger), and J. H. Hofmeyr to part company with thinkers like Hoernlé in the 1930s. Their case was made even clearer after 1948. But had they a workable alternative prescription for the country's ills?

This question can best be answered after one has considered the grounds on which their position has been attacked. A revisionist school of academics emerged during the 1960s, who argued cogently that the liberals had done a disservice to the cause of black liberation by diverting their energies into non-viable lines of activity aimed at goals which would not in fact bring about black liberation. In 1970 F. A. Johnstone argued that, so far from economic forces threatening to pull down apartheid (or merely leave it alone, as Blumer had argued), 'the relations between capitalist development, apartheid policies and the core structure of white supremacy are essentially collaborative', so that 'quite contrary to the prevailing thesis, white supremacy is continually being reinforced by economic development'. He saw the growing urbanisation and the upward occupational mobility of blacks in industry, not as proof of the failure of apartheid, but merely as signs of an artful attempt by the Government 'to maximise economic development both for the sake of white prosperity and for the material protection of white supremacy'. Because white security and white prosperity seemed to be interlocked, Johnstone went on to argue that white policy was designed to restrict black opportunity by ensuring that blacks were not enabled to make use of their industrial bargaining power, or acquire power either through education, or through the accumulation of wealth.

Members of the revisionist school, in subjecting the South African economic system to Marxian analysis, began to develop the argument that the *apartheid* system was designed primarily to assist the capitalist mode of production under South African conditions rather than to protect the interests of the white race as such (though the interests of the white race as a whole happened to coincide with the interests of South African capitalism). Thus, for Johnstone, the failure and lack of concern on the part of the protagonists of *apartheid* to achieve separation of the races in practice was relatively immaterial. It was not intended to do that, Johnstone urged, but to ensure – if necessary by the controlled bending of its own rules – that industry could remain in white hands and continue to produce under conditions of industrial peace. A further assertion, that South African industrial prosperity was attributable to cheap labour made cheap through the calculated impoverishment of the African Reserves – a variant on the theory of under-development – pointed in the same direction. The South African economy, these writers were saying in effect, corresponded closely to the Leninist model of an imperialist economic system, with the exploiter class located partly in South African business, partly in overseas bodies which financed South African economic development, and partly in the white workers whose privileged position in the economy gave them a parasitic relationship to the business interests. The revisionists saw no necessary antagonism between *apartheid* and economic growth, thus parting company with the O'Dowd school, and substituting an opposite near-determinist theory of their own.

Their attack on the liberal position was extended across the whole front, casting doubts on the liberals' analysis of the South African problem, on their prescription for change, and in the final resort on their bona fides (for if liberals were wrong in their diagnosis, and wrong in their prescription, did it not follow that they desired no cure?)

Rejection of the liberals' analysis that racial prejudice was the root cause of South Africa's disequilibrium can be seen in their critique of the MacCrone thesis on the origins of white race attitudes, but above all in their attribution of economic causes to South African racism. Martin Legassick has cogently argued that whereas the earlier policy of segregation was at bottom an attempt to apply a system of extra-economically controlled labour to mining and farming, *apartheid* was the application of a cheap forced labour policy to secondary industry, which came into its own after the Second World War as the main growth sector in the economy. Manufacturing, he argued, required the recruitment of semi-skilled operatives for factory employment on a large scale. Some employers advocated a government-sponsored policy for the settlement of African workers in towns, with houses, amenities and pension rights. Others, who enjoyed the support of the white working class, advocated the intensification of black labour migrancy as an alternative. The Nationalist victory in 1948, Legassick continues, was a victory for the latter group, who derived support from the mining and farming interests – the former traditionally dependent on migrant labour, the latter satisfied with increased control on urban influx (which checked the labour drain from their farms) and increasingly dependent on convict labour (often men who had fallen foul of the influx control regulations) and their own organised recruitment direct from the Reserves.

The liberals' prescription came under attack as well, on several grounds. Their pressure to secure the economic emancipation of the black was condemned as emanating from an element in the population whose wealth or education made it safe from black competition – a debating point on which the revisionists and the Nationalists agreed. Their insistence on keeping their protests within the law, which amounted under the circumstances to a refusal to take an effective part in the overthrow of the system, was taken to mean that they adhered in the last resort to the system which the law protected. Indeed, Janet Robertson's *Liberalism in South Africa* (1971) describes the stresses felt within the Liberal Party on this very point. Meanwhile adherents of political pluralism attacked the liberal position as politically unrealistic, and – without necessarily being Nationalists – were drawn towards a multi-state model. The Spro–Cas Report, *South Africa's Political Alternatives* (1973), followed this line.

To outline the growing ideological debate seems an appropriate way to end a history of South Africa written in the 1970s. The debate is still in full flow, and seems likely to be increasingly influenced by the pressure of political events as it takes its course. David Yudelman, in 1975, attempted a bird's-eye correlation of the liberal-reformist and revisionist arguments, and in an article which is a model of clarity assailed some of the revisionists' main arguments about the role of industrialisation and the role of the state in South Africa, as well as their assumptions about the nature of political change. Leo Kuper, a sociologist, and Norman Bromberger, an economist, took issue with them in the early 1970s on a number of points. Kuper's *Race, Class and Power*, in which he brought together articles written at intervals since 1966, gave a wide-ranging critique of the neo-Marxist model (while accepting the central relevance of class factors) and suggested that Marxism might be 'simply a rhetoric in a racial movement for liberation'. Bromberger argued that even if Johnstone's thesis were true in the short run, in the longer term the two goals of white prosperity and white security might prove to be incompatible with each other. Where Johnstone argued that there had been a calculated attempt by the white authorities to destroy black bargaining power on the industrial, educational and income levels, Bromberger attached importance to Africans' upward mobility in employment as something likely to make them less replaceable, more ambitious, and less deferential socially. He argued that there had in fact been significant black educational advance. He attacked the revisionists' view that capital in general demands cheap labour, and stressed the importance in any discussion of wage policies of taking the factor of population growth into account. (Poverty datum figures calculated on families of five need drastic upward revision if the average family is found to have seven people.) He also asked why it should be necessary (as Legassick once put it) to 'decode' the language of political racism in order to find an inner economic explanation. If racial fears are expressed, there was at least a reasonable chance that those who expressed them were governed by racial fears – the fears of a white community, because they were white, that they might not always be welcome in a predominantly black continent. For Bromberger, therefore, the Bantustan policy was not a propaganda device designed to conceal a system of exploitation, but 'a risky strategy seriously undertaken in the hope of averting long-run disaster'.

At bottom, the debate over South Africa was a debate over the possibility of evolutionary change. Both domestic and external considerations were important here – the willingness of the South African Government to change its policies in the light of experience and informed criticism, and in response to pressure, and the preparedness of the outside world to allow it time to do so. Domestic and international issues could not easily be separated, for both featured regularly on the agenda of the U.N. The colour bar in Johannesburg was as repugnant to Washington, London, Delhi and Moscow as the colour bar in Windhoek, and in Windhoek the world body found legal grounds for intervention. The sheer difficulty of unwinding so elaborate a system as separate development, after decades of propaganda in its support, needs to be stressed. The fact that the Tomlinson blueprint had been shown to be unworkable might be an excellent argument for scrapping the system; but the conversion of its supporters required an emotional as well as an intellectual *volte-face*. The danger of a powerful white backlash against any attempt to unscramble the system was considerable. The difficulty of containing pent-up black feelings once emancipation were embarked upon was equally great. As the crisis over Angola, South West Africa and Rhodesia moved towards a climax in 1975–6, the Government showed a certain flexibility in its international relations, but little evidence of intention to move either fast or far on the home front. Liberal policies recommended to Rhodesia were not regarded as suitable for South Africa – perhaps even for South West Africa. At home there was an apparent decision to relax the harsher features of the system in areas not regarded as critical to the apartheid policy. Thus mixed theatre audiences were increasingly permitted under licences individually applied for, and mixed sporting activities even at club level became safer to organise without police intervention. The job market was also thrown open more widely to blacks, save in critical areas controlled by strong white unions. The one clear line of advance was towards Homeland independence – a slow move towards (or perhaps away from) the solution of a small part of a much bigger problem.

Opinion leaders outside South Africa were therefore given good reasons for concluding that the Government would not attempt to change its direction. This gave force to the plea for violent change; but violence, it had to be recognised, would involve threats not only to public order but also to the resources on which human survival depended. As South Africa was still the breadbasket for much of sub-Saharan Africa, this was a very serious consideration. The issues were delicately poised, for as Kuper expressed it, against 'the atrocities of civil war, in massacre, torture, slitting of throats, disembowelment, impaling, rape, desolation' had to be placed 'the continuing atrocities of racial domination in the form of high infant mortality rates, low expectation of life, malnutrition, disease, poverty, and the denial of human rights and human dignity'. The greater the threat of violence from outside, the greater was the danger that public opinion in white South Africa would be distracted from its task of reconciliation across the colour line by the escapist cry of 'the nation in danger'. The laager served Andries Pretorius well at Blood River, but it served Cronje at Paardekraal extremely badly. Never was the country in more urgent need of justice, courage and a sense of history.

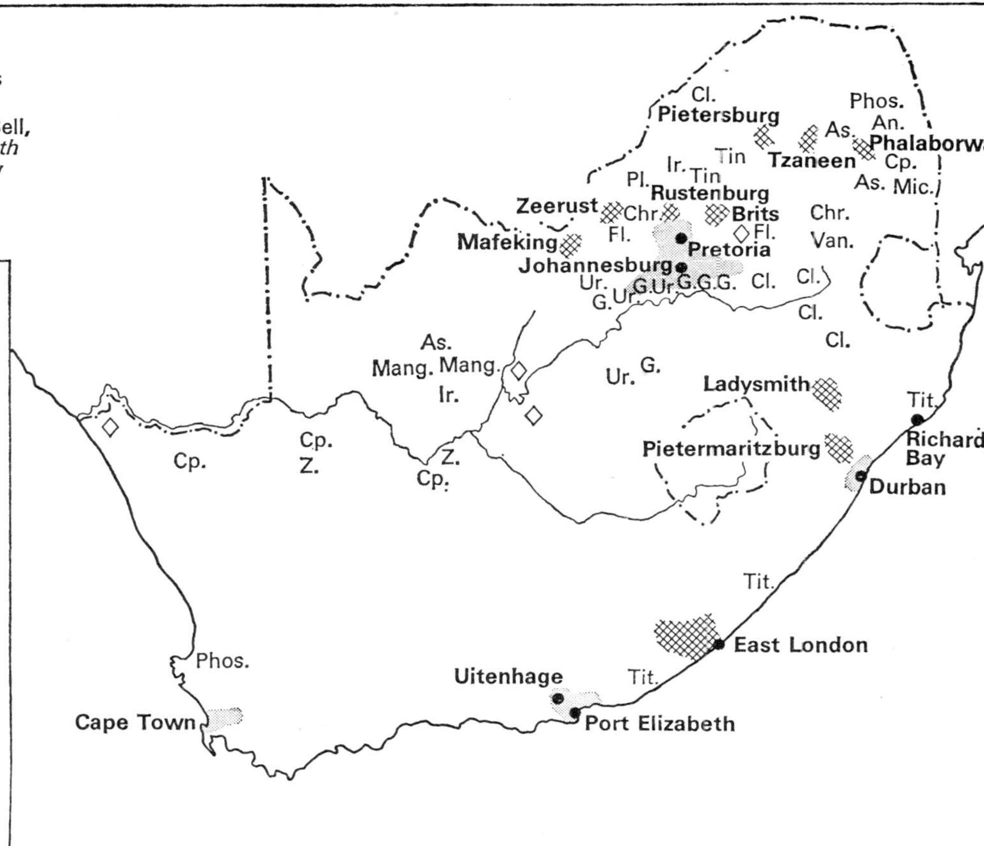


Established industrial regions

Proclaimed industrial growth points

Sources: *Development Atlas* (1966), R. T. Bell, *Industrial Decentralization in South Africa* (1973), and information by courtesy of Dr. Max Mehliss.

Key to minerals

| | Mineral | 1975 production values (millions of Rands) |
|---|---|---|
| An. | Antimony | 22·3 |
| As. | Asbestos | 91·5 |
| Cl. | Coal | 316·1 |
| Cp. | Copper | 146·3 |
| Chr. | Chrome | 40·8 |
| ◇ | Diamonds | 174·0 |
| Fl. | Fluorspar | 7·8 |
| G. | Gold | 2560·0 |
| Ir. | Iron ore | 42·1 |
| Mang. | Manganese | 100·4 |
| Mic. | Mica | 0·4 |
| Pl. | Platinum | Not available |
| Phos. | Phosphates | 24·8 |
| Tin | Tin | 12·7 |
| Tit. | Titanium | Not available |
| Ur. | Uranium | Not available |
| Van. | Vanadium | 39·0 |
| Z. | Zinc | 14·9 |
| | Other | 539·9 |
| | TOTAL | 4134·0 |

Map 5 Mineral production and industrial development

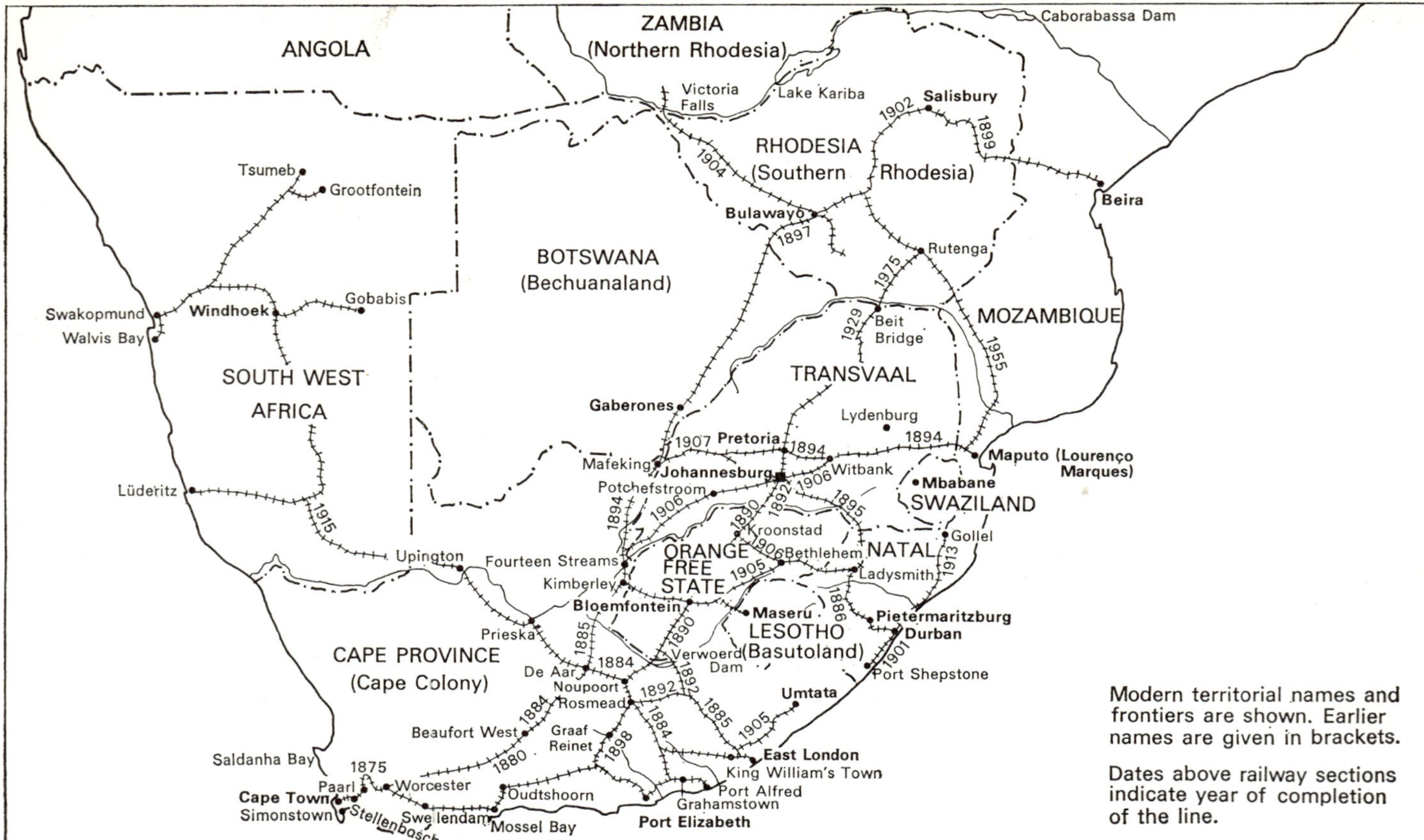


Map 6 Political boundaries and railway communications

# Bibliographical Notes

The references given in these pages represent a compromise between a conventional bibliography and conventional footnotes. They are designed primarily as a guide to further reading. In the case of books, the date given is generally that of the most recent edition, modern reprints of older works being indicated where appropriate. Notes in square brackets refer back to an earlier note giving more detail.

The following abbreviations are used in the notes:

| | |
|---|---|
| *A.Y.B.* | *Archives Year Book for South African History* |
| *Butterworths* | *Butterworths's South African Law Review* |
| *C.A.H.A.* | *Central African Historical Association* |
| *C.H.A.* | *Cambridge History of Africa* |
| *C.H.B.E.* | *Cambridge History of the British Empire* |
| *D.S.A.B.* | *Dictionary of South African Biography* |
| *Eth. Pub.* | *Ethnological Publications* (Department of Native Affairs) |
| F.A.K. | Federasie van Afrikaanse Kultuurvereniginge |
| *I.C.S.* | Institute of Commonwealth Studies, London: collected seminar papers, Societies of Southern Africa |
| I.S.E.R. | Institute of Social and Economic Research, Rhodes University |
| *J.A.H.* | *Journal of African History* |
| *J.M.A.S.* | *Journal of Modern African Studies* |
| *J.S.A.S.* | *Journal of Southern African Studies* |
| *O.H.S.A.* | *Oxford History of South Africa* |
| *Q.B.S.A.L.* | *Quarterly Bulletin of the South African Library* |
| *Rhod. Hist.* | *Rhodesian History* |
| *S.A.B.R.A.* | *South African Bureau of Racial Affairs* |
| *S.A.H.J.* | *South African Historical Journal* |
| *S.A.I.R.R.* | *South African Institute of Race Relations* |
| *S.A.J.E.* | *South African Journal of Economics* |
| *S.A.J.S.* | *South African Journal of Science* |
| *S.A.L.J.* | *South African Law Journal* |
| *Spro-Cas* | *Study Project on Christianity in Apartheid Society* |
| *U.G.* | *Union Government* |
| UNISA | University of South Africa |
| V.R.S. | Van Riebeeck Society |

# Bibliographical Notes

CHAPTER I

1. For recent interpretations of the Khoi–San relationship, see R. H. Elphick, *The Cape Khoi and the First Phase of Race Relations in South Africa* (unp. th., Yale, 1972); G. Harinck, 'Interaction between Xhosa and Khoi . . . 1620–1750', in L. M. Thompson (ed.), *African Societies in Southern Africa* (1969) pp. 145–69; S. Marks, 'Khoisan Resistance to the Dutch in the 17th and 18th centuries', *J.A.H.* XIII, 1 (1972) 55–80; S. Marks and R. Gray in *C.H.A.* IV (1975) pp. 419–20; I. Schapera, *The Khoisan Peoples of South Africa* (1930); E. M. Thomas, *The Harmless People* (1959); P. V. Tobias, 'Physical Anthropology and somatic origins of the Hottentots', *African Studies* 14, 1 (1955) 1–15; E. O. J. Westphal, 'The linguistic pre-history of Southern Africa: Bush, Kwadi, Hottentot and Bantu linguistic relationships', *Africa* XXXIII, 3 (1963) 237–65; A. R. Willcox, *The Rock Art of South Africa* (1963); M. Wilson in *O.H.S.A.* I (1969) pp. 40–74; J. B. Wright, *Bushman Raiders of the Drakensberg* (1971).
2. Archaeological evidence for the early history of southern Africa is discussed in J. D. Clark, *The Pre-History of Southern Africa* (1959); R. M. Derricourt, 'Archaeological Survey of the Transkei and Ciskei, Interim Report for 1972', *Fort Hare Papers* 5 (1973) 453–5; B. M. Fagan, *South Africa during the Iron Age* (1965); R. R. Inskeep, in *O.H.S.A.* I pp. 31–9; R. J. Mason, 'The first early iron-age settlement in South Africa, Broederstroom, 24/73, Brits District, Transvaal', *S.A.J.S.* 69 (1973) 324–6; R. Oliver and B. M. Fagan, *Africa in the Iron Age* (1975).
3. For early trading activities, see R. Gray and D. Birmingham, *Pre-Colonial African Trade* (1970); A. Smith, 'The Trade of Delagoa Bay as a factor in Nguni politics, 1750–1835', in Thompson (ed.) [n. 1 above] pp. 171–89.
4. On the early history of Bantu-speaking peoples in southern Africa, see P. S. Garlake, *Great Zimbabwe* (1973); W. D. Hammond-Tooke (ed.), *The Bantu-speaking Peoples of Southern Africa* (1974); M. Legassick, 'The Sotho-Tswana peoples before 1800', and S. Marks, 'The traditions of the Natal Nguni: a second look at the work of A. T. Bryant', in Thompson (ed.) [n. 1 above]; S. Marks and R. Gray in *C.H.A.* IV 384–468; I. Schapera (ed.), *The Bantu-speaking Tribes of South Africa* (1956); P. E. N. Tindall, 'Great Zimbabwe in recent literature', *Rhod. Hist.* 4 (1973) 93–104; N. J. van Warmelo, *A Preliminary Survey of Bantu Tribes in South Africa* (1935); M. Wilson in *O.H.S.A.* I pp. 75–186, and 'The early history of the Transkei and Ciskei', *African Studies* 18, 4 (1959) 167–79.
5. For the Mfecane/Difaqane generally, see M. How, 'An alibi for Mma

Nthatisi', *African Studies* 13, 2 (1954) 65–76; W. F. Lye, in Thompson (ed.) [n. 1 above], pp. 190–206, and 'The Difaqane: the Mfecane in the south Sotho area', *J.A.H.* VIII, 1 (1967) 107–31, and 'The Ndebele kingdom south of the Limpopo river', *J.A.H.* x, 1 (1969) 87–109; M. Mainga, *Bulozi under the Luyana Kings* (1973); J. D. Omer-Cooper, *The Zulu Aftermath* (1966); P. B. Sanders, *Moshoeshoe, Chief of the Sotho* (1974); L. M. Thompson, *Survival in two Worlds: Moshoeshoe of Lesotho, 1786–1870* (1975).

6. For the Zulu revolution in particular, see J. B. McI. Daniel, 'A geographical study of pre-Shakan Zululand', *S.A. Geographical Journal* 55, 1 (1973) 23–31; M. Gluckman, 'The rise of the Zulu Empire', *Scientific American* CCII, 4 (1960) 157–67, and 'The Kingdom of the Zulu in South Africa', in M. Fortes and E. E. Evans-Pritchard, *African Political Systems* (1940) pp. 25–55; F. N. Okoye, 'Tshaka and the British traders', *Trans-African J. of History* 2, 1 (1972). The Zulu political system is handled in Chapter 4.

CHAPTER 2

1. Recent works on the Portuguese exploration and early settlement of southern Africa include E. Axelson, *The Portuguese in South-East Africa, 1600–1700* (1960); C. R. Boxer, *The Portuguese Seaborne Empire* (1969); R. Raven-Hart, *Before Van Riebeeck* (1967).
2. For the Dutch Company period, see especially A. J. Böeseken, in C. F. J. Muller (ed.), *500 Years* (1969) pp. 16–63; C. R. Boxer, *The Dutch Seaborne Empire* (1965); M. Katzen, in *O.H.S.A.* I (1969) pp. 187–232; R. Raven-Hart, *The Cape of Good Hope, 1652–1702* (1971); M. W. Spilhaus, *South Africa in the Making, 1652–1806* (1966); H. B. Thom (ed.), *The Journal of Jan van Riebeeck, 1651–62* (1952–58).
3. On the Huguenots and other immigrants, see C. G. Botha, *The French Refugees at the Cape* (1919); C. C. de Villiers, *Geslacht-Register der Oude Kaapsche Familien* (1893–94); J. A. Heese, *Die Herkoms van die Afrikaner, 1657–1867* (1971); J. Hoge, *Personalia of the Germans at the Cape, 1652–1806* (*A.Y.B.*, 1946); and *Bydraes tot die Genealogie van ons Afrikaanse Families* (1958); N. Nathan, *Huguenots in South Africa* (1939).
4. For works on the Dutch Reformed Churches, see Chapter 5 n. 6.
5. Works on the architecture and cultural achievements of the Company period include M. G. Atmore, *Cape Furniture* (1965); C. de Bosdari, *Cape Dutch Houses and Farms* (1964); H. Franzen and M. A. Cook, *The Old Houses of the Cape* (1965); G. E. Pearse, *The Cape of Good Hope, 1652–1833: an account of its buildings and the life of its people* (1956).
6. On Cape slavery, see V. de Kock, *Those in Bondage* (1963); I. E. Edwards, *Towards Emancipation: a study in South African Slavery* (1942); A. F. Hattersley, in *C.H.B.E.* VIII (1963) pp. 266–78; J. S. Marais, *The Cape Coloured People* (1937); *Report of De Chavonnes and Van Imhoff* (*V.R.S.* vol. 1, 1918).
7. The following works are helpful for the study of socio-economic aspects of Company rule: H. J. Mandelbrote (ed.), *O. F. Mentzel's Description of the Cape of Good Hope* (*V.R.S.* vols. 4, 6, 25, 1921–44); J. S. Marais, *The Cape Coloured People* (1937); D. Moodie, *The Record* (1960 reprint);

S. D. Neumark, *The South African Frontier* (1957); H. M. Robertson, 'Some doubts concerning early land tenure at the Cape', *S.A.J.E.* III, 2 (1935) 158–72, and '150 years of economic contact between black and white', *S.A.J.E.* 2, 4 (1934) 403–25 and 3, 1 (1935) 3–25; P. J. van der Merwe, *Die Trekboer in die Geskiedenis van die Kaapkolonie* (1938), and *Die Noordwaartse Beweging van die Boere voor die Groot Trek, 1770–1842* (1937).

8. For the early political relationship between the Company and the free burghers, see W. J. de Kock, 'Etienne Barbier', in *D.S.A.B.* I p. 53; L. Fouché (ed.), *The Diary of Adam Tas* (*V.R.S.* 2nd series vol. 1, 1970); I. D. MacCrone, *Race Attitudes in South Africa* (1937).

CHAPTER 3

1. For the political relationship between the Cape authorities and the free burghers after 1776, see works listed in Chapter 2 n. 8, and J. J. Badenhorst, 'H. C. D. Maynier', in *D.S.A.B.* II pp. 456–9; C. Beyers, *Die Kaapse Patriotte, 1779–95* (1967); L. C. Duly, *British Land Policy at the Cape, 1795–1844* (1968); W. Freund, *Society and Government in Dutch South Africa: the Cape and the Batavians, 1803–06* (unp. th., Yale University, 1971). H. Giliomee, 'Democracy and the Frontier', *S.A.H.J.* 6 (1974) 30–51; J. A. Heese, *Slagtersnek en sy Mense* (1973); P. J. Idenburg, *The Cape of Good Hope at the Turn of the Eighteenth Century* (1963); H. Lichtenstein, *Travels in South Africa* (*V.R.S.* vols. 10, 11, 1928–30); J. S. Marais, *Maynier and the first Boer Republic* (1944); H. A. Reyburn, 'Studies in Cape Frontier History', *The Critic*, Oct 1934 to June 1935; P. J. van der Merwe, *Die Kafferoorlog van 1793* (1940).
2. The political and constitutional issues involved in the transition from Dutch to British rule in 1795–1830 are handled in M. Donaldson, *The Council of Advice at the Cape of Good Hope, 1825–34* (unp. th., Rhodes University, 1974); S. F. N. Gie (ed.), *The Memorandum of Commissary J. A. de Mist* (*V.R.S.* vol. 3, 1920); V. T. Harlow and W. M. Macmillan, in *C.H.B.E.* VIII (1963) pp. 169–238, 249–65; G. M. Theal, *Records of the Cape Colony, 1793–1835* (1897–1905); J. P. van der Merwe, *Die Kaap onder die Bataafse Republiek, 1803–06* (1926).
3. For the 1820 Settlement and the British impact on the Cape in the early nineteenth century, see J. M. Berning, *A Select Bibliography of the 1820 Settlers and Settlement* (1970); F. G. Butler (ed.), *The 1820 Settlers: an illustrated commentary* (1974); Sir G. Cory, *The Rise of South Africa* (1965 reprint); I. E. Edwards, *The 1820 Settlers in South Africa* (1934); H. E. Hockly, *The Story of the British Settlers of 1820 in South Africa* (1957); K. S. Hunt, *Sir Lowry Cole* (1974); R. F. M. Immelman, *Men of Good Hope ... the Cape Town Chamber of Commerce, 1804–1954* (1955); R. Lewcock, *Early nineteenth century Architecture in South Africa* (1963); A. K. Millar, *Plantagenet in South Africa: Lord Charles Somerset* (1965); E. Morse Jones, *Roll of the British Settlers in South Africa* (1971); A. M. L. Robinson, *None daring to make us Afraid* (1962).
4. On the various aspects of the humanitarian movement as it affected the Cape; see I. E. Edwards, *Towards Emancipation* [Chapter 2 n. 6]; H. A.

Gailey, 'John Philip's role in Hottentot emancipation', *J.A.H.* III, 3 (1962) 419–33; J. S. Galbraith, *Reluctant Empire* (1963); T. Kirk, 'The Kat River Settlement', *J.A.H.* XIV, 3 (1973) 411–28; W. M. Macmillan, *The Cape Colour Question* (1927), and *Bantu, Boer and Briton* (1963); J. S. Marais, *The Cape Coloured People* (1937); G. R. Mellor, *British Imperial Trusteeship* (1951). See also works on the missionary factor listed in Chapter 7 n. 10.

5. The related questions of frontier policy and the origins of the Great Trek can usefully be approached through the following authorities: C. Beyers, *Die Groot Trek met betrekking tot ons Nasiegroei* (*A.Y.B.* 1941); J. S. Galbraith, *Reluctant Empire* (1963); C. F. J. Muller, *Die Britse Owerheid en die Groot Trek* (1948), and *Die Oorsprong van die Groot Trek* (1974); M. Nathan, *The Voortrekkers of South Africa* (1937); H. A. Reyburn [see n. 1 above]; J. du P. Scholtz, *Die Afrikaner en sy Taal, 1806–75* (1964); G. M. Theal, *History of South Africa since 1795* (1908–10); H. B. Thom, *Die Lewe van Gert Maritz* (1965); E. A. Walker, *The Great Trek* (1948).

CHAPTER 4

1. General discussions of African government are to be found in M. Fortes and E. E. Evans-Pritchard, *African Political Systems* (1940); W. D. Hammond-Tooke, 'Segmentation and Fission in Cape Nguni politics', *Africa* XXXV, 2 (1965) 143–67; J. B. Peires, 'The rise of the "Right-Hand House" in the history and historiography of the Xhosa', *History in Africa* 2 (1975) 113–25; B. Sansom, in W. D. Hammond-Tooke (ed.), *The Bantu-Speaking Peoples of Southern Africa* (1974) pp. 246–83; I. Schapera, *Government and Politics in Tribal Societies* (1956); J. Vansina, 'A comparison of African kingdoms', *Africa* XXXII, 4 (1962) 324–35; N. J. van Warmelo [Chapter 1 n. 4].
2. H. Ashton, *The Basuto* (1952) p. 216.
3. On the Tswana peoples, see Z. K. Matthews, 'The Tshidi Rolong: a short history', *Fort Hare Papers* 1, 1 (1945) 9–28; B. A. Pauw, 'Some changes in the social structure of the Tlhaping', *African Studies* 19, 2 (1960) 49–76; I. Schapera, *Handbook of Tswana Law and Custom* (1955); A. Sillery, *Founding a Protectorate: a history of Bechuanaland, 1885–95* (1965), and *Sechele: the story of an African chief* (1954).
4. On the Pedi, Venda and Lobedu, see D. R. Hunt, 'An account of the Bapedi', *Bantu Studies* (1931) 275–326; E. J. Krige, 'The place of the northern Transvaal Sotho in the southern Bantu complex', *Africa* XI, 3 (1938) 265–93; E. J. and J. D. Krige, *The Realm of the Rain Queen* [Lobedu] (1943), and 'The Lobedu of the Transvaal', in D. Forde (ed.), *African Worlds* (1954); J. D. Krige, 'Traditional origins and tribal relations in the northern Transvaal', *Bantu Studies* (1937) 321–56; H. Mönnig, *The Pedi* (1967); G. M. Pitje, 'Male Education among the Pedi', Part 1, *African Studies* 9, 2 (1950) 53–9; G. P. J. Trümpelmann (ed.), *Maleo en Secoecoeni...van Th. Wangemann* (*V.R.S.* vol. 38, 1957); T. S. van Rooyen, *Die Verhoudinge tussen die Boere, Engelse en Naturelle in die Geskiedenis van die Oos-Transvaal tot 1882* (*A.Y.B.* 1951); N. J. van Warmelo, 'Contributions towards Venda history, religion and tribal ritual', *Eth. Pub.* vol. III (1932), and in Hammond-Tooke (ed.), *Bantu-Speaking*

*Peoples* (1974); G. P. Lestrade, 'Some notes on the political organisation of Venda-speaking tribes', *Africa* (1930) 306–21.

5. On the southern Sotho, see works by Sanders and Thompson in Chapter 1 n. 5, and C. C. Saunders, 'Early knowledge of the Sotho', *Q.B.S.A.L.* (1966); G. Tylden, *The Rise of the Basuto* (1950).
6. On the southern Nguni, see P. A. W. Cook, *The Bomvana* (n.d.); E. J. de Jager, 'Geskiedenis van die AmaXhosa en AmaThembu', *Historia* 9, 3 (1964) 215–27; W. D. Hammond-Tooke, *Bhaca Society* (1962); M. Hunter, *Reaction to Conquest* (1961); J. H. Soga, *AmaXosa Life and Customs* (1931), and *The South-Eastern Bantu* (1930); M. Wilson, in *O.H.S.A.* I (1969).
7. On the northern Nguni, see J. R. D. Cobbing, *The Ndebele under the Khumalos* (unp. th., Lancaster University, 1976); E. J. Krige, *The Social System of the Zulus* (1950); H. Kuper, *An African Aristocracy* [Swazi] (1952); S. Marks, 'Traditions of the Natal Nguni', in L. M. Thompson (ed.), *African Societies in Southern Africa* (1969) pp. 126–44; J. S. M. Matsebula, *A History of Swaziland* (1972); F. N. Okoye, 'Dingane . . . a reappraisal', *J.A.H.* x, 2 (1969) 221–35; J. D. Omer-Cooper, *The Zulu Aftermath* (1966); E. A. Ritter, *Shaka Zulu* (1955).
8. For age-regiments, see E. J. Krige, [works cited in n. 4 above]; H. Kuper, *An African Aristocracy* (1952); H. Mönnig, *The Pedi* (1967); I. Schapera, *Handbook of Tswana Law and Custom.*

CHAPTER 5

1. There is a long tradition of Afrikaner writing on the republican theme. See J. A. Coetzee, P. J. Meyer and N. Diederichs, *Ons Republiek* (1941); E. F. W. Gey van Pittius, *Staatsopvattinge van die Voortrekkers en die Boere* (1941); D. F. Malan, *Afrikaner Volkseenheid en my Ervarings op die Pad daarheen* (1959); G. D. Scholtz, *Die Ontwikkeling van Politieke Denke van die Afrikaner* (1967– ); F. A. van Jaarsveld and G. D. Scholtz, *Die Republiek in Suid-Afrika: agtergrond, ontstaan en toekoms* (1966); M. C. E. van Schoor and J. J. van Rooyen, *Republieke en Republikeine* (1960); P. A. C. Wieringa, *De Oudste Boeren Republieken in Zuid-Afrika* (1921); A. Wypkema, 'Die Volkstemidee in Suid Africa', *Historiese Studies* I, 1 (1939).
2. The history of Voortrekker constitutionalism can be consulted in the following works: J. S. du Plessis, *Die . . . Amp van Staatspresident in die Z. A. Republiek* (*A.Y.B.* 1955); H. J. Mandelbrote in C.H.B.E. VIII (1963) pp. 391–9; G. Preller (ed.), *Voortrekker-wetgewing* (1924); G. D. Scholtz, *Die Konstitusie en die Staatsinstellinge van die Oranje-Vrystaat, 1854–1902* (1937); L. M. Thompson, 'Constitutionalism in the Boer Republics', *Butterworths* (1954) 49–72; G. N. van den Bergh, 'Die Drie-en-Dertig Artikels: Grondwet of regsprekende handleiding?', *S.A.H.J.* I (1969) 5–14; J. J. van Heerden, *Die Kommandant-Generaal in die Geskiedenis van die Z.A. Republiek* (*A.Y.B.* 1964); F. A. van Jaarsveld, *Die Veldkornet . . . in die Opbou van die Z.A. Republiek tot 1870* (*A.Y.B.* 1950). The political relationship between the Boer republics and the Imperial Government is handled in Chapter 8.
3. For early Voortrekker disputes and the Republic of Natalia, see H. Cloete,

*A History of the Great Boer Trek* (1900 reprint); A. J. du Plessis, *Die Republiek Natalia* (*A.Y.B.* 1942); J. Bird, *Annals of Natal* (1965 reprint); F. A. van Jaarsveld, *Die Eenheidsstrewe van die Republikeinse Afrikaners* I, 1836–64 (1951); *Voortrekker Argiefstukke, 1829–49* (1937).

4. Transvaal developments are handled by R. Cornwell, 'Land and politics in the Transvaal in the 1880s', *I.C.S.* 4 (1974) 29–40; J. S. du Plessis [n. 2 above]; C. T. Gordon, *The Growth of Boer Opposition to Kruger* (1970); W. A. Kleynhans, *Volksregering in die Z.A. Republiek; die rol van Memories* (1966); D. W. Krüger, *Paul Kruger* (1961–3); J. S. Marais, *The Fall of Kruger's Republic* (1961); J. A. Mouton, *Generaal Piet Joubert in die Transvaalse Geskiedenis* (*A.Y.B. 1957*); F. J. Potgieter, *Vestiging van Blanke in Transvaal, 1837–86* (*A.Y.B.* 1958); G. S. Preller, *Andries Pretorius* (1938); S. Trapido, 'The S.A. Republic: class formation and the State, 1850–1900, *I.C.S.* 3 (1973) 57–65; J. J. van Heerden [n. 2 above]; F. A. van Jaarsveld [n. 2 above]; F. A. F. Wichmann, *Die Wordingsgeskiedenis van die Z.A. Republiek, 1838–60* (*A.Y.B.* 1941).
5. Orange Free State republicanism can be approached through W. W. Collins, *Free Statia, or Reminiscences... 1852 to 1875* (1907); Sir J. G. Fraser, *Episodes in my Life* (1922); J. H. Malan, *Die Opkoms van 'n Republiek... tot 1863* (1929); H. P. N. Muller, *Oude Tyden in den O.V.S.* (1907); J. M. Orpen, *Reminiscences...from 1846 to the present day* (1908); G. D. Scholtz, *President J. H. Brand, 1823–88* (1957); M. C. E. van Schoor, *Politieke Groepering in die Transgariep* (*A.Y.B.* 1950), and *Nasionale en Politieke Bewuswording van die Afrikaner in...Transgariep tot 1854* (*A.Y.B.* 1963), and in C. F. J. Muller (ed.), *500 Years* (1969) pp. 203–20.
6. For the politics of the Dutch Reformed Churches, see B. Booyens, *Kerk en Staat, 1795–1843* (*A.Y.B.* 1965); A. Dreyer, *Die Kaapse Kerk en die Groot Trek* (1929); S. P. Engelbrecht, *Geskiedenis van die Nederduitsch Hervormde Kerk van Afrika* (1953); G. B. A. Gerdener, *Ons Kerk in die Transgariep* (1934); T. N. Hanekom, *Die Liberale Rigting in Suid-Afrika* (1951); A. Moorrees, *Die Nederduitse Gereformeerde Kerk in Suid-Afrika, 1652–1873* (1937); G. D. Scholtz, *Die Geskiedenis van die Nederduitse Hervormde of Gereformeerde Kerk van Suid-Afrika* (1956–60); B. Spoelstra, *Die 'Doppers' in Suid-Afrika, 1760–1899* (1963).
7. The domestic divisions in the Transvaal resulting from the Uitlander immigration are handled in G. Blainey, 'Lost causes of the Jameson Raid', *Economic History Review* 2nd Series, XVIII (1964–65) 350–66; F. J. Dormer, *Vengeance as a Policy in Afrikanderland* (1901); J. P. Fitzpatrick, *The Transvaal from Within* (1899); J. A. Hobson, *The War in South Africa* (1900); A. H. Jeeves, 'The Rand capitalists and the coming of the S.A. War, 1896–99' (unp.); R. V. Kubicek, 'The Randlords in 1895: a reassessment', *Journal of British Studies* XI, 2 (1972) 84–103; J. S. Marais, *The Fall of Kruger's Republic* (1961).

CHAPTER 6

1. On Cape liberalism, see T. N. Hanekom [Chapter 5 n. 6]; P. B. Hinchliff, *J. W. Colenso* (1964); J. H. Hofmeyr, *Life of J. H. Hofmeyr* (*Onze Jan*) (1913); P. Lewsen, 'The Cape liberal tradition, myth or reality?', *Race* XIII,

I (1971) 65–80, and 'J. X. Merriman', *D.S.A.B.* II pp. 463–69; W. M. Macmillan, *Bantu, Boer and Briton* (1963); L. Marquard, *Liberalism in South Africa* (S.A.I.R.R., 1965); J. Rose Innes, *Autobiography* (1949); W. E. G. Solomon, *Life of Saul Solomon* (1948).

2. The grant of self-government to the Cape is handled in A. H. Duminy, *The Role of Sir A. Stockenström in Cape Politics, 1848–56* (*A.Y.B.* 1960); A. K. Fryer, *The Government of the Cape of Good Hope, 1825–54* (*A.Y.B.* 1964); A. F. Hattersley, *The Convict Crisis and the Growth of Unity* (1965); B. A. le Cordeur, *Robert Godlonton as Architect of Frontier Opinion* (*A.Y.B.* 1959); H. J. Mandelbrote in *C.H.B.E.* VIII (1963) pp. 367–99; S. Trapido, 'The origins of the Cape franchise qualifications of 1853', *J.A.H.* V, I (1964) 37–54.

3. The main issues in Cape political history are covered in M. F. Bitensky, *The South African League* (unp. th., *Witwatersrand University*, 1951); W. B. Campbell, *The South African Frontier, 1865–85* (*A.Y.B.* 1959); T. R. H. Davenport, *The Afrikaner Bond* (1966); and in *O.H.S.A.* I (1969) pp. 297–333; A. E. du Toit, *The Cape Frontier . . . 1847–66* (*A.Y.B.* 1954); J. H. Hofmeyr [n. 1 above]; T. Karis and G. M. Carter, *From Protest to Challenge: Documents of African Politics in South Africa, 1882–1964* I (1970) Part I; R. Kilpin, *The Romance of a Colonial Parliament* (1938); J. G. Lockhart and C. M. Woodhouse, *Rhodes* (1963); J. L. McCracken, *The Cape Parliament* (1967); T. Ranger, 'The last word on Cecil Rhodes?', *Past and Present* 28 (1964) 116–27; J. Rutherford, *Sir George Grey, 1812–98* (1961); J. du P. Scholtz, *Die Afrikaner en sy Taal, 1806–75* (1964); N. H. Taylor, *The Separation Movement during the Period of Representative Government at the Cape, 1854–72* (unp. th., University of Cape Town, 1938); S. Trapido, 'African divisional politics in the Cape Colony, 1884–1910', *J.A.H.* IX, I (1968) 69–98, and 'The origin and development of the A.P.O.', *I.C.S.* I (1970) 89–111; F. A. van Jaarsveld, *The Awakening of Afrikaner Nationalism, 1868–81* (1961); E. A. Walker, *W. P. Schreiner: a South African* (1937); P. Walshe, *The Rise of African Nationalism in South Africa: the African National Congress, 1912–52* (1970); B. Williams, *Cecil Rhodes* (1938); D. Williams, 'African nationalism in South Africa, origins and problems', *J.A.H.* XI, 3 (1970) 371–83; M. J. Zeeman, *The Working of Representative Government at the Cape under Sir P. Wodehouse, 1862–70* (unp. th., University of Cape Town, 1940).

4. Works on the early history of Colonial Natal include J. Bird, *Annals of Natal*, (1965 reprint); E. H. Brookes and C. de B. Webb, *A History of Natal* (1965); N. Isaacs, *Travels and Adventures in Eastern Africa* (*V.R.S.* vols. 16, 17, 1936–37); D. J. Kotze, *Letters of the American Missionaries, 1835–38* (*V.R.S.*, 1950); F. Owen, *The Diary of the Rev. Francis Owen, Missionary with Dingaan in 1837–38* (*V.R.S.* vol. 7, 1926); J. Stuart and D. McK. Malcolm, *The Diary of H. F. Fynn* (1950); M. C. van Zyl, *Luitenant-Goewerneur M. West en die Natalse Voortrekkers, 1845–49* (*A.Y.B.*, 1955); L. M. Young, *The Native Policy of Benjamin Pine in Natal, 1850–55*.

5. On Shepstone's native policy, see O. Geyser, *Die Bantoe-beleid van Theophilus Shepstone* (*A.Y.B.* 1968); W. Rees (ed.), *Colenso Letters from Natal* (1958); S. Trapido, 'Natal's non-racial franchise, 1856', *African Studies* 22, I (1963) 22–32; D. Welsh, *The Roots of Segregation, 1845–1910* (1971).

6. Problems relating to the government of Natal are handled in T. R. H. Davenport, 'The responsible government issue in Natal, 1880–82', *Butterworth's* (1957) 84–133; J. Lambert, *Sir J. Robinson and Responsible Government, 1863–97* (unp. th., University of Natal, 1975); A. Preston (ed.), *Sir Garnet Wolseley's South African Diaries, Natal 1875* (1971); C. J. Talbot, *Harry Escombe and the Politics of Responsible Government in Natal 1879–85* (unp. th., University of Natal, 1974).
7. On Indians in Natal, and in South Africa generally, see E. Bradlow, 'Indentured Indians in Natal and the £3 tax', *S.A.H.J.* 2 (1970) 38–53; G. H. Calpin, *Indians in South Africa* (1949); J. J. Doke, *M. K. Gandhi* (1909); M. K. Gandhi, *Satyagraha in South Africa* (1954); W. K. Hancock, *Smuts* vol. I (1965) pp. 309–47, vol. II (1968) pp. 128–49, and *Four Studies in War and Peace in this Century* (1961); R. A. Huttenback, *Gandhi in South Africa* (1971); P. S. Joshi, *The Tyranny of Colour* (1942); B. Pachai, *The International Aspects of the S.A. Indian Question, 1860–1971* (1971); M. Palmer, *History of the Indians in Natal* (Natal Regional Survey, vol. 10, 1957); L. M. Thompson, *Indian Immigration into Natal, 1860–72* (*A.Y.B.* 1952).

CHAPTER 7

1. For conflict on the San frontier, see R. Collins in G. M. Theal (ed.), *Records of the Cape Colony* (1897–1905) vol. VII pp. 98–139; J. S. Marais, *The Cape Coloured People* (1937); D. Moodie, *The Record* (1960 reprint); J. B. Wright, *Bushman Raiders of the Drakenberg* (1971).
2. For the subjection of the chiefdoms in general, see L. M. Thompson in *O.H.S.A.* vol. II pp. 245–86. For the history of the Cape eastern frontier, see W. B. Campbell [Chapter 6 n. 3]; G. B. Crankshaw, *The Diary of C. L. Stretch* (unp. th., Rhodes University 1960); R. Derricourt and C. C. Saunders (eds.), *Beyond the Cape Frontier* (1974); A. E. du Toit [Chapter 6 n. 3]; W. Freund, 'The Eastern frontier of the Cape Colony during the Batavian period', *J.A.H.* XIII, 4 (1972) 631–45; J. S. Galbraith, *Reluctant Empire* (1963); A. Gordon Brown (ed.), *The Narrative of Private Buck Adams* (*V.R.S.* vol. 22, 1941); W. M. Macmillan, *Bantu, Boer and Briton* (1963); J. W. Macquarrie, *Reminiscences of Sir Walter Stanford, 1850–1929* (*V.R.S.* vols. 39, 43, 1958–62); J. Roxborough, *Colonial Policy on the Northern and Eastern Frontiers of the Cape of Good Hope, 1834–45* (unp. th., Oxford University, 1954); J. Rutherford, *Sir George Grey* (1961); C. C. Saunders, *The Annexation of the Transkeian Territories, 1872–95, with special reference to British and Cape Policy* (unp. th., Oxford University, 1972); M. Wilson in *O.H.S.A.* vol. I (1969) pp. 233–71.
3. On the Griqua frontier, see J. A. I. Agar-Hamilton, *The Road to the North* (1937); C. W. de Kiewiet, *British Colonial Policy and the South African Republics, 1848–72* (1929); S. J. Halford, *The Griquas of Griqualand* (1949); W. M. Macmillan, *The Cape Colour Question* (1927); J. S. Marais, *The Cape Coloured People* (1937); W. P. Morrell, *British Colonial Policy in the Age of Peel and Russell* (1930), and *British Colonial Policy in the Mid-Victorian Age* (1969).

4. On the frontier between the south Sotho and the Orange Free State, see works by De Kiewiet and Morrell in n. 3 above, and J. A. Benyon, *Basutoland and the High Commission, 1868–84* (unp. th., Oxford University, 1968); P. B. Sanders, *Moshoeshoe, Chief of the Sotho* (1975); G. M. Theal (ed.), *Basutoland Records* (1964 reprint); L. M. Thompson, *Survival in Two Worlds: Moshoeshoe of Lesotho, 1786–1870* (1975); G. Tylden, *The Rise of the Basuto* (1950); J. van der Poel, *Basutoland as a Factor in South African Politics, 1852–70* (*A.Y.B.* 1941).
5. On the South African Republic's frontier with the Pedi, Lobedu, Venda and Transvaal Ndebele, see J. A. I. Agar-Hamilton, *The Native Policy of the Voortrekkers* (1928); J. B. de Vaal, *Die Rol van João Albasini in die Geskiedenis van die Transvaal* (*A.Y.B.* 1953); D. R. Hunt [Chapter 4 n. 4]; A. M. Ncube, 'The Venda, and the Mphephu war of 1898' (unp., *C.A.H.A.*, 1972); A. Preston (ed.), *Sir Garnet Wolseley's South African Journal, 1878–80* (1973); J. I. Rademeyer, 'Die Oorlog teen Magato', *Historiese Studies* 2 (1944) 79–122; K. W. Smith, *The Campaigns against the Bapedi of Sekhukhune, 1877–79* (*A.Y.B.* 1967), and 'The fall of the Bapedi of the north-eastern Transvaal', *J.A.H.* x, 2 (1969) 237–52; G. P. J. Trümpelmann [Chapter 4 n. 4]; C. J. Uys, *In the Era of Shepstone* (1933); T. S. van Rooyen, [Chapter 4 n. 4]; N. J. van Warmelo, *Transvaal Ndebele Texts* (*Eth. Pub.* vol. I, 1930).
6. On the Swazi frontier, see N. G. Garson, *Swaziland and a Road to the Sea, 1887–95* (*A.Y.B.* 1957); P. Bonner, in *I.C.S.* 2 (1971); H. Kuper, *An African Aristocracy* (1947).
7. On the Natal–Zululand frontier, see E. H. Brookes and C. de B. Webb, *A History of Natal* (1965); C. W. de Kiewiet, *The Imperial Factor in South Africa* (1937); S. Marks, *Reluctant Rebellion* (1970); D. R. Morris, *The Washing of the Spears* (1964); M. C. van Zyl, *Die Uitbreiding van Britse Gesag oor die Natalse Noordgrensgebied* (*A.Y.B.* 1966).
8. On the Transvaal–Tswana border, see J. A. I. Agar-Hamilton, *The Road to the North* (1937); J. A. Mouton, *Generaal Piet Joubert in die Transvaalse Geskiedenis* (*A.Y.B.*, 1957); A. Sillery, *Founding a Protectorate* (1965), and *Sechele: the Story of an African Chief* (1954).
9. On the Ndebele frontier north of the Limpopo, see J. R. D. Cobbing, 'Lobengula, Jameson and the Occupation of Mashonaland', *Rhod. Hist.* 4 (1973) 39–56; A. Dorey, 'The Victoria Incident and the Outbreak of the Ndebele War' (unp., *C.A.H.A.*, 1972); S. Glass, *The Matabele War* (1968); V. W. Hiller, *Guide to the Public Records of Southern Rhodesia* (1956); P. Mason, *The Birth of a Dilemma* (1958); T. O. Ranger, *Revolt in Southern Rhodesia* (1967), and 'The role of the Ndebele and Shona religious authorities in the rebellions of 1896 and 1897', in E. Stokes and R. Brown (eds.), *The Zambesian Past* (1965); S. Samkange, *The Origins of Rhodesia* (1968); P. Stigger, 'Volunteers and the profit motive in the Anglo-Ndebele war of 1893', *Rhod. Hist.* 2 (1971) 11–23.
10. For the role of the missionaries on the southern African frontier, see A. J. Dachs, 'Missionary imperialism: the case of Bechuanaland', *J.A.H.* XIII, 4 (1972) 647–58; J. du Plessis, *History of Christian Missions in South Africa* (1965); J. S. Galbraith, *Reluctant Empire* (1963); N. Majeke, *The Role of the Missionary in Conquest* (1952); S. Marks, *Reluctant Rebellion*

(1970); J. Roxborough [Chapter 7 n. 2]; I. Schapera (ed.), *Apprenticeship in Kuruman . . . Journals and Letters of Robert and Mary Moffat* (1951), and *David Livingstone: South African Papers 1849–53* (*V.R.S.* 2nd series vol. 5, 1974); D. Williams, *The Missionaries on the Eastern Frontier of Cape Colony, 1799–1853* (unp. th., Witwatersrand University, 1959).

CHAPTER 8

1. For the modern debate on the meaning of imperialism in Africa, see especially J. A. Benyon, 'The Cape High Commission: another neglected factor in British Imperial expansion', *S.A.H.J.* 5 (1973) 28–40; D. K. Fieldhouse, *Economics and Empire, 1830–1914* (1973); J. A. Hobson, *Imperialism: a Study* (1902); R. E. Robinson and J. Gallagher, *Africa and the Victorians* (1961); E. T. Stokes, 'Late nineteenth century colonial expansion and the attack on the theory of economic imperialism: a case of mistaken identity?', *H.J.* XII, 2 (1969) 285–301.
2. For British colonial policy in southern Africa down to 1870, see works by Du Toit, Rutherford and Galbraith [Chapter 7 n. 2], De Kiewiet and Morrell [Chapter 7 n. 3] and M. V. Jackson-Haight, *European Powers and South-East Africa* (1967).
3. On the period 1870–86, see Agar-Hamilton [Chapter 7 n. 8]; R. L. Cope, 'Shepstone, the Zulus and the Annexation of the Transvaal', *S.A.H.J.* 4 (1972) 45–63; C. W. de Kiewiet, *The Imperial Factor in South Africa* (1937); W. H Dunn, *J. A. Froude* (1961); S. P. Engelbrecht, *President T. F. Burgers* (1946); C. F. Goodfellow, *Great Britain and South African Confederation* (1966); M. Macmillan, *Sir H. Barkly* (1969); J. J. Oberholster, *Die Anneksasie van Griekwaland-Wes* (*A.Y.B.* 1945); D. M. Schreuder, *Gladstone and Kruger* (1969); A. Sillery, *John Mackenzie of Bechuanaland* (1971); F. A. van Jaarsveld, *Vaalrivier, Omstrede Grenslyn* (1974).
4. On the period 1886–99, see works by Blainey, Kubicek and Marais [Chapter 5 n. 7], Cobbing, Hiller, Mason and Stigger [Chapter 7 n. 9] and E. Axelson, *Portugal and the Scramble for Africa* (1962); J. Butler, *The Liberal Party and the Jameson Raid* (1968); J. S. Galbraith, *Crown and Charter* (1974); E. Pakenham, *Jameson's Raid* (1960); J. van der Poel, *Railway and Customs Policies in South Africa, 1885–1910* (1933), and *The Jameson Raid* (1951); P. J. van Winter, *Onder Krugers Hollanders* (1937); P. R. Warhurst, *Anglo-Portuguese Relations in South-Central Africa, 1890–1900* (1962); R. H. Wylde, *Joseph Chamberlain and the S. A. Republic 1895–99* (*A.Y.B.* 1956).
5. On the Anglo-Boer War of 1899–1902, see J. H. Breytenbach, *Die Tweede Vryheidsoorlog* (1969); J. P. Brits (ed.), *The Diary of a National Scout, P. J. du Toit* (1974); C. R. de Wet, *Three Years' War* (1902); J. F. C. Fuller, *The Last of the Gentlemen's Wars* (1937); E. Hobhouse, *The Brunt of the War and where it fell* (1902); G. Jordaan, *Hoe zij stierven* (1915); R. Kipling, *The Five Nations* (1917), and *The Science of Rebellion* (1900); R. Kruger, *Goodbye Dolly Gray* (1959); G. H. L. le May, *British Supremacy in South Africa* (1965); P. Lewsen, *Selections from the Correspondence of J. X. Merriman* vol. III (*V.R.S.* no. 47, 1966); L. Marquard (ed.), *Letters from a Boer Parsonage* (1967); S. T. Plaatje, *Boer War Diary* (ed. J. Coma-

roff, 1973); G. Preller (ed.), *Scheepers se Dagboek* (1938); D. Reitz, *Commando* (1931); J. C. Smuts, 'Memoir of the Boer War', in W. K. Hancock and J. van der Poel (eds.), *Selections from the Smuts Papers* vol. I (1966) pp. 537–663; J. H. Snyman, *Rebelle-Verhoor in Kaapland ... 1899–1902* (*A.Y.B.* 1962); S. B. Spies, *Roberts, Kitchener and Civilians* (unp. th., Witwatersrand University, 1974); C. J. S. Strydom, *Kaapland in die Tweede Vryheidsoorlog* (1937); B. Viljoen, *My Reminiscences of the Anglo-Boer War* (1903).

CHAPTER 9

1. On the peace negotiations of 1901–2, see C. R. de Wet, *Three Years' War* 1902); W. K. Hancock, *Four Studies in War and Peace in this Century* 1961); and *Smuts* vol. I (1962); C. Headlam, *The Milner Papers* vol. II (1933); J. D. Kestell and D. E. van Velden, *The Peace Negotiations between Boer and Briton* (1912); G. H. L. le May, *British Supremacy in South Africa* (1965); P. Magnus, *Kitchener* (1958).
2. On Cape and Natal politics in 1902–10, see Brookes and Webb [Chapter 6 n. 4]; P. Cuthbert, *The Administration of Dr Jameson as Prime Minister of the Cape Colony, 1904–08* (unp. th., University of Cape Town, 1950); T. R. H. Davenport, *The Afrikaner Bond* (1966); P. Lewsen, *Selections from the Correspondence of J. X. Merriman* vols. III and IV (*V.R.S.* nos. 47, 50, 1966–9); L. M. Thompson, 'The Colony of Natal and the Closer Union Movement', *Butterworths* (1957) 81–106.
3. On the Transvaal and Orange River Colony under Milner's governorship, see D. J. N. Denoon, *A Grand Illusion: the Failure of Imperial Policy in the Transvaal Colony during the period of Reconstruction 1900–05* (1973), and 'Capitalist influence and the Transvaal Government during the Crown Colony period', *H.J.* XI, 2 (1968) 301–31, and 'The Transvaal labour crisis, 1901–06', *J.A.H.* VII, 3 (1967) 481–94; Headlam [n. 1 above]; A. Jeeves, 'The control of migratory labour in the South African gold mines in the era of Kruger and Milner', *J.S.A.S.* 2, 1 (1975) 3–39; A. Mawby, *The Political Behaviour of the British Population of the Transvaal, 1902–07* (unp. th., Witwatersrand University, 1969), and 'Capital, Government and Politics in the Transvaal, 1900–07', *H.J.* XVII, 2 (1974) 387–415; A. P. Newton, *Select Documents on the Unification of South Africa* (1924); E. T. Stokes, 'Milnerism', *H.J.* V, 1 (1962) 47–60; M. Streak, *Lord Milner's Immigration Policy for the Transvaal, 1897–1905* (1969); B. Synge, *The Story of the World* (1903).
4. On relations between black and white during the Milner years, see T. R. H. Davenport, *The Beginnings of Urban Segregation in South Africa* (I.S.E.R., 1971); R. A. Huttenback, *Gandhi in South Africa* (1971); S. Marks, *Reluctant Rebellion* (1970); G. B. Pyrah, *Imperial Policy and South Africa, 1902–10* (1955); *Report* of the South African Native Affairs Commission (1905); C. M. Tatz, *Shadow and Substance in South Africa* (1962).
5. On the Afrikaner political revival after 1902, see Davenport [n. 2 above]; N. G. Garson, 'Het Volk: the Botha–Smuts party in the Transvaal, 1904–11', *H.J.* IX, 1 (1966) 101–32; J. Kirstein, *Some Foundations of Afrikaner Nationalism* (unp. th., University of Cape Town, 1956); 'Knop' [G. Preller],

*Agt Jaar s'n Politiek: skoon geskiedenis van die Suid Afrikaanse Nasionale Party, 1902–10* (1910); A. E. G. Trollip, *The First Phase of Hertzogism* (unp. th., University of Witwatersrand, 1947).

6. On the Transvaal British, see works by Denoon, Jeeves and Mawby in n. 3 above.
7. On self-government for the Transvaal and O.R.C., see W. K. Hancock, *Smuts*, vol. I (1962); W. K. Hancock and J. van der Poel, *Selections from the Smuts Papers*, vol. II (1966), pp. 215–27; R. Hyam, *Elgin and Churchill at the Colonial Office, 1905–08* (1968); R. Hyam and G. Martin, *Reappraisals in British Imperial History* (1975); Le May [n. 1 above]; N. Mansergh, *South Africa, 1906–61: the price of Magnanimity* (1962); Newton [n. 3 above]; Pyrah [n. 4 above].
8. On railway and customs questions and on the National Convention, see A. R. Booth, 'Lord Selborne and the British Protectorates, 1902–10' *J.A.H.* x, 1 (1969) 133–48; R. H. Brand, *The Union of South Africa* (1909); R. Hyam, 'African interests in the South Africa Act, 1908–10', *H.J.* XIII, 1 (1970) 85–105; F. S. Malan, *Konvensie-Dagboek* (*V.R.S.* no. 32, 1951); L. M. Thompson, *The Unification of South Africa* (1960); J. van der Poel, *Railway and Customs Policies in South Africa, 1885–1910* (1933); E. A. Walker, *W. P. Schreiner, a South African* (1937); E. H. Walton, *Inner History of the National Convention* (1912).

## CHAPTER 10

1. For the political history of the Botha and Smuts ministries and the Nationalist breakaway, see F. V. Engelenburg, *General Louis Botha* (1929); B. Friedman, *Smuts: a Reappraisal* (1975); O. Geyser, *Geskiedenis van die Nasionale Party* (1975); W. K. Hancock, *Smuts* vol. I, *The Sanguine Years* (1965), vol. II, *The Fields of Force* (1968); W. K. Hancock and J. van der Poel, *Selections from the Smuts Papers*, vols. I–IV (1966), V–VII (1973); D. W. Krüger, *South African Parties and Policies, 1910–60* (1960); P. Lewsen, *Selections from the Correspondence of J. X. Merriman, 1905–24*, vol. IV (*V.R.S.* no. 50, 1969); M. P. A. Malan, *Die Nasionale Party van Suid-Afrika, 1914–64* (1964); A. H. Marais (ed.), *Politieke Briewe 1909–12* (1971–3), and 'Aspekte van die 1915-Verkiesing', *S.A.H.J.* 5 (1973) 61–93; L. M. Thompson, *The Unification of South Africa* (1960); C. M. van den Heever, *General J. B. M. Hertzog* (1946).
2. For the Government's relationship with African political movements, see notes to Chapters 18 and 19, and the following: M. Benson, *The Struggle for a Birthright* (1966); A. M. Davey, *The Bondelswarts Affair* (UNISA, 1961); R. Freislich, *The Last Tribal War* (1964); W. K. Hancock, *Smuts* vol. II (1968) pp. 88–110; C. Kadalie, *My Life and the I.C.U.* (ed. S. Trapido, 1970); P. Kallaway, 'F. S. Malan, the Cape liberal tradition, and South African politics, 1908–24', *J.A.H.* XV, 1 (1974) 113–29; T. Karis and G. M. Carter, *From Protest to Challenge* vol. I (ed. S. Johns III, 1972); S. T. Plaatje, *Native Life in South Africa* (1915); E. Roux, *Time longer than Rope* (1964); H. J. and R. Simons, *Class and Colour in South Africa* (1969); B. Sundkler, *Bantu Prophets in South Africa* (1961); C. M. Tatz, *Shadow and Substance in South Africa* (1962); P. Walshe, *The Rise of African*

*Nationalism in South Africa, 1912–52* (1970); P. L. Wickins, *The I.C.U.* (unp. th., University of Cape Town, 1973).

3. On relations between Botha, Smuts and the Indian community, see Chapter 6 n. 7.
4. On white labour unrest in 1913–14 and 1922, see G. V. Doxey, *The Industrial Colour Bar in South Africa* (1961); W. K. Hancock, *Smuts* vol. I (1965) pp. 348–74, vol. II (1968) pp. 62–88; F. A. Johnstone, *Class, Race and Gold* (1976); H. J. and R. Simons [n. 2 above]; D. Ticktin, 'The war and the collapse of the S.A. Labour Party', *S.A.H.J.* I (1969) 59–80; I. L. Walker and B. Weinbren, *2000 Casualties* (1961).
5. On the upsurge of Afrikaner nationalism and the Afrikaner rebellion of 1914, see T. R. H. Davenport, 'The South African rebellion of 1914', *English Historical Review* LXXVII, 306 (1963) 73–94; N. G. Garson, 'The Boer rebellion of 1914', *History Today* XII, 2 (1962) 132–9; J. C. G. Kemp, *Die Pad van die Veroweraar* (1946); D. F. Malan, *Glo in u Volk* (1964) pp. 90–5; S. G. Maritz, *My Lewe en Strewe* (1939); J. D. Naude, *Generaal Hertzog en die Ontstaan van die Nasionale Party, 1913–14* (1970); *Report* of the Judicial Commission on the Rebellion (*U.G.* 46 of 1916); G. D. Scholtz, *Generaal C. F. Beyers* (1941), and *Die Rebellie* (1942); S. B. Spies, *The Rebellion in South Africa, 1914–15* (unp. th., University of Witwatersrand, 1963); J. Steinmeyer, *Spykers met Koppe* (1946); A. E. G. Trollip, *The First Phase of Hertzogism* (unp. th., University of Witwatersrand, 1947).
6. On the First World War and the S.A. Party–Unionist merger, see J. Buchan, *The South African Forces in France* (1920); W. K. Hancock, *Smuts* vol. I (1965); S. B. Spies, 'The outbreak of the first world war and the Botha Government', *S.A.H.J.* I (1969) 47–57; Union Government, *The Union of South Africa and the Great War, 1914–18* (1924); P. F. van der Schyff, *Die Unionistiese Party in die S.A. Politiek*, 1910–21 (unp. th., Potchefstroom University, 1964).
7. On the peace conference, the League of Nations, the Commonwealth and the politics of expansion in Africa, see G. Curry, 'Woodrow Wilson, Jan Smuts and the Versailles Settlement', *American Historical Review* LXVI, 4 (1961) 963–86; L. H. Gann, *History of Southern Rhodesia to 1931* (1965); Lord Hailey, *The Republic of South Africa and the High Commission Territories* (1963); W. K. Hancock, *Smuts* vol. II (1968), and *Four Studies in War and Peace in this Century* (1961), and *Survey of British Commonwealth Affairs* vol. I (1937); H. C. Hummel, *Sir Charles Coghlan* (unp. th., London University, 1975); R. Hyam, *The Failure of South African Expansion, 1908–48* (1972); B. K. Long, *Drummond Chaplin* (1941); C. Palley, *The Constitutional History and Law of Southern Rhodesia* (1966) pp. 1–214; J. C. Smuts, *The League of Nations, a practical Suggestion* (1917); J. van der Poel, *Selections from the Smuts Papers* vols. IV and V (1966–73), esp. vol. V, pp. 65–77; J. P. R. Wallis, *One Man's Hand: the Life of Sir Charles Coghlan* (1950); P. R. Warhurst, 'Rhodesian–South African Relations, 1900–23', *S.A.H.J.* 3 (1971) 92–107.
8. On the Nationalist–Labour Pact and the fall of the Smuts Government, see D. W. Krüger, *South African Parties and Policies, 1910–60* (1960); M. Creswell, *An Epoch in the History of South Africa: Life of F. H. P. Creswell* (1956); C. E. M. O'Dowd, 'The general election of 1924', *S.A.H.J.* 2 (1970) 54–76.

CHAPTER 11

1. For literature on Hertzog's colour bar policy, see notes to Chapter 19.
2. On dominion status, the flag issue, external relations, the High Commission Territories, and other domestic issues, see the works by Hailey, Hancock and Hyam [Chapter 10 n. 7] and L. Blackwell, *African Occasions* 1938); T.R.H. Davenport, 'Nationalism and Conciliation: the Bourassa–Hertzog posture', *Hertzog-Annale* x, 16 (1963) 72–87, and *Canadian Historical Review* XLIV, 3 (1963) 193–212; R. M. Dawson, *The Development of Dominion Status, 1900–36* (1937); D. W. Krüger, *The Making of a Nation* (1969); W. M. Macmillan, *Complex South Africa* (1930); D. F. Malan, *Afrikaner Volkseenheid en my Ervarings op die Pad daarheen* (1959); N. Mansergh, *Survey of Commonwealth Affairs, 1931–39* (1952), and *Documents and Speeches on Commonwealth Affairs, 1931–52* (1953); A. Paton, *Hofmeyr* (1964); O. Pirow, *J. B. M. Hertzog* (1957); D. Reitz, *Trekking On* (1933); H. Reitz, *The Conversion of a South African Nationalist* (1946); *Report* of the Carnegie Commission on Poor Whiteism (1932); *Report* of the Native Economic Commission (*U.G.* 22 of 1932); G. D. Scholtz, *Hertzog, Smuts en die Britse Ryk* (1975), and 'Generaal Hertzog en die internasionale politiek', *Hertzog-Annale* (1954); J. C. Smuts, *Africa and Some World Problems* (1929); C. M. van den Heever, *General J. B. M. Hertzog* (1946); K. C. Wheare, *The Constitutional Structure of the Commonwealth* (1960).
3. For Hertzog's relations with the Indian community, see works listed in Chapter 6 n. 7.
4. On the 'Native Bills' and Hertzog's relations with blacks, see works by Kadalie, Simons, Tatz, Walshe and Wickins listed in Chapter 10 n. 2, and W. K. Hancock, *Smuts* vol. II (1968) pp. 259–66; T. Karis and G. M. Carter, *From Protest to Challenge* vol. I (1972) Part III; E. Roux, *Time longer than Rope* (1964); C. M. van den Heever [n. 2 above]; J. van der Poel, *Selections from the Smuts Papers* vol. V (1973) pp. 368–77 and vol. VI.
5. On the Great Crash, Coalition and Fusion, see S. H. Frankel, 'South Africa's monetary policy', *S.A.J.E.* I, I (1933) 79–87; C. S. Richards, 'Economic revival in South Africa', *Economic Journal* XLIV (1934) 616–30; C. G. W. Schumann, *The World Depression: South African and the Gold Standard* (n.d.), and *Structural Changes and Business Cycles in South Africa* (1938).

CHAPTER 12

1. On the political history of the Fusion era, and of the 'Native Bills' see works by Karis and Carter, Roux, Simons, Tatz, and Walshe in Chapters 10 n. 2 and 11 n. 4, and the following: M. Ballinger, *From Union to Apartheid* (1969); T. R. H. Davenport, 'The triumph of Colonel Stallard', *S.A.H.J.* 2 (1970) 77–96; G. Heaton Nicholls, *South Africa in my Time* (1961); D. B. Molteno, 'The Betrayal of Native Representation', (*S.A.I.R.R.*, 1959); A. Paton, *Hofmeyr* (1964); *Report* of the Cape Coloured Commission (*U.G.* 54 of 1937); *Reports* of the Joint Select Committee on the Native Bills, 1930–4 and 1935; *Report* of the Native Affairs Commission (*U.G.* 48 of 1937); Union of South Africa, *Joint Sitting Debates* (1936).

2. For black politics in the years after 1936, see works by Roux, Simons and Walshe cited in Chapter 10 n. 2, as well as T. Karis and G. M. Carter, *From Protest to Challenge* vol. II (1973) parts I and II.
3. For the rise of Purified Nationalism, see A. C. Cilliers, *Quo Vadis?* (1939); J. A. Coetzee, *Nasieskap en Politieke Groepering in Suid-Afrika, 1651–1968* (1969); E. P. du Plessis, *'n Volk staan op* (1964); D. F. Malan, *Afrikaner Volkseenheid* (1959); O. Pirow, *J. B. M. Hertzog* (1958); M. Roberts and A. E. G. Trollip, *The South African Opposition, 1939–45* (1947); N. M. Stultz, *Afrikaner Politics in South Africa, 1934–48* (1974); J. F. J. van Rensburg, *Their Paths Crossed Mine* (1956); W. H. Vatcher, *White Laager: the rise of Afrikaner Nationalism* (1965).

CHAPTER 13

1. For South Africa's external policy and participation in the Second World War, see J. A. I. Agar-Hamilton and L. C. F. Turner, *Crisis in the Desert* (1952) and *The Sidi Rezegh Battles* (1957); J. A. Brown, *Eagles Strike* (1974); N. Mansergh, *Survey of Commonwealth Affairs, 1939–52* (1958), and *Documents and Speeches on Commonwealth Affairs, 1931–52* (1953); N. Orpen, *The East African and Abyssinian Campaigns* (1968), and *War in the Desert* (1971); L. C. F. Turner, *War in the Southern Oceans* (1961).
2. On party politics and political events in 1939–48, see works by Ballinger and Heaton Nicholls listed in Chapter 12 n. 1, and works by Malan, Pirow, Roberts and Trollip, Stultz, Van Rensburg and Vatcher listed in Chapter 12 n. 3, as well as L. Blackwell, *Farewell to Parliament* (1946); W. K. Hancock, *Smuts* vol. II (1968); K. Heard, *General Elections in South Africa, 1943–70* (1974); B. K. Long, *In Smuts's Camp* (1945); A. Paton, *Hofmeyr* (1964).
3. On United Party racial policy, see works by Karis and Carter, Roux, Simons, Tatz and Walshe cited in Chapter 10 n. 2, and M. Ballinger, *From Union to Apartheid* (1969); T. R. H. Davenport, 'The Smuts Government and the Africans 1939–48', I.C.S. Seminar Papers (1974); C. R. Diamond, *African Labour Problems on South African Gold Mines, with special reference to the Strike of 1946* (unp. th., University of Cape Town, 1969); E. Hellmann (ed.), *Handbook on Race Relations* (1949); S. Johns III, 'The birth of non-white trade unionism in South Africa', *Race* IX (1967) 173–92; *Report* of the Inter-Departmental Committee on the Social, Health and Economic Conditions of Urban Natives (1942); *Report* of the Native Laws Commission (*U.G.* 28 of 1948); *Report* of the Witwatersrand Mine Natives' Wages Commission (*U.G.* 21 of 1944).
4. On Indian affairs, see works listed in Chapter 6 n. 7, by Calpin, Joshi, Pachai and Palmer; also W. K. Hancock, *Smuts* vol. II (1968); G. Heaton Nicholls, *South Africa in my Time* (1961); A. Paton, *Hofmeyr* (1964); M. Webb, and A. M. Keppel Jones, in E. Hellmann (ed.), *Handbook on Race Relations* (1949) pp. 206–28.
5. For works on the concept of *apartheid*, see Chapter 18 n. 1.

CHAPTER 14

1. The white politics of the period are handled from various viewpoint in M.

Ballinger [Chapter 13 n. 2]; L. Blackwell, *Blackwell Remembers* (1971); G. M. Carter, *The Politics of Inequality* (1958); K. Heard [Chapter 13 n. 2]; D. F. Malan [Chapter 12 n. 32]; M. P. A. Malan, *Die Nasionale Party van Suid-Afrika* (1964); J. Robertson, *Liberalism in South Africa, 1949–63* (1971); B. Schoeman, *Van Malan tot Verwoerd* (1973).

2. On the legislative programme of the Malan and Strijdom governments, and the controversies which it aroused, see B. Beinart, 'Sovereignty and the law', *Tydskrif vir Hedendaagse Romeinse–Hollandse Reg*, 15 (1952) 101–34; D. V. Cowen, *Parliamentary Sovereignty and the Entrenched Clauses of the South Africa Act* (1951); M. Horrell, *Survey of Race Relations* (*S.A.I.R.R.*, annual volumes 1948– ); H. J. May *The South African Constitution* (1955); L. M. Thompson, *The Cape Coloured Franchise* (1949); *Report* of the [Tomlinson] Commission for the Socio-Economic Development of Bantu Areas (*U.G.* 61 of 1955); White Paper on the Tomlinson *Report* (*W.P.* F of 1956). For Bantu Education see Chapter 18 n. 6, and for Group Areas see Chapter 18 n. 8.
3. On the opposition of black communities to government policy, see works by Benson, Karis and Carter, Simons and Walshe cited in Chapter 10 n. 2, as well as the Bloemfontein Charter of the Inter-denominational African Ministers' Federation, *Africa South* 1, 2 (1957) 22–6; E. Feit, *South Africa: the dynamics of the African National Congress* (1962); L. Kuper, *Passive Resistance in South Africa* (1957); A. Luthuli, *Let my People Go* (1963); J. K. Ngubane, *An African explains Apartheid* (1963); P. N. Raboroko and D. Nokwe, 'Congress and the Africanists', *Africa South* 4, 3 (1960) 24–38; J. Robertson [n. 1 above]; G. Watson, *Passing for White* (1970); M. Webb and K. Kirkwood, *The Durban Riots and After* (*S.A.I.R.R.*, 1949).

CHAPTER 15

1. For unrest during this period, see M. Ballinger, *From Union to Apartheid* (1964); E. Feit, *Urban Revolt in South Africa, 1960–64* (1971); M. Horrell (ed.), *Survey of Race Relations 1956–57* pp. 66–72, *1957–58* pp. 48–76, *1958–59* pp. 122–46, *1959–60* pp. 39–68, *1961* pp. 42–61, *1962* pp. 11–25, *1963* pp. 11–21, *1964* pp. 25–33; C. Hooper, *Brief Authority* (1960); G. Mbeki, *The Peasants' Revolt* (1964); A. Reeves, *Shooting at Sharpeville* (1960); The official report on the Sharpeville shootings (An. 25 of 1961) was not published.
2. For political developments among blacks, see works by Benson, Feit, Karis and Carter, Luthuli, Ngubane, Robertson and Simons listed in Chapter 14 n. 3.
3. For the trial of political offenders, in particular the Treason Trial, and questions relating to the rule of law, see B. Beinart, 'The rule of law', *Acta Juridica* (1962) 99–138; E. H. Brookes and J. B. Macaulay, *Civil Liberty in South Africa* (1958); D. V. Cowen, *The Foundations of Freedom* (1961); T. R. H. Davenport, 'Civil rights in South Africa, 1910–60', *Acta Juridica* (1960), 11–28; H. H. W. de Villiers, *Rivonia: Operation Mayibuye* (1964); L. Forman and E. S. Sachs, *The South African Treason Trial* (1957); M. Horrell (ed.), *Survey of Race Relations 1956–57* pp. 41–5, *1957–58* pp. 34–7, *1958–59* pp. 44–7, *1959–60* pp. 37–9, *1961* pp. 62–3; H. Joseph, *If*

*This be Treason* (1963); T. Karis, 'The South African treason trial', *Political Science Quarterly* LXXVI, 2 (1961) 217–39, and *The Treason Trial in South Africa: a guide to the microfilm record* (1965); N. Mandela, *No Easy Walk to Freedom* (ed. R. First, 1965); A. Sampson, *The Treason Cage* (1958); N. M. Stultz, 'The politics of security: South Africa under Verwoerd', *J.M.A.S.* VII (1969) 3–20.

4. On Dr Verwoerd and the policies associated with his name, see n. 1 above and A. Hepple, *Verwoerd* (1967); A. N. Pelzer, *Verwoerd Speaks* (1966); G. D. Scholtz, *Dr H. F. Verwoerd* (1974); H. F. Verwoerd, in *Senate Debates 1951* cols 2203–35, *1952* cols 3587–614, *1954* cols 2595–620, *1955* cols 4527–46, *1956* cols 3861–908 [policy motions].
5. On the Homeland policy and its adoption, see W. W. M. Eiselen, 'Harmonious multi-community development', *Optima*, Mar 1959, pp. 1–15; N. J. Rhoodie, *South African Dialogue* (1972) pp. 113–210; B. Schoeman, *Van Malan tot Verwoerd* (1973) pp. 224–33; H. F. Verwoerd in *House of Assembly Debates* (1959) cols 6214–27. G. Buthelezi, 'White and Black Nationalism, Ethnicity and the Future of the Homelands' (*S.A.I.R.R.*, 1974).
6. On developments within the 'white' political parties and the events connected with the founding of the Republic of South Africa, see A. R. Delius, *The Last Division* (1959); K. Heard [Chapter 13 n. 2]; A. Hepple [n. 4 above]; E. Kahn, *The New Constitution* (1962); H. Macmillan, *Pointing the Way* (1972); N. Mansergh, *Speeches and Documents on Commonwealth Affairs, 1952–62* (1963) pp. 306–400; N. J. Rhoodie [n. 5 above] pp. 211–54; G. D. Scholtz [n. 4 above]; S. Uys, 'The White opposition splits', *Africa South* 4, 2 (1960) 12–19; F. J. Wessels, *Die Republikeinse Grondwet* (1962); K. C. Wheare, *The Constitutional Structure of the Commonwealth* (1960).

CHAPTER 16

1. For information on the main domestic issues of the Vorster era, see H. Adam, *Modernising Racial Domination* (1971); A. Baldwin, 'Mass removals and separate development', *J.S.A.S.* 1, 2 (1975) 215–27; R. T. Bell, *Industrial Decentralisation in South Africa* (1973); C. Desmond, *The Discarded People* (1970); R. First, J. Steele and C. Gurney, *The South African Connection* (1972); K. Heard [Chapter 13 n. 2]; D. A. Kotze, *African Politics in South Africa, 1964–74* (1975); G. M. E. Leistner, *Economic and Social Forces affecting the Urbanisation of the Bantu population of South Africa* (1972); A. S. Mathews, *Law, Order and Liberty in South Africa* (1971); E. Potter, *The Press as Opposition* (1975); P. Randall, *A Taste of Power: the final co-ordinated Spro-cas Report* (1973); N. Rhoodie [Chapter 15 n. 5] J. L. Sadie, *Projections of the South African Population, 1970–2020* (n.d., based on 1970 Census); B. Schoeman, *Vorster se 1000 Dae* (1974); J. H. P. Serfontein, *Die Verkrampte Aanslag* (1970); *The State v. the Dean of Johannesburg* (*S.A.I.R.R.*, 1972); D. Worrall, *South African Government and Politics* (1971).

CHAPTER 17

1. For South Africa's role in the establishment and history of the United

Nations, see C. J. R. Dugard [n. 5 below]; W. K. Hancock, *Smuts* vol. II (1968); R. Higgins, *International Law and the U.N.* (1963).

2. For the South African Indian question at the U.N., see works by Joshi, Pachai and Palmer listed in Chapters 6 n. 7 and 13 n. 4.
3. For South African foreign policy generally in the period 1948–76, see D. Austin, *Britain and South Africa* (1966); J. Barber, *South Africa's Foreign Policy, 1945–70* (1973); G. Cockram, *Vorster's Foreign Policy* (1970); C. J. R. Dugard and G. G. Lawrie, 'The Simonstown Agreement', *S.A.L.J.* LXXXV, 1 (1968) 142–77; K. W. Grundy, *Confrontation and Accommodation in Southern Africa: the limits of independence* (1973); M. Horrell (ed.), *Surveys of Race Relations* (1948– ); E. H. Louw, *The Case for South Africa* (1963); C. S. Nolutshungu, *South Africa in Africa: a study in ideology and foreign policy* (1975); J. Seiler, 'South African perspectives and responses to external pressures', *J.M.A.S.* 13, 3 (1975) 447–68; T. M. Shaw, 'Southern Africa: cooperation and conflict in an international sub-system', *J.M.A.S.* 12, 4 (1974) 633–55; J. Spence, *Republic under Pressure* (1965), and in *O.H.S.A. vol.* II (1971) pp. 477–528; A. Vandenbosch, *South Africa and the World: the foreign policy of Apartheid* (1970).
4. For South Africa and the High Commission Territories (later Lesotho, Botswana and Swaziland), see Lord Hailey, *The Republic of South Africa and the High Commission Territories* (1962); R. Hyam, *The Failure of South African Expansion, 1910–48* (1972); M. Perham and L. Curtis, *The Protectorates and South Africa* (1935).
5. On the South West African issue at the U.N., see R. B. Ballinger, *South Africa and the United Nations: myth and reality* (1963); A. A. d'Amato, 'The Bantustan proposals for South West Africa', *J.M.A.S.* 4, 2 (1966) 177–92; C. J. R. Dugard, *The South West Africa (Namibia) Dispute* (1973); R. First, *South West Africa* (1963); I. Goldblatt, *The Mandated Territory of South West Africa in relation to the U.N.* (1961); R. W. Imishue, *South West Africa* (1966).
6. For the relationship between South Africa and (Southern) Rhodesia, see works by Gann, Hummel, Hyam, Long, Palley, Wallis and Warhurst in Chapter 10 n. 7, and J. Barber, *Rhodesia: the Road to Rebellion* (1967); L. H. Gann and M. Gelfand, *Huggins of Rhodesia* (1964); P. Mason, *1960: Year of Decision* (1960).

CHAPTER 18

1. On the interpretation of the terms 'segregation' and '*apartheid*', see E. H. Brookes, *Apartheid: a documentary study of modern South Africa* (1968); G. Cronje, *'n Tuiste vir die Nageslag* (1945), and *Regverdige Rasse-Apartheid* (1947); E. P. Dvorin, *Racial Separation in South Africa: an analysis of the Apartheid theory* (1952); W. W. M. Eiselen, 'The Meaning of Apartheid', *Race Relations* (1948) 69–86; J. B. M. Hertzog, 'Toespraak ... op Smithfield, 13 Nov 1925, *Hertzog-Annale* x (1963) 2–16; R. F. A. Hoernlé, *South African Native Policy and the Liberal Spirit* (1939), and *Race and Reason* (1945); L. E. Neame, *The History of Apartheid* (1962); N. Rhoodie and H. J. Venter, *Apartheid* (1959); S.A.B.R.A., *Integration and Separate Development* (1952); C. M. Tatz, *Shadow and Substance in*

*South Africa* (1962); L. M. Thompson, 'Afrikaner Nationalist historiography and the policy of Apartheid', *J.A.H.* III, 1 (1962) 125–41; P. van Biljon, *Grensbakens tussen Blank en Swart in Suid-Afrika* (*c.* 1947).

2. On racial separation in central and local government, see Tatz [n. 1 above] and works cited in Chapters 11 n. 4 and 12 n. 1.
3. On territorial separation, together with the problem of squatting and the establishment of resettlement villages, see A. Baldwin [Chapter 16 n. 1]; C. Bundy, 'The Emergence and decline of a South African Peasantry', *African Affairs* 71, 285 (1972) 369–88; T. R. H. Davenport and K. S. Hunt, *The Right to the Land* (1974); C. Desmond [Chapter 16 n. 1]; M. E. Elton Mills and M. Wilson, *Land Tenure*, vol. IV of the Keiskammahoek Rural Survey (1952); S. T. Plaatje, *Native Life in South Africa* (1915); *Report* of the Commission of Inquiry into European Occupancy of the Rural Areas, 1959–60; *Report* of the Natives Land Commission (*U.G.* 19 of 1916); E. Roux and A. M. Keppel Jones, in E. Hellmann (ed.), *Handbook on Race Relations* (1949) pp. 171–205.
4. On the separation of the races in the urban areas, see Anon., 'Off to Meadowlands', *Bantu* 4 (1955) 3–24; T. R. H. Davenport, 'African townsmen?', *African Affairs* 68, 271 (1969) 95–109, and *The Beginnings of Urban Segregation in South Africa* (I.S.E.R., 1971), and 'The triumph of Colonel Stallard', *S.A.H.J.* 2 (1970) 77–96; G. Davis, L. Melunsky and du Rand, *Urban Native Law* (1959, with supplements); E. Hellmann in Hellmann (ed.), *Handbook on Race Relations* (1949) pp. 229–74; T. Huddleston, *Naught for Your Comfort* (1956); J. E. Mathewson, *The Establishment of an Urban Bantu Township* (1957); *Report* of the Native Laws Commission (*U.G.* 28 of 1948); *S.A.I.R.R.*, 'The Western Areas – Mass Removal?' (1953); A. Steward, *You are Wrong, Father Huddleston* (1956); A. S. Welsh, *Natives in Urban Areas* (1946); D. Welsh, in *O.H.S.A.* vol. II (1969) pp. 172–244.
5. On the pass laws and influx control, see E. Kahn, in E. Hellmann (ed.), *Handbook on Race Relations* (1949) pp. 275–91; M. Horrell, *The Pass Laws* (*S.A.I.R.R. Fact Paper*, 1960).
6. On educational segregation, see P. A. W. Cook in E. Hellmann (ed.), *Handbook on Race Relations* (1949) pp. 348–86; Federasie van Afrikaanse Kultuur-Vereenigings, *Christelike Nasionale Onderwys Beleid* (1948); R. F. A. Hoernlé, *South African Native Policy and the Liberal Spirit* (1939) pp.123–45; R. Hunt Davis, *African Education in the Cape Colony: a historical analysis* (unp. th., University of Wisconsin, 1969); C. T. Loram, *The Education of the South African Native* (1917); E. G. Malherbe, *History of Education in South Africa* (1925), and *Education and the Poor White* (1932), and *The Bilingual School* (1946), and *Bantu Manpower and Education* (*S.A.I.R.R.*, 1969); *Report* of the Phelps–Stokes Commission on Native Education (1922); *Report* of the Inter-Departmental Committee on Native Education (*U.G.* 29 of 1936); *Report* of the Native Affairs Commission (*U.G.* 48 of 1937); Report of the Bantu Education Commission (*U.G.* 53 of 1951); Universities of Cape Town and the Witwatersrand, *The Open Universities in South Africa* (1957).
7. On cultural *apartheid*, see M. Horrell, *Surveys of Race Relations* (1948– ); A. Paton, *Apartheid and the Archbishop* (1973) pp. 275–88; D. Welsh,

'The cultural dimension of Apartheid', *African Affairs* 71, 282 (1972) 35–53; and references listed in n. 1.

8. On Group Areas, see M. Horrell, *The Group Areas Act: its effect on Human Beings* (*S.A.I.R.R.* 1956), and *Group Areas: the emerging pattern* (1966), and *Survey of Race Relations 1967* pp. 191–213, *1968* pp. 190–209, *1969* pp. 162–80, *1970* pp. 186–201, *1971* pp. 155–71, *1972* pp. 128–51, *1973* pp. 111–26, *1974* pp. 156–64, *1975* pp. 66–80.

CHAPTER 19

1. On the history of the South African economy in general, see N. N. Franklin, *Economics in South Africa* (1954); J. A. Henry, *The First Hundred Years of the Standard Bank* (1963); D. Hobart Houghton, *The South African Economy* (1976), and in *O.H.S.A.* vol. II (1971); D. Hobart Houghton and J. Dagut, *Source Material on the South African Economy* (1972–3); H. M. Robertson, *South Africa – Economic and Political Aspects* (1957); C. G. W. Schumann, *Structural Changes and Business Cycles in South Africa* (1938).
2. For labour patterns in the diamond and gold mining industries, see works by Denoon, Jeeves and Mawby in Chapter 9, n. 3, and R. F. Siebörger, *The Recruitment and Organization of African Labour for the Kimberley Diamond Mines, 1871–88* (unp. th., Rhodes University, 1976); J. Smalberger, 'I.D.B. and the mining compound system in the 1880's', *S.A.J.E.* 42, 4 (1974) 398–414; S. T. van der Horst, *Native Labour in South Africa* (1942), and in E. Hellmann (ed.), *Handbook on Race Relations* (1949); P. R. Warhurst, 'Rhodesian–South African Relations, 1900–23', *S.A.H.J.* 3 (1971) 92–108; G. F. Williams, *The Diamond Mines of South Africa* (1902); F. Wilson, *Labour on the South African Gold Mines* (1972).
3. On the history of collective bargaining and trade union formation, see G. V. Doxey, *The Industrial Colour Bar in South Africa* (1961); E. Kahn, 'The right to strike in South Africa: an historical analysis', *S.A.J.E.* 11, 1 (1943) 24–47; H. J. Simons, in E. Hellmann (ed.), *Handbook on Race Relations* (1949); *Report* of the Witwatersrand Natives Mine Wages Commission (*U.G.* 21 of 1944).
4. The issue of job reservation is handled in G. V. Doxey [n. 3 above]; W. H. Hutt, *The Economics of the Colour Bar* (1964); *Official Yearbook* [of the Union of South Africa] No. 29 (1956–57) pp. 858–67; *Report* of the Industrial and Agricultural Requirements Commission (*U.G.* 40 of 1941); *Report* of the Low Grade Mines Commission (*U.G.* 34 of 1920); *Report* of the Cape Coloured Commission (*U.G.* 54 of 1937); *Report no. 282* of the Board of Trade and Industries (1945); S. T. van der Horst [n. 2 above]; F. Wilson [n. 2 above].
5. On labour migrancy, influx control and the restriction of the economic opportunities of urban blacks, see T. R. H. Davenport, 'The triumph of Colonel Stallard', *S.A.H.J.* 2 (1970) 77–96; T. R. H. Davenport and K. S. Hunt, *The Right to the Land* (1974), documents 119–26; G. Hart, *Some Socio-Economic Aspects of African Entrepreneurship* (*I.S.E.R.*, 1971); D. Hobart Houghton [n. 1 above]; E. Kahn, in E. Hellmann (ed.), *Handbook on Race Relations* (1949) pp. 275–91; R. B. Savage, *A Study of Bantu*

*Retail Traders in certain areas of the Eastern Cape* (I.S.E.R., 1956); F. Wilson, *Migrant Labour* (1972).

CHAPTER 20

1. The following works all have a bearing on the modern South African debate: H. Adam, *Modernising Racial Domination* (1971); M. Ballinger, *From Union to Apartheid* (1964); H. Blumer, in G. Hunter (ed.), *Industrialization and Race Relations* (1965) pp. 220–53; N. Bromberger, in A. Leftwich (ed.), *Economic Growth and Political Change* (1974) pp. 61–124; E. H. Brookes, *White Rule in South Africa* (1974); R. F. A. Hoernlé, *South African Native Policy and the Liberal Spirit* (1939), and *Race and Reason* (1945); R. Horwitz, *The Political Economy of South Africa* (1967); F. A. Johnstone, 'White prosperity and white supremacy in South Africa today', *African Affairs* LXIX, 274 (1970) 124–40; L. Kuper, *Race, Class and Power* (1974); M. Legassick, 'Legislation, ideology and economy in post-1948 South Africa', *J.S.A.S.* 1, 1 (1974) 5–34, and 'South Africa: capital accumulation and violence' (unp.); I. D. MacCrone, *Race Attitudes in South Africa* (1937); W. M. Macmillan, *My South African Years* (1975); L. Marquard, *Peoples and Policies of South Africa* (1962); M. C. O'Dowd, 'South Africa in the light of the stages of economic growth', in A. Leftwich (ed.), *Economic Growth and Social Change* (1974) pp. 29–43; A. Paton, *Hofmeyr* (1964); N. J. Rhoodie (ed.), *South African Dialogue* (1972); H. M. Robertson, '150 years of economic contact between black and white in South Africa', *S.A.J.E.* 2, 4 (1934) 403–25, and 3, 1 (1935) 3–25; J. Robertson, *Liberalism in South Africa* (1971), Spro-cas, *South Africa's Political Alternatives* (1973), and *Power, Privilege and Poverty* (1972); S. T. van der Horst, 'The effects of industrialisation on race relations in South Africa', in G. Hunter (ed.), *Industrialisation and Race Relations* (1965); H. Wolpe, 'Capitalism and cheap labour-power in South Africa: from segregation to apartheid', *Economy and Society* 1, 4 (1972); D. Yudelman, 'Industrialisation, race relations and change in South Africa', *African Affairs* 74, 294 (1975) 82–96.

# Appendixes

## TABLE 1

### *HEADS OF STATE, 1652–1976*

1. *Governors of the Colony during the Dutch East India Company Period, 1652–1795*

| | | |
|---|---|---|
| 1652 Jan van Riebeeck | 1708 L. van Assenburgh | 1751 R. Tulbagh |
| 1662 Z. Wagenaar | 1711 W. Helot* | 1771 J. van Plettenberg |
| 1666 C. van Quaelberg | 1714 M. P. de Chavonnes | 1785 C. van der Graaff |
| 1668 J. Borghorst | 1724 J. de la Fontaine* | 1791 J. I. Rhenius* |
| 1670 P. Hackius | 1727 P. G. Noodt | 1792 S. C. Nederburgh and S. H. Frykenius |
| 1672 I. Goske | 1729 J. de la Fontaine | |
| 1676 J. Bax | 1737 A. van Kervel | |
| 1679 S. van der Stel | 1737 D. van den Henghel* | 1793 A. J. Sluysken |
| 1699 W. A. van der Stel | 1739 H. Swellengrebel | |

2. *Governors during the First British Administration, 1795–1801*

| | | |
|---|---|---|
| 1795 Gen. J. H. Craig | 1798 Gen. F. Dundas* | 1801 Gen. F. Dundas* |
| 1797 Earl Macartney | 1799 Sir G. Yonge | |

3. *The Batavian Administration, 1803–5*

1803–5 J. A. de Mist (Commissioner), J. W. Janssens (Governor)

4. *Governors under the Second British Occupation, 1805–47*

10 Jan 1805 Gen. Sir D. Baird†
17 Jan 1807 Gen. H. G. Grey†
22 May 1807 Earl of Caledon
6 Sep 1811 Gen. Sir F. Cradock
18 Oct 1813 Gen. G. R. Meade†
6 Apr 1814 Gen. Lord Charles Somerset
[13 Jan 1820 to 30 Nov 1821 Gen. Sir R. Donkin†]
5 Mar 1826 Gen. R. Bourke†
9 Sep 1828 Gen. Sir G. L. Cole
10 Aug 1833 Col. T. F. Wade†
10 Jan 1834 Gen. Sir B. D'Urban
22 Jan 1838 Gen. Sir G. T. Napier
18 Mar 1844 Gen. Sir P. Maitland

* Acting governors.
† More important acting governors.

5. *Heads of State in Divided South Africa, 1847–1910*

(a) *White Regimes*

| | *Cape Colony* | *Natal* | *Orange River Sovereignty* | |
|---|---|---|---|---|
| 4 Dec 1845 | | M. T. West | | |
| 27 Jan 1847 | Gen. Sir H. E. Pottinger | | | |
| 1 Dec 1847 | Gen. Sir H. G. W. Smith | | | |
| 8 Mar 1848 | | | Maj. H. D. Warden | |
| 19 Apr 1850 | | B. C. C. Pine | | |
| 31 Mar 1852 | Gen. the Hon. G. Cathcart | | | |
| 23 July 1852 | | | H. Green | |
| | | | *O.F.S.* | *Transvaal* |
| 5 Dec 1854 | Sir G. Grey | | | |
| 15 May 1854 | | | J. P. Hoffman | |
| 27 Aug 1855 | | | J. N. Boshoff | |
| 5 Nov 1856 | | J. Scott | | |
| 5 Jan 1857 | | | | M. W. Pretorius |
| 8 Feb 1860 | | | M. W. Pretorius | |
| 9 Oct 1860 | | | | S. Schoeman |
| 15 Jan 1862 | Sir P. Wodehouse | | | |
| 2 Apr 1862 | | | | W. J. van Rensburg |
| 17 June 1863 | | | J. J. Venter* | |
| 2 Feb 1864 | | | J. H. Brand | |
| 24 May 1867 | | R. W. Keate | | |
| 31 Dec 1870 | Sir H. Barkly | | | |
| 1 Dec 1872 | *J. C. Molteno* | A. Musgrave | | |
| 1 July 1872 | | | | T. F. Burgers |
| 22 July 1873 | | Sir B. C. C. Pine | | |
| 1 Apr 1875 | | Gen. Sir G. Wolseley | | |
| 3 Sep 1875 | | Sir H. E. Bulwer | | |
| 31 Mar 1877 | Sir H. B. E. Frere | | | |
| 12 Apr 1877 | | | | Sir T. Shepstone |
| 6 Feb 1878 | *J. G. Sprigg* | | | |
| 4 Mar 1879 | | | | Col. W. O. Lanyon |
| 28 June 1879 | Sir H. B. E. Frere | Gen. Sir G. Wolseley | Sir H. B. E. Frere | Gen. Sir G. Wolseley |
| 2 July 1880 | | Gen. Sir G. P. Colley | | Gen. Sir G. P. Colley |
| 22 Jan 1881 | Sir H. Robinson | | | |
| 27 Feb 1881 | | Gen. Sir E. Wood* | | Gen. Sir E. Wood |
| 9 May 1881 | *T. C. Scanlen* | | | |
| 8 Aug 1881 | | | | Triumvirate |
| [27 Feb 1881 to 6 Mar 1882 | | Gen. Sir E. Wood* *et al.*] | | |

| | *Cape Colony* | *Natal* | *O.F.S.* | *Transvaal* |
|---|---|---|---|---|
| 6 Mar 1882 | | Sir H. Bulwer | | |
| 8 May 1883 | | | | S. J. P. KRUGER |
| 13 May 1884 | *T. Upington* | | | |
| 18 Feb 1886 | | Sir A. E. Havelock | | |
| 25 Nov 1886 | *Sir J. G. Sprigg* | | | |
| 1 Dec 1889 | | Sir C. B. H. Mitchell | | |
| 11 Jan 1889 | | | F. W. REITZ | |
| 13 Dec 1889 | SIR H. B. LOCH | | | |
| 17 July 1890 | *C. J. Rhodes* | | | |
| 28 Sep 1893 | | Sir W. Hely-Hutchinson | | |
| 10 Oct 1893 | | *Sir J. Robinson* | | |
| 30 May 1895 | SIR H. ROBINSON | | | |
| 13 Jan 1896 | *Sir J. G. Sprigg* | | | |
| 21 Feb 1896 | | | M. T. STEYN | |
| 15 Feb 1897 | | *H. Escombe* | | |
| 5 May 1897 | SIR A. MILNER | | | |
| 5 Oct 1897 | | *Sir H. Binns* | | |
| 14 Oct 1898 | *W. P. Schreiner* | | | |
| [2 Nov 1898 to 14 Feb 1899 | GEN. SIR W. F. BUTLER]* | | | |
| 9 June 1899 | | *Sir A. H. Hime* | | |
| 18 June 1900 | *Sir J. G. Sprigg* | | | |
| 6 Oct 1900 | | | SIR A. (LORD) MILNER† | |
| 6 Mar 1901 | Sir W. Hely-Hutchinson | | | |
| 13 May 1901 | | Sir H. McCallum | | |
| Jan 1901 | | | Sir H. Goold-Adams | |
| 29 Sep 1902 | | | | Sir A. Lawley |
| 18 Aug 1903 | | *G. M. Sutton* | | |
| 22 Feb 1904 | *Dr L. S. Jameson* | | | |
| 2 Apr 1905 | | | LORD SELBORNE | |
| 15 May 1905 | | *C. J. Smythe* | | |
| 28 Nov 1906 | | *F. R. Moor* | | |
| 4 Feb 1907 | | | | *L. Botha* |
| 2 Sep 1907 | | Sir M. Nathan | | |
| 27 Nov 1907 | | | *A. Fischer* | |
| 3 Feb 1908 | *J. X. Merriman* | | | |
| 17 Jan 1910 | | Lord Methuen | | |

* More important acting heads of state. †Also Governor of O.R.C. and Transvaal.

*Note:* Names of High Commissioners and Republican State Presidents are given in capitals, governors and lieutenant-governors in lower case, prime ministers in italics.

(b) *Black Regimes*

| *Chiefdom* | *Rulers* | | |
|---|---|---|---|
| Bhaca | Ncaphayi (d. 1845) | | |
| Griqua (Griquatown) | Andries Waterboer (*c.* 1790–1852) | | |
| | Nicholas Waterboer (1852–78) | | |
| (Philippolis) | Adam Kok II (d. 1835) | | |
| | Adam Kok III (1835–75) | | |
| Hlubi | Langalibalele (1818–89) | | |
| Hurutshe | Ikalafeng (1850–93) | | |
| Kgatla | Lentswe (1875–1924) | | |
| Kololo | Sebetwane (*c.* 1823–51) | | |
| Kwena | Setshele I (*c.* 1829–92) | | |
| | Sebele I (1892–1911) | | |
| Lete | Mokgosi I (*c.* 1820–86) | | |
| | Ikaneng (1886–96) | | |
| Lobedu | Modjaji (*c.* 1860–94) | | |
| Mpondo | Faku (d. 1867) | | |
| | Mqikela (d. 1887) | Ndamase (d. 1876) | |
| | Sigcawu (d. 1905) | Nqiliso | |
| | | Poto | |
| Mpondomise | Mhlonhlo (1837–1906) | | |
| Mthethwa | Dingiswayo (d. 1818) | | |
| Ndebele (Khumalo) | Mzilikazi (1821–68) | | |
| | Lobengula (1868–93) | | |
| | Nyamanda (1893) | | |
| (Transvaal) | Ndzundza | | |
| | Mabhogo (fl. *c.* 1860–85) | | |
| | Nyabela | | |
| Ndwandwe | Zwide (fl. 1820) | | |
| Ngwaketse | Gaseitswe (*c.* 1846–89) | | |
| | Bathoen I (1889–1910) | | |
| Ngwane | Matiwane (d. 1829) | | |
| Ngwato | Sekgoma I (*c.* 1835–57, 1859–66, 1872–75) | | |
| | Kgama III (1872, 1875–1923) | | |
| Pedi | Thulare (d. 1824) | | |
| | Malekutu | Sekwati (d. 1861) | |
| | Mampuru (1862, 1882–3) | Sekhukhune I (1862–81) | Kholoko I (1883–93) |
| | | Morwamotsa II | |
| | | Sekhukhune II (1893–) | |
| Phuti | Moorosi (d. 1879) | | |
| Rolong (Ratlou) | Moswete (1821–1904) | | |
| (Tshidi) | Tawana (d. 1849) | | |

| *Chiefdom* | *Rulers* |
|---|---|
| Rolong (Ratlou) | Monthsiwa (1849–96)<br>Besele (1896–1903) |

**Sotho**

Mokhachane
|
Moshweshwe (*c.* 1823–70)
|
Letsie (1870–91)
|
Lerothodi (1891–1905)
├ Letsie II (1905–13)
└ Griffith (1913–39)
  |
  Seeiso (1939–40)
  |
  Moshweshwe II (1960– )
  (MaNtseko regent 1940–60)

**Swazi**

Sobhuza I (1815–36)
|
Mswati II (1838–65)
|
Ludvonga II (1868–72)
├ Bhunu (Ngwane V) (1889–99)
│ |
│ Sobhuza II (1899– )
└ Mbandzeni (Dlamini IV) (1875–9)

**Tawana**

Letsholathede (d. 1874)
Moremi II (1876–91)
Sekgoma (1891–1906)

**Thembu**

Ngubencuka (d. *c.* 1830)
├ Mthikrakra
│ |
│ Ngangelizwe (d. 1884)
│ |
│ Dalindyebo (d. 1920)
│ |
│ Jongelizwe
│ |
│ Sabata
└ Matanzima

**Tlhaping**

Molehabangwe
├ Mothibe (d. 1836/8)
│ ├ Gasebone (d. 1897)
│ │ |
│ │ Botlhasitse (d. 1887/95)
│ │ |
│ │ Galishiwe (1887/95–1927)
│ └ Jantji
├ Molale
│ |
│ Mankurwane (1869–92)
│ |
│ Molale (1892–1920)
└ Mahura (d. 1869)

**Venda**

Ramabulana (d. 1864)
Machado (d. 1895)
Mphephu (exiled 1898)

| *Chiefdom* | *Rulers* |
|---|---|

**Xhosa**

- Phalo
  - Gcaleka
    - Khawuta
      - Hintsa (d. 1835)
        - Sarhili (1835–93)
          - Sigcawu (1893–1902)
  - Rharhabe
    - Mlawu
      - Ngqika (d. 1829)
        - Sandile (1829–78)
        - Maqoma (d. 1873)
    - Ndlambe (d. 1828)

**Zulu**

- Senzangakhona
  - Shaka (d. 1828)
  - Dingane (1828–40)
  - Mpande (1840–72)
    - Cetswayo (1872–84)
      - Dinuzulu (1884–1913)

6. *The Union of South Africa, 1910–61: Governors-General, Prime Ministers and Imperial High Commissioners*

| | *Governor-General* | *Imperial High Commissioner* | *Prime Minister* |
|---|---|---|---|
| 31 May 1910 | Viscount Gladstone | Viscount Gladstone | Gen. L. Botha |
| 8 Sep 1914 | Viscount Buxton | Viscount Buxton | |
| 3 Sep 1919 | | | Gen. J. C. Smuts |
| 20 Nov 1920 | Prince Arthur of Connaught | | |
| 21 Jan 1924 | Earl of Athlone | Earl of Athlone | |
| 30 June 1924 | | | Gen. J. B. M. Hertzog |
| 26 Jan 1931 | Earl of Clarendon | | |
| 6 Apr 1931 | | Sir H. J. Stanley | |
| 7 Jan 1935 | | Sir W. H. Clark | |
| 5 Apr 1937 | Sir P. Duncan | | |
| 5 Sep 1939 | | | Gen. J. C. Smuts |
| 24 May 1941 | | Lord Harlech | |
| 17 July 1943 | N. J. de Wet (acting) | | |
| 23 June 1944 | | Sir W. Huggard | |
| 27 Oct 1944 | | Sir E. Baring | |
| 1 Jan 1946 | G. B. van Zyl | | |
| 3 June 1948 | | | Dr D. F. Malan |
| 1 Jan 1951 | E. G. Jansen | | |
| 2 Oct 1951 | | Sir J. le Rougetel | |
| 2 Dec 1954 | | | J. G. Strijdom |
| 4 Mar 1955 | | Sir P. Liesching | |
| 3 Sep 1958 | | | Dr H. F. Verwoerd |
| 12 Jan 1960 | C. R. Swart | | |

7. *The Republic of South Africa, 1961–76: State Presidents and Prime Ministers*

| | *State President* | *Prime Minister* |
|---|---|---|
| 31 May 1961 | C. R. Swart | Dr H. F. Verwoerd |
| 13 Sep 1966 | | B. J. Vorster |
| 31 May 1967 | J. F. T. Naude (acting) | |
| 10 Apr 1968 | J. J. Fouché | |
| 19 Apr 1975 | Dr N. Diederichs | |

# TABLE 2

## *COMPOSITION OF THE HOUSE OF ASSEMBLY, 1910–75*

| *Election Year* | *Total Seats* | | | *Unionist Party* | *South African Party* | *Labour Party* | | | | *Independent* |
|---|---|---|---|---|---|---|---|---|---|---|
| 1910 | 121 | | | 39 | **67** | 4 | | | | 11† |
| | | | | | | | | *National Party* (Hertzog) | | |
| 1915 | 130 | | | 40 | **59** | 4 | | 27 | | |
| 1920 | 134 | | | **25** | **41** | 21 | | 44 | | 3 |
| 1921 | 134 | | | [Unionists absorbed in S.A.P.] | **79** | 9 | | 45 | | 1 |
| 1924 | 135 | | | | 53 | **18** | [*'Pact' Govt.*] | **63** | | 1 |
| | | | *Labour* (National Council) | | | *Labour* (*Creswell*) | | | | |
| 1929 | 148 | | 3 | | 61 | **5** | | **78** | | 1 |
| 1933 | 150 | | 4 | | **61** | [*'Fusion' Govt.*] | | **75** | | 10 |
| | | *Socialist* | | *Dominion Party* | | *United Party* | | | *National Party* (Malan) | |
| 1938 | 153 | 1 | 3 | 8 | | **111** | | | 27 | 4 (3*) |
| 1943 | 153 | | **9** | **7** | | **89** | | | 43 | 5 (3*) |

| | | | | | | | | | | |
|---|---|---|---|---|---|---|---|---|---|---|
| | | *Communist Party* | | | | | *Afrikaner Party* | | | |
| 1948 | 153 | 1* [Party banned, 1950] | | **6** | 0 | 65 | **9** | **70** | | 2* |
| 1953 | 159 | 1* [unseated] | | **5** | | 57 | [Afrikaner Party absorbed by Nationalists] | **94** | | 2* |
| | | *Liberal Party* | | | *Federal Party* | | | | | |
| 1958 | 159 | 2* | | 0 | 0 | 53 | | **103** | | 1* |
| | | | *Pro-gressive Party* | | | | | | | |
| 1961 | 159 | | 1 | | | 49 | | **105** | | 4‡ |
| 1966 | 166 | | 1 | | | 39 | | **126** | | |
| | | | | | | | | | *'Herstigte' National Party* | |
| 1970 | 166 | | 1 | | | 47 | | **118** | 0 | |
| 1974 | 171 | | 7 | | | 41 | | **123** | 0 | |
| 1977 | 165¶ | | *Progressive Federal Party* 17 | | | *New Republic Party* 10 | *South African Party* 3 | **134** | | |

* Elected under the Representation of Natives Act, 1936.
† Mainly Natal Unionists not yet amalgamated with the Unionist Party.
‡ Elected under the Separate Representation of Voters' Act, 1955.
¶ No elections held in South West Africa
Figures in **bold** indicate that the party participated in the Government.

# Index of Persons

# General Index